SUFFOLK'S
ANCIENT SITES - HISTORIC PLACES

SUFFOLK'S
ANCIENT SITES - HISTORIC PLACES

Written & Compiled by

Mel Birch

a castell publication

ISBN 0948134 50 X *(Paperback)*
ISBN 0948134 51 8 *(Hardback)*

First Published April 2004

Published in Great Britain by
Castell Publishing Mendlesham Suffolk IP14 5RY

Printed by
Biddles Book Manufacturers Kings Lynn Norfolk

Sources . . .

WITH AROUND six thousand listings it has unfortunately not been practical to specify the sources from which each has been obtained. The majority are known to exist, or to have existed from evidence on the ground or verified in documentary records, but there are those that cannot be substantiated either because they have come down the generations by word of mouth as 'tradition asserts . .' or as supposition based on the limited and inconclusive information at hand.

For this reason I have tried to blend the material retrieved through excavation and research by the professional archaeologists going back to Basil Brown - augmented by the work of amateur individual and group enthusiasts through field work, and recorded in the Suffolk Archaeological Unit and the Suffolk Record Offices - with the valued work carried out by local historians, both professional and amateur. Subsequently, I have given weight to the conclusions of such eminent people as Vincent Redstone, Claude Morley, W. G. Arnott and Norman Scarfe. I make no apology for promoting Morley's often controversial analysis of earthworks and, in particular, place-name meanings, for while the recognised authorities such as Skeet and Ekwall have been used throughout this book, Morley's greater local knowledge and willingness to investigate 'on site' allows me to give weight to his findings for the more obscure translations.

I have used extensively the range of books written on Suffolk's history by such authorities as Nicholas Pevsner *'The Buildings of England - Suffolk'*, P. G. M. Dickinson *'Suffolk'* (based on Dutt's *'Little Guides'*); Arthur Mee *'The King's England - Suffolk'*; Norman Scarfe *'The Suffolk Landscape'* and *'Suffolk in the Middle Ages'*; William White *'General History & Description of the County of Suffolk 1844'*; the two Suffolk volumes of *'Victoria County History'*; Kirby *'Suffolk Traveller'*; William Copinger *'Suffolk Records & Manuscripts'*; David Dymond and Peter North East *'The History of Suffolk'*; W. G. Arnott and his works on the history of Suffolk's rivers *'Suffolk Estuary'*, *'Alde Estuary'*, and *'Orwell Estuary'*; Eric Sandon *'Suffolk Houses'*; E. Farrar *'Suffolk Houses' in 'East Anglian Miscellany'*; Brian Flint *'Suffolk Windmills'*; Rowland Parker *'Men of Dunwich'*; augmented by the Suffolk Archaeological unit's *'Sites & Monuments Record'*; the numerous volumes of *'The Proceedings of the Suffolk Institute of Archaeology and History'*; *'A Survey of Suffolk Parish History'*; *'Pocket Histories of Suffolk Parishes'*; *'East Anglian Miscellany'*; *'East Anglian Notes & Queries'*; *'The Gentlemen's Magazine'*; *'The East Anglian Magazine'*; *Faden's 1783 map of Suffolk surveyed by Joseph Hodskinson*; *The 1st Edition Ordnance Survey maps 1836*; other old county and estate maps; the current *Ordnance Survey Pathfinder Series* and the two volumes of the *'Suffolk Domesday Book'*, plus local references in national works such as Oliver Rackham's *'The History of the Countryside'*, and Maurice Beresford's *'The Lost Villages of England'*. Material has also been gleaned from research being carried out for my forthcoming books *'Suffolk's Lost Villages & Deserted Settlements'* and *'The Castles of Suffolk & other Fortified Earthworks'*.

Acknowledgements & Credits . . .

Cover - The River Deben below Waldringfield *(George James Rowe - Ipswich Borough Council Museum & Galleries Collection)*. p13 - Roman Fort at Burgh Castle from the air *(©Norfolk Museums & Archaeology Service)*. p137 - Walton Castle Roman Fort *(from an old print)*; Burgh Castle *(from an old print)*. p138 - Eastlow Hill, Rougham *(Suffolk Parish Histories, reprinted from the old Suffolk Chronicle & Mercury)*; Roman Villa at Standon Chare *(East Anglian Magazine)*. p139 - The Black Ditches *(© Crown Copyright/ MOD - Reproduced with the permission of the Controller of Her Majesty's Stationery Office)*; Romano-British Camp, Clare *(© Crown Copyright/MOD - Reproduced with the permission of the Controller of Her Majesty's Stationery Office)*. p140 - Sutton Hoo *(Copyright Reserved - Cambridge University Collection of Air Photographs)*; Old Minster, South Elmham St. Cross *(©Norfolk Museums & Archaeology Service)*. p141 - Bury Abbey before the Reformation *(East Anglian Magazine)*; Original Leiston Abbey ruins *(East Anglian Magazine)*. p142 - Flixton Abbey *(Suffolk Parish Histories)*; Priory of Crutched Friars, Little Whelnetham *(Suffolk Parish Histories)*. p143 - St. Olaves Priory, Herringfleet *(Suffolk Parish Histories)*; Redlingfield Nunnery *(Suffolk Parish Histories)*. p144 - Alnesbourne Priory, Nacton *(Suffolk Parish Histories)*; Kersey Priory *(East Anglian Magazine)*. p305 - St. Petronella Leper Hospital, Bury St. Edmunds *(East Anglian Magazine)*; The West Gate, Ipswich *(from an engraving by Godfrey, published by Hooper)*. p306 - St. Gregory's Church, Sudbury *(East Anglian Magazine)*; Sudbury Grammar School in 1700 *(East Anglian Magazine)*. p307 - Wolsey's College, Ipswich *(from an old print)*; The Market Cross & Moot Hall, Ipswich *(from an old engraving)*. p308 - Little Wenham Castle *(East Anglian Magazine)*; Ruins of Walton Old Hall *(Suffolk Parish Histories)*. p309 - Livermere Hall *(from an old print)*; Brightwell Hall *(Suffolk Parish Histories)*. p310 - Oakley Park *(from an old print)*; Assington Hall *(Suffolk Parish Histories)*. p311 - The Lowestoft High Light *(from an old print)*; Flixton Hall *(Suffolk Parish Histories)*. p312 - Rushbrook Hall *(East Anglian Magazine)*; Tudor Bridge, Westhorpe Hall *(Suffolk Parish Histories)*.

I am indebted to Wendy Birch for providing publications from the Suffolk Library Service, and to the Bury Records Office and Archaeological Unit for making their records available for my perusal with their usual friendly and helpful advice. Finally, to Eve Vongswang for taking on the daunting and unenviable task of proofreading this work. I apologise to her in advance for errors which may well have arisen and remain as a result of my continually and frustratingly updating and amending material after she had finished.

In such an extensive project as this, mistakes in the information provided may occur for which I take full responsibility. I therefore welcome any constructive criticism or new information which will augment any future revised editions.

An Introduction . . .

IT IS NOT my intention here to present a history of Suffolk from earliest times; this has been done on many occasions by others more qualified than I, and approached from various perspectives and with particular objectives. Rather my aim is to bring together for the first time, in one popular publication for the mutual benefit of all, as many of the county's archaeological and historic sites that I could research within each parish. Not all are proved - many being purely conjectural - and not all still remain today in a county with such a high agricultural emphasis where much has been ploughed to extinction. Many, including whole towns and villages, have been lost to coastal erosion - the most notable, Dunwich, which in early medieval times was a city of wealth and importance - while coastal changes have reduced other busy medieval ports such as Walberswick, Blythburgh and Orford to villages, or to seaside towns like Aldeburgh and Southwold. Rivers have changed course or become silted up after years of inactivity, and with sea levels thought to have been much higher in pre-Conquest times it is difficult to visualise how the landscape must have looked when quite large boats were able to sail up to Debenham, Otley, and to Rattlesden where, according to the poet John Lydgate, stone was barged along the river Rat to build Bury Abbey. It is also thought that in early times much of the north-west of the county lay beneath the Old Fen Sea and had thriving fishing industries.

The sites described cover all periods of history from Mesolithic to the early 19th century. Not all are of international importance like Sutton Hoo, or even of particular national or even local interest, yet all have their place in mapping a picture of Suffolk's chequered past.

It is accepted that Suffolk's geological topography means that early man settled in the west of the county in far greater numbers than in the east, and pre-historic sites are therefore more in evidence there. At the time dense forest covered the uplands of mid-Suffolk, whilst to the west open chalk and sandy heathland predominated. This was poor land agriculturally but early man was a hunter and found enough meat without resource to farming to any degree. This would only prove a temporary situation, for as the population grew it could not be fed by this haphazard method alone and a planned farming system evolved. The fertile agricultural land lay on the boulder clay to the east in the area known as High Suffolk and this is to where the population later drifted, clearing the forest as they went. So it is in west Suffolk that the best of the early pre-historic sites remain. We marvel at the prowess of Stone-Age man at Elveden where excavations have revealed a perfectly preserved flint tool industry, and Barton Mere where, during a drought in 1831, the 10-acre lake revealed evidence of a Bronze Age settlement and a wooden structure created for catching fish. It was also a time of conflict with ancient tribes establishing and contesting their boundaries. Before the coming of the Romans, 'Grimsditch', now traced by a ditch and lane crossing the old Roman road at Thornham Parva, may have been dug to form a territorial division between the two great East Anglian tribes, the Trinovantes (from Essex) and the Iceni (from Norfolk). Few forts or 'camps' of the period survive in Suffolk, but one still of impressive size and belonging to the transitional period before the great Roman invasion is Erbury at Clare, a small town with a surplus of great monuments. Even earlier is the Iron-Age fort at Barnham, one of only two identified in the county. East Anglia was also the destination for the great trackway known as the Ickneild Way which dates back to Neolithic times (4,000-2,000 B.C.). It formed the easiest route for communication and trade from southern England to the Wash following the open chalk ridge between impenetrable forest. The way passes through Suffolk from the river Kennett crossing at Dalham, north-east to Knettishall Heath Country Park and the river Little Ouse. Another fascinating site relating to this period (and awaiting further research on the ground) was discovered on aerial photographs at Fornham All Saints. It may be an ancient cursus - a ceremonial way - possibly dating back to 3,000 B.C. and used for ritual functions in much the same way as Stonehenge. It follows the west bank of the river Lark and may extend over a mile towards Bury St Edmunds.

The Roman conquest of Suffolk, as in the country as a whole, can best be seen in their network of roads. A number still remain in evidence traced by modern highways or in tracks and field boundaries. The task of mapping and looking for evidence of the sections still to be identified remains one of the joys of the amateur archaeologist. Roman camps, forts, towns and villas are all to be seen in the county, some still as earthwork banks, others solely in crop marks on aerial photographs as with the extensive villa at Lidgate. A magnificent monument to the troubled times in late Roman Britain remains in the great Saxon Shore fort of Burgh Castle near Great Yarmouth. It still has walls standing to 15' and covers 5 acres. Taken into Norfolk in 1976 for no better reason than to tidy up the county boundaries, it is included here as one of Suffolk's most impressive sites. The most famous find of the period is the Mildenhall Treasure, a hoard of sumptuous silverware, now one of the major exhibits in the British Museum.

The Saxon period brought Christianity to Suffolk through three notable saints; Furvey, Felix and Botolph. Evidence of their first sanctuaries in an inhospitable land can be seen in the Roman fort at Burgh Castle and on an isolated promontory at Iken on the river Alde; the debate as to whether Felix's See was at Walton Castle (another Roman Saxon Shore Fort) or at Dunwich is now irrelevent as both potential sites lie beneath the North Sea. The Minster at South Elmham lies in another isolated spot. It is thought to have been the seat of the East Anglian Bishopric some time after it was first founded by St Felix around 630 A.D., although it has not so far been dated with any confidence. In 1939 the lonely heathland barrows at Sutton Hoo revealed possibly Britain's greatest archaeological discovery when Basil Brown unearthed the great ship burial of one of the kings of the East Anglian royal dynasty, the Wuffangas. The site of their palace, said by Bede to have been at Rendlesham, has still to be located. Over at West Stow the remains of a Saxon village and burial ground which survived for over 250 years - part of that time in apparent harmony with a Romano-British settlement nearby - has been re-created. Excavations over recent years at Brandon have uncovered an extensive occupation site covering all archaeological periods and is proving one of the most important Middle Saxon sites yet discovered in Britain. Evidence unearthed in Ipswich (*Gipeswic* c975) suggests that the town has had trading links with the Continent since the late C6 and that it could well have been one of the largest known early trading communities in NW Europe. Its pottery, commonly known as 'Ipswich ware' was being distributed from Kent to Yorkshire between around 625 and 850 A.D. Bury St. Edmunds is another important Suffolk town with ancient origins. The former Saxon settlement of *Beodericworth* became the fortified town of *Byrig* in 1038, and later, the burial place of King Edmund. Apart from scattered ruins, all that remains are the two great gatehouses of its abbey which was once one of the greatest in England. Its fame had been assured when the body of the East Anglian king, Edmund, killed by the Danes (at Hoxne?), was buried here and canonised. This lead to a steady procession of royalty and dignitaries visiting the abbey to pay homage at his shrine. Bury Abbey has another claim to fame, for it was here at the high altar in 1215 that the most powerful barons of the day met to plan how they might compel

King John to ratify the liberties of England. This led to Runnymede and the signing of Magna Carta. Sudbury (*Southburgh*) was probably a place of considerable importance as early as 570 A.D. It was mentioned in the Anglo Saxon Chronicle in 797 A.D, and already an urban centre by the late Saxon period with its own mint. Exning is thought to be the birthplace of St. Etheldreda who founded Ely Abbey in the mid 7th century; she was the daughter of the East Anglian King Anna, killed by the pagan Mercian king Penda near Blythburgh. Asser, the biographer of Alfred the Great, claims that Hadleigh was the burial place of the Danish king Guthram in 889 A.D.

Suffolk has its fair share of important and innovative castles from the Norman period. Framlingham and Bungay belonged to one of the county's most formidable families, the Bigods. Framlingham was the first castle in Britain designed to be defended from a series of towers set in the curtain wall rather than from an inner keep. The future Queen Mary was staying here when she received the call to return to London to claim the throne of England from the unfortunate Jane Grey. Orford was another new design in defence. Henry II built a castle here with an eight-sided keep, making it easier to defend, but it was never tested. The little known motte at Haughley is the largest earthwork in the county, some 80' high. Haughley was one of the Suffolk honors - great estates owned by the most powerful lords - others being at Clare and Eye. A mighty battle was fought in 1173 between the royal army of Henry II and one of Flemish mercenaries under the command of the Earl of Leicester. After initial successes including the total destruction of Haughley castle, the earl was intercepted while trying to cross the river Lark at Fornham St Genevieve by the Chief Justicair of England, Richard de Lucy, and a terrible slaughter took place. The Seven Hills in the adjoining parish of Fornham St Martin are said to be the burial mounds of those who lost their lives.

As the Normans gradually eased into the English way of life or, more accurately, as the local inhabitants began to grudgingly accept their presence, the barons' need for personal defence deminished and their castles became fortified houses and eventually manor houses and mansions. Examples of this gradual change can be seen at Little Wenham Hall, the earliest known use of homemade brick in a fortified house. The age of the lords of the manor also saw domestic changes in towns and villages with the granting of rights to hold markets and fairs. With less opportunity to leave their mark on the battlefield, the great lords and barons attempted to seek immortality, and salvation in the hereafter through 'good works'. They donated part of their wealth to building and enhancing churches and founding priories, chapels, colleges and hospitals; and later free schools and almshouses. One very inconspicuous brick gatehouse on the edge of docklands is all that remains of Cardinal Wolsey's great college at Ipswich. If it had not been for his sudden demise it may well have rivalled Oxford and Cambridge in size and importance. Today, ironically, Suffolk is one of only two English counties without a university. Many great houses have gone - notably Rushbrook, Flixton and Hawstead - demolished during the irresponsible two decades which followed the Second World War - but many others remain as at Helmingham, Long Melford, Ickworth, Hengrave, Somerleyton and Heveningham. Only the moat and 3-arch Tudor bridge remain of another great mansion, that of Mary Tudor and Charles Brandon in my own village of Westhorpe. Mary was the brother of Henry VIII and one-time Queen of France. Moats, first built with defence in mind during the uncertain times following the Conquest, still continued to be constructed, but now mainly for fashion. Suffolk has the greatest number of moats of any county in the country apart from Essex.

Justice was still being meted out without sensitivity, and most parishes and large town had their own gallows. There are records of where many stood, and other sites can be identified from field, wood or lane names. A description of the procedure makes gruesome reading: 'The body was bound round with hoops of iron and hung up by a loop of iron over the head. It often hung twelve months or more, and as the flesh rotted, the bones often fell to the ground and were collected and buried by the victim's friends and family.' It is thought that initially some may not even have been dead when they were first hung. The accession of Queen Mary - often referred to as 'Bloody Mary' - led to the persecution of many Protestants. Some died as martyrs - often burned at the stake. Dr Rowland Taylor, a Hadleigh rector, met this end in 1555 and his monument stands on Aldham Common. Others are remembered in memorials in Ipswich and Bury St. Edmunds. Though it is thought between a third and a half of the population died of The Black Death in the 14th century, little remains today to show the effects in Suffolk. Only Wordwell is known to have been depopulated and deserted solely due to plague deaths, but in the name Chainhouse Road in Needham Market we have a reminder of the time when the town suffered the pestilence and was barricaded at either end with chains to stop the townspeople entering and leaving.

With several important rivers emptying their waters along the 50 plus miles of coastline, Suffolk has always nurtured vital trade links with the continent but at the same time been susceptible to invasion. King Alfred's navy was involved in skirmishes with the Danes in the Orwell Estuary in 885 A.D., and Ipswich was twice attacked and sacked by these hostile invaders. During the Dutch Wars two great sea battles were fought off the Suffolk coast, at Lowestoft and Sole Bay off Southwold.

A notable feature of the post-medieval period was the change in the appearance of the countryside effected by the great landowners. Many of the greens, commons and heaths which had adorned the landscape for centuries and provided common grazing, were enclosed; nothing now remains of Allwood Green which once extended over five mid-Suffolk parishes. Even villages dating back to Saxon times were lost, forcibly removed or reduced to accommodate great parks. One of the best examples is Little Livermere where aerial photographs show the former village still laid out in earthworks. Much later still we would see this destruction repeated when the new farming techniques of the 20th century were to destroy much of the remaining ancient woodland and hedgerows.

The Civil War and the threat from Napoleon also left their own indelible marks on the Suffolk landscape through sconce earthworks and the round martello towers dotted along the coast. Pill boxes and abandoned airfields will, in their turn, become the historic reminders of a more recent conflict.

Whilst this book attempts to bring us up to date with the archaeological sites in Suffolk, the work continues. Whether by accident or design, discoveries will still be made; professional archaeologists, the enthusiastic amateur just fieldwalking his local parish, and those working on the land as farmers, developers or maintenance workers will slowly fill the gaps in our knowledge of the past. However small and insignificant they may at first appear, all play their part in completing the complex jigsaw. Perhaps no future find will attain the magnificence of Sutton Hoo, Mildenhall or Hoxne; then again . . .

Mel Birch
Westhorpe 2004

Gariannonum, the Roman Saxon Shore Fort at Burgh Castle built to protect the vunerable Waveney approach from invading Saxons around AD 290.

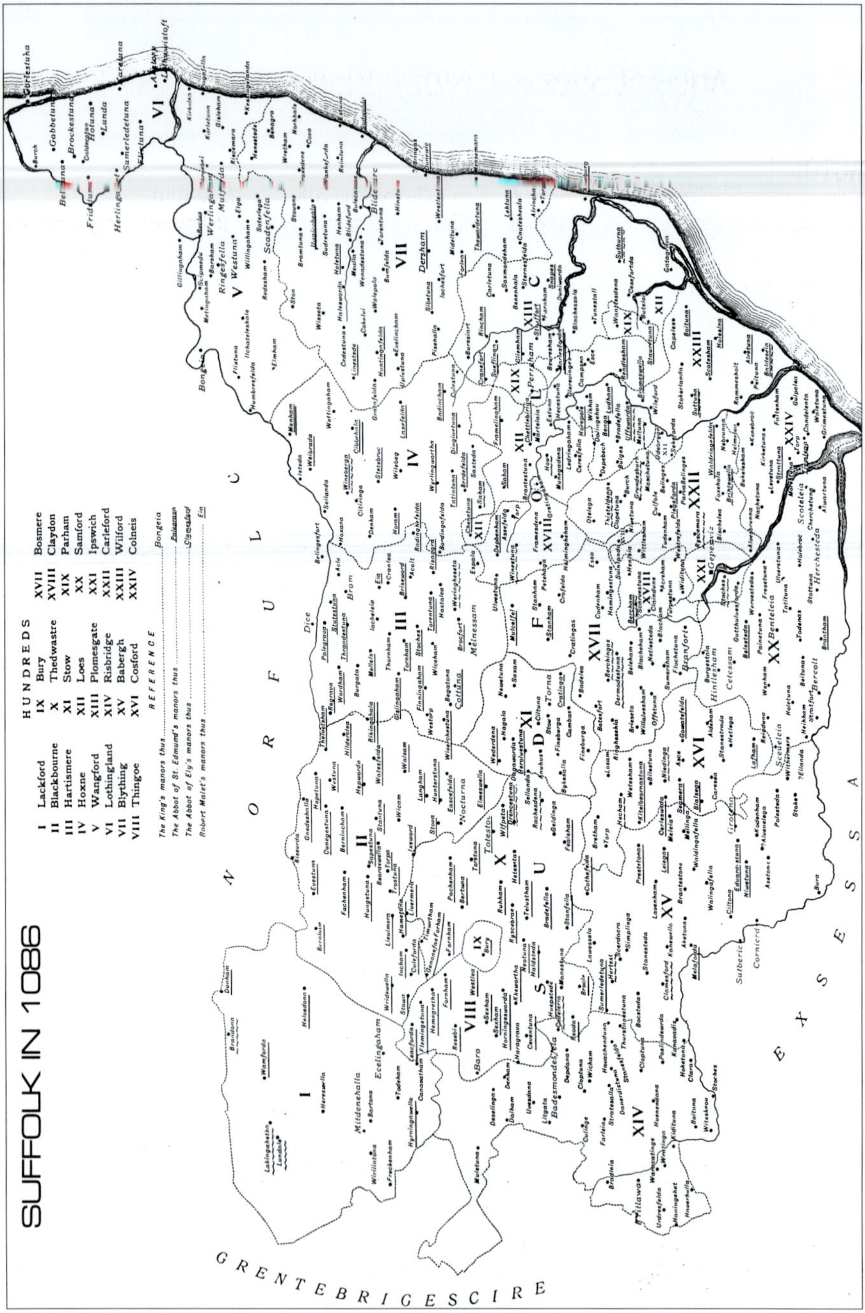
SUFFOLK IN 1086
HUNDREDS
I Lackford
II Blackbourne
III Hartismere
IV Hoxne
V Wangford
VI Lothingland
VII Blything
VIII Thingoe
IX Bury
X Thedwastre
XI Stow
XII Loes
XIII Plomesgate
XIV Risbridge
XV Babergh
XVI Cosford
XVII Bosmere
XVIII Claydon
XIX Parham
XX Samford
XXI Ipswich
XXII Carleford
XXIII Wilford
XXIV Colneis
REFERENCE
The King's manors thus
The Abbot of St. Edmund's manors thus
The Abbot of Ely's manors thus
Robert Malet's manors thus
NORFULC
SUDFULC
EXSESSA
GRENTEBRIGESCIRE

Ancient Sites & Historic Places by Parish

ACTON *(3 miles NE of Sudbury)*

Babergh Hundred. 'Farmstead or village of a man called Ac(c)a' (OE) *Achetuna* (DB)
Manors. Acton Manor (1301 de Hodeboville family.) *Sub-Manors.* Clerbeck; Rokewoods; Leys; Tolemach.

Ancient Woodland.
Paradise Wood and Hawk's Grove, NW of the parish, form the remains of ancient woodland.

Palaeolithic Settlement.
In 1920, Palaeolithic implements were found in gravel pits N of Acton Place.

Ancient Enclosure.
A large double-ditched irregular enclosure of Iron Age/Romano-British date has been discovered in the parish.

Roman Roads.
A Roman road enters the parish SW of School Farm as a footpath to Slough Farm. From here the track makes a sweeping arc before regaining the line of the ancient road again to meet the Melford road at exactly the point where another Roman road heading for Bridge Street comes from the SE to cross it - its course traced by a footpath across the fields. After a diversion caused by sand and gravel workings, Bull Lane likely continues the line to Long Melford street, part of another Roman road heading NNE to Bridge Street (the present A143).

Gospel Oak.
A Gospel Oak stood where two concrete World War II pillboxes now stand beside the Lavenham to Bridge Street road.

Ancient Mound.
To the W of the site of Acton Place, what appeared to be an artificial mound of unknown date and purpose was partially removed by the USAF during World War II, and the remainder has since been destroyed by the construction of a business park.

Medieval Green.
The triangular road junction at Newmans Green marks the site of a small green shown on Faden's 1783 map.

Historic Houses & Ancient Moated Sites.
The manor was anciently called Aketon and held by Robert de Bures whose brass of 1302, in Acton Church, is one of the best preserved in England. The site of the ancient Acton Place, ½ mile W of the village and former seat of the Daniels, now comprises a modern Business Park. The sumptuous mansion which Robert Jennens built later to replace the old house, within its great park, was pulled down in 1825. Acton Hall, N of the church and standing on the site of the former hall, still possesses parts of its ancient moat in the form of a horseshoe. Balesden Hall, on the northern parish boundary and now little more than a cottage, stands on a magnificent moated site. A narrow moat encloses a large quadrangular site with fish-ponds to the S, with another square moat to the NE.

AKENHAM *(3 miles NW of Ipswich)*

Bosmere & Claydon Hundred. 'Homestead of a man called Aca' (OE) *Acheham* (DB)
Manors. Akenham Manor (anciently held by Brewse family.) *Sub-Manors.* Rous/Rice Hall; Stoneham Manor.

AKENHAM *(continued)*

Historic House.

Rise Hall, near the church, is a late Georgian building on the site of an ancient manor house, formerly the residence of the Le Ruse or Rous family in the C13.

ALDEBURGH

Plomesgate Hundred. 'Old fort or stronghold on the river Alde' (OE) *Aldeburc* (DB)

Manors. Aldeburgh (1155 William Martel). *Sub-Manors.* Vicarage Manor.

Roman Fortified Town & Ancient Port.

The town was once a fortified place; finds suggest Roman, with a settlement and fort to the E of the present town. As recently as the C16 it was an important port centred on a haven to the NE at Thorpehithe - still remembered in 'The Haven'. Both settlements are now under the sea as is the bulk of the present town which was considerably larger than now with fairs, a market and 'denes' similar to Yarmouth. The Moot Hall which stood in the market place is now isolated on the edge of the beach. The town gained borough status in 1529 and a map of 1588 shows five streets running parallel with the coast; now there are but two. Aldeburgh built three ships for Sir Francis Drake at the time of the Armada, and returned two members of Parliament from 1571 until 1832 when it was disfranchised. Nearly half the houses stood empty in 1674 and the local poet George Crabbe saw eleven houses destroyed by the high tides of 1779. Aldeburgh's decline was arrested when several influential families moved their summer residences here and it became a 'fashionable' seaside resort.

Roman Roads (?)

Both the A1094 (from Stratford St Andrew) and Leiston Road (from Dunwich) may be Roman in origin.

Site of Ancient Priory.

St Marys Priory, founded by William de la Pole and mentioned in 1448, was dissolved in 1525. The site is unknown and probably lies under the sea.

Lost & Deserted Medieval Villages.

Now lost to the sea, Slaughden or 'Slawtinge', shown as a village of some 20 houses standing well back from the beach on Appleton's map of 1588, prospered with new quays when Thorpehaven became blocked (*see above)*. Dramatic photographs show the sea's destruction of 'The 'Three Mariners' Inn last century. Hazlewood was once a separate parish with its own church NW of the town. This church was ruinous by the C17 when part of the parish was ecclesiastically united with Friston; the remainder became part of Aldeburgh in 1934. Villagers were said to have married and been buried here from the days of King John. Slight traces remain of the church W of the Leiston road and the parish is remembered in Hazlewood Hall Farm, Hazlewood Common, and Hazlewood Marshes to the S bordering the river Alde.

Medieval Market & Fairs.

The late market grant of 1547 was probably inherited from nearby Aldringham which was being depopulated along with neighbouring Hazlewood (*see above*). A further grant for an additional market due to an increase in population was made in 1568. The market was obsolite by 1891. The town had several fairs: Fishing Fair (1679); Toy Fair (1759) and Pleasure Fair (1885). Oakley Square formed the site of the fairs until it became too riotous; it was then moved to a site S of the town. The last of the fairs had closed by 1912.

Medieval Market Cross.

Market Cross Place marks the former site of an ancient Cross.

Stocks & Whipping Post.

The whipping post remained in use until 1631 and the stocks were removed to the end of the Town House in 1741.

Site of old Windmill.

A post mill which stood in Station Road dates back to at least 1724. It was demolished in 1924.

ALDEBURGH *(continued)*

Almshouses.
Repairs to almshouses recorded in 1626 and 1643.

Free School.
Land for a Grammar School was incorporated in 1638.

Historic Fortifications.
There is a Martello Tower at Slaughden in the S of the parish. These round towers, of which there are several dotted along the Suffolk coast, were the idea of Sir David Dundas following his experience in Corsica, where a round tower on Point Mortella with walls 18' thick had succeeded in driving off several man-of-war. Erected as a panic measure when invasion by Napoleon seemed imminent, they were less strongly constructed with walls 9' thick at the front and 5' at the rear; nevertheless each tower comprised some 700,000 bricks. Completed in 1812, like the pill-boxes and tank defences of two world wars, they were never needed.

Historic Houses.
The Moot Hall is timber-framed of c1520-40 with brick-nogging on the upper floor inserted in 1654. Its site once occupied the market place and at one time the ground floor housed a prison. The Old Customs House in High Street was erected after 1585 following fierce competition with neighbouring Orford. Ye Old Cross Keys Inn in Crabbe Street is C16 and the White Lion Inn dates from 1563.

ALDERTON *(8 miles SE of Woodbridge)*

Wilford Hundred. 'Farmstead by the alder trees' (OE) *Alretuna* (DB)
Manors. Alderton Hall (1113 William de Glanville). *Sub-Manors.* Boville's; Peche's; Manor of Alderton Comptis/Earls Alderton Hall.

Iron-Age Settlement.
Aerial photos show a complex series of small enclosures in the N of the parish probably associated with Iron-Age occupation.

Site of Earthworks (?)
The Mount, S of the village on a strategically placed knoll above the marshes, is suggestive of being the site of a former defence or lookout post. Faden shows an undefined round object (topped by a cross?) in this position on his 1783 map. A Domesday manor here was called 'Litelcros' (Little Cross).

Site of old Windmill.
A smock mill which stood just S of the village dates back to at least 1796. It was demolished in 1956.

Historic Fortification.
At Shingle Street, SE of Buckenay Farm, is a Martello Tower built in 1812 to defend the coast against the threat of invasion by Napoleon. It has now been converted into a private house.

Historic Houses & Ancient Moated Sites.
Naunton or Alderton Hall was the major of four manors here. It was formerly the seat of the Naunton family who owned most of the parish including two of the other manors. They had already been here 'some hundreds of years' before their move to Letheringham in the reign of James I, at which time one of the family, Robert Naunton, was Secretary of State. In an outbuilding of Alderton Hall Farm, which now stands on the site, are remnants of the earlier C15 Naunton Hall in the form of dressed stone arches and a buttressed angle. There are also remains of the very unusual and ancient moat system which once encompassed it. Stangrove Hall, S of the village, stands by the site of the other main Alderton manor, Earls Alterton Hall. The Swan Inn is C15/C16.

ALDHAM *(2 miles NE of Hadleigh)*

Cosford Hundred. 'The old homestead' or 'homestead of a man called Ealda' (OE) *Aldeham* (DB)
Manors. Aldham (-1462 de Vere family.)

ALDHAM *(continued)*

Ancient Woodland.
Wolves Wood, a managed Nature Reserve, and Aldham Park Wood are ancient woodland.

Ancient Moated Mound.
The Saxon church of St Mary is built on a mound partly surrounded by a moat of undetermined age and purpose.

Medieval Market (?)
A receipt is on record from John Corder, Clerk of the market of Aldham 'for use of market boards'. The date is unfortunately illegible.

Almshouses.
Almshouses were believed sited in Holly Lane.

Deserted Medieval Village.
Berisford includes Aldham in his list of lost Suffolk villages and although there is a settlement in the parish, lying beside the roads to Elmsett and shown on Faden's map of 1783, this is of later date. The same map shows not a single property other than the hall and church to the SW, but evidence in the form of faint earthworks on the valley side W of the church, which may date from late Saxon times, point to an earlier medieval village in this area. Twenty-three households were assessed, in all probability on this earlier site, in 1327.

Historic House.
Aldham Hall is of ancient origin and areas of water, some created from the Brett river which flows past along the valley bottom, may be remains of fishponds. Aldham Priory Farm has the remains of an ancient moat. Although the surrounding field names on the tithe map of 'Moated Platform', 'Friar's Piece' and 'Ploughed Friars' are suggestive, there is no record of a priory here or of a manor in Aldham in ecclesiastical ownership.

ALDRINGHAM-CUM-THORPE *(5 miles SE of Saxmundham)*

Blything Hundred. 'Homestead belonging to Aldhere's people' (OE) *Alrincham* (DB)
Manors. Aldringham Manor (1180 Ranulph de Glanvile, Lord Chief Justice); Thorpe Manor (C12 Granted to Thetford Priory).

Tumuli.
A group of Bronze Age round barrows (overgrown but in good condition) are situated behind the village inn. A Bronze Age round barrow, cut into by a golf bunker by the old railway track, lies on the N side of the road to Thorpeness. In Square Plantation, S of the Thorpeness road, is a single overgrown Bronze Age round barrow.

Site of Ancient Chapel.
Skeletons from a cemetary probably associated with the medieval Chapel of St Mary, Thorpe, a chapelry of Snape Priory in use in 1477, were unearthed in an enclosure called 'Chapel Field'. According to Kirby in 1734, the chapel was 'standing since the restoration but is now in ruins.' It was dismantled in 1820 and the site ploughed.

Medieval Market & Fair.
Hamo de Masey obtained a grant for a market and fair here in 1319, but its importance was eventually undermined by both neighbouring Aldeburgh (who themselves obtained a grant in 1547) and its own hamlet, Thorpe, which was developed by Stuart Ogilvy early in the C20 into the 'garden suburb' of Thorpeness. A fair was held on Goldfair Green. It was obsolite by 1891.

Medieval Greens & Commons.
Faden's 1783 map shows three open spaces: Coldford (Goldfair) Green, on the western parish boundary in the fork of the present B1069 and B1353 roads, now enclosed and developed; Aldringham Common commenced from E of the crossroads and extended S as a wide linear green, past the long-gone Hazlewood

ALDRINGHAM-CUM-THORPE *(continued)*

Church and tapering down to end at The Red House just outside Aldeburgh. Thorpe Common still covers most of Thorpeness.

Historic House.
Aldringham, being a quiet little village situated within easy reach of the coast, became a centre for smuggling. Many a cargo of contraband was landed on the sandy beach in the hamlet of Thorpe (now Thorpeness) and taken across the lonely heath to be held in secret until it could be moved on. Inns played a prominent part in these exercises and the local 'Parrot and Punchbowl' (previously 'The Case is Altered') was no exception. The ancient beamed building, formerly thatched, was in the same family from 1604 until the early C19.

ALPHETON *(6 miles N of Sudbury)*

Babergh Hundred. 'Farmstead/village of a woman called Aelfflad or Aethelflaed' (OE) *Alflede(s)ton* (DB)
Manors. Alpheton (C12/C13 Walter de Barnham).

Ancient Woodland.
Alpheton Hall Wood, N of the parish by Shimplingthorne, is remains of ancient woodland.

Roman Road.
The Roman road from Long Melford to the Bradfields headed NNE through the parish; its route, not evident on the ground, probably deviated from the normal direct line to negotiate Chadbrook.

Site of Roman Building & Late Saxon Settlement.
In the S of the parish, by the Roman road passing through the hamlet of Bridge Street, evidence of Roman and late Saxon occupation along with considerable C1 pottery led to the discovery of a substantial Roman building.

Medieval Green.
The right hand bend in the A134 traces the eastern boundary of the former triangular Alpheaton Tye Green shown on Faden's 1783 map and now partly redeveloped.

Workhouse.
A workhouse was listed in Alpheton with 35 inmates in 1766.

Historic Houses & Ancient Moated Sites.
Mill House, by Chad Brook at Bridge Street on the southern boundary, dates from 1574. Alpheton Hall, by the church, was formerly moated and earthworks to the W of the church may be the remains of former fish ponds.

AMPTON *(5 miles N of Bury St Edmunds)*

Thedwestry Hundred. 'Farmstead or village of a man called Amma' (OE) *Hametuna* (DB).
Morley suggested that this may have been the home of Anna, the East Anglian Saxon king, and that the river had been artificially diverted here, N of Knight's Grove, to form a fortified enclosure.
Manors. Ampton (1269 Richard de Flempton).

Tumulus.
A round barrow on the W side of the Timworth road, S of the church and beside the course of the Roman road, was described as 15' in diameter and 3' high (1950) but has now been ploughed out.

Roman Road.
A Roman road bisects the parish virtually W-E from the dismantled railway S of Oak Covert, to near the S end of Ampton Water. It is not evident on the ground.

Ancient Chapel.
A Chapel dedicated to St Mary was founded by John Crocket in 1478. Dissolved 1547, its site is unknown.

Free School/Hospital.
A hospital/school was founded in 1702 by James Calthorpe for six boys.

AMPTON *(continued)*

Almshouses.

The charming almshouses were founded by Dorothy Calthorpe in 1693 for six poor women.

Historic House.

Ampton Hall is an 1885 rebuild of the old hall of the Calthorpe family built c1700. It stands in an extensive park of over 700 acres which includes Livermere Park and Lake.

ASHBOCKING *(7 miles N of Ipswich)*

Bosmere & Claydon Hundred. 'Place at the ash-tree(s)' (OE) *Assa* (DB), *Bokkynge Assh* (1411). Bocking later added to original name Ash following the acquisition of the manor by the de Bocking family in the C14. *Manors.* Ashbocking Manor/Ash Hall/Bocking Hall (1281 Philip Hervey held of the Honor of Eye). *Sub-Manors.* Harney's/Harvey's; Ashbocking Green or Kitts de Decampo.

Ancient Mere (?)

The parish reputedly anciently stood beside a large mere or lake covering 100 acres.

Site of Romano-British Camp (?) and Medieval Buildings.

In a field near Poplar Farm, NW of the village, "Feoffee Moat", a banked rectangular enclosure about 140' by 120', contained medieval sherds; another, 200 yds E contained floors, walls and traces of timber and plaster from a number of buildings round a central court. Between these two enclosures was evidence of another group of buildings with a general scatter of pottery sherds dating from the Iron Age into the Roman period.

Roman Road.

The course of a Roman road is traced by the B1078 through the parish SW-NE forming the parish boundary from Hare and Hounds Corner to E of the crossing with the B1077.

Medieval Green.

Faden's map of 1783 shows a rectangular Ash Green occupying either side of the present B1077 just N of its junction with the B1078, bounded on the W by Manor Farm and Feoffes Farm, and on the E by Green Farm and Walnut Tree Farm.

Historic Houses & Ancient Moated Sites.

The C16 timber-framed manor house of Ash Hall, situated near the church, occupies the site of the former hall of the Bocking family (1338-1585) who gave their name to the village. It still retains a small portion of its once extensive moat. Feoffee Farm, on the eastern parish boundary, also retains part of its ancient moat. The Manor Farm, on the SW edge of the former green, may be the site of the smaller manor of Kitts de Campo or Ashbocking Green. S of Blosses and NW of the church is a rectangular and linear earthwork in a meadow which may be a former moat or an enclosure with a linking ditch. Walnut Tree Farm is C16.

ASHBY *(6 miles NW of Lowestoft)*

Mutford & Lothingland Hundred. 'Aski's farmstead' (OScand). No Domesday entry, which Morley suggests may be due to it being Crown lands seized by William through resistance after the Conquest, and not assessed in 1086.

Manors. Ashby Manor (1269 Sir John de Askby).

Ancient Lake Settlement (?)

A hard chalk platform surrounded by woodwork of some description at Fritton Decoy has similarities with the ancient Lake Dwelling discovered at Barton Mere (*see* Great Barton).

Ancient Boat Burial.

A boat burial, more primitive than those found at Snape and Sutton Hoo, was discovered in the parish in 1830. It was thought unlikely to be earlier than 600 A.D.

ASHBY *(continued)*

Medieval Common.
The medieval common was enclosed by John Wentworth in 1599.

Deserted Medieval Village.
In 1599 the tenants whose properties formed the medieval village around Ashby Common were bought out by John Wentworth who enclosed the 40 acres, not to enlarge the adjacent Somerleyton Park, but for 'productive purposes'. St Mary's Church, Ashby Hall Farm, and two isolated farms are all that remain.

ASHFIELD-CUM-THORPE *(3 miles E of Debenham)*

Threadling Hundred. 'Open land where ash-trees grow' (OE) *Assefelda* (DB). 'Thorpe' means hamlet of.
Manors. Ashfield Manor (1313 Ivor de Kenton).

Ancient Woodland.
Great Wood on the western parish boundary is a fragment of ancient woodland.

Tumulus.
'Mill Mount', at Thorpe Hall in the hamlet of Thorpe, is a flat-topped Bronze Age round barrow with encircling ditch where 'human bones have been disinterred'. As its name suggests, it was later used for a post-mill.

Roman Road.
The A1120 follows the course of a Roman road SW-NE from Swiss Cottage on the SW parish boundary to just NE of Stonehouse Farm on the NE boundary.

Ancient Cross.
A medieval Cross once stood in the parish.

Deserted Medieval Village (?)
Thorpe Hall and the ruined round tower of St Peter's Church, are all that remain of Thorpe. Its church, which had long been in ruins, was rebuilt in 1739 to provide the spiritual needs of Ashfield's parishioners when their own church fell into decay. Faden illustrates this reversal in fortunes on his map of 1783 which shows Thorpe church complete and Ashfield's as 'in ruins'. However, in 1853 former status was restored with Ashfield's church rebuilt and returned to use and Thorpe's again abandoned and left to decay. Foundations in the grounds of the hall show that the earlier church was of very ancient origin and larger than that which replaced it. This suggests that it at one time served a large community, but there is now no evidence of this former settlement.

ASPALL *(5 miles S of Eye)*

Hartismere Hundred. 'Sheltered spot by the stream where aspens grow' (OE) *Aspala* (DB). The brook separating the hall from the church indicates the place where the original aspens grew over one thousand years ago.
Manors. Aspall Manor (1352 De la Pole family).

Ancient Woodland.
Aspall Wood, just NE of Aspall Hall, is part of ancient woodland.

Mill.
A cyder mill was built by the de Chevallier family in 1728. It originally produced '25 hogsheads' of cyder. The original press still exists as a museum piece at Aspall Hall where cyder production continues to this day.

Ancient Fair.
An annual fair once held here was one of only two mentioned in Domesday.

Medieval Green.
Aspall Green is shown on Faden's map of 1783 as a rectangular green running W-E from the present B1077, bounded on its southern side by Aspall House and a public footpath. A ditch marks its eastern boundary.

ASPALL *(continued)*

Historic House & Ancient Moated Site.
The manor house of Aspall Hall situated NE of the church dates from *c*1580. It has a magnificent ancient oval moat of great strength which must originally have surrounded an even earlier building, probably the seat of the de Aspall family who took their name from the parish and were later resident in Stonham Aspal. Another moat is at Aspall House to the N. The house gained recognition through the Chevallier family first as a dairy centre, and later for its production of cider which so impressed the great agriculturalist Arthur Young on a visit in 1786. Later the family developed a particularly fine strain of barley which became known as the 'Chevallier barley' and was marketed throughout the Continent and America.

ASSINGTON *(4 miles ESE of Sudbury)*

Babergh Hundred. 'Farmstead where Assa's people live' (OE) *Asetona* (DB) *Assintona* (1175)
Manors. Assington (C12 William Lungespeye). *Sub-Manors.* Levenya Strattons; Shimplingford; Aveley/ Alvingley.

Ancient Woodland.
Part of Assington Thicks is ancient woodland, as was Birch Avery, now destroyed and arable.

Site of Former Medieval Village.
When Assington Park was landscaped and extended E to engulf the church and green in 1750, the village moved further S. The 1817 tithe map shows dwellings in the park still evident in the form of house platforms S of the church.

Medieval Greens.
Assington Green, shown in 1783, was a small triangular green NW of the church; enclosed in 1817 it was incorporated into Assington Park. Marshalls Green stood on the S side of the present A134 opposite Assington House, and Darking Tye, SW of the parish, was a triangular green at the road junction by Dorking Tye House.

Workhouse.
A workhouse with 20 inmates is recorded in 1776.

Historic House & Ancient Moated Site.
Within the remnants of its former park is the site of Assington Hall, a Tudor mansion (burned down in 1957) with an impressive red-bricked towered and castellated doorway. Cromwell lodged here during the Civil War as a guest of the Parliamentarian Gurden family whilst laying siege to Colchester. A story relates how the local incumbent, the Rev. Thomas Walker, threatened to throw himself across the path of a member of the family who was intent on hastening to London to sign the warrant which would send Charles I to the block. He is alleged to have sworn that if he drove on it would be over his dead body. The Hall had been home to the Gurdens since the C16 and itself replaced an earlier hall, seat of the Corbets from the C13. To the S is a moat called 'The Island' on the tithe map. The field to the N named 'Stew Banks' suggests these were fish-ponds connected with the hall.

ATHELINGTON *(4½ miles SE of Eye)*

Hoxne Hundred. 'Town of the aethelings' or 'of the princes or nobles' (OE) *Alinggeton* (1219). The name suggests there may once have been a great house here belonging to the royalty of the East Angles with elaborate earthworks and moats. Athelney is now a hill rising conspicuously from broad surrounding marsh flats; its name perhaps originally Aethelinga, i.e. Princes Island.
Manors. Athelington Manor (C13 Roger de Huntingfield).

Historic Houses & Ancient Moated Sites.
Three moats survive at the early C17 Athelington Hall, W of the church. Meadow Farm, E of the church, has three sides of an oblong moat. Church Farm dates from 1682.

BACTON *(6 miles N of Stowmarket)*

Hartismere Hundred. 'Farmstead of a man called Bacca' (OE) *Bachetuna* (DB)
Manors. Bacton (anciently in the hands of the Bishop of Norwich who had a grant of free warren here in 1318). *Sub-Manors.* Boys/Horinger's Manor.

Roman Site (?)
Terra sigillata of the C1-C2 has been found in the area of Russell's Hill, an isolated spot in the SE corner of the parish with the earthwork remains of a moat.

Ancient Tracks.
A track called Boy's Entry from the Haughley road to Old Bells Farm, which forms the southern parish boundary and the ancient Hundred boundary between Stowe and Hartismere, goes back at least to Saxon times.

Medieval Greens.
Carters Green, shown on Faden's map of 1783, is now named Cow Green (N section) and Canham Green (S section). The manorial records show Cow Green as Calcote Green. Although the original green has been mostly enclosed and infilled, the former boundaries are largely preserved as ditch lines and a few old properties of unknown age are sited around its edge. Smiths Green originally led up from Boys Hall by the present Green Lane track to join Carters Green at Pepper Hill. Bacton Green ran NE from the lane leading to Bacton Hall - which also comprised the parish and hundred boundary - tapering off towards the road, then as a narrow linear green along the NW side heading towards the village. At Lodge Farm it turned left following the line of the Wyverstone road and then came back on itself in a loop to Earls Green, then called Alice Green. The church stands on the edge of Tailors Green (unnamed by Faden), its situation now obstructed by a modern bungalow.

Site of old Windmill.
A post mill which stood E of Ducks Eye dated back to at least 1798. It was burned down c1900.

Medieval Guildhall.
A guildhall housing the guilds of St. Peter and St. John is mentioned up to the C16. Its site is unknown.

Historic Houses & Ancient Moated Sites.
A narrow, many-angled moat surrounds the ancient Bacton Hall, W of Bacton Green. Manor House Farm was built in 1715 by the Pretyman family who owned the manor from 1568. It retains three sides of a quadrangular moat from the previous manor house, the S side filled-in. An oblong moat, now only defined in earthworks, can be clearly traced at Russell's Hill (*see above*). There is another, perfect quadrangular moat at Redhouse Farm, Earls Green, and another of curious shape at Pulham's Farm, ¼ mile S of the church, rectangular on the W side but almost circular on the E. The site of the ancient rectory, 1 mile SW of the church at the Grange, is marked by the remains of a moat, quadrangular in plan, and there are traces of two adjacent rectangular moats on the site of Kerry's Farm at Cow Green. West House was built in 1530 and the thatched Bull public house is also of ancient origin.

BADINGHAM *(4 miles NNE of Framlingham)*

Hoxne Hundred. 'Homestead or village associated with a man called Beada' (OE) *Badincham* (DB)
Manors. Badingham Hall/Carbonel (1314 William de Bovile). *Sub-Manors.* Okenhill Hall/Saxhams; Colston Hall.

Roman Road.
A Roman road runs SW-NE through the parish traced (where a footpath follows its course SW of Stone Cottages) by a central bank with ditches either side, then along the line of the A1120 to Boundary Farm.

Ancient Mounds.
The church stands on the slope of a hill known as Burstonhaugh (and later, Derhaugh), the effect of which causes the nave floor to rise towards the E. SSE of the church and W of The Old Rectory is another mound, date and origin unknown. It overlooks the course of the old Roman road and may have held a beacon. The road

BADINGHAM *(continued)*

at Castle Farm traces a suspicious curve round the farm buildings before turning N to form the parish boundary with Dennington. Intriguingly, the site was previously called Mottshall. Perhaps one or more of these mounds may have been associated with the Saxon Beada and later the powerful early Norman families who resided here (*see place-name*).

Ancient Chapels.
There were two chapels here, one founded by Sir Walkelin de Hardricshall in 1330 and dissolved in 1536, and another which was in being from 1298 to 1518. The sites of both are unknown.

Medieval Cross.
Twenty pounds was bequeathed towards the erection of a Cross at Colston Cross in 1523.

Medieval Greens.
Bowling (or Brabling) Green, now represented by Bowling Green Farm, may have already been enclosed by 1783 when Faden's map, although naming it, failed to show its form. Pound Green is now marked by Pound Green Cottage and Pound Green Road. Badingham Green is shown as a tiny green bordered by Pikes Farm and Lime Tree Farm on the NW side of the Roman road.

Site of old Windmill.
A post mill which stood in Low Street in 1783 was demolished c1913.

Historic Houses & Ancient Moated Sites.
The site of the main manor, Badingham Hall, 1½ miles NE of the church and 1 mile NW of the Roman road, dates to Norman times and may have been Beada's first Saxon residence (though more likely on the rise by the church *see above)*. Although never themselves seated here, the De Bovilles who inherited the manor from the first Norman lord, William Malet, no doubt built a dwelling here, as pottery sherds from the site go back to the C13. The Carbonells who followed probably built a fortified manor house surrounded by a strong moat. The Rous family later erected a red-brick Tudor house on the flint foundations, and it was this, considerably reduced to a simple farmhouse, which was pulled down in the 1960s. The site has now been ploughed out but a fragment of flint walling remains and, in places, the outline of the old moat can still be traced. The other manor house, Colston Hall, SE of the village, was home to the Derehaughs or Verehaughs in the mid-C14 when they also held Badingham Hall Manor, and Burstonhaugh, one of two additional manors added since 1086. Colston Hall was later the residence of the Holts. Okenhall Hall (the fourth manor), 1 mile S of the village, dates from 1552. Ancient Moat Farm, NE of Brabling Green, has a large irregular oblong moat, the SE side now mostly destroyed. The White Horse public house dates back to the C15.

BADLEY *(2 miles NW of Needham Market)*

Bosmere & Claydon Hundred. 'Bada's meadow' (OE) *Badeleia* (DB)
Manors. Badley Manor (C13 Geoffrey de Badele held of the Honor of Clare).

Ancient Woodland.
Upper and Lower Badley Woods, SW of the hall, are fragments of ancient woodland.

Ancient Well.
The place-name may have derived from a meadow S of the hall which contains a spring called Our Lady's Well. Here is the source of the Bat Stream, an affluent of the river Gipping.

Tumulus (?)
Cropmarks near Badleybridge Farm may indicate the site of a long barrow, now ploughed out.

Ancient Track.
The tree-lined Badley Walk, which ran from the Ipswich road to Badley Hall and still exists as a public footpath, is said to be part of a former pack road which ran to West Creeting and onwards to the Roman Norwich road. Elizabeth I probably rode upon it when she visited the Pooleys at the hall.

BADLEY *(continued)*

Site of Chantry.

A Chantry, founded in 1492 by Edmund Alcoke and dissolved in 1546, was situated on the south side of Badley Hall in rough pasture cut by a tree-fringed stream. It was given to the Knights Hospitallers (at Battisford) by Robert Fitz Jefferey.

Deserted Medieval Village (?)

Only the isolated church and hall remain of what may be a lost village. A likely site is just to the SW where Badley Green is shown on Faden's 1783 map. Two parallel earthworks 15 yds. wide running E-W, N of the church are the likely outline of the original carriageway to the Hall. Badley Walk, a grassy track 130' wide, runs for nearly a mile from the Stowmarket road.

Anglo-Saxon Cemetery (?)

Finds claimed at Gateford by the river Gipping in 1865 during the construction of the railway consisted of a copper alloy Byzantine bowl, a bronze 'hanging' bowl, and a possibly unrelated Roman vessel full of denarii.

Medieval Green.

Badley Green, a small green SW of the hall and church, was shown and named on Faden's map of 1783. It still remains in an area probably little changed since its royal visit in the C16.

Historic House & Ancient Moated Site.

Isolated with its church, Badley Hall, now but a shadow of its splendid former self, is a late C15 timber-framed Manor House, two-thirds of which was pulled down *c*1759. Part of the ancient moat remains, with a fish-pond on the hill to the N which provided water to tanks in the basement of the hall. It was in the hands of Ralph de Badley until 1424 when it passed to the Mortimers and then the Alcocks. Before the end of the century the Poleys were resident here and it remained with that family until the early part of the C18. Doves Hill Farm is another old residence.

BADWELL ASH (formerly Little Ashfield) *(4 miles SE of Ixworth)*

Blackbourn Hundred. 'Bada's spring by clearing where ash-trees are felled' (OE) *Badewelle Asfelde* (C13) *Manors.* Little Ashfield (C14 William Criketot). *Sub-Manors.* Stikeland/Shakerland Hall; Brushes al Brokeshull; Tiptofts al Wyverstone Tiptod's.

Ancient Spring.

An ancient spring - possibly Bada's (*see place-name*) - can still be seen in a wood N of Mill House on the western parish boundary.

Prehistoric Settlement & Anglo-Saxon Cemetery.

A prehistoric settlement with a possible palisaded ditch, along with a Saxon cemetery of a little after 450 A.D. was discovered in gravel workings in 1922. Findings included urns, 30-40 skeletons, shield bosses and spearheads. Later trenching uncovered the edge of an ancient mere which ran roughly parallel with Ashfield Road. There was evidence of prehistoric and Roman settlement alongside it.

Ancient Track.

The ancient Hundred Lane runs N-S to form the parish boundary between Badwell Ash and Wyverstone from the crossing with Madge's Lane to the crossing with Braziers Lane, themselves both ancient tracks forming the northern and southern parish boundaries with Walsham-le-Willows and Great Ashfield.

Medieval Green.

The small, rectangular Badwell Green is shown E of the hall in the area of Moat House on Faden's 1783 map.

Site of old Windmill.

A post mill stood SW of the church on the W side of the road to Hunston. It dated from at least 1783 and was demolished c1930.

BADWELL ASH *(continued)*

Historic House & Ancient Moated Sites.
The impressive manor house of Ash (or High) Hall was built c1500. It was probably at one time quadrangular in design, with towers at the corners of a former substantial moat. Fragments of a very broad moat survive at Green Farm, Badwell Green. At Cutchey's Farm, near the parish boundary with Great Ashfield, is an oblong moat widening into a pond on the W; other moats are at Moat Farm and Moat House, Badwell Green. Tiptofts Farm in the hamlet of Long Thurlow stands on the formerly moated site of the manor house of Tiptofts al Wyverstone Tiptod's.

BALLINGDON-CUM-BRUNDON *(To the W of, and now a part of Sudbury)*

Babergh Hundred. 'Rounded hill' (OE) *Baldinigcotum, Belidune, Balydon, Baliton.*
Formerly separate parishes, Ballingdon SW, and Brundon NW of Sudbury, now form part of its outer suburbs.

Ancient Woodland.
Brundon Wood, W of the parish, is all that remains of a section of ancient woodland.

Prehistoric Site & Roman Cemetery.
A settlement site covering the Palaeolithic, Neolithic and Iron-Age periods was discovered at Brundon. Nearby, in 1948, an Early Roman cemetery was unearthed.

Site of Ancient Chapel.
Situated at the bottom of Ballingdon Hill, Ballingdon Chapel of the Brothers of St Thomas the Martyr was purchased in 1120 together with All Saints Church Sudbury by Adam the Monk.

Deserted Medieval Village.
In the C12 Brundon was a parish in its own right, but in a letter of 1678 William Windham stated that little use was being made of the church as there was but one dwelling left in the parish. The church was in ruins by 1740 and has now long gone. It stood just E of Brundon Wood by a track which leads to the Hall and watermill. The original village was probably sited in the area of this track. There were originally two water mills here, one described as a fulling mill in a Latin account of the Manor of Brundon-cum-Molendino.

Historic House.
Ballingdon Hall, built *c*1593 by Sir Thomas Eden, attracted national attention in 1972 when its owners moved the timber-framed building en-bloc 200 yds further up Ballingdon Hill to a new site after acquiring an industrial estate as neighbours. Successfully completed, they now enjoy again their peaceful solitude. The Bull Inn, built in 1540, stands by Ballingdon Bridge. The name probably comes from the heraldic bull of the De Clares, once lords of the manor. The yard was once a venue for the 'sport' of bull-baiting.

BARDWELL *(2½ miles N of Ixworth)*

Blackbourn Hundred. 'Spring or stream of a man called Bearda' (OE) *Berdeuuella* (DB). Includes the Domesday vill of Wyken.
Manors. Bardwell Manor (c1097 granted to Ralph de Bardewell in fee [land belonging to Abbot of St. Edmunds]). *Sub-Manors.* Wykes/Wicken; Wyken Hall.

Ancient Woodland
Wyken Wood (formerly Great Wood) and Ash Grove, in Wyken hamlet to the S, are ancient woodland.

Site of Ancient Spring (?)
Spring Road and Spring House suggest that the site of the ancient spring from where Bardwell took its Old English place-name was in the vicinity. The ancient hall of the Berdewells was also sited here (*see below*).

Tumulus.
A large barrow lies in a field N of Bowbeck House, on the former Bardwell or Bowbeck Heath.

Pre-Historic Track & Roman Road.
Field boundary hedges from TL951 752 - TL944 784, trace the course of Peddars Way, a prehistoric track used

BARDWELL *(continued)*

by the Romans. Its course runs SSE-NNW through the parish passing the Roman villa site at Stanton Char. NE of Barningham Park Farm, an 800' length survives in good condition at the edge of a field of old pasture. The E ditch is under a hedge and forms the parish boundary, and the W ditch emerges 18" deep. A section of the road crosses a meadow in Barningham Park where it is about 15 paces wide. The village itself is suggestively enclosed within an apparent planned rectangular road system near the crossing of two Roman roads.

Ancient Track.
Wood Lane is an ancient track which forms a part of the western parish boundary from the SE corner of Fakenham Wood, N along the wood's eastern edge, and beyond to the track leading to Sparrow Hall in Euston Parish. It is suggested that this was part of an alternative route for Peddars Way until 1671 when it was blocked by an Act of Parliament and abandoned.

Medieval Archery Practice.
An old document makes mention of 'Payd for bread and cheese and ale to making of the butte'.

Deserted Medieval Village.
Posters Lane and the hedge and ditch line trace the route of the former Podd Street and Rush Green where field evidence in the form of substantial scatters of C11-C14 pottery sherds place the site of Wyken, a possible medieval village which once existed along the northern boundary of the detached section of Bardwell parish on the Stanton border. Wyken Hall, mentioned in Domesday, stands close by.

Medieval Green & Heath.
Bardwell Green was named and shown on Faden's map of 1783 as a very small green centred at the junction of Spring Road, Stanton Road, and Davey's Lane. The same map shows the great expanse of Bardwell Heath extending N to join Barningham Heath and W and S to incorporate parts of Sapiston and Stanton parishes. Missing from the map and probably already lost by this time is Rush Green (*see above*) which lay beside and is remembered in Rushgreen Grove.

Site of old Windmill.
A post mill stood on the S side of the Davey's Lane-Knox Lane crossroads. It dated from at least 1783.

Former Guildhall.
The village still contains its former Guildhall - a Guild of St. Peter existed here c1474. The building was later used as a poor house (accommodating 11 females in 1844).

Historic Houses & Ancient Moated Site.
The still impressive C15 Bardwell Hall stands on the site of the ancient hall of the Berdewells. They were seated here from the time of the Conquest until the middle of the C15 and gave their name to the parish. Although it still retains its ancient domestic chapel, it is unrecognisable as the old manor house of the judge Sir William Lee shown on an old estate map of 1730 and mostly demolished later that century. It had a moat, D-shaped and some 360' square, with fish-ponds. The moat was bulldozed in 1959 leaving only a shallow depression, and the fish-ponds filled in. Wyken Hall, S of the parish, has fragments of the medieval house and retains its ancient barns. Pelham House dates from the C15.

BARHAM *(5 miles NNW of Ipswich)*

Bosmere & Claydon Hundred. 'Homestead or enclosure by the (burial) hill' (OE) *Bercham* (DB)
Manors. Barham Manor (-1536 Abbot of Ely, 1545 John Southwell). *Sub-Manors.* Shrubland Manor.

Ancient Woodland.
Rede Wood in the SE of the parish, and Borley's Wood in the NE, are ancient woodland.

Site of Tumuli.
The place-name suggests an enclosure ('ham') beside a cast-up hill ('barrow' or 'burgh'). A manuscript

BARHAM *(continued)*

of 1818 describes two such barrows. They were said to lie in the hamlet of Sharpstone Street on the W of Sandy Lane - the road running NE to Coddenham from the old A140 Norwich Road N of Claydon - in an area known as The Dentings and Dentings Plantation. The largest was on the turning itself, and the other a little further along the lane. Nothing of them now remains. Sharpstone is said to come from *Sceaf*, a Pagan Saxon settlement.

Iron-Age Settlement.
Perhaps relative to the place-name, a circular post-built house was uncovered on a hill-top here in 1979 associated with two furnaces or ovens.

Roman Roads.
Six Roman roads converged at Barham, the avenues and vistas of Shrubland Hall gardens tracing the course of some. Evidence remains of one leading to Coddenham Church and another to Baylham. A coin of Domitian A.D. 81-96 was found on the surface of the former. A track leading to Shrubland Hall from just N of Sandy Lane lies in an area known as Sharpstone Street, 'Street' being Roman for road.

Site of Battle (?)
Local tradition speaks of a battle fought between Saxons and Danes in the parish. Three skeletons (face down) were found in Chapelfields c1934.

Medieval Green.
Barham Green, named and shown in 1783, remains E of Green Farm.

Workhouse.
The Bosmere & Claydon Union Workhouse stood on the W side of the old Norwich Road opposite Shrubland Park near the junction with Sandy Lane. It was built in 1766 and extended in 1835 to accommodate 500.

Historic Houses & Ancient Moated Sites.
Barham Hall, near the church, retains a doorway and coat of arms from the previous Hall, home of Robert Southwell (d.1554). Barham Manor, by Manor Farm, dates from the C16 and retains part of its ancient moat. The present Shrubland Hall was built in Italian style by Sir Charles Barry in 1851 and stood in a 300 acre park initially stocked with deer (1909). It occupies the site of an earlier Elizabethan house which Sir Nicholas Bacon built for his younger son, Edward; one side only of the broad moat of this earlier house remains. In the grounds N of Shrubland Hall, just outside the parish boundary, are the remains of an even earlier hall possibly built by Sir Philip Booth c1507. It had a private chapel which was used as a garage in 1934. The Sorrell & Horse Inn once stood on the opposite side of the road (the site now marked by a row of cottages converted from the old stables). It was moved when the new hall was built.

BARKING *(1 mile SW of Needham Market)*

Bosmere & Claydon Hundred. 'Settlement of the family or followers of Berica' (OE) *Berchingas* (DB)
Barking had a Domesday mill and weir of another, showing the parish then extended to the river Gipping.
Manors. Barking-cum-Needham (-1536 Bishop of Ely, 1561 vested in Crown, 1611 Sir Francis Needham).
Sub-Manors. Overhall.

Ancient Woodland.
Priestly Wood, Bonny Wood and Titley Hill were identified in a survey of the Bishop of Ely's estates in 1251. Priestly Wood still has the boundary banks shown on a map of c1641. Park Wood and Oak Hills are further sections of ancient woodland.

Roman Road.
The projected line of the Roman road from Bildeston passing WSW-ENE through Barking to Coddenham to join that heading N (A140), is evident as a metalled lane from Middle Farm and a footpath from Lower Farm to the Needham road. From here it is lost in arable fields as it heads for the Gpping crossing at Sharmford.

BARKING *(continued)*

Ancient Gospel Oak.

In the rectory grounds are three cedars planted in 1712 by Robert Uvedale whose son was rector here for fifty-two years. Close by is what remains of an old Gospel Oak of great age.

Ancient Way.

Needham Market was once only a hamlet and its church merely a chapel-of-ease to Barking without a graveyard. The Causeway, a hollow way enclosed by ancient overhanging hedgerow, once provided a funeral way, transporting coffins from Needham for burial at Barking.

Site of Gallows.

In May 1781, workmen digging on the turnpike road just outside Needham Market (the present B1113) at a place called Gallows Hill found the skeleton of a man with the irons in which he had been gibbeted.

Medieval Market & Fair.

The Bishop of Ely had the grant for a market and fair here in 1226. With the decline of Barking and expansion of the better situated Needham (formerly merely a hamlet of the former), Sir Francis Needham later moved the market to a more commercially viable site in the NE corner of the parish by the main Bury-Ipswich road. Needham eventually encompased both the area and market.

Medieval Green.

Barking Tye, now a hamlet, still retains the large green mostly on the western side of the road. Faden's map of 1783 shows the road to Bildeston crossing the green diagonally NE-SW rather than skirting it as now.

Site of old Windmills.

Two mills are recorded which predate the C19. A smock mill which stood in Mill Lane dates back to at least 1792 and was taken down in 1918. A post mill stood on the green in the hamlet of Barking Tye from at least 1783 until its demolition in 1910.

Guildhall.

A guildhall which stood in the parish incorporating the guilds of Holy Trinity, St. John the Baptist and St. Thomas (1458), and St. Margaret (1546), was dismantled in 1632 and the materials used to build the Free Grammar School at nearby Needham Market (*see* Needham Market).

Almshouse (?)

Notice of intention to build an almshouse was given by Lord of the Manor Sir Francis Needham in 1637 although, by this date, he could have intended it to be sited in adjoining Needham.

Historic Houses & Ancient Moated Sites.

Barking Hall, former seat of the Earls of Ashburnham (and recorded with 22 hearths in 1674 when the home of Sir Francis Theobald), stood within a park on the site of an earlier hall. It was later (c1836) divided into tenements and occupied by the poor. The hall was demolished in 1926 leaving only the (now converted) stable block. Home Farm, to the SW, occupies the site of Fairfax, formerly the ancient Spaldings Hall. Tarston Hall, E of Bonny Wood, stands on the site of an earlier manor house and has an extensive moat. Other moats are at Moat Farm in Barking Tye, Middle Farm, and a moated rectangular enclosure on the corner of Bonney Wood.

BARNARDISTON *(5 miles NW of Clare)*

Risbridge Hundred. 'Farmstead of a man called Beornheard' (OE) *Cileburna* (DB) *Bernardeston* (1194)
Manors. Barnardiston (c12-1347 Barnardiston family). *Sub-Manors.* Chilborne.
Interestingly, the parish was known by the name of its sub-manor at Domesday.

Ancient Saxon Meeting Place (?)

114 acres which comprise Monks Risbridge (now part of Barnardiston) were formerly extra-parochial, without church, house or population. It provided the meeting place for the Hundred to which it gave name.

BARNARDISTON *(continued)*

Workhouse.

A workhouse is recorded in the parish with 30 inmates in 1776.

Historic Houses & Ancient Moated Sites.

In the grounds of the Victorian rectory, NE of the church, is the moated site of the original Manor House; three sides of the moat remain. The modern Barnardiston Hall, 1 mile N of the village on the parish boundary, retains fragments of the extensive moat of the former hall.

BARNBY *(4 miles SE of Beccles)*

Mutford & Lothingland Hundred. 'Barni's farmstead' (OScand) *Barnebi* (DB)

Waveney Marshes occupy half the parish of Barnby, one of only four Danish settlements in Suffolk.

Manors. Barnby appears in a Mutford grant although evidence for an actual manor here has not been established. 'The manor, if it ever existed here, has long since become extinguished'. (Copinger)

Medieval Commons.

Barnby Common, named on Faden's 1783 map, covered an area SE of the Beccles road, N of Mutford Big Wood. Northall, an extension, ran SW from N of Pond Farm, W of Mutford Big Wood, and partly in Mutford parish. Immediately E of the church the map marks an area 'Common'. This stretched E to Eade's Farm and S across Mutford parish boundary. When enclosed, 13 acres of the common were allocated to the poor of the parish in lieu of their right to cut furze for fuel. Later it was let and the income used to purchase winter coal.

BARNHAM (St Gregory & St Martin) *(9 miles N of Bury St Edmunds)*

Blackbourn Hundred. 'Warrior homestead'/'Beorn's homestead' (OE) *Byornham* (*c*1000) *Bernham* (DB)

Manors. Barnham al Pleyfords (Reginald le Brun gave to the monks of Thetford). *Sub-Manors.* Calthorpe; Baggotts.

Tumuli.

There are several barrows situated in the parish: one of Bronze Age date is located at Mill House, with another in the same field originally much larger but now mostly removed to 'facilitate the passage of farm carts entering the gate'; on Barnham Heath a barrow lying under pasture 37 yds in diameter and 3' high, showed no sign of a ditch, but post-holes were found; SW of Blackbird Spinney; S of Duke's Ride - 144' in diameter and 1' 6" high; one in the village at the junction of the A134 and the Elveden road; another of Palaeolithic/ Bronze Age date ½ mile N of the village, E of the A134; and a barrow (?) in a plantation on Thetford Heath *c*27 yds in diameter and *c*10' high.

Stone Age Flint Industry.

Excavations by the British Museum in the late 1990s revealed upwards of fifty tool implements along with large quantities of animal bones including bear, rhino and straight-tusked elephant dating back around 400,000 years.

Ancient Settlement Sites.

A site by the Icknield Way and excavations at East Farm Pit have revealed Lower Palaeolithic and Early to Middle Bronze Age settlement sites along with fortified Iron-Age enclosures.

Iron-Age Fort.

Probably identifying Beorn's 'warrior homestead' *(see place-name)*, this Iron-Age fort is one of only two belonging to the period discovered so far in Suffolk. Measuring 105 yds by 77 yds. and surrounded by a double rampart and ditches, it is only one-third the size of the other at Burgh. Excavations revealed the ditches to be 23' wide and 10' deep.

Ancient Way.

The pre-historic Ickneild Way, from Wiltshire to the Wash, forms the western parish boundary from Shelterhouse Corner, NE to the southern edge of Thetford Forest.

BARNHAM *(continued)*

Ancient Battle (?)
The parish is the reputed site for a battle between the East Anglian King Edmund and the Danes in c870 AD.

Ancient Cross.
On Barnhamcross Common, on the northern bank of the Little Ouse, the base remains of what was known as the 'Franchise Cross' marking the boundary between the Liberty of St Edmund and the Liberty of Thetford.

Site of Historic Moated House & Deserted Medieval Village.
Barnham originally comprised two villages, Barnham St Gregory and St Martin, each with its own church suggesting populous early settlement in the area. St Gregory remains, but St Martin has been lost but for its ruined church and the distinctive outline of a moated site E of the sewerage works with possible fish ponds to the N. This site, seen most clearly from an aerial photograph of 1946, is marked 'Hall Meadow' on the tithe map. Also on the Common are further earthworks of house platforms and trackways associated with the former village.

BARNINGHAM *(6 miles NNE of Ixworth)*

Blackbourn Hundred. 'Homestead or village of the family or followers of Beorn' (OE) *Bernincham* (DB) The parish boundary runs down the centre of Coney Weston village leaving half the village in Barningham. *Manors.* Barningham/Barningham Hall al Senclers Manor (C13 John de St. Clare). *Sub-Manors.* Netherhall; Holdens al Haldens.

Roman Road.
The course of the Peddars Way heads SSE-NNW to form the western parish boundary from a pond at TL948 765 to a small grove at TL945 784. The aggar, now forming field boundaries, marks part of its route.

Medieval Heath.
E and S of Barningham Park was extensive heathland named Barningham Heath and Bardwell Heath on Faden's map of 1783. The heath also extended into Bardwell, Sapiston and Stanton parishes.

Site of old Windmill.
A post mill stood on the E side of the B1111 road to Hopton, NE of the village, in 1783.

Historic House & Ancient Moated Site.
There is a moat in Moat Plantation, NE of the present Hall, connected by a channel to the site of the old Hall, seat of the Shelton family.

BARROW *(6 miles W of Bury St Edmunds)*

Thingoe Hundred. 'Place at the wood or grove' (OE) *Baro* (DB)
Manors. Barrow Manor (C13 Thomas de Barwe). *Sub-Manors.* Feltons; Wolf Hall/Mundefords.

Ancient Woodland.
Higham Grove, on the western parish boundary, and the extensive Wilsummer Wood and the smaller Barnfield Wood SE of the village, are ancient woodland. Wylesmere Wood, shown on a map of 1597, has been lost and there is only a fragment of Great Papeley Wood remaining on the eastern parish boundary.

Site of Tumuli (?)
A tumulus was opened at Barrow Bottom in 1813 and dated as Saxon. In another mound 'in Barrow', a Celtic 'leaf-shaped' bronze sword was discovered. A mound has been described as once standing in the same field as the site of Barrow Hall.

Ancient Moated Mound.
In the grounds of Barrow Lodge, ½ mile NW of the village on the parish boundary with Denham, is a moated mound known as Mote Hill. Its origin is conjectural, for although there is evidence that it was at one time used as the base for a post-mill, its name suggests a much earlier use possibly as the ancient meeting place

BARROW *(continued)*

or, as the moat suggests, a small motte castle which preceded the fortified site at Barrow Hall.

Medieval Market & Fair.

In 1267 Maud Passelewe was granted "a market every week on Saturdays at her manor of Barewe, and a fair every year for three days . . . unless it were to the injury of the neighbouring markets and fairs." About twenty-two years earlier her husband, Hamon, had been granted free warren in Barrow.

Medieval Greens.

Two greens are shown in Barrow on Faden's map of 1783; Barrow Green (Barroughe Greene 1597), a small triangular green, still traced by the original roads at the southern end of the village with ponds along the green edge, and Burthorp Green to the NE, larger, and again outlined by present roads. Both greens have been built upon.

Gallows.

In 1275, the King's Justices found that the bailiffs of Maud Passelewe and William Giffard (her son in law) had erected a gallows in Barrow on which they had put to death a thief, apparently without trial. Its site is unknown but likely occupied one of the burial mounds reported in the parish.

Workhouse.

The parish had a workhouse with 30 inmates in 1776.

Site of old Windmill.

A post mill stood S of Hatchery House in c1730. It was demolished c1883.

Historic Houses & Ancient Moated Sites.

An impressively large, rectangular, ramparted moat, S of the church, marks the site of Barrow Hall. In the second half of the C16, Sir Clement Heigham, former Member of Parliament for Ipswich and Speaker of the House of Commons during the reign of Elizabeth I, built a new hall here which was demolished towards the end of the C18. This may also have been the early C13 site of the fortified manor house of the de Barewe and de Passelewe families. Fish-ponds run N of the site towards the church. Wolfe Hall, S of the village, is Tudor. A rectangular moat on the W side of the former Burthorp Green is now mostly dry with a causeway to the N. It is marked on a map of 1597 as 'Site of Felton's Manor'.

BARSHAM *(2 miles SW of Beccles)*

Wangford Hundred. 'Homestead of a man called Bar (or 'boar' as a nickname)' (OE) *Barsham* (DB)
Manors. Barsham Hall (1534 Blennerhesset family). *Sub-Manors.* Barsham.

Medieval Greens.

A chain of greens is shown running from Barsham in the direction of Ilketshall St Andrew on Faden's map of 1783, but none are named. Clarkes Lane, on the SW parish boundary, had a linear green now marked as High Common on the OS map.

Historic Houses & Ancient Moated Site.

The moated manor house of Barsham Old Hall, N of the parish, built by the Etchinghams (the last of whom died in 1527), has been largely pulled down. The great hall 44' by 28' occupied the height of the building. The remains of what became known as Blennerhassett Tower, from the Blennerhassett family who later resided there, is now represented by a flint range 300' long with fireplaces, now used as a barn but still bearing the family coat of arms and the date 1563. Part of the Rectory is C16, and Ashman's Hall is another old building.

BARTON MILLS *(1 mile SE of Mildenhall)*

Lackford Hundred. Barton - 'Outlying farm or grange where corn is stored' (OE) *Bertuna or Bartona* (DB). It is suggested that the original two Bartons in the county were distinguished by being named Great Barton and Little Barton (or Barton Parva) - now Barton Mills. The latter later derived the name from its very early mills beside the river Lark (*see below*).

BARTON MILLS *(continued)*

Manors. Barton Mills/Monks Hall (-1553 Abbot of St. Edmunds, Bury). *Sub-Manors.* Shardelowes; Pooley Barton; W. Bonners and Torkleys.

Tumulus.
On Chalk Hill, N of Chalk Hill Farm by the Newmarket road, is a Bronze Age barrow, one of an original group of four in line. Excavations in 1923, along with two others excavated in 1869, revealed inhumations and a cremation along with Beaker pottery.

Site of Roman Villa (?)
Claims were made by workmen of a Roman villa, complete with mosaic floor, discovered and destroyed during quarrying at Chalk Hill many years ago.

Site of Ancient Water Mills.
The village, formerly known as Little Barton or Barton Parva, took its present name from the important fulling mill and fishery leased by Bury Abbey and situated where the Newmarket road crosses the river Lark. The industry lasted until 1285 when it was converted to a grain mill. There was at least one other corn mill here belonging to another lord.

Site of Grange & Ancient Moated Site.
A grange of the abbots of Bury Abbey is known to have been situated in Little Barton. Although the exact site is unknown it was likely to have been close to the present Grange Farm where some buildings were shown on Faden's map of 1783. It was described as having chalk-clunch and lime-washed walls and a thatched roof. Just S of Barton Hall are three sides of a narrow rectangular moat, with fish-ponds to the NE.

Templars Preceptory (?)
There is some evidence to support the possible site of a Templars Preceptory of St. Mary here in 1312.

Medieval Market & Fair (?)
The grant of a market and fair to 'Tuwand' in 1220/21 could refer to Barton Mills.

Historic Houses.
Wealda Hall House has C15 origins, and a set of cock-spurs and a fighting hood are preserved at the C17 Bull Inn.

BATTISFORD *(3 miles SW of Needham Market)*

Bosmere & Claydon Hundred. 'Ford of a man called Baetti' (OE) *Betesfort* (DB). The ford in question would appear to have been at the bottom of Hascot Hill where the road crosses the Bat stream rising from the ancient Lady Well spring in the adjoining parish of Badley.
Manors. Battisford/Bishop's Hall (C12 William Gernon). *Sub-Manors.* Lyngges/Ling's; Commandry of St. Johns; Milding Hall.

Ancient Woodland.
A small part of ancient woodland in the form of Great Newton Wood remains on the NE parish boundary.

Site of Preceptory or Commandery of the Knights Hospitallers.
The old moated St John's Manor House, built in the 1570s-80s, stands on the site (and is thought to have been partly built from the materials of) the major command post in Suffolk of the Knights Hospitallers founded *c*1154. This military order originated in a hospital in Jerusalem about 1050 for the tending of sick and weary pilgrims. Battisford had two subordinate members attached to it at Coddenham and Mellis. The knights were granted a market, fair and free warren (*see below*), and in 1275 William de Batesford granted them 40 acres of land and 6 acres of woodland. Further acquisitions included half the church of St. Mary in Battisford in 1338. After the Dissolution it was granted to Andrew Judde, Alderman of London. Remains of a terracotta plaque bearing the arms of Sir Giles Russell, Master of the Preceptory in 1529, was found in the cellar, and an early Tudor terracotta plaque bearing the head of St John the Baptist formerly built into the base of the chimney stack is now over the fireplace.

BATTISFORD *(continued)*

Medieval Market & Fair.
In 1271, Henry III granted these knights a market, fair and free warren on their lands at Battisford.

Medieval Greens.
A large linear green shown as Battisford Tye on the 1783 map was enclosed c1812. It ran E from a short way along Bow Road, bordered by Rookery Farm and Woodlands Farm, to Tyelay Pond and Tye Farm and was later bisected by the present Battisford Straight Road.

Historic House.
Battisford Hall, rebuilt c1655 by Martin Slater, stands beside the site of the former Manor House known as Bishop's Hall, demolished 1757.

BAWDSEY *(10 miles SE of Woodbridge)*

Wilford Hundred. 'Island, or dry ground in the marsh, of a man called Baldhere' (OE) *Baldereseia* (DB). The place-name indicates that this coastal parish must once have been an island. It includes the former smuggling haunt of Shingle Street.
Manors. Bawdsey Manor (1290 Butley Priory and Robert de Ufford). *Sub-Manors.* Bawdsey Antley al Glover's/Bawdsey Willoughbys.

Medieval Market & Fair.
In 1283 Robert de Ufford, Lord of the Manor and twice Chief Justice of Ireland, obtained a license for a weekly market and a 3-day fair. The market was discontinued in 1797, and the fair in 1835.

Historic Fortifications.
A Martello Tower, built in 1812 to defend the coast against a possible invasion from Napoleon, stands by the beach at TM355 397, and there is another further N at TM358 411. A Martello Tower E of Bawdsey Manor on the E bank of the Deben was demolished in 1819 and there is documentary evidence of a fourth at one time situated on the beach E of the church, now demolished or eroded into the sea.

BAYLHAM *(3 miles SSE of Needham Market)*

Bosmere & Claydon Hundred. 'Enclosure or water-meadow at a river-bend' (OE) *Beleham* (DB)
Manors. Baylham Manor (C13 William de Burnavile).

Ancient Woodland.
Ditch Wood, Spink's Wood, Tuttonhill Wood, Knotting Grove, Hulverhill Covert and Raven's Grove are all parts of extensive ancient woodland.

Roman Road.
The Roman road running S-N from Colchester to Caister-by-Norwich and crossing the river Gipping at Sharmford, SSE of Baylham House Farm, is visible on aerial photographs.

Site of Roman Villa.
The Roman town of *Combretorium,* centred on Coddenham, extends into Baylham where a possible Roman villa was discovered in the hamlet of Baylham Stone.

Medieval Green & Common.
A square area lying W of the Baylham to Nettlestead road and bounded by footpaths immediately S of the hamlet of Baylham Stone, is named Newmans Green on Faden's map of 1783. Baylham Common occupied a large portion of the SE of the parish.

Historic Houses & Ancient Moated Site.
Baylham Hall retains a fragment of the T-shaped C16 Manor House of the Acton family and a much levelled former strong moat enclosed by a narrow outer one except on the SE side. Mill House, attractively situated by the old hump-back bridge over the Gipping, has a central core which is thought to date back to pre-Reformation times.

BECCLES

Wangford Hundred. 'Place by the stream in a pasture' (OE) *Becles* (DB)

The place-name may refer to a tributary of the Waveney to the west of the town. Situated in an enviable position on a bold promontory above the river, Beccles was an important town even in the days of the Conqueror when the river could accommodate large herring fleets who used the quays here. Its position might well have led to its becoming a Norman fortress town had it not been for its acquisition by Bury Abbey during the second half of the C10, for whom it provided 60,000 herring a year. Four disastrous fires of 1586, 1662, 1667 and 1669 destroyed virtually all the town's old and notable buildings, but sympathetic rebuilding at the end of the C17 and a programme of careful conservation since then has helped preserve its character. The market dates back to Anglo-Saxon times and its old streets still betray their C11(or earlier) origins through the name 'gate' (Scandinavian *gade* or *gata* meaning 'street').

Manors. Beccles Manor (-1536 Abbot of St. Edmunds, Bury; 1539 William Rede). *Sub-Manors.* Roos/Rose Hall al Jerald's; Ashman's; Pismere/Piswell Castle.

Ancient Tracks.

The street known as Puddingmoor is thought to have once been a very ancient pre-historic track. An ancient packway, still called 'The Packway' and running from Cromwell Road Crossing to Oak Lane, forms the southern parish boundary.

Ancient Earthwork.

Aerial photographs show a substantial enclosure of unknown origin on Beccles Common and Golf Course just NE of the town. It has c328' sides and an inner enclosure with c164' sides. A suggestion of a trackway or bank runs E-W along and beyond the northern edge. Its purpose and origin are unknown.

Ancient Oak & Gibbet (?)

In the medieval park of Roos Hall stands the famous 'Hanging Oak' reputedly over 500 years old. It is so-called from the tradition that in medieval times criminals were executed by being hung from its branches.

Medieval Chapel.

C18 St Peter's House in Saltgate, stands on the site of the C12 St Peter's Chapel. A small portion of its flint fabric remains in a cupboard, and fragments of early stained glass in a rear building may also have come from the chapel. It was used by the fishing community and Divine service was still being performed here in 1470.

Site of Medieval Leper's Hospital & Ancient Chapel.

The Lazer House, a lepers' hospital dedicated to St. Mary Magdalen and St. Anthony, was founded in 1267. It was re-founded in 1361 by Sir R. de Walkfare, and granted with 3 acres of land and an ancient chapel (then disused) by Charles II to the Corporation of Beccles Fen in 1675. The hospital was also described as 'wasted' by this time. St Mary's Hill marks the site and is remembered in Hospital Road which leads off St Mary's Road

Site of Hermitage Chapel.

Hermitage Inn stands on the site of a Hermitage Chapel at the crossing of the Waveney N of the town. Founded before 1458 and dedicated to St Mary, it was dissolved c1546. The site was later used for a public house called 'The Hermitage'. With travel often a hazardous occupation in those times, many chapels were sited at major road and river crossings for travellers to pray for a safe journey.

Medieval Common.

Much of Beccles Common, shown on Faden's map of 1783 as stretching from the Waveney to the Lowestoft road, is now a golf course. The southern part has been lost to Beccles development into Worlingworth parish. The enclosure of the part granted to William Rede in 1540 caused many disputes regarding the rights and useage of the common land.

Site of Martyrdom.

Near the spot where the Baptist Martyrs' Memorial Chapel stands, three townspeople - Thomas Spicer, John

BECCLES *(continued)*

Denny and Edmund Poole - were burnt at the stake in 1556 during the Marian persecutions. A tablet marks the event.

Site of old Windmills.

Bullock's Mill, a post mill dating back to at least 1737 lay S of the town centre, and Ingate Mill, recorded in 1783 in the hamlet of Ingate, was still standing in 1882.

Ancient Market & Fair.

Beccles had one of the few markets already listed as existing at the Conquest. At this time the Abbot took three parts of every customary due from the market and the King a fourth part. The Abbot was granted the right to hold a fair in 1205 and the charter renewed in 1259.

Site of Market Place.

Old Market near St. Peter's Chapel marks the site of the original market. A new site was acquired in the C14 at New Market where it still exists today.

Recreation.

Beccles Races held two meetings annually in the early C18 on the Common. A stand and other buildings were erected for spectators in 1769. Cockfighting often provided an added attraction. Meetings declined and were finally abolished in the 1840s.

Free Grammar School.

Leman House in Ballygate was formerly a free grammar school for 51 boys founded by Sir John Leman, Alderman of London in 1631, and endowed with 100 acres of land. The house, 'beautified' in 1762, dates from the C16.

Almshouses & Workhouse.

Almshouses in Puddingmoor Street for eight poor widows were later used as a workhouse (c1684) and House of Correction (1787).

Gaol.

A charter granted the town right of a gaol in 1584. Impliments of hard labour were retained here till 1879.

Medieval Guildhall.

During riots in 1584 over peoples' rights to pasture their livestock on Beccles Fen, the windows of the 'Guildhall' were broken. This may have been the Old Town Hall and former Court House near the church, rebuilt in 1726. It housed the guilds of HolyGhost, St. Michael, Ascention, Holy Trinity, Holy Name of Jesus and St. Nicholas. The Guildhall was used as an entertainment centre in 1663.

Historic House & Ancient Moated Site.

Roos Hall is situated ½ mile W of the town centre and 500 yds. from the river Waveney. It is conjectured that the earlier hall of Sir Robert de Roos (1321) stood within what was once an encircling moat, only part of which remains. The present hall, built by Thomas Colby in 1583, occupies only a small part of the moated area, but it was once much larger and one of the finest of its period in Suffolk. The Waveney House Hotel has parts dating back to c1592. The White Lion was mentioned as a coaching stop in 1743.

BEDFIELD *(4 miles NW of Framlingham)*

Hoxne Hundred. 'Open land of a man called Beda' (OE) *Berdefelda* (DB)

Manors. Bedfield (-1538 Eye Priory; 1538 Charles Brandon). *Sub-Manors.* Bull Hall/Bullyshall.

Ancient Track.

Hollow Way forms the larger part of the southern parish boundary.

Medieval Greens.

The 32 acres of Bedfield Long Green, shown and named by Faden in 1783 as a linear green running from Bonds Farm to Poplar Farm, were enclosed in 1849; the present road marks its western side. Little Green,

BEDFIELD *(continued)*

SE of the last, still exists as a 13-acre common. An encroachment on the N side was recorded as 'Old Womans Yard'.

Historic Houses & Ancient Moated Sites.
Late C16 Bedfield Hall has a small moat which extends to the W to form another moat originally enclosing a large area. At Bedfield House, Bedfield Little Green, there are three parts of a quadrangular moat, and a moat partly surrounds Low Farm (formerly Pipe's Farm) in Dogs Lane on NE parish boundary, with a smaller one enclosing the grounds. By the T-junction in the centre of the village a small rectangular moat surrounded the former rectory shown on the 1842 tithe map.

BEDINGFIELD *(4 miles SE of Eye)*

Hoxne Hundred. 'Open land of the family or followers of a man called Beda' (OE) *Bedingefelda* (DB)
Manors. Bedingfield Hall (1099 given by William Martel to Abbot of St. John's, Colchester to found Snape Priory; 1524 Cardinal Wolsey). *Sub-Manors.* Flemings/Buck's Hall.

Medieval Greens.
Ducks Green, a semi-circular green shown and named by Faden in 1783, lay S of Bedingfield Street bordered by Bucksgreen Farm; it is now named Buck's Green. Just to the SE, a small square green was called Bedingfield Green. It was enclosed in 1864 and is today marked by Green Farm and Bedingfield Green.

Historic Houses & Ancient Moated Sites.
Flemings Hall lies 1 mile SE of the church. The Manor of Flemings or Bucks Hall can be traced back to the reign of Henry III when the lord was William or Adam de Fleming. The present house, built c1586, stands on an island site approx. 100 yds. square surrounded by a strong moat with brick-lined walls. The site is likely to have encompassed the fortified home of the Bedingfields who lived here for over three centuries from c1309, and even the de Flemings who preceded them. Bedingfield Hall, immediately SE of the last, is encompassed by one of the strongest moats in Suffolk. It measures over 219 yds on each side and contains an area of about four acres; it had a drawbridge until about 1834. The Hall comprises two individual wings, one earlier and possibly once an aisled hall. Evidence suggests it was never a residential manor. In 1069, the Earl of Arundel held his manor of Bennold and by Domesday it was in the possession of Ralph de Limesi as Tenant in Chief. The 1327 Subsidy List shows Peter de Bedingfield as residential owner followed by Adam de Fleming of Flemings Hall. There are three parts of an irregular moat at Bedingfield House, S of Bedingfield Street; and at 'Moated Yards', ½ mile NW of the church, is a well-formed oblong moat.

BELSTEAD (formerly Belstead Parva) *(4 miles SW of Ipswich)*

Samford Hundred. 'Place in a glade'/'place of a funeral pyre'/'Bele's place' (OE) *Belesteda* (DB). Neighbouring Washbrook was anciently Belstead Magna. The place-name meaning is uncertain. Belstead Brook runs through the parish, and the light sandy soil provides conditions for a former Bronze-Age burial mound - two gold torques were found N of Belstead Brook in the 1960s (*see* Ipswich).
Manors. Belstead (C13 William Goldingham).

Ancient Woodland.
Old Hall Wood which runs over the southern parish boundary is part of ancient woodland.

Ancient Way & Ford.
Stone Lodge Lane crossed Belstead Brook just below Gusford Hall at the Domesday *Gutthulvesforda* 'Guthwulf's Ford' in St. Mary, Stoke parish in Ipswich. The manor, however, appears to lie mainly in Belstead.

Historic Houses.
Belstead Hall, N of the church, may stand on the site of the earlier hall of the Goldinghams. One, John, who died in 1518, is commemorated in an armoured brass effigy in the church. Lord of the Manor, William de Goldingham, had "paid fines to Ipswich for freedom from toll for himself and his villeins." in the reign of King John. Belstead House, which is mainly C17 with later additions, has a C16 core.

BELTON *(5 miles SW of Yarmouth)*

Mutford & Lothingland Hundred. 'Place in a glade' or 'an area of dry land surrounded by fen' or 'place of a funeral pyre' (OE) *Beletuna* (DB). Includes the Domesday vill of Gabton *(Gabbetuna).*
Manors. Belton Manor/Gapton Hall (C12 Baruli de Bosco).
The parish registers records a severe outbreak of plague in Belton in 1665.

Tumulus.
Roman pottery has been found in a round barrow at Mill Hill S of the village and 1½ miles S of the Roman fort at Burgh Castle. It is possible that this burial mound is that which gave the parish its name (*see above*).

Medieval Market & Fair.
Leigh Priory obtained a grant of a market and fair here in 1270.

Medieval Common.
Belton Common is shown in 1783 covering all the western side of the parish and running N into Bradwell.

Historic Houses.
Browston Hall, in the hamlet of Browston SE of the village, is a C17 Manor House and former home of the Symonds and the Le Gryce families. Old Hall hides behind a Georgian facade.

BENACRE *(7 miles SE of Beccles)*

Blything Hundred. 'Cultivated plot where beans are grown' (OE) *Benagra* (DB)
Manors. Benacre (C11 Godefridus de Petro Ponti/Pierrepont; 1237 Simon de Pierpont had 'wreck of sea' [claim on cargo washed up from wrecks on the shore] in Benacre). *Sub-Manors.* Flemings/Buck's Hall.

Coin Hoards.
In 1786, at a spot now called Moneytree Clump beside the present A12, a workman engaged in 'cutting the turnpike' skirting the park of Benacre Hall, home of the Gooch family, unearthed a stone bottle containing about 900 silver coins, claimed to be Roman and no later than C1. About twenty years prior to this, an earthen jar containing some 400 pieces of silver from the reigns of Edward I and II had been found in the parish.

Gallows.
In the C13 Robert de Pierpont had free warren and right of gallows in Benacre. The site is not known.

Deserted Medieval Villages.
Although there is now no village in Benacre, it would appear that there have previously been two centres of population. The manor was purchased from the Carthew family in the mid-C18 by Sir Thomas Gooch. The family proceeded to enclose the southern half of the parish, building a mansion, Benacre Hall, within a great park. A scatter of pottery, building flint, burnt clay and field systems S of the isolated church and within the park, suggests that the main settlement was formerly situated here. However, the fact that the pottery was of C13/C14 date and the church bears a tablet on the W wall stating that it was 'decayed through length of time and falling into ruins' when Sir Thomas virtually rebuilt it in red brick, suggests the village had already long been abandoned. The road E of the church is called The Street and is shown to continue to the beach just S of Benacre Sluice on Faden's map of 1783 - its line marked by a public footpath today. In 1065, just prior to the Norman Conquest, Beorngares was a fair sized manor belonging to Wulfsige, Lord of Mutford. It contained 180 arable acres, 10 acres of meadow and enough woodland for eight swine. Also here were two watermills and a saltpan. Apparently an important port in early Norman times when it carried the Domesday name Bringas, it is thought to have been situated by the Hundred river estuary near Benacre sluice.

Historic House.
Benacre Hall was built c1721 on the site of an earlier hall. It was destroyed by fire in 1926 and restored by 1981.

BENHALL *(1½ miles SW of Saxmundham)*

Plomesgate Hundred. 'Nook of land where beans are grown' (OE) *Benenhala* (DB). Includes the Domesday vill of Carlton which, for a time, became a separate parish (*see* Carlton).
Manors. Benhall Manor (c1160 Ralph de Glanvile). *Sub-Manors.* Benhall St. Roberts.

Ancient Woodland.
The extensive Dodd's Wood and the smaller fragments of Benhall Wood, Crane's Wood and Archer's Covert, are ancient woodland.

Anglo-Saxon Industrial Site.
An Anglo-Saxon pottery site was discovered S of Kiln Cottage in the former settlement of Kelton.

Site of old Windmills.
Two mills were standing in the parish in 1736: one occupied the green and was demolished in 1921. Another stood E of Rose Hill House.

Medieval Green.
Benhall Green, named by Faden in 1783, and shown forming a virtual market place just W of Stansfield Church, appeared to have been well populated as it is again today with modern properties.

Medieval Market & Fair.
The C13 Lord of the Manor of Kelton, Guido Kerr (*see below*), obtained the grant for a market and fair in 1282. Only some ten years later these privileges appear to have been transferred to Guy Frere, Lord of the adjoining Manor of Benhall who is recorded as holding a market and fair in Benhall from 1292.

Deserted Medieval Village.
The hamlet of Benhall Green in the SE corner of the parish forms the only village settlement. However, an area W of Benhall church was formerly a settlement of some considerable size known as Kelton. It lay S of Dodd's Wood and was enclosed by country lanes forming an irregular rectangle bordered by disused clay pits in the NW, Silverlace Green on the E, Kelton End and Benhall Street at the SE and Benhall Place at the SW.

Free School.
William Corbold's will in 1746 provided for the education of four poor children of Saxmundham at the school in Benhall.

Historic Houses & Ancient Moated Site.
The earlier Benhall Lodge was built by Sir Edward Duke 38 years after he purchased the manor in 1600. Edward Hollond demolished this building and built the present residence on a different site in 1815 with an extensive park of 130 acres. Manor Farm, S of Benhall Green, has two sides of a quadrangular moat. It is shown on Faden's 1783 map approached by a wide avenue of trees from the Aldeburgh road. This avenue has been lost to the construction of the railway line to Lowestoft.

BENTLEY *(5½ miles SW of Ipswich)*

Samford Hundred. 'Woodland clearing where bent-grass grows' (OE) *Benetleia* (DB). Includes the Domesday vill of Dodnash.
Manors. Bentley Hall (C13 Hugh Talmache). *Sub-Manors.* Old Hall Bentley/Church House; Bentley Fastolfs; Dodnash.

Ancient Woodland.
Great Martin's Hill Wood (which falls partly in the parish) and Dodnash Wood in the S, and Old Hall Wood and Bentley Long Wood in the N, are remains of ancient woodland.

Roman Road.
A length of the Roman road from Colchester to Caister-by-Norwich forms the parish boundary with Copdock.

Medieval Deer Park.
Saxton's map of 1575 shows a deer park at Bentley Hall, parts of which remain in what is now Bentley Park.

BENTLEY *(continued)*

Site of Priory.
A farmhouse situated on the banks of a stream on the southern parish boundary stands on the site of Dodnash Priory. This Augustinian Priory which owned land in fifteen Suffolk parishes, took its name from one of the four Saxon manors here. Founded in 1188 by Maurice de Dodenes for a prior and three Austin canons and dedicated to St Mary, it was suppressed by Cardinal Wolsey in 1525 to help finance his ill-fated college at Ipswich. Nothing remains of the buildings except for a few re-used stones in the walls of the present farmhouse which occupies the site, and a large pond may be the remains of a former fish-pond.

Historic Houses.
The Manor House of Bentley Hall, N of the church, contains a beautifully carved beam with the initials L.T. and S.T. and the date 1528. The initials are believed to be those of Lionel and Susan Tollemache whose family goes back to pre-Norman times. A couplet states 'Before the Normans into England came, Bentley was my seat and Tollemache was my name'. Opposite is the timber-framed Long Barn, Tudor in origin, and at 60 yds, said to be the longest historic barn in Britain. Old Hall, close to the northern parish boundary, is the site of their earlier manor house. In the NE corner of the parish, Hubbards Hall dates from 1591. The old Tankard Inn was the first changing place for horses on the Ipswich-London stage coach.

BEYTON *(5½ miles SE of Bury St Edmunds)*

Thedwestry Hundred. 'Farmstead of a woman called Beage or a man called Baega'? (OE) *Begatona* (DB)
Manors. Beyton (1276 Adam de Ratlesden).

Medieval Green.
The green, in the centre of the village and shown but not named on Faden's map of 1783, remains today.

Historic House & Ancient Moated Site.
C17 Brook Farm, E of the church, has a small square moat of considerable width, its inner side brick-lined.

BILDESTON *(5 miles NW of Hadleigh)*

Cosford Hundred. 'Farmstead (or hill/promontory) of a man called Bildr' (Oscand+OE) *Bilestuna* (DB)
Manors. Bildeston (c1200 Godfrey de Loveyn/Lovaine).

Roman Road.
The Wattisham road, heading NE from the high street, follows the course of a minor Roman road (only 15' wide) until it turns left, from which point the Roman road continues ahead as field boundaries and then along the right side of a small wedge of woodland.

Site of Ancient Chapel.
On the site of the rectory, on the S side of Church Lane (formerly Chapel Lane), was a chapel with Anglo-Saxon origins dedicated to St Leonard, which, before the Reformation, contained the Edrington Chantry. It had possible connections with the priory at Great Bricett and was in existence in 1446. It fell into disuse c1640 but reopened in 1680 as a place of worship because of the distance of the church from the town. It was last mentioned in 1723 and demolished early in the C19.

Site of old Windmill.
A post mill stood SE of the village in 1798. It was gone by 1887.

Medieval Market & Fair.
In 1264, the de Loveynes, Lords of the Manor, obtained the grant for a weekly market and annual fair. With the loss of the manufacture of blue cloth and blankets for which the town was once famous, support dwindled and the market finally closed in the C18; the last fair took place towards the end of the C19.

Site of Deserted Medieval Village (?)
To the S and E of the church and old hall site, linear depressions may represent hollow ways associated with a deserted medieval village - the present village lies in the valley some ½ mile E of the church. These earthworks

BILDESTON *(continued)*

were levelled and ploughed in 1973 but quantities of C13 pottery are now appearing. The de Loveynes were lords of the manor at that time, and the place-name suggests that the earliest settlement was on the hill around the church and hall, probably moving down into the valley of the river Brett with the town's rise to wealth during the height of the cloth industry.

Workhouse.

A workhouse in the village housed 30 inmates in 1776. In 1829 it occupied a large house called Bridewell which was demolished c1864.

Historic House & Ancient Moated Site.

Fragments of an ancient circular moat W of the church, c246' in diameter and now dry, mark the site of the old Hall, the probable residence of the de Lovelynes who held the manor from 1219 until 1397. The earthworks of possible fish-ponds are just to the S. The Crown Inn dates from 1495 when it was a wool merchant's house. Later it became a coaching inn and was used for the Petty Sessions for Hiring Servants.

BLAXHALL *(4 miles SW of Saxmundham)*

Plomesgate Hundred. 'Nook of land belonging to a man called Blaec' (OE) *Blaccheshala* (DB)
Manors. Blaxhall Manor al Ashe Bigots (c1280 Thomas de Weyland). *Sub-Manors.* Valence.
There is a tradition that the population was virtually wiped out by the Black Death in the C14 to be largely replaced by gypsies.

Ancient Woodland.

Documentary evidence of ancient woodland at Long Grove on the SW parish boundary.

Tumuli.

A round barrow 4-5' high and situated on Blaxhall Common ¾ mile E of village, was reported in 1827 to contain 'Roman urns'. Forty years later, in 1867, several Roman coins and urns were unearthed at Grove Farm, suggesting the site of another barrow ½ mile further N.

Roman Pottery Industry.

Roman pottery kilns were discovered at Grove Farm.

Medieval Commons.

The triangular Blaxhall Common, shown and named by Faden in 1783, lay at the E end of Church Road and is now completely built over; the OS map marks the area Mill Common. Water Common lay on the NE side of Farnham Road near the junction with the road going SW to Stone Common and was bordered by Glebe Farm and Gorse Farm.

Site of old Windmill.

Dykes Mill, a post mill dating from at least 1783, stood on Mill Common. It was burned down in 1883.

Historic House.

The Ship public house dates from c1700 and was reputedly involved in smuggling.

BLUNDESTON *(3 miles NW of Lowestoft)*

Mutford & Lothingland Hundred. 'Blunt's farmstead' (OE) *Blundeston* (1203)
Manors. Blundeston Hall (C13 Henry de Blundeston). *Sub-Manors.* Gunvilles al Blunston Gunviles.

Medieval Common.

Blundeston Common is shown on Faden's 1783 map, the northern section bordered by Rectors Wood, Great Wood and Brickhill Wood to the N and Heath Lane to the S. Common Farm marked the northern limit of the irregular southern section and has been enclosed and infilled with major housing development.

Free School.

A school house with one acre was bequeathed by Rev. Gregory Clarke to support a school in 1726.

BLUNDESTON *(continued)*

Historic House & Ancient Moated Site.
At Blundeston Hall, SE of the church, three sides remain of the ancient rectangular moat which formerly surrounded the old hall, seat of the Blundestons. It is connected to a stream.

BLYFORD (or Blythford) *(2½ miles SE of Halesworth)*

Blything Hundred. 'Ford over the Blyth (river-name for 'the gentle or pleasant one)' (OE) *Blideforda* (DB)
Manors. Blyford (C12 De Criketot family).

Ancient Woodland.
Blyford Wood in the N of the parish is part of ancient woodland.

Ancient Lane.
King's Lane is a narrow lane running due N and S from the Halesworth-Southwold road, from Blyford nearly straight to Beccles. Tradition names it as the route taken by King Anna with his East Anglian army to fight King Penda of Mercia in 654 A.D. It is also possible that Anna's body was later borne down this same lane to Blythburgh Church for his internment after he had been mortally wounded. *(see Blythburgh)*

Site of Ancient Earthworks.
Aerial photographs show a large area of enclosures, straight ditches, etc., E of Walnut Tree Farm.

Historic House & Ancient Moated Site.
S of the present Hall is the site of a small rectangular moat with a causeway at the NW corner and attached to a larger irregular moated enclosure; the site has now been destroyed. In the early C17, a house - probably the former hall - was shown within the enclosure. The thatched Queens Head public house dates from the C17.

BLYTHBURGH *(4½ miles W of Southwold)*

Blything Hundred. 'Fort or stronghold on the river Blyth' (OE) *Blideburh* (DB)
Manors. Blythburgh Manor (C12 Bishop of Norwich; mid-C12 John Fitz Robert). *Sub-Manors.* Blythburgh Late Priory; Hinton Late Priory; Westwood.
While there is conjecture over Blythburgh's early origins, there is no doubt that it was well established in Saxon times when a flourishing port with a considerable fishery and its own market (*see below*). By Norman times the Quarter Sessions serving the whole of the Beccles division were held here. Blythburgh reached the height of its prosperity in the C15 and its subsequent decline resulted from the demise of nearby Dunwich, the silting up of the river and the suppression of its priory. It once possessed several streets of houses (which scatters of Medieval pottery sherds suggest also extended N of the river) but a terrible fire in 1676 destroyed most of its fine buildings. In 1679 Blome said of Blythburgh: 'Tis now a poor decayed town'.

Ancient Woodland.
Documentary evidence of ancient woodland remains at Haw Wood, Hinton Long Spring, and near Common Wood in the S of the parish. Broom and Lodge Coverts and Spring and Ling Hill are possibly part of the ancient Bulcamp Wood, location for the bloody battle of 654 A.D.

Tumulus (?)
A possible round barrow was reported on the Nature Reserve SW of Westwood Lodge. A low mound 49' to 66' in diameter and 2' to 2' 6" high was located under heathland.

Roman Fort (?)
It has been erroneously thought that the place name indicates the presence of a Romano-British fort in the vicinity, but although there is evidence of Roman occupation here, there is nothing to support this theory.

Roman Industrial Sites.
Along the length of the shoreline of Bulcamp Marshes from Mile Walk Covert to Wolsey's Creek the Romans had salt and tile production sites.

BLYTHBURGH *(continued)*

Roman Cemetery.
Following the great fire of 1676, a number of Roman urns were dug up among the old buildings and more, along with coins and pottery sherds, have continued to be unearthed.

Site of Ancient Battle.
Tradition says that Anna, the Christian Saxon King of the East Angles, and Firminus, his son, were slain by the heathen King Penda of Mercia in Bulcamp Forest, about 1 mile NW of the village, in 654 A.D. A report in 1763 stated that some five hundred bodies had been unearthed in a field near the church, reputedly from the battle.

Site of Saxon Minster & East Anglian Royal Tomb.
The East Anglian King Anna is said to have been buried at Blythburgh in 654 A.D in 'a church of wood, thatch and mud' on the site of the present church. In the C11 his body was removed to Bury Abbey where he was canonised.

Priories.
In the garden of a house called The Priory, NE of the church, are the scant remains of the Augustinian Priory founded as a cell to the important priory of St Osyth, near Clacton in Essex, possibly by de Chesney, and dedicated to St Mary. Excavations in the mid-C19 indicated that the priory church was cruciform in design with a central tower. Although it was partially independent from St Osyth and possessed considerable property, it remained a small community never appearing to exceed four canons in residence. In 1528 it was granted to Cardinal Wolsey for his college at Ipswich. There was also a priory or hospital of Black Friars who moved here in 1384 from Dunwich when their original site was threatened by the sea.

Site of Ancient Chapel.
Blythburgh Bridge carries the present A12 road over the river Blyth. A wayside chapel called the Chapel of the Holy Cross is mentioned on the N side of the main street leading to the 'great bridge' between 1482-1572, and some walls of this chapel remained standing in 1760. It was quite the normal practice in medieval times to provide a chapel for travellers on the bridges at major river crossings.

Medieval Park.
Westwood Lodge is a former lodge of the park which Sir Owen Hopton is said to have created by enclosing the common land of Blythburgh 'with pail and dyke and laid into his park' in 1567.

Site of old Windmill.
A post mill stood on Priors' Hill in 1736.

Ancient & Medieval Markets & Fairs.
The king owned a market here in 1066, one of the few mentioned prior to the Conquest, and William de Norwich was granted a licence in the C12, privileges conferred on the Lord of the Manor, John de Clavering around 1324. The market was obsolite by 1679. The medieval Market Place stood opposite the priory. Blythburgh also had three annual fairs, one held in the hamlet of Hinton.

Site of Execution.
Toby's Walk and Toby's Barn, S of the village, commemorate the scene of the execution in 1750 of Toby Gill, a 'black drummer' with Sir Robert Rich's Regiment, who was tried and convicted at Bury St Edmunds for the murder of Anne Blackmore on Blythburgh Heath.

Gallows.
A gibbet is recorded as standing by Hulver Heath in 1400.

Gaol.
The House of Correction was said to be in great decay in 1641 and a gaol to be in existence in 1754.

Deserted Medieval Village.
In the S of the parish, on the N bank of Dunwich River, Hinton Hall, Hinton Grange, Hinton Lodge and

BLYTHBURGH *(continued)*

Hinton Long Spring, identify the area of the former parish of Hinton, still shown as such on Faden's map of 1783.

Guildhall (?)

There was likely a guildhall here (probably destroyed in the great fire), which housed the four recorded guilds of St. Barbara, The Blessed Virgin Mary, St. Andrew and St. John.

Almshouses.

Almshouses stood E of the church in 1500.

Workhouse.

The Union Workhouse was built at Bulcamp in 1766. Whilst under construction it was partly destroyed by a mob who had to be dispersed by the military. Although opened 'to house 56 paupers', 352 inmates were recorded a year later and it still housed 264 in 1843.

Historic House.

Westwood Lodge, 2 miles S of the village, stands on the site of the former Manor House of Westwood which was destroyed by fire. Leases for the former hall date from 1573. Blythburgh Lodge is a C16 manor house extended in the C17. The Inn of the Hart was in existence in 1520 on the site of the present White Hart public house. It doubled as a courthouse in the C16.

BOTESDALE *(7 miles NW of Eye)*

Hartismere Hundred. 'Valley of a man called Botwulf' (OE) *Botholuesdal* (1275)
Ecclesiastically a hamlet of Redgrave it became a separate civil parish in 1866.

Ancient Woodland.

Stubbing's Wood, Jacobites Wood and The Grove are parts of ancient woodland.

Roman Pottery Industry.

A Roman pottery kiln was discovered in the parish.

Ancient Chapel.

Situated in The Street, St Botolph's Chapel, founded in Anglo-Saxon times, overlooked the valley of a small rivulet. From it, the village was named Botolph's Dale, now corrupted to Botesdale. The present simple, single-cell chapel was built c1500 and later refounded as a chantry by John Sherife, his wife and Bridget Wykys. It was later used as a chapel-of-ease to neighbouring Redgrave.

Site of old Windmills.

Three mills are recorded dating back to at least the C18: one stood in the village W of Street Farm in 1764; another, a post mill of pre-1777, can be traced to Mill Road, E of the village (demolished c1916), and one is recorded in 1783 by the A143, N of the village.

Medieval Greens.

Common Road now runs down the middle of what was Botesdale Green - named and shown on Faden's map of 1783 - in a SSW direction from just N of Lodge Farm to just S of Potters Lane. Another long green shown but not named on the same map lay behind the street running N from the church bordered on the W by the stream and the parish boundary. Both greens were enclosed in 1818 but not developed.

Medieval Market & Fair.

The village formerly had a market, granted in the C13 to the Abbey at Bury as lords of Botesdale, Redgrave and Gislingham. There was also a fair by a charter of Henry III on a two-acre site known as Black Hills. Both were obsolete by 1844.

Free School.

A Free School was founded by Sir Nicholas Bacon in a house adjoining the chapel in 1576. Later, it became a grammar school before closing in 1883.

BOTESDALE *(continued)*

Historic House.

Hamblyn House (1508), is one of several old houses in the street reflecting its more prosperous past.

BOULGE *(2½ miles N of Woodbridge)*

Wilford Hundred. 'Uncultivated ground covered with heather, etc.' (OE) *Bulges* (DB). Odo de Campania held Bulges and Depebeck (Debach) at Domesday when it is likely that Debach was under forest and Boulge the main centre of settlement.

Manors. Boulge Manor (c1267 Bovile family; 1281 Queen Margaret [annexed to Debach]).

Ancient Track.

An ancient packway, probably that which ran between Bigod's castles at Walton, Framlingham and Bungay, passed through Boulge now as a public footpath from Horse Covert NNE to the road and then (from a short distance SE along the road) NE as a track to the parish boundary.

BOXFORD *(5 miles SW of Hadleigh)*

Babergh Hundred. 'Ford where box-trees grow' (OE) *Boxford* (C12)

Manors. Coddenham (1086 Ralph of Linesy); Boxford Manor (1275 Godfrey de Bellomonte). *Sub-Manors.* Peyton Hall; Coddenham Hall; Boweshowse al Bornhouse; Calthorpe Hall; Badleys/Badley Hall; Georges.

Cremation Cemeteries.

Two Belgic cremation cemeteries have been discovered in the parish on a tributary of the river Stour.

Roman Road.

As its name suggests, the hamlet of Stone Street on the W side of the stream lies on the course of a Roman road running SE - NW, to Bridge Street, N of Long Melford.

Site of old Windmills.

A post mill recorded at Cherry Ground in 1783 was still standing in 1885. A smock mill recorded at the same time was burned down in 1901; it stood on the S side of Boxford Lane, SE of the village.

Medieval Market.

Boxford had an early market for which it did not obtain an official grant.

Workhouse.

A workhouse with 30 inmates is recorded in 1776.

Free School.

A Free Grammar School was established in the village by a charter of Queen Elizabeth I in 1596. The site is now a private house called The Old School House.

Historic Houses.

Peyton Hall, 1½ miles S of the village and SW of Whitestreet Green, was the Manor House of the ancient family of Peyton from whom came the Uffords, Earls of Oxford. The Elizabethan Coddenham Hall is now a farmhouse. It is built near the site of the ancient manor house, formerly the seat of the Brands and the Bennetts. The White Hart public house dates from the C16 and the Fleece is a former coaching inn.

BOXTED *(6 miles NE of Clare))*

Babergh Hundred. 'Place where beech-trees or box-trees grow' (OE) *Boesteda* (DB)

Manors. Boxted Manor (C12 Forfeited by Roger Poictou and held by William Hervey). *Sub-Manors.* Troketts al Truckets; Mores.

Ancient Woodland.

There is documentary evidence of ancient woodland W of the church at Longley Wood, Lownage Wood, Park

BOXTED *(continued)*

Wood and Oak Grove, and at Rochester Wood just NE of the village.

Tumulus.

An old map shows a round barrow to the E of Boxted Hall on the right of the present B1066 and immediately S of a footpath heading NE towards Nine Acre Plantation.

Site of Water Mill (?)

N of Lodge Farm where the northern parish boundary with Somerton meets at a ford, the former site of a water mill is suggested by field names of 'Mill Meadow' and Mill Field'.

Site of old Windmill.

A smock mill is recorded at Fenstead End in 1783.

Historic Houses & Ancient Moated Sites.

Situated in the valley below the church, Boxted Hall, dating from the C16, has a strong moat crossed by an old Tudor bridge. The inner site is oblong but the external bank assumes an oval form. The house was built by William Poley in a 90 acre park on a manor originally belonging to the Abbey at Bury. There is a curious moat, irregular in size and plan, at Moat Farm in the hamlet of Felstead End one mile W of the village. Truckett's Hall, formerly a sub-manor, S of the parish, is also moated, and NE of this are remains of a moat on the site of Tittle Hall.

BOYTON *(7½ miles SE of Woodbridge)*

Wilford Hundred. 'Farmstead of a man called Boia' (OE) *Boituna* (DB)

Manors. Boyton/Boyton Hall Manor (-1538 Belonged to Butley Priory; 1538 Anne of Cleeves).

Tumuli.

A flat-topped round barrow c54' in diameter and 4' high, lies W of Valley Farm, and another mound or small barrow is attached to the parish boundary bank between Boyton and Capel St Andrew.

Iron-Age Find.

SE of Boyton Hall Farm on the bank of the River Ore, near Boyton Marshes, a fine gold torque some 18" long was found 12' down in a loom pit in 1835. It is now on display in the British Museum.

Medieval Heath.

Boyton Heath, named on Faden's map of 1783, lay on the W side of the present A12, SW of the village.

Old Dock.

An old barge jetty remains on the river Butley at Boyton Dock, E of Dock Farm. From here a quality clay, discovered in the parish and used for fine pottery, was shipped. The dock was also used during two brief spells of a short-lived brickmaking industry and also for the import of coal from Newcastle.

Almshouses.

The imposing Warner almshouses situated near the church were provided by the will of Mary Warner who held the manor and died in 1757. It was initially intended for 6 poor men and 6 poor women each to have 4s a week; the men also to have annually 'suits of brown warm clothes' comprising a coat, waistcoat and breeches, and the women new gowns and petticoats. The income of the trust was such that in 1835 and 1847 wings were added to the original building to double the accommodation.

BRADFIELD COMBUST (formerly Little Bradfield) *(5 miles SE of Bury St Edmunds)*

Thedwestry Hundred. 'Broad clearing' (OE) *Bradfelda* (DB). Bradfield was a single township until Domesday, its sole church lay in what is now Bradfield St. George. This was given to Bury Abbey and it became Monks' Bradfield. The second manor was also given to the Abbey and its later grange burned in the Peasants' Revolt of 1329 when a subsidy termed it Parva Bradfield, later Brent Bradfield and later still Bradfield Combust - the *Victoria County History* states that it was also known as Bradfield Manger, and there is a public house of that name in the village. The manorial chapel of the third emerged in 1317

BRADFIELD COMBUST *(continued)*

'ascribed to Saint Clare' - it had been founded by the Seyncler family.
Manors. Bradfield Combust al Roos Manor (1314 Thomas Fitz Talbot). *Sub-Manors.* Sutton Hall. Copinger noted another manor in Bradfield held by William de Ufford in the C14.

Ancient Woodland.
Field patterns now outline what was ancient woodland now lost at Sutton Hall Wood. An unnamed wood N of Oldhall Green may represent a remaining fragment.

Roman Road.
The course of a Roman road runs S-N through the parish on the line of the present A134 road from the parish boundary S of Bradfield Loft Farm to the Inn where the modern road leaves it by veering NW. Its approximate line is continued for a short way by a country road which then swings E at the northern parish boundary.

Historic Houses & Ancient Moated Sites.
The strong square moat of the abbot's grange (*see above*) is still outlined in earthworks just W of the present hall in Bradfield Park, itself only built in 1857 to replace a previous hall. Bradfield House is C17 and The Manger public house C16. Sutton Hall, SE of the village, has a quadrangular moat, the S side in Cockfield parish, with other features to the NE.

BRADFIELD ST CLARE *(5 miles SE of Bury St Edmunds)*

Manors. Manor of Bradfield (1207 Gerebert de St. Cleer and 1253 John le Seycler held the manor by the service of 1½ knights fees from the Abbot of St. Edmunds at Bury).

Ancient Woodland & Deer Park.
The manorial seat was said to be 'situate in a noble park'. Bradfield Woods, comprising Monks' Park Wood and Felsham Wood in the adjoining parish, were owned by Bury Abbey. Founded within seventy years of the Conquest, the abbots created a deer park of some 220 acres called Monks' Park, well documented back to 1252. The wood's boundary which is still demarcated by a mighty bank remained virtually unaltered until the 1960s when nearly two-thirds of the woodland within the park was destroyed. Its saviour was the Suffolk Trust for Nature Conservation who purchased what remained and now manage it exactly as in Medieval times.

Martyrdom of St Edmund (?)
Whilst the legend of St Edmund and his death at the hands of the Danes and subsequent martyrdom has brought great wealth and interest to those with whom it is associated, much has been accepted as no more than legend adding colour and spice to a sordid and cruel event. Claims for the site of his execution and intitial burial are still no more than conjectural. The only clear facts we have are that 'Edmund led his forces into battle at a place called 'Haegelisdun' and was defeated. He was taken prisoner, cruelly put to death and buried nearby at Sutton'. Hoxne's claim to be the site has been widely accepted since Medieval times (*see Hoxne*). Now investigations by Dr. Stanley West have made a case for Bradfield: in this parish, is a field called 'Hellesden' and one mile S, in the adjoining Bradfield Combust, is Sutton Hall; both sites are only five miles from Bury St Edmunds and its Abbey where Edmund's body was later taken.

Medieval Greens.
Maypole Green, named by Faden in 1783, lay across the parish boundary with Bradfield St George within an area now defined by a curving lane heading SW from Felsham Road, SE to Bishop's Farm, returning by a field boundary to Felsham Road. Pitcher's Green, named on the same map and also on the OS, is not shown on either, and Bradfield Bush presumably marks the tiny triangular (green ?) on the junction of the entrance drive to Bush Green Farm with Bury Road, and named Bush Green on the present OS map.

Deserted Medieval Village (?)
Though there is no village settlement in the parish, one may have existed in medieval times around the now isolated church. Here a spread of medieval occupation pottery and a small patch of burnt clay may indicate

BRADFIELD ST CLARE *(continued)*

the presence of former dwellings, whilst remains of an early hall in the form of ancient moated earthworks (*see below*) lie just NE of the church. Just NE of this site, old properties (now gone) are shown abutting the lane between Bush Green and Pitcher's Green on Faden's map of 1783.

Historic House & Ancient Moated Sites.

St Clare Hall, one mile E of church, marks the site of the Hall, formerly used as a grange for the monks of Bury Abbey. In the C12 Gerebert de St. Cleere, a Norman knight from St Clare-sur-Epte, held this place, and the church was presumably first dedicated to him, their patron. A century later, Clare, St Francis's friend, was canonised and the Bradfield dedication and allegiance switched to her. This site may have been the first post-Conquest home of this family, although an alternative site is within a curiously irregular moated site just E of the church at Pitcher's Green, where a C14 guilded bronze seal die of the Earden of the Friars Minors (Franciscans) of Canterbury was found. Only the S and W sides which broaden in places to 30' and 60' remain, although the outline of the E side can still be traced. Church Farm is another fine old timber-framed house.

BRADFIELD ST GEORGE *(4½ miles SE of Bury St Edmunds)*

Manors. St. George/Monks Bradfield (Held by the Abbot of St. Edmunds, Bury).

Ancient Woodland.

Bradfield Woods Reserve, a pre-Conquest wood coppiced since at least the C13, is protected and managed by the Society for the Promotion of Nature Reserves. It may be visited on application to the warden at Felsham.

Roman Road.

The course of a suspected minor Roman road follows a short section of sunken lane N from Laurel Farm on the Felsham road and then as a public footpath following the hedge line to cross the river Blackbourn at TM923 596. From here the route goes E of Free Wood to meet the parish and district boundary at Freewood Farm. When sectioned, the road was found to be 23' wide.

Medieval Greens.

Bradfield Green, shown in 1783 as a square green on the S side of Chapel Road, adjoined Kingshall Green, Rougham, to the N. Another small green ran SW from this, to the E of the church. The small rectangular Smallwood Green lay SW-NE and has been replaced by the road in the hamlet of Smallwood Green.

Historic Houses & Ancient Moated Sites.

Hall Farm, adjoining the church, incorporates reused components from an earlier aisled hall house; traces of the earlier moat remain. Cargate Farm, in Cargate hamlet, SE of the parish, retains a fragment of its moat.

BRADWELL *(8 miles NW of Lowestoft)*

Mutford & Lothingland Hundred. 'Place at the broad spring or stream' (OE) *Bradewell* (1211) Includes the Domesday vill of Browston.

Manors. Bradwell Hall (C13 Osbert de Daggord). *Sub-Manors.* Caxton Hall; Browston Hall; Hubland Hall/Habbelond's; Gapton Hall. Caxton Hall (owned by the prior of St. John's of Jerusalem) and Gapton Hall (owned by the prior of Leigh Priory in Essex) were granted to the Cavendish family at the Dissolution. The township of Hornes is possibly represented by Hobland Hall which occupies a possible Danish site. Inexcusably transferred to Norfolk in 1976 boundary changes, the parish is now partially enveloped by the western sprawl of Great Yarmouth suburbs.

Tumulus (?)

A possible tumulus stood in the SE angle of Hobland Hall Park.

Medieval Commons.

Bradwell Common is shown in the area of Bradwell Hall in the N of the parish on Faden's 1783 map. Another common now appears to be occupied by housing and a school.

BRADWELL *(continued)*

Site of old Windmill.
A post mill recorded in 1736 was still standing NE of the church in 1903.

Market & Fair.
The granting of a market and fair was made in 1252, possibly to Osbert de Daggord who held the manor in the C13. The market was probably sited in the area of Market Road.

Historic Houses.
Hobland Hall, on the southern parish boundary, is a late C18 house in a well-wooded park of 36 acres (1844). Gutted by fire in 1961, it possibly occupies the site of the old manor house.

BRAISEWORTH *(2 miles SW of Eye)*

Hartismere Hundred. 'Enclosure infested with gadflies' or 'belonging to a man nicknamed Briosa' (OE) *Briseworde* (DB)
Manors. Old Hall Manor (C11 Sir Robert Sackville held of the Honor of Eye). *Sub-Manors.* Newhall; Bowell's Hall/Boville's; Barnies/Rooky's.

Ancient Woodland.
Steggall's Wood, on the NW parish boundary, is a part of ancient woodland.

Ancient Linear (Boundary/Defensive?) Ditch.
Grimm's Ditch, referred to in field names and in a C13 charter relating to Thornham Parva, runs W-E through the village of Thornham Parva (not evident on the ground here except in field alignments), then after crossing the A140 Ipswich - Norwich (Roman) road, enters Braiseworth where it forms the parish boundary on the line of the B1117 as far as Ash House, then straight on along a track called Put Lane. The purpose of the ditch is unknown. It may have once formed a division between the northern Iceni tribe and the southern Trinovantes, or even a defensive ditch dug by the Iceni to delay the Roman forces progress N to establish their headquarters at Caister St Edmund, just outside Norwich. Notwithstanding, the Romans eventually took this Iceni stronghold and made their base there, naming it *Venta Icenorum.*

Roman Road.
The modern A140 follows the course of the Roman road to form the western parish boundary.

Deserted Medieval Village.
Berisford lists Braiseworth as a deserted medieval village. Seven taxpayers were assessed here in 1327. A medieval village settlement may have occupied either side of the lane running N from the Norman remains of St Mary's Church roughly parallel to the river. At least four properties lined this now barren former route to Eye with traces of property boundaries still evident.

Historic House & Ancient Moated Site.
The two main manors here were Old Hall and New Hall. C19 and current OS maps name the site beside the river Dove on the southern parish boundary 'Braiseworth Hall' and 'Braiseworth Old Hall Farm'. Whilst marking but not naming a building in the same position, Faden's 1783 map shows a 'Braiseworth Hall' E of Gardiner's Hall, on the eastern side of the road just N of the road junction, a site not shown or suggested on recent OS maps, but marked as a small square in a rectangular plot and unnamed on the C19 OS. There are remains of a moat at The Orchards (formerly Rectory Farm). Potters Farm (Church Farm?) of c1580, on the right side of the lane leading to the site of the old church, has unusual mouldings.

BRAMFIELD *(2 miles S of Halesworth)*

Blything Hundred. 'Open land where broom grows' (OE) *Brunfelda* (DB)
Manors. Bramfield (1269 John de Vallibus). *Sub-Manors.* Brookhall.

Ancient Woodland
Kingstall Wood, SW of the village, and Bramfieldhall Wood, SE, are ancient woodland.

BRAMFIELD *(continued)*

Roman Road.

In no place is the Roman Stone Street ,which passes NNW-SSE through the parish, evident on the ground.

Ancient Earthworks.

'Castle Yard', S of Castle Farm and E of Bramfield Hall, is a circular enclosure in pasture on an elevated site approached by a possible causeway. It comprises a slightly raised platform c71 yds. in diameter enclosed by a circular ditch of no great size or strength, and little to suggest any form of defensive bank. Although in recent times only a single sherd of possibly C12 date has been found on the site, there are claims of Roman and pre-Roman finds here which, if they could be varified, would suggest a possible small Romano-British hill fort protecting two Roman routes. A few miles to the E is Roman Stone Street, with another possible Roman road running from Halesworth to Dunwich which would have passed even closer. It may have later been adapted to provide a residence for the de Bramfields who held the manor of Bramfield as tenants of the Honour of Richmond in the C12. Earl's Way, part of Dunwich Lane, an ancient packway also appears to pass directly by the site (*see below*).

Ancient Oak.

'When the Baily had ridden to Bramfield Oak, Sir Hugh was in Ilketshall bower; When the Baily had ridden to Halesworth Cross, He was singing in Bungay tower . . .' So went part of an ancient ballad describing Earl Hugh Bigod's retreat before Henry II's men to the comparative safety of his castle of Bungay in the C12. Amazingly the tree to which this refers only fell in 1843 leaving the stump of this ancient oak - which once stood beside the old highway - incorporated into Bramfield Park where it still remains, S of Bramfield Hall.

Ancient Track.

An ancient track known as the Earl's Way enters the parish from the Peasenhall Road at Earlsway Farm, running NE passing S of Kingstall Wood to Castle Yards. The name refers to the Earls of Richmond, one of whom, Earl Alan of Richmond, held the manors of Bramfield and Kettleburgh at Domesday, through which the track appears to run. It pointedly skirts the boundary of the manor of Peasenhall, held by the prosperous Bigods, the family with which the track has often been mistakenly associated.

Ancient Stone Circle (?)

The parish is said to contain twelve large stones and eight smaller stones arranged in a circular pattern. Site and origin are unknown.

Ancient Chapel.

A chapel over which the Priory of St. Osyth had rights was mentioned in 1281. Its site and history are not known.

Medieval Market & Fair.

John de Vallibus obtained the grant for a market, fair and free warren in 1270.

Former Almshouse.

The will of Thomas Neale, lord of the manor of Bramfield cum Brook Hall in 1701, left orders for the erection and endowment of an almshouse for four single persons, providing for each a room and half a rood of land. This was duly built in 1723 for eight poor people. It was demolished in 1968.

Historic Houses & Ancient Moated Sites.

Bramfield Hall, former seat of the Rabett family who resided here for 400 years, is Tudor behind a Georgian facade. Holly Farm, ¾ mile NE of the village, is timber-framed and probably early C17. The site of the former Tudor manor house of Old Brook Hall, demolished in 1805, may be NNW of the village where the present hall stands, or at Broad Oak Farm SW of this which was named 'Bramfield Old Hall' by Faden in 1783. It was the residence of Arthur Coke, third son of Sir Edmund Coke, Lord Chief Justice of England in the reign of James I. A 1629 inventory lists 24 rooms. A map of 1745 shows a moat, now gone, at Bunkers Hill Farm, S of Kingstall Wood, SW of the village.

BRAMFORD *(2½ miles NW of Ipswich)*

Bosmere & Claydon Hundred. 'Ford near where broom grows'(?) (OE) *Branfort* (DB). Includes the hamlet of *Runcton* N of Sproughton and represented by Runcton Farm.
Manors. Bramford/Carlton (C13 Robert de Rheims). *Sub-Manors.* Lovetot; Normans with Beverlies; Overtye; Fricketts; Weylands; Kentons.

Ancient Woodland
Round, Bullen and Miller's Woods, and Bushey, Fore and Gobert's Groves, are ancient woodland.

Tumuli (?)
Two barrows (now ploughed out) were situated on a terrace to the W of the river Gipping, E of Lower Dairy Farm. A possible long barrow is suggested by oval crop marks S of Bullen Farm.

Roman Road.
The B1113, known here as Loraine Way, passes S-N through Bramford tracing the course of the C3 Roman road from Stratford St Mary to Caister St Edmund. It follows the left bank of the Gipping before crossing at Baylham.

Ancient Lane.
Grindle Lane marks the Anglo-Saxon boundary between Bosmere and Samford Hundreds as well as the parish boundary between Bramford and Sproughton. The name Grindle means 'stream by a track', exactly as it remains today.

Ancient Ford.
The B1067 road crosses the river Gipping near the church, site of the ancient ford of the place-name.

Site of Ancient Chapel.
A chapel was mentioned here in 1338. Its site is unknown.

Medieval Greens.
A square green called Bramford Tye lay immediately N of Tye Farm in Tye Lane, W of the parish, and is shown on Faden's map of 1783. Further S, the L-shaped Bulling (Bullen) Green was sited on the N side of Bullen Lane between Bushey Grove to the N and Bullen Wood to the S.

Site of Historic Houses.
Approached by Hall Walk from the B1113, Bramford Hall, built by John Acton in the C17 and shown on Faden's 1783 map, stood in a 300-acre park to the W of the village. It has gone, as has Bullen Hall their earlier residence. Bullen Lane and Bullen Wood remain, whilst Bullenhall Farm may occupy the original site.

BRAMPTON *(5 miles NE of Halesworth)*

Blything Hundred. 'Farmstead where broom grows' (OE) *Bramtuna* (DB)
Manors. Brampton (1270 Alan de Wymondale). *Sub-Manors* Hales Hall (1325 Walter Hales).

Site of Ancient Cross.
'In a field in the parish' was the base of an ancient cross said to mark the spot where the Court Leets were originally held.

Site of Ancient Chapel.
An ancient chapel, founded by Robert Seffeld in 1310 and dedicated to St Bartholomew, was situated in the parish. Its site is unknown.

Medieval Market & Fair.
There was a grant to hold a market and fair in 1251 and Lord of the Manor, Alan de Wymundale, obtained a further grant in 1271.

Moated Mound.
W of Station Road, which runs between Brampton and Redisham, a circular moat surrounds a mound some 88' in diameter and 9' above the water level. The moat varies between 9' and 15' in width. The

BRAMPTON *(continued)*

entrance is of the SW and there is a dog-leg extension running in a NW direction for 9'. The outer bank of the moat is ramparted. C13-C14 pottery sherds, and a few Roman, have been found on the mound. It is only a short distance from the old moated Brampton Hall with which it was perhaps once associated.

Workhouse.
A workhouse is recorded in the parish accommodating ten inmates in 1776.

Historic House & Ancient Moated Sites.
Brampton Old Hall, now a farmhouse, was built in 1796 on the site and within the ancient moat of an earlier hall, destroyed by fire in 1733. It was long the residence of the famous Leman family, one of whom was Lord Mayor of London. The moat has banks 4' above the water with an entrance on the W. To the W of this moat, another encloses a small island. Interestingly, another smaller manor here, that of Hales Hall, was the residence of another Lord Mayor of London, Roger Duke, who held the office for four consecutive years 1227-1230. The remains of a moat at Manor Farm, NW of the church and rectory, may be the site of the manor house of Hales Hall. Faden possibly wrongly named it 'Brampton Hall' on his map of 1783. NW of the village at Holly Bush Farm are three sides of a narrow moat. The Rectory retains fragments of its former moat, and Hill Farm, by the southern parish boundary, had a moat (probably square) backfilled in 1971.

BRANDESTON *(4 miles SW of Framlingham)*

Loes Hundred. 'Farmstead of a man called Brant' (OE) *Brantestona* (DB)
Manors. Brandeston (C13 Alan, Lord Burnell). *Sub-Manors.* Brandeston Ryboffs.

Ancient Woodland.
Jubilee Wood, Kiln Wood and Whin Covert are parts of ancient woodland.

Ancient Track.
Friday Street is thought to have been an ancient green lane.

Quakers' Burial Ground.
A Quakers' burial ground was located at Friday Street in c1704.

Site of Moated Mound (?)
In Friday Street, just 300 yds. W of Monewden Hall, 'on the top of the hill stands a distinct mound which is circular and enclosed by a moat obliterated on the S by the garden of an old cottage which is built on the mound'.(Morley) This mound, no longer evident, may have held (and pre-dated?) a post-mill, noted in 1836, but not located.

Pound.
The village Pound was formerly situated opposite the forge.

Almshouses.
Almshouses are recorded here in 1674 occupied by five poor persons. There was a Town House recorded in 1754.

Historic Houses & Ancient Moated Sites.
Brandeston Hall, now a school, lies to the S of the church. It was home to the Revetts from 1543 to 1845. Mostly destroyed by fire in 1854, it was rebuilt in Elizabethan style with the E wing remaining from the old house. The original vicarage, situated at The Broadhurst, has a C13 central core. Moat Farm, NW of the village, is a manor house still within its ancient moat. The Priory, ¾ mile to the N, dates from 1586. The Queens Head public house dates from c1447; The Yews, formerly the Seven Bells public house, is C17; Number 32, The Street, is C17 and Number 50, The Street, C16. Willow Lodge dates from c1700 and is a former chapel. Three sides of an isolated, dry, oblong moat remain on the SW parish boundary, E of Tabie's Wood in Friday Street.

BRANDON *(8 miles NNE of Mildenhall)*
Lackford Hundred. 'Hill where broom grows' (OE) *Brandona* (DB)
Manors. Brandon Manor (1250 granted to the Bishop of St. Etheldreda, Ely).
A small town on the border with Norfolk surrounded by heathland, warrens and conifer forests. Flint found here in large quantities is said to be the best in the world and the town became known for the making of gun-flints and general flint-knapping. Many of the local houses are built or ornamented in flint. The famous Grimes Graves, where these flints were mined in prehistoric times, are a mile or so away across the border. There were also extensive warrens in the area producing a considerable trade in rabbit skins and furs, and the river was at one time navigable for barges. The area is rich in archaeological material.

Tumuli & other Mounds.
A round barrow in Mount Plantation to the W of Lingheath Farm is 50' in diameter and 1'-2' high. Another is in Conifer Plantation and is 22 yds in diameter and 5' high; a third close by is 33 yds in diameter, flat-topped and 5' high (mutilated on the N side), and a fourth, at North Court in the area of the other barrows, could also be a garden feature as a former owner of North Court is believed to have been buried in a tomb in the garden! A circular mound, 56' in diameter and just over 3' high, is situated in woodland between Brandon Park House and Lodge on the B1106 - this may be another ornamental feature(?) There are other mounds of unknown date and origin at White Hill, S of the town, and just to the E of this.

Site of Roman Building.
A Romano-British settlement site NE of the Little Ouse extends S into Suffolk where a Roman building and Terra Sigillata of C1-C2 A.D. was found near Fenhouse Farm.

Lower Palaeolithic - Middle Saxon Settlements.
Excavation work over recent years between the church and the river has revealed an extensive occupation site covering all archaeological periods. This site is claimed to be one of the most important of the Middle Saxon period yet discovered in Britain.

Site of Battle and Norman Encampment (?)
It is known that heavy fighting took place near Brandon when the Conqueror's army was subduing the Saxons who were holding out under Hereward in the 'Camp of Refuge' on the Isle of Ely. In 1868 some human remains were found and townspeople talk of skeletons of tall, fine-limbed men along with swords and head-pieces unearthed during 1878-80 on the water meadow between the church and Little Ouse, just S of the staunch across the river. Examination showed the site had been irregularly and perhaps hastily moated on all sides.

Ancient Chapel.
The possible remains of the Chapel of St Andrew, mentioned in a 1251 terrier of Brandon Manor, was discovered during excavation work on the Palaeolithic-Middle Saxon settlement site (*see above*).

Site of Medieval Bridge.
Brandon Bridge, one of the few Medieval bridges which remained in the county, was demolished in the C20. A wooden bridge here in 1487 had replaced a ferry - High Street being once known as Ferry Street.

Site of Hermitage Chapel.
The remains of a wayside chapel dating from 1180-1280 which stood by the medieval Brandon Bridge, may still be seen to the rear of Brandon House Hotel on the N side of the river.

Site of old Windmill.
A mill is recorded on Mill Hill in 1736. Its fate is not known.

Medieval Market & Fair.
The Bishop of Ely obtained the grant for a market and fair here in 1271. They were obsolete by 1679.

Free School.
A free grammar school for forty scholars was endowed by Robert Wright of Downham Hall in 1646. The

BRANDON *(continued)*

school was demolished in 1877.

Guildhall (?)

The fact that the guilds of Holy Trinity, St. Mary, St. Peter and St. George (1471), and St. Cross (1469) are recorded in the town strongly suggests that a guildhall once existed here.

Workhouse.

A workhouse is recorded with 21 inmates in 1776. It was converted to a National School in 1843.

Amshouses.

A cottage adjoining the church, given in trust by Mrs Anne Curtis in 1675 for three poor families, was rebuilt in 1840. Halls Almshouses in High Street (1698) were rebuilt in 1877 and destroyed in a fire of 1894.

Historic House.

Brandon Hall, ½ mile W of the town, was built in 1690. The Ram Hotel probably dates from the C14 when many pilgrims to the shrine at Walsingham broke their journey here.

BRANTHAM *(8 miles SW of Ipswich)*

Samford Hundred. 'Enclosure or water-meadow of a man called Branta'? (OE) *Brantham* (DB)

Manors. Brantham (-1547 Given to Battle Abbey along with the berewicks (sub-manors) of Bercold, Scotlege, Meelflege and Benetlege; 1547 Earl of Oxford). The parish includes the hamlet of Cattawade.

Ancient Woodland.

Spooner's Wood, The Haugh and Braham Wood, N and NW of Braham Hall, are ancient woodland.

Site of Hermitage Chapel.

A wayside travellers' chapel, built c1350 and situated on Cattawade Bridge which spans the Stour between Suffolk and Essex, was mentioned by Kirby in 1764.

Historic Houses & Ancient Moated Sites.

Brantham Hall, situated E of the village and now a farmhouse, was the seat of Sir Humphrey Wingfield during the first half of the C16. The 1839 tithe map shows that it once had a rectangular moat adjoining the S side of the present hall measuring 65½ yds N-S and 71 yds E-W; it has now been filled in. Braham Hall in the hamlet of Cattawade also had a rectangular moat and is now a farmhouse. It was the residence of the Braham family (Sir John Braham was mentioned in 1460) and the C16 home of Thomas Tusser, the agriculturist, whose widely aclaimed work *Hundred Good Points of Husbandry* was first published in 1557. Brantham Bull, E of the village, is a timber-framed inn dating back to the C16.

BREDFIELD *(3 miles N of Woodbridge)*

Wilford Hundred. 'Broad stretch of open country' (OE) *Bredefelda* (DB)

Manors. Bredfield Manor (pre-1199 Peche family, 1308 Queen Margaret). *Sub-Manors.* Unnamed (1298 Robert de Ufford); Bredfield Campsey.

Ancient Woodland.

Queen's Wood and Oak Grove in the NW corner of the parish are ancient woodland.

Ancient Way.

An old Packway which ran from the Bigod's castle at Walton near Felixstowe to their castle at Framlingham was known as Walton Lane or 'Earl's (Bigots) Way'. It crossed the parish forming part of the northern parish boundary N of Oak Grove, and the southern boundary of the extra-parochial strip of land called Dallinghoo Wield. The track then passed to the NW of 'Bredfield Castle' (*see below*).

Site of Ancient Moat and Fortified Earthworks.

NE of Poplar Farm and S of Pound Lane, the remains of earthworks known as 'Bredfield Castle' on an old estate map. It comprises a roughly rectangular platform enclosed by a deep, wide, oval moat called 'Oliver's

BREDFIELD *(continued)*

Ditches' (believed to be of earlier date). The earthwork is now little more than undulations in a cultivated field. The site occupies 'Yard', 'Moat Yard', 'Great Castle Field', and 'Little Castle Field' on the tithe map. Although the mound is now only some 3' high and the moat 3' deep, in the early C20 it still had a depth of about 8'. Considerable pottery and oyster shells from the site suggest it was occupied between the C11 and C14. Its builder and former residents are unknown, but Roger Bigod held four acres in Bredfield and a certain Norman held 12 acres, the approximate size of the whole site. Bigod's way also ran close by the site. In the past often described as the site of a castle, this is based on nothing more than the field names. It does, however, suggest a fortified building of some substance once stood here.

Quakers' Burial Ground.
Land was purchased for a Quakers' burial ground in 1720.

Medieval Greens.
Bredfield Green, named and shown on Faden's map of 1783, was a small green covering the junction with Caters Road W of the church and marked by Green Farm. An extension to the E is named Hopwell Green in the area of Moat Farm but its extent is not shown.

Historic Houses & Ancient Moated Sites.
Bredfield House, built in 1665 and formerly the seat of the Jenny family and birthplace of Edward FitzGerald (translator of the *Rubaiyat of Omar Khayyam)*, was demolished c1950. High House, W of the village and now a farmhouse, is C16. There is a fragment of a moat remaining at Moat Farm, N of the village.

BRENT ELEIGH *(2 miles SE of Lavenham)*

Babergh Hundred. 'Illa's clearing in a wood' (OE+ME) *Illeleia* (DB) *Brendeylleye* (1312). Eleigh is a derivative of Illeigh the ancient lords of the manor prior to the Sheltons. The name Brent, meaning 'burnt', appears to have been added to the original name following a fire in 1254 which destroyed the former village. *Manors.* Brent Eleigh Manor (C13-C17 Shelton family). *Sub-Manors.* Abbot's Hall; Fenhall.

Ancient Woodland.
Camps Wood and The Grove, in the S of the parish, are parts of ancient woodland.

Roman Road.
A Roman road passes SW-NE bisecting the parish. It is nowhere evident on the ground except where a short section of road traces its course W of Tye Farm across the parish boundary.

Medieval Market.
Sir Henry Shelton obtained the grant for a market here in 1260.

Almshouses.
Dr Edward Coleman of Trinity College Cambridge founded the two-storey almshouses in 1731. Some years earlier he had provided the parish with a parochial library of some 1,500 books which were housed in the church until 1859.

Historic Houses & Ancient Moated Sites.
Brent Eleigh Hall, near the church, is Elizabethan but occupies the site of the ancient hall of the Shelton family who held the manor for over 300 years from the C13. The moated Wells Hall, former home to the Shorehams, retains a fine Tudor gatehouse, and the impressive Corner Farm dominates the road junction.

BRETTENHAM *(5 miles NE of Lavenham)*

Cosford Hundred. 'Homestead of a man called Bretta' (OE) *Bretenhama* (DB)
Manors. Brettenham (C13 Richard de Clare). *Sub-Manors.* Ryses; Stanstead al Stanstreet Hall; Willisham's.

Ancient Woodland.
Devil's Hill Wood, Morieux Wood and Ram's Wood are parts of ancient woodland.

BRETTENHAM *(continued)*

Roman Camp (?)
A field now under the plough SW of the church still shows traces of earthworks in the form of a rectangular ditched enclosure. Roman finds suggest a camp W of the Roman road which skirts the village. The parish has been suggested as the possible site of the Roman station *Combretonium*.

Roman Cemetery (?)
A new library at Brettenham Park was built in 1902, 'on the site of an old burial ground - probably Roman.'

Roman Road.
The parish boundary between Brettenham and Buxhall, and District boundary between South Suffolk and Mid Suffolk, follows the course of a Roman road N from TL980 542 to Pie Hatch Farm on the boundary with Rattlesden.

Site of Saxon Priory.
A priory founded by Leofstan c1066 and dedicated to St Leonard is said to have stood in the parish. It was dissolved in 1414 and its site has not been identified.

Medieval Green.
Oxes Green, a tiny triangular green on the northern parish boundary, was shown and named on Faden's map of 1783. It stood SE of Castle Farm at a junction formed by the present road to Felsham and another road (shown by Faden but lost to the creation of a second world war airfield) heading NE to meet a right-angled bend in a road heading S from Hollybush Farm.

Workhouse.
A workhouse is recorded in Brettenham with twenty inmates in 1776.

Historic Houses & Ancient Moated Sites.
In the C16 Brettenham Hall, seat of the Wenyeve family for more than two centuries, resided for a time Joseph Bonaparte, Napoleon's brother and ex-King of Naples and Spain. The hall stands in a park extending to some 150 acres and there is evidence of a possible earlier moated site to the N. The lake in Devil's Hill Wood may have at one time been a fish-pond to an earlier hall. Church Farm SE of the church is C16. The C15 timber-framed Popples is situated 1½ miles SW of the village and has fragments of a small moat. There are other moated sites at The Poplars which dates from the C15 (a small square moat now cut by a road), Rose's Farm, SW of the church (three sides traceable of an oblong moat), the Rectory, N of the church (the N and W sides 20' wide, the other sides filled in but still traceable), Ryece Hall, NW of the church, and a moated site N of Lower Farm, N of the village. N of Pound Farm and E of Molieux Wood, a moat 230' square with an entrance causeway in the SE associated with a small enclosure to the NE, has been ploughed out. There was a sub-triangular moat in a small plantation NW of Spains Plantation in 1980 which also appears to have now gone.

BRIGHTWELL *(5½ miles SE of Ipswich)*

Bosmere & Claydon Hundred. 'Bright or clear spring' (OE) *Brihtewella* (DB). Springs from which the parish no doubt gained its name lie to the NE of Dairy Farm.
Manors. Brightwell Manor (-1234 Abbot of St. Etheldreda, Ely; 1234 Richard de Gossebek).
State papers reputedly hold a complaint of Thomas Toyser in 1538 'against illdoers who dig for gold and treasure in this parish'. He further promised to hand all treasure over to the King if he was granted a licence to mine for gold himself.

Tumuli.
One of the two round barrows situated W of Foxburrow Plantation, has now been covered by farm buildings.

Medieval Park.
The parish is said to have once held a medieval park probably associated with the hall (*see below*).

BRIGHTWELL *(continued)*

Medieval Fair.
A fair was held in the village on Mid-Summer Day in 1618.

Historic House.
The Manor House of Brightwell Hall was rebuilt in 1663 'at great expense' by Sir Samuel Barnardiston after he acquired the manor from John Essington. In 1664 it was listed as having '24 hearths'. It was mostly demolished in 1760 and converted to pasture land, leaving the present small brick farmhouse, once part of the stable block of the former mansion.

BROCKLEY *(6½ miles SW of Bury St Edmunds)*

Thingoe Hundred. 'Woodland clearing by a brook' (OE) *Broclega* (DB)
Manors. Brockley Hall (1167 Peter de Brockley). *Sub-Manors.* Talmages and Wyfolds; Inghams.

Ancient Woodland.
A small strip of ancient woodland remains at Long Gove, S of the parish.

Medieval Greens.
Faden shows several greens in 1783. The northern limits of Pound Green, N of Brockley Hall and W of Bury Road, are outlined by Hawks Lane. The brook from where the parish took its name formed the southern limits and then crossed the green heading NW at a spot called Shepherd's Nap. The square Gurland Green on Bury Road at the junction with Sadler's Lane, still retains a number of ponds. Cages Green, a small linear green running S from Manston Hall, replaced part of Tuffield Road. Brockley Green, on the southern parish boundary, covered the junction of four ways - Bury Road (NE and S), Cooks Lane (W), and a track to Brockley Church (N).

Site of old Windmill.
A windmill at Mill Hill House was recorded as standing in 1783.

Historic Houses & Ancient Moated Sites.
Ancient Brockley Hall which adjoins the church is a former aisled manor house of c1300. It was originally surrounded by an oblong moat with an entrance to the N, parts of which remain. Close by on the N side of the church, a smaller, stronger moat is fed by a stream, with, further to the W of these, the remains of another moat, the northern side straight, the eastern forming an arc. In the hamlet of Gulling Green, N of the parish, are two sides of a moat at Gulling Green Farm and fragments of a moat to the NE on the site of the Rectory. At Brockley Green, a small part of the moat remains at Glasshouse Farm, and at an isolated square moat just N of Bevan's Farm on the eastern parish boundary, split half logs, described as 2' in diameter, were found during de-silting in the 1980s, probably from the revetment. They were carbon-dated to the C8 but it is not known whether this date referred to when they were planted or when they were felled and used.

BROME *(2 miles N of Eye)*

Hartismere Hundred. 'Place where broom grows (in abundance)' (OE) *Brom* (DB)
Manors. Brome Hall/Davillers (C13 Bartholomew D'Avilers). *Sub-Manors.* Ling Hall; Monk's Brame.

Roman Road.
The present A140 road from Ipswich to Norwich follows the course of the old Roman road SE-NE through the parish, forming the western parish boundary from the junction by The Devil's Handbasin service station.

Deserted Medieval Village (?)
The present parish comprises scattered farmsteads, an isolated church beside the site of its ancient hall, and a small settlement in the hamlet of Brome Street. Nick's Lane, which runs SW from the church to the B1077

BROME *(continued)*

road to Eye, has been suggested as the site of a now lost medieval village settlement. Faden's map does not show this lane but does show a number of properties along the road W of the church.

Remains of Wayside Cross.
The remains of an old stone Wayside Cross stood *in situ* at the junction of Stuston Lane (by The Devil's Handbasin) until a complaint that it was 'an object likely to cause an unbroken colt to shy' resulted in its removal to a new site in the courtyard at Brome Hall. The junction was also reputedly the site of a tollgate where the keeper made travellers drop their money into a bowl of vinegar before passing to prevent the spread of plague.

Medieval Common.
A large common, bisected by the Roman road running SW-NE, is shown and named on Faden's map of 1783. It extended S to Chestnut Farm in Eye parish, and W just into Thrandeston and just N of the present Grange Motel. It was enclosed in 1808 and, after being partly destroyed in the construction of the second world war airfield, is now an industrial site.

Medieval Market & Fair.
The grant of a market and fair was made in 1253, possibly to Bartholomew D'Avilers.

Historic Houses & Ancient Moated Site.
Brome Hall, an impressive mansion built c1550, was much reduced before 1840 and finally demolished in c1959. It stood on a site S of Brome Street previously occupied by an Elizabethan Hall built by Sir Thomas Cornwallis, who died in 1590. It is said at that time to have held a private chapel. An earlier Thomas Cornwallis, founder of this noble knightly family which held high office during the reigns of several monarchs, was Sheriff of London in 1378 and seated at the ancient Ling Hall immediately SE of the church. Here the original oval moat (now mainly dry) still remains with, close by the south-western side, another of oblong formation. Post holes found on the moated site have identified an aisled hall 80' by 35'. Brome Avenue, formerly an impressive double avenue shown on Faden's map, leads from the hall site to the the B1077 on the northern outskirts of Eye. Ling Hall was referred to in 1445, but a Bernard de Ling owned land in Brome as early as 1209 and a Joan de Lyng is mentioned in 1327. The earliest house was claimed to be the C12 manor house of the Davillers. Parke's Farm, W of the church, has a surviving wet fragment of a sub-rectangular moat.

BROMESWELL *(2 miles NE of Woodbridge)*

Wilford Hundred. 'Rising ground where broom grows' (OE) *Bromeswella* (DB)
Manors. Bromeswell Manor (C13 William de Caniso). *Sub-Manors.* Staveton with Bromeswell.

Tumulus (?)
A mound, 33' in diameter and 5' high, in the grounds and N of Sutton Hoo Mansion, may be a round barrow.

Site of Ancient Hundred Moot & Gallows.
The ancient meeting place of Wilford Hundred was situated at the junction of the Orford and Bawdsey roads, its site now occupied by Woodbridge Golf Club. It is marked 'Gallows Hill' on the 1843 tithe map and human remains have been unearthed here showing it was later used for a gallows.

BRUISYARD *(4 miles NE of Framlingham)*

Plomesgate Hundred. 'Peasant's enclosure' (OE) *Buresiart* (DB)
Manors. Bruisyard/Roke Hall (C13 Henry Hoe).

Ancient Woodland.
The great stretch of Bruisyard Wood, and to the E of this the small rectangular Hernsey Wood, are remains of ancient woodland.

BRUISYARD *(continued)*

Chantry College & Nunnery.
In 1346 Maud, Countess of Ulster, founded a perpetual chantry for a warden and four chaplains in the Abbey at Campsea dedicated to the Annunciation of The Blessed Virgin Mary. Eight years later this chantry was removed to Rokehall in Bruisyard and refounded by Nicholas Gernun. It had only a short life, however, for in 1364 it was dissolved and converted for the use of the abbis and sisters of the Nuns Minoresses of the Order of St. Clare, who took over the building in 1366. The nunnery should have been suppressed in 1536, but on payment of a £60 fine was exempted from the act and continued for another three years. In the grounds of the present Hall *(see below)* are traces of the former buildings, and in the house itself is a carved stone mantelpiece which must once have formed part of the monastic buildings.

Site of old Windmill.
A windmill is recorded standing E of the church in 1783.

Historic House & Ancient Moated Site.
The Hall, now a farmhouse, dates from 1610. It is a rebuild (probably for Michael Hare) of the former Manor House known as Rokehall which at one time was occupied by a Convent of Franciscan Nuns of St Clare (*see above*). There are remains of an extensive moat which must have enclosed a large area, and to the N, a possible fishpond. The Grange was mentioned in the parish register of 1633 when referring to a footbridge over the river at 'the Graunge' being 'utterly decayed'. It was replaced by a felled oak which was laid across the river. A C17 beamed Tithe Barn is also preserved.

BRUNDISH *(4½ miles N of Framlingham)*

Hoxne Hundred. 'Enclosed pasture/park on a stream' (OE) *Burnedich* (DB). The stream referred to is the river Alde, which at this point near its source, is only a stream.
Manors. Brundish with Firnhall (1221 Alkia de Brewes). *Sub-Manors.* Rodestrate/The Chantry/Pieshall's/Pyeshall; St. Edmund's House; Rounton's; Wilbies.

Ancient Chantry.
A famous Chantry, dedicated to St Mary, was founded in 1385 by Sir John de Payshall, rector of Caston and one of the executors of Robert de Ufford, Earl of Suffolk. Within it, six chaplains were to pray for the soul of the said Earl following his death. At the Dissolution it was granted to Richard Fulmerston. The site is unknown but may be marked by Chantry Farm, Chantry Hill, just S of the church, and the site of Brundish Hall.

Medieval Green.
A long narrow linear green is shown but not named on Faden's map of 1783 running the length of what is now Brundish Street from the Wilby road NE to Dairy Farm.

Site of old Windmill.
A post mill called Upper Mill stood N of Yew Tree House in 1783. It was demolished c1914.

Historic Houses & Ancient Moates Sites.
On the site of Brundish Hall, adjoining the churchyard on the E side, is half of an almost square moat with fish-ponds to the E. The hall was occupied by the Wyard and Gooch families in the C17-C19 before being dismantled and shipped to America in the 1920s. Brundish Manor, in the hamlet of Brundish Street, is a former aisled hall dating from c1500. It retains part of its ancient moat where excavations have revealed mid C13 to mid C14 occupation. Close by and SW of Potash Farm, are two sides of a strong moat 50' wide and, to the S of this, in The Street, St Edmunds Farm (the probable site of St. Edmund's manor house) has portions of a moat formerly enclosing three square sites - one side of each being common with one of another. In the extreme S of the parish on the boundary with Dennington is Runton's Moat, a rectangular moat divided into two parts, now surviving only as a dry earthworks. This is the site of the Manor of Runton's or Rungeton's held by the de Rungeton family in the late C13 and early C14. William de Rungeton was Lord

BRUNDISH *(continued)*

of Tannington and Brundish in 1316. The manor house is said to have been destroyed by fire together with the manorial court books. Since then all the lands in Brundish and Tannington have been free. Brundish Lodge, on the eastern parish boundary, has major sections of a strong moat with another isolated but complete moat to the S. Other moats are at Yew Tree House, W of the village (two moats adjoining each other), The Woodlands, near the SW parish boundary, (N and E sides of a large moat), a narrow isolated moat N of this at Potash Yard, and finally the outline of a large isloated and very ancient oval moat, now dry, opposite and E of Tannington Long Road. The Poplars dates from the C15.

BUCKLESHAM *(6 miles SE of Ipswich)*

Colneis Hundred. 'Homestead of a man called Buccel' (OE) *Bukelesham* (DB). The parish was anciently known as Bulechamp. It includes the Domesday vill of Kembroke (*see below*) with its church of All Saints, which may have been sited in Chapel Road which runs W from Kembroke Hall.
Manors. Bucklesham Manor (C13/C14 John Cordeboef). *Sub-Manors.* Kembroke; Tyrellshall al Tyrrels Feltwell-cum-Foxhall.

Site of Prehistoric Settlement & Cemetery.
Bucklesham Hall, one mile E of the village, stands on the site of a pre-historic settlement and cemetery.

Late Iron Age Enclosure.
A substantial quadrilateral Late Iron Age enclosure lies S of the village.

Medieval Heath.
The south of the parish is covered by Levington Heath which is shown and named on Faden's map of 1783.

Medieval Watermill & Clothing Industry.
A watermill called 'Fullyngmyll' suggests cloth fulling was carried out here in 1460. Fulling is the process of cloth finishing by which wet woollen cloth is passed between vertical rollers to shrink it in the direction of the weft. It is then stored in an enclosed space by which process it shrinks to about half its length and width. The cloth then assumes a felted appearance making it warmer and comparatively impervious to moisture. It can then be used to make overcoats and heavy suits.

Historic House.
Kembroke Hall in the E of the parish stands on the site of the manor house of Kembroke, one of the lesser Bucklesham manors. It is shown and named on Faden's map.

BUNGAY

Wangford Hundred. 'Elevated island' (Scand.) or 'Island of the followers of Bunga' (OE) *Bunghea* (DB). The river Waveney forms a loop around Outney Common virtually making an island (and formerly probably did) of the N of the town. A silver penny of Offa, King of Mercia (757-796 AD) was dug up in the osier ground near the castle ramparts in 1813.
Manors. Bungay Burgh (Bigot family, Earls of Norfolk). *Sub-Manors.* Bungay Soke; Bungay Priory.
Bungay was originally in two parishes: Bungay St. Mary and Bungay Trinity and is still dominated by these two fine churches (one of Norman date), the twin towers of the Norman castle, and fragments of its priory. Unfortunately, only a few of the old medieval properties have survived the disastrous fire of 1688 when the town lost 190 houses, the church of St. Thomas, the grammar school, three almshouses, two market crosses and the major part of the priory. Bungay holds a claim to fame being the only town in England still with a Town Reeve, an office which pre-dates even that of mayor. Although not a 'borough' at Domesday, the fact that it then possessed three churches is suggestive of urban status even then. A Mint was established by the 'Jews at Bongeye' in 1158. An Act was passed in 1669 to make the Waveney navigable for barges with four locks being constructed between the town and Barsham. This brought great trade to the town which reached a peak in the 1760s -'70s, but with the coming of the railways in 1860 the river trade declined and eventually ceased.

BUNGAY *(continued)*

Roman Road.

Wainford Road now bridges the Waveney carrying the old Roman Stone Street into Norfolk and forming the NE parish boundary. The old Roman road formerly crossed the river by a 'Waggon Ford' - the Saxon 'wain ford'.

Ancient Site.

Pagan Anglo-Saxon remains have been discovered at Stow Fen SW of the town on the S side of the river Waveney.

Ancient Hundred Meeting Place.

The ancient meeting place of Wangford Hundred was probably at the former Roman waggon ford over the Waveney (*see above*).

Ancient Camp (?)

The *Victoria County History* in the early part of the C20. described it thus: 'On the N side of the railway on common land are three parts of a simple rectangular enclosure. The longest part running NE-SW is 200', and the other sides are at SW and SE with a short bank 12' long turning at right-angles towards the SE. The greatest height of the rampart is now 2' but is greatly trodden down by cattle. Flint flakes and arrow heads have been found on the site.'

Ancient Fortress Town.

The origins of Bungay, as previously shown, suggest the town may have at one time been a virtual island settlement. The fact that it was once called Bungay Burgh also indicates that it was fortified long before the erection of the castle in the C12. Indeed, land called Ollands to the S of the town is described as the 'Campo de Ilketshale' in a deed in the time of Edward III, suggesting it may have been headquarters to Ulfcytel, the Danish King of East Anglia c1000 A.D. The castle may even have been erected on an earlier earthworks - the course of the Roman Stone Street appearing to pass both sites.

Norman Castle.

In a superbly defensive position above the Waveney, at a point where the river forms a great horseshoe bend, is what remains of a formidable fortress. The foundations and basement of what was once a mighty stone keep, 90' high, with walls 18' thick lie just W of the yard of the Kings Head Hotel. Of the forebuilding, described as one of the strongest in England, the gatehouse, comprising two massive semicircular flint towers, still remains along with meagre fragments of the curtain wall and some earthworks known as 'Castle Hills', now a public recreation area. The castle was built in the C12. by Roger Bigod, one of William the Conqueror's chief barons and procurer of 117 manors after the Conquest. The family's continual misdemeaners led to conflicts with first King Stephen who took the castle in 1140 and subsequently his successor Henry II to whom the Earl was forced to surrender it in 1155. An old ballad confirms the continuing haughty boasts of Hugh Bigod in 1174: "Were I in my Castle of Bungay, Upon the Water of Waveney, I would ne care for the King of Cockney." However, he was forced to eat his words and pay a 1,000 marks fine to stop royal troops demolishing the keep - evidence of their initial attempts to undermine the walls is still evident today, and a unique survival in England. The castle later came into the possession of the Uffords and Howards, and was purchased in 1800 by Charles Howard, Duke of Norfolk, from whose descendant it was leased by Bungay Town Trust in 1934.

Town Defences.

The town was anciently defended by a ditch, fragments of which still remain near Trinity Church, along Outney Road, by the old railway sidings, and along the length of Nethergate Street. A trial trench dug during excavations in 1983, N of Quavers Lane, revealed the Town Ditch 59' wide and 13' deep backfilled in the late C13 or early C14.

Nunnery.

St Mary's, now the parish church, once formed the church of the Benedictine Nunnery founded around 1160

BUNGAY *(continued)*

by Roger de Glanville and his wife the Countess Gundreda and dedicated to The Blessed Virgin Mary and The Holy Cross. By 1287 it supported a prioress and sixteen nuns but this number had dropped by half by the time it was dissolved in 1537 and granted to Thomas, Duke of Norfolk. The great fire of 1688 subsequently destroyed most of the priory buildings. What remains comprises some walling, part of the arch of the former chapel in the churchyard, and some flint precinct walling in St Marys Street and Trinity Street.

Medieval Hospital.

A hospital dedicated to St John stood on Flixton Road S of the town.

Sites of Ancient Chapels.

The ancient chapel of St Mary Magdalen, founded by Roger Rose in 1373 and dissolved in 1536, stood to the W of Upper Olland Street where a modern house incorporates walling encasing a flattened arch. It was probably associated with St John's Hospital (*see above*). Stow Park, a house one mile SW of the town, stands on the elevated site of an ancient chapel founded in the C12 or C13. Some remains have been unearthed. A Hermitage Chapel existed near the E end of the bridge on the S side of the river Waveney. It was demolished in 1733.

Medieval Mills.

In the C14 the town recorded four watermills and two windmills. Three windmills were listed in the late C18: one by the B1435 S of the town (still standing in 1826); one listed in 1764 by the B1435 E of the town, and a post mill near the school SE of the town (still there in 1824).

Medieval Green & Commons.

Upland Green is shown and named on Faden's map of 1783 lying S of the town and running NE from St Margarets Road (in place of the present track), as far as Manor Farm. A number of ponds mark its former outline. Outney Common, named and shown on the same map remains today in a northern horseshoe loop of the Waveney river. It covers 402 acres and was formerly extra-parochial and placed under the management of common-reeves who allowed 150 townspeople common-rights to pasture two head of cattle here. Part is now a golf course. The 88 acres of Stow Fen, SW of the town, which also provided common grazing, was managed by Fen-reeves.

Medicinal Spring.

Chalybeate Spring, in the castle grounds, was believed to possess medicinal properties. In 1700 a Mr. King devised a scheme to make the town a bathing and watering place without success.

Medieval Market & Fairs.

The town obtained the grant for a market in 1228, regranted in 1384 to Margaret, Countess of Norfolk. Fairs were in existence in 1199 when Hugh Bigot gained permission to extend the privileges of his fair.

Medieval Market Crosses.

The Butter Cross, an open octagonal structure situated in the Market Place was erected in 1689 to replace one of the market crosses destroyed in the great fire the year previous - an event for which it stands as a memorial. It has Tuscan columns and arches and a dome surmounted by a handsome figure of Justice added in 1754. It apparently originally held a prisoner's cage complete with wrist irons and whipping post. There was another market cross here called the Corn Cross, taken down in 1810.

Recreation.

The Corpus Christi Pageant was held on Trinity Sunday at Holy Trinity Church. It was not uncommon for such festivities to end in riots as took place in 1514 and again in 1537. Games are recorded as having taken place in the two churchyards of the parish churches 1560-67 and in Castle Yard in 1568. Camping (a ball game similar to football) was held on Bungay Common.

Almshouse & Former Infirmary (?)

The earliest house remaining in town to survive the fire is in St Mary's Street, opposite the church. This house, now converted into shops, dates from 1500. There are some curious Elizabethan carvings on the windows and merchant's marks in several places suggest that it was the home of a wealthy merchant. Its origins appear

BUNGAY *(continued)*

earlier, however, as it is supposed to have been at one time an infirmary for the nunnery, and stone steps within probably date from this time. The wooden figure of a crusader found in the town and thought to represent Ranulph Glanville, the nunnery's founder who accompanied Richard I to the Holy Wars, is supposed to have come from this house. Later it formed part of the trust of Thomas Popeson who, in addition to founding the free grammar school, gave this building as an almshouse for four 'impotent widows' of St Mary's parish. Five tenements comprised Wharton's Almshouses in 1577, one of the three lost in the great fire.

Site of Pest House.
The town's pest house stood on Outney Common N of the town. It was pulled down in 1771 and the foundations were still visible in 1846.

Workhouse.
The town's workhouse had 25 inmates in 1776.

Free Grammar School.
Churchwarden's Accounts mention a chapel in the churchyard converted to a school in 1565 by Thomas Popeson. In 1568 the Priory paid 2s. 4d. for 50 'poplying borde' for the schoolhouse. In 1580 a new purpose-built Grammar School was founded in Earsham Street by Thomas Wingfield which was subsequently destroyed in the fire of 1688. New buildings were erected within two years which continued in use until 1865 when they were extended. A new school was built in St John's Road on the outskirts of town in 1924.

Historic Houses.
Most of the old medieval houses of the town were lost in the great fire of 1688. One notable exception is a property remaining in St Mary's Street just opposite the church which dates from c1500 (*see above*). The Fleece is a C16 coaching inn and The Three Tuns, another old coaching inn, was erected after the fire on the site of an older building - the well in the cellar dates from 1540. It was a calling point for the Yarmouth-London via Ipswich stage coach in 1743.

BURES ST MARY *(5½ miles SE of Sudbury)*

Babergh Hundred. 'The dwellings or bower' (OE) 'St Mary' is the church dedication. *Bura* (DB)
Manors. Bures Manor (C13 William de Aguillon). *Sub-Manors.* Overhall al Ropers; Netherhall/Silvesters; Smallbridge; Cornerth al Cornhall al Northall; Tanys.

Ancient Woodland.
Nayland End Wood and Arger Fen are ancient woodland on the eastern parish boundary.

Tumuli (?)
The outline of two possible long barrows have been identified W of Smallbridge Farm on the N bank of the river Stour. Interestingly, it has been suggested that a ring ditch, recognised on aerial photographs, may have been a defended earthworks and not a tumulus as originally thought.

Ancient Chapel.
St Stephens Chapel, 1 mile NE of the village, founded by Sir Gilbert de Tany and dedicated to Stephen Langton Archbishop of Canterbury in 1218, was said by Galfridus de Fontibus to occupy the site of the Saxon church in which Edmund was crowned King of the East Angles on Christmas Day 855. It had long been used as a barn before being restored to house the magnificent tombs of three of the de Vere family, Earls of Oxford, brought here in 1935 from Colne Priory, Earls Colne in Essex. Timber-framed with a thatched roof, the building has a good E window and three Early English lancets. The tombs are thought to contain: the 5th Earl, Robert de Vere - a stone effigy of c1296 on a tomb chest of c1340; the 11th Earl, Richard de Vere, Commander at Agincourt with his wife Alice - large alabaster tomb; and the 8th Earl, Thomas de Vere, 1371 -alabaster tomb with the lower half of a mid-C12 coffin lid (probably that of Alberic, Great Chamberlain and first de Vere, who died 1141).

Medieval Market & Fair.
Robert Aguillon obtained the grant for a market in 1271, and for a fair which would continue until 1871.

BURES ST MARY *(continued)*

Gallows (?)

A gibbet is once thought to have stood at the top of St Edmunds Lane, locally known as Deadman's Lane.

Workhouse.

A workhouse here was recorded as accommodating 50 inmates in 1776.

Historic Houses & Ancient Moated Sites.

Standing 1½ miles SE of the village on the banks of the Stour, Smallbridge Hall, surrounded by fragments of its ancient moat (the river Stour provides the S side), was home to the Waldegrave family from 1380 to 1700. Aerial photographs show a complicated pattern of possible former defensive works. The hall was visited by Elizabeth I in 1561 and again in 1579. The expenses incurred in entertaining her entourage during one of these two day visits amounted to £250, a staggering sum in those days. Great Bevills, a spectacular house of c1500 situated in a great park off the road to Sudbury and ½ mile N of the village, was built as a second home for the Waldegraves. Once part of Tawneys Manor, centred at the top of Cuckoo Hill, Bevells is thought to have originated from Beauvilles, a Norman family. Sawyers Farm in the N of the parish is a very ancient house dating from c1400, and Moat Farm, NE of the village, has fragments of two sides of a narrow moat.

BURGATE *(5 miles NW of Eye)*

Hartismere Hundred. 'Gate of a fortified settlement' (OE) *Burgata* (DB). A suggestion that it means 'Burial gate(road)' where the body of King Edmund lay for one night on its journey to Bury Abbey seems unlikely. *Manors.* Burgate Manor (C14 Robert de Burgate). *Sub-Manors.* Higham.

Ancient Woodland.

Burgate Wood, E of the old hall site and within which is an earthwork (*see below*), is ancient woodland.

Mound.

The small mound in a field NNE of a dry moat called the Moatyards may be a related feature or a round barrow.

Iron Age Settlement.

There are signs of Iron Age occupation near Hill House, NE of the church.

Ancient Way.

'Ikelyngge Weye', mentioned on a deed of 1410 as running from Redgrave to Burgate, can be traced on the ground from the A143 at Red Bridge, along Bugg's Road to Little Green, Furze Way and Stonebridge Lane. It may well have connected with the Roman road (A140) and the ancient Grimm's Ditch in Thornham Parva via Cowpasture Lane in Mellis. Morley suggests that Ikelynnge refers to Icel of the Mercian family of Icelingas whose Saxon home was at Icklingham in west Suffolk.

Ancient Moated Earthworks.

The place-name may refer to an earthwork known as Foxhills in Burgate Wood, W of the church. Enclosed by earthen banks and surrounded by a moat some 5' deep (now mostly dry), the width bank to bank is about 180' by 210', with the banks being about 26" wide and the moat 16' to 26' wide. A deep depression or ditch runs E-W for a short distance from the earthwork and may be associated with it. An investigation by Basil Brown spoke of a small mound SE of the moated area. Burgate's main manor was held by Adelhelm under Aubrey de Vere at Domesday, but by the C13 it was the seat of the de Burgates who held as tenants of the de Veres, Earls of Oxford. William de Burgate has a tomb in the chancel of the church dated 1409. Situated just W of the present moated Hall, the earthworks, may be an early Norman ring-works (simple type of castle) and represent the site of their former residence. This is suggested by C11-C12 pottery found in the concave enclosure, and while claims of earlier finds of a Saxon date must be taken with caution, if true they would suggest an even earlier origin for the site, one which may identify the place-name (*see above*).

Medieval Market.

The de Burgate family obtained the grant of a market here in 1272.

BURGATE *(continued)*

Medieval Greens.

Faden's map of 1783 shows three greens in the parish. Burgate Great Green survives complete S of Bury Road, as does Burgate Little Green at the southern end of Bugg's Road. Stubbings Green, on the parish boundary, is shown as a rectangular green and named Reydon Slough.

Historic House & Ancient Moated Sites.

W of the church, Burgate Hall, built in 1587 by Sir Nicholas Bacon and now a farmhouse known as Hall Farm, retains three sides of an ancient moat. An irregular moat at Stubbing's Entry at the W end of Stebbing's Green, S of the parish, encloses a large area with an extension towards the E forming three sides to another moat. Basil Brown suggests that a pavement he discovered on the site at a depth of 13" covering several feet and created from oyster shell points to a pre-Conquest date for the site, whilst stonework unearthed within the moated enclosure shows the former house here was fortified or semi-fortified. Adam de Stebing had possession in the early C13, but a charter of 1315 speaks of land of the Abbey of Bury St Edmunds called 'Stulbyng', a name it has carried in a corrupt form ever since. Two sides still survive of the rectangular moat which surrounded Glebe Farm on the site of the former rectory. Hill House, further N and formerly known as 'Hills' or 'The Hille', dates from the mid C16. Although owned by Robert Coppins in 1563, it takes its name from another Robert, Robert Hill who held the property in 1653. Part of a moat shown on the 1847 tithe map can be traced in a meadow near Waveney Lodge.

BURGH *(3½ miles NW of Woodbridge)*

Carlford Hundred. 'Fortified place' (OE) *Burc* (DB)

Manors. Burgh Hall (C13 John de Crek). *Sub-Manors.* Thistleton Hall; Cleve's al Blomviles.

Fortified Iron Age Enclosure & Roman Settlement.

The site of the place-name is situated at Castle Field beside the B1079 and extending either side of Drabs Lane. An important Belgic Iron-Age fortified site belonging to the Trinovantian tribe from which much fine pottery has been obtained is overlayed, in the northern corner, by an early Roman settlement with considerable building material. Continual ploughing has obliterated much of the site which comprises a rectangular earthworks with double banks and ditch measuring 675' by 660'. Excavations in the 1950s revealed a hypocaust and coins dating the Roman occupation from Tiberius 14-37 A.D. to Valentinian 364-75 A.D. This has been suggested as an alternative site to Brettenham for the Roman station *Combretonium*. It was at one time thought that a Norman motte occupied the NE corner of the enclosure where the field name Old Motte is suggestive, but excavations appear to have now ruled this out. St Botolph's Church stands within the earthworks.

Site of Ancient Chapel.

In much the same way that the missionary St Fursey had associations with the Roman fort of Burgh Castle in the N of the county (and perhaps St Felix with the Roman fort, now under the sea at Walton near Felixstowe), a chapel is said to have once occupied the site of the church in the SW corner of this Roman enclosure and to have held the body of another of the Christian missionaries, St Botolph, from 680 A.D. until its removal to Bury Abbey. The little church retains the saint's dedication. An alternative site has been suggested opposite Manor Farm where excavations on a house platform visible on aerial photographs revealed Thetford ware and tile fragments.

Ancient Track.

The Packway, a section of the ancient Bigod packway which connected his castles of Walton, Framlingham and Bungay, runs from Looms Farm N to a drive leading to Loomswood Farm, then E along the drive to Horse Covert.

Medieval Green.

A small linear green shown and named Sky Green on Faden's map of 1783 ran S from Brickwall Farm to the road junction and was lined with old properties on its western side.

Historic Houses & Ancient Moated Sites.

The site of C16 Thistleton Hall, a Manor House situated one mile NE of the church and demolished c1955, is

BURGH *(continued)*

marked by a complicated triple moat. The former hall stood on a small island enclosed by a strong moat of great width. This in turn was protected by two outer moats, one of which is irregular and also appears of very ancient origin. It was possibly the seat of William de Burgh whose widow, Maude de Lancaster, gave the manor to the chantry she founded at Campsea and soon after transferred to the nuns of Bruisyard. Sadly the hall ended its days within the confines of a second world war airfield. Moat Farm, ½ mile W of Boulge Park, has three sides of an oblong moat and N of this, fragments of a former square moat. There is a moat at Loom's Farm, just N of this.

BURGH CASTLE *(4 miles SW of Great Yarmouth)*

Mutford & Lothingland Hundred. 'Fortification/stronghold' (OE) *Burch* (DB). The parish was formerly known as *Cnobersburg* after the Saxon chief who lived here.
Manors. Burgh (1246 The Prior of Bromholm who had right of wreck, view of frankpledge and assize of bread and beer in Burgh).

Roman Saxon Shore Fort.
Situated above the marshy ground where the river Waveney joins Breydon Water is the spectacular remains of *Gariannonum*, a Roman Fort built around 290 A.D. and garrisoned by a body of Cavalry - the Stablesian horse. The Fort was one of a series built along the east coast under the command of the Count of the Saxon Shore to defend this outpost of the Roman Empire against attack from northern invaders. It overlooked the Roman commercial harbour of Caister-on-Sea and was situated to the N of a small creek (now Belton Fen) where it is thought lay a naval dockyard which the fort defended. It is roughly quadrangular in plan with standing flint walls 9' thick alternating with courses of tile and interspersed with massive bastions, added later and intended to carry ballistas (catapults for hurling stones). The enclosure measures 640' x 300' x 325' and covers some five acres. The side facing the marshes is now undefended, but footings of a fourth wall have been found showing that the material on this side has been robbed, taken away by boat and much of it used in the churches here and at Burgh St Peter and Reedham. The remaining walls still have an average height of 15'. The fort was in use for a little over a hundred years. Traces of buildings, probably of Roman date, have been identified lying just N of the fort.

Site of Saxon Monastery.
In about 635 A.D., in the N corner of the abandoned Roman Fort, the Irish missionery St Fursey established his Saxon monastery. Though nothing remains of the buildings, excavations found evidence of oval huts (apparently monks' cells) and what was probably a tiny church. A cemetery lay at the S end of the fort beneath the Norman motte.

Site of Norman Motte.
At the S corner of the abandoned Fort the Normans raised an early castle motte over the Saxon cemetery and surrounded it with a moat. The builder of the castle was probably Ralph the Engineer, mentioned in Domesday, and it likely had a timber tower and stockade. The mound was removed in 1839.

Medieval Commons.
Faden shows a rectangular Burgh Common NE of the church in part of the area now covered by Burgh Castle Marshes. To the W, in an area now called Churchfarm Marshes, were two small areas of unnamed common.

Medieval Archery Practice (?)
Butt Lane, near the school, is suggestive of a field nearby used formerly for archery practice.

Recreation.
Based on the custom of 'beating the bounds', the Great Water Feast became an annual event of 'perambulation of the waters' and aquatic sports. It began c1670 and continued irregularly in 1777 and 1779 and was revised in 1816. The event was last staged in 1889.

Historic Houses.
Burgh Hall dates back to the mid C17 with Georgian additions. The Grange is a house of great antiquity situated at the SE end of the old common in the N of the parish.

BURSTALL *(4 miles W of Ipswich)*

Samford Hundred. 'Site of a fort or stronghold' (OE) *Burgestala* (DB)

Manors. Brokes Hall ([no dates] Lady Catesby and Mr. Broke held the manor of the Honor of Clare). *Sub-Manors.* Harrold's/Horrold's; Langston's/Langton's/Lingston's.

Site of 'fort' (?)

Though no site has been identified in connection with the place-name, the village may have stood 'at the site of a burh' - perhaps of Romano-British date - the earthworks of which were then visible but have since been lost. There is a Fort Cottage, right on the parish boundary in an elevated position beside the road SE of the church and village.

Ancient Chapel.

In the C15 it was said that the 'Chapel of St. Albert (Ethelbert) was maintained by the Abbot of Battle Abbey'. The site of the chapel is not known.

Medieval Green.

The road heading SE from the church, the lane running NE-N to Burstall Hall, and a footpath NNW appear to trace the outline of Burstall Green, named on Faden's map of 1783. The site has been mostly infilled.

BURY ST EDMUNDS

The Saxon settlement of *Beodericeworth* became the fortified town of *Byrig* in 1038, and Bury St Edmunds in 1065, after the C9 East Anglian King *Sancte Eadmundes* (Saint Edmund), following his internment here. This ancient borough was capital of the former West Suffolk and of the Liberty of St Edmund. Its unusually formal grid-pattern street plan was the result of influences acquired by Abbott Baldwin (1065-1098) following a visit to Rome. Bury's growth and fame centred on its great Abbey - at its height one of the four or five most powerful and wealthy Benedictine monasteries in England; its influence reflected in all the historic aspects of rural life throughout this half of the county. Despite its subsequent fall and destruction, two great gateways remain to remind us of its former glory. The Georgian period saw a great revival in Bury's fortunes and it has settled into its role as a busy, yet stylish market town and centre for the west Suffolk farming community.

Roman Road (?)

It is suggested that the A14 from Newmarket traces the course of a Roman road which passed N of the site of the medieval town heading E to Ixworth. Early maps of Fordham and Barton mark it 'Peddars Way' and Margary states this 'may well be' a road linking the Icknield Way to the main Roman Peddars Way.

Tumulus - Ancient Hundred Courts.

Outside the Northgate on the W side of the road to Fordham, an ancient round barrow was used by the people of Bury for their ancient hundred court. The name is retained in Thingoe Hundred. Three internments were unearthed following C19 excavations, although the centre of the mound was never reached.

Early Saxon Cemetery (?)

A probable early Anglo-Saxon cemetery was discovered on Tollgate Lane.

Saxon Monastery & Benedictine Abbey

Bury's origins began in 633 A.D., when Siegbert, King of the East Angles, founded a church and monastery at Beodericeworth. In 903 A.D. the body of the martyred King Edmund was brought here to a specially prepared wooden church after he was killed at Hoxne (although this location for his demise is constantly being questioned). King Cnut founded a Benedictine abbey on the site in 1020 beside the river Lark and St Edmund's shrine made it a place for universal pilgrimage (*see below*). The great Norman church was commenced in 1095, and a new Norman town was constructed west of the abbey. The wealth that ensued gave the abbotts great power, not only over the town but over a considerable area of the county, and kings and queens paid visits to the shrine (*see below*). Not surprisingly, over the years the abbots were in constant conflict with the townspeople over their power and high-handedness (*see also 'markets & fairs'*) and this led to attacks on

BURY ST EDMUNDS *(continued)*

the abbey when it was burnt and plundered both in 1327 and during the Peasants' Revolt in 1381. Many of the monastic buildings were destroyed in a disastrous fire of 1465 - this time accidental - and the full reconstruction had barely been completed before the Dissolution saw the end of what has been described as 'the finest abbey in the kingdom with the exception of Glastonbury'. The major remains comprise: St James's Church (now the Cathedral), St Mary's Church, the Abbey Gate, and the magnificent Norman Tower, but there are fragments of other buildings including the High Altar attractively encapsulated in the beautiful Abbey gardens.

Abbey Gates.

The Norman Tower was erected about 1090 in the time of Abbot Baldwin and is the finest building of its kind in Europe. It is 86' high and 36' square. The Abbey Gate, the main entrance gate to the Abbey, was completed about 1377 to replace the orginal gate destroyed by the townspeople in the disturbances of 1327. It is some 50' long, 40' broad and 62' high, and one of the finest examples of Decorated style.

Shrine of St Edmund.

The shrine of St Edmund was visited by kings and great nobles throughout the land, and Edward the Confessor held St Edmund in such reverence that he always insisted on travelling the last mile to the Abbey on foot. In 1132 Henry I was caught in a violent storm whilst returning to England from a visit to Chartres to meet Pope Innocent III. Considering this a judgement on his sins he headed straight for Bury where he made a solemn vow at the shrine of St Edmund to amend his life. Unfortunately another king, Soon after Eustace, son of King Stephen, had sacked and burned the Abbey's farms and granaries when the abbots refused to provide him with money and provisions to assist his fight against Maude for the English throne, he was seized with a fever from which he died at Ipswich. A similar fate befell Henry III during a visit in 1272, whilst Edward I often visited Bury and in 1296 held a parliament here. The shrine brought great wealth to the abbey and the abbots did all in their power to capitalise on its 'pulling power'. Stories and legends abounded concerning its powers, many of dubious origin and emanating from the abbots: Leofstan, the second Abbot, had the temerity to open the shrine to inspect the remains of the Saint after which it is said his hand withered and needed the attention of the King's own personal physician. Frequently faced with financial difficulties through over indulgences, the abbots obtained a charter for certain stipulated fair days, not only to promote the shrine but also to advertise the other impressive relics which they possessed - some again rather dubious: the Abbey boasted the alleged coals on which St Lawrence was toasted, the parings of St Edmund's nails, a knife and the boots of St Thomas of Canterbury, and a portion of the True Cross. They also displayed several skulls reputed to have the power of removing headaches, along with relics producing rain and preventing weeds growing amongst corn.

Magna Carta.

On 20th November 1215 , the High Altar at Bury Abbey was the scene of a gathering at which Cardinal Langton and the leading barons of the time swore to compel King John - by force if necessary - to ratify the liberties of England. This led to the signing of Magna Carta the following year at Runnymeade.

Town Defences.

The town had three forms of defence of which there are scant remains. The W was protected by a wall which extended from Westgate to Northgate. The N and S sides by banks and ditches, and the eastern side by the precinct walls of the abbey and the river Lark. In a district called Harberdeen, between Southgate Street and the river, the only remaining earthwork defences lie in a field. The line of the Grindle running due W from Southgate was over 33' wide at the top and 10' deep and most likely a part of the medieval or even earlier defences - possibly of C11 or earlier date. Tayfen Road has replaced Tayfen Water, a stream which once formed part of the defences; part of this area also appears to have been protected by a flint rubble wall uncovered during excavations in 1968 and 1995. The town gates, mentioned in 1194 by Joselin de Brakelond, were mostly pulled down soon after 1760 to improve access. The East Gate adjoined the Abbots Bridge guarding a ford and a footbridge - a chimney gap in the wall identifies the position of a gatetower. Roundabouts now occupy the sites of the North and South gates - foundations of the former, demolished between 1761-5, were exposed during 1993 roadworks. A fifth gate, Risbygate, was sited at a point where Risby Street meets Brentgovel Street and St Andrews Street.

BURY ST EDMUNDS *(continued)*

Site of Medieval Archery Practice (?)

The Butts, on the S bank of the Linnet and N of Cullum Road, is the probable meadow where medieval archery practice once took place.

Franciscan Priory.

The power exerted over the town by the great Benedictine monastery prohibited other religious houses from setting up here. Only one tried it and this was while the Abbey was 'between abbots'. An order of Franciscan or Grey Friars moved in and set up in the N part of town. Their stay was shortlived however for no sooner had a new Abbot been appointed at the Abbey than he ordered them out. Receiving no response he had their buildings destroyed and the friars removed. They appealed to Rome and were granted another site in the W of the town but the abbots, still fearful of encroachments on their privileges, continued to hassle the monks to such an extent that Henry III was forced to intervene to protect them. Following the death of the Pope, the abbots appealed to his successor who commanded the Franciscans to demolish their buildings on pain of excommunication and to leave the town within one month. The monks were forced to concede and moved their monastic possessions the short distance to Bebwell on the banks of the river Lark, just beyond the bounds of Bury (*see* Fornham All Saints).

Medieval Hospitals.

The town had six hospitals, all founded by abbots from the abbey and situated at points covering the five entrance gates to the town where the alms of travellers could be collected. St Nicholas's Hospital stood about a quarter of a mile beyond the old East Gate. It was founded c1200 by a Bury abbot and first mentioned in 1226 when Henry III granted the hospital a fair. It was dissolved c1539. The site is represented by Chapel Farm at the junction of Hollow Road and Barton Road which contains a C14 church window said to have come from the former Leper Hospital of St Petronilla. To the N of the window is the buttressed end of a building with the outline of a large W window. St Stephen's Hospital was situated in Eastgate Street on the N side of the road between East Bridge and St Nicholas's Hospital; some fragments of old wall remained into the C19. St Petronilla's leper hospital was founded c1200 by Abbot Samson and dissolved 1539. It stood on Southgate Green near the hospital of St John just beyond the South Gate. St John's or 'Domus Dei' Hospital, situated in Southgate Street outside the South Gate, was founded 1248-56 by Abbot Edmund 'for supplying hospitality and refreshment to Christ's poor without any fraud or diminutation'. If any of the poor in the hospital fell into any grave sickness and were not able to depart, they were to 'tarry till strong enough to go on their way.' No brother or sister was to be admitted except they were approved by two wise and discreet wardens who were to act under the guidance of the almoner. Mass was not to be celebrated in the house, nor any altar erected, but a room was to be provided for private prayer. This hospital also came to an end at the Dissolution. St Peter's Hospital stood beyond Risby Gate and was for infirm, leprous or invalided priests. It was founded c1130 by Abbot Anselm and dissolved in 1582 - St Peter's Barn was built with materials from the ruins. St Saviour's Hospital, founded 1184-5 by Abbot Samson but not fully endowed until the reign of King John, stood in Northgate Street just beyond the North Gate and said to have been of such magnitude that it housed a parliamentary assembly in 1446. In this hospital Humphrey, Duke of Gloucester, is said to have been murdered following his arrest by order of Parliament. The so-called gatehouse which remains is, in fact, the W end of a range formerly 100' long. It is probably of C14 date with a two-centred entrance arch. Of the large window above, only the lower half of the frame survives. A small part of the precinct wall still stands. It was dissolved in 1542.

Sites of Medieval Chapels.

There were at least eight independent chapels in the town: St Mary's at Eastgate Bridge; Our Lady's at Westgate; Stone Chapel at Risbygate on the site of the Grapes Inn; St John's on the Hill; St Thomas's at Northgate; St Botolph's in Southgate Street; St Denis's; and St Margaret's, dating from the C12 - parts of which can be seen in the exterior S wall and the interior of the early Georgian St Margaret's House which is attached to Shire Hall. There were also a number of other chapels connected to hospitals and establishments: St Michaels, in the infirmary; St Andrews, in the cemetery of the monks; St John's-ad-Fortem; St Anne's-in-Cryptis; St Lawrence's, in

BURY ST EDMUNDS *(continued)*

the Courtyard; St Giles', near the nave of the Abbey Church; and St Edmund's (or Round Chapel), in the churchyard. There was also a Hermitage Chapel at the West Gate.

Medieval Colleges.
Dhodeni College was founded in 1020 by King Cnut; Glemsford College in 1389, and Jesus College, by John Smith 'two furlongs' from the parish church of St Mary's' in 1480 for a warden and six priests.

Medieval Bridges.
The Abbot's Bridge, which crosses the Lark from the Abbey Gardens, dates from the late C12 with two added C14 breakwaters. The ancient Southgate Bridge was discovered beneath successive road widening.

Site of old Windmills.
Eastgate Mill stood in Mount Road before 1597 and was still standing in 1688. A mill which stood in Kings Road in 1675 was moved to Walberswick. Four windmills are recorded standing in Bury in the C18: One in Mill Road (1783), still standing in 1867; Southgate Mill (1783), N of the school and S of Hardwick Lane, disused by 1903; a post mill (1740), by Hardwick Lane, disused by 1845 and West Mill (1783), by Horringer Road, demolished 1918.

Site of 'Witches' Executions.
In 1644 forty townspeople were hanged on the 'Thinghoe' during the purge by the witch-finder Hopkins. Two widows executed for witchcraft in 1664 proved to be the last recorded in England.

Medieval Markets & Fairs.
A market, already established here in Anglo-Saxon times, was moved to a more prominent position on Angel Hill in front of the Abbey entrance and developed under the abbot's control. The October fair, lasting over three weeks and held by a charter granted to the Abbot in 1272, became one of the most fashionable and frequented in the land 'not so much for merchandise as for company'. It was visited by many of the highest personages in the kingdom. In the C15, Charles Brandon, Duke of Suffolk and Mary Tudor, sister of Henry VIII and former Queen of France, had a magnificent tent erected on the fairground for themselves and their retinue. The fair continued in being for exactly 600 years. The Abbey jealously guarded its privileges and control over the markets and fairs held within the town and in 1201 when the Bishop of Ely attempted to set up a Market in Lakenheath, some 15 miles away, he was met by 600 armed men headed by the Abbot of Bury's bailiff who overturned the stalls and took away the cattle. James I granted an Easter fair in 1609 along with confirmations of the grants to other fairs and markets including the Calf's Tail Fair.

Site of Market Cross.
The Town Hall on Cornhill, rebuilt in 1620 and converted into a theatre in 1734 before being completely remodelled from the designs of Robert Adam, stands on the site of the medieval Market Cross erected in 1583 and destroyed by fire in 1608. Celia Fiennes, on visiting Bury during her travels through East Anglia in the C17, described 'Ye Market Cross with a dyal and lanthorn on ye top.' There were four 'Town Crosses' of stone marking the boundaries of the wards and a 'Weeping Cross' on Sunny Hill 'which we ascend towards Hardwick'.

Free Grammar School.
In 1550 Edward VI ordained that there should be a Grammar School in Bury to be called the Free Grammar School of King Edward VI. This was duly begun on a site in Eastgate Street. In 1665 it moved to Northgate Street where its buildings, now a Girls' High School, still remain.

Medieval Guildhall.
The Guildhall in Guildhall Street, said to have been given to the town by Jankyn Smith about 1473, and much altered and restored, retains a C15 kingpost roof. A doorway of c1300 origin is thought to have been inserted later.

Historic House.
On the Cornhill, Moyse's Hall, a two-storey Norman domestic building of c1180 constructed of flint and stone, is one of the earliest surviving domestic Norman buildings in the country. Said to have been built by a rich Jewish merchant, it was still probably connected with the Abbey. The Hall now houses a museum. Cupola House in The

BURY ST EDMUNDS *(continued)*

Traverse was built in 1690 for the wealthy apothecary Thomas Macro. The Manor House dates from the late C17, and Number 7 Northgate Street was formed from two early C16 timber-framed buildings. The Shire Hall, fronting the churchyard, stands on the site of St Margaret's Church. It was given by Thomas Badby in 1578 to use for public meetings and assizes. It was formerly a thatched building, rebuilt in 1803, and remodelled in 1841. The present Angel Hotel was built in 1779 but has occupied the site since at least 1452. Medieval arched vaults, supported by low, sturdy pillars which comprised the cellars may have formed a charnel house to which priests would retire to sing masses. The two inns called The Castle and The White Bear anciently also occupied this site standing side by side; The Castle is mentioned in 1418 as 'le In atte Castell'. The Greyhound was rebuilt as the Suffolk Hotel in 1833 but has a history going back to the days when it was owned by the Abbey. They owned a house on the site in 1295 and it has been an inn since at least 1539 until recent times.

BUTLEY *(7 miles E of Woodbride)*

Loes Hundred. 'Woodland clearing of a man called Butta' (OE) *Butelea* (DB)
Manors. Butley/Brochons (c1180 Theobald de Valoines). *Sub-Manors.* Tangham.

Ancient Woodland.
Carmen's Wood, in the N of the parish, and Water Wood, NW of Butley Abbey, are areas of ancient woodland.

Multi-period Settlement Sites & Cemetery.
Finds at Big Mount Field, E of Neutral Farm in the N of the parish, include two hoards of Bronze-Age socketed axes, much Iron-Age and Roman occupational material, and a Saxon rectangular hut floor. NE of Butleyferry Farm, E of Stonebridge Marshes and S of Butley Marshes, not far from the mouth of the Butley River where it joins the larger river Ore, rises a solitary rounded hill surrounded by marshes called Burrow Hill. During the early part of this century while digging for gravel on the wide platform on top, heaps of human and animal bones were said to have been constantly unearthed along with metal fragments lying not far below the surface. Archaeological excavations have since revealed evidence of occupation covering Bronze Age, Iron Age, Roman, and Mid-Saxon (C8) in the form of post-hole structures and an inhumation cemetery.

Ancient Ferry.
Burrow Hill's medieval name was Insula de Burgh. It was owned by the Priory 'for whom the island was the main stepping-stone in their ferry route to Orford . . .' The ferryhouse constructed on it (which lay on the S foot of the hill) was sufficiently important to be marked on a C16 chart. The island was connected with the mainland by a causeway. On the far side of Butley River in Gedgrave parish is Ferry Cottage.

Ancient Quay.
At the end of the C16, Stonebridge Marshes were finally enclosed leaving the former Butley Priory Quay derelict and grass-covered in a meadow just S of the ruined monastic buildings.

Site of Ancient Moated Priory.
At Five Cross Ways, Church Road, the C14 gatehouse remains of the Priory which formerly covered 20 acres. It was founded in 1171 by Ranulph de Glanville, Justicair to Henry II, as a house for Augustinian Canons and dedicated to The Blessed Virgin Mary. The heraldry displayed proves a date of about 1320-5, the earliest dateable building with flushwork decoration, and described as 'one of the most ambitious and interesting C14 buildings in Suffolk' and 'one of the finest in its class in England'. The Priory was richly endowed with many possessions including at least 23 churches in Suffolk and 11 in Norfolk plus 14 manors. It consisted of 36 canons in 1200. At the Dissolution the Prior was suspected of aiding the escape of a canon imprisoned for treason and he also initially refused to sign the surrender of the priory but was finally forced to capitulate. Nothing remains of the church except an arch of c1300 which led out to the S transept, though excavations in 1930-3 revealed its plan, showing it was about 270' long, consisting of an aisled nave, transepts, and a large choir with wide aisles, beyond which projected a Lady Chapel. The original C12 nave had been aisleless. Michael de la Pole who fell at Agincourt was buried in the priory church. In 1737, George Wright converted the gatehouse into an attractive mansion. Part of the extensive moat still survives.

BUTLEY *(continued)*

Site of Gallows (?)

Gallows (Galloise) Hill in Butley parish is mentioned in a lease of the ferry to Robert Morse in 1632.

Medieval Green.

Capel Green is named on Faden's map of 1783 but not shown. An area W of the priory is named Capel Green on the OS map where there is a Green Farm.

Site of old Windmill.

A post mill recorded at Butley Mills in 1783 was burned down at an unknown date.

Workhouse.

A workhouse/town house was in existence in 1731, demolished 1840.

Historic House.

The Oyster public house is first recorded in 1732 but the interior dates to the C16.

BUXHALL *(3½ miles SW of Stowmarket)*

Stow Hundred. 'Bucc's corner of land' (OE) *Buckeshala* (DB)

Manors. Buxhall (Late C13 John Copinger). *Sub-Manors.* Cockerells Hall; Leffey Hall; Fenn Hall.

Ancient Woodland.

Pie Hatch Wood, a small wood in the SW corner of the parish, is a section of ancient woodland.

Roman Road.

The course of a Roman road running S-N provides the western parish boundary. Its course is traced by a country road from the southern parish boundary to N of Pie Hatch Wood; here the road bears right and the line continues as field boundaries to the W of Manor Farm. Mitchery (formerly Misery) Lane then traces it to the northern boundary. Its great drainage ditch survives like a length of moat along the E side.

Ancient Mound (?)

In the grounds of Buxhall Rectory, later home of the Copingers, a mound about 39' in diameter and just over 3' high may be a garden feature, but it is said to have been associated with Maypole Hall and called 'Moot Hill' on early maps possibly suggesting a former function as the meeting place for the manor court.

'Anti-Highwayman Trench'.

A unique feature remains at Pye Hatch Wood. An 'anti-highwayman trench' - a cleared strip of land between the wood and the Roman road - giving warning of attacks upon travellers by highwaymen hiding in the trees.

Medieval Chapel.

A chapel which marked the burial place of several generations of the Copinger family was situated near Fasbourn Hall; it fell into ruin in 1441.

Site of old Windmill.

A post mill shown E of Mill Green in 1783 was burned down in 1814. It was said to occupy the site of a mill recorded here at Domesday.

Stocks.

The medieval stocks were originally situated by the Great Finborough-Rattlesden road junction.

Medieval Green.

On Mill Green (Buxhall Tye) Henry Sowgate was allowed half a rod to build a cottage in 1583, and the Rector of Buxhall was fined 3d. for playing bowls in 1603. Property boundaries trace the green's outline at the T-junction.

Historic Houses & Ancient Moated Sites.

Fasbourn Hall, originally known as Copinger Hall or Court, approached by an ancient double-arched bridge one mile S of the church, was the manorial seat of the Copingers from 1428 to 1948. Here in 1512, Sir William Copinger was born. He became Lord Mayor of London and was noted for his wealth and hospitality; to 'live like

BUXHALL *(continued)*

a Copinger' became a proverbial expression throughout the county. A curious grant, given by Henry VIII in 1512 and still in existence, allowed Walter Copinger to wear his 'bonnet' even in the presence of the king because he was 'so deseased in the hede'. The house still retains part of its quadrangular moat. In the C17 Buxhall Hall became a manor house. It was taken down c1700 and its site is marked by an avenue of trees. C16 Maypole Farm near the church is timber-framed; objects pertaining to Roman Catholic religious devotion were found hidden here. There are moats at the site of the former manor house of Cockerell's Hall (quadrangular - its course marked by a series of ponds), and at Fenn Hall, another former manor house, NW of the church.

CAMPSEY ASH *(2 miles E of Wickham Market)*

Loes Hundred. Campsey or Campsea: 'At the ash near Campi's promontory' (OE) *Campeseia* (DB) *Esce* (DB). Two quite distinct settlements at Domesday. The original ash-tree doubtless grew at the island in the middle of the splay of the river Deben where Ash Abbey was situated. Campsey refers to a tongue of upland jutting out into this river expansion - possibly at the present Quill Farm.

Manors. Campsey Manor (1293 John de Moese). *Sub-Manors.* Priory of Campsey; Morehall Hall; Ash.

Ancient Woodland.

Copperase Wood in the SW ,and The Oaks in the W of the parish are fragments of ancient woodland.

Site of Nunnery & Chantry College.

Ash Abbey farmhouse, one mile SW of the village, is the site of St Mary's Nunnery for Augustinian Canonesses and College. The Priory of Campsea was founded c1195 by Theobald de Valoines who gave all his estate in that parish to his two sisters Joan and Agnes to build a monastery in honour of the Blessed Virgin for themselves and other religious women. This they did with Joan becoming the first prioress of the house for Austin nuns and Agnes succeeding her; the grant was confirmed by King John in 1203. During its long history it always bore a good reputation and at the Dissolution there were 20 nuns in residence. Ash College, founded by the Countess of Ulster (who obtained a licence from Edward III), began in 1347 with a warden and four secular priests. Only 7 years later, in 1354, it was removed to Bruisyard (*see* Bruisyard). Of the religious buildings remaining at the Dissolution, only part of the W range survives in the barn along with what was formerly the C14 Dwelling House, now known as Ash Abbey (*see below*). Inside are the remains of a splendid timber building with a raised aisle-type roof which formerly housed the small college. Flint foundations remain under the lawns, along with a large fish-pond across the lane. Six stone coffins were dug up near the house in 1842.

Medieval Water Mill.

Situated beside the stream is a water mill. This mill is of ancient origin and originally associated with the nearby nunnery.

Site of Windmill.

A mill is shown N of the Abbey in 1783.

Medieval Green & Common.

'Aysshe Green' is recorded in 1433 and shown as Ash Green on Faden's 1783 map. It lay on the S edge of Campsea Ash Park to the W of the country lane which skirts the SW edge of the park; Ashgreen Farm marks the green's NE corner. On the same map the church is shown lying on Ash Common which covered the southern road junctions in the village.

Recreation.

A Camping Field is recorded here which provided the site for a medieval football game.

Town House.

A town house comprising two tenements adjoining Pinstead Lane is recorded in 1794.

Historic Houses.

Ash Abbey is a magnificent C14 type of hall house. As Norman Scarfe explains . . .'it is as if the truss of an aisled hall were lifted up to the first floor, and supported on a gigantic tie-beam . . a massive tree-trunk'. Chantry Farm,

CAMPSEY ASH *(continued)*

SW of the church, was attached to the Nunnery and, perhaps, the chantry-house. It was the seat of Theophilus Howard, Earl of Suffolk, and afterwards purchased by John Braham (or Brame). It retains a carved chimney piece of C13 date. The site of High House, built c1600 by John Glover, servant to Thomas, Duke of Norfolk, or his son William "who was unhappy slaine" in 1641, is shown on Faden's map standing to the S of its 175 acre deer park approached by a great avenue of lime and elm. It was rebuilt in Elizabethan style in 1865 by J. G. Sheppard, but demolished in the 1950s. This avenue still remains running SSE from the present B1078.

CAPEL ST ANDREW *(7 miles E of Woodbride)*

Wilford Hundred. 'St Andrew's Chapel' from *Capel* (ME) meaning 'Chapel' plus dedication. *Capeles* (DB)
Manors. Capel St. Andrew (1310 Simon de Ratlesden).

Ancient Mounds or Tumuli

Tangham Mount in Tangham Forest, 30' in diameter and 5' high with traces of a ditch, may be a burial mound or ancient defensive post. There is a low round mound, possibly a barrow, some 59' in diameter and 4½' high in Tangham Forest on the southern boundary, and a circular mound 98'-115' in diameter and 4' high, also in Tangham Forest between Tangham House and Tangham Cottages which may also be a possible round barrow.

Site of Ancient Chapel (Church?)

The place-name suggests an ancient chapel in the parish but this may have been a reference to the Saxon church mentioned in Domesday. A church, dedicated to St. Andrew, later given to Butley Priory, existed here in 1529. Its site may have been opposite Home Farm where many human bones have been dug up.

Deserted Medieval Village (?)

Without its former church, manor house and green, it is conjectural whether the parish ever possessed a village settlement of any consequence; much is now hidden beneath the conifer plantation of Tangham Forest.

Medieval Green.

Bordered by Water Wood to the N and Oak Wood to the S, Capel Green is shown on Faden's 1783 map just W of Butley Priory. It was square and lay on the right side of the lane to Green Farm which stood on its NW corner.

Site of Historic House.

Tangham Cottages stand on the site of the old Tangham Manor House.

CAPEL ST MARY *(5½ miles SE of Hadleigh)*

Samford Hundred. 'Chapel' (ME) plus dedication. *Capeles* (DB)
Manors. Boitwell Hall/ Boyton Hall with Groats/Grot's Deny's and Helhouse Lands al Beames (C13 Jeffrey de Capell held as Honor of Heningham). *Sub-Manors.* Churchford Hall; Thorney; Castel's; Rembrow.

Ancient Woodland.

Great Martin's Hill Wood is a stretch of ancient woodland to the S of the parish.

Roman Settlement & Site of Roman Villa.

There was a Roman settlement here, and a possible villa was discovered in 1928 on a council estate known as Windy Hill. The site overlooks the valley above Lattinford Bridge on the parish boundary. Further excavations found painted plaster, glass and pottery sherds of C1-2. A cobbled yard was uncovered in 1967 partly overlaid with the floor of an outbuilding.

Roman Road.

The parish boundary traced the line of the Roman road from Colchester, now the A12.

Roman Industrial Site.

Near the villa site are signs of a local Roman pottery and tilemaking industry.

Ancient Chapel.

The place-name suggests an ancient chapel here dedicated to St Mary. One of the three manors is called Churchford

CAPEL ST MARY *(continued)*

and is situated in the N of the parish through which flows a brook and is represented by Churchford Hall and Churchford Farm. This may be a clue to the site of the former chapel.

Travellers' Cross (?)
Cross Green on the old London road suggests the former site of a roadside Travellers' Cross.

Medieval Green.
Cross Green is shown and named on Faden's map of 1783 as a triangular widening of the Old London Road. Its site remains at the eastern end of the section of Old London Road now cut off by the present A12 dual-carriageway. Bush Farm stands on its northern corner, but the site has been completely infilled.

Historic Houses & Ancient Moated Sites.
The parish comprised three manors, Boynton Hall, Churchford Hall and Vaux-and-Jermyn's. Boynton Hall, situated on the S side of the former Cross Green, still retains parts of the ancient C14 moated manor house. Churchford Hall, NW of the church, marks the site of the former manor house, and Jermyns Farm, near the northern parish boundary represents the third manor, with the site of Vauxhall manor house to the NW, now in the adjoining parish of Wenham Magna. Vine House, shown surrounded by a moat on the C19 tithe, is now lost beneath a modern housing estate.

CARLTON *(1 mile N of Saxmundham)*

Hoxne Hundred. 'Farmstead or estate of the freemen or peasants' (OScand) *Carletuna ?* (DB)
Formerly a separate parish, now joined with Kelsale to create Kelsale-cum-Carlton.
Manors. Carlton Manor (1281 Alice, Countess of Norfolk; accquired in 1334 by Prioress of Campsey).

Site of Ancient Chantry.
John Framlingham founded a chantry here in 1332 for three chaplains to pray for the soul of Alice of Hainault, Countess of Mareschall, the first wife of Thomas de Brotherton, Earl of Norfolk. In 1546, after the Dissolution, it was granted to William Honing. Its site is unknown.

Medieval Green.
Carlton Green is named and shown by Faden as a linear green replacing part of the present road to Peasenhall. It commenced at a point where it forms a fork with a footpath (named Carlton Green on the present OS map) and ran WNW to Green Farm, turning N to Trust Farm.

CARLTON COLVILLE *(3½ miles SW of Lowestoft)*

Mutford & Lothingland Hundred. Carlton - 'Farmstead or estate of the freemen or peasants' (OScand) *Carletuna* (DB) *Carleton Colvile* (1346). It was once known as Est Carlton (East Carlton) but became Carlton Colville many years after the acquisition of the manor by Robert de Colvile in 1227.
Manors. Carlton Hall (1227 Robert de Colvile). *Sub-Manors.* Broomholm Priory; Fastolf's Manor.

Neolithic-Early Bronze-Age Site.
An extensive Neolithic to Early Bronze-Age site found by the Beccles Road, produced a hoard of Neolithic axes.

Roman & Anglo-Saxon Settlement and Cemetery.
Digging on a barrow on Bloodmoor Hill on the Carlton - Gisleham parish boundary in 1768 unearthed a skeleton around whose neck was hung a gold medal and an onyx set in gold (*see* Gisleham). Recent excavations in the area have produced material from two main periods; C1-C2 Roman and C6-C8 Anglo-Saxon including post-holes of buildings, etc. 6,000 Roman and 4,000 Saxon pottery sherds were collected along with large quantities of metal working debris, and there was evidence of an extensive multi-phased Roman field system underlaying the Anglo-Saxon settlement.

Site of Ancient Chapel.
There was a chapel in the parish dedicated to St Mary but nothing is known. A Chapel Road runs NW from St Peter's Church.

CARLTON COLVILLE *(continued)*

Medieval Market & Fair.
Roger de Colvile obtained the grant for a market and fair here in 1267, and of free warren when it was still known as Est Carlton.

Medieval Ferry or Ford (and site of Hundred Court ?)
The parish adjoins Oulton Broad/Lake Lothing in an area known as Mutford Bridge. This is believed to be the site of a medieval ferry or ford (and, perhaps, the Hundred Court for Mutford). The waters were later bridged but this was swept away in 1717 to be replaced by another.

Medieval Green.
A major housing development and the B1384 now cover the very irreguar-shaped Carlton Green shown and named on Faden's map of 1783 running in a NE arc to join the green at Pakefield. Another long green, named Whitton Green, is shown running NE in the area of The Uplands in the N of the parish.

Ancient Moated Sites.
Carlton Hall, N of the church, stands on the site of the manor house of Carlton Hall destroyed by fire in the first half of the C18. The original seat of the de Colville's may be represented by the isolated horseshoe moat with a NE entrance, immediately S of the village. Another ancient circular moat named The Mardles (from the Old French Mardelle meaning 'brink of the well'), a name applied to the spot where gathered hemp is placed to soak, used to be situated in the Street. It was said to have been water-filled from several springs within the area with a central island of fairly hard ground. A few bricks lay on the surface but there appeared no foundations. The site was destroyed by gravel extraction between 1927 and the 1960s and later infilled. This could possibly be related to another Carlton manor, Fastolf's, first mentioned in the reign of Edward III and called after Hugh Fastolf, lord here in 1378.

CAVENDISH *(6 miles NW of Sudbury)*

Babergh Hundred. 'Cafna's enclosure' or 'Cafa's late pasture' (OE) *Kauanadisc* (DB)
Manors. Overhall (C12 divided between David de Lindsey and Sir Hugh de Odyngseces). *Sub-Manors.* DeGrays/Coltshall; Netherhall; Newhall; Houghton Hall; Bulley Hall; Impey or Impsey Hall/Quipsey Hall; Kensings/Kessings Hall; Poytons; Peche's/Peychy's; More Hall; Collingham Hall; Stansfield Hall.

Ancient Woodland.
Northy Wood and Houghton Grove in the N, and the larger Easty Wood in the centre of the parish, are all parts of ancient woodland.

Tumulus (?)
'Inside Blacklands Park' entrance gate, a round barrow was named but not shown on any maps.

Ancient Earthworks.
Excavations in 1983 on earthworks in a pasture covering 3.6 hectacres at Colts Hall identified hollow-ways, banks and ditches and an oval enclosure 153 yds by 109 yds having a shallow ditch and traces of an internal bank. An C11 date has been suggested for the enclosure which may possibly identify the original Cafna's Hall and its associated settlement (*see above place-name*).

Hermitage Chapel.
Medieval manuscripts speak of a Hermitage Chapel situated here, later incorporated into Clare Priory.

Free Grammar School.
A free grammar school was founded in 1696 under the will of the Rector of Cavendish, Thomas Grey, for a master to teach 15 poor children in English, Latin and Greek. It was endowed with a farm in Pentlow just across the border in Essex.

Medieval Fairs.
Until the late C19, Cavendish had two annual fairs, one for cattle and one for 'pleasure'.

CAVENDISH *(continued)*

Medieval Green.

The much photographed Cavendish Green remains today bordered by old properties exactly as it did on Faden's map of 1783.

Workhouse.

A workhouse accommodating 30 inmates in 1776 was situated on the N side of Stow Street, formerly Workhouse Street. Accounts date from 1758.

Almshouses.

Nationally known from their features in many books and magazines, five thatched almshouses form a picturesque composition with the church and green at Hyde Park Corner. They were badly damaged in a fire in 1971 but have since been restored.

Historic Houses & Ancient Moated Sites.

The Gernons, a family of some note in Norfolk and Essex, were seated here. They later assumed the name of the parish and their residence Cavendish Hall, now divided into three cottages, retains the arms of this powerful family. One, Sir John Cavendish, born here in 1373, became Chief Justice of the Court of King's Bench, an office he filled with distinction until decapitated by rebels under Jack Straw in 1382 on Bury Market Hill. This act was in reprisal for the actions of Sir John's youngest son, also a John, who had assisted in dispatching another rebel leader, Wat Tyler, whilst in the service of Richard II. Colts Hall, W of the village, replaces an ancient hall once home to Thomas Colt, Chancellor of the Exchequer in the mid-C15. Nether Hall, N of the church, formerly a manor house and now a farmhouse, is C16, as is the timber-framed Old Rectory. Houghton Hall, on the site of the manor house and in the same area, retains part of its quadrangular moat. There are other moats at Blacklands Hall (built in 1576 , restored and enlarged in 1850), a long curved channel graduating from 20' wide at the NE to 60' at the SW, and SE of Houghton Grove, where there is an isolated square moat, now dry. There is also a moat at the site of Over Hall manor house W of the church which was locally known as 'Pockey Hall', a reference to its use in 1767 as an isolation hospital for smallpox victims. "When the railway was built around 1860, foundations were found about the site of the present station indicating the site of a 'big house' ". Faden's map of 1783 marks 'Cavendish Place' approximately in this position adjoining the A1092 to the N by Pentlow Bridge.

CAVENHAM *(4½ miles SE of Mildenhall)*

Lackford Hundred. 'Cafa's homestead/enclosure/water-meadow' (OE) *Kanauaham* (DB) *Cauenham* (1198) *Manors.* Cavenham al Canham (C11/C12 Gilbert de Clare). *Sub-Manors.* Shardelowes.

Ancient Track.

The Ickneild Way passes SW-NE through the southern part of the parish crossing the tributary of the river Lark at Stone Bridge, SE of the village.

Tumuli.

A round barrow stands at the intersection of the Ickneild Way with Risby Road, 300 yds S of the church; another lies on the NE parish boundary W of the river Lark, and a third from documentary evidence only, contained a cremation internment of probable Bronze-Age date.

Neolithic Settlement Site.

A Late Neolithic domestic site dating from 2000-3000BC was discovered during quarrying for gravel. The site was perched above the flood plain of the river Lark. The density and nature of the features were suggestive of a domestic settlement. There is also evidence of earlier Mesolithic presence in the area.

Ancient Linear Ditch.

The Black Ditches, a possible ancient boundary ditch and bank, is visible in two sections with a marshy (originally) central break. The S section, forming the eastern parish boundary, runs from the Ickneild Way N to its crossing of the Lark at Lackford, and is traceable for 1½ miles across Risby Poor Heath to the S along the edge of Long Plantation, extending over the parish boundary. The N section lies on Cavenham Heath extending from S of

CAVENHAM *(continued)*

Oak Plantation 1,100 yds to the Lark. The date and purpose of the earthwork is unknown but it is probably post-Roman.

Roman Town(?)
The Roman town of *Camboricum* may be sited in the area, either here or in the parish of Icklingham to the N.

Ancient Chapel.
A chapel dedicated to Our Lady was mentioned in 1363. Its site is unknown.

Ancient Preceptory.
It has been suggested that Cavenham can be identified as the *Togrynd* where a Preceptory of the Knights Templars of St John was established. Its site is probably represented by Temple Bridge in the extreme N of the parish by the river Lark. Its foundation is unknown but it was likely dissolved by 1312.

Guildhall (?)
There were four guilds here - St. Andrew, St. Mary, Holy Trinity (1389) and St. John Baptist (1446) - suggesting that the parish formerly held a guildhall.

CHARSFIELD *(5½ miles N of Woodbridge)*

Loes Hundred. *feld* 'tract of open country' (OE) possibly with Celtic river name *Char* *Ceresfelda* (DB)
Manors. Charsfield Manor (C11 Roger Bigot; C13 William de Weyland).

Roman Road.
The B1078 Ipswich Road follows the course of a Roman road SW-NE to form the parish boundary from Debach House to Valley Farm.

Site of old Windmill.
A post mill stood S of King's Farm in 1783.

Medieval Green.
Boardy Green in the N of the parish is now a hamlet.

Lost Medieval Village (?)
The village of Charsfield Parva appears to have lain alongside the Deben's affluent running E from Charsfield. Domesday Book called it *Parva Ceresfella* with 'a church with 36 acres' but it is not heard of again.

Historic Houses & Ancient Moated Sites.
William de Weyland anciently held the manor which later passed to the Bedingfields. It was Sir Henry Bedingfield who held his first manor court in Charsfield but he may not have resided here. The first known resident lord was John Leman. Charsfield Hall is C16, and Park Farm, to the SE, which has portions of a square moat mostly now dry, with part of another to the N, may have been the site of the original manor house. Another ancient property is Redhouse Farm, ¾ mile NW of the village, which retains a large part of a moat of irregular plan. A carved beam from Rectory House, demolished in 1861, is dated 1385.

CHATTISHAM *(5 miles E of Hadleigh)*

Samford Hundred. 'Homestead or water-meadow/enclosure of a man called Ceatt'? (OE) *Cetessam* (DB)
Manors. Chattisham/Chattisham Hall (1275 Priory of Wykes, Essex).

Historic House & Ancient Moated Site.
There are remains of a moat at Chattisham Hall.

CHEDBURGH *(7 miles SW of Bury St Edmunds)*

Risbridge Hundred. 'Hill of a man called Cedda' (OE) *Cedeberia* (DB). Norman Scarfe considers it may refer to a mound connected with Cedd, the founder of Christianity in Essex, who died on 26 October 664 A.D.
Manors. Chedburgh Hall and Arneboroughe (1315 Thomas Verdon).

CHEDBURGH *(continued)*

Medieval Green.
A linear green shown unnamed on Faden's 1783 map, ran from the road junction NNE, gradually tapering down to become the road. The green also extended SW into Depden parish. There was no village settlement here at this time and all the later development appears to have been created by the upgrading of the main road (A143) heading E to Horringer, and the later construction of a road NW to Chevington.

Historic House & Ancient Moated Site.
Chedburgh Hall, now a farmhouse near the church, stands on the site of the ancient manor house and still retains traces of an earlier moat.

CHEDISTON *(2 miles W of Halesworth)*

Blything Hundred. 'Stone of a man called Cedd' (OE) *Cedestan* (DB) The name should be Chedistone, and the erratic from which it took its name lies near Rockstone Manor Farm in neighbouring Cookley. *(see Cookley)*
Manors. Bavants al Norton Bavents (1263 Hubert de Bavent). *Sub-Manors.* Wrights al Glemham's; Hovells.

Romano-British Occupation Sites.
At Chediston Grange, ½ mile S of the church, there is evidence of a metal working site and tile and pottery kilns indicating a Romano-British occupation site. Just E of the church in the area of Herne Hill Farm, wall footings of a Romano-British building were unearthed during trial trenching.

Ancient Tracks.
The Packway forms the NW parish boundary from Christmas Lane. Another packway running N from Walpole, crossing Low Road (B1123) and passing Packway Farm to Duke's Farm, is likely to be a part of Earl Bigod's highway connecting his great castles of Walton, Framlingham and Bungay.

Medieval Green.
Faden's map of 1783 shows 'Cheddiston Green' as a largish oblong green running WNW from a footpath E of Ash Farm to Chediston Grove along a road leading from the church to Town Farm.

Medieval Fair.
A licence to hold a fair was granted to Wrights al Glemham's Manor in c1276.

Almshouse.
By a deed of Henry Claxton in 1575 three tenements were occupied by three poor families. The almshouses were rebuilt in 1832.

Historic Houses & Ancient Moated Sites.
South of Grove Farm in a field called 'The Grove', 2 miles W of the church, are two dry moated manorial sites with traces of associated earthworks. The larger moat at the NW measures 200'x150', and the smaller 135'x104'. Finds suggest an early C14 date for the site, the same period as the church. This may have been the site of the third Chediston manor, Wrights, or more likely, the earlier residence of Hubert de Bavent who owned the main manor in 1263. Later called Norton Bavents, it was moved to Chediston Hall, some distance E of the site of the E-shaped Chediston Hall, which was demolished in 1955 and shows traces of a moat on the tithe map and a possible fish-pond immediately to the N. Although rebuilt in the 1830s in Jacobean style, it was Tudor in origin and owned by Sir John Pettus in 1674. Chediston Grange stands within an ancient rectangular moat 186' by 218-226' with strong defences and two entrances. It was the original manor house site of the Hovell family. There are two sides of a square moat at Hill Farm and there was a moat with subsidiary enclosures near the western parish boundary at the former Westend Farm which was destroyed when a bomb dump exploded at nearby Metfield Airfield in 1944. The whole site has been bulldozed leaving only an isolated pond.

CHELMONDISTON *(6 miles SSE of Ipswich)*

Samford Hundred. 'Farmstead of a man called Ceolmund (OE) *Chelmundeston* (DB)
Manors. Chelmondiston (-1316 Crown property; 1316 Sir John de Holbroke).

CHELMONDISTON *(continued)*

Industrial Sites.
There were salt pans at Pin Mill beside the river Orwell, and Pringle's or Clamp House Hard indicates a place where peat or turf for fuel was once cut and stacked.

Medieval Archery Practice.
Butt Meadow indicates the probable site of medieval archery practice.

Ancient Water Mill.
At Pin Mill the mill pond banks remain from the C14 water mill.

Site of old Windmill.
Elmer's Mill stood S of Church Lane in 1783. It was pulled down in 1913.

Historic Inn & Ferry House (?)
The Butt & Oyster Inn, dating from c1500 and picturesquely situated on a hard by the river Orwell in the hamlet of Pin Mill, may once have been a ferry house. The Water Bailiffs and Burgesses of the Port of Ipswich held their Admiralty Courts here between 1546 and 1552.

CHELSWORTH *(5 miles NW of Hadleigh)*

Cosford Hundred. 'Enclosure of a man called Ceorl' (OE) *Ceorleswyrthe* (962) *Cerleswrda* (DB)
Manors. Chelsworth (-c1527 Abbot of St. Edmunds, Bury; c1527 Sir Anthony Wingfield).
Chelsworth was another of south-west Suffolk's flourishing cloth centres and its larger than average church is a remnant of its former industrial prosperity.

Roman Road.
Two Roman roads must have crossed Chelsworth parish. Land boundaries given in 962 A.D. refer to a 'street' - a Roman road. The course of one, heading ENE crossing the river Brett to enter the parish of Kettlebaston by Wagger Farm, must have clipped the N of the parish before traced on the ground at Bildeston by the road to Wattisham.

Ancient Watermills.
The 'Upper Mill' or fulling mill stood in or near the orchard of the Grange, perhaps at the weir to the S of the island 'which is called Mill Hill'. Lower Mill, which was pulled down c1754, was possibly situated near Mill Tongs.

Ancient Bridge.
A two-arched bridge of ancient origin leads to the hall and Chelsworth Common.

Medieval Archery Practice.
Butt Field (part of Chelsworth Park) identifies the site of possible medieval archery practice. In the C16 the parish boasted of having 'seven able archers'.

Medieval Common.
Chelsworth Common lay S of Chelsworth Hall and Park, on the country road which joins the present A1141. It is shown as a small triangular area but not named on Faden's map of 1783, by which time it may have already been considerably reduced in size. The present field boundaries may trace part of its original extent.

Historic Grange.
Chelsworth Grange, long used as the rectory, is an old half-timbered C16 house close by the church. It was here that Tom Killigrew, banished from the court of Charles II, ended his days. The Prior of Kersey is known to have once had free warren here.

Historic House & Ancient Moated Site.
Joined here by two tributary streams, the Brett skirts the rising ground called Park Fields, now Chelsworth Park. The present hall is modern but traces of the ancient Hall were said to have been seen within the park in the C19

CHELSWORTH *(continued)*

on an island site near the Grange with the river forming the S side. Here, C16 court rolls talk of 'Le Mote and Hall Gardens', and a description in 1605 states 'No mention where the mannour house stoode. Yet at the W end of the churche appeareth the seate of a most ancient house environed with ditches and moates . . .' The knightly family of Blakenham lived here for several generations until 1302 when it became the manor of Hugh de St Philibert. The tomb of Sir John de St Philibert who died in 1359 lies in the church. The last residential medieval lord was Sir John de Plays who died in 1387. In 1485 the then lord, Sir John Howard, gave a legacy of twenty shillings to repair "my church" at Chelsworth, and it is traces of his hall which remained in Park Fields. The timber-framed Grange dates from c1450 and The Peacock Inn contains wood carvings from 1410.

CHEVINGTON *(6 miles SW of Bury St Edmunds)*

Thingoe Hundred. 'Estate associated with a man called Ceofa' (OE) *Ceventuna ?* (DB)
Manors. Chevington Manor (-1539 Abbot of St. Edmunds, Bury; 1539 Sir Thomas Kytson).

Ancient Woodland.
Park Wood and Jennison's Plantation, part of the park of the abbots' manor house, are ancient woodland.

Ancient Way.
An ancient green way ran from the abbots' hall towards their Abbey at Bury. It is shown on Faden's map of 1783 and can still be traced following the N bank of the stream E from the hall, then turning NNE passing through Chevington Field Plantation and W of Downter's Wood; then N following the western boundary of Ickworth Park before bearing E by the river Linnet to Bury.

Deer Park.
The abbots of St. Edmundsbury had a deer park here associated with their country retreat. It lay to the N and NW of the hall.

Site of old Windmill.
A post mill stood NW of the Broad Green crossroads in 1783. It was disused by 1900.

Medieval Greens.
Two greens are shown and named in Chevington on Faden's map of 1783 lying side by side. Broad Green and College Green extended from the Hargrave Road-Mill Road junction to incorporate most of the village. The area was at least partly enclosed in 1816 and is now built over. Just S of these greens, connected by the road to Chedburgh, another large green is shown but unnamed by Faden's map. It covered the area now known as Tan Office Green.

Historic Houses & Ancient Moated Sites.
The present C17 Chevington Hall, standing on the N side of the church, occupies an exceedingly strong, ramparted and irregular ancient moated camp, which was later the site of the fortified manor house of the abbots of Bury. The massive horse-shoe moat, 60' wide and 14' deep, has a rampart rising to 9'. A mound beyond the N side may have been used as an outpost or observation platform, while on the E side lie possible fish-ponds. The site, which may well be that described in the place-name, formed part of the estate of Britwulf the Saxon, conferred on Bury Abbey at the Conquest at the express wish of Abbot Baldwin. It later became a favourite retreat of the abbots who used the earthworks to protect the country house they built within and mentioned in 1309. A stone coffin of a C13 ecclesiastic was found at the church in 1838. At the Dissolution, the manor and park were granted to Sir Thomas Kytson, builder of Hengrave Hall. Despite the magnificence of that property, the Kyson family spent considerable time here at Chevington which they described as their "favourite possession", staying at the Hunting Lodge rather than the hall itself. Chevington Lodge Farm to the NW, named 'Chevington Lodge' by Faden in 1783, probably marks its site . The Rectory retains the NW half of a square moat and, just NW of this and North Plantation, a square 'moat' was marked on the OS 1st Ed. map of 1865 with a stream or drain joining at the centre of the NE and SW sides. A fragment of the moat remains at Moat Farm, a former C15 hall house near the SE parish boundary.

CHILLESFORD *(9 miles NE of Woodbridge)*

Plomesgate Hundred. 'Gravel ford' (OE) *Cesefortda* (DB). The original ford was probably at the northern extremity of Butley River just S of the church.
Manors. Chillesford (1280 Sir Thomas de Weyland). *Sub-Manors.* Russell's.

Tumuli.
A round barrow lies in Tunstall Forest on the N side of the B1078, and another on the extreme NE parish boundary with Iken and Sudbourne. There are two further barrows on Wantisden Heath, on the western parish boundary, lying either side of the footpath crossing Round Hill.

Ancient Track.
Friars Walk is an ancient pathway leading to Gedgrave and Orford.

Medieval Watermill.
Carlton Watermill, built in 1530, was still in existence in 1908.

Historic House.
Froize/Friars Inn was in existence in 1734 when it was known as Decoy House.

CHILTON *(1 mile NE of Sudbury)*

Babergh Hundred. 'Farm of the young (noble)men' or 'Ceola's farmstead' (OE) *Ciltona* (DB)
Formerly united with Waldingfield as Waldingfield-cum-Chilton, it is now a separate parish.
Manors. Chilton al Waldingfield Hall/Carbonels with Chilton Manor (C12 William Carbonels).

Iron-Age Enclosure.
Two sides of an Iron Age enclosure have been discovered at County Farm.

Roman Road.
The eastern parish boundary follows Valley Road, tracing a length of Roman road from N of Valley Farm to the outskirts of Great Waldingfield where a field boundary may mark its line until lost under the site of the disused airfield.

Deserted Medieval Village.
The expansion of business parks in neighbouring Sudbury is eating into the SW corner of Chilton parish. There is no longer a village here, only an isolated church, the impressive Chilton Hall and an odd farm or two. However, C13-C15 pottery has been found around the church, and trial trenching revealed trackways, medieval field boundaries and ditches, plus that of an Iron Age enclosure which contained not only prehistoric artefacts but Late Saxon and Early Medieval pottery including Thetford ware. This suggests an early settlement here and the remains of a deserted medieval village and green of which the Norman church was a focal point.

Medieval Common (?)
White states that Chilton Common was enclosed in 1813, though no green or common is shown in Chilton on Faden's map of 1783 and no name on the present OS maps is suggestive of one.

Historic House & Ancient Moated Site.
There was a hall here at Domesday, probably on the same site and possibly connected with the 'young noblemen' to which the place-name may refer. The present isolated Chilton Hall is situated on high clay lands NE of the church and some quarter of a mile from the Waldingfield road. It stands on the C13 site of an earlier fortified manor house which was long the seat and stronghold of the powerful knightly family of Crane, one of whom, Sir Robert, lies in a magnificent tomb in the nearby church. Much of the hall was destroyed in a fire of c1800, but a substantial fragment of their great Early Tudor brick mansion of c1430-1643 still remains. Its battlemented observation tower is still here, approached from a bridge spanning the perfectly preserved moat, some 40' wide, which still surrounds it. Its former gatehouse has now gone.

CLARE *(8 miles E of Haverhill)*

Risbridge Hundred. Perhaps originally an old river-name of Celtic origin meaning 'bright stream' (Clare is on a tributary of the river Stour). *Clara* (DB)

Manors. Clare Manor descended through the Earls of Clare, Hereford & Gloucester to the Mortimers. *Sub-Manors.* Stone Hall al Stonehouse al Manse Manor.

Clare derived its importance in Saxon times from its position on the frontier of the kingdom of East Anglia and this importance continued after the Norman Conquest. William gave the town along with many other estates to Richard FitzGilbert, Earl of Brionne in Normandy, and these lands became known collectively as the Honour of Clare. The town is noted in the Domesday Survey as a borough with 43 burgesses, 2400 acres of arable land, a vineyard of five acres, a market and a church. During this period the town was almost an island - To the S and E were rivers (Stow and New River) and Chilton Dyke, and to the W ran the Hawedych, and a stream ran from this across Gosford Street (Callis Street) into the Chilton ditch. Though Clare's status is now much diminished, it still retains great monuments to its noble past.

Tumulus.

A round barrow lay in a field at Chilton Street, E of Folly Road and Mott's Farm (probably named after it).

Romano-British Fortified Camp.

N of the town and just W of Bridewell Street on Lower Common, a D-shaped camp covering 13 acres is enclosed by fragmentary double banks and ditches which are more perfect on the N and SE sides. The inner bank is 9' high on the N and there are entrances to the NE and E. The earthwork is the best of its kind in Suffolk and probably constructed c300 A.D. to defend the Iceni frontier against the Catuvellauni. The manor of Clare-cum-Chilton (Chilton hamlet is 1¼ miles N), was established within the camp in the mid-C13 and aerial photos show an extensive manorial complex with at least four structures and possible fish-ponds. The manor was known as Erbury and recorded as *Erdebir* c1232. It represents the old-English *Earthburh*, meaning 'earth fortification'.

Roman Road (?)

A Roman road is thought to have followed the Stour valley passing through Clare to connect the two major Roman settlements at Wixoe and Long Melford, though the present A1092 shows little evidence of its course.

Norman Castle.

Situated S of the town, now within a country park, the huge earthworks of Clare Castle occupy an area of some 20 acres. They consist of a Norman motte 53' high and 850' in diameter surrounded by the remains of a deep moat. E of the motte are two baileys enclosed by ramparts. In the C19 the railway station was constructed within one of these. A wide ditch divides the baileys from one another and also encircles them joining up with the moat round the motte - a perfect example of a motte-and-bailey castle. Most of the masonry has now disappeared but there are fragments of a shell keep of C13 date atop the motte, and some flint walling. This very early castle is first recorded in 1090 when Richard, Earl of Hertford, made the castle his residence, retitling himself Earl of Clare, but the initial earthworks here may comprise a pre-Conquest fort, held in the early C10 by the Saxon Earl Aluric, son of Withgar, later adapted and extended by the Normans.

Priories.

Early in the C10, Earl Aluric, who held the castle site, founded a church dedicated to John the Baptist within what is now the N bailey. In 1090, after the Conquest, Gilbert de Clare founded an alien Benedictine Priory and gave it as a cell to the abbey of Bec in Normandy. In 1124 it was moved to Stoke-by-Clare. Many burials associated with the priory have been found in the castle precincts. 'The Priory', standing in a secluded position to the S of the town close to the castle, forms a part of the extensive remains of the first house of the Order of Augustinians established in England. It was founded by Richard de Clare, Earl of Gloucester, in 1248 and it was here that Joan of Acres, second daughter of Edward I, was buried with great ceremony in 1305, and also Lionel, Duke of Clarence and son of Edward II, in 1377, adding greatly to the prestige of the priory. It was made indigenous by Richard II in 1396 and given by him as a cell to St Peters at Westminster. In 1406 Edmund, Earl of Marsh and heir of the founders, converted the priory into a college for a priest and secular canons. It was dissolved

CLARE *(continued)*

in 1538 and the site granted to Robert Frende. Succession went full circle in May 1953 when the Augustinian friars returned to their ancient home and the priory was re-established. The priory church is 160' long with the S wall standing to its full length. At the E end are the remains of the magnificent sedelia, to the W of which is the site of the tomb of Joan of Acres and the blocked doorway to St Vincent's Chapel. The Prior's House is complete, as is the infirmary.

Hermitage.
Faden's map of 1783 shows a hermitage beside the Chilton Stream, just NE of the town, to the W of the present Hermitage Farm and N of Hermitage Close.

Ancient Chapels & Chantry.
In the hamlet of Chilton, on the S bank of the Chilton Stream at the junction with the Poslingford road, stands the former Chilton or Wentford Chapel of St Mary Magdalene, converted into a house c1550. It is Norman in date and retains the N doorway with Norman ornamentation, plus remains of two blocked contemporary windows over the E gable. It was granted to the Guild of St. John Baptist in Chilton by Richard, Duke of York, in 1444. The hamlet of Wentford is situated in the S of Poslingford parish. In the C17, a Wayside Chapel, now represented by Chapel Cottage, was used as a powder magazine in the Civil War. The site of Clare Chantry was adjacent to 'Highfields' E of the town, S of the Cavendish road and opposite the school.

Ancient Bridge.
Gosford, the ancient ford across Callis Street, was spanned by a wooden bridge in 1387 using timber from Hundon Park.

Mills.
A malt watermill was recorded in 1381 and another was in existence in 1770. Four windmills (said to be valued at £10) are recorded here c1295. Later, a postmill stood on Mill Hill in 1678. N of Mill Farm, on the southern parish boundary, a mill was shown in existence in 1783 standing beside the River Stour; it was blown down in 1875.

Medieval Commons.
In 1553/4, Queen Mary granted Upper and Lower Common (formerly known as Houndwall and Erbury Garden) 'for the use of such inhabitants of the borough that did not own 15 acres, to graze their horses and cows upon'.

Pillory & Ducking Stool.
A pillory existed near the Moot Hall, and the town's bailiffs were ordered to repair 'Le Cuckyngstol' in 1357.

Medieval Market & Fairs.
Clare already boasted a market in Saxon times which continued after the Conquest. A grant for a fair was obtained in 1226 (with a further grant for a market and fair in 1250) and there were later two annual medieval fairs, with the important Wentford Fair held in the adjoining field to Wentford Chapel. Both abolished by 1891.

Site of Market Cross.
The old Market Cross, replacing an even earlier one ('in need of repair' in the C16), once stood on Market Hill. It was taken down in 1838 when a new Corn Exchange was erected and a number of 'unsightly' buildings in the Market Place were removed.

Pest Houses.
Two pest houses were erected on the common c1724 to accommodate small pox victims.

Prison.
Bridewell prison was mentioned in 1700. In 1787 it was converted to a private house.

Free School.
A free grammar school is recorded in 1443. In 1550 it was reputedly being housed in the former Guildhall and, at some time, in two rooms above the Market Cross. In 1668 the will of William Cadge provided for a schoolmaster to teach ten poor boys of Clare. Free places were abolished in 1856.

CLARE *(continued)*

Almshouses.
Almshouses consisting of three cottages by the church, and three acres of land in Bridewell Meadow were founded by James Bingley in 1462 to provide for six poor widows.

Moot Hall.
The Moot Hall, first mentioned in 1481, was reputedly sited on the S side of the Market Place. It was said to be in need of repair in 1650 and the upper stage fell down in 1664.

Guildhall.
The former guildhall stands opposite the church. There were four guilds in the town: Corpus Christi (c1462); St. Augustin in Convent of Clare (1488); St. Peter (1524); St. John Baptist (1524).

Historic Houses.
Beneath a C15 timber-framed building at the W end of Market Hill is a well-preserved C14 stone-vaulted undercroft, its massive groined roof supported by a central octagonal pillar. Among other historic houses are: The Ancient House, situated at the SW corner of the churchyard - a former priests' house of 1473 with fine C17 pargeting, and Stone Hall, in Nethergate Street, mentioned in documents since 1307. Cliftons, which has a beautiful C16 central chimney, and the impressively timbered Nethergate House in Nethergate Street, is the finest of the C17 period. The Bell Hotel (formerly called The Green Dragon) and the Peppermill Restaurant are both housed in C16 buildings. The Swan Inn was formerly Quylters, a tenement mentioned in Court Rolls of 1361. It features a carved inn sign depicting the royal arms of England and France which possibly came from Clare castle. A John Norfolk left his son an alehouse called 'le Swan' in 1498. An inventory of 1549 mentions The Half Moon, formerly known as The Moon Inn. In Callis Street, The Grove is said to have been built in 1420. In Chilton hamlet, Lodge Farm and Motte's Farm are two interesting old houses.

CLAYDON *(4 miles NW of Ipswich)*

Bosmere & Claydon Hundred. 'Clayey hill' (OE) *Clainduna* (DB)
Manors. Claydon/Claydon Hall (c1274 Adam Aula de Cleiden held of half a fee of Honor of Lancaster).

Site of old Windmill.
A post mill is shown N of the village in 1783. It was still working in 1892.

Historic Houses & Ancient Moated Site.
Claydon Hall, now a farmhouse SE of the church, was built c1621 and stands within the northern side of what remains of a strong moat some 70 yds by 50 yds with an entrance on the NW corner. The 1926 OS map shows Claydon Hall 'on the site of a castle' and it is this description of the earliest dwelling here that pervades from all early authorities. If it was indeed a castle, or at least (from the obvious former strength of the earthworks) a fortified manor house, it could well have been the seat of an Adam Aula de Cleiden who held the manor in the middle of the C13. He died in 1274 and his successor, William de Cleydon, was granted free warren here in 1302. Mockbeggers Hall, also known as Mock Hall or The Old Hall (there is also a possibility that it was formerly called 'Byrches'), half a mile S of the village, was the seat of the Aylemar family. Like Claydon Hall, the present house was built c1621. Its strange name is said to have originated from the fact that beggars making the long walk up to the hall from the road often left empty-handed after finding the hall unoccupied.

CLOPTON *(4 miles NW of Woodbridge)*

Carlford Hundred. 'Farmstead on a hill' (OE) *Clopetuna* (DB)
Manors. Clopton Hall al King's Hall (1127 William, 3rd Earl of Albermarle). *Sub-Manors.* Brentha al Brendhall; Rouse Hall; Wascolies al Westelyes.

Roman Road.
The B1078 traces the course of a Roman road ENE from the parish boundary at Debach House to Clopton Green. From here the present road turns S and the Roman road is lost in fields as it heads for Otley Bottom.

CLOPTON *(continued)*

Early Settlement.
The parish comprises an isolated church and scattered farms but there was once a medieval market and fair here (*see below*). A possible former nucleated village site NW and NE of the church has been identified by extensive scatters of early Saxon and Middle Saxon Ipswich ware pottery. Further evidence of early settlement may come from a small stream which rises here to form the southern parish boundary before becoming the river Lark. It was said to have once been navigable to Clopton and a field through which it runs is still called Clopton Dock.

Ancient Chapel.
St Margaret's Chapel, founded by Walter de Cokefield in 1329 and dissolved c1546, was situated in the parish. Its site is unknown.

Medieval Market & Fair.
In 1303 Sir John de Weyland, resident Lord of Rouse Hall Manor, obtained a grant for a market and fair here. Described as long obsolete in 1844, the site may be marked by Market Hill, NW of the church.

Medieval Green.
The area marked Clopton Green on the present OS map was shown as a green and named 'Clapton Green' on Faden's 1783 map. It lay between boundary ditches just N of Cats Hill, bordered by Green Farm. The line of the Roman road cuts across its south side.

Historic Houses and Ancient Moated Sites.
Behind its C18 frontage, Clopton Hall, NW of the church, dates from around 1500 and probably stands on the site of an earlier manor house. There is a moat at Moat Hall in the N of the parish.

COCKFIELD *(6 miles SSE of Bury St Edmunds)*

Babergh Hundred. 'Open land of a man called Cocca(Cohha)' (OE) *Cochanfelda* (DB)
Manors. Cockfield Manor (-c1535 Abbot of St. Edmunds, Bury; c1535 Robert Drury). *Sub-Manors.* Earls Hall; Butlers al Jacobbies; Pepers al Colchesters.

Ancient Woodland.
Bull's Wood on the eastern parish boundary is a part of ancient woodland.

Ancient Defensive Ditches.
The Warbanks, in the SW corner of the parish and extending into Lawshall and Shimpling parishes, are of very ancient origin. They comprise long ramparts and ditches crossed by a Roman road running between Alpheton and Bradfield Combust, just N of Thorn Corner. They once formed a single defensive system but have now been reduced to three sections. A small bronze bust of a woman was found within the earthworks.

Roman Road.
The boundary between Babergh and St Edmundsbury Districts follows the line of a Roman road running almost due N, its course traced by the present A134 from Shrub Farm to just S of Block Farm on the northern parish boundary. It is lost S of Shrub Farm and returns as the A134 on the parish boundary at The Warbanks.

Ancient Mounds.
At Colchester Green 1 mile NE of the village 'some mounds were to be seen' and 'some Roman tile found' in 1834.

Ancient Boundary Stone.
Formerly inscribed 'This marks the bounds of three Hundreds and three towns' - Babergh, Thredwastry & Cosford (Hundreds); Cockfield, Felsham & Thorpe Morieux ('towns'). 'Close to this stone is a pond by the road-side called the Hundred-Stone Pond through which flows a stream' (1886). The stone survives today on the verge on the E side of the Felsham Road - Bury Road junction, although the inscription is no longer visible.

Gallows (?)
Gallow Lane runs W from the A1141 to the now lost Smithwood Green which may once have held a gibbet.

COCKFIELD *(continued)*

Site of old Windmills.
Two post mills are shown in the parish in 1783: one, W of Cockfield Hall, was demolished after 1902, and the other, SW of the hall, blew down in 1860.

Medieval Market & Fair.
A grant for a market and fair was made in 1254.

Medieval Greens.
A widely scattered village round seven greens, called Windsor, Colchester, Smithwood, Great Cross, Old Hall, Parsonage and Button. All the greens are shown on Faden's map of 1783, and the sites of all except Parsonage named on the present OS. Windsor was a rectangular green on a curve in the road running NE from the Roman road on the western parish boundary; Colchester, a small rectangular green at the eastern end of Bird's Lane on the NE parish boundary; Smithwood, possibly a small square green lay on the southern parish boundary W of Gallow Lane and was destroyed during the construction of the World War II airfield; Great Cross is named Pepper Green in 1783 and shown as just a widening of the road on a bend W of Pepper Hall (the OS names the site Cross Green); Oldhall Green is shown running S as an inverted triangle from the site of the hall on the NW parish boundary; Parsonage was a small triangular green at the junction with the lane to Bull's Wood, marked by Tuns Farm and an ancient moat; and Button was a small square green near the SE parish boundary opposite High Hall Farm, and now infilled.

Workhouse.
A workhouse with 30 inmates is recorded in 1776.

Historic Houses & Ancient Moated Sites.
Cockfield Hall, S of the church, is the site of the Manor of Cockfield Hall recorded from 967 A.D. It belonged to the abbots of Bury Abbey as long ago as 1275, later to the wealthy cloth merchants, the Springs of Lavenham, and later still, the Herveys. The present hall has much reused material from the old hall which stood near Oldhall Green in the N of the parish where a part of the ancient moat survives. Earl's Hall, S of the village and now a farmhouse, takes its name from the de Veres, Earls of Oxford, who once owned the manor. A moated site here was owned by the King family in the C15 when various buildings and 28 acres belonging to the manor of Earls Hall were recorded. After being purchased by the Herveys of Peppers Hall in the C18, it was allowed to decay. Knightshill Farm near Button's Green is situated below the intriguingly named Knight's Hill, and is of C17 date. Peppers (formerly Pepperall's) Hall at Cross Green, E of the village, formerly the residence of the Harvey family, has a moat and is shown approached by an impressive tree-lined avenue in 1783. Kirby described it as 'a handsome mansion' in 1764. Church House is a Grade II listed building. There is a large, isolated square moated site NW of this with the W side of another beyond. The greater part of a large and very ancient moat lies just NE of Tuns Farm and E of this, Palmers Farm has a perfect rectangular moat. The Three Horseshoes public house is thought to date from 1470, The Coaching House (on the A134) from the C15/C16, and Thatchers Restaurant is housed in an early C17 building.

CODDENHAM *(3 miles ESE of Needham Market)*

Bosmere & Claydon Hundred. 'Cod(d)a's homestead or water-meadow/enclosure' (OE) *Codenham* (DB)
The parish includes the Domesday vill of Olden.
Manors. Denney's with Sackvill Rents (1285 Roger de Prydeton). *Sub-Manors.* Vesseys al Veises otherwise Priory/Manor of Coddenham Vicarage (granted to the Priory of Royston); Bridge Place; St. John of Jerusalem; Pipps; New Hall.

Ancient Woodland.
Coddenham Wood, Long Strops (formerly Priory Grove), and Blower's Pightle Grove are parts of ancient woodland.

Early Fortified Enclosure & Major Roman Fort & Posting Station.
In the vicinity of Baylham House Farm are two superimposed forts lying on the NE side of the river Gipping.

CODDENHAM *(continued)*

The smaller of the two dates from the pre-Roman Trinovantians and is rectangular with four ditches bisected by the major Roman road from Colchester to Caister-by-Norwich. The larger is a parallelogram with three ditches and has been identified as the early Roman military fort of *Combretonium* situated at a ford across the river and at an intersection of four Roman roads. It later became a Roman posting station. Since its discovery in 1823 much material has come from the fields on the E side of the river N and S of Baylham Mill where a plan was uncovered of extensive building dating back to the C1. A statuette of Emperor Nero (now in the British Museum) and medallions, all of Late C1, indicate a possible imperial shrine.

Roman Settlement.

Excavations are continuing on a Romano-British farmstead site discovered in the area of Valley Farm just NW of the village beside the Roman Stone Street. The site was occupied throughout the Romans period.

Roman Roads & Ancient Ford.

Roman roads pass through the parish to cross the Gipping. Excavations have provided evidence that they crossed at Sharmford (Old English for 'dirty ford', a reference to the local mud). Stone Street is evident in a section of straight road coming in NNE-SSW from Pettaugh to Choppins Hill, and may be traced again by a footpath which appear to follow its course past the village and from Walnut Tree Farm Cottages through Shrubland Park to the present A14 dual-carriageway. Mill Lane which passes the major Roman site at Baylham House Farm may also trace its course. The old disused section of the A140, now used as a slip road near the Beacon Hill interchange, probably marks the old Roman Pye Road between Stratford St Mary and Caister-by-Norwich (*Venta Icenorum*). It was sectioned here at Coddenham and found to be 32' wide with an agger 1'6" high. It postdated a mid-C1 pit and was suggested as having been constructed around 70 A.D.

Roman Beacon Site (?)

Beside the Roman Pye Road (the present A140), at the junction with the present A14 in the SW corner of the parish, is a circular mound shown on Faden's map of 1783 and the 1837 OS map. It is situated on a high wooded hill known as 'Beacon Hill' (Faden names it 'Bacon Hill'). This may have been the site of a Roman look-out station associated with this major road.

Saxon Settlement & Cemetery

A Saxon industrial(?) site, and a burial ground of the same period, occupy opposing slopes of the valley through which runs a tributary of the river Gipping to Gosbeck - perhaps formerly known as 'Goose Brook'(?)

Site of Nunnery (?)

A Cistercian Nunnery is thought to have existed for a short period somewhere in the parish. Founded c1160 by Eustachius de Mere, it appears to have been destroyed some 24 years later. Its dedication to St. Mary suggests that the parish church may have been used as the monastic church. In 1774 an alabaster cross said to have come from this priory was discovered in the manor house 'which connects by a tunnel' with the church opposite. Although a site is suggested by an ancient fragment of woodland formerly called Priory Grove, William White adds to the confusion by stating that de Mere gave Coddenham Church to Royston Priory about 1220.

Knights Hospitallers.

The Knights Hospitallers from the Commandry at Battisford held land in the parish. They may have also had a chapel on this land which extended into neighbouring Hemingstone. (*see* Hemingstone)

Lost Medieval Village (?)

Olden (the Domesday *Uledana* or *Wledana)* was 1 league long and 3 furlongs broad with a church. It had numerous small arable holdings, woodland and meadow. It was last mentioned in 1650 - 'a leet (meeting place for the manorial court) in Coddenham called Olden.' Its shape suggests it lay in the west of the parish.

Site of old Windmill.

A post mill is recorded NE of the A1120/B1078 road junction in 1785.

Old Parish Library.

The widow of Balthazar Gardemau (1656-1739), who was born in Poitiers and came to England as a

CODDENHAM *(continued)*

refugee and was appointed to the living in Coddenham in 1690, bequeathed 361 volumes of Anglo-French Literature to found a parochial library here in 1757. It was moved to the Cathedral Library in Bury St. Edmunds in 1964.

Free School.

A school established here in 1753 was endowed by the same Lady Catherine Gardemau (*see above*) for teaching 15 poor boys and 15 poor girls to read, write and cast accounts. The girls were also taught knitting and sewing.

Workhouse.

A workhouse in the parish is recorded in 1776.

Historic House & Ancient Moated Sites.

Choppins Hill Farm, ¾ mile N of the village, is C14 with an aisled medieval timber-frame. Jordaines manor house was built c1450. The Crown Inn, formely known as The Gryffon, was built in 1559 by the Woodhouse family as a Dower House. Wodehouse was an archer from nearby Crowfield knighted by Henry V after the Battle of Agincourt. Licensed c1620, the inn closed c1969 and was divided into two houses. The Dukes Head public house was built in 1500. The shop and post office, in the centre of the village, occupies part of the timber-framed former Live and Let Live public house which dates back to the C15 and has C17 pargetting. At Birch Farm, NW of the parish, is part of a moat, its plan difficult to determine, and ¼ mile SE of this, Dial Farm has an imperfect oblong moat. Ivy Farm, just E of the village, is also moated.

COMBS *(1 mile S of Stowmarket)*

Stow Hundred. 'The hill-crests or ridges' (OE) *Cambas* (DB)

Manors. Combs (1206 Bartholomew de Glanville). *Sub-Manors.* Bavents.

Ancient Woodland.

Combs Wood, E of the hall and church, is ancient woodland recorded in Domesday and now managed.

Moated Mound.

'Mill Mound' is a small circular mound much mutilated and overgrown situated in the SW corner of a small plantation known as Jack's Grove. A shallow ditch and outer bank remain around the northern half and the whole is some 98' in diameter with a causeway across the W side of the ditch. The mound may never have been of great height as the site is on a ridge giving command over a considerable area. Pevsner believed it to be the site of a small motte with no signs of a bailey. The cruciform ditch on the flat summit of the mound confirm its (later) use for a post-mill, but the moat leaves considerable doubt as to its original purpose.

Holy Oak.

Holyoak Farm, near the church, is said to take its name from the tree under which the local Protestants met during Queen Mary's reign to hear the scriptures read from a bible chained and concealed in the trunk.

Site of Former Medieval Village (?)

Earthworks of the private road and tenements of an alleged shrunken medieval village in the vicinity of the church were first seen in a pasture survey of 1978 and subsequently in aerial photographs. A probable roadway leads W from the church across the front of the present 'Combs Hall' (the earthworks of the original hall and garden lie to the S) and other agricultural buildings to link with the N-S road to Holyoak Farm. Further evidence of an original settlement around the church comes from an old chronicle which states that one Nigell, a servant of Count Robert the Domesday tenant, 'took away twelve socmanni (small farmers) who were before this time parishioners of the church of Stow and attached them to the church in Combs; this being duly confirmed by the Commissioners.'

Ancient Chapel (?)

'Combes Chapel' was mentioned in 1337 but its site is unknown. It may possibly have been a reference to the church itself, in medieval times sometimes named 'chapel'.

COMBS *(continued)*

Medieval Greens.

Old Mill House and Westend Farm mark the NE side of the former Brastead Green which lay on the W side of Mill Lane, shown and named on Faden's map of 1783. Also shown just N of this, an inverted L-shaped green lay across the junction of Mill Lane with the road to Little Finborough and extended round to Model Farm in the village centre. It was named as Trickers Hill and bordered by old properties of which the Old Rectory appears one of the few survivors today. Another large green is shown near the SE parish boundary; this was Moats Tye which lay on the SE side of Bradley Lane and ran from the junction with Deadman's Lane, NE to the T-junction along the line of the hundred boundary between Stow and Bosmere; White House Farm lay on its SE side. It is still marked Moats Tye on the OS map.

Site of old Windmills.

Two post mills are recorded in the parish in 1736: Upper Mill stood E of Cockrill's Farm, and the site of Brastead Mill, which stood on Brastead Green and was demolished after 1931, is marked by Old Mill House.

Workhouse.

A workhouse is recorded with 36 inmates in 1776.

Historic Houses & Ancient Moated Sites.

The original Combs Hall which lay S of the church was the seat of the wealthy Dandye family in the early C15 and later the Bridgemans, one of whom, Orlando, rebuilt it c1710. On his death c1730 it was sold to the Crawleys who for some reason immediately demolished it. All that remains are traces of ancient foundations and a series of fish-ponds. Edgar's Farmhouse, a C14 aisled hall, has been rescued from a housing estate development and moved to the East Anglian Life Museum in Stowmarket. It was owned by the Adgor family in 1342. Boyton Hall has an ancient pear-shaped moat, lying across the Great Finborough parish boundary, and Ebb's Farm has three separate portions of a once extensive moat, now divided by a road. There is a moat at Holyoak Farm, whilst Kimberley Hall, in the hamlet of Moats Tye 1 mile S of the village, has two sides of a narrow moat. In the SW corner of the parish, Moat Farm retains three sides of a rectangular moat.

CONEY WESTON *(6 miles NE of Ixworth)*

Blackbourn Hundred. 'The king's manor - the royal estate' (OScand) *Cunegestuna* (DB). Its name suggests that it was one of the earliest royal estates in Suffolk, perhaps preceding the creation of the Hundreds.
Manors. Coney Weston Manor (-1545 Abbot of St. Edmunds, Bury; 1545 Francis Lovell).

Tumulus.

A Bronze Age barrow is recorded in the parish.

Roman Road.

A country road from Knettishall enters the parish NE of the village tracing the course of a Roman road SSW from East Harling in Norfolk. Near Broom Barn it bears SSE and is then lost. It no doubt passed through Barningham and is roughly traced again by Stanton Road (B1111) then the A143 to Ixworth. Another, Peddars Way, passes SSE-NNW through the W of the parish from a small plantation W of Crossways Cottage, but its course is nowhere evident on the ground. A bank surviving along the line of the western parish boundary by Park Covert, Thirty Acre, and Rookies Coverts, has been described as the conjectural and alternative route for Peddars Way prior to 1671.

Medieval Heath.

The village developed along the road to Hopton just N of the parish boundary. When the massive Barningham Heath - which extended S from the northern parish boundary to join the equally extensive Bardwell Heath - was enclosed by Private Acts in 1777 and 1799, a new road was created along its former northern edge connecting the villages of Barningham and Coney Weston. Residential development in Coney Weston was then created along this road just to the S of the old village leaving the strange effect of the old half of the village within the parish and the newer half in Barningham parish. Both heaths have now been enclosed.

COOKLEY *(2½ miles WSW of Halesworth)*

Blything Hundred. 'Clearing of a man called Cuca' (OE) *Cokelei* (DB)
Manors. Cookley (mid-C13 Robert de Ludham). *Sub-Manors.* Cookley Grange; Rughagh.

Ancient Packway.
A packway identified in Walpole to the S and Chediston to the N must have passed through Cookley. It is likely to have entered the parish by the river crossing in Walpole village and followed the line of the present road to Cookley Street then the footpath passing High Farm and leaving the parish to enter Chediston past Chediston Grange, continuing N past Packway Farm and Duke's Farm.

Sacred Stone (?)
Rockstone Manor Farm, 1 mile NE of the church, assumes its name from a huge standing block of stone lying nearby. Tradition asserts that the erratic - a stone washed down from the north with the waters following the end of the last Ice Age - has Druidical associations. Neighbouring Chediston(e) takes its name from the stone.

Medieval Green.
Cookley Green is shown and named by Faden on his 1783 map as a linear green widening as it ran N replacing the Huntingfield to Linstead Parva road, which forms the western parish boundary from its junction with Mary's Lane to the NW boundary. From here it continues N as Linstead Green; Green Farm and Valley Farm stood on its eastern edge. The width of the road at this time, S of Mary's Lane with properties set back, may have given rise to another property being named Green Farm and the naming of Cookley Green to this section on the present OS map.

Medieval Grange.
The manor house of Cookley Grange near the northern parish boundary stands on the site of a grange built by the Cistercian Abbey at Sibton, founded in the C12.

Historic House.
In the area of Cookley Street, Buck's Farm and Hill Farm are timber-framed and date from the C17. A little further E, Walnut Tree Farm is C16.

COPDOCK *(3 miles SW of Ipswich)*

Samford Hundred. 'Pollarded oak-tree' (OE) *Coppedoc* (1195).
The place name seems to refer to a single oak tree obviously of some stature, even though its top had been removed.
Manors. Copdock with Barons (1286 Robert Copedoc [part may have been held by the Holbroke family]). *Sub-Manors.* Copdock Hall al Fitz Raffes.

Roman Road.
The slip road to Copdock village off the A12 dual-carriageway opposite Bentley Long Wood, and the old London Road running SSW-NNE through the parish, follow the course of the major Roman road from Colchester *(Camulodunum)* to Caister by Norwich *(Venta Icenorum)*. Its line leaves this road opposite Copdock Hall and is lost in the present village emerging as Swan Hill in the adjoining parish of Washbrook heading for Sproughton as the B1113.

Medieval Green.
Mace Green, shown and named on Faden's map of 1783, covered a T-junction on Wenham Road. Barrens Farm marks its northern extent.

Historic Houses.
Copdock Hall, W of the church, was the residence of the Fosters in the mid C16. Whilst the present house is mainly modern, a spectacular barn remains from the earlier house. Barrens Farm occupies the site of the former Barons manor house.

CORTON *(3 miles N of Lowestoft)*

Mutford & Lothingland Hundred. 'Farmstead of a man called Kari' (OScand) *Karetuna* (DB)
Manors. Corton (1313 Geoffrey de Corton). *Sub-Manors.* Newton.

Roman Signal Station (?)
In 1812 a building 75' square with walls constructed of flint and rubble on a base of oak planks, was said to have fallen from the cliff and been lost to the sea - the cliffs are some 70'-80' high here. It may have been a signal station added to the shore defences in the C4.

Medieval Chapel.
A chapel, traces of which could still be seen in the late C18, once stood in the parish. The site may well now be under the sea. Nothing is shown on Faden's map of 1783.

Lost Medieval Village.
The sea has taken most of the parish and what remains has been gradually abandoned over the years. Foundations of old dwellings have been discovered and some centuries ago there was a parish E of Corton called Newton. Its church was lost in 1350 and little of the parish survived beyond the end of the C14. By 1854 all that remained was the stone base of Newton Cross on a small piece of ground known as Newton Green. The Cross, along with the final piece of land were submerged by 1873. Continuing cliff falls have, over the years, exposed a number of antiquities of both man and beast. The manors of Corton and Newton-with-Stalhams-in-Lound were anciently held by the De Herling family who had free warren here.

Medieval Green & Cross.
Newton Green and its medieval village cross had been washed away by 1873.

Site of old Windmill.
A post mill is recorded as standing in the village prior to 1793 and was still there in 1848. It s site is unknown.

Almshouse.
An almshouse accommodating eight poor people is recorded here in 1674.

COTTON *(6½ miles N of Stowmarket)*

Hartismere Hundred. 'Codda's farmstead' (OE) *Codestuna* (DB)
Manors. Cotton Braisworth (C13 William Briseworth). *Sub-Manors.* Cotton Hempnall/Caldecott; Campine's/Champains/Cumpyns; Gipswich.

Ancient Track.
The old Hundred Lane, dividing Hartismere and Stow Hundreds, runs from the southern end of Swilltub Lane (which forms the western parish boundary) to just SW of Redhouse Farm (part of the southern boundary) where it turns away SW to form the Mendlesham and Gipping parish boundaries.

Medieval Green.
Faden shows a green replacing the present road E and N of the church on his 1783 map. He names it merely 'Green' and shows a windmill immediately to the N.

Site of old Windmill.
A post mill is shown NW of the church in 1783. It was pulled down c1915.

Guild House.
A Guild House is recorded in Cotton in 1477, and one guild in 1524.

Almshouse.
An almshouse which housed ten poor people in 1674 was that probably converted to a workhouse in 1840.

Historic Houses & Ancient Moated Sites.
There are a number of moated sites in the parish. Cotton Hall, a manor house of ancient origin in the S of the parish, has a series of moats and fish-ponds; a gold cup was found in the largest moat to the S in the C18. The moat, mainly oblong in form, is deep and wide and appears to be walled on either side. To

COTTON *(continued)*

the NE is a perfect small, square moat. Cotton Lodge, 1 mile SE of the village, has a strong square moat. The Lodge, built c1580, was reputedly used as a meeting place by conspirators in the Gunpowder Plot - one of the main conspirators was Ambrose Rokewood, a Suffolk man of Coldham Hall, who was executed on Tower Hill for his part in the plot. The Trowel and Hammer public house dates from the C16. Other moated sites are at the Elizabethan Hempnalls Hall, ¾ mile NE, which still retains its C16 brick bridge; the right-angle of a moat remains at the Rectory, S of the church; a perfect narrow moat encloses a large area in a small plantation SW of Hayes Farm and W of the Stonham road; and another isolated moat, now dry, lies in a field E of Hill Farm between Stonham Road and Mendlesham Road. There are remains of a moat S of Willow Farm by Mendlesham Road and another on the road junction N of Hill Farm.

COVEHITHE (formerly North Hales) *(4½ miles NNE of Southwold)*

Blything Hundred. 'Harbour near (South) Cove' (OE) *Coveheith* (1523)
Manors. Nothales called Oulstede Manor (c1286 John de Vallibus).
The splendid ruins of a later church (no part older than 1380) still makes a bold statement to the former wealth of the one-time medieval port of North Hales, now completely lost to the North Sea along with its original church. The port was shown to be double the size of Saxmundham in the 1327 Subsidy, and what remains is a final fragment of a manor or hamlet called Covehithe which inherited the parish status after 1523. It takes its name from the manorial lords as, according to Kirby ,"John and Walter Cove were lords here in the time of Edward I (1272-1307)and had a hithe or quay for loading and unloading small vessels; for here the river formerly emptied into the sea." Johanne de Cove was shown to be the town's wealthiest inhabitant in 1327. The port's demise was not only due to coastal erosion but was hastened by an outbreak of plague in 1603 when 82 inhabitants died.

Ancient Woodland.
Erosion of the unstable cliff is gradually eating away the ancient woodland of Easton Wood.

Ancient Chapel.
St Peter's Chapel, founded by William Yarmouth in 1494, probably lies beneath the North Sea.

Medieval Quay.
The hithe or quay here, which loaded and unloaded vessels in the time of Edward I (1272-1307), must have stood some distance E of the present Covehithe Broad which was created from the flooding of the heath sometime after Faden's map of 1783 *(see below)*.

Medieval Market & Fair.
John and Walter Cove had the grant of a market, and a fair on St Andrews Day, in 1298. The fair was disused by 1844.

Civil War Incident.
In 1643 the nave of St Andrew's Church was destroyed by the parishioners.

Medieval Common.
The extensive Covehithe Common is shown by Faden in 1783 lying N and W of the church and extending W to a modern track called Green Lane. The westward limit of a square extension is marked by a footpath and Field Farm. It also extended a considerable way SE and S from the church but has since been breached and more than half lost to the sea. Much of the remainder has been flooded to create the present Covehithe Broad.

COWLINGE *(8 miles NNW of Clare)*

Risbridge Hundred. 'Place associated with Cul or Cula's people' (OE) *Culinge* (DB)
Manors. Cowlinge (C11/C12 William de Eureux, Earl of Salisbury). *Sub-Manors.* Shardelowes.

Ancient Chapel.
St Margaret's Chapel was mentioned in 1297 and dissolved in 1546. Its site is unknown.

COWLINGE *(continued)*

Former Gallows (?)

In 1658, Ann Higham of Cowling, widow, bequeathed to Anne Mortlock, her neice, 'Gallow Croft, held of the Manor of Cowling'.

Medieval Greens.

The four tiny greens of Hobbies, Lambsfair, Fairstead and Pound Green, shown on Faden's 1783 map, are still marked on the present OS. Mill Green identifies the site of a former windmill.

Medieval Fairs.

The grant of a fair was made to Alainora, Countess of Salisbury, in 1225. A second fair was granted the next year. Both were for sheep and lambs (one in July, the other October) and took place on Lambsfair Green.

Historic Houses & Ancient Moated Sites.

The manor was the seat of William Longsword, Earl of Salisbury and Somerset, and son of Henry II. The moated enclosure of his ancient manor house lie in the wood near the entrance to Branches Park. Parsonage Farm in the village is C16. Ballards Place dates from c1574. There are several moated sites in the parish: Cowlinge Hall, SW of Farley Green and seat of Francis Dickens, lord of the manor and a great benefactor of the parish, has a fine quadrangular moat with two entrances; there are three sides of a rectangular moat at Shardelows Farm on the NE parish boundary; Fairstead Farm, E of the village, has a well-defined moat and three sides of another in Island Wood to the NE; Dowell's Farm in Beeton's Plantation W of the village has a nearly square narrow moat with, just to the E of this, the site of another rectangular moat with a partly moated forecourt on the E side (now gone) named 'Moat Yards' on the 1846 tithe map; in a field at Pound Green are portions of a small quadrangular moat; there is a small perfect oblong moat in a field SW of Brigg's Farm; and there were three sides of an irregular moat at Hobbies Green.

CRANSFORD *(3 miles ENE of Framlingham)*

Plomesgate Hundred. 'Ford frequented by cranes or herons' (OE) *Craneforda* (DB)

Manors. Cransford al Cransford Hall (1316 Robert de Ufford). *Sub-Manors.* Vicedelence/Visdelieu/Fidlers Hall.

Medieval Green.

A tiny linear green named Cransford Green in 1783 is shown as little more than a widening of the road to Bruisyard Street just N of High House Farm; it now shows as a kink in the road.

Historic House & Ancient Moated Sites.

The moated manor house of Fiddlers Hall, S of the village, has an Elizabethan chimney and bears the C14 name, 'Visdelieu' from its early lord, Thomas Visdelieu. It was later the residence of the well-known family of Rous. There are remains of a rectangular moat just S of St Peter's Church.

CRATFIELD *(6½ miles WSW of Halesworth)*

Blything Hundred. 'Open land of a man called Craeta' (OE) *Cratafelda* (DB)

Manors. Cratfield (c1140 manor divided with part granted to St. Neots Monastery). *Sub-Manors.* Cratfield Le Roos.

Roman Road.

A Roman road runs diagonally NW-SE through the centre of the parish. Its course is evident on the ground in a road entering the parish just SE of Manor Farm and running straight to Church Farm where it veers right. It is noticed again in Tongs Lane which traces it in parts to Silverley's (Silver Lace) Green where it continues as the road to and beyond the parish boundary.

Earthworks.

In a field S of the village are broad banks c4' high forming three sides of a square; date and purpose unknown.

CRATFIELD *(continued)*

Medieval Greens.

Faden's map shows several greens in the parish in 1783: Westhall Green was a long narrow green on the western parish boundary. It ran S from Moat Farm to an extension of Deadman's Grave, which originally curved E following the parish boundary - OS names the area Swan Green; Bell Green, which ran NW covering the area of the present village with old properties lining its SW boundary, is now enclosed and infilled; Goostead Green, a tiny green by the course of the Roman road, is now incorporated in a nursery; Northward (Norwood) Green is now largely arable but in 1842 was divided between 72 commoners grazing 'one beast each of any age' - it was enclosed under General Acts of 1846; Silver Lace (Silverley) Green, where 24 commoners once pastured one-year-old beasts or colts, comprised a large green, now enclosed but clearly outlined in a curving field boundary lying NE and SE of a new road between North Green Farm and Old Hall Farm - Cratfield Hall lies on the NE edge of the green; to the S of this, a narrow linear green called Barfile Green lay between Sponge and Larters Farm.

Guildhall & Almshouses.

Close to the church is the Guildhall built in 1563. Later it was converted to almshouses occupied rent free by poor persons and named the Town House.

Historic Houses & Ancient Moated Sites.

The moat at Moat Farm, Swan Green, is rectangular on the N and W but from the NW makes a sweeping arc extending far beyond the southern angle. There are several other moated sites in the parish: Moat House Farm, North Green, and at Rose's Farm, SW of the village; at Lodge Farm where there is one each side of the parish boundary with Laxfield, and cropmarks NE of this suggest a lost moat or rectangular enclosure; to the SW of these, the eastern half of a water-filled rectangular moat survives at Red House Farm with a causeway or bridge to the W, plus the S and E sides of a double moat further S; Church Farm has remnants of a small square moat, and three sides of an isolated square moat remain to the E of this close to the parish boundary; the possible moat of the medieval parsonage lies in a small field adjacent to the vicarage; Manor Farm is also moated.

CREETING ST MARY *(2 miles NE of Needham Market)*

Bosmere & Claydon Hundred. 'Settlement of the family or followers of a man called Craeta' (OE) plus church dedication. *Cratingas* (DB).

Manors. Creeting St. Mary (c1414 Abbot of Bernay granted to Eton College). Creeting St. Olaves otherwise Gratinges/Wolney Hall al Wonhall with Mickfield and Cooks Upon Cranes (-C14 Greistein Abbey; C14 William de la Pole). Creeting All Saints (1299 Eva, widow of Robert de Tybetot.

Site of Hundred Court.

Bosmere, in the grounds of Bosmere Hall, is a deep lake (or mere) of some 9 acres from where the Hundred takes its name. It lies on the southern parish boundary in the former Creeting All Saints.

Tumulus, Ring Ditches & Mesolithic Occupation Site.

A Ring Ditch was discovered from aerial photography close to Needham Lake recreation area. Whilst it has been identified as the outline of a possible Early Bronze Age round barrow, finds on the site in the form of 232 items of worked flint pre-date the earthworks and are probably from the Mesolithic period. Aerial photographs have also shown two ring ditches by the Gipping at Ravens Farm.

Roman Road.

The A140 road to Norwich traces the line of the old Roman road from Colchester to Caister St. Edmund (*Venta Icenorum*) which crosses the parish N-S.

Alien Priories.

The more important of the two Creeting priories, St Mary, was founded c1156 as a cell to the abbey of St Mary of Bernay, in Normandy. It later became a joint priory with Everdon in Northants, and so continued until its suppression in 1462, when it was granted, with other possessions, to form part of the endowment of Eton College; the Provost and Fellows still hold much of the land in the parish. The site of the priory

CREETING ST MARY *(continued)*

is unknown. The church and priory of Creeting St Olaves stood 1 mile NW of St Mary's on the E side of Low Lane leading to Woolney Hall. Robert de Mortain, Earl of Cornwall, gave the manor of St Olaves with its priory to the Benedictine Abbey of Grestein in Normandy c1070. In 1345 Edward III granted the manor to Tydeman de Lymbergh, but in 1360 allowed it to be sold to Sir Edmund de la Pole. No trace remains of the priory which only appears to have had one prior and went into decay in the C17, or of the church which was still in existence in 1532 when John Pinkeney was buried in the chancel. However, 'men when ploughing years ago frequently turned up bits of masonry, bones and skulls in the valley at the E end of the bye lane across the stream from Fen House to Creeting St Peter.' Low Lane changes its name to The Lord's Highway from the priory-church site as it heads NE, crossing a stream by Lady Bridge to meet the main road opposite Earl Stonham church.

Lost Medieval Villages.

The history of Creeting has come full circle. Initially it was the single settlement of Cretta. That it became extensively settled before the Conquest is evident from its eight Bosmere entries in Domesday under *Gratinga, Cratinga* and *Cratingh*. The parish became Cretinge by 1215 and Cretyngge Magna and Cretyngge Parva by 1327. Later two became three: St Mary, with a church and priory; All Saints, with a church (sharing St Mary's churchyard), and St Olaves, also with a church and priory. After the demise of St Olaves, St Mary and All Saints parishes became commonly known as Creeting-two-Churches. When the long disused church of All Saints was taken down In 1795, it was discovered to have no foundations. In 1884 the churchless parishes of All Saints and St Olaves were consolidated with St Mary to become one large parish again. Although difficult to define with any accuracy, it would appear that All Saints parish comprised the area to the SE extending to the river Gipping - where the expanse of water known as Bosmere with its hall and mill gave name to the Hundred - along with the strip of land forming the NW boundary as far N as All Saints Hall opposite St Mary's church (and the site of All Saints Church). St Olaves carried on N from here to Creeting Bottom incorporating the site of St Olaves church and priory in the area of the manor house of Woolney Hall. It is difficult to know where exactly the divisions between St Olaves and St Mary were in the rest of the parish. Only one part of Creeting parish was situated on the S side of the Gipping; this was the extensive manor of Newton which extended SW beyond the railway and road to Stowmarket to incorporate Great and Little Newton Woods S of Badley and now incorporated in Needham Market and Barking parishes.

Watermills.

'It (Newton) is a large farm including a wood called Newton Wood and dwellings called Newton Cottages; here were two (water?) mills three centuries ago'. Bosmere mill was built in 1768. It was converted into flats in 1976.

Site of old Windmills.

Two windmills are recorded in the parish in the C18: one stood at Creeting Bottoms in 1764 and the other, a post mill (for which the buck remains) was sited NW of Sally Wood's Lane.

Medieval Green.

Jack's Green, named on Faden's 1783 map, is shown lying E of the present Church Lane and S of the two Creeting churches of St Mary and All Saints. The road from Duche's Lane through Creeting St Olaves to Creeting Bottom appears on Faden's map as a narrow linear green.

Almshouse.

Called 'The Mercho', this almshouse was purchased from the parish in 1768 by Samuel Uvedale. Its site is not known.

Historic Houses & Ancient Moated Sites.

At Vale Farm, near the eastern parish boundary is an unusually wide moat surrounding a small area and extending 300' towards the S. Fox's Farm, 1 mile E, retains two sides of a square moat and there are three water-filled arms of an isolated moat at Broadgates Farm NE of the village. There is another small portion of a moat near the schoolhouse. Bosmere Hall in Creeting All Saints was built by Samuel Uvedale c1768.

CREETING ST PETER (Formerly West Creeting) *(2½ miles ESE of Stowmarket)*

Stow Hundred. Creeting: 'Settlement of the family or followers of a man called Craeta' (OE) plus church dedication. *Cratingas* (DB). St Peter, although adjacent, is situated in a different Hundred to the other Creetings.
Manors. Creeting St. Peter (1275 John de Bovile). *Sub-Manors.* Brasin's/Brasier's Hall al Thorney Mumpliers.

Ancient Earthworks & Ford.

Situated in an arable field between West Creeting Hall and the river Gipping, ¾ mile S of the church, is a roughly circular site discovered in aerial photographs. Although ploughing has reduced the earthworks to a ringed depression, a description of the site prior to its loss to ploughing in 1959 states that it was a raised area surrounded by a bank and wet moat with an entrance on the NE. An abundance of oyster shell, pottery sherds and metal objects from the plough field has suggested a settlement date for the earthworks of C12-C13. The site is probably a Norman ring-works - a fortified earthworks with similar objectives but simpler specifications to the more recognised motte castle. It was probably hurriedly constructed to defend the 'Gate Ford' known to have existed by the Gipping in this vicinity - a field called Gateford Fen lies S of the river in Badley - and later modified perhaps to contain an early residence belonging to William de Boville, the probable sub-tenant here in 1264. The river makes a loop opposite the site which may once have led to silting and provided the likely place to ford.

Medieval Green.

West Creeting Green is shown on Faden's map of 1783 as a mere widening of the road through the village centre and is remembered in Green Farm. The present road now passes along the right side.

Historic Houses & Ancient Moated Sites.

The main Creeting manor was held by William de Boville as sub-tenant of Geoffrey de Magnaville, and West Creeting Hall, a C19 farmhouse, with Tudor origins, no doubt occupies the site of a former Manor House (pre-dating the ring-works). The family owned manors in Badingham, Dennington, Dallinghoo, Thorpe, Alderton, and Boulge, and although William's son John claimed free warren, view of frankpledge, and assize of bread and beer in West Creeting in 1275, there is no evidence that the family ever used Creeting as its main residence. It did, however, become the residence of a daughter, Mary de Bovile, who married Thomas de Latymer in 1327. Roydon Hall at West Creeting Green, was built in the 1590s by Robert Flicke and retains the NE side of a very wide moat.

CRETINGHAM *(4 miles WSW of Framlingham)*

Loes Hundred. 'Homestead of the people who lived in a sandy or gravely district' (OE) *Gretingaham* (DB)
Formerly comprised the two parishes of Great and Little Cretingham.
Manors. Cretingham al Tye's (1251 Nicholas de Cretingham). *Sub-Manors.* Harolds; St. Margaret; Kettlebars; Little Cretingham; Cretingham al Sulyards; St. Peters.

Site of Early Iron-Age Farmstead.

Unexcavated earthworks and sites of huts are visible about 1 mile S of the village on the E of the Otley-Cretingham road. These may form the original settlement from which the parish was named.

Roman Road.

The line of the Roman road from Coddenham to Peasenhall is traced by the A1120 SW-NE from The Homestead to just SW of Lodge Villas.

Deserted Medieval Village & Chapel.

Hollow ways and outlines of properties suggest the site of the former medieval settlement of Little Cretingham (or Over Cretingham) which lay in the long southern extension to the parish by the Otley road In Henry III's time the manor was held by a certain Nicholas and contained 'a messuage with sixteen acres of Land, Meadow and Pasture'. The site of this 'messuage' may perhaps be identified in Home Farm. There was at one time a small church or chapel here, lost before 1291. It probably lay in the area of Chapel Hill, a modern country road connecting a former road (now a public footpath) which ran parallel with the road to Otley from Kittle's Corner.

Historic Houses & Ancient Moated Sites.

Timber-framed Moat Farm, ¾ mile NE of the village, dates from 1602 and replaces a much earlier building. It

CRETINGHAM *(continued)*

has a fine moat with an irregular outer bank and an entrance on the N. The Potash is also timber-framed and dates from the C16 and early C17. The New Bell Inn is another old building. The outline of one arm of a moat remains just S of Manor Farm, and there is part of a small square moat at Sparks Farm N of the village. S of Cretingham Lodge, earthworks showing as shadow marks form the outline of an enclosure - a possible lost moat measuring c230' by 131'.

CROWFIELD (cum Bocking) *(2½ miles ENE of Needham Market)*

Bosmere & Claydon Hundred. 'Open land near the nook or corner' (OE) *Crofelda* (DB). Crowfield is sited at the head of a valley and includes the Domesday vills of Bocking and Horswold.
Manors. Crowfield Hall (C13 John de Bocking). *Sub-Manors.* Bocking Hall.

Roman Road.

A fine length of Roman road known as Stone Street runs SSW-NNE from S of Clay Cottage to N of Walnutree Cottage.

Medieval Greens.

Field boundaries trace the outline of the former Crowfield Green on the N side of Church Road. Brook Hall Farm stands on the northern side. The green is shown and named by Faden in 1783, as is Stonham Green which extended S into Crowfield parish tapering down to end at Crowfield church near the junction with Church Road and predating the present road.

Historic Houses & Ancient Moated Sites.

Close to the churchyard is a perfect sub-rectangular moated enclosure with the remains of another - in the form of two arms - to the SW. There were two manors in Crowfield - Crowfield Hall and Bocking Hall - and the parish was known in 1743 as Crowfield-cum-Bocking. A survey in 1665 which states 'Croffeld Hall, which stood anciently within the mote by the chappell', and Bocking Hall, which was built within less than a hundred years, were for a long time in the possession of the family of Woodhouse . . .', suggests that no house stood (at that time) within the moat by the church but that there was a house called Bocking Hall on another site - the one with the remains of a moat further SW (?) This house appears to have become the seat of the Middleton family who, in 1728, rebuilt and renamed it Crowfield Hall. This was pulled down in 1829 and a new hall erected to the W. At New Hall, in the NE corner of the parish, three sides remain of a small rectangular moat c66' by 98' with a NE entrance.

CULFORD *(4 miles NNW of Bury St Edmunds)*

Blackbourn Hundred. 'Ford of a man called Cula' or 'Ford at the hollow' (OE) *Culeforda* (DB)
Manors. Culford (-1541 Abbot of St. Edmunds, Bury; 1541 Christopher Coote). *Sub-Manors.* East Hall al Syfrewats.

Tumuli.

In Brockley hamlet, NE of Culford Park, is a large round barrow known as the 'Hill of Health'. A fine example of a large Bronze-Age 'bowl' barrow is situated on the S edge of Dixon's Covert on the N side of the West Stow to Fornham St Genevieve road. Its diameter was measured as 150' with a height of 8'.

Deserted Medieval Settlements.

The site of the original Culford village lies near the church in Culford Park. The layout is shown on an estate map of 1793 and a Highways Diversion Order of 1804. The village was cleared in 1825-8 after Richard Benyon de Beauvoir purchased the estate from the Cornwallis family and extended the park. The only surviving buildings are the church and Home Farm which stands at the extreme SE of the old village site. Chimney Mills, formerly a separate parish on the southern parish boundary by the river Lark, has twice been annexed to Culford, the final time in 1897. One property plus the mill on the river were all that survived of the former parish by the 1930s. Chimney Mills and Chimney Street come from the medieval latin word *Chimnagium* which was a toll charged for wayfarage through forests.

CULFORD *(continued)*

Ancient Water Mill.
The Ancient watermill (*see above*) was later operated by steam as well as water. It was called Hardles Mill in 1700.

Site of old Windmill.
A post mill was shown in 1783 SE of Chimney Mill.

Historic Houses & Ancient Moated Site.
Culford Hall, now a school, was built in 1591 by Sir Nicholas Bacon and stands in a magnificent park of some 500 acres. It was the principal seat of the Marquis of Cornwallis. who had the hall completely rebuilt 1790-96. A rectangular moat with an entrance causeway on the N is shown on estate maps of 1742, 1791 and 1793. It was probably filled-in when Culford Park was rebuilt and may represent the site of the previous Hall before 1591. Lodge Farm in the extreme N of the parish marks the likely site of the medieval warrener's lodge.

CULPHO *(5 miles W of Woodbridge)*

Carlford Hundred. 'Cuthwulf's spur of land' (OE) *Culfole* (DB)
Manors. Culpho al Verdons and Wachesham (C13 John de Wachesham held 4 fees of the Honor of Lancaster).
Sub-Manors. Culpho Abbatis/Culpho Regis.

Early Settlement.
Scatters of Ipswich ware pottery suggest a pre-Conquest settlement close to the church.

Historic House & Ancient Moated Sites.
A fine quadrangular moat of ancient origin, 120 yds N-S and 87 yds E-W, with considerable fragments of foundations mark the site of Abbey Farm, just NW of the church. There is no record of any monastic building in the parish but the manor was given by William de Valoines to Leiston Abbey, so as the likely Manor House, Abbey Farm would probably have acquired this title. The tiny church with its churchyard and ancient dedication to St Botolph shows signs that it may at one time have been moated.

DALHAM (formerly Dalham with Dunstalls) *(6 miles ESE of Newmarket)*

Risbridge Hundred. 'Homestead in a valley' (OE) *Dalham* (DB)
Manors. Dalham with Dunstal's (C12 William Peche held of the Honor of Clare).

Ancient Woodland.
Fragments of extensive ancient woodland still exist in Hawson Hills, Coy's Grove, Leipsic Wood, Blocksey Wood, Glade Wood, Brick Kiln Wood, the delightful Bluebutton Wood, Alderfield Plantation and Dunstall Green Wood; the latter now only outlined in ancient field boundaries in the hamlet of Dunstall Green.

Ancient Track.
Old Suffolk Road, a track from the SW parish boundary to a point where it joins Dalham Road just W of the village, is a Hundred Lane forming the county boundary with Cambridgeshire and dating back to Saxon times.

Medieval Green.
Dunstall Green is shown as a roughly inverted triangle on Faden's map of 1783 where it named 'Tunstall' (no doubt in error). It ran S from from Jillings Farm to Stud Farm and is now replaced by the straight Denham Road; the area is now the hamlet of Dunstall Green. The properties of the village itself lay around the edges of a narrow unnamed linear green which ran N-S replacing the present road from Malting Farm to The Sounds. The area has been totally infilled with properties to create the present village.

Site of old Windmill.
Lower Mill, a smock mill situated W of the village, was built c1790 and restored in 1981.

Workhouse.
A workhouse here was recorded as housing 14 inmates in 1776.

DALHAM *(continued)*

Historic House.

Dalham Hall, former seat of the Affleck family, was built in 1704 by Simon Patrick, Bishop of Ely and stands serenely in its park above the delightful dale village. It once belonged to Cecil Rhodes, founder of Rhodesia, who died before he could take up residence. The present house stands on the site of an earlier hall and among the monuments in the church is one from the early years of the C17 to Thomas Stuteville, "Late lord of this towne and patron of this churche." It goes on to inform us that he and his wife "continued and kept hospitalitye in the manor place here 40 years together . . ." The manor, formerly known as Dalham with Dunstalls, had come into the possession of the Stutevilles in the early years of the C15 and remained with them for nearly three hundred years before the Afflicks became lords. The Affleck Arms public house dates from the C17.

DALLINGHOO *(4½ miles N of Woodbridge)*

Wilford & Loes Hundreds. 'Hill-spur of Dalla's family' or 'The dalemen's promontory' (OE) *Dallingahou* (DB) Incorporates Dallinghoo Wield, an extra-parochial parish covering 38 acres without house or population. It claimed to be the smallest parish in England.

Manors. Dallinghoo Manor (C12 De Glanville family). *Sub-Manors.* Dallinghoo Campsey; Earls Dallinghoo; Bast Brodish.

Ancient Woodland.

Only a fragment remains of the once extensive Dallinghoo Wood, while there are parts of further ancient woodland in the N of the parish at Page's, New and Home Coverts.

Quaker's Burial Ground.

Land was purchased in the parish for a Quaker's burial ground in 1703.

Historic House & Ancient Moated Sites.

The very fine mansion of Dallinghoo Hall which stood some distance SE of the church was destroyed by fire in 1729. The original house had been built for William Churchill who sometimes resided here and, after rebuilding, became for some time the seat of his son-in-law, Francis Negus. Only two sides now remain of a fine moated site at Moat Farm near the eastern parish boundary, and 'A broad moat in the midst of a weird and gloomy wood in the wild and formerly extraparochial area of Dallinghoo Wield bears no name'.

DARMSDEN *(1 mile SW of Needham Market)*

Bosmere & Claydon Hundred. 'Deormod's hill' (OE) *Dermodesduna* (DB)

Once a separate parish, it has from an early period been a hamlet of Barking under the name Barking-cum-Darmsden. When it separated ecclesiastically in 1901, it failed to regain its civil parish status and forms a part of the manor of Tarston Hall.

Manors. Darmsden Manor (C13 William Burnaville). *Sub-Manors.* Darmsden Hall/Taston Hall.

Iron Age Settlement.

S of Darmsden Hall are a series of large Early Iron Age storage pits suggesting a long settlement period from c400 B.C. to the first century A.D.

Ancient Mere.

Just E of Darmsden Hall, on the parish boundary, is an area of water named Liver Mere on Faden's map of 1783. The present OS map names it 'Baylham Fish Pond' which probably refers to a service it once provided for the hall.

DARSHAM *(5½ miles NNE of Saxmundham)*

Blything Hundred. 'Homestead or village of a man called Deor' (OE) *Dersham* (DB)

Manors. Darsham cum Yoxford (C11/C12 Roger Bigot). *Sub-Manors.* Abbot's; Austins; Gerrards.

Ancient Woodland.

Sillett's Wood and Oak Spring are a part of ancient woodland.

DARSHAM *(continued)*

Medieval Greens.

China Green is named and shown on Faden's map of 1783 as a tiny triangular green bordered by properties W of the church, and Bristle or Brussells Green as a largish rectangular green E of the church.

Site of old Windmill.

A post mill is shown just SW of Darsham House in 1783. It was pulled down in 1937.

Historic House & Ancient Moated Sites.

Darsham Hall, now a farmhouse, was built in the C15 by Edward Hemmings. Darsham House dates from 1679 with Georgian additions. NE of Darsham railway station is the greater part of a small rectangular moat, and there is another moat on the W of the A12 Ipswich-Lowestoft road, S of White House Farm. Cropmarks of an infilled moat known as Cheney Moat, with adjacent ditch and possible internal features, is situated on the S side of The Street.

DEBACH *(4 miles NNW of Woodbridge)*

Wilford Hundred. 'At the deep valley through which flows a stream' (OE) *Debenbeis* (DB). The present tiny parish comprises only large flat uplands. Originally it may have been virgin forest, and the adjoining parish of Boule (which meets the place-name description), once a part of Debach containing its original church of St Michael on the site of the pre-Conquest church mentioned at Domesday. The present Debach church was built in 1851.
Manors. Debach Burgh (1316 Queen Margaret; 1329 Gilbert de Boulge). *Sub-Manors.* Bast Struttings (situated mainly in Boulge parish).

Roman Road.

The course of a Roman road is traced by the present B1078 as it forms the northern parish boundary from just NE of Poplar Farm to Brook Farm.

Historic House & Ancient Moated Site.

Debach House on the northern parish boundary is early C17. The C19 Moat House stands on the moated site of the Old Rectory with fishponds. NW of this in All Saints churchyard is the northern half of an egg-shaped enclosure with a bank N of the church.

DEBENHAM *(8 miles W of Framlingham)*

Thedwestry Hundred. 'Settlement by the river between steep banks' (OE) *Depbenham* (DB)
Manors. Crows Hall al Woodwards (1221 Robert Aguillers). *Sub-Manors.* Ulveston Hall; Debenham Priory; Bludhall; Sackvilles; Harborough Hall cum Aspall or cum Debenham; Giesting al Gostings/Gostlinges Hall al Gostelens Hall; Scotnetts with The Haugh.
The town, which suffered severely from a fire in 1744 which destroyed 30 houses at the N end of town, is now little more than a large village. In Saxon times, however, it was considerably more important. The Saxon kings of East Anglia occasionally held their courts here, and tradition says that the river Deben was at that time navigable up to the town, despite the fact that it rises only one mile W at Brice's Farm. This would appear to be borne out by its name (*see above*) and the fact that an anchor was found embedded in the sand at a place called the Gulls in the last century. The church has evidence of Saxon origins and was one of two recorded here at Domesday; the other may have been situated in Gracechurch Street where flint footings have been discovered on the site of a present house.

Tumulus.

A round barrow lies near Brice's Farm (now renamed The Firs) W of the village.

Site of Battle (?)

Blood Hall on the NE parish boundary is the manor house of Bludhall Manor. Tradition says that the previous Old Hall was built on the site of a battle with the Danes. Surrounding fields are suggestively named Mount Piece, First Blood Hill, Second Blood Hill, Great Blood Field, Second Blood Field, Knights Close, etc.

DEBENHAM *(continued)*

Ancient Track.

Waddlegoose Lane - also called Waddledickie (Suffolk dialect for donkey) - was probably an ancient packway.

Site of Priory (?)

Finds in Priory Field (off Priory Lane) suggest a former unrecorded Augustinian priory may have been sited here. A less exciting possibility is, however, that the manor house of Priory Manor may have stood here; so named because it was vested in Butley Priory.

Site of Moated Earthwork.

NW of the town and 200 yds N of a ford across the river Deben is a site ploughed out in 1967 but examined by Elizabeth Owles of Ipswich Museum. The original earthwork comprised an area of ½ acre, 55 yds in diameter enclosed by a circular moat which was 10' below the centre of the enclosure and ramparted. At some time a Victorian cottage had been built in the bottom of the dry moat which had been widened at this point to accommodate a garden. Field names described the enclosure as Mount Piece. Pottery sherds dated from the C13-C14.

Site of Civil War Skirmish(?)

Crows Hall (*see below*) is said to have been attacked during the Civil War.

Medieval Greens.

Camps Green, shown on Faden's 1783 map, lay within the curving outline of Thorpe Lane and Kenton Road and is remembered in Camp Green Farm on its northern limits. Small, square Rumble Green lay on the bend in the road at the northern end of Roamwood Green Lane.

Site of old Windmill.

A post mill named Page's Mill stood at Mill Farm, NE of the village, in 1736. It was demolished about 1917.

Medieval Market & Fairs.

Its Saxon origins and royal connections suggest that there may have already been a market here at the Conquest. A grant for a market was made to Robert Aguillers in 1221. There were also two fairs - Camps Green the probable veune for the great Midsummer Fair - but all have long ceased.

Recreation.

Camps Green was the former site of the town's entertainment ground, The Angel and The Buck controlling its two entrances. A timber-framed house in the street still retains a room at one time used as an Elizabethan theatre.

Market Cross.

A Market Place was in existence with a Market Cross, the lower part being later used as a police station.

Guildhall.

Situated in the high street, the former guildhall dates from c1500.

Free School.

The former timber-framed Free School for twenty children, endowed by Sir Robert Hitcham in 1648, stands along the high street.

Workhouse.

A workhouse is recorded here accommodating 40 inmates in 1776.

Historic Houses & Ancient Moated Sites.

Crow's Hall, 1 mile E of the town, was built in 1508 and had a chapel in 1519. It was home to the Framlinghams and the Gawdys. It incorporates parts of a fortified manor house raised in 1310 which itself replaced the stronghold of C13 owner John Crow, constructed on a defensive site above the Deben Valley. The moat system is complex; the only portion completely intact is that forming the island on which the hall stands which is 98 yds square and crossed by a picturesque four-arched brick bridge; there are remains of fish ponds to the N. There may have been up to three moats here protecting buildings and stock. With a manorial history going back to its first Norman owner, Ranulph Peverel, the site has been occupied since the earliest times. Debenham Hall is an ancient house surrounded by a moat. Ulverston Hall, W of the town, retains three portions of a quadrangular moat, and Blood

DEBENHAM *(continued)*

Hall to the NE of the parish stands on the moated site of an earlier hall. Other moats are at Esther's Moat, ½ mile to the W; at Hill Farm, which has part of a moat with an artificial cutting containing water which probably formed part of a defensive work; at Old Hall, NW of the parish; and at White Hall to the SW. In the town itself, much was lost in a fire of 1744, but among the survivors, The Angel is C16 and The Red Lion dates from c1600.

DENHAM (St. Mary) *(7 miles WSW of Bury St Edmunds)*

Risbridge Hundred. 'Homestead in a valley' or 'Home of the Danes' (OE) *Denham* (DB)
Manors. Denham Manor (1275 Sir John de Say). *Sub-Manors.* Abbotts.

Ancient Woodland.
Hockerhill Wood, in the centre of the parish, and Denham Thicks, now in three separate fragments E of the church, are parts of ancient woodland.

Site of Priory (?)
Denham Priory, close to the SW parish boundary and originally on the edge of Tunstall Green, and nearby Denham Abbots and Abbot's Farm, are suggestive of a former monastic building in the vicinity. However, as William White states, "In Edward III's time, Denham belonged to the Hethe family and was afterwards appropriated to 'some monastic institution'". This may well be the origin of the appendages of 'priory' and 'abbots' to various local properties.

Medieval Green.
The large triangular-shaped Tunstall Green, shown mainly in Dalham parish, extends into the SW corner of Denham, its original limits - the eastern point of the triangle - traced by property boundaries running NE past Denham Priory to Denham Abbots and then ESE behind a row of properties bordering the road to Dalham.

Ancient Mill.
A water or wind mill is recorded in existence in 1339.

Almshouse.
The Townshend family, continuing the tradition of the Lwekenors, became great benefactors to the parish, Lady Mary Townsend providing £100 in 1662 which was used to purchase a house for poor parishioners.

Historic House & Ancient Moated Site.
Late Georgian Denham Hall stands in the middle of a large moated platform; the ivy-clad corner tower of the previous hall, built c1570 and formerly the seat of the Lewkenors, stands above the water. The Lewkenors were granted the manor and were in residence here from the time of the Dissolution. Sir Edward Lewkenor is said to have furnished part of the hall with a large table at which the poor were fed three times a week (the dairy is the possible site). Sir Edward and his wife, Susan, both died of smallpox at the hall in 1605 within two days of each other. The estate was carried by marriage to the first Lord Viscount Townshend, who died in 1687.

DENHAM (St John) *(3 miles E of Eye)*

Hoxne Hundred. 'Homestead in a valley' (OE) *Denham* (DB)
Manors. Denham Manor (1245 Thomas de Muton).

Ancient Woodland.
Coldham Wood and Deal Plantation are parts of ancient woodland.

Site of College (?)
The moated site of College Farm, situated by the church, may have been a collegiate of priests connected with Hoxne Priory and founded c1495 by Sir Edmund Bedingfield.

Medieval Greens.
A narrow linear green, named Denham Green on Faden's 1783 map, follows the eastern parish boundary S from the junction at Clubbs Farm to a E-W footpath N of The Lodge. Now replaced by the present road.

DENHAM (St John) *(continued)*

Site of old Windmill.

A post mill stood on the former Denham Green in 1783. It was pulled down in 1910.

Historic House & Ancient Moated Sites.

Denham Hall has a fine oblong moat of considerable width, with a narrow channel connecting it with another smaller moat to the S. College Farm still retains portions of its moat.

DENNINGTON *(2½ miles N of Framlingham)*

Hoxne Hundred. 'Farmstead or village of a woman called Denegifu' (OE) *Dingifetuna* (DB). Denningworth, anciently a part of Dennington, is named from the OE *Denegifuworth* meaning Denegifu's enclosure i.e. the actual home of the woman called Denegifu (*see above*). The site is unknown.

Manors. Dennington Manor (C12 Sir John de Bovile).

Ancient Woodland.

Dennington Wood in the E, and Parsonage Wood in the S, are sections of ancient woodland.

Roman Road.

The course of a Roman road running SW-NE through the parish is traced in a road from Dennington Corner, then as a country lane from Church Farm to Parkgate Farm, then as a track with a central bank and ditches on either side to TM296 667. A stone layer was visible in a section cut by the local farmer in the 1970s.

Ancient (?) Mound.

An earthen mound of undetermined date and purpose lies at the N end of Dennington Wood.

Site of Ancient Deer Park.

Parkgate Farm, SE of the village beside the Roman road, marks the site of the entrance to one of the three great deer parks noted in Domesday Book - others were at Bentley and Ixworth, whilst the Malets had one at Eye soon after. Dennington park was later merged with the vast Bigod park at Framlingham.

Ancient Chantries.

Two chantries were situated in the church here at different times; St. Mary's, known as Our Lady's Chantry, founded by Sir John Boville in 1306, and St Margarets, called Philip's Chantry, founded in 1437 by Sir William Philips, Lord Bardolf, for two priests to celebrate mass daily for the welfare of himself and his wife during their lifetime and for their souls after death. Both were granted to Richard Fulmerston. A small farmhouse which stood in front of the present Queens Head public house became The Chantry. It was later used as a school and, sometime before the last war, dismantled and re-erected at Princes Risborough in Buckinghamshire.

Medieval Greens.

A road or track originally ran NW from the present A1120 near Wash Farm to Frostley Bridge at the junction of the B1118 following the course of a tributary of the river Alde. At its southern end, Capens Green is named but not shown in detail on Faden's 1783 map. The area is now marked by Capons Green Farm. The same map also names Maypole Green W of the church, but again it is not outlined. It may have occupied the area now enclosed N of Saxtead Road by a track N from the water tower to Redhouse Farm, Severalls Lane, and a country lane heading SSE back to Saxtead Road. Owls Green lay in the N of the parish by the road to Laxfield near the junction with the B1116 road to Fressingfield.

Historic Houses & Ancient Moated Sites.

The present strongly moated farmhouse of Dennington Hall, former seat of the Earls of Stradbroke, occupies a site which was long the seat of the Rous family. As Leyland said: 'All the Rouses that be in Suffolk come, as far as I can learn, out of the House of Rous at Dennington' where 'divers of them lie in the church under flat stones'. An earlier incumbent was Sir John Phelip who served at Agincourt with distinction under Henry V and died in 1441. His successor, Sir William, became Lord Bardolf. The ancient moat is a perfect square with signs of a slight inner bank and some flint walling; there are fish-ponds to the SE. C16 Dennington Place, 1¼ miles W of the village, has the greater part of a quadrangular moat fed by a channel with fish-ponds known as The

DENNINGTON *(continued)*

Lays to the S. Moat Farm on the northern parish boundary is the site of the ancient manor house of Pyeshall where C12-C14 pottery has been found in a pit. It still has its ancient moat with adjacent fishponds and an estate map of 1627 shows the old house within the moat. E of the last, Grange Farm has two joined moated enclosures, the smaller one early, the larger C16-C17 with an earthen (prospect?) mound within the SE corner. The records of The Queens Head public house date from 1483, and another public house, The Royal Oak, was reputedly situated in the parish in 1620. There are more moats in Dennington than in any other Suffolk parish, with further sites at: Trust Farm, SE of Dennington Place - two sides of an irregular moat; The Chestnuts, formerly Moat House, NW of the last - the remains of a rectangular moat; Red House, Maypole Green - the greater part of a narrow square moat surrounds a large area; Maypole Green - fragments of another moat a short distance W of the last; Pound Farm, ¾ mile NW of the village - a small square moat with an extension from the NW corner; Glebe Farm, S of the church - square moat, somewhat irregular, enclosing a large area with a wide pond on the northern side; Elm Hall, ½ mile SE of the village - small oblong moat; Whitehouse Farm , SW of the village - well-proportioned oblong moat; another small moat at Brown's Farm just E of the last; Fentons Farm, Maypole Green - a small rectangular moat (the moat in Dennington, the house in Tannington); Wood Farm, E of the village; an isolated moat, now dry, at Jubilee Wood, W of Dennington Wood; fragments of a moat at Office Farm and cropmarks of a possible moated site at Street Field, W of the village and S of Saxtead Road.

DENSTON *(6 miles N of Clare)*

Risbridge Hundred. 'Farmstead of a man called Deneheard' (OE) *Danerdestuna* (DB)
Manors. Denston Hall (C13/C14 Thomas de Grey). *Sub-Manors.* Beaumonds; Stonehall/Shepcote.

Ancient Woodland.
Hollybud Wood, and Elm and Redfield Groves are part of ancient woodland.

Ancient Mound.
On the W side of the road to Wickhambrook, just S of the Wickham Street crossroads, is an ancient scheduled mound 66' in diameter and 4' high. It may be a round barrow. There is no trace of a ditch or any central mutilation. Local legend claims the mound covers the dead from a Civil War battle near Wickhambrook.

Medieval Green.
On Faden's 1783 map, the small triangular area of green formed by a T-junction of lanes on the S side of the church was shown edged by a number of old properties.

Site of College of Chantry Priests.
In 1474 Edward IV presented Sir John Howard, John Denston and John Broughton the Younger with "Denston's Chauntery" in the "town of Denardiston," endowed with the manor of Beaumonds in Lindsey. It was formed of 'three chantry priests to sing in the parish church of Denston . . . their mansion house adjoins the church'. The chantry or college for a warden and priests was never very important, for when it was dissolved in 1548, the staff only consisted of a warden and two priests. Chantry Farm which lies to the SE of the church is suggestive of the site and may contain a relic from it (*see below*), but an estate map of 1676 marks 'The College' as a building set back on the W side and names Chantry Farm as 'The Parsonage House'.

Guildhall (?)
There may have been a Guildhall here. In the particulars of grants in 1549, a house called 'le Guildehall' is mentioned.

Workhouse.
The parish had a workhouse where 10 inmates were listed in 1776.

Historic Houses & Ancient Moated Sites.
Denston Hall in Denston Park is mainly C18, but a square moated site to the S, shown on estate maps of 1676 and 1778, contained the former hall of c1500, seat of the Robinson family from 1591; their monuments adorn St Nicholas Church. The illustration of 1676 shows a tall brick C15 gatehouse in the middle of the E side attached

DENSTON *(continued)*

to a timber-framed range fronting the moat. Stretches of crenellated walling linked this range with two small brick turrets at the NW and SW corners. The gatehouse was demolished in 1778 and the W arm only of the moat was surviving in 1958. E of The Thatchers, on a footpath which follows the parish boundary with Stradishall, a linear pond marks the site of Old House Yards, a small roughly square enclosure 66 yds by 55 yds - probably a former moat; a 1778 estate map shows a building within the enclosure. Chantry Farm, formerly known as 'The Parsonage House' (*see above*), probably dates from the early C16. It still contains a beam carved with the crests of the Broughton and Everard families (Henry Everard married Margaret Broughton).

DEPDEN *(7 miles SW of Bury St Edmunds)*

Risbridge Hundred. 'Deep valley' (OE) *Depdana* (DB) Includes the Domesday vill of Clopton.
Manors. Depden (1528 Anthony Gournay/Gurney).

Ancient Settlement Site.
Cropmarks in the area of the disused airfield have revealed a number of circular, oval and irregular enclosures.

Deserted Medieval Settlements.
Beresford included Depden as one of his lost English villages and there is not only evidence of a possible former settlement near the isolated church, but Faden's map of 1783 shows what was probably its replacement around the extensive Depden Green N of the Hall. This latter settlement was also doomed to failure for whilst the limits of this green can still be traced and it remains in its entirety N of the road, the many properties shown on the map lining the green, particularly along its eastern and northern sides have gone. Their demise may have been a consequence of the erection of the modern Depden Hall which overlooks the site.

Medieval Green.
Depden Green is shown by Faden covering an extensive area from N of the hall and beyond the present road. Whilst the area S of the road has been subject to enclosure and some redevelopment - especially the new houses which follow the western boundary - that to the N of the road still retains its former rectangular shape and form edged by old ponds and water courses. A linear green is shown but not named by Faden running NE from Shop End at the junction with the lane to Elms Farm now replaced by the road to Chedburgh.

Site of old Windmill.
A post mill which stood on the green in 1783 was demolished c1910.

Historic House & Ancient Moated Sites.
Depden Hall is modern, but three sides of a large moat nearby mark the site of the former hall where excavations have revealed a brick wall (pre-1660?) with two courses of Ashlar blocks at its base and traces of an earlier Tudor wall. The hall was the seat of the Jermyns in the second half of the C16 and also formerly home to the Coel, Thornhill and Mures families. Soil marks of an enclosure c38 yds square (with flattened outer earthworks?) next to the site of the isolated St Mary's Church suggest a possible former moat. Strangely, Faden's map shows a group of buildings here but omits the normal illustration for a church.

DRINKSTONE *(7½ miles SE of Bury St Edmunds)*

Thedwestry Hundred. 'Farmstead of a man called Dremic' or 'Soldier's farm' (OE) *Drincestuna* (DB)
Manors. Drinkstone Hall/Lovayne's (C13 Matthew de Lovaine). *Sub-Manors.* Halls al Timperley's.

Ancient Woodland.
There are four fragments of unnamed ancient woodland in the S of the parish.

Roman Road.
The course of a minor Roman road has been identified by in a footpath entering the SE corner of the parish and forming the boundary between Drinkstone and Woolpit for a short distance. It continues straight over an open field and then follows the field edge past Hill Farm. It is probably picked up again as Deadman's Lane, then as the parish boundary just NE of the windmill, continuing straight on past woodland before the footpath and

DRINKSTONE *(continued)*

boundary bear right to meet the road by Bridge Farm.

Ancient 'Ridge & Furrow' ploughland.
Just SW of Home Farm, in meadowland in the Black Bourne valley, are signs of the former 'Ridge-and-Furrow'.

Former Medieval Deer Park (?)
The mansion of Drinkstone Park is said to have been built in 1760 by Joshua Grigby who was High Sheriff of Suffolk in 1810. Faden's map of 1783 shows it with a great 230 acre park extending W from Park Road, the majority in the adjacent parish of Hessett. Its northern boundary is marked by the lane running W to Elm's Farm in Hessett from the junction by Meade Farm, and it extended S to a lane which connected Park Road with Manor Road in Hessett, part of which remains on the southern side of Clayhill Wood. It is thought to have formerly been a medieval deer park.

Medieval Green.
The diamond-shaped Drinkstone Green covered the entire area of the present hamlet and extended N as a linear green almost to Drinkstone church. Arms also ran SE, as a wide linear green to a point just N of Rattlesden River and Felsham Road, now marked by a kink in the present road, and S as a stepped linear green to just N of Gedding Hall; again its course is clearly marked by that of the present road. The main Drinkstone Green, which was formerly edged with properties, was enclosed in 1854 and completely built over to form the present hamlet and main centre of population, almost completing the drift S of the former village based near the church. Faden's map also shows a rectangular green NE of Drinkstone Green called Marsh Green. It lay S of Burts Farm and a footpath from Gedding Road, its outline now completely obliterated.

Medieval Market & Fair.
The de Lovaine family had the grant of a market, fair, pillory, ducking stool and view of frankpledge in 1267. Frankpledge was a system by which a group of freemen (later unfree men were admitted to the system) were held responsible by the state for each other's misdeeds. Sheriffs held periodical 'views' of frankpledge, i.e. courts to see that the law was being obeyed. These were later replaced by manorial court leets which served the same purpose.

Sites of old Windmills.
NE of the village is a windmill dated 1689, one of three existing C17 mills in Suffolk. Two others were recorded here in the C18; a smock-mill, first mentioned c1780 and last worked c1900, survives nearby in ruins, and the other, a post mill, was recorded as standing by Mill Farm before 1780.

Historic Houses & Ancient Moated Sites.
At Hall Farm, Drinkstone Green, an oblong moat c76 yds by 60 yds remains from Drinkstone Hall, built in 1760 on a much earlier site and demolished c1953; the area N and E of the moat is marked 'warren' on a map of 1702. Ticehurst House on the northern parish boundary - now apparently stranded in Tostock by the moving of the Drinkstone boundary S to follow the line of the Woolpit bypass - dates from 1599. The hall may occupy the site of that recorded in Domesday as '2 horses at hall'. Rookery Farm, S of the village, has a moat; there is a rectangular moat c91 yds by 37 yds NW of the village at Park Cottages, and Home Farm has a small square moat. Lost moats include a small square moat which stood on the W of the Gedding Road just N of Rookery Farm - gone by 1904, and a semi-circular moat abutting the SW side of the road between Deadman's Lane and Gedding Road.

DUNWICH *(8 miles NE of Saxmundham)*

Blything Hundred. Celtic name meaning 'deep water' to which the 'wic' meaning 'harbour' was later added making the probable meaning 'deep water harbour' (OE) *Domnoc* (636?) *Duneuuic* (DB). Includes the Domesday vill of Alneterne.

Manors. Dunwich (Crown property); Manor of the Temple (-1561 The Preceptory of Knights Templars in Dunwich and later those of Battisford; 1561 Thomas Andrews).

Lost Ancient East Anglian City & Seaport.
Seated upon a high hill composed only of loose textured loam and sand beside the hostile North Sea, Dunwich

DUNWICH *(continued)*

was, despite its initial power and fame, always a doomed city. The Saxon place-name suggests that Dunwich was a Saxon trading post like Ipswich, Norwich and Hamwich (Southampton). Certainly it was the sea which first brought the ancient city to fame and prosperity and has, over the centuries, proceeded to destroy it, leaving only a tiny hamlet and the merest fragments of its illustrious past. It is first noticed in c632 A.D. as the probable site where the Burgundian missionary St Felix first established his See, although there seems little doubt from coins and other finds that the Romans had been here and probably built a station or fort. Unfortunately, if they were, like virtually everything else the evidence is now under the waves along with its churches, chapels, monasteries, hospitals, etc. While the claims for thirteen churches here is an exaggeration, and tales of their bells still ringing beneath the waves, a whimsical fancy, Dunwich had about eight or nine medieval churches (with probably up to six existing at any one time), still a considerable number. The main manor of Dunwich had two caracutes (240 acres) of land in the time of Edward the Confessor, but by Domesday in 1086 this had been reduced by half - "the sea made off with the other". In 1066 there were 120 burgesses in the town, a figure which had increased to 236 by 1086. In the early years of the reign of Henry II it became the demesne of the crown and had a mint; it was described as 'a town of good note, abounding with much riches, and sundry kinds of merchandise'. King John granted the town its first charter in 1199 and, in the reign of Edward I, although already in decline, it had eleven ships of war, sixteen 'fair' ships, twenty vessels trading to the North Sea, Iceland, etc., and twenty-four small boats for the home herring industry. In 1295 (till disenfranchised by the Reform Act of 1832) Dunwich provided two Members of Parliament. From 1296 the town's craftsmen built, at their own cost, and equipped for the defence of the realm, eleven ships of war, carrying up to 72 men each. Meanwhile, the sea had been continually eating away at the cliffs. Only ten years earlier the violence of the sea had overthrown three churches, but January 1328 proved decisive when a great storm finally choked the harbour. A new one was built, and when this too was lost in 1464, a third. Yet in between these catastrophies the town continued to play an active part in international affairs. In 1334 it was recorded as having 54 shops and bakeries, and in 1347 the port sent six ships with 102 mariners to assist in the siege of Calais, during the war with France, losing most of the ships, the lives of some 500 townspeople and goods and merchandise to the value of £1000. But the writing was now inexorably on the wall. By 1540 three-quarters of the town had been lost, and before 1600 the chapels of St Anthony, St Francis and St Katherine together with the South Gate and Gilden Gate were under water. By 1677 waves washed the Market Place. In 1680, all the buildings north of Maison Dieu Lane were demolished, and in 1702 the sea reached St Peter's Church which was dismantled and soon undermined. The Town Hall shared the same fate. In 1715 the jail was submerged, and in 1729 the farthest bounds of St Peter's churchyard were washed away. The end came in December 1740. The wind, blowing very hard from the north-east, and continuing for several days, occasioned terrible devastation. Great parts of the cliff were carried away by the violence of the waves which destroyed the last remains of the churchyard of St Nicholas, together with the great road formerly leading from the quay to the town, leaving several naked walls, the tokens of ancient buildings. King's Holm, otherwise called Leonard's Marsh, was laid under water and covered with such quantities of shingle and sand 'as to be ever since of little value'. Cock and Hen hills which, the preceding summer, were forty feet high, 'had their summits levelled with their bases and the ground around them was so rent and torn that the foundation of the chapel of St Francis, situated between them, was exposed to view'. The remains of the dead were washed from their repositories, and several skeletons appeared scattered upon the beach. For many years the haunting ruin of All Saints, its last remaining medieval church, stood precariously on the edge of the cliff but in time this too was swept to an eternal grave. In the earliest map of Dunwich, dated 1587, the surviving part of the town had been about 500 yds E-W and nearly a mile N-S; by 1977, this was down to less than 55 yds E-W and 525 yds N-S.

Ancient Woodland.

The final fragment of the ancient Dunwich Wood is now disappearing over the cliff to the E of the friary, and roots and stumps of the old wood are sometimes seen at low tide. Thomas Gardner, the C18 local historian, spoke of the former extent of woodland: 'A wood called East Wood, or the King's Forest, extended several miles south-east of

DUNWICH *(continued)*

the town, but it has been for many years destroyed by the sea. The land must have stretched far out, and have formed the southern boundary of the bay of Southwold, as Easton Ness did the northern. In an eruption of the sea in 1739, the roots of a great number of trees were exposed, which appear to be the extremity of some wood, which was in all probability part of this submerged forest, which also encompassed another wood called West Wood.'

Ancient Well.
An ancient well named St James's Well was situated just W of St James Church.

Tumuli.
A round barrow lies W of Fen Covert in the NW corner of the parish. Frederick's Mount is a suggestively named site in Dunwich Forest by Dunwich River. It is possible that Cock and Hen Hills, once a prominent feature on early maps of the town and described at the time of their demise as being 40' high, may have been large Roman burial mounds of the type still in existence at Bartlow on the Essex-Cambridgeshire border.

Site of Roman Town & Fort (?)
Finds of the period including excavations in 1970, the suggestive Cock and Hen hills (*see above*), and the possible termination of more than one Roman road here, appear to make Dunwich the probable site of a Roman civil or military settlement. It may possibly be the site of the Roman town of *Sitomagus* mentioned on Inter 1X as being thirty-two Roman miles from *Venta Icenorum* (Caister St Edmund, just outside Norwich) in the Antonine Itinerary - a fourth century Roman road-book - although the known Roman settlement at Hacheston also meets these criteria, as does Knodishall with Buxloe near Aldeburgh. Norman Scarfe suggests that there may have been a Saxon Shore fort here similar to Burgh Castle and Walton (Felixstowe), suffering the same fate as the latter.

Roman (?) & other Roads.
At least two possible Roman roads are thought to have terminated here: Stone Street, coming in from Bungay, and the Roman road which came originally from Coddenham and is roughly traced as far as just NW of Yoxford by the A1120. The main road into town from the S was eroded away by the sea in 1609 and an order made for the construction of a new road. Kings Road/Kings Highway/King Johns Road, part of which remains in the form of a chalky track through the heather, is said to have run from Dunwich to Bury St. Edmunds.

Saxon Meeting Place.
Leets Hill, the Saxon meeting place, was situated just outside the town's defences. It has been suggested that the two extraordinary hills which still exist here, Dingle Great Hill and Dingle Little Hill at one time provided the meeting place of the Things of Suffolk - one for the shire and the other for Blything Hundred.

Town Defences.
Described in the C12 as having 'a great and strong defence, environed with great dykes and banks, with many sundrye high hills about and within the said town and libtie'. Gardner described Dunwich as 'encompassed by a ditch encircling a huge rampart of earth crowned with a high and strong palisade of timber. Its approaches were through gatehouses strong enough to keep out great numbers of people so that the town was a great force.' So it would appear, for in 1173 they were tested by a rebel army under the Earl of Leicester who demanded the town's submission: 'That day you could see tradesmen and trusty knights hurrying out to man their defences, each knowing his job, some as bowmen, others with lances, the strong helping the weak to have frequent spells of rest. Inside the town there was not a girl or a woman who was not carrying stones to be hurled from the palisade . . . The Earl of Leicester retired, humiliated.' These defences remained perfect until the reign of Edward I (1272-1307) when a portion was removed to enable the monks to extend the precincts of Greyfriars. Today the sea has done what the Earl could not, and only the last vestiges of Pales Dyke - the town's defensive ditch, originally 40' wide and 15' deep, with its earthen ramparts - can be seen beside the flint walls of Greyfriars precinct; this too has mostly fallen from the cliff into the insatiable North Sea. A walk along the cliff path past Greyfriars will bring you to the site of the town's Middle Gate. Here a wooded sunken way heads away from the cliff along what was once the old Midgate Street.

DUNWICH *(continued)*

Ancient Mounds (Defensive Look-out Posts?)

In Greyfriars Wood, W of Greyfriars and just S of the Middle Street (now a public footpath) is an ancient mound marked as such on the OS maps. Its closeness to the town defences may suggest a possible lookout post. This is strengthened by the fact that another mound, known as Temple Hill from the fact that it stood near the Knights Templars preceptory and which formerly lay beside Middleditch to the E (now lost over the cliff), was originally identified in the early OS as a tumulus but on excavation in 1935 was shown to be built *over* the Pales Dyke (town ditch). This mound was 20' high and 60' in diameter and revealed C13-C14 pottery.

Castle (?)

In the Patent Rolls under 1217 there is a reference to Eustace de Vescy's custody of 'the castle and town of Dunwich'. Norman Scarfe considers the possibility that a small Norman castle once stood within a Roman fort as was the case at both Burgh Castle and Walton (Felixstowe). All would now be long lost to the North Sea.

Ancient Chapels.

There were at least four chapels in Dunwich. St Mary & St John lay to the S of the town, and was mentioned in 1340. Its ruins were still standing in 1587 and probably in 1753. St Francis stood at the N end of the town, between Cock and Hen hills in the hamlet of Dingels, and was lost in the storms of 1740. St Anthony's was lost very early and little is known of it; and St Catherine's appears to have been a guild chapel situated in St John's parish.

Monasteries & College (?)

The Burgundian missionary St. Felix is thought to have first established his East Anglian See here in c632 AD, possibly within a Roman fort (*see above*), as did the other missionaries Fursey and St. Botolph (*see* Burgh Castle and Iken). Here Felix established a college/seminary for promotion of Literature and Christianity (the oldest recorded school in the county). The Franciscan Monastery of Greyfriars was founded c1265 by Richard FitzJohn and his wife Alice. It had 20 friars in 1277. Due to the erosion of the cliffs it was moved further inland to its present site in 1289. The precinct wall enclosing some 7 acres remains (although now itself starting to crumble over the cliff) with an archway and smaller doorways of the gatehouse, along with part of the S range of the monastic buildings. The precinct originally had three gates but that on the E facing the sea was 'quite demolished'. The north wall has buttresses and windows but the S wall is fragmentary. It stood along the S side of the cloister and its ground floor provided the cloister walk. The Priory of Dominican Friars stood in the parish of St John and was 'but 120 rods distant from the house of the Franciscans'. It was founded before 1256 by Sir Roger de Holesle and had 24 friars in 1277. They had a licence to move their friary to Blythburgh in 1384 but for whatever reason did not take this up and were still in Dunwich when the house was dissolved in 1544. Its ruins were still showing in 1587 but were lost to the sea soon after. A Benedictine Monastery which existed as a cell to the Priory of Eye was founded sometime after 1080, but it too had mostly been lost by 1300.

Hospitals.

The Norman apse of the chapel of St James Hospital, founded by John, Earl Moreton, remains in the churchyard SE of St James Church which dates from 1830. Being a Leper hospital it had been built outside the town c1150 on the lower slopes of Leets Hill and, at that time, consisted of a master and several 'leprous brethren and sisters'. In 1754 Gardner described how the once great income of the hospital had dwindled away so that the residue maintained only three or four indigent people 'who reside in one poor old house, being all that remains of the buildings, except the shells of the (once great) church and chapel'. Maison Dieu Hospital of the Holy Trinity was founded before 1200. By 1631 the church had been pulled down and the hospital described as being decayed; foundations lay beneath Dunwich's present main car park. The eight-acre site of the Preceptory of Knights Templars (Hospitallers) stood in Middlegate Street in the W part of the town, just inside the ramparts and about '55 rods' (just over 300 yards) from All Saints (the last church to fall from the cliff). It was established in 1185 on land granted by Henry II. In 1312, on the suppression of the Templars, it was transferred to the Knights Hospitallers and became known as 'the hospital'. The Order in Dunwich accumulated great wealth and its church was described in 1631 as being a 'fine building', although their methods in obtaining revenue

DUNWICH *(continued)*

was not always true to their vows. However, they survived to the Dissolution and in 1562 it was granted by the Crown to Thomas Andrew.

Site of Gallows.
The 'Conde' (wooden tower or large gallows) were formerly sited on Cock Hill.

Site of old Windmills.
John Cove granted messuage and windmill for rent of ½ mark in 1185, possibly associated with 'Temple Mount', and windmills were among the losses in the great storm of 1347. Two post mills were shown in Dunwich on a map of 1587.

Medieval Market & Fair.
Dunwich had a market in the C12, and one had almost certainly existed here from Saxon times. The market was formerly held daily, decreasing to weekly on a Saturday as the fortunes of the borough declined. Even as a weekly market it was described as 'small' in 1679. St. Leonard's Fair was first mentioned in the C11 as a 3-day fair and feast. St. James Fair was held annually on the Feast of St. James. Although the Market Place was washed away in 1677, a market and fair were still surviving in the town in Kirby's day (1734).

Market Cross.
A Cross formerly stood in the Market Place, but when the sea reached the spot by 1677, the townspeople had it removed. Lead and other materials were used to build butchers shops and other retail outlets providing supplies for the market.

Gaol.
The town gaol was lost to the sea in 1765.

Almshouses.
A large number of almshouses existed in Dunwich, all now gone. A warrent to reduce 'almshouses called tippling houses to eight in number' was issued in 1633. Maison Dieu became an almshouse prior to its final demise. It was recorded as having six inmates in 1636.

Town House.
The Town House was 'made dangerous by force of sea' and moved to a new site (between the Ship Inn and the Museum) in 1716.

Guildhall.
Known at different times as the Guildhall, Tollhouse and Court House, it stood in the SW corner of the Market Place until 1677. It held the guilds of Jesus (1525), Our Lady (1521), St. John Baptist and St. Katherine (C16).

Historic House.
The Ship Inn (formerly Barne Arms), situated in The Street, is well over 300 years old.

EARL SOHAM *(3½ miles W of Framlingham)*

Loes Hundred. 'Homestead by a pool' (OE) *Saham* (DB) *Earl* after the manorial Lord Bigod, Earl of Norfolk.
Manors. Earl Soham Manor (1140 Hubert de Montcheney; 1177 Hugh Bigot, Earl of Norfolk).

Ancient Pool & Site of early 'Homestead'.
Norman Scarfe has suggested the pool from which the parish obtained its name is still in existence as the big reedy bog, S of Soham Lodge, later adapted by the Bigods as fish ponds for their Lodge. Aerial photographs have probably identified the site of the original 'homestead'.

Roman Road.
The modern A1120 road follows the course of a Roman road running from the parish boundary SW of Hill Farm to Mill House, and NE of the village from the old police station to the Saxtead parish boundary just before the green. The road is lost where it passes through the village, but when a trench was dug across the line of the road N of the church a layer of large flints was discovered 6-9" thick and 25-30' wide.

EARL SOHAM *(continued)*

Ancient Tracks.

Earl Bigod's manor with its deer park and hunting lodge is connected with Framlingham Castle by a medieval trackway. It runs as a footpath from the Lodge to the modern A1120 road; then as a country road up beside the church to Mill Lane, just E of Dial Farm; then as Earl Soham Lane, a footpath track to meet a road at Apsey Green; then straight over along a country road into Framlingham. It is likely that Mill Lane itself which carries the line of the parish boundary is of ancient origin, as is Hollow Lane which forms a part of the northern boundary between Bedfield Road and Bullswood Lane.

Deer Park.

The deer park and warren (in existence 1635) probably originated from the C13 when the Bigots were lords here.

Site of old Windmills.

Two windmills are recorded in the parish in the C18: Ashfield Mill stood at Old Mill Farm on the western boundary before 1739, and a post mill was shown at Mill House beside the A1120 on Mill Hill in 1783. Both were pulled down in 1947.

Charity Tenements.

A document gives particulars of five charity tenements erected between 1581-3 and called 'Black Dames'. They are sited in the N of the parish near Soham Town Corner.

Medieval Market & Fair.

Roger Bigod obtained grants for a market and fair in Earl Soham in 1292; these were confirmed on Thomas de Brotherton by Edward II in 1313.

Historic Houses & Ancient Moated Sites.

The present Earl Soham Lodge is an C18 house with traces of the former C16 manor house of the Cornwallis family. It stands within the very strong, circular moat, 104 yds in diameter and 6½' to 8' deep, which once encircled the original C13 manor house of the Bigods, which was used as their hunting lodge whilst seated at Framlingham Castle. The moat is crossed on the S side by a C16 brick bridge and the S end of the system has an earthen bank 1½' high. 33 yds E is a flight of three parallel rectangular fish ponds. These earls of Norfolk held the manor from 1140 to 1547. Fragments at Moat Farm beside the Roman road suggest a former rectangular moat some 98 yds by 55 yds. Now a private house, The Falcon Inn dates from the C16.

EARL STONHAM *(2½ miles NE of Needham Market)*

Bosmere & Claydon Hundred. 'Homestead by a stone, or with stony ground' (OE) *Stanham* (DB) *Earl* after the Manorial lords, the Earls of Norfolk.

Manors. Earl Stonham (1107 William Bigot, Earl of Norfolk). *Sub-Manors.* Creeting Apud Montem al Derebolt's; Filloils Manor.

Roman Tumulus.

Many years ago it was said that there was, to the N of the church and within the churchyard, 'an extensive barrow in the vicinity of which urns of a grey colour are found'. Although illustrated on an old map in Ipswich Museum, nothing remains today. The fact that the church lies between the Coddenham to Caister St Edmund Roman road (the A140) and Forward Green (*see below*), suggests it would not be unreasonable to find a burial mound of the period in the vicinity.

Roman Settlement/Cemetery (?)

Considerable Roman finds in the way of coins and pottery were discovered in 1865, 1870 and 1881 in the area of Forward Green.

Roman Road.

The Roman road from Colchester to Caister St. Edmunds crosses the eastern sector of the parish N-S.

Ancient & Medieval Tracks.

Old Hundred Lane forms the western end of the northern parish boundary with Mendlesham, and the boundary

EARL STONHAM *(continued)*

of the ancient Saxon Hundreds of Stow and Hartismere, dating back at least to this period and may even be pre-Roman. The 'Lord's Highway' runs from the church to the priory at Creeting St Olaves, crossing a brook by Lady Bridge. Its likely association with the manorial lords, the Earls of Norfolk, suggest an early origin.

Medieval Greens.

Faden's map shows Middlewood Green occupying a rectangular area now enclosed on the northern and western sides by the roads from Saxham Street to Stonham Parva. Forward Green, shown and named by Faden, remains today as a triangular green with Green Farm marking its eastern corner. The narrow linear Tidymans Green which extended Forward Green W in place of the present road to Bell's Cross, and Broad Green, which enclosed the southern part of this triangular area (the two greens connected by Ball's Way and extended half way to Roydon Hall, the termination marked by a kink in the track), have been replaced by a recreation ground. A small square northern extension of Tidyman's Green, unnamed by Faden, is marked Wick's Green on the present OS map.

Medieval Market.

The Duke of Norfolk had the grant of a market and fair here in 1327.

Guildhall.

Timber-framed Waylands Cottages at Wick's Green, which dates from the C15, is probably the former Guildhall 'settled in the 15th of Edward IV (1476) for the benefit of the parishioners' according to William White, who added that it was now used as a schoolhouse (1844).

Historic House & Ancient Moated Sites.

Georgian Deerbolts Hall, NW of Creeting Bottoms in the SE corner of the parish, stands on the irregular one acre moated site of the old manor house, seat of the Drivers and Thomas, High Sheriff of Suffolk (1726). It was named Dear Bought Hall on Faden's 1783 map. The hall was the birthplace of the poet James Bird (1788-1839). At Moat Farm, near Westwood Hall and N of the parish in Middlewood Green, is a large oblong moat, the southern side of which has been destroyed.

EAST BERGHOLT *(6 miles SE of Hadleigh)*

Samford Hundred. Bergholt: 'Wood on or by a hill to the east of another' (OE) No ancient woodland remains in the parish but the wood referred to may have been east of King's Wood, Stratford St. Mary. *Bercolt* (DB)
Manors. East Bergholt Manor (1315 Philip de Orebyn); Illarius/New Hall (C14 Philip Tilney). *Sub-Manors.* Oldhall/Adehall; Spencers; Commadry's al St. John's.

Roman Road.

The present A12 follows the course of the Roman road from Stratford St Mary to Coddenham SW-NE across the northern part of the parish from Four Sisters to the Lattinford Bridge.

Roman Cemetery

Ackworth House stands on the site of a Roman cremation cemetery.

Monastery.

St Mary's Abbey was formerly a Benedictine Nunnery originally established by Lady Mary Percy in 1598 for English Ladies in Brussels. At the time of the French Revolution the community returned to England, and after settling first in Winchester in 1794, they purchased the Old Hall in East Bergholt and created a monastery here in 1857. It is now occupied by Franciscan friars.

Site of Knights Templars (?)

It is likely that the Templars, who held a sub-manor here and in the C12 claimed free warren, view of frankpledge and assize of bread and beer, established a residence and/or chapel here.

Site of Chapel (?)

Cropmarks just NE of Valley Farm may relate to an ancient Chapel once reputedly sited here (*see above*). The wayside Chapel of St. Mary which stood on Cattawade Bridge was founded by Hugh, Rector of Bergholt in the C13.

EAST BERGHOLT *(continued)*

Medieval Greens/Heaths.

Faden's 1783 map shows East Bergholt Heath covering much of the parish. One section ran SW either side of East End Road and W of the length of B1070 heading S; Mill Road marks the western side of a large green/heath heading NW and connected to the former, its northern extent marked by the end of a modern development and Rookery Farm. Another green/heath lay S of the village street between Flatford Road and Hog's Lane. The Heath was enclosed in 1815 - one of John Constable's paintings shows a part being ploughed the following year.

Ancient Watermills.

There were three water mills here in 1562. Flatford Mill, now a Field Centre, was a water or fulling mill in 1536 (made famous in the paintings of John Constable).

Site of old Windmills.

The Black Mill and The White Mill were both in existence before 1779 and again received immortality through John Constable's paintings. They stood in close proximity near Old Mill House, S of Mill Road.

Medieval Market & Fair.

This large village formerly had a market and fair, referred to in 1459. They appear, however, to have fallen on hard times during the C16-C18 when many houses were pulled down and a number of legacies towards rebuilding the church remained uninstigated.

Free School.

A free grammar school was founded by Mrs. Lettice Dykes and Edward Lamb in 1588. It was rebuilt in 1831.

Workhouse.

A workhouse was first mentioned in 1734. The inmates were transferred to Tattingstone in 1768.

Almshouse.

In 1720 the will of Edward Clarke provided three cottages on East bergholt Heath for the use of three poor industrious widows.

Historic House & Ancient Moated Sites.

To the E of Old Hall (*see above*) is a virtual circular earthwork, c98 yds in diameter with banks c6½' high, now occupied by a car park. This is probably the site of an even earlier hall as the area to the SE is named Old Hall Park. S of Flatford Mill, a small oblong moat lies close to the river Stour from which water is obtained via a short channel.

EASTON *(3½ miles S of Framingham)*

Loes Hundred. 'Farmstead or village to the east of another*' (OE) *Probably Kettleburgh. *Estuna* (DB). Includes the Domesday vill of Martley.

Manors. Easton Manor (c1273 Sir William Charles). *Sub-Manors.* Martley Hall.

Ancient Woodland.

Maid's Wood, Ralph's Wood and Ash Grove are parts of ancient woodland.

Lost & Relocated Villages.

Moated Martley Hall, N of the present village, was a distinct township at Domesday named Mertlega or Martele. It would appear that when the earls of Rochford built a new Hall and created a park at Easton in the C18 (*see below*), the emparking involved diverted the Kettleburgh road to the S away from the church, with the subsequent loss of the former village houses. The village properties are shown on Faden's map of 1783 lining the new realigned road S of the park. Times and fashions have changed again for today this forfeited land has been reclaimed and infilled with a new residential housing development.

Medieval Fair.

A fair was held on Hallowmas Day in 1618.

EASTON *(continued)*

Historic House & Ancient Moated Sites.

An enclosure near the church known as 'The Wilderness' may be that of the White House, the first manor house from at least the C14. It may also be the site of the rebuilt house of the Wingfields who made their seat here in the C16. After acquiring Easton in 1708, the earls of Rochford built a new house, probably on a different site, and created a park, in existence by 1783. The Duke of Hamilton massively rebuilt this house in the C19 calling it The Mansion. It was demolished in 1925. C17 Bentries Farm, to the E of Easton Park, stands on the E side of an island c48 yds square surrounded by a moat 33'- 39' wide and up to 10' deep. The SE arm of the moat is bordered by a bank mounded at the E end. Martley Hall, another ancient manor house N of the village *(see above)*, has an irregular hexagonal moat. The White Horse public house in the centre of the village dates from the C17.

EASTON BAVENTS *(N of Southwold)*

Blything Hundred. Easton - 'Farmstead to the east of another*' (OE) *Possibly Reydon. 'Bavents' relates to the de Bavents who owned the manor in the C13. *Estuna* (DB)

Manors. Easton Bavents (1237 Thomas Bavent).

Lost Medieval Village.

This once extensive parish was called Exoche by the Romans. Sited on the edge of the crumbling cliffs, it comprised 770 acres in 1815, half this in 1881, and now a strip of land just over 1½ miles long but only on average about 250 yds wide. It formerly had a bold promontary called Easton Ness, said to have projected more than two miles out to sea forming the northern boundary of Southwold Bay, and at that time Britain's most easterly point. Like Dunwich, all has been lost to the sea - church, chapel and village settlement. St Nicholas Church, shown standing in 1638, was gone by c1666. It was shown in the sea on a map of 1753 with the caption 'ruins of a church destroyed by the sea'. The parish's demise can be seen in its diminishing population: 1524 - 60 taxpayers; 1603 - 46 adults; 1674 - 7 households; 1801 - 17 inhabitants, 1881 - 13.

Ancient Chapel.

The ancient chapel dedicated to St Margaret, which stood to the W of the church and said to have held a special relic which made it a place of pilgrimage had, by 1754, fallen into 'irreparable decay' and was being used as a barn. This too has long since been submerged.

Medieval Market & Fair.

A descendent of Thomas de Bavent (Lord of the Manor in 1281) obtained the grant of a weekly market and annual fair in 1330.

Sea Battle.

The promontary of Easton Ness formed the northern bounds of Southwold (Sole) Bay. The Battle of Sole Bay was fought off Easton Bavents on 28 May 1672 when the English and French fleets, under the Duke of York and the Count d'Estrees, at anchor here with over 100 ships to water and refit, were attacked by a Dutch fleet under De Ruyter who had taken them offguard. A fierce battle ensued during which the French broke off the engagement and the Earl of Sandwich was killed on board the *Royal James* which was blown up. The result was indecisive with both sides claiming victory. An 11' bronze cannon made around 1530 and raised by marine archaeologist Stuart Bacon, is believed to be from the wreck of the *Royal James*, the 1,426 ton flag ship of the English Navy which had only been completed the previous year.

EDWARDSTONE *(5 miles E of Sudbury)*

Babergh Hundred. 'Farmstead of a man called Eadweard' (OE) *Eduardestuna* (DB)

Manors. Edwardstone Manor (C11 Hubert de Munchensi/Monchesney). *Sub-Manors.* Lynnes al Algoods; Tewes/Tues al Tendring.

Ancient Woodland.

Park Wood, Stallington Wood, Cowper's Wood, and Bull's Cross Wood are fragments of ancient woodland.

EDWARDSTONE *(continued)*

Ancient Priory (& Chapel?)

The priory here was a short-lived cell of the Benedictine Abbey of Abingdon near Oxford, founded in 1114 by Hubert de Monchesney and transferred to Colne Priory, Essex, in 1160. A St John's Chapel, mentioned in 1160, may have been connected with it. The priory was, according to Bowen's map of 1755 and Faden's of 1783, a substantial building and occupied the site now known as Priory Farm at Priory Green N of the village. Reused material from its demise may be incorporated in the gatehouse of Edwardstone Hall.

Medieval Greens.

Faden's map of 1783 shows Whistlers Green as a long triangular green sited at the junction N of Edwardstone Hall, and Mill Green as a small rectangular green covering the T-junction NE of the Hall. This same map marks Priory Green on the northern parish boundary. Although not naming it, Faden shows a possible green in the area now marked by a loop in the lane and track in the same spot, now enclosed and built over. Old properties were formerly shown lying along the northern side but only Priory Farm remains.

Site of old Windmill.

A smock mill stood on Mill Green in 1783.

Medieval Market.

A grant was made for a market in 1240.

Workhouse.

A workhouse is recorded here with 40 inmates in 1776.

Historic House & Ancient Moated Site.

The church and the site of Edwardstone Hall (taken down in 1952) are approached by a drive which commences from the remaining ornate brick gatehouse. The Hall stood in a park which would appear to have at one time been very extensive and to have stretched beyond the river Box and the western parish boundary. It also oocupied the site of an ancient hall recorded at Domesday, seat of the wealthy De Monte Canisio or Montechensy family. Lynn Hall, at Priory Green, belonged to Waldingfield clothiers, and is C16, and Sherbourne House, in the S of the parish, while considerably altered, dates from later in the same century. Moat Farm, at Mill Green, retains the N side of a small moat.

ELLOUGH (or Willingham All Saints) (see also Willingham St Mary) *(3½ miles SE of Beccles)*

Wangford Hundred. 'Place at the heathen temple' (OScand) *Elgar* (DB)
Manors. Ellough Manor (-C13 Crown property; 1345 Sir Robert Wachesham).

Ancient Woodland.

Two fragments of Ellough Wood are part of ancient woodland.

Site of Ancient Heathen Temple (?)

Elgr is the Norse word for temple. The church may have replaced a heathen temple, possibly on the same site.

Medieval Moor.

The site of Ellough Moor was shown and named on Faden's map of 1783. It lay mostly to the N of Benacre Road in Worlingham parish and was enclosed in 1797. It was later used for a second world war airfield.

Lost Settlements.

Whilst there is no village as such nor written evidence that one ever existed, there are signs of a former medieval settlement around the isolated church on the southern parish boundary. Here a lane from the church (now a footpath) heads NW to join the country road heading for Beccles and another NNE to connect with Ellough Hall on the Hulver road (now lost). Still in the S of the parish but over to the E, an area of c9.5 ha. was evaluated prior to development. Documentary evidence show the sites of Warrens Lane and Potters Farm to have been in existence when Ellough Mooor was enclosed in 1797 and immediately W of the farm on the W side of Warrens Lane, a quantity of C13-C14 pottery sherds were

ELLOUGH *(continued)*

recovered from a brick kiln and a series of ditch-like features.

Site of Historic House (?)

Part of Sandpit Lane which ran NW through the moor from Benacre Road mainly in Worlingham parish, is shown on Faden's 1783 map as a tree-lined avenue to a point where the lane swings right before resuming its original course. An entrance leads off this avenue to a large building within a rectangular enclosure marked 'Ruins' on the C19 tithe. The site, which may be that of the Wachesham's manor house, stands beside the Benacre road on the northern parish boundary and now on or under the disused World War II airfield. This part of Sandpit Lane is now covered by industrial works.

ELMSETT *(4 miles NNE of Hadleigh)*

Cosford Hundred. 'Dwellers among the elm-trees' (OE) *Elmeseta* (DB)
Manors. Elmsett (C13 Sir John de Bathan/Bathonia).

Ancient Woodland.

Elmsett Park Wood and Borley's Wood are parts of ancient woodland.

Ancient Well.

By a footpath in the valley at the southern end of Elmsett Park Wood is an ancient spring and dropping well which is said to possess medicinal properties.

Medieval Fair.

Elmsett Green probably provided the site for the annual medieval fair once held in the village.

Medieval Green.

Faden shows narrow wedge-shaped Elmsett Green running along the northern side of Whatfield Road from a curve in the road near Corn Mill, past Maltings Farm, and terminating at its widest in the village by a large moat.

Workhouse.

A workhouse, situated at Cobb's Bridge, recorded 12 inmates in 1776.

Historic Houses & Ancient Moated Sites.

The C15 Rectory House has a large ancient moat, now half of an ellipse, with straight northern and eastern sides, but Faden's 1783 map shows it as very large and roughly circular. Elmsett Hall retains a small part of its moat, and there is a moat at Church Farm which, although itself of C18-C19 date, stands on the site of the former Hall, possible seat of Edward Sherland who died in 1609 and has an impressive monument in the nearby church. A fragment of a moat remains at Elmsett Gate Farm (formerly the 'Moated House'), S of the village, and a large part of the moat at Mill Farm was levelled and built over in 1969. Parts of Rookery Farm date from the C16.

ELMSWELL *(5 miles NW of Stowmarket)*

Blackbourn Hundred. 'Spring or well where elm-trees grow' (OE) *Elmeswella* (DB). Elmer being a known surname in the area, Morley considers 'Elm' to be a personal name i.e. 'Aelfmaer's Well'.
Manors. Elmswell (-1536 Abbot of St. Edmunds, Bury; 1536 Sir Thomas Darcy).

Ancient Spring.

The spring from which Elmswell obtained its name is probably that at Hawks End just before the right hand bend in School Road N of the church where early maps show elm trees.

Roman Pottery Industry.

A Roman kiln was discovered in Kiln Lane in the 1960s, evidence of a one-time pottery industry here.

Roman Road (?)

The line of a probable Roman road heading for Ixworth is traced by the dead straight line of the present A1088 from the junction with the road to Tostock, running NNW to the parish boundary and beyond to Norton village. Another (very conjectural) road may be traced by the parish boundary and old county boundary between East and

ELMSWELL *(continued)*

West Suffolk which heads NNE from a section of the old by-passed A45 at TL9946 6256 (here undetected on the ground), by Warren Mill House (where a footpath follows its course to the Wetherden road) and then by field boundaries to just beyond the railway track at TL9990 6385. From this point its line is again lost on the ground.

Ancient Cross.

In the churchyard of St John the Baptist is the shaft of an ancient Saxon Cross with a modern top.

Ancient Boundary.

An old ditch and bank called The Franchise Bank divided the Franchise of St Edmund from the geldable, otherwise called the Hundred Mere. It was also the Procession Way dividing the parishes of Elmswell and Wetherden. It is evident on the ground as a track from the Wetherden road to Warren Mill House, then as a footpath to the old main road which forms the boundary with Woolpit parish.

Ancient Way.

A short stretch of the ancient highway from Bury to Ipswich remains as 'Earthfield Lane' beside the A14 dual-carriageway at the interchange with the A1088. Traces of a bridle path leading from Penny Lane by Norton Wood are still called the Lord's Highway or Abbot's Walk. The Way once led from Bury Abbey and was used by the abbots to reach their grange at Elmswell Hall.

Medieval Green.

Boten Haugh Green is named and shown on Faden's map of 1783 as one of the largest greens in Suffolk at 195 acres. Regretably now enclosed and broken up, it leaves little obvious evidence of its former existence. The road N to Great Ashfield which cuts through it (as it did then) is now bordered by modern houses but a closer examination shows several of the old farmsteads which lined the green still surviving in their original positions with evidence of former C13-C14 dwellings in the form of house platforms, boundary ditches, field boundaries, footpaths and concentrated pottery scatters. Together they help to rediscover the green's extent. Button Hoo Green, as it was later known, was fish-shaped and curved to the W. The square 20 acre 'tail' section, Little Green, is now occupied by School Lane, the railway station and a factory - the latter built over the northern edge. It is shown on an early C19 map edged with many old properties . The 'body' of the green lay either side of the Ashfield road widening as it went - its eastern edge marked by Grove Farm and Lea Farm (in Great Ashfield parish), and its western by Willow Farm, Green Farm and Dagwood Farm. It curved westwards towards the 'head', S of the line of the road to Norton (which is modern), and terminated at Norton Little Green. An arm went off NW to end at Hunston Green. White Gates (in Great Ashfield) appears to be the northern limit of the main green.

Abbot's Warrens.

To the SE of the parish were the extensive warrens for the Abbot of Bury Abbey's country seat here. They are remembered in Warren Farm, Warren Mill House and The Warren, S of the parish boundary in Woolpit.

Ancient Windmills.

Two windmills (valued at 26s. 8d.) were recorded in the parish in 1283.

Almshouses.

In a commanding position on the ridge of a hill, a row of delightful almshouses form a picturesque scene beside the church. They were founded in 1614 by Sir Robert Gardener, Chief Justice of Ireland, for six poor widows, three from Elmswell and three from Woolpit. They received a pension of 16d per week plus a yearly supply of 'ready-made gowns of coarse blue cloth/stuff'. Gardener died in 1619 and has a large, majestic monument in the church. The almshouses were restored in 1967.

Historic Moated Grange.

Until the reign of James I, when it passed to Sir Robert Gardener, the Abbot of Bury Abbey held the manor. A fragment of the square moat (now largely infilled and ploughed) which once formed an island site for his original Grange and country seat, remains at Elmswell Hall. The present house sits within the outer moat. Henry VI was entertained here in 1433 and, prior to the Dissolution, the Abbot often held his Great Court of St. Edmund in the parish.

ELVEDEN *(5 miles S of Brandon)*

Lackford Hundred. 'Swan valley' or 'Valley haunted by elves and fairies' or 'Aelfa's valley' (OE) *Eluedena* (DB) *Manors.* Elveden Manor (1252/80 Sir Richard de Lerling had free warren). *Sub-Manors.* Stanes al Monks Hall; Gelham al Hastings.

Lower Palaeolithic Industrial Site.

In the late 1990s, the British Museum carried out excavations on a major settlement site of the Lower Palaeolithic Period at Brickyard Pit. It has proved a significant site internationally, showing some of the earliest evidence of human industrial activity - a Stone Age tool industry dating back 400,000 years. Nearly 24 sq.yds of perfectly preserved work area has produced several dozen flint tools, hand-axes, scrappers, etc., along with the bones of several animals long since extinct in this country.

Course of Prehistoric Trackway.

The course of the Icknield Way, one of Britain's oldest known trackways, runs SSW-NNE to form the parish boundary and the Hundred boundary between Lackford and Blackbourne; Margary also includes it in his list of Roman roads. It is not evident on the ground through the parish, but its line is marked by the edge of woodland. It was still a working road in 1783 when Faden shows it heading SW from Thetford and names it The Old London Road. At that time Old Elveden Gap, where the present Elveden Road crosses the parish boundary (and Icknield Way), formed a major junction with roads and tracks, all now lost, spiralling out in all directions.

Tumulus.

The remains of a round barrow, S of Duke's Ride and W of the Icknield Way, are marked as 'John Mann's Clump' on the 1841 tithe map. Situated in the centre of a cultivated field and much mutilated it is 60 paces in circumference and 2' high.

Romano-British Settlement & Coin Hoard.

In this parish in 1953 sherds, quern stones and other occupational material were found together with a spouted flask covered by a small dish which contained 1,146 silver coins, the majority early C3 A.D. and ranging from Antoninus Pius to Philip II.

Historic House.

Elveden Hall stands on an ancient site once appropriated to Bury Abbey and later given by Henry VIII to the Duke of Norfolk. During 1863-70, after he became Lord of the Manor, Prince Duleep Singh converted the present Hall from a modest Georgian house of c1768 into a sumptuous Indian palace. This theme was continued on an even grander scale by Lord Iveagh between 1899-1903. The hall stands in a small park adjoining the ancient 1,000 acre rabbit warren, once a part of the former hall. King Edward VII and George V were frequent visitors.

ERISWELL *(3 miles N of Mildenhall)*

Lackford Hundred. 'Spring or stream of a man called Here' or 'Efer's well' (OE) *Hereswella* (DB). Includes the Domesday vill of Coklesworth. Morley suggests the the Old Fen Sea which once covered the (now drained) fens, isolating Ely, would account for the two fisheries recorded here at Domesday.

Manors. Eriswell Manor (C13 Ralph de Rouetustre [Rochester]). *Sub-Manors.* Chamberlains.

Tumuli.

There are several burial mounds in the parish: two round barrows E of Dalehole Plantation stand beside the A1065, with another S of these, again right beside the road, excavated c1927 and now ploughed out; one on the western edge of Gibson's Slip, c82' in diameter, 2½' high; one formerly NW of this S of Partition Belt and known as Gibson's Gate, a mound 4' high; one E of Foxhole Heath, known as Galley Hill; a Bronze-Age barrow 65½' by 60½' by 1' high with surviving ditch at Chamberlain's Buildings Farm; a round barrow S of Chestnut Court known as Blood Hill, 85' in diameter and 5' high; another 87 yds from this a mound oval to triangular in shape c131' x 82' and just over 3' high; finally, a very distinct rise in a flat arable field W of the last and Cranhousefield Belt identified from aerial photos as a probable barrow which in 1946 was c98' in diameter and 2½' high.

ERISWELL *(continued)*

Deserted Village.

Two separate pagan Anglo-Saxon settlements developed here beside two wells or streams. The northern, Coclesworda, formerly a berewick (secondary manor), became Cocilsworth with its own hall and church; the southern, Eriswell, also had its own church. Already in severe decline with its hall and church in ruins, Cocilsworth was eventually completely swamped by the construction of the Lakenheath airbase, leaving a small hamlet now known as Little Eriswell. The village of Eriswell, near the western boundary, was then left to oversee this massive parish of fen edge and Breckland heath and fir.

Ancient Chapel.

The ancient Chapel of St Lawrence which stood beside Cocilsworth Church was probably founded by the de Tuddenhams who held the manor from c1296.

Site of Ancient Water-mill.

Domesday listed two water-mills in Eriswell. At least one of these was sited to the W of the site of the old manor house and chapel where an intricate system of moats and waterways used the watercourse still in existence today. Meadows to the W are named 'Mill Meadow' on the 1839 tithe map which also shows a circular island in the centre of the water with three arms - the possible mill? Some distance to the E, now within the area of buildings connected with Lakenheath Airfield, is Caudle Head, the only remaining of five areas of water shown on Faden's map of 1783 at the tip of branches leading from a water course which itself leads directly from the moat and Eriswell Load.

Medieval Rabbit Warrens.

When the New England Company purchased the manor of 'Eereswell cum Chamberlains' in the mid C17, it noted two free warrens here containing some 2,000 acres. These were presumably at High and Low Warren with a lodge situated in each. High Lodge marks the site of the former, first mentioned in 1309.

Historic Houses & Ancient Moated Site.

A half circular moat immediately W of Eriswell Hall Farm in the N of the parish, relates to the site of the former manor house beside the ruins of the earlier church of St Peter. An avenue of trees marked on Faden's 1783 map on an E-W alignment on the eastern side of the main Erisell-Lakenheath road (B1112) stretches to the Brandon Road (A1065) a distance of some 1.05km. At the western end two buildings are shown situated either side of the road. The presence of the avenue suggests that these were buildings of some importance. The easternmost building has gone and the site built over, but parts of the westernmost may have been incorporated into two surviving buildings at Chamberlain's Farm. One of the two Erisell manors was called Chamberlains and this may be the site of the former manor house. A single line of the former avenue still survives.

ERWARTON (formerly Arwarton) *(9 miles SE of Ipswich)*

Samford Hundred. 'Eoforweard's farmstead' (OE) *Eurewardestuna* (DB)
Manors. Erwarton (C13 Bartholomew Davillers).

Ancient Way (?)

Lanes are rarely named on Faden's 1783 map, so his naming of Taylors Lane connecting Crouch House, on the NW parish boundary, with The Street, just W of the church, may suggest its antiquity and importance. Although now lost, its line is still marked by tracks, footpaths and field boundaries. Surprisingly, from N of Crouch House the lane met the main road just E of Chelmondiston village, not by one of the two present footpaths, but by a staggered route running between them, marked now only by field boundaries.

Ancient Chapel (?)

St Mary's Chapel was mentioned in 1269. It may have been a chapel connected with the C13 Daviller family. Their tombs lie in St Mary's Church which dates from the C14, suggesting their monuments were originally housed in an earlier church on the site of which this chapel was a part.

ERWARTON *(continued)*

Ancient Wharf.
Arwarton Ness is an ancient wharf by the river Orwell. It was used extensively by vessels 'during all times of the tide' for transporting coprolite (fossilised animal dung at one time used as a fertiliser) which was raised extensively in the parish and elsewhere along the estuary.

Civil War.
It is believed that five bells were removed from the church and broken up for shot to defend the hall from Fairfax's soldiers during the Civil War.

Medieval Market & Fair.
A grant for a market was made to Arwarton in 1254. Sir Robert Bacon was later granted a market and fair in 1347, long discontinued.

Almshouses.
Sir Philip Parker founded almshouses in the village in 1740.

Historic Houses.
Erwarton Hall was anciently the seat and manor of the Daviller family. The present Hall was built by Sir Philip Parker after he purchased the manor from the Drurys c1577. An earlier owner was Sir Philip Calthorpe who married Anne Boleyn's aunt. It was said that Anne was a regular visiter to the hall and that after her execution her heart was taken from London and buried in a casket within the walls of the church here. The authenticity of this tradition was strengthened when workmen found a heart-shaped casket during restoration in 1837. The hall still retains a curious gatehouse with cylindrical turrets constructed for the earlier hall soon after Calthorpe's death in 1549. Faden's map does not show the hall but illustrates the 'Parsonage' as a large house on the site of Arwarton Hall Farm on the NE parish boundary. The Queens Head public house dates from the C16.

EUSTON *(4 miles SE of Thetford)*

Blackbourn Hundred. 'Farmstead of a man called Eof' (OE) *Euestuna* (DB). Now includes Little Fakenham. *Manors.* Euston Manor al Little Hall or Verleys (Late C11 Robert de Verley); Fakenham Parva Manor (1320 Comyn family. *Sub-Manors.* Cockfield Hall (?)

Tumuli.
There is a round barrow on Rushford Heath by the Roman Peddars Way in the NE corner of the parish. A ring of chalky soil about 2' wide around an area raised 1½' high revealed by ploughing in 1939 S of Rushford Road, is a probable round barrow with, NE of this, another barrow. On the other side of the road in Great Furze Plantation, two ill-defined mounds, one 66' in diameter and 3' high, and the other 197' x 126'. NW of Park Farm in the S of the parish is a partly ditched bell-barrow 143' in diameter and 9' high. It comes within the area of the deserted village of Little Fakenham and may well have been later used for a mill mound.

Roman Road & Ancient Ford.
Euston incorporates that part of the parish of Rushford S of the Little Ouse river which includes the Hall. The course of the Roman Peddars Way, which is diverted to form the eastern parish boundary, returns to its original course by making a sharp re-alignment again at the northern county boundary with Norfolk to cross the Little Ouse by a ford - hence the place-name Rush-ford, 'ford where rushes grow'. This shows that the ford probably pre-date the Romans and is of prehistoric origin.

Deserted Village.
The Medieval village of Little Fakenham formerly lay on the N bank of the river Blackbourn in Euston parish. A park was created and landscaped for Euston Hall in 1671 (*see below*) which resulted in the village - in all probability already in decline - being deserted and gradually resettled S of the river by the Saxon church of St Peter. This was one of two churches listed in Fakenham at Domesday, and when the park was extended and modified in the C18, the old village with its now ruined church of St Andrew was totally obliterated - this second of the Domesday churches has now been revealed by cropmarks on the eastern bank of the Blackbourne S of Park

EUSTON *(continued)*

Farm. Other earthworks of the former village show irregular house 'platforms' with parallel banks to the NE forming a wide 'hollow way'. To the SE can be seen a sunken track running from N of the Blackbourn to S of The Racing Stables with either side of this an area of terracing up the hillside with six or seven platform areas.

Old Coach Way.
Duke's Ride, an old coachway which ran W from Euston Hall, seat of the Duke of Grafton, to join the Icknield Way to London, and E to connect with the Icknield Way Path NW of Coney Weston, remains in the form of a long track. Faden names a part of it 'Coach Way' on his map of 1783.

Former Deer Park.
The park associated with Euston Hall was initially landscaped in 1671 to form a deer park which in 1677 was encompassed by a pale fence nine miles in length. The park was extended and re-designed between 1730-1748, and modified by Capability Brown 1767-1783. Although it was described as richly wooded and stocked with 700 head of deer in 1844, it was disparked before 1867.

Historic House.
Euston Hall, in a great park of c1400 acres, is the seat of the Dukes of Grafton. The present hall, built by Lord Arlington c1666-70 and radically rebuilt 1750-6, was badly damaged by a fire in 1902. It stood on the site of an earlier hall where Elizabeth I lodged in 1578 just prior to her host, a Mr. Rokewood, being committed to prison.

EXNING *(2 miles NW of Newmarket)*

Lackford Hundred. 'Settlement of Gixa's family or followers' (OE) *Essellinge* (DB) *Exningis* (1158)
Manors. Exning Manor (C12 Matthew, Count of Boulogne). *Sub-Manors.* Well Hall al Coggeshalls; Jardens al Gardeners al Jardins.
Exning was a town when Newmarket was only a hamlet. The later growth of Newmarket through royal patronage and strategic siting beside the main road led to Exning's demotion and the loss of its market to its neighbour - hence (New)market. In minor county boundary changes in 1994, the small hamlet of Landwade, formerly in Fordham, Cambridgeshire, was taken into Suffolk, with the sole excuse of 'tidying up' the NE Exning parish boundary.

Bronze-Age Burials.
The multiple burial of a Bronze-Age family of eight people unearthed in 1979 in a heavily built-up area of the village suggests they were originally covered by a barrow destroyed during this urban development.

Ancient Well.
St Wendred's Well, whose waters are said to be good for ailments of the eyes, is situated in a small wood called the Seven Springs, ¾ mile S of the village (and unfortunately just E of the busy A14 Newmarket bypass).

Roman Wells.
A group of natural springs N of St Wendred's Well are supposed to have been used as baths by the Romans and were indeed marked 'Roman Baths' on the 1927 OS map (and as 'Roman Remains' on that of 1959). No building material has been found in the vicinity.

Roman Villa & Settlement Site.
A Roman aisled hall discovered in the hamlet of Landwade, ¾ mile SW of Landwade Church and E of the disused railway, was excavated in 1904-6 and 1957-8. It had been 100' long and later rebuilt in flint and mortar on a timber frame. A small bathhouse had been added in the later C2, and a further hypocausted room added shortly before the building was destroyed by fire at about the beginning of the C4. Alongside was an earlier C1 ditch. A group of inhumations with associated pottery (findings from two wells) along with a tessellated pavement showed settlement in the area from C1-C4.

Ancient Fishing Industry.
Further evidence that the Old Fen Sea reached as far as Exning as recently as the C11 comes from the Domesday record of a fishery here producing 8,200 eels.

EXNING *(continued)*

Site of Birthplace of Saxon Queen of East Anglia.
The A14 Newmarket by-pass may have covered The Island, a moated earthworks site S of the church, which has been confidently suggested as the birthplace of St Etheldreda. To the N and untouched by the motorway are remains of an ancient dovecote and fish-ponds. The site was examined prior to the construction of the bypass. It consisted of a rectangular mound c89' N-S by 39' E-W surrounded by a moat. There was no trace of a building on the mound, but pottery found here was of C14 date whilst underneath the mound and outside the moat were traces of a Late Saxon settlement of about Conquest date. The fish-ponds, severely damaged by dredging by the owner in 1991, consisted of two linear ponds running NW-SE, linked by a short ditch. Their date is unknown but probably Medieval and although divided by a stream, connected to the moat 230' E (The Island).

Site of Baptism of St Etheldreda.
St Wendred's Well (*see above*) marks the site where, supposedly, in 630 A.D., St Etheldreda, third daughter of Anna, King of the East Angles, was baptised by St Felix of Burgundy. Although she was canonised by the Pope as a virgin, according to Bede she had survived two husbands: Tonbert, Prince of East Anglia and Egfrid who became King of Northumbria c670. Later she took the veil at Coldingham Monastery in Scotland. In 673 she founded the convent at Ely and in due course became its abbess. Here she died in 679. She is often called St Audrey, from which name the expression 'tawdry' is derived. It was originally used to describe the magnificence of her shrine at Ely but for some reason later became a term of derision.

Scene of Norman Conspiracy.
The manor was held by Ralph de Guader on whom the Conqueror conferred the title Earl of East Anglia. However, after an abortive conspiracy against William in 1075 with others including the Earls of Hereford and Northumberland, he was forced to flee, first to France, then to Denmark, leaving behind his possessions. Perhaps his residence in Exning once occupied the moated earthworks site known as 'The Island'? (*see above*).

Medieval Commons.
Exning Common is shown and named on Faden's map of 1783 occupying all the area W of the termination of Landwade Road to the parish boundary which also determines its northern and southern limits. The map also shows another extensive, but unnamed common running along the E side of the present Fordham Road, N into Snailwell parish in Cambridgeshire. Today the area is part of Plantation Stud.

Site of Mills.
A water course remains from an old watermill mentioned in a deed of 1600 which formerly stood by the Mill House, SE of Rose Hall. It was shown on Faden's map of 1783 which also shows a windmill beside Windmill Hall, NE of the village.

Medieval Market & Fair.
Exning apparently had a market as early as c1200, but it was William de Valence, Earl of Pembroke, who obtained the official privilege of holding a market and fair here in 1258. Tradition asserts that a medieval pestilence in Exning was responsible for its later removal to a site away from the village, although Newmarket's more strategic position beside the main thoroughfare seems a more likely reason.

Site of Deserted Village & Chapel.
Traces of a deserted medieval village can be seen in earthworks N and W of Landwade Church. The remains are visible as hollow ways running from the moat of the old hall, and in house platforms and the faint remains of another moat or possible fish-ponds. Although not recorded in Domesday, Landwade was first mentioned in 1060 when it was known as *Landuuade*, an OE word probably meaning 'estate or district ford'. There were 15 households at its height in 1327, but these had dwindled to 4 by 1674. A chapel also existed here.

Guildhall (?)
There was possibly a guildhall in Exning as the parish had four guilds: Holy Trinity (1452), The Blessed Mary and St. Christopher (1456) , and St. Mildred (1524).

EXNING *(continued)*

Historic House & Ancient Moated Site.

E of Landwade Church a square moat enclosing a large area with an entrance on the W is the site of the former Landwade Hall. It was described thus: 'The remains of the old mansion which are within a moated site, in a retired spot surrounded with woods, exhibit the architecture of the early part of the C16 and C17. The original entrance appears to have been a bridge crossing the middle of the S arm of the moat, but access is now given by a C17 brick bridge'. The last house on the site was pulled down 1850-60. There is a painting of the old hall in Anglesea Abbey.

EYE *(5 miles SSE of Diss)*

Hartismere Hundred. 'Dry ground (island) in the marsh' (OE) *Eia* (DB)

Manors. Eye/Eye Sodemere (C12 Stephen, Earl of Boulogne). *Sub-Manors.* Netherhall; Flemworth; Cranley/Cranley Hall; Eye Hall/Eye Priory Manor. As its name suggests, the town was once a virtual island, described in the latter part of the C10 by Abbo Floriacencis as situated in the midst of a marsh and navigable from the Waveney. This was confirmed by finds of boating artefacts in its southern marshes then covered by water from the Yaxley road to Eye Park. In virtually every respect the history of Eye follows much the same course as that of Clare. Eye was also an Honor (comprising some 220 estates) and a small borough at Domesday, and had its great castle and a priory. Both towns were in the hands of powerful lords, Richard FitzGilbert at Clare and William Malet here in Eye. It later received a charter confirming its borough status from King John and regularly sent two members to Parliament from 1570.

Ancient Linear (Boundary/Defensive?) Ditch.

Grimm's Ditch, referred to in field names and in a C13 charter relating to Thornham Parva, runs W-E through the village of Thornham Parva, crosses the A140 Roman road and enters Braisewaith, its course traced by the line of the B1117 as far as Ash House. The road bears left here and the line of the ditch is continued across the parish boundary into Eye by a firm track called Put Lane which can be followed straight to a country road, known in its northern unmade section as Rapsy Tapsy Lane (*see* Braiseworth).

Site of Roman Villa (?)

'The remains of the hypocaust of a possible villa' were claimed to have been discovered during 1857 in 'Camp Field' close to the Roman road from Colchester to Casiter St Edmund (the present A140). However, investigations by Basil Brown were not able to confirm the site as Roman.

Roman Hoard.

In 1781 a leaden box was found containing several hundred Roman gold coins dating to Arcadius and Honorius.

Roman Cemetery.

The finding of a Roman cemetery containing upwards of 150 cremation urns N of Abbey Farm was reported in 1818.

Anglo-Saxon Cemetery.

An Anglo-Saxon cemetery was discovered N of the town by the river Dove.

Norman Castle.

Eye castle, built by William Malet and completed by his son Robert, consists of a high mound, a bailey covering 2 acres to the SW, traces of ditches in Buckshorn Lane to the W and the remains of a flint wing wall ascending the motte on the N. The whole is enclosed by Church Street, Castle Street and the market place which together appear to form a larger outer bailey. After attaining the title of Great Chamberlain of England under Henry I, Robert lost all his possessions including the castle for plotting against the king and was banished, the fortress being taken into the hands of the Crown. Destroyed in 1655 (*see below*), the present ruin of a 'shell-keep' atop the motte is a mere C19 folly; it replaced a windmill which had stood there until after the Battle of Waterloo.

Priory.

The Priory (or Abbey Farm), E of the town, is the site of a Benedictine priory founded as a cell to the Abbey of

EYE *(continued)*

Bernay in Normandy by Robert Malet soon after the Conquest, and dedicated to St Peter. Malet's position ensured that the priory was always well endowed. Its possessions included the episcopal see at Dunwich, and when this was lost to the sea, St Felix's 'Book of Gospels' was brought here from the stricken city and, under the name of the 'Red Book of Eye', the common people were accustomed to swear. The priory was released from its dependence on Bernay by Richard II, and dissolved in 1536, at which time the book was supposedly removed to the Continent. All that remains above ground is part of the S transept, some masonry of the walls of the church in the W wall of the present C18 farmhouse, and a separate oblong building to the NW. Of brick and assigned to the early C16, excavations suggest this may have been a guest house. Extensive fish-ponds associated with the priory lie to the E.

Site of Lepers' Hospital.

The Lepers' Hospital, probably founded in the C12, was first mentioned in 1329 during the reign of Edward III when protection was granted 'to Adam Fraunceis, master, and the brethren of the leper hospital of St Mary Magdalen without the town of Eye for their messengers collecting alms about the realm, as they had nothing of their own whereon to live'. The hospital continued until the dissolution. Its exact site is unknown but like all lazer hospitals would have been situated away from the main centre of population. Two fields shown on the 1839 tithe (now part of a cemetery) are called Magdalen Field and their location would fit the 1329 description.

Ancient Deer Park.

Domesday speaks of a great deer park here, its site still identifiable in Park Lane and Park Farm S of the town.

Medieval Archery Practice.

A butt for archery practice was formerly sited just before Moorhall Causeway, at the southern end of Town Moor.

Civil War Skirmish.

In 1655 the Parliamentarians captured and demolished the castle which was being defended by Lord Cornwallis.

Medieval Greens.

Faden's 1783 map shows and names the triangular Langton Green running SE from Broome Common. The extensive Cranley Green, SE of Eye, is now traced by field boundaries, its southern side from S of Gate Farm to Kiln Farm; then N three fields, W one field and N to the footpath - this footpath follows the former northern boundary of the green W to just before Cranley Farm; then S to the Eye-Redlingfield road; then E along the road back to Gate Farm. Two fields immediately S of Cookley Barn trace the southern extent of the arrow-shaped Cookley Green, a road and footpath forming its eastern side and the parish boundary N to South Green Farm; the area is marked South Green on the present OS map. Town Moor, a willowy common SW of the town, is thought by Norman Scarfe to have been artificially created when thousands of tons of soil were removed to build the castle motte and at the same time produce a natural marshy defence against attack.

Site of old Windmills.

A post mill stood on the castle motte in 1783; it was dismantled in 1917 and moved to Cranley Green. Victoria Mill stood beside Castleton Way at the W end of the town in 1779; it collapsed in 1955.

Medieval Market & Fairs.

The town already had a market at Domesday and a fair in 1135. Two further fairs were granted but sited outside the borough, at Thrandeston and Finningham. In the C18 the Manor of Eye held a court of 'pie poudre' - a summary court formerly held at fairs and markets to administer justice among itinerant dealers, etc.

Recreation.

Annual horse race meetings formerly held in the hamlet of Cranley Green were revived in 1839 and held in Eye Park until 1855.

Historic Free School.

A Free Grammar School was established here before 1548 when Francis Kent left a house and 26 acres of land for the maintenance of an usher to teach writing and grammar to the children of Eye, Horham, Athelington and Bedfield. The school was later accommodated in the old Guildhall (*see below*).

EYE *(continued)*

Guildhall.

The Guildhall of St Mary, a fine timber-framed building delightfully situated beside the beautiful church, was founded in 1536. There were two guilds established in Eye: Our Lady and St. Peter (1524). From 1598 it was used to accommodate the Grammar School. Although much rebuilt and enlarged in the late C19, it retains much of its original C15 work.

Almshouses.

Nicholas Bedingfield erected the Bedingfield Almshouses in Lambseth Street for the free habitation of four poor widows or old maids of Eye. His will of 1636 endowed them with property in trust to provide 2s monthly, a new gown of grey cloth every two or three years, and a cart-load of firewood every year. The almshouses were rebuilt or repaired in 1780. The Town Houses formerly standing in Magdalen Street and given by Edward Golding in 1576 to be occupied by poor families rent-free, were pulled down in the C19.

Market Cross.

Eye Cross stood in 'The Shambles' on the square still called 'The Cross'. Hexagonal and built of studs, brick and tile, it was occupied every Saturday by two men 'who sold meat at all corners'. Close by were the town stocks.

Historic Houses & Ancient Moated Sites.

The C16 former White Lion Hotel in the centre of town was never a coaching inn as it lay off the main highway. The Queens Head public house dates from the C16. Cookley Farm, E of the town, is a C15 hall-house. In the hamlet of Cranley, SE of the town, the ancient timber-framed manor house of Cranley Hall has ponds which may be remnants of its former moat; another small rectangular moat can be identified on a map of 1626 (and on an estate map of 1726) just SE of the hall. No buildings are shown on the moat but a bridge crosses it on the N. The hall was sold by Henry Grey to Myles Edgar shortly before 1626 and remained in this family until 1705. In the same area, timber-framed Flimworth Hall has an irregular oblong moat with a general width of 22', but the northern side widens to 75'. This is the site of Flemworth Hall Manor recorded from the C15. A survey of 1651 states that the house had been built 'not long since' by Thomas Lucas 1584-1664. At Gate Farm (formerly Kiln Farm) is another oblong moat mutilated at the NE, and there are three sides of a moat at King's Farm further S. About ½ mile SW of the town, Rook Hall has the remains of an open timber roof of C15-C16, and an ancient barn.

EYKE *(3½ miles NE of Woodbridge)*

Loes Hundred. 'Place at the oak-tree' (OScand) *Eik* (1185). Includes the Domesday vill of Staverton. A Norman church was built c1150 in Eyke, 'which had only just come into existence''. It may however have been earlier represented by Staverton, now merely a Butley hamlet.

Manors. Eyke Manor (1286 William de Montcaniso). *Sub-Manors.* Staverton; Rectory Manor.

Ancient Woodland & Deer Park.

Staverton Park is situated here and in the adjoining parish of Wantisden. It was from this ancient woodland, once much more extensive, that Eyke attained its Scandinavian place-name. It was probably created as a deer park C11-C13 - the earliest reference being in 1178 - and was said to be marked by a medieval boundary bank. C13 records of the park show that bark was stripped from the felled trees and sold for tanning leather, acorns sold for fattening pigs, wood for timber and fuel, and also grazing rights let for sheep and stock. In 1528 the monks of Butley Abbey took the Queen of France (Henry VIII's sister Mary Tudor) and her husband Charles Brandon, Duke of Suffolk, for 'a picnic under the oaks with fun and games'.

Site of Ancient Chantry.

Bennet's Chantry was dedicated to St Mary. Lands it owned in Eyke and Rendlesham were granted to Sir Michael Stanhope and John Delle in 1275. Its site is unknown.

Site of Mills.

A watermill existed on the bank of the river Deben between 1601 and c1747. A post mill stood on the W side of The Street at the N end of the village in 1783. It was dismantled in 1910.

EYKE *(continued)*

Recreation.

An accusation was made against the parish priest in 1644 that he had been present at Camping (playing a kind of football) on the Lord's Day. The site of the Camping field is not known.

Site of Historic House.

Staverton Hall, home of John Staverton and shown on Norden's 1601 map, was arable land by 1845 and now part of Rendlesham Forest. The house was attacked and ransacked during the Peasants' Revolt of 1381. The Elephant and Castle public house in Eyke Street dates from 1627.

FAKENHAM MAGNA *(5½ miles SE of Thetford)*

Blackbourn Hundred. 'Facca's enclosure' (OE) *Fachenham* (DB). Fakenham Magna (1283)

Manors. Fakenham Magna (1243 Beatrice, Countess of Provence). *Sub-Manors.* Ringsmere Grange or Manor.

Tumuli.

On the southern end of Larkhall Heath, SW of the village, were two round barrows now covered by Honington airbase. One was a bowl barrow 120' in diameter and 6½' high before levelling. Another barrow is described in a letter from Rainbird Clark to W F Grimes in the 1950s as being between Honington village and the W bank of a brook which flows towards Euston (doubtless the Blackbourne), and c50yds from the water on low ground.

Multi-period Settlement Site.

A settlement was discovered N of the bridge in 1946 in a field known as Hercules Went. It comprised c200 mainly circular huts many with hearths or fire holes, covering an occupation period from Palaeolithic to Anglo-Saxon. The site extends along a gravel terrace overlooking a length of the river Blackbourne called Broad Water. Later excavations revealed a 'wharf'.

Site of Ancient Battle (?)

A large Viking force under Thurkill the Tall landed at Ipswich in 1010 and, according to the *Saxon Chronicle*, went "straight to where they heard that the Saxon Ulfcytel was with his levies", near Thetford. Following a bloody battle in which Ulfcytel, Earl of the East Angles, was defeated ,"Hringmara (Ringmere) Heath was a bed of death".

> "Thought me, when I spied them, Thorkel's folk were fain,
> (The song of the sword they never shirk) to tread the battle-plain;
> And awhile ago at Ringmere Heath we passed into the fray;
> We stood the storm of iron, with our hosts in war-array . . ."

Rymer, 4 miles S of Thetford and one of the most isolated spots in Suffolk, is thought to have been the site so described. It was extraparochial until 17 December 1881 when it was annexed to Fakenham. Its correct name is Ringmere ('Ryngemere Graunge', 1320), and remains as Rymer Point *(see below)*.

Ancient Ringworks & Site of former Earthworks.

An earthworks known as Burnt Hall Plantation lies in a meadow on the N bank of the river Blackbourne ¼ mile S of the church. A near-dry outer ditch or moat encircles an enclosure with banks up to 8' high. The rampart broadens on the northern side apparently for purposes of defence and there is an original entrance on the NW. The circumference around the top of the bank is 257 yds and the diameter c88 yds (although the enclosure is not a true circle). The interior is low lying and saucer-shaped. There are traces of an outer bank under grass in the surrounding meadow especially towards the river. Although the site is light sandy soil, no finds have been made here. The Saxon Manor of Fakenham was held by Alestan and given by William I to his nephew Peter de Valoines after the Conquest. The field names and Saxon place-name are suggestive of Facca's pre-Conquest defensive 'enclosure' (*see place-name*), and/or a later Norman ring-works (a form of early castle) perhaps occupied by the Valoines' who held the manor for some time. The poet Robert Bloomfield, who was born in the village, wrote a poem called 'Broken Crutch' in which he described a hall destroyed by fire which once stood within the earthworks encircled with elms - hence the name Burnt Hall Plantation. Basil Brown has identified the course of an ancient road which is seen now as field boundaries and a footpath running from Bardwell Road SE past

FAKENHAM MAGNA *(continued)*

the earthworks to the Sapiston road by George Cottage. 600yds N of Burnthall Plantation, cropmarks show a roughly circular enclosure with an entrance to the NE, with which it may in some way be connected. 165' in diameter, it is unbanked but has a shallow ditch and causeway to the N and a possible second to the SW. The site is low lying in pasture 110yds E of the river and no internal features or artefacts have been found. Neither the 1767 or 1839 tithe maps show the earthwork although both name the pasture 'Castle Fen', and an area of woodland c550yds to the NNE, 'Castle Oaks'. The sites may be connected with the Battle of Ringmere in 1010.

Ancient Mere & Grange.

Uniquely, nine parishes meet at Rymer Point like the spokes of a wheel. Here was once a great mere in an area of light, dry, waterless land to where the local inhabitants formerly had a shared right of way. Rymer Farm, situated in the extreme W of the parish by what remains of the mere, probably stands on the site of the ancient Rymer Grange. Documents relating to the land of Edmund Comyn (1320) describe a tenant, the Abbot of Tilley, as holding the tenement called 'Ryngem Graunge', and a Crown grant to Charles, Duke of Suffolk, in 1539 records 'the farm called Ryngemere Graunge, Suffolk belonging to the suppressed priory of Tylley, Essex.' It is not known if any fragments of the old grange are incorporated in the present farmhouse. Rymer was a separate extra-parochial parish, abolished in 1885, and consolidated with Fakenham Magna in 1931.

FALKENHAM *(9 miles SE of Ipswich)*

Colneis Hundred. 'Falta's enclosure' or 'Falcon's enclosure' (OE) *Faltenham* (DB)
Manors. Falkenham/Falkenham Dodnash (-1525 vested in Dodnash Priory; 1525 Cardinal Wolsey). *Sub-Manors.* Russell's.

Ancient Port.

An important district in 1086, with a church dedicated to St. Aethelbeorht (perhaps dating it to c793). Before the reclamation of the marshes the river Deben presented a very different picture from today. When under flood the river was often four times wider than now and the higher gravel lands stood out as numerous creeks and havens. The long lost port of Goseford (or Gosford), already long established when the Normans came, was once the most important in Suffolk and became a focal point for the old Hundred of Colneis. It was not a single place but a district covering the Deben from its estuary through Falkenham to just short of Kirton Creek and comprised several small creeks and landing places along the banks of the 'Fleet' called Holgate, Mergate, Micklegate, Wangate and Northgate. The Kingsfleet was a drainage system which provided sheltered water along the river and can still be seen today, though now much narrower. The port reached the zenith of its importance after the Bigods became lords of Walton, and when taken into royal hands during the wars of Edward III in 1338, it became an assembly point for the royal fleet towards which it contributed 15 ships compared with Ipswich's 10 and Orford's 5. Gosford's demise came in the C15, with the rise of Woodbridge, and later Harwich and Ipswich with their deep water facilities catering for the ever-increasing size of vessel.

Site of Historic House.

Russell's Farm in Lower Falkenham is the probable site of the former manor house of Russells, a Falkenham Manor held in the C16 by the Waller family.

FARNHAM *(3 miles SW of Saxmundham)*

Plomesgate Hundred. 'Homestead or enclosure where ferns grow' (OE) *Ferneham* (DB)
Manors. Farnham (C12 Sir Robert de Sackville). *Sub-Manors.* Claydon.

Site of Roman Villa & Industrial Site.

A Late Roman villa was discovered near Burnt House Farm, N of Langham Bridge, and excavated in 1971. It was a small structure, roughly cruciform, and interpreted as a bath house 15' x 9' with projecting bays to E and W and walls made originally of coralline crag. There was evidence of extensive robbing in medieval times, but coins dated the occupation from the C3-C4. Adjoining the villa was an iron-working site.

FARNHAM *(continued)*

Deserted Medieval Village (?)

Whilst the parish now comprises little more than the church, hall, rectory and a cluster of properties on the northern boundary, the original settlement may well have centred around the river Alde crossing at Langham Bridge (*see also above*). Here an ancient island site known as Farnham Bottley may have housed the first 'enclosure', whilst a C13-C15 pottery scatter point to continued medieval settlement in this area.

Workhouse.

A workhouse was recorded here with six inmates in 1776.

FELIXSTOWE

'Colneis Hundred. 'A place of felled tress or a clearing' (OE) *Filchestou* (1254)

Manors. Felixstowe/Walton St. Felix (c1105 Priory cell dependent on Monastery of St. Andrews at Rochester and founded by Roger Bigot). *Sub-Manors.* Felixstowe Priory (Roger Bigot).

The Manor of Walton, held by Roger Bigod, once extended over the greater part of the present Felixstowe parish forming the main peninsular limb of the important port of Goseford. *For this reason all the major historical sites now within Felixstowe parish are listed under Walton.* The earliest settlement was in the area now known as 'Old Felixstowe' called simply *Burch* at Domesday. Part was known as Fylthestowe in the C14 and not unnaturally this was later adapted to Felixstowe through Walton's associations with St. Felix, the first Bishop of East Anglia. In a total role reversal, Felixstowe, a C19 village is now a major international port whilst Walton has been reduced to little more than a suburb of the former.

Site of old Windmill.

A windmill which stood on Ferry Road had gone by 1740.

Historic Fortfications.

Eight Martello Towers were built along the coast between Walton Ferry and Felixstowe Ferry in 1806. Three remain complete: at the W end of the seafront near the docks; at the S end of the golf course, and at Felixstowe Ferry (derelict by 1981). Of the remainder: one at TM2992 3426 appears to have survived as part of a larger building; another at Walton Ferry port TM2765 3404 was still standing as a prominent mound in 1972; one at TM2870 3194 has eroded into the sea; one at TM371 350 was abandoned as unsafe in 1835 (and presumably met the same fate), and one described as being on the crest of the cliff with a moat was demolished in the early 1900s.

FELSHAM *(8 miles SE of Bury St Edmunds)*

Thedwestry Hundred. 'Faele's homestead or village' *Faele* means 'pleasant' (OE) *Fealsham* (DB)

Manors. Felsham Hall/Capels (1268 William Peche). *Sub-Manors.* Brookhall al Lovaynes; Maiden Hall.

Medieval Green.

Faden's 1783 map shows the tiny triangular Oxes Green, just S of Castle Farm, situated at the point where the country road was originally met by another (now lost during the construction of a World War II airfield) heading SSW from a sharp bend in the lane SW of Maltings Farm in Rattlesden. The road junctions immediately NW and NE of the church still retain tiny triangular areas, shown in 1783 as larger unnamed areas.

Medieval Market & Fairs.

William Peche had the grant for a market in 1268, and a fair for livestock. This market appears to have failed, for in 1608 another licence was granted to William Risby to keep a market and two yearly fairs at Maydenhall in Felsham. The last fair was abolished in 1871 because it was said to be 'the cause of great immorality'.

Historic Houses & Ancient Moated Sites.

The *Victoria County History* describes Castle Farm W of Hightown Green, which is partly surrounded by a moat, as 'built on the remains of the old castle'. The previous mansion, seat of the Reynolds family, was indeed called The Castle, but this name derived more from its decorative castellations than from any ancient associations.

FELSHAM *(continued)*

John Wesley on a visit in 1771 described it as 'the best contrived and most beautiful I ever saw'. Shortly afterwards it was demolished. Felsham Hall stands within the ancient quadrangular moat of the old hall, its great wood situated entirely in the neighbouring parish of Bradfield St George. Just S of the hall, at Maiden Hall, cropmarks have identified a square moat and an outer enclosure with various external subdivisions of the former manor house, a sub-manor of Felsham owned by Hugh de Morieux in 1234. It is shown as a very large mansion on Faden's map of 1783. Some time later it was absorbed into the main manor. Capel Farm, 1¼ miles SW on the parish boundary, has a good double rectangular moat with a possible fish-pond. The house is probably C17 but is built on the site of an earlier C13 structure formerly known as Felsham Hall. In 1469 Baldewin Coksedge, in one of the earliest Wills written in English, mentions 'fysshynge in the moote'. Other moated sites are at Moat Farm, SW of the village - perfect; Valley Farm - two pieces of an undefined moat; the western side of a moat at Brook Hall with an extension to the E, with a perfect oblong moat, in good condition, to the NE of this, and three sides of an isolated moat to the S; and at Moore's Farm, the W side and the NW angle remain. Hill Farm, on the NE parish boundary, is a notable half-timbered building.

FINNINGHAM *(7½ miles N of Stowmarket)*

Hartismere Hundred. 'The homestead belonging to Fina's people' or 'Fenmen's home' (OE) *Finingaham* (DB) It has also been suggested that it means 'belonging to the Finborough people' in other words 'the ham of the Finborough people' a group who detatched themselves from the main nucleus at Finborough and moved north to form a new settlement at Finningham.

Manors. Finningham Hall/Coniers (1239 Conyers family). *Sub-Manors.* Necton Hall/Norton Hall.

Ancient Saxon Cemetery.

While digging a cutting near the station for the railway in 1848-9, a number of cremation urns were discovered along with 'various ornaments of brass and the heads of spears'.

Ancient Earthworks.

In the N of the parish, on the boundary of Finningham, Gislingham and Walsham-le-Willows (the former two bisecting the site), Cromwell's Plantation hides an earthworks once locally known as Fapes Hill (a local dialect word for gooseberry/ies). It comprises an enclosure encircled by strong ramparts and surrounded by a water-filled outer moat. Oval, with a broad entrance exactly to the NW, the centre is 111' E-W by 84' N-S with an enclosing bank 10' high and 51' broad at the base and 12' at the top. This in turn is surrounded by a moat 12' broad. Basil Brown visited the site in 1961 when it was being drained and revealed a hearth with sandy pottery later identified as C10-C12. The earthworks is similar in size and plan to those at Burgate, Fakenham Magna and Creeting St Peter, and is likely to be a simple early Norman castle - known as a ring-works. The *Victoria County History* named it Sto(ke)land or Sto(ne)land Abbey, a name they probably applied to a building which stood W of the earthworks and marked 'cottage' on an enclosure map of 1819. It appeared again on a map of 1886 but was gone by 1904. This building may have been a shooting-box or lodge built by lord of the manor, John Hookham Frere (1769-1846), for his own use. Morley considers 'Abbey' should read 'Abbot(of Bury)'s'. Before enclosure, the earthworks stood on the extensive Allwood Green. Perhaps it was also used by the Knights Templars who set up in Gislingham in the C12. (*see* Gislingham).

Medieval Green.

Church Green, which forms a delightful setting for the church and several old properties, is not shown or named on Faden's 1783 map. The great Allwood Green covering parts of 5 parishes, extended S into Finningham from the Cromwell's Plantation earthworks to the Walsham road and E to just beyond the B1113 at Rob Hall.

Medieval Fair.

An important pedlary fair was formerly held annually on Church Green under the auspices of Eye. The fair was obsolite by 1891.

Site of old Windmill.

A post mill stood between Mill Farm and Mill Cottage in 1783; it was pulled down in 1877.

FINNINGHAM *(continued)*

Guildhall.
The Old Guildhall still existed in Mill Street in the C20.

Historic Houses & Ancient Moated Sites.
Finningham Hall, ½ mile NW of the church, was the seat of the knightly family of Frere who lived in Suffolk from at least the C13; John Frere is known to have settled in Finningham in1598. It still retains part of the ancient moat of the former Hall of Robert Conyers who held the manor in 1239 and in whose family it remained for some time. Green Farm beside Church Green also has associations with the Frere family. Yew Tree House, N of the church, is decorated with some of the most handsome late C17 pargetting in Suffolk. The White Horse public house has C16/C17 origins.

FLEMPTON *(5 miles NW of Bury St Edmunds)*

Thingoe Hundred. 'Farmstead belonging to the fugitives'? (OE) *Flemingtuna* (DB)
Manors. Flempton/Geodings (C13 Sir Benedict de Blakenham).

Ancient Woodland.
Brick Kiln Plantation, Brakey Pin and Old Broom are parts of ancient woodland.

Tumuli.
Remains of four ancient barrows lie on Risby Poor's Heath, on the western parish boundary.

Site of Ancient Mill.
A water mill once stood by the river Lark in the NE corner of the parish. The site dates back to the C13 when land was purchased from Richard de Ickworth by Sir Benedict de Blakenham (who died in 1282) consisting of "a messuage, a mill, one carucate of land (approx. 120 acres), and ten acres of meadow" for one hundred silver marks.

Medieval Green.
Flempton Green bordered by a number of old houses is not shown on Faden's map of 1783.

FLIXTON *(2½ miles SW of Bungay)*

Wangford Hundred. 'Farmstead or village of a man called Flik' (OScand) *Flixtuna* (DB). Norman Scarfe believes it possible that the place-name may refer to Saint Felix rather than a man named Flik from the way in which Felixstowe is often pronounced 'Flickstoo' in East Anglian dialect.
Manors. Flixton Manor (C13 Bartholomew de Creke; 1252 Flixton Nunnery). *Sub-Manors.* Boyse's.

Ancient Woodland.
Abbey Wood, Long Plantation, Buck Plantation, Oak Grove, Coombe's Wood, Heavyland Wood, and Packway Wood are all sections of ancicnt woodland.

Ancient Track.
The Packway runs as a public track ENE from Grange Road along the southern edge of Packway Wood, past Sternacre Farm to the eastern parish boundary. It may be a part of Earl Bigod's route connecting his strongholds of Walton, Framlingham and Bungay, sections of which still appear in several parishes.

Romano-British Site.
Excavations in Flixton Park on the site of a ring ditch identified by aerial photos revealed C1 Late Iron Age/ Roman pits, trough-like features, and a perfect circle of closely-spaced post-holes c80' in diameter.

Saxon Cemetery.
Excavations in Flixton Park also revealed 43 inhumation burials including grave goods, dating from the C6.

Site of Moated Nunnery.
An Augustinian Nunnery of Our Lady and St Catherine was founded in 1258 by Margery, the daughter of Geoffrey de Hanes and widow of Bartholomew de Creke, for a prioress and six or seven nuns. Evidence suggests it was

FLIXTON nr. Bungay *(continued)*

begun as a Benedictine nunnery and later became Augustinian. It also appears to have had its problems. In 1349 the effects of the Black Death reduced the nuns to a state of poverty causing the church to fall into disrepair, and there were 'bad reports' on several of the nuns in 1478. In 1528 it was offered to Cardinal Wolsey towards the endowment of his College at Ipswich but, following his fall from grace and the subsequent abandonment of his 'grand scheme', it was granted to John Tasburgh in 1532. Part of one wall survives SE of the church with an arch incorporated into Abbey Farm, along with the greater part of its ancient moat 16-22' broad with banks rising c4'6" above the water. There is a fish-pond within the enclosure.

Deer Park.

Before building Flixton Hall, Sir John Tasburgh would appear to have created a deer park, for there is reference to a 'newe parke' in 1611. In 1892 this park comprised nearly 600 acres.

Site of Watermill & Ancient Road.

A watermill was situated near a ford over the river Waveney in 1264. The remains of an ancient road to South Elmham was also detected at this spot in the C20.

Site of Former Gallows (?)

In this parish a George Carver suffered the death penalty in 1593 on Gallows Hill.

Deserted Medieval Settlement.

Five messuages, existing in 1607 and removed to make way for the new park, have been discovered from aerial photographs in the S of Flixton Park, N of Park Road. These include two ditched house platforms each with about ¼ acre and almost certainly farmstead sites. Later fieldwork revealed C13-C15 pottery. The lack of any finds of a later date may suggest these homes were already deserted or in decay when the park was created.

Historic Houses & Ancient Moated Sites.

S of the church and E of Flixton Hall park, the moated site of Boys Hall with its strange triangular plan of a straight S side 50' wide with ends converging to meet at the N in a rounded angle, and a curved cross-channel dividing the enclosure into two unequal parts, may well have preceeded that of Flixton Hall which stood close by. Flixton Hall, long the seat of the Tasburgh family, was the last magnificent house built in Elizabethan style by Sir Nicholas Tasburgh c1615. It may have been a rebuild of the existing Bateman House as he appears to have created his new park prior to building the hall. On December 13th 1846 the mansion, which was formerly surrounded by a moat crossed by an ancient drawbridge, was gutted in a fire which entirely destroyed the interior leaving only the bare walls remaining. Despite being sympathetically rebuilt its days were numbered, for in 1950 one of the finest houses in Suffolk was finally and scandalously demolished. There are portions of another moat at Starknaked Farm 1 mile SE.

FLIXTON *(3 miles NW of Lowestoft)*

Mutford & Lothingland Hundred. 'Flik's farmstead'* (OScand) *Flixtuna* (DB) * Note the comment on Flixton, Bungay.

Manors. Flixton Manor (1240 Bartholomew de Creke; 1316 Edmund Bacun). *Sub-Manors.* Lawneys.

Medieval Industry.

As with the Norfolk & Suffolk Broads, Flixton Decoy was created through 'turbary' - the extraction of peat. According to the Account-Rolls this medieval industry accounted for thirty-one per cent of the manorial income for Flixton in 1355-7.

Medieval Common.

Flixton Common, named and shown on Faden's map of 1783, lay SE of the ruined St Andrew's Church and immediately S of Oulton Hospital, the former workhouse. It was roughly rectangular with an extension W from Laurel Farm to Wood Lane either side of the road to Blundeston. It has now been largely enclosed.

Deserted Medieval Village.

Flixton once included Oulton in its parish, but fortunes have changed and whilst Oulton, due in no small

FLIXTON nr. Lowestoft *(continued)*

measure to the Norfolk & Suffolk Broads, has grown and thrived becoming an independent parish and an important part of Lowestoft, Flixton has shrunken in size and status. Its church stands, now a ruin, on the ridge of a field beside the old hall. It is also likely, as Norman Scarfe suggests, that St Michael's Church, now the parish church of Oulton, was once the mother church of Flixton and the ruined St Andrew's merely of chapelry status. Berisford lists Flixton in his *Lost Villages of England,* and whilst it certainly meets the criteria - only two inhabitants, a farmer and a shepherd, recorded here in 1602 - little is known of its earlier population.

Medieval Market.
The de Creke family obtained the grant for a market here in 1253.

Historic House.
Morley suggests Old Hall, the former manor house situated by the ruined church, stands on a Danish site.

FLOWTON *(6 miles NW of Ipswich)*

Bosmere & Claydon Hundred. 'Floki's farmstead' (OScand+OE) *Flochetuna* (DB)
Manors. Flowton (1428 William de Clopton). *Sub-Manors.* Archers.

Ancient Woodland.
Flowtonhall Grove, S of the hall, is a part of ancient woodland.

FORNHAM ALL SAINTS *(2½ miles NW of Bury St Edmunds)*

Thingoe Hundred. 'Forna's home' or 'Enclosure by trout stream' (OE) plus church dedication *Fornham* (DB)
Manors. Fornham All Saints (-1536 Abbot of St. Edmunds, Bury; c1539 Sir Thomas Kytson). *Sub-Manors.* Aldreds.

Ancient Cursus (?)
Aerial photographs have revealed what appears to be a cursus - a 'Ceremonial Way' - running parallel to the river Lark, just above the flood plain on its left (W) bank, E of the A1101 road. It crosses SE-NW through the parish whose church may have been sited 'with reference to some remote memory or tradition of it'. It stops short of a field in Hengrave which aerial photos show to be full of the marks of (presumably) pre-historic occupation - ring ditches and more complex furrows. The whole site may date back to 3,000 BC and may have been used for ritual functions in much the same way as Stonehenge. Cropmarks indicate where timbers or palisades might have stood, while the four ring-ditches lie at the end of a mile-long double-ditched enclosure up to 130' wide and known as a cursus. Unfortunately, no excavations have as yet been carried out on the site but some believe the monument which runs under the church may continue for at least a mile further towards Bury St Edmunds.

Site of Tumulus (?)
Named in 1926 as 'tumulus' and shown as an oval mound c60' x 30' at the end of (and directly on the alignment of) a post-medieval tree-lined avenue, the earthwork was destroyed during the creation of a golf course - the remains forming a bunker on the 7th green. However, it may have been a landscape feature or the remains from a collapsed building feature (of the former lodge?).

Roman Settlement (?)
Excavations have revealed a possible Roman settlement site in the parish.

Roman Road (?)
It is suggested that the A14 road approaching Bury St Edmunds from Newmarket and forming the southern parish boundary to the Westley roundabout is a former Roman road, and that its line is traced from here by the straight hedgeline to the SE parish boundary. David Dymond has noticed that in early manuscript maps of Fordham and Barton it is marked as 'Peddars Way' and, as the authority on Roman roads, Margary considers this may well be a road linking the Icknield Way to the main Roman Peddars Way.

Tumulus, Court of Judication & Gallows.
On Shire Hall Heath, a burial mound called 'Henhoe' became the Hill of Judication for the town of Bury St.

FORNHAM ALL SAINTS *(continued)*

Edmunds when the local court was transferred from Catteshill, E of the town, in 1305. It would appear that it was later used for the town's gallows.

Site of Saxon Battle (?)

A battle is said to have been fought in this parish between King Alfred's son, Edward the Elder (who reigned from 899 to 924), and Ethelwald, his cousin, 'over whom he gained a complete victory'. Site and date are unknown.

Site of Friary.

A Franciscan house, founded by Gilbert de Clare, Earl of Gloucester, arrived in 1257 and established themselves at the N end of Bury St Edmunds. In 1262, aroused by such impudence, the Abbot at Bury Abbey ordered them to pull down the buildings they had erected. The friars appealed to Rome and as a result they were granted a new site at the W side of the town. Unimpressed, the Abbey again forced their removal. They then approached Henry III for assistance and as a result of his intervention they returned to the western side of the town and built a monastery. This time the Abbey appealed to Rome and Pope Urban IV reversed the decision and ordered the friars to pull it down and abandon the place. This the friars did and after a reconciliation with the monks in 1263 they were given a fresh site by the abbot beyond the north gate at a place called Babwell, where they remained until the Dissolution. It was here in 1289 that the Chief Justice of the Common Pleas, Sir Thomas Weyland, sought refuge after being convicted of felony. He was admitted as a novice but discovered and sent to the Tower. The popularity of the Babwell friars is evident from the bequests to them and the number of notables who chose to be buried in the friary church; these included Sir William de Clopton, Sir William Drury, Sir Walter Trumpington, and Robert, Bishop of Emly in Ireland. The friary was situated on the southern parish boundary, just outside Bury by the Tollgate crossroads at the southern end of the A1101 road from Mildenhall. Nothing of the friary stands above ground but some remains of the building have been incorporated in the house known as Babwell House which was built on the site (now the Priory Hotel), and much of the boundary wall also remains.

Medieval Green.

Faden's map shows the church standing on the widest part of a triangular green running S to the crossroads. It is not named, and although described in 1929, has now been enclosed and built over by residential housing.

Site of Watermill.

There was a water mill for grinding corn associated with Babwell Friary, N of Tollgate Bridge where Jocelin de Brakeland, commenting on Abbot Samson's faults, stated 'he has so raised the level of the fish pond at Babwell for the new mill that . . .' etc. The mill is shown on Bowen's map of 1755 but not Faden's of 1783.

Guildhall (?)

There were five Fornham guilds recorded: The Blessed Virgin Mary and St. Martin (1480), Holy Trinity (1481), St. Peter (1483) and St. Genevieve (1490). It is likely these were held in a guildhall in either All Saints or St. Martins, though it is not recorded.

Historic Houses & Ancient Moated Sites.

Aldridges, an important moated grange and manor house since converted into cottages, has an irregular oblong moat. It was the occasional retreat of Abbot Boon. There is a moat at Fornham Hall Farm on the NE parish boundary, site of the former manor house where manorial courts were held in 1539.

FORNHAM ST GENEVIEVE *(2½ miles NE of Bury St Edmunds)*

Thedwestry Hundred.

Manors. Fornham St. Genevieve (-1536 Abbot of St. Edmunds, Bury; 1539 Sir Thomas Kytson).

Site of C12 Battle.

In 1173 an army of Flemings under the command of Robert Beaumont, Earl of Leicester, landed at Walton and, after laying seige to Dunwich and resting up at Bigod's castle at Framlingham, over-ran the royal castle at Haughley. On proceeding towards Bury St Edmunds, Leicester received reports of a welcoming committee being formed there comprising a royal army under the command of Richard de Lucy, Chief Justicair of England, and

FORNHAM ST GENEVIEVE *(continued)*

his aid Humphrey de Bohun. Outnumbered and anxious to avoid confrontation, Leicester decided to skirt the town. Leaving the track from Haughley they passed through Great Barton and reached the river crossing SW of Fornham St Genevieve Church. It was October 17th when Leicester's troops, still under the euphoria of their success at Haughley, began crossing the Lark in great disorder (probably around the site of the present footbridge at Ducksluice Farm). Watching from the walls at Bury, de Lucy saw his chance and ordered de Bohun to launch a mounted attack. The rebels were taken by surprise and overwhelmed; the carnage was said to be terrible. Many died trampled under the hooves, others were drowned, and those who tried to escape across the marshes were either pursued and cut down or hacked to pieces with pitchforks and flails by the locals who had joined the battle intent on revenge for the rebels' riotous pillaging. The Countess was captured but the Earl escaped to St Genevieve Church with the remnants of his army where he made a final stand. Defeated, he accompanied his wife to Bury as prisoners before being handed over to Henry II. Doubtless following much hard bargaining, they later managed to negotiate their freedom. It is said that copper pennies of Henry II, rotted out of the pouches of slain soldiers, along with an antique ring (suggested by some to have been thrown away by the Countess in her flight), have been found in the river. A C12 sword, 3' 5" long inlaid with silver, was also discovered in mud at the bottom of a ditch here in 1933 and is now displayed in the Moyses Hall Museum in Bury.

Site of Abbot's Grange & Park.

The Abbot of Bury Abbey had an estate here known in medieval times as Abbot's Mill. Following the Dissolution, it was granted to Sir Thomas Kytson of Hengrave, and in 1789 purchased by B E Howard, the 12th Duke of Norfolk who died in 1842. He it was who completely rebuilt the abbot's grange which stood near the church and which itself has now been pulled down, leaving only the stables. The hall's removal is said to have been due to the creation of Fornham Park sometime between 1769 and 1788 (certainly before 1783). The park boundary bank known as 'Park Bank' is still seen as earthworks running SW-NE to the N of the site of the Hall.

Site of Mills.

The Abbot of Bury Abbey had a water mill for corn on his estate. One miller is recorded in the parish in 1550-99 and two between 1600-1649. One mill was shown as a 'Floer Mill' in 1769, but this would appear to have gone by 1783. Faden shows a windmill beside the road which crosses the River Lark NE of Mill Farm on the northern parish boundary in 1783.

Deserted Medieval Village.

Listed as one of his 'lost villages of England' by Berisford, only the ruined tower of St Genevieve's Church (destroyed by fire in 1775) still stands close by the site of the Hall, demolished in 1950 and itself on the site of the Abbot's grange. Park Farm remains as a monument to the cause of the demise of this tiny parish, namely the creation of Fornham Park.

Recreation (?)

A site known as Le Camping Close may refer to a field used for medieval ball games, or perhaps this time, in total contrast, to a site connected with the great battle fought here in 1173 (*see above*).

FORNHAM ST MARTIN *(N of Bury St Edmunds)*

Thedwestry Hundred.

Manors. Fornham St. Genevieve (-1536 Abbot of St. Edmunds, Bury; 1539 Sir Thomas Kytson).

Tumuli.

Seven Hills, locally known as 'John's Hill', SE of the river bridge in John's Hill Plantation in the extreme NW corner of the parish, are burial mounds believed by some to mark the graves of leaders killed in the Battle of Fornham St Genevieve in 1173. They could also be round barrows of Celtic origin, though they have been so mutilated by the transplanting of trees that their original form is lost and it is even impossible to discover their exact number. Excavations on one in 1826 appear to identify them with the battle as it was said to have revealed a circular mound containing no less than forty skeletons in a heap, piled in order tier above tier 'wonderfully complete, all radiating from a centre, faces upwards, feet inwards, with many heads cleft or

FORNHAM ST MARTIN *(continued)*

with arrow holes'. Unfortunately, nothing remains as proof of these 'finds'.

Roman Road (?)

It is suggested that a Roman road (traced by the A14 from Newmarket) passed through Bury St Edmunds and then Fornham St Martin and Great Barton parishes to connect with the Peddar's Way to Ixworth. It may also be traced by the road E from Tollgate Bridge (*see* Fornham All Saints).

Site of Mills.

There was a medieval watermill here. Abbot's Mill, Mill Lane, was situated near where the club house of the present golf course stands. A windmill stood on the southern parish boundary on the W side of Hollow Road near Hollow Road Farm in 1783.

Medieval Bridge.

Tollgate Bridge which carries the A134 over the river Lark and divides Fornham from Bury was rebuilt in 1890. The foundations of the original medieval bridge on the same site, belonging to the abbots of Bury Abbey, was discovered during pipe laying. The abbots maintained a lucrative trade levying tolls on travellers crossing here.

Historic Houses.

Faden's map of 1783 illustrates two large houses here. The one shown nearly opposite the church may be Fornham House, whilst the site of the other, N of the village on the W side of the present B1106 and N of the A134 junction, appears to now be occupied by three modern properties.

FOXHALL *(2 miles SE of Ipswich)*

Carlford Hundred. 'Foxes burrow' (OE) *Foxehola* (DB). The parish probably includes the former Domesday vills of Ingulveston, Darnford and Neckemara.

Manors. Foxhall al Caswell's (C13 William de Holbroke). *Sub-Manors.* Foxhall; Feltons.

Tumuli.

A round barrow, now under the plough, lies E of Dobb's Lane, near Foxhall Road. Another 'bowl' barrow lies at the W end of Pole Hill on the N side of Foxhall Road, whilst an oval 'mound' is sited NNE of Tyrrells Hall now known as Lodge Farm.

Ancient Enclosure & Settlement.

An Iron-Age enclosure with an adjacent Anglo-Saxon Settlement was discovered near Lodge Farm beside the Mill River which meanders through the tranquil valley from Kirton Creek.

Chapel (?)

It is thought that Foxhall once had a medieval wayside chapel.

Deserted Medieval Village (?)

Formerly a separate parish but now merely a hamlet of Brightwell, Foxhall was a Domesday vill but, being comprised mostly of sandy heathland, it may never have had a village or been a very populous parish despite the close proximity of Ipswich. It has long lost its church of All Saints (decayed by 1530 and unfit for services soon after), the living transferred to the adjoining parish of Brightwell. The small portion which still stands is attached to Hall Farm and used as an outhouse.

Medieval Heath.

The road from Woodbridge through Martlesham to Trimley and Felixstowe runs along the edge of Levington Heath and Foxhall Heath which together formed a band of heathland stretching all along the southern boundaries of Bucklesham and Foxhall parishes. Shown and named on Faden's map of 1783, the 760 acres were enclosed by a private Act of 1803 and turned into arable fields.

Historic House.

Lodge Farm stands on the site of Tyrrell's Hall, the Manor House of one of the Bucklesham manors. It belonged to the Prior of Ely in 1316.

The remains of the Roman Saxon-Shore fort of Walton Castle from a print of 1786.

The magnificent Roman Saxon-Shore fort at Burgh Castle has changed little since this old print.

(Above) Eastlow Hill Roman burial mound, Rougham.

(Below) The excavated hypocaust of the Roman Villa at Stanton Chare.

The Black Ditches cutting diagonally through Oak Plantation at Cavenham.

Erbury, the Romano-British Camp at Clare.

(Above) The Wuffingas Royal East Anglian burial site at Sutton Hoo with the river Deben beyond.

(Below) The isolated Old Minster at South Elmham St. Cross which possibly represents the first Bishopric of St. Felix built within a Roman moated camp.

An impression of Bury Abbey before the Reformation.

A photograph of the remains of the original Leiston Abbey taken before the second world war.

(Above) Remains of the Priory of Augustinian Nuns at Flixton Abbey founded in 1258.

(Below) The Tudor building on Chapel Hill, Little Whelnetham, containing fragments of the Priory of Crutched Friars founded in 1273.

St. Olaves Augustinian Priory, Herringfleet, founded in the early C13 by Roger FitzOsbert.

The C14 barn at Redlingfield Hall, probably the former guest house or infirmary of the small Benedictine nunnery founded in 1120.

(Above) This old barn at Priory Farm, Nacton was the former Chapel of Alnesbourne Augustinian Priory, founded c1200.

(Below) Remains of the Augustinian Priory's C13 cruciform church at Priory Farm, Kersey.

FRAMLINGHAM

Loes Hundred. 'Homestead of the family or followers of Fram' (OE) *Framelingaham* (DB)
Manors. Framlingham Manor (1101 Roger Bigot; 1312 Thomas de Brotherton). *Sub-Manors.* Clubald's al Clarvals al Clarvaald Le Clarbolds.
The town, at one time considered a borough, lies on either bank of the small river Ore which rises close by, and was said to have been anciently navigable for small crafts from Snape and the river Alde. An anchor and two elephant tusks have been discovered in the sand below the present river channel. The town has strong links with medieval England providing home to the powerful baronial family of Bigod who resided in the great castle and were continually in conflict with the Crown. 'Bloody' Mary was proclaimed Queen of England whilst staying here and the great church contains 'one of the best series of mid-C16 Early Renaissance monuments in England', mainly devoted to the Howards, Dukes of Norfolk. Another tomb contains the remains of Henry Fitzroy, Duke of Richmond and natural son of Henry VIII.

Iron-Age Site.
An Iron-Age site was discovered on top of a spur of land overlooking the river Ore.

Roman Road.
A part of the northern parish boundary, in the form of a road, follows the course of a Roman road SW-NE from Dennington Corner to Parkgate Farm from where it continues as a footpath. SW of Dennington Corner the course of the ancient road is across open fields and crossing the river Ore, but is now nowhere evident on the ground. However, Faden's map of 1783 shows a road, now lost, tracing the course of the Roman road from just above the fork in Peppers Wash Lane N of Oak Farm, SW over the parish boundary to the green at Saxtead.

Town Defences.
A track running WNW from the B1120, N of the castle, traces the line of the Town Ditch.

Saxon Stronghold & Cemetary (?)
Tradition would have us believe that the castle was built on an existing mound which had held a Saxon stronghold in the time of King Edmund; and that the king fled here in 870 A.D. and was besieged by the invading Danes before his eventual martyrdom at Hoxne(?) Whilst an attractive thought, there is no evidence for this and a cemetery discovered in the outer bailey in 1954 which was claimed to be Saxon, is more probably Medieval.

Norman Castle.
The first evidence we have of settlement here is a manor house (fortified, but no doubt built of wood) erected around 1100 on the site of the present castle, when the first of the great Bigod barons, Roger I, was given the manor of Framlingham by Henry I. His second son, Hugh, who succeeded him was created Earl of Norfolk c1152 by Stephen as a reward for his attesting that Henry I had, on his deathbed, declared Stephen his successor in preference to his daughter, Maude (or Matilda). Whether true or not - and the proceeding fortunes of this notorious family would leave some doubt - Hugh then erected the first stone castle. In 1173, true to their ongoing turbulant relationship with the crown, another Roger was caught supporting the rebel Earl of Leicester and lost his privileges and his fortress which was then dismantled. Roger Bigod III rebuilt the castle sometime between 1189 and 1213, and the existing curtain walls 48' high with its revolutionary thirteen towers we see today are from this period, along with pieces of what still remained from the previous C12 work. 'The Mere' was probably created deliberately to extract material for the castle earthworks and a fish-pond, and also for added security on the western side of the castle in the C12. 1215 saw the Bigods once again on the wrong side of the King who besieged and took the castle; but the pendalum was to swing again in 1246 when the same Roger was made Marshal of England. The ownership of the castle alternated between Crown and Lord over the centuries and in 1553 Henry VIII granted it to his daughter, Mary. It was while staying here that she was informed of the death of her brother, Edward VI, and Lady Jane Grey's claim to the throne. Quickly gathering an army comprising loyal local followers she marched from the castle to London. Once she became queen, her over-enthusiastic purge to restore the Catholic faith was to bring her the contemptuous title of 'Bloody Mary'. One of its last owners, Sir Robert Hitcham, is responsible for the absence of related buildings within the curtain walls, as he

FRAMLINGHAM *(continued)*

bequeathed the castle in his will to Pembroke Hall, Cambridge, with the condition that they dismantle all the buildings within and erect a poor-house. This request was carried out after his death and the subsequent poor-house, a single storey building of c1200 built on the site of the Great Hall, continued until 1837. Now under the protection of English Heritage, the castle site comprises three fortified enclosures of great strength; the central enclosure, which includes the castle, lies in the NW angle of a larger bailey and is surrounded by a massive ditch - the bailey is also moated. Attached to the castle, on its NW side, is a third enclosure called 'The Lower Court' which was protected by ramparts and the great mere - found to be a natural lake adapted and extended for the defence of the castle in the Middle Ages when soil was removed to construct much of the great motte and outworks.

Ancient Deer Park.

The Bigods had a great deer park here N of the castle. A survey of Edward VI in the C16 described it as containing 600 acres and being three miles in circumference. Evelyn says that Suffolk, in particularly Framlingham, was famous for producing the largest and tallest oaks - perhaps in the world, and Miller informs us that the oak which afforded the beams of the *Royal Sovereign* grew at Framlingham and was 4'9" in diameter and yielded 4 beams, each 44' long. The park has gone but there are reminders in fragments of woodland called Lodge Wood, Ash Grove, Oak Grove; and in Great Lodge Little Lodge, and Parkgate Farm on the Dennington boundary.

Site of Hermitage.

St Bennett's Hermitage was mentioned in 1385. It was situated on the W side of College Road where several human skeletons were unearthed while digging foundations at a house called The Hermitage in the C19. The Hermitage was still in existence in 1547 adjoining six acres of glebe land called Hermitage Close.

Site of Chapel (?)

At the end of Gipsey's Lane by Pepper's Wash where the River Ore flows under the road from Framlingham to Saxtead Bottom, is a site right by the river and beside the line of the Roman road (here not visible on the ground). Much building debris, C17 pottery and re-used C15 masonry including a tomb fragment in the form of a knight's knee, have come from what was an old building c40' by 20'. Nothing is known of its history or purpose. Faden's map of 1783 shows a lane (now lost) which traced the Roman road SW to the green at Saxtead, and also the outline of a building, probably that described above.

Medieval Greens.

Babling Green is named and shown on Faden's map of 1783 as a rectangular green on the N side of the loop in the B1120 heading NE from Framlingham town and castle. It is marked now by Brabling Green Farm. Apsey Green, formerly known as Herbshaw Green, is also named and shown as a triangular green running E-W from the junction of New Street and the lane going W past D'Urban's Farm - the lane initially traces the northern outline of the green. Cole's Green is named on the map but not shown and may already have gone by then. It is marked as being on the fork of a lane running SE to Cole's Green and a track to Edward's Farm.

Site of Mills.

A watermill, in existence c1340, was probably situated N of the bridge in Bridge Street, whilst another was said to have stood in the area of Station Road. A post mill which stood on Mount Pleasant in 1736 was later moved to Tannington, and a smock mill was recorded in Victoria Mill Road in 1714.

Site of Medieval Archery Practice.

Butt Pightle and a record from 1632 of 'carpenters work about the Butts' implies the existence of a site for archery practice in the parish.

Medieval Market & Fair.

The Bigods had the grant of a market in 1286, but it was Thomas de Brotherton, created Earl of Norfolk and Marshall of England when the Bigods temporarily fell from favour, who procured a licence for a fair and a charter

FRAMLINGHAM *(continued)*

of free warren for all his demesne lands in Framlingham.

Site of Ancient Market Cross.
The Market Place originally held an ancient Market Cross housing a boys' school on the upper floor (*see below*). It was taken down in 1788.

Medieval Guildhall.
The Mansion House, called the Guildhall, which stands on the N side of Market Hill its walls secluding St Michael's Church from the Market Place, occupies the site of a hall which belonged to the Guild of the Blessed Virgin Mary, founded here at an early period and dissolved c1537.

Almshouses & Workhouse.
Sir Robert Hitcham acquired the manor and castle of Framlingham for £14,000 in 1635. His will of 1636 settled his estate on Pembroke College, Cambridge with the stipulation that a part be appropriated for the foundation of almshouses at Levington and Framlingham, and for the foundation of schools in Framlingham, Debenham and Coggeshall (*see below*). The material for the erection of the almshouses in Framlingham 'for twelve poor people', a workhouse and the school, he deemed should come from the demolition of the buildings within the castle. This is why nothing remains today within the great curtain walls. The workhouse was erected within the castle grounds and the almshouses at the western extremity of what was the castle mere. Further well-endowed almshouses for eight poor people were erected in Feak's Pightle in 1703 under a bequest of Thomas Mills, former Grundisburgh tailor and later wheelwright at Framlingham, who was buried beside his almshouses. The workhouse within the castle, which had 100 inmates in 1776, was converted to public rooms c1844.

Free Schools.
Framlingham College, attractively situated N of the town, has developed from a school house recorded in 1564 and the initial endowment of Sir Robert Hitcham in 1636 for a school for the poor of Framlingham, Debenham and Coggeshall (Essex). Sir Robert died within seven days of executing his Will but a dispute with his heir resulted in Pembroke College being kept out of the manor and lands till 1653 when Cromwell ordered the will to be fully implemented making separate orders for schools at Debenham, and particularly Coggeshall, which he considered inpractical to combine with Framlingham due to their distance from the town. The school was housed initially within the castle, then in the Guildhall. In 1878 an impressive new college was erected in College Road for 350 children. A Boys' Free School, originally held in a room over the Market Cross, was moved to new premises built near the almshouses when the Cross was taken down in 1788.

Historic Houses & Ancient Moated Sites.
Framlingham Hall, 1½ miles NNW, dates from the C16 but was much altered c1860; it still retains fragments of its ancient moat. The old Tithe Barn stands in the grounds of the rectory. Moat Farm still has its moat and there is part of a moat at Hill Farm, S of the town. Boundary Farm, on the western parish boundary, still retains fragments of a moat and rectilinear enclosures. A field just NE of Edward's Farm and SE of the town shows cropmarks of a square moat (a surviving arm was shown on the 1957 OS map); darker areas to the N may indicate fish-ponds. The Crown Hotel goes back to c1553 and The Crown & Anchor Inn and The White Horse public house also date from the C16. A deed of 1686 describes The Griffin Inn as lying between the Crown Inn and the Lion Inn yard. The Castle public house occupies the site of a former brewery.

FRAMSDEN *(11 miles NE of Ipswich)*

Thedwestry Hundred. 'Fram's valley' (OE) *Framesdena* (DB)
Manors. Framsden (C13 Roger de Montalt).

Roman Road.
A short section of the A1120 follows the course of a Roman road running SW-NE from E of Peats Corner near the

FRAMSDEN *(continued)*

junction with the B1077 to the parish boundary at the crossing of the Deben, only a few miles from its source and here, as yet, little more than a stream.

Old Windmill.

The preserved post mill lying N of Hill Farm beside the B1077 road dates from c1760.

Workhouse.

A workhouse was recorded here in 1776 with 40 inmates.

Historic Houses & Ancient Moated Sites.

Framsden Hall, built by the Radcliffe family c1480, stands to the W of the former manor house. Nothing remains of this previous hall except the NE part, and a piece of the SW end of its long oblong moat. It was certainly here in 1282 when the Monteulto or Montalt family held the manor, for we learn from the Patent Rolls that Joan de Montalt and her son were attacked and assaulted by night in her house at Framsden. Close by the present hall is a fine barn some 200' long, the upper floor C16 timber-frame and the ground floor late C17 or early C18 brick. Boundary Farm on the western parish boundary is a medieval hall-house, its Elizabethan summer-house now used as stables. It is one of the few places in Suffolk where Fritillaries grow. An interesting irregular moated site roughly 70 paces by 40 (now dry) lies isolated SW of Yew Tree Farm and S of Birds Lane. 1½ miles SE of the village part of a moat (now dry) remains N of Basting's Hall in which C12-C13 pottery was found; and in a field an equal distance S is a perfect square moat connected by channels with the Hall and with the road to the E. Moat Farm still retains fragments of its moat. There is part of a moat at the strangely-named Highrow Trinangle in Highrow Wood on the SW parish boundary. This is the former site of Highrow Farm, all the buildings of which were gone by the late 1970s.

FRECKENHAM *(4 miles SW of Mildenhall)*

Lackford Hundred. 'Homestead or village of a man called Freca' (OE) *Frekeham* (895) *Frakenaham* (DB) The parish was situated on the edge of the Old Fen Sea which covered a large extent of NW Suffolk in ancient times. This led to a suggestion that the place-name rmay instead refer to 'the enclosure of a band of warriors/ pirates', a reference, perhaps, also to the earthworks in Mount Meadow (*see below*).

Manors. Freckenham (-1536 Bishop of Rochester; 1537 Sir Ralph Warren). *Sub-Manors.* Beck/Bek/Beckhall; Burton/Burtyus.

Site of Tumulus.

A barrow once stood about 110 yds. inside the parish boundary.

Roman Hoard.

A hoard of some 600 Roman coins dating from the period 306-361 AD was unearthed in the parish in 1948.

Fishing Industry.

The parish anciently enjoyed a considerable fishing industry from its position on the edge of the Old Fen Sea. In 1086 Domesday Book records two fisheries here.

Motte & Bailey Castle.

The curving, sunken road running from the village centre to the church follows the line of the bailey ditch of Freckenham Castle. Mount Meadow comprises a large circular chalk motte still well over 16' high with a surrounding moat and two baileys. Excavations have revealed the tooled cornerstone of a substantial building and several pieces of dressed stone still remain. Freckenham Manor was granted to Lanfrec, Archbishop of Canterbury in 1071 and it was held by the Bishop of Rochester 16 years later, remaining in the Bishop's hands until the mid C19. Yet if we are to believe the alternative interpretation of *Frakenaham (see place-name)* the site may have an earlier origin (later adapted by the Normans) as the Saxon King Anna's daughter, Etheldreda, was born only three miles away at Exning. Although the 'Castel' at Freckenham was mentioned in a document of c1115 (which claimed to be a copy of a charter of 896 A.D.), there is no mention of a castle or any substantial building here in 1185. At the time Bishop

FRECKENHAM *(continued)*

Gilbert was intent on clearing the 'miserable hovels and houses' he claimed the village was comprised of at that time, and 'levelling them with the ground'.

Site of Ancient Chapel.

A chapel was first recorded here in a document of c1281 when 'Lord John was chaplain to the chapell of the Blessed Mary of Freckenham'. It was said to be in existence in 1185. Its location was believed to have been in either North Street or Mortimer's Lane. In 1924 'foundations in Three Corners Close might, by their position to the Pilgrims' Way and by the character of their brickwork, suggest the site of the chapel'. Three Corners Close was situated between North Street and the river opposite the 'Pilgrim Field'. The foundations are of very early brick. The chapel was last mentioned in 1548.

Gallows.

A convention between the Bishop of Rochester and the Abbot of St Edmunds that "the gallows at Frakenham in future shall be on the boundary between the lands of the said Bishop (Freckenham) and Abbot (Herringswell) and their successors, provided that one gallows shall stand on the lands of the said Bishop at Frackenham, and the other gallows on the lands of the said Abbot at Heryngesville, and on these gallows shall be hung all the robbers caught on the lands of the said Bishop of Frakenham." The gibbet was probably sited on the tumulus which stood on the parish boundary (*see above*).

Site of old Windmill.

A smock mill stood on the W side of the Freckenham to Chippenham road SW of the church before 1781. It was demolished c1910.

Medieval Market & Fair.

In 1218 the Bishop of Rochester obtained the grant for a market, and in 1249 for a fair and free warren. There is record of a dispute between the Bishop and the Abbot of St. Edmunds regarding damage done to the Bishop's market at Freckenham in 1221. The Abbots made every effort to prevent markets establishing themselves within an area they considered (often unreasonably) constituted a trade threat to their own in Bury. Those that did exist were constantly being harried.

Historic Houses & Ancient Moated Site.

Freckenham Hall, a red-brick Tudor manor house, is situated opposite the castle. It probably stands on the site of the medieval manor house. The building was evidently much more extensive than it is now, for in the garden that surrounds it can be seen solid blocks of masonry which probably mark its former limits. It would appear that the present outer walls of the house were once inner walls yet they are obviously strong enough to serve their purpose. The owner in 1537 was Sir Ralph Warren, a former Lord Mayor of London. The manor house of Burtin or Burtyus Manor, a sub-manor of Freckenham, may have stood on the site of the Village Hall. The 'Pightell', an enclosed meadow some 200 yds up Mortimer's Lane, was known in 1277 as 'Morty's Pightell' and belonged to William de Mortimer, the Crusader, who let it for the sum of '6d per annum together with the buildings on it'. These may have included the present farmhouse on a site which may possibly date from that period. There are remains of an isolated dry, rectangular moat in the suggestive Mot Meadow to the E of Mortimers Lane which runs N from the village. It has now been ploughed out.

FRESSINGFIELD *(9 miles W of Halesworth)*

Hoxne Hundred. 'Open ground covered with furze' or 'Open ground of Frisian's people' (OE) *Fessefelda* (DB) Includes the Domesday vills of Chippenham and Whittingham.

Manors. Veales with Launce's & Thykbrome Veales cum Membris (C13 William de Veal); Whittingham with Wakelyns (1201 Ernold Fitz Roger Le Rus). *Sub-Manors.* Chippenhall Hall/Chevenhall; Fressingfield Hall; Wakelin's; Ufford Hall; Fressingfield; Launces.

Roman Road.

The course of a Roman road bisects the parish running NW-SE. The B1116 traces its line from the parish boundary

FRESSINGFIELD *(continued)*

SE of Rookery Farm to the point where the modern road turns S toward Fressingfield village. Its line continues, passing the Romano-British farm site at Peartree Farm, unseen on the ground until picked up again by a country road at Little Whittingham Green which continues to the parish boundary at Silverley's Green.

Site of Earthworks.

On Chippenhall Green a slight mound enclosed by a circular ditch is shown on a map of 1927 to contain a windmill with two rectangular structures, one within and one without the enclosure. The earthworks may well be medieval and pre-date its use as a windmill base.

Medieval Chapels.

There were two chapels here; Whittingham Chapel, mentioned between 1325 and 1482 and probably associated with, and sited within, the moats of the former Whittingham Hall. St Margaret's Chapel, was mentioned in 1458.

Deserted Medieval Village.

Great Whittingham and Little Whittingham were former parishes later incorporated into Fressingfield. Fieldwalking has revealed the sites of six medieval homesteads on the southern edge of the former Great Whittingham Green, in the NE corner of the parish. These were spaced at about 110 yd intervals and produced pottery of C12-C14 date. Whittingham Hall Manor obtained the grant of a market in the C13, probably initially on the green, which seems to indicate a notable green-edge settlement of Great Whittingham here in the C12 with a period of maximum activity in the C13-C14 and gradual decline in the C15-C16.

Deer Park.

Whittingham Hall had a large rectangular deer park near the northern parish boundary, the northern half of the area marked on a map of 1702 as 'The Deere Parke'. Tracks around the edge of the former park are known today as The Gallops and The Chase. The park probably existed by 1596.

Medieval Greens.

Of the seven former greens and commons in Fressingfield only the extensive Chippenhall Green near the parish boundary remains today much as it was. Hussey Green, SE of the village, which covered 51 acres and belonged to the Manor of Chippenhall, was enclosed under an Award of 1796 and converted to arable. No peripheral buildings remain and a substantial part of the green outline has also been obliterated. Footpaths still lead from Laxfield Road and the Roman road to meet, now without purpose, at the site. The outline of Little Whittingham Green to the E, enclosed some time ago, is preserved in the surrounding roads. The name 'Whittingham Green' is marked against this road pattern in 1783 and 'Little Whittingham Green' across the area on the 1837 1st Ed. OS map. The Roman road appears to run through the centre of the green. The larger Great Whittingham Green in the NE corner of the parish was already partly enclosed by 1646. By 1702 its 67.5 acres had been divided into nine fields - The Great Greene, The Greene, Hop Greene, Pound Greene, Home Greene, The Long Greene, The Square Greene, The Court Greene, and Borrett's Great Greene. Four farmsteads adjoin the former green but fieldwalking has revealed sites of other houses around the margins. The site of the tiny Caterpole Green is marked by Caterpole Corner. A hamlet in the S of the parish is called Ufford Green and contains the manor house of Ufford Hall. It suggests there was formerly a green here, long gone by 1783 when Faden made no mention of it.

Site of old Windmill.

A post mill is shown on Chippenhall Green in 1783. It was pulled down in 1936.

Medieval Market.

The grant of a market to the manor of Whittingham Hall was obtained in 1267. In 1275 the market was held on the manor of Launces by John Launce. On the demise of Great Whittingham this was transferred to a new site in Fressingfield village where the former market place is situated opposite the Swan public house. A lease preserved in the Swan and dated 1741 refers to 'the common street sometime being the market place'.

Almshouses.

Three tenements were given by Edward Bohun in 1497 and occupied by poor families.

FRESSINGFIELD *(continued)*

Workhouse.

In 1615 the (old)? guildhall was converted to a workhouse which housed 26 inmates in 1776.

Free School.

A Free School was founded by Archbishop Sancroft (1616-93) in 1685. It was housed in the upper room of the Guildhall. William Sancroft, who was made Archbishop of Canterbury in 1677, was imprisoned in the Tower of London in 1688 for refusing to take the oath of allegiance. Deprived and expelled from the church in 1690 he returned to Fressingfield until his death.

Medieval Guildhall.

The Old Guildhall, now The Fox & Goose, a restaurant, was in existence in the C15. It was apparently sold c1510 when situated on the line of Cratfield Road to the S, packway leading towards 'le Croche' (Crouch Hill) to the W, land belonging to St. Mary's College to the N and John Goldwyn's land to the E - possibly the site of Bridge Cottage. The New Guildhall, S of the church, which replaced it the same year, was formerly the timber-framed Church House. It housed the Guild of St. Margaret of Antioch (1465). In 1704 William Sancroft gave the building with land towards the repair and maintenance of the church of St Peter and St Paul.

Historic Houses & Ancient Moated Sites.

Ufford Hall on the southern parish boundary consists of a much-altered C16 timber-framed open hall standing on the remains of its moated site. The Ufford family held the manor here with the Abbot of Bury's manor of Chippenhall in the C12-C13, and the present hall was home to the Sancrofts in 1565 and for several generations. William Sancroft, Archbishop of Canterbury , who died in 1693, was one of this family. A sadly mutilated moat remains at Fressingfield Hall. Despite being very fragmented the plan of the land it formerly surrounded appears square. The hall was owned by William Grudgefield c1650. There were two rectories here in the Middle Ages. These may well have been at Church Farm, W of the church, where the stables contain the timbers of a former C14 aisled hall, and at Tithe Farm, just SE of the village, where there are two sides of an oblong moat and the T-shaped farmhouse is a much altered mid C14 raised-aisled hall with, nearby, the remains of a C14 barn which was also once aisled. Chippenhall Hall is a fine old manor house. An impressive outbuilding of the former Whittingham Hall, 1 mile NE of the village and N of Whittingham Green, carries the date 1653. It stands beside the moated site of the earlier manor house, home to Thomas Baker. The moat is large and square and there is a portion of another which apparently enclosed a small area along the southern side of the first; there are entrances to subterranean passages here. Three sides of a moat remain at Home Farm near the eastern parish boundary. There is the greater part of a large moat at Vales Hall Farm, site of the manor house; there are two moats at Fressingfield Lodge, one oblong, the other to the W divided into two parts; two pieces of a quadrangular moat remain at Hill House, SW of the Lodge. A portion of a moat enclosing both a large and small area survives at Moat Farm, 2 miles SE of the village, and there are other moats or parts of moats at Pear Tree House, Nunnery Farm, Pinkneys Farm, Lawn Farm, and an isolated moat surrounding a small grove NW of the last.

FRESTON *(3½ miles S of Ipswich)*

Samford Hundred. 'The Frisian's farmstead or village' (OE) *Fresetuna* (DB)
Manors. Freston (1234 Philip de Freston). *Sub-Manors.* Bonds/Bonds Hall.

Ancient Woodland.

Freston Wood and Cutler's Wood are parts of ancient woodland.

Coin Hoard.

In 1828 a hoard of Roman coins was found in the parish.

Historic House.

Freston Hall was anciently the seat of a family which took its name from the parish. Philip de Freston was admitted a free-burgher of Ipswich in 1233 and the estate continued with the family until the time of Henry VIII when it passed to the Latimers. All that now remains on the site, delightfully situated on the S bank of the

FRESTON *(continued)*

Orwell, is Freston Tower, a quaint folly designed by William Latimer and built c1550 as (so the story goes) 'a pleasant retreat' for his daughter Ella's studies. It comprises a brick tower of six floors measuring 10' by 12' with polygonal angle buttresses terminating in pinnacles and with a polygonal stair turret to the estuary rising above the pinnacles. According to his instructions, the Lower Room was to be devoted to Charity from 7 in the morning to 8, the second for Tapestry 9-10, the Third to Music 10 till noon, the Fourth for Painting noon-1, the Fifth to Literature 1-2, and the Sixth, appropriately enough, to Astronomy in the evenings. Later, between 1772-79, it was used as an isolation hospital for those afflicted with smallpox. The fine timber-framed Bonds Hall, in the centre of the parish, represents the site of the other Freston manor and was home to Nicholas Bond in the first half of the C14. During the time of Elizabeth, Thomas Gawdy, Judge of Common Pleas, was in possession.

FRISTON *(2¼ miles SE of Saxmundham)*

Plomesgate Hundred. 'The Frisian's farmstead or village' (OE) *Frisetuna* (DB)
Manors. Friston (-1524 Snape Priory; 1524 Cardinal Wolsey). *Sub-Manors.* Becklings/Biecking Hall/Blicking.

Site of Tumulus (?)
Kirby names the crossroads N of Friston decoy 'Polsborough Gate' in 1735, a strong reference to a conspicuous Pfol's Barrow long since swept away and unmentioned on modern maps of the area.

Roman Settlement.
At Barber's Point S of the parish on the banks of the river Alde, sherds, bones and debris of a Roman villa or small settlement was first discovered in 1907.

Medieval Greens.
Friston Green was named and shown on Faden's map of 1783 as a small triangular green lying at a fork in the road S of the church. It has now been completely infilled with residential development and called 'The Common'. Friston Moor was shown on the same map as a large area of common NW of the church. It ran from the present B1121 road NE from Moor Farm in line with the parish boundary with Clouting's Farm and Pattle's Farm, forming the northern limit. Another Moor Farm and Little Moor Farm trace the S side of the inverted L-shape.

Historic House.
Friston Hall, approached by a half-mile long drive from the A1094 road, is shown with a tree-lined avenue running S for well over a mile on Faden's map of 1783 to the W of Black Heath Wood. It was built in the C16 by Michael Hare, and was owned by Thomas Bacon in 1674 when it was recorded as having 20 hearths.

FRITTON *(8 miles NE of Beccles)*

Mutford & Lothingland Hundred. 'Farmstead offering safety or protection' (OE) or 'Frithi's farmstead' (OScand) *Fridetuna* (DB). Includes the Domesday vill of Caldecott.
Manors. Fritton al Fritton Paston's (C13 Nicholas de Freton). *Sub-Manors.* Caldecot Hall.

Tumulus or Ancient Defensive Post.
Two minor hills have been left on the summit of the large Bell Hill mound as a result of digging into what was thought to be a burial mound. However other suggestions have been voiced as to the origin of this large hill or mound. One suggestion is that it is in fact a Danish earthwork created by cutting through a natural ridge to create a defensive post 120 paces E-W by 45 paces N-S with a maximum height of 20' and situated some 30 paces from reclaimed cattle marshes. The name has been taken from the adjoining village of Belton (*Beletuna* at Domesday). Beli, a Viking, it is further speculated, first took this fort by assault and subsequently settled in the township which now bears his name. It was noted that there was a large percentage of Norse place-names in Lothingland Hundred. Ordnance Survey also appear to be changing their opinion; once naming it a tumulus, they now identify the hill as an ancient battery.

Early Settlement.
Fritton shows signs of continual settlement from Roman times. The extraordinary church of St Edmund the

FRITTON *(continued)*

Martyr, perhaps founded by King Canute (Knut), has one of the earliest Saxon towers in the country incorporating Roman tile and features from several periods, whilst the mere also has Viking associations.

Medieval Commons.

Herringfleet and Belton Commons are shown on Faden's map of 1783 linking and covering the western side of Fritton parish. They are now mostly covered by Waveney Forest. Fritton Common covered an area from Crossways lying either side of Beccles Road and extending to Fritton Decoy. It continued SW to a point where a finger from the lake extends NW. This area is also now under plantation.

Medieval Industry.

The extensive expanse of Fritton Decoy (or Lake), nearly 3 miles in length and in places ¼ mile wide, was anciently part of a large estuary. Tradition asserts that it was formerly called Gunhilde's Mere and named after Gunhilda, sister of Sweyn and aunt to the Danish King Canute (Knut). The modern appearance of the lake was created by turbary - the extraction of peat in medieval times - and the Account Rolls show that half a million sods of peat were extracted in 1318 making up seventy-six per cent of the income of Fritton Manor.

Medieval Market & Fair.

Henry de Caldecot, lord of the Manor of Caldecot, obtained the grant for a market and fair in 1269.

Historic Houses.

Old Hall, E of the church and the former house of the main manor, is situated in Fritton Lake Country Park. Caldecott Hall, now a farmhouse in the N of the parish, stands on the site of the other manor.

FROSTENDEN *(4½ miles NW of Southwold)*

Blything Hundred. 'Valley frequented by frogs' (OE) *Froxedena* (DB)
Manors. Frostenden (1267 Gilbert Frostenden). *Sub-Manors.* Coldham; Kings Manor.

Site of Ancient Dock and Quay.

Now under the plough but clearly visible, a circular mound (just across the parish boundary - *see* South Cove) overlooks to the W what remains of a possible ancient dock and quay dug out of the E side of the river entering at Easton Broad. Domesday designated *Froxedena* a sea-port (Portus Maris), and Suckling suggests that this was in the area of Frostenden Bottom through which a small stream winds its way by South Cove to Easton Broad, tracing the parish boundary with South Cove - The river would have been much wider and deeper in earlier times. It may have Danish origins, but its purpose and that of the adjacent mound have yet to be confidently established.

Medieval Salt Industry.

Domesday records a saltworks in the parish, probably at Frostenden Bottom. This was discontinued soon after, suggesting that the sea-port was already well in decline by this time.

Medieval Common.

An extensive linear common called Frostenden Clay Common is shown on Faden's 1783 map. It extended S from Green Lane track by Primrose Wood (now replaced by Primrose Lane), curving E and ending in line with Wash Lane. The area is still marked Clay Common on the present OS map but has been enclosed. On the same map, Frostenden Common lay by the road at Frostenden Corner, whilst Frostenden Hall is shown standing on the edge of the smallish square Frostenden Green.

Historic Houses & Ancient Moated Sites.

Little remains of the original manor house of Frostenden Hall situated near the church. It was purchased by John Glover who died in 1573 and in whose family it remained for many years. The Hermitage near the southern parish boundary is an historic building, and Green Farm on the western boundary, N of the road to Stoven, still retains part of its moat. In Gough's Wood, W of the A12 on the southern parish boundary, C13 pottery has been recovered from a moated site; and at Frostenden Spring, a wood on the northern boundary, a quadrangular moat was mapped in 1840, preserved in plantation.

GAZELEY *(5 miles SE of Newmarket)*

Risbridge Hundred. 'Gaeg's woodland clearing' (OE) *Gaysle* (1219). Gazeley was not a parish at Domesday, but the extensive manor of Desning which covered some 4,400 acres.
Manors. Gazeley Manor (-1348 de Clare family). *Sub-Manors.* Desning Hall al Castle Hall; Higham Hall; Gazeley Rectory; Althorpe's/Applethorpe's al Bovill's; Talmags al Talmyties and Passelowes.

Ancient Way.
A short section of the ancient Icknield Way, one of the oldest recorded trackways in the country, passes SW-NE through the N of the parish from the A14 slip-road towards Cavenham.

Tumuli.
Excavations on a Bronze-Age bowl barrow* NW of Pin Farm near the northern parish boundary (ploughed out by 1986) revealed 16 burials, whilst another, NW of this and formerly known as Blackhill round barrow* is now under the plough. Three barrows lie together S of the Icknield Way by the B1506 slip-road from the A14 to Newmarket. One is 100' in diameter and 4½' high, another 92' in diameter and 1' high; the third is now ploughed out. SE of Pin Farm, Mount Plantation and the tithe names of 'The Mount' and 'Little Mount' fields suggest the site of at least one other former barrow.

Motte & Bailey Castle.
Denham Castle on the border with Denham but actually in Gazeley parish, colloquially known as 'Castle Holes', comprises a much mutilated motte now 10' high enclosed by a wide moat still wet on the N and E. There is an oval bailey to the SW with remains of an inner rampart. The site which lies in rough pasture was excavated in 1861 when the foundations of a Norman tower which once flanked the outer entrance were discovered along with coins and a spur. There are a number of stone corbels built into one of the old flint farm buildings which may have come from the site. Richard FitzGilbert was Lord of the Manor of Deselynge at Domesday and it is to this family that the site, a military outpost of Clare, is attributed. The seat of the manor later moved to Desning Hall.

Medieval Green.
A linear green edged by properties, shown but not named on Faden's map of 1783, ran the length of, and predated, the present street. This has now been infilled to the road with modern housing.

Site of Medieval Gallows (?)
Both the barrows (*see above* *) are sited in a field named on the tithe map 'Gallows Field' suggesting one of the mounds was used to hold a gibbet in medieval times.

Guildhall (?)
There may at one time have been a guildhall here as the parish formed three early guilds: All Saints, St. James and St. Margaret (1389).

Historic House & Ancient Moated Sites.
Desning Hall (1845), SE of the village, stands beside the great moated site of the ancient manor house of 'Deselynge'. To the W of it is another very broad water-filled trench which may have formed one side of a similar enclosure.

GEDDING *(8 miles W of Stowmarket)*

Thedwestry Hundred. 'The place belonging to Gydda's people' (OE) *Gedinga* (DB)
Manors. Gedding Manor al Gedding Hall (1196 Adam de Geding).

Moated Church.
The little Norman church of St Mary, just S of Gedding Hall on the Drinkstone road, was once encircled and defended by an ancient moat, parts of which can still be traced. On the NW it is about 16' wide being continued in a westerly direction into the adjoining field. On the N it is 27' wide, but the E and S sides have gone. Nicholas Pevsner considers them moat-sized boundary ditches.

Lost Medieval Settlement.
The former settlement of Little Gidding (or Gedding) was amalgamated with Felsham in 1883.

GEDDING *(continued)*

Site of old Windmill.
A post mill stood in the SE corner of the parish by Mill House in 1783. It was pulled down c1904. A mill, moved here from Felsham in 1867, required 18 shire horses and took two days.

Historic House & Ancient Moated Site.
Gedding Hall lies isolated N of the church in a defensive situation on the summit of rising ground. The only trace of the original fortified manor house first built on the site by Sir John de Geddynge in 1273 - 'quadrangular, of great strength and moated' - is the strong wide moat. The present Hall, a part restoration of 1897 and part rebuild of the C15 Hall of the Chamberlaynes, is still nevertheless very impressive with its C16 Tudor brick gatehouse, and drawbridge (now immovable) crossing the moat at the main S entrance. The moat measures overall c 82yds E-W by c87yds N-S and is still wet on the E and S sides. A connecting series of four fish-ponds lie to the E fed by a stream to the S, and a sluice ditch connects the moats to the ponds. There are possible traces of an earlier enclosure in front of the Hall. The Chamberlaynes' period of greatest wealth was under Sir Robert Chamberlayne, born c1435 and a leading Yorkist, who eventually fell from grace under Henry VII and was beheaded in 1491. He probably built the gatehouse and perhaps the whole moated complex. If he did, the buildings must date from the 1480s. The Hall was later the seat of the Bokenham family.

GEDGRAVE *(½ mile SSW of Orford)*

Plomesgate Hundred. 'Goat's grove' (OE) Morley suggests 'Great graef' (Ditch of passage). *Gategraua* (DB). Gedgrave was extra-parochial until 1958 when it gained civil parish status.
Manors. Gedgrave (c1171 Ralph de Glanville).

Medieval Salt Industry.
Faden's map of 1783 marks the site of salt pans by Gedgrave Marshes, in the estuary of Butley River.

Ancient Ferry.
Ferry Cottage marks the site of the former ferry house of the medieval ferry which was owned by the Prior of Butley Abbey and plied across the Butley river from Burrow Hill (*see* Butley).

Medieval Chapel & Deserted Medieval Village (?)
Despite a population of 66 in 1881, the parish is now churchless and sparsely populated with only a hall, farm and two cottages. It formerly had a chapel dedicated to St Mary and St George where, it is said, seamen's wives prayed for their husband's safety (1679). There was also an old hall called the 'Holy House'. The church, which had fallen into disrepair, was dismantled *c*1550, but the chapel was still standing in the C17.

GIPPING *(4 miles NE of Stowmarket)*

Stow Hundred. 'The place of Geppa's people' (OE) *Gippinges* (C12). The river Gipping takes its name from the parish, although it rises just across the parish boundary in the adjoining hamlet of Mendlesham Green. Until 1866 when it became a separate civil parish, Gipping was a hamlet of Old Newton.
Manors. Gipping (1316 Arnold de Mountensey).

Ancient Woodland.
Gipping Great Wood, Little Wood and the plantations of Guidepost, Deal, Ash and Corner are possible remains of ancient woodland. They formed a part of the Tyrell's 600-acre park.

Ancient Track.
A track called Old Hundred Lane and dating from at least Saxon times marks the northern and eastern parish boundary with Cotton and Mendlesham, and the hundred boundary between Stow and Hartismere. It commences at TM068 646, runs E to a junction of tracks SW of Redhouse Farm, then SE to Palgrave Farm.

Site of Moated Mound.
Described in 1924 as being a circular mound 40' in diameter and about 5' high, enclosed by a moat, partially filled in, and situated in the corner of a pasture some 200 paces NW of Hill Farm. Sherds of C13-C14 pottery were

GIPPING *(continued)*

found from the old turf line below the mound during limited excavations in 1960. Its position suggests a mill mound but there is no documentary evidence to support this, and the enclosing moat which shows as being quite large on the early OS map may suggest a defensive origin. The site has been completely destroyed by ploughing, leaving no indication now as to its exact position.

Ancient Chapel.

Now the parish church, the Chapel of St Nicholas was believed to have been in existence in 1340 and was referred to in 1446. It was rebuilt c1483 by Sir James Tyrell, who died in 1502, as a private chapel to his adjoining Hall, and the quantity and quality of the decorative flintwork is probably not exceeded on any building in the county. Throughout history the Tyrells appear a rather tainted family. It was Sir James who is thought to have carried out, as Shakespeare so dramatically put it, 'the most arch act of piteous massacre that ever yet this land was guilty of', namely the murder of the princes in the Tower. An inscription in the splay of the vestry door of the chapel bears the somewhat pathetic plea to 'Pray for Sir Jamys and Damr Anne his wyf', but on the NE buttress, a more defiant motto in French translates to 'Let him complain who will'. Almost inevitably Sir James met his end on the block at Tower Hill, this time for assisting Edmund de la Pole's flight to Flanders. Their claimed notoriety goes back much further still, for after the knight Sir Thomas Tyrell had accompanied William the Conqueror to England, he was said to have been responsible for 'accidentally' firing the fateful arrow which took out the eye of William Rufus, the Conqueror's son and successor. They also had their honourable members; a Sir John Tyrell fought at Agincourt and was Speaker of the House of Commons.

Historic Houses & Ancient Moated Sites.

The Tyrell family have been associated with Gipping since Domesday when Sir Walter Tyrell held the manor. The moated manor house of Gipping Hall, their manorial seat which lay E of the chapel, was demolished in 1860 when Sir Charles Tyrell was lord, leaving an empty space in a meadow still marked by a well. A house called Gipping Lone stands ½ mile further N on a moated site originally occupied by the Old Vicarage or Coppings, a house probably built at the same time as the chapel for priests who served the Tyrell family. Parts are embellished with the Tyrell coat of arms which may suggest that it later became a personal residence. It is probable that a large portion of the ancient moat was in-filled in the C16. Another moat lies at Grange Farm.

GISLEHAM *(5 miles SW of Lowestoft)*

Mutford & Lothingland Hundred. 'Gisli's homestead' (OE) *Gisleham* (DB)
Manors. Gisleham Hall/Gisleham with Pyes (1270 Alan de Wymenhale). *Sub-Manors.* Pyes Hall.

Tumulus.

In 1768 a Saxon barrow on Bloodmoor Hill on the northern parish boundary revealed a skeleton around whose neck hung a gold medal, a copy of a coin of Justinian I (527-65), and an onyx set in gold. On the medal was D.N.T.AVITVS, and on the reverse a helmeted head with VICTORIA AVGGG, exergue CONOB. On the onyx a helmeted man stands by his horse holding the reins.

Ancient Battle (?)

A battle was said to have been fought between the Saxons and Danes on Bloodmoor Hill, a sandy hoh half a mile NNE of Bludmer Farm and 775 paces N of Sandpits Covert, at the junction of three parishes.

Saxon Watch Tower (?)

It is believed that the round tower of Holy Trinity Church with its immensely thick walls may have originated as a watch tower in the days of Athelstan, the first Saxon King of England.

Medieval Common.

A massive common, named Runhill Heath on Faden's map of 1783, extended S from Heath Farm in a narrow linear form either side of the old main road before widening to cover an area extending W to Duck's Entry (in Rushmere) and S to the junction of Primrose Lane near The Elms; then across to a line with Pond and Laurel Farms in the E.

GISLEHAM *(continued)*

Medieval Market & Fair.
In 1270 Alan de Wymenhale obtained a grant for a market and fair on his manor in Gisleham.

Historic Houses & Ancient Moated Sites.
On the site of the Manor House, S of the church, is one of the most interesting homestead moats in Suffolk. It consists of a very perfect double moat, one inside the other; the outer one c167yds square. A drawbridge was removed c1794. The manor formerly belonged to the knightly Garney family. On the opposite side of the road the site of Gisleham Hall has one side of its original moat. Chestnut Farm has part of a moat.

GISLINGHAM *(5 miles SW of Eye)*

Hartismere Hundred. 'The enclosure of Gisli's people' (OE) *Gyselingham* (1060) *Gislingaham* (DB). Prior to the Norman Conquest, a group of Gysela's family or followers appear to have moved about fifty miles from their initial home at Gisleham just S of Lowestoft to form this new settlement called Gyselingham.
Manors. Swatshall Hall (C13 William de Gislingham). *Sub-Manors.* Rushes; Jennies; Gislingham/Goldingham/ Goldingham Hall; Lawford and Collesford; Gislingham and Heighams.

Ancient Road.
From W of the church an ancient road to Burgate, known as the Impaugh Way, passes N through the parish. Its route S of the village follows the road to Finningham beyond where it is named MillGate Way on Faden's 1783 map.

Preceptory of Knights Templars.
A Preceptory of Knights Templars of St John is known to have existed in the parish, and the fact that Brother Alan Martell 'Master of the Knights Templars' was fined in Gislingham during 1225 shows that it was founded some time before this. They appear to have held the Manor of Lawford and Collesford where, in 1286, they claimed view of frankpledge and assize of bread and beer. Brother Thomas de Stamford was Preceptor in 1305 and it was likely terminated at the Templar's suppression in 1312 at which time there appears ample evidence that they possessed a virile house here under Simon de Heyford. However, by the time the Knights Hospitallers finally took possession of the site in 1338, little was left and they appear never to have maintained it. In 1554, after the Dissolution, it was granted to John Green and Robert Hall. Its site could be the earthworks in Cromwell's Plantation which sits astride the parish boundary with both Finningham and Walsham and called erroneously 'Stoland Abbey' by the *Victoria County History*. (*see* Finningham). Basil Brown offered two more likely candidates with significant field names. The remains of a moat, still wet, W of Lady Margaret Farm, on the site of the former Street Farm, retains the chalk spread of possible floors of buildings along with C13 pottery sherds. The site is close to, and E of, fields named Further Temple Field, Great Temple Field, New Temple Field and Middle Temple Field. Another possible site in the same area is by Lady Margaret Farm and New Manor Hall Farm where traces of two arms of a moat, rammed clay areas, stone floors with grouted-in clay, wall footings, building debris and C13-C14 pottery lies on Temple Close Field adjoining Temple Lane (now Northlands).

Medieval Green.
The massive Allwood Green which lay partly in Walsham, Finningham, and both Rickinghall parishes also covered the western extension of Gislingham parish (to the earthworks in Cromwell's Plantation (*see* Finningham), from Highways down to Homa-Gen, and a short distance E of the B1113 - most of its eastern edge still marked in field boundaries. A small triangular Green is shown and named Rush Green on Faden's map. It is now enclosed and its site marked by Rush Green Farm S of the village. Another long narrow Green, marked Park Way on the same map, ran from Broad Dock on the eastern parish boundary (now a strip of woodland), W past Green Farm and connecting to the present Green Lane. A curve in the road from Allwood Green to the village is marked 'Little Green' on the current OS map, but although a triangular

GISLINGHAM *(continued)*

junction of roads is shown at this point on Faden's map it does not show it as a Green; it may already have gone by this time.

Site of old Windmill.

A post mill said to date from 1615 stood on Allwood Green in 1783.

Free School (?)

A will of 1636 refers to repairs to school. Four schoolmasters/tutors are recorded 1672-1733.

Guildhall.

The Old Guildhall in Mill Street is situated to the W of the village and is now divided into cottages. It dates from the C15 and has a fine roof.

Historic Houses & Ancient Moated Sites.

A perfect isolated moat with an entrance to the SW in Moatyard Plantation in the NE corner of the parish, is the probable site of Heigham Hall the C13 manor house of the de Belliecampo family. There was a moat at Proctors Barn, SW of this, but both moat and building (formerly known as Old Black Barn) have gone. A part of a probable square moat remains at Manor Farmhouse, Little Green, which has been identified by Edward Farrer as Brands, a C15 timber-framed house first mentioned in a deed of 1597 "wherein one Thomas Hubberd doth now inhabit". The site of the manor house of Swattisfield Hall or Swatshall (shown by Faden in 1783) is marked by part of a strong moat S of Duchess Wood on the eastern parish boundary; it had been rebuilt, allegedly, by Charles Bedingfield at the beginning of the C18. N of the church, at Ivy House Farm, is one arm of a moat which may have belonged to the Old Rectory. It was situated to the E of the present early Tudor farmhouse where many large stones and Early Medieval to Tudor sherds have been found. A possible ploughed-out moat at Rush Green Field, opposite the rectory, has revealed building material and Early Medieval sherds.

GLEMSFORD *(5 miles NE of Clare)*

Babergh Hundred. 'Ford (perhaps) where people gathered for revelry or games' or 'Ford over the gleaming river' (OE) *Glemesford* (c1050) *Clamesforda* (DB)

Manors. Glemsford Manor (1361 Bishop of Ely). *Sub-Manors.* Methold's and Wimbolds; Callis al Tylnes; Glemsford al Peverells.

Glemsford thrived on the back of the cloth industry in the C16 and C17, and later the silk, velvet,horsehair and flax industries - the latter remembered in Flax Lane.

Ancient Woodland.

Court Wood and Lumpit Wood are fragments of ancient woodland.

Ancient Ford.

Could the ancient ford referred to in the place-name and dating back at least to Saxon times have been where Scotchford Bridge now carries the B1065 over the river Glem, here little more than a stream? Two roads and a footpath from Stanstead Church meet here at the river.

Saxon College of Priests.

In the time of Edward the Confessor a college for a dean and priests invested in numerous privileges was founded and flourished till the reign of Henry III. Strangely, nothing is known of them from this time and it is likely the college with its probable connections with the See of Ely was moved c1272 when records ceased. The site is thought to be opposite Peverells, W of the village, and while there are no visible remains, a well from the period is said to have survived.

Site of Chapel (?)

A chapel dedicated to Our Lady was mentioned here in 1520. Its site is unknown and this could, in fact, be a reference to the church which carries the same dedication and in early times was often referred to as 'the chapel'.

GLEMSFORD *(continued)*

Medieval Green.
Faden's map of 1783 shows the triangular Tye Green lying in the junction of Skate's Hill and Cavendish Lane on the W side of the village bordered by properties on the SW and E sides. The village has now been extended E and the Green enclosed and completely redeveloped.

Site of Mills.
A watermill known as Weston Mill was shown on Faden's map of 1783 standing by the river Stour S of the junction of the B1065 and A1092 roads near the site of the old railway station. A windmill is recorded in 1799 W of Park Lane and E of the village.

Medieval Fair.
The village, an important wool trade centre in the C15 and C16, formerly had an annual fair 'for pedlery and toys', obsolite by 1912.

Workhouse.
A workhouse is recorded here with 50 inmates in 1776.

Historic Houses & Ancient Moated Site.
Timber-framed Angel House in Egrement Street has a C15 carved corner post. Peverells at the W end of the village dates from 1614, the same date as Monks Hall in Low Street ¼ mile NE of the village. The former home of the Kerrington family, it has now been converted into cottages. The Angel Inn dates from the C16. The moat at Park Farm, just S of the church, has now been ploughed out.

GOSBECK *(7½ miles N of Ipswich)*

Bosmere & Claydon Hundred. 'Stream frequented by geese' (OE) *Gosebech* (1179). The parish was originally called Easton. To distinguish it from two other Eastons in Suffolk it assumed the name Easton Gosbeck in 1174. In the C17 it finally dropped the name Easton altogether to become Gosbeck - hence its ommission under this name at Domesday, where it is recorded with 14 acres as Easton in Bosmere Hundred.
Manors. Gosbeck/Gosbeck with Newton (1234 Richard de Gosbeck). *Sub-Manors.* Childs; Ketsalfield.

Ancient Woodland.
Gosbeck Wood is a part of ancient woodland.

Late Iron-Age Settlement.
A Late Iron-Age settlement was discovered in the parish.

Roman Road.
The A1120 road forms a short section of the NW parish boundary following the course of the Roman Stone Street from Gosling's Farm NE to Tollgate Farm.

Ancient Track.
To the SE and parallel to the Roman road is an ancient (possibly Saxon) track called Green Way which runs from Greenway Farm to Pettaugh Lane. It then turns N forming the eastern parish boundary and joining the Roman Stone Street, here known as Ipswich Way.

Ancient Moated Mound.
N of Gosbeck Wood, NW of the church and on the boundary with Crowfield, is a double rectangular homestead moat, now dry, with a third parallel, water-filled arm to the SE. This is shown on a map of 1748 with 'Cottage Yards' to the S and a circular moated area called 'Ye Mount' attached to the SW corner and linked to a second, smaller circular area called 'Round Hole'. Whilst the mount may at one time have carried a windmill it is unlikely that this formed its original purpose. Finds date the site from the late C13 to the C17. A survey of the Manor of Gosbeck in 1641 refers to 'the wood of the lord, formerly built with the site of the Manor of Gosbeck; 'Castle Yard' and 'the wood of the lord formerly built with the site of the castle'. These would all seem to apply to Gosbeck Wood and the moats on the N side of it.

GOSBECK *(continued)*

Medieval Green.

The 1641 survey (*see above*) also indicates that the area to the N of Gosbeck Wood was called 'Loosegrene'. The 1748 map shows this as a narrow strip-green but only part of the Green edge survives today. It ran from the church NE to Greenway Farm. The present road traces its SE side and, at its northern end, a track called Green Way continues on NE.

Historic Houses & Ancient Moated Site.

The Moat, now Moat Farm a timber-framed house with ancient barns, has the remains of an ancient moat. There is a fragment of a moat at Rye Farm on the eastern parish boundary. Gosbeck Hall, The Manor House and Newton Hall all occupy historic sites.

GREAT ASHFIELD *(8 miles NW of Stowmarket)*

Blackbourn Hundred. 'Clearing where ash trees are felled' (OE) *Eascefelda* (DB)

Manors. Ashfield Magna (-1264 Le Blund family; 1264 William de Criketot). *Sub-Manors.* Abriwicks al Allred Wykes.

Ancient Woodland.

Parker's Grove to the W of Castle Hill, and Brown's Wood to the S, are surviving ancient woodland.

Ancient Lane.

A broken section of the ancient Hundred lane which dates back at least to Saxon days, forms a part of the eastern parish boundary running S from E of Brook Hall.

Ancient Cross.

An ancient carved cross, 10'6" high and made of Barnack stone, bears an inscription of c1250 on the E side panel 'REG DOURIVIAG'. The cross is probably Saxon, dating from the C8. It once served as a churchyard footbridge before being moved by Lord Thurlow to Ashfield House, his home on the parish boundary. Unfortunately, when being re-erected, it broke into three pieces and had to be repaired. Another fragment of the cross appears to have been built into the exterior fabric of the church above an old Saxon dial.

Motte & Bailey Castle.

Half a mile SW of the church is the imposing moated area of Castle Hill. It comprises a very rotund mound, 130' in diameter and 11½' high, overgrown in trees and surrounded by a water-filled moat 16½' wide. The whole is in a perfect state of preservation. An irregular circle in plan, the mound has a slightly depressed oval summit c49' across. The curving hedge and ditch which originally formed the boundary of the field in which the earthworks stands in all probability traces the line of the former bailey for scatters of early medieval pottery have been found here. The earthworks has been identified as a C12 'adulterine' motte and bailey castle raised without royal approval in the uncertain times when Stephen and Maude fought for the English throne. Its builder is likely to be a descendent of the Domesday tenant Robert le Blund.

Medieval Greens.

The northern limit of the massive medieval Boten Haugh (Button Hoo) Green just extended into the southern edge of the parish bordered by Lea Farm (Ashfield Lee), Haugh Lane, White Gates (which lay at the entry to the Green) and Schoolhouse Farm. Days Green is named on Faden's 1783 map at the meeting of Hantons Lane with Brazier Lane which forms a part of the northern parish boundary - it appears to have been little more than a green area formed by the junction. The area is named Daisy Green on the present OS map.

Recreation.

One acre of church lands formerly situated near the church and called 'Camping Field' suggests the former site of the medieval ball game.

Site of old Windmill.

A post mill stood on Button Haugh Green in 1783. It was pulled down c1917.

GREAT ASHFIELD *(continued)*

Historic Houses & Ancient Moated Site.

Lea Farm, on the southern parish boundary and formerly on the NE edge of Button Haugh Green, was once a manor house known as The Lee or Ashfield Lee. It was long the seat of the Smiths and still retains fragments of its small rectangular moat. The Smiths were formerly known as the Hovells and it was two of the sons from the marriage of Eliza Smith to the local vicar Thomas Thurlow who achieved the pinnacle of their appointed careers. Edward, born in 1735, rose to the position of Lord Chancellor in 1778, taking the title Lord Thurlow of Ashfield. It is said his talents were so splendid that it was Dr Johnson no less who said, 'I would prepare myself for no man in England but Lord Thurlow; when I am about to meet him I should wish to know a day before.' His brother, Thomas, embracing his father's profession, was elevated to Bishop of Durham in 1787. Hall Farm, between the church and castle, has a square moat with an extended W arm probably once forming another. In an isolated position E of the church and N of a track called Hantons Lane, is a small but perfect square moat with associated cropmarks, and in the SE corner of the parish is a fragment of a moat by Ashfield Haugh. White Gates on the southern parish boundary is C15 in origin. Its name suggests that perhaps it once controlled the entrance (gate) to the former extensive Button Haugh Green which ran S through Elmswell and part of Norton.

GREAT BARTON *(2½ miles NE of Bury St Edmunds)*

Thedwestry Hundred. 'Barley farm, outlying grange where corn is stored' (OE) *Bertuna* (DB)
Manors. Great Barton (Abbot of St. Edmunds, Bury until the Dissolution when it passed to the Crown).
Sub-Manors. Necton Hall/Conyers Hall.

Ancient Field Boundaries, Track (?) and Woodland.

The NW parish boundary is marked by nearly two miles of straight field edges cutting through a virtually continuous line of probable ancient woodland from Colton's Wood in the S to Blackmoor Bottom in the N. Here it forms Back Lane and sweeps E to join Brand Road from Thurston to Great Livermere. Barton Shrub in the SE of the parish is also ancient woodland.

Ancient Lake Settlement.

Barton Mere lies to the E at the junction of three parishes - Great Barton, Pakenham and Thurston, and is equally divided into two parts NW-SE by the former two. When full it covers 10 acres and has a maximum depth of 7'. In 1831, during a drought, deer bones and wolf tibia were exposed, and in 1868 during similar conditions labourers claimed that 'bayonets (bronze spearheads?), round brass things like soldiers wear on their hats', and 'stakes sticking up out of the bottom about as thick as the thin part of a man's leg about 6' or 7' long' were also found, plus animal bones, flint flakes and fragments of hand-made pottery. Also discovered at the same time was a wattle structure 5'7" by 3'10" with 14 uprights 2-3" thick, lying 28" below the surface of the deepest part of the mere. Twigs and sticks were worked into these like the sides of a basket. This structure was supposed to have been used for catching fish and the whole general scene suggested associated items of an ancient lakeside settlement of possibly Bronze-Age date.

Ancient Well.

An ancient well is shown on the present OS map situated in the village on the NW side of the A143, SW of its junction with the East Barton road.

Roman Roads.

The course of a short length (third of a mile) of Roman road marks the SE parish boundary from a minor road N of Rougham Park at TL9105 6460 to just S of a major housing estate in the adjoining parish of Thurston at TL9122 6515. It crosses an open field and is not evident on the ground. The course of another Roman road is thought to be traced by the straight field boundaries running S of the Bury to Barton village road past Hollow Road Farm. It has been noticed that in early manuscripts of Fornham and Barton it is marked as 'Peddars Way', and as Margary states in his work on Roman roads in Britain, 'this may well be' a road linking the Icknield Way to the main Roman Peddars Way (*see* Fornham All Saints).

GREAT BARTON *(continued)*

Ancient Midden, Saxon Meeting Place & Gallows (?)

'Catteshill', a mound which once stood at Cattishall Farm, Cattishall, N of Mount Road, became the judicial assembly point for Bury following the acquisition of its predecessor, the tumulus 'Thingoe', by the convent of Bury Abbey. It is no longer marked on the OS map and may now lie beneath the railway which crosses the area of Cattishall E-W. It was originally thought to be a burial mound but excavations have revealed that it was an Iron-Age/Roman midden (mound of refuse) containing C1 sherds, lava quern fragments and food bones. The mound may also at one time have been used for a gallows.

Medieval Greens.

A large residential development occupies a part of the formerly extensive Conyard Green shown and named on Faden's map of 1783. Its very irregular shape and the completely new road network created over the area makes it impossible to trace its former boundaries on the present landscape with any accuracy. It is remembered in Conyer's Green. Catshall Green, a northern extension of the extensive Blowthorn Heath and also shown and named on the same map, lay on either side of the lane connecting Green Lane with Mount Road and was bordered by Catshall Farm and Tyburn Barn. Church Green lay near the church.

Ancient Cross.

An ancient stone Cross known as Pleiste was mentioned in 1613 as being situated on Church Green, to the S of the churchyard.

Site of old Windmill.

A post mill is shown beside The Mill House on the S side of Mill Road, N of the village in 1783. It was demolished in 1920.

Historic Houses & Ancient Moated Sites.

Necton Old Hall stood on the edge of a very large common called Conyard Green, N of the village. A later farmhouse on the site was described in 1910 as situated up a 'loke' entered from the road which bounded the W side of the park of Barton Hall. It was surrounded by a square moat, with a portion of a former strong earthen rampart 100' long indicating a former defensive addition. The moat was crossed on its northern side where a bridge was previously sited, and the house itself stood 'as it has stood for the last 350 years, facing W and touching the edge of the moat on its western side'. Though previously a manor house and later a farmhouse, it was by this time divided into three cottages. John Maunsell died 'seized of the manor of Necton Hall or Conyers Hall' in 1271 and it was subsequently vested in the Nectons and the Conyers. Nicholas Conyer held in 1375. Today the Hall has gone and only the western moat, reasonably complete, with two short extensions to the E and a small remnant to the S, remains. Barton Hall, built by Robert Audley c1624, was destroyed by fire in 1914, though the NW corner of the Hall ruins still stand to their full height. The Hall had a park with a herd of deer but this has now largely been built over. The original manor house on the site known as Barton Old Hall was built by Thomas Folkes and was later the seat of the Bunbury family, one of whom was a celebrated caricaturist. An entry in a Terrier of 1566 describes it as including a hall, private chamber, buttery, 2 rooms called 'le maydschamber' a solar over the parlour, a kitchen and kitchen chamber, another solar over the kitchen and a servant chamber. It is thought to be represented by the present Manor Farm S of the village.

GREAT BEALINGS *(2½ miles W of Woodbridge)*

Carlford Hundred. 'Settlement of the dwellers in the glade or by the funeral pyre' or 'Clearing of the Ingas (OE) *Belinges* (DB). Includes the Domesday vill of Seckford.

Manors. Great Bealings (C13 Sir Hugh de Peche). *Sub-Manors.* Seckford Hall.

Tumulus & Ancient Industrial Site.

In the park NE of Rosary Farm and S of Bealings House, 'an ancient mound which has yielded up pottery, two urns and flint tools, and is supposed to have been British, has been found in the parish', suggesting that the alternative place-name of 'Settlement of the dwellers by the funeral pyre' would, in this case, seem appropriate.

GREAT BEALINGS *(continued)*

In 1978 a furnace used for smelting iron ores was discovered on 'Rookery Mound' as it was known, along with Iron-Age pottery and flint implements. This is probably the same site.

Ancient Ford.
The name of Seckford comes from Sedgeford, an ancient ford which crossed the river Finn in the parish.

Ancient Wayside Cross.
It was said that 'near this tumulus is the pedestal of an ancient Wayside Cross'. (*see above*)

Free Chapel.
The last reference to the Free Chapel of St Peter situated in the parish was when the last chaplain, a certain Robert Wright, was instituted in 1596.

Medieval Market & Fair.
There was the grant of a market and fair to Bealings in 1271. Whilst the grant does not specify whether it applied to Great or Little Bealings, it was likely to the de Seckford family who resided here.

Historic Houses & Ancient Moated Site.
Seckford Hall, 1½ miles E of the church, is an Elizabethan mansion incorporating an early Tudor timber-framed building. It was the former home of Woodbridge's great benefactor, Sir Thomas Seckford, Master of Requests in the reign of Elizabeth I. The Seckfords were seated on this ancient site from the time of Edward I to that of Charles I. The parish boundary between Bealings and Martlesham passes through the Hall and the doorposts were used for the customary 'bumping' ceremony when the bounds were beaten at Rogationtide. The derelict mansion was rescued in the late 1940s by Sir Ralph Harwood who restored it to its former glory and created a high-class hotel. The manor house of Bealings Hall which stood near the church was taken down c1780. It was the seat of Hugh Petches and later John Pitt moved here from Crows Hall, Debenham.

GREAT BLAKENHAM *(5 miles NW of Ipswich)*

Bosmere & Claydon Hundred. 'Blaca's homestead or enclosure' (OE) *Blac(he)ham* (DB)
Manors. Great Blakenham Manor (C11 William Gifford, Earl of Buckingham gave the manor towards the foundation of the alien priory [*see below*]).

Ancient Woodland.
Great Wood, W of the church, is a part of ancient woodland.

Roman Road (?)
Until it turned N to cross the Gipping at Sharmford, the old Roman road from Colchester to Caister St Edmund via Coddenham may possibly be traced by the old Ipswich-Stowmarket road (B1113) NW through the parish.

Site of Priory.
In this parish a small alien priory was established as cell to the great Benedictine Abbey of Bec c1092 during the time of William Rufus; this followed the gift of the manor to the abbey by Walter Gifford, Earl of Buckenham. By 1291 it was under the control of Ogbourne St George Priory in Wiltshire when it served merely as a grange. In 1442 after the dissolution of the alien priories it was granted to Eton College.

Medieval Green.
Recent building development has uncovered medieval pottery and ditch features associated with the former edge of a green which once occupied an area S of the church and NW of Hackney's Corner. It is not named or shown on Faden's map of 1783 and may already have gone by this time.

Historic House.
The Manor was given by Walter Gifford, Earl of Buckingham, to Bec Abbey in Normandy. The former manor house which stood SE of the church and close by the river Gipping, has gone; the site covered by industrial works.

GREAT BRADLEY *(6 miles N of Haverhill)*

Risbridge Hundred. 'Broad clearing' (OE) *Bradeleia* (DB)
Manors. Great Bradley (C12/C13 Bigot family ?).

Ancient Woodland.
Hart Wood in the S of the parish is part of ancient woodland, as are Bradley Park Wood, College Grove and Bases Wood in the N. Bradley Park Wood is enclosed by an external ditch with traces of an internal bank along the S boundary where established hedges suggest the wood has a possible C9-C10 origin and was probably later a part of large park associated with the former Hall. While parks were rarely shown in any detail, Faden's map of 1783 does name Park Wood and shows it as extensive woodland.

Medieval Greens.
Pound Green and Ever Green formed a linear green extending S from (and incorporating) the main village (Pound Green), to Ever Green Farm, and W nearly to the spring, source of the infant river Stour (Ever Green). East Green, a triangular green E of the village, covered the area of College Farm and extended along the track SSW to the Bradley road. Another tiny triangular green called Longacre Green occupied the area on the northern parish boundary marked by tracks running NW and W from Longacre Green Farm.

Medieval Fair.
The village formerly had an annual September fair.

Site of old Windmill.
A windmill is shown by Mill Farm on the B1061 road N of the village in 1783. It was demolished in 1949.

Historic Houses & Ancient Moated Sites.
The moated site of the ancient Hall adjoins the churchyard. Its large rectangular moat is now dry but its defences must have been very strong judging by the huge ditch which runs along the S side. Another, later C16 moat, joins it to the E. The manor was anciently held by the Somerie family. Two wet arms of a moat survive in a T-shaped earthworks beside Ever Green Farm. C18-C19 brick rubble lies on the surface within the enclosure. The Fox & Goose public house has C16 origins.

GREAT BRICETT *(7 miles S of Stowmarket)*

Bosmere & Claydon Hundred. 'Fold or stable infected with gadflies'? (OE) *Brieseta* (DB)
Manors. Great Bricett Manor (1096 the manor was given to the church on the foundation of the alien priory; 1444 granted to Kings College, Cambridge).

Ancient Park & Woodland.
Park Wood (formerly Bricet Park) and Out Wood to the S, are the only remaining fragments of the ancient woodland no doubt associated with a great park belonging to the Augustinian Priory. Part was destroyed during the creation of the airfield runways.

Roman Road.
The course of a Roman road runs ESE-WNW forming a part of the northern parish boundary through Wattisham Airbase. It can be traced on the ground along the road through the base and then the public road from W of Three Releet Farm to Broad View Farm. The old road was found to be 16' wide and 40' between the flanking ditches.

Pre-Historic, Roman & Medieval Settlement Site.
Fieldwalking in two arable fields S of the line of the Roman road on Wattisham Airbase, prior to housing development in 1993, revealed significant amounts of medieval pottery including C12 glazed Stamford ware (exceeedingly rare on rural sites in Suffolk and even in towns like Ipswich) suggesting occupation of the site from at least the C12 to C14. Trial trenching revealed a cobbled track, Roman ditches and pottery, including prehistoric, with beaker pottery of the Early Bronze Age and sherds of Neolithic ware. A number of medieval post-holes associated with buildings were also discovered. The features and early pottery were in the area of the guardhouse which was known to have overlain a C1-C2 Roman site. All features on the ground in this northern part of the parish, apart from a remaining section of Park Wood, have been obliterated by the airfield.

GREAT BRICETT *(continued)*

Site of Priory, Chantry and Ancient Defensive Monastic Earthworks.

The site of a priory of Augustinian Canons, founded in 1110 by Ralph FitzBrian and his wife Emma and dedicated to St Leonard, stands W of the church at a place known as 'Nunnery Fields'. It was richly endowed with the manor and tithes of Bricett and of Smithfield in London, along with other property. Americ Petche, a descendant of the founder, later founded a chantry in the chapel. Although originally independent, sometime in the C13 it became a cell of the Abbey of Nobiliac in France and placed under the protection of Herbert de Lozinge, 1st Bishop of Norwich. It maintained 4-6 canons in 1291 and suffered a major fire in 1416. As an alien priory it was dissolved in 1427 and in 1444 granted to the Provost and fellows of King's College, Cambridge. The priory church survives as a part of the parish church, and of the monastic buildings, a farmhouse on the site of the former Hall immediately adjoining the church incorporates most of the W range of the cloister buildings. The site of the refectory and dormitory can still be traced. Around the site of the Priory is a defensive system comprising twin circular moats adjoining one another, whilst to the W of the church stands Nunnery Mount, 82yds in diameter enclosed by a moat c14yds wide and 2'6" to 8' deep. Building debris on the island suggests it once held the priory's domestic buildings.

Medieval Greens.

Wallow Lane forms the southern parish boundary and the S side of a former linear green shown and named Green Street Green on Faden's map of 1783. Its eastern limit is shown in field boundaries just E of the B1078 road and Wallow Farm in Offton parish formed the western termination. A small green, not marked on this map, stands opposite the church of St Mary and St Lawrence.

Site of old Windmill.

Mill House, W of the B1078, marks the site of a windmill shown by Faden in 1783. It was demolished in 1954.

Medieval Market & Fairs.

The grant of a market to be held on Tuesdays, and two fairs held on the festivals of St. Leonard and St. Lawrence, was made (probably to the Priory who held the manor) in 1135.

Historic House.

Finds during an investigation in 1956 within the farmhouse which incorporates the former manor house (*see above*) has identified it as a very early aisled hall-house. Some structural woodwork of the highest interest was discovered - a wall with bold cross-bracing and, at its foot, four arched doorways of timber, three of the same size and a smaller one with dog-tooth ornament on jambs and arch. That alone dates the oak to some time before 1300 and makes it one of the oldest wooden houses still standing.

GREAT CORNARD *(1 mile SE of Sudbury)*

Babergh Hundred. 'Cultivated land used for growing corn' (OE) *Cornerda* (DB). Cornard was anciently called 'Corn-earth' and became the property of a family who assumed the name.

Manors. Cornard Magna/Abbas Hall (C12 Serlio de Cornerthe). *Sub-Manors.* Greys.

Ancient Woodland.

Abbas Hall Wood is ancient woodland associated with the Hall.

Roman Road.

Valley Road traces the course of a Roman road providing the parish boundary with Newton SSE from TL905 419 to the junction with the A134 Sudbury road. From here its course is marked by field boundaries to Newton Leys.

Roman Tile Industry.

The Romans had a tile industry in the parish.

Medieval Green & Common.

Cornard Heath, a large common on the NE corner of the parish, was named and shown on Faden's map of 1783 as occupying the triangle created by the junction of the Sudbury road and the RomanValley Road. It was enclosed in 1813 and part is now incorporated into a nursery. Upper Tye was a long narrow green now

GREAT CORNARD *(continued)*

replaced by the road from Poplars Farm at Cornard Tye, S to Little Cornard passing to the E of Abbas Hall Wood.

Workhouse.

A workhouse was recorded here with 20 inmates in 1776.

Historic Houses & Ancient Moated Site.

Abbas Hall, possibly dating from 1290, is situated E of the main residential area of the parish. Abbas stems traditionally from 'Abbess', the property being in the ownership of the Abbey of Mallings in Kent during the reign of Henry VIII. The present Elizabethan house hides the C14 two-bay aisled hall-house of the manor of Abbas. Great Greys in the SE corner of the parish is on the site of the former manor house of Greys Hall, residence of the de Greys, lords of the manor of Greys (which included land in the adjoining parish of Newton) from the early C14; they were to hold the manor for the next 450 years. Poplars Farm in Cornard Tye NE of the parish is an old house, and S of the parish on a road junction by the school, in an area known as The Wrongs, is an irregular quadrangular moat.

GREAT FINBOROUGH *(2½ miles SW of Stowmarket)*

Stow Hundred. 'Heaped-up mound' (OE) *Fineberga* (DB)

Manors. Finborough Magna (1254 Robert Musgrove). *Sub-Manors.* Finborough al Ardens al Arders al Adders; Cantilupe's al Cantelowes al Cantelo's; Boyton Hall.

Ancient Woodland.

Of three sections of ancient woodland still remaining in the N of the parish in the 1950s - Temple Grove, Middle Grove and Whites Grove - only the former remains.

Site of Iron-Age/Roman Settlement (?)

Field-names and a small trial excavation strongly suggest the possibility of an Iron-Age/Romano-British settlement in the parish.

Ancient Earthworks & Site of Battle (?)

A hill or mound called Devil's Hill is situated on a golf course in Finborough Park in the NW corner of the parish. Tradition states that a part of this natural rise is artificial (*see above)*, raised as a defence in Saxon times. The 'Battle of Finnesburn' is said to have been fought out here when Danes falling back from Thetford in 1005 encountered the Saxon army. "For five long days the battle's sound was heard by Finburghe's earth-raised mound." Eventually, the determined force of defenders won the day. The wounded leader of the attackers withdrew his battle-stained forces declaring that "they had never met a worse hand-play" and left behind a tiny but victorious garrison, its members weary and wounded, but with spirits "undiminished and unquell'd." Unfortunately, tradition is all we have to go on as there is no evidence for the event. A similar story is told of a Saxon-Danish battle at Old Newton only a few miles away (*see* Old Newton). Is this another suggested site for the battle or another incident in the same conflict ?

Medieval Green.

A triangular green, named and shown as Hoistead Green on Faden's 1783 map, lay on the eastern side of High Road. Cagman's Lane entered the green from the W and left it heading SE past High Street Green Farm (the name given to the area on the present OS map). Only the southern end survives as grassland; the narrow N end is now incorporated into neighbouring fields and private gardens.

Historic Houses & Ancient Moated Sites.

The present Finborough Hall in its 200 acre park was rebuilt by Roger Pettiward in 1795 following the fire which destroyed the former Elizabethan house. The manor was granted by Elizabeth I to Henry Gilbert and an ornamental carved bressumer in the stables bears the initials 'HG'. Boarded Barn Farm at High Street Green, (now known as West End Farm), has three sides of a moat. It was anciently called Adders Hall and was the manor house of Finborough Magna. Its name was a corruption of the de Arden family who held the manor as a knight's fee belonging to the Bishop of Ely's manor of Hitcham in the C13.

GREAT GLEMHAM or Glemham Magna or North Glemham *(4 miles W of Saxmundham)*

Plomesgate Hundred. 'Homestead or village noted for its games and revelry'? (OE) *Glaimham* (DB)
Manors. North Glemham al Glemham Magna (1263 Hugh de Cressy). *Sub-Manors.* Great Glemham/ Lowdham Hall.

Ancient Woodland.
High Grove Wood by Low Road in the W of the parish, and Haw Wood in the E, are fragments of ancient woodland.

Site of Watermill (?)
Mill Farm was the later name of Mansion House (*see below*). The fact that the site is beside what appears to be a millpool on a tributary of the river Ore suggests a former watermill here. The house and the probable mill have long gone.

Historic Houses.
Hall Farm on the northern parish boundary stands on the site of Great Glemham Hall, the 'Manor of Great Glemham or Lowdham Hall' belonging to Butley Priory and after the Dissolution granted to Anne of Cleeves by Henry VIII. After Anne's death it was granted to William Edgar whose family continued to live at the Hall until the C18. From 1796 to 1801 it was occupied by the poet George Crabbe as a tenant of the North family of Little Glemham Hall. The E-shaped hall was probably demolished after Samuel Kilderbee built the new Hall, known as Glemham House, for the Duke of Hamilton in 1814. The eastern part of the parish comprising some 200 acres was then emparked and laid out by Humphrey Repton. Samuel himself lived at 'Mansion House' E of the church and N of The D Wood.

GREAT LIVERMERE or Livermere Magna *(5 miles NNE of Bury St Edmunds)*

Thedwestry Hundred. 'Pool with thick (muddy) water' or 'Liver-shaped pool' or 'Lake where rush or iris grow' (OE) *Leuuremer* (c1050) *Liuermera* (DB)
Manors. Livermere Magna al Uphall al Brome Hall (C13 Matthew de Thelnetham). *Sub-Manors.* Livermere Magna/Grange.

Ancient Woodland.
Slades Covert, N of the village, is a part of ancient woodland.

Ancient Mere.
The ancient liver-shaped muddy pool referred to in the place-name still exists as the mere now transformed into a landscaped serpentine lake (*see below*).

Roman Road.
The course of a Roman road has been traced in cropmarks WNW-ESE from Ampton Water, crossing the road to Timworth N of Wadgate House, passing through Fox Spinney, crossing the road to Thurston, and leaving the parish just N of Puttockshill

Village Emparking
In 1709 Thomas Lee of Kensington purchased Little Livermere (Livermere Parva) - to the N of the mere referred to in the place-name - from the Coke family and in 1715, Great Livermere (Livermere Magna) to the S. He was succeeded by Baptist Lee in 1724 who, after coming into great wealth sometime in the 1730s, created a 1,000 acre deer park in the centre of the two parishes. Joined by James Calthorpe from the adjoining parish of Ampton, he created a serpentine lake of some 60 acres running through the park 'for their mutual convenience as well as for ornament and pleasing views and prospects' from their respective lands and grounds. The park was enclosed with a pale fence, and scattered strips of glebe and town land in Great Livermere were exchanged for enclosing outside the park. (*see also* Little Livermere)

Free School.
Calthorpe's Charity School was founded in 1692 by James Calthorpe for six boys from Ampton, Great and Little Livermere, Ingham and Timworth. They were to wear blue caps and coats, the latter monogrammed 'J. C.'. The site of the school is not known.

GREAT LIVERMERE *(continued)*

Historic House & Ancient Moated Site.
A wooded site SW of the church, partially surrounded by an impressive moat, is the probable site of Brome Hall which was succeeded by Livermere Hall. The manor, also known as Uphall as early as the C13, was owned by the Thelnethams in 1327. The Claxton family were Lords in the 1670s - Elizabeth Claxton who died in 1683 is listed as having a house with 17 hearths in 1674. William Sakings, its next owner, died in 1689 and is buried in the churchyard; he was falconer to three monarchs, Charles I, Charles II and James II. The manor and hall then came into the hands of the Coke family, one of whom, Arundell, was hanged for the attempted murder of his brother-in-law in 1722. It was then purchased by the Lee family who presumably built the new hall or enlarged the existing one. The hall was demolished in 1923.

GREAT SAXHAM *(5 miles SW of Bury St Edmunds)*

Thingoe Hundred. 'The Saxons' (or Seaxa's) homestead' (OE) *Saxham* (DB)
Manors. Saxham Magna (Abbot of St. Edmunds, Bury; 1541 Sir Richard Long). *Sub-Manors.* Wodethorpe Hall.

Ancient Woodland.
Hearse Wood, The Park, and Little Papeley Wood N of the parish, are ancient woodland.

Medieval Green.
An area named Frizzeler's (or Fressel's Green) on the present OS map, situated S of the church and E of Hearse Wood, is not named or shown on Faden's 1783 map. It did show the whole area encompassed by the great 140 acre park connected with the hall, and it may well be that the green was lost during the park's creation. The green took its name from the family of Frezill who anciently held the manor.

Deserted Medieval Village (?)
No village exists here, only modern development either side of the country road leading from the church and hall to the Little Saxham to Barrow road. Maurice Beresford includes it in his list of lost medieval villages of England, and if indeed a medieval village did once exist centred on the church it may well have been removed when the hall's park was created. This park is shown by Faden totally enveloping the parish from the Barrow road in the N to Frogsend Farm on the southern parish boundary.

Historic Houses.
The manor was held for several generations by the Eldred family, one of whom, John, built Nutmeg Hall, naming it after the nutmegs and other spices he first introduced into England. In the park near the rectory is an ancient thorn known as 'Eldred's Thorn'; the tradition being that beneath this thorn was John's favourite seat. The old hall was accidentally burned down in 1779. Its site lies to the SE of Saxham Hall, a late C18 mansion standing in a fair sized park said to have been 'embellished' by Capability Brown. On Frizzle's Green (a corruption of Fressel's Green), S of the church near Herstwood, stood the moated manor house of Sir Walter de Fressel who retained it until 1368. This family were listed here as early as 1286 when a Walter Fresel held a house and 60 acres for a rent of seventeen shillings from the Abbot at Bury Abbey. Part of the moat remains.

GREAT THURLOW or Thurlow Magna *(4 miles NE of Haverhill)*

Risbridge Hundred. 'Burial mound of the warriors (or nobles)' (OE) *Tridlauua* (DB). Claude Morley translates it as *thrythe hlaw* - 'Lady Thryth's Tumulus'.
Manors. Great Thurlow (1272 Sir Gilbert Peche). *Sub-Manors.* Wadgell's Hall; Temple End.

Ancient Woodland.
There are areas of ancient woodland E of the village at Wadgell's Wood, Grove Wood and Trundley Wood, and W of the village at The New Plantation.

Site of Tumulus (?)
Both its place-name and ancient spelling 'Tritlaw', meaning famous tumulus or assembly hill, indicate a large

GREAT THURLOW *(continued)*

burial mound situated in the parish, probably later utilised as a meeting place. It may have been used as an administrative centre for the rural community of what became in 1044 the 'Liberty of St Edmund', but which had been the same administrative area (measured as 8½ Hundreds) that had been in operation well before this time. The adjoining parish of Little Thurlow has a mound beside the Great Bradley road N of the village which later supported a windmill, but the most likely suggestion comes from Norman Scarfe who suspects a possible ritual cursus in the area. Little Thurlow again provides the probable site in the parish itself which is linear, running almost due E-W and widening to a spot known as Temple End by Temple Stream. Low Farm here was named 'Temple' on Faden's map. Although the Knights Templars had a preceptory in the area, what was actually sited at this spot is not known and would reward investigation.

Alien Hospital or Free Chapel.

A small hospital or free chapel was sited here subordinate to the foreign hospital of Hautpays. It was dedicated to St James and founded in the reign of Richard II for the poor, aged and infirm by the Earl of Boulogne. As an alien house it was taken by the Crown in the C14, and in 1463, Edward IV included it among the numerous endowments to the Maison de Dieu in Cambridge, now part of Kings College. Its site is not known.

Medieval Green.

Sowley Green, shown but not named on Faden's map of 1783, lies on the junction of Bury Road and the present A143 road, E of the village.

Medieval Market & Fair.

A grant was obtained by Sir Gilbert Peche for a market here in 1272, and later an annual toy fair.

Historic Houses & Ancient Moated Sites.

Great Thurlow Hall is mid-Georgian in date but stands on the site of an earlier hall. Wadgell's Farm, 1½ miles E of the village, is surrounded by a very strong embanked moat of unusual type, now mostly infilled. There is a perfect quadrangular moat on the Withersfield road on the site of Glebe Farm at the western end of Glebe Plantation SW of the village near the vicarage, and another, partly drained, square moat at Sowley Green.

GREAT WALDINGFIELD or Waldingfield Magna *(3 miles NE of Sudbury)*

Babergh Hundred. 'Open land of the forest dwellers' (OE) *Wealdingafeld* (c995) *Waldingefelda* (DB)
Manors. Carbonels or Butlers (1275 Thomas Carbonel). *Sub-Manors.* Badley al Peyton Hall; Brandeston Hall; Moreves al Morefes al Sarres with Storkenest; Sandesfords al Stanford; Dowres/Dowayres.

Roman Road.

Valley Road follows the course of a Roman road SSE-NNW to form the parish boundary with Chilton. Its course is lost under the disused airfield just N of White Hall Farm but continued NNW to join the Roman road from Bridge Street in Long Melford. Another Roman road from Long Melford crossed NE to form the northern parish boundary, its course marked by School Farm Lane and a short length of hedgerow E of Washmere Green.

Hundred Meeting Place.

Barrow Hill, on the former Babergh Heath, was the probable meeting place for the Hundred Court in Saxon times. The heath takes its name from Badan Beorh meaning the hill mound or tumulus of Bada and has given name to the Hundred.

Medieval Heath & Green.

On Faden's 1783 map, Babergh Heath is named and shown covering an area approximately from Babergh Hall and Babergh Place in the N, tapering down to the junction of Valley Road and Waldingfield Road in the S. Its western limits roughly following the parish boundary and its eastern, Waldingfield Street, plus an extension now occupied by a development known as The Garrison. Old properties originally lined its edge, few if any of which appear to remain today. The northern section of the former heath has been enclosed and the southern section is now mainly covered by a housing development which traces its original shape either side of the road. Dyer's Green is unnamed on Faden's map but shown as a long rectangular green replacing the present road SW

GREAT WALDINGFIELD *(continued)*

towards the village from the junction of the present B1071 and B1115 roads to Babergh Place. Upsher Green, named on the present OS map but not on that of 1783, is shown on the latter as little more than a widening at a right-angle bend in the country road from Waldingfield Church to Edwardstone just to the W of Powers Farm. Properties and gardens now occupy and define the former area.

Historic Houses & Ancient Moated Sites.

C17 Babergh Hall, former seat of the Keddingtons, lords of the manor, is situated on the road to Acton. Brandeston Hall in the N of the parish and dating from the C16/C17, stands on the site of the former manor house and retains a large part of the former moat. Brandeston Manor Hall was held by Ralph de Curbespine of the Bishop of Bayeux in the C11-C12. In the time of Edward I it belonged to the Bavent family and was given to the Nunnery of Dartford in Kent c1360. Dyer's Green Farm, SW of Holbrook Park, has two sides of an oblong moat, and a series of other earthworks and cropmarks seen in aerial photos. High Trees, close to the church, is of C16 date, as is White Hall, 1 mile SW. Gable Cottage is believed to date from the C14.

GREAT WENHAM or Wenham Magna *(4½ miles SE of Hadleigh)*

Samford Hundred. 'Homestead or enclosure with pastureland' (OE) *Wenham* (DB). Kirby calls it Wenham Magna and Burnt Wenham in the C18. It has also taken the name Wenham Combusta.
Manors. Wenham Magna/Brent Wenham (1281 Priory of Leights, Essex; 1536 Sir Richard Cavendish). *Sub-Manors.* Boyton Hall.

Ancient Woodland.

Brimlin Wood in the N of the parish is ancient woodland, at one time probably associated with the ancient manor house at Vauxhall just to the W.

Historic Houses & Ancient Moated Sites.

The timber-framed houses of Priory Farm, NE of the church, and Wenham Hill Farm and Wenham Place to the S, all date from Tudor times; the former taking its name from the fact that the manor was later appropriated to Leigh Priory in Essex. There is an ancient circular moat at Vauxhall, about 1½ miles N, site of the original manor house of the Vaux family and named Farce Hall on Faden's 1783 map. The rectory is Elizabethan (enlarged 1869), and cropmarks E of The Robins, S of the parish, may be those of a former medieval moat.

GREAT WHELNETHAM or Welnetham Magna *(4 miles SSE of Bury St Edmunds)*

Thedwestry Hundred. 'Enclosure frequented by swans near a water-wheel (or some other circuar feature)' (OE) *Hvelfiham* (DB) *Weluetham* (1170). The place-name probably refers to the ancient mere at Sicklesmere, a hamlet to the N of the parish (and a possible ancient watermill?).
Manors. Whelnetham Magna (C13 Edmund de Welnetham). *Sub-Manors.* Sicklesmere/Sygelsmer; Copdock's/Cobdoes/Copdoes.

Roman Road.

The course of a Roman road running virtually S-N bisects an eastern extension of the parish from TL893 581 to Water Lane at TL894 591. It is not evident on the ground.

Site of Large Roman Settlement & Cemetery.

A large Roman settlement and burial site dating from the C1-C4, which included the foundations of a Roman villa, have been discovered in the N of the parish in the hamlet of Sicklesmere by the river Lark. Camden talks of 'great quantities of potsherds and platters of Roman manufacture, also ashes and bones of sheep and oxen, many horns, a sacrificial knife, urns and other relics'. At the beginning of the C18, Sir Richard Gipps of the manor house found the head of a Roman spear, a sacrificial knife, vessels, coins, bricks and paterae, one of which was inscribed *'anisim'.*

Site of Roman Camp (?)

The *Victoria County History* states under Great Whelnetham in its listing of unidentified earthworks: 'To the E

GREAT WHELNETHAM *(continued)*

of the hamlet of Sicklesmere, the base of a rounded slope is scarped to a depth of 8', upon which a fragment of a rampart 3' high remains. This looks towards the S across the site of the ancient mere - formed by the waters of the river Lark - and confronts another site which has yielded abundant relics of Roman occupation *(referring to above)*. Around the N and W sides of the area from which Roman relics have been excavated, and extending far towards the SW, is a manorial bank'. Basil Brown suggested it may have been a camp by quoting G. B. Barham who many years ago described 'considerable remains of the ramparts on the S and SW sides' as being 'still visible'.

Ancient (?) Mounds.
Three small mounds lie in the parish: one, situated by the Stanningfield to Great Whelnetham road just N of Moor Green Farm, is c33' x 16½' in size; another is further N and W of the same road, by Grove Cottages; and there is a third along Bell Lane by Brook Green. Their age and purpose are unknown.

Medieval Green.
Moor Green is named and shown as a rectangular green on Faden's 1783 map running NNW from Smithies Farm in Stanningfield Parish, past the junction with Old Lane, and replacing the present road to Great Whelnetham village which forms the SW parish boundary. Its northern limit was marked by a windmill which stood at the point where a track called Mill Lane crosses the road. Cocks Green and Cocks Green Lane, shown and named on the present OS map SE of the village, whilst appearing of ancient origin, are not shown in 1783.

Site of old Windmill.
A post mill which stood to the N of Moor Green in 1783 with Mill Lane (now a track) leading off SW, was dismantled c1949.

Site of Workhouse (?)
Great Workhouse Field on the 1843 Tithe map suggests a workhouse once existed here; Church Cottages are a possible site.

Historic Houses & Ancient Moated Sites.
The C16 timber-framed Great Whelnetham Hall, seat of the Gipp family for several generations, retains a complicated but incomplete system of ancient defensive moats from an earlier hall. This hall was home to the de Whelnethams - in 1365 Simon de Sudbury, Bishop of London, granted "forty days pardon" to anyone who cared to pray for the soul of Sir John de Whelnetham, Knight, and Lady Alice, his wife. The rectory dates from Elizabethan times. Copdoe's Farm probably occupies the site of Copdoes Manor House. Thomas de Weyland held this manor in the latter years of the C13, and in 1369 it passed through marriage to the De Spencers, one of whom, Thomas, became the husband of Constance, daughter of Edmund Plantaganet, Duke of York. The Rushbrooke Arms public house in the hamlet of Sicklesmere dates from the C16.

GREAT WRATTING or Wratting Magna *(2½ miles NE of Haverhill)*

Risbridge Hundred. 'Place where crosswort or hellebore grows' (OE) *Wratinga* (DB) Also formerly known as Tallow Wratting.
Manors. Wratting Magna (-1184 de Clare family; c1184 Gilbert de Vere).

Ancient Woodland.
Abbacy Wood and Ganwick Wood are parts of ancient woodland.

Site of Roman Building.
The *Gentleman's Magazine* of 1804 reported the discovery of great quantities of Roman pottery, coins, urns, etc. in a field belonging to Sotterly Green Farm.

Site of Battle (?)
Red Field is reputedly the site of the Battle of Risbridge fought in 635 A.D. between Sigeburt, King of East Anglia, and Penda, King of Mercia.

GREAT WRATTING *(continued)*

Medieval Green.

Wratting Green is named by Faden in 1783 and shown as a small green lying at the angle where a track from Burton Ley Plantation joins Witherfield Road, W of the village. It is now edged with modern properties.

Site of Gallows (?)

Fields named 'Gallows Field', 'Little Gallows Field' 'Long Gallows Field' and 'Gallows Field Bottom', N of Gravel Pit Plantation, suggest the site of a former medieval gibbet.

Site of old Windmill.

A windmill and Millhouse which stood SW of Ganwick Farm in 1780 had gone by 1840 leaving only a mound.

Workhouse.

Vernons Workhouse was in existence in 1747 and disused by 1840 (apart from one section 'occupied rent-free by one person of the parish'). It was located in a messuage called Weathercock Farm.

Historic Houses & Ancient Moated Site.

'The Ganwick' was the oldest house in the village dating back to the C13. Ganwick Farm, on the eastern parish boundary, occupies the small quadrangular (now dry) moated site. Old maps mark the site 'Ancient Remains'. The Red Lion public house dates from the C15/C16.

GROTON *(6 miles W of Hadleigh)*

Babergh Hundred. 'Sandy or pebbly stream' (OE) *Grotena* (DB)

Manors. Groton Manor (C11/C12 Abbot of St. Edmunds, Bury - leased to Robert de Cokefeld in 1286. Apparently the ownership was determined by a most unlikely duel between the Abbot and Cokefield which the Abbot lost).
Sub-Manors. Castelins/Castelyns.

Ancient Woodland.

Groton Wood in the NE of the parish, and Winding Wood and Mill Wood on the western parish boundary, are parts of ancient woodland.

Ancient Motte & Meeting Place (?)

Three footpaths meet at Pitches Mount in Groton Park where an earthen mound c20' high with a ramparted flat top c143 yds in circumference, stands on an elevated site with expansive views over the surrounding countryside. The base is stepped out to form a ring and create a narrow platform. The mound has been mutilated on the NE for the extraction of gravel. Though the light soil has led to land slip and infilling, there is still evidence of a moat and there also appears signs of a possible small bailey to the NW, but the ground has been considerably disturbed. In the late C12, Jocelin de Brakelond recorded that in the time of King Stephen the vills of Groton and Semer were granted for life to Adam de Cockfield because he could defend the vills against the holders of the neighbouring castles at Milden and Offton as he had his own castle at Lindsey. The Cockfields continued to hold Groton down to c1198 after which it was held under the Abbot of Bury by Gilbert Peccatum (Peche or Pecche). The name Pitchers may date back to the Pecche family, for although Groton House was occupied by a John Pytches from c1804, and it was no doubt he who turned the mound into a garden feature (making the stepped platform?) when he created the park around it, the fact that two fields which predate his purchase of the house are named 'Pitches Field' would suggest that its likely origin is with a medieval lord and therefore more ancient. The meeting of what may be ancient footpaths at this point - coming in from the N, E, and W (which includes one from the S) via a ford or bridge across the stream, and the presence of Parliament Heath, a small green to the N, suggest an ancient meeting place for the judicial court, later adapted by the Normans.

Medieval Greens.

Parliament Heath, named on Faden's 1783 map, was shown as a small green situated in the N of the parish with houses on its N and S sides. It is now enclosed. Castlings Heath to the E of this comprised 29 acres

GROTON *(continued)*

belonging to a John Webb on the tithe map. It was shown in 1783 edged with properties on most sides. The western half is now enclosed and the southern extant, towards Gosling Green, has now been infilled with houses. The green took its name from Castlings Hall which stood on its northern edge (*see below*). In his diary for 1595, Adam Winthrop records " . . . and on Munday in Witsunweeke ther did come a swarme of bees flyeing ouer Castleynes heathe into Carter's grounds." The present OS map shows Butcher's Lane running N from Boxford village entering Groton parish and turning NE at the hamlet of Horner's Green, then heading to Gosling Green before turning N to Castling's Heath. Faden does not show a green at either place or indeed even the lane. If there were greens here, they may have already gone by 1783.

Almshouses.
Almshouses comprising four tenements were recorded here in 1702.

Workhouse.
A workhouse in the village had 30 inmates in 1776.

Historic Houses & Ancient Moated Sites.
The Elizabethan Groton Hall was home to the Winthrop family, one of whom, John, led the main local exodus to New England in America in 1629, becoming the first governor of Massachusetts. At Moat Farm, Parliament Heath, are the remains of three sides of a quadrangular moat, and there is also a moat at Castlings Hall in the NE of the parish, the site of Castelins or Castelyns Manor owned by Sir Gilbert Chastelyn in 1292. Manor Farm dates from the C16 and was extended into an L-shaped house in the C17. Farrer suggests that Adam Winthrop (*see above)* may have lived here for some time around 1595 at the time his brother resided at Groton Hall.

GRUNDISBURGH *(3½ miles NW of Woodbridge)*

Carlford Hundred. 'Stronghold at Grundi' or 'Stronghold near the foundation of a building' (OE) or 'Stronghold of Grundi' (OScand) where Grundi is a common name. *Grundesburch* (DB). 'The Stronghold' (Iron-Age Camp) 'near the foundation of a building' (Roman settlement) refer to the adjoining parish of Burgh (*see* Burgh) once a part of Grundisburgh, i.e. 'Grundi's - burgh'.
Manors. Grundisburgh Hall (1270 Sir Hugh Peche).

Medieval Market & Fair.
Sir Hugh Peche obtained the grant of a market here in 1285 and a fair during Whitsun week, both long obsolite.

Historic Houses & Ancient Moated Sites.
Grundisburgh Hall, standing in a small park with a lake 1 mile S of the church, was rebuilt c1500 on the site of the ancient manor house. This had long been the seat of the Blois family. In 1668 they moved to Cockfield Hall, Yoxford. The church has a brass monument to John A'wall who died in 1501. He lived at Bastes, an ancient timber-framed hall-house E of the church and rebuilt by his son, Thomas, c1520. The family of Bast were living in and around Grundisburgh from as early as the C14 - a William Bast is mentioned in 1327. Bridge Farmhouse, 1 mile SE of Grundisburgh Hall, dates from Tudor times and there are three sides of a rectangular moat lying on the S side of the crossroads at Bond's Corner with an 'Island and pond' (tithe map).

GUNTON *(1½ miles N of Lowestoft)*

Mutford & Lothingland Hundred. 'Gunnin's farmstead' (OE) *Guneton* (1198).
Once a separate parish, Gunton has now been enveloped in the urban sprawl of Lowestoft.
Manors. Gunton (C12 Church of St. Michael, Norwich; 1287 Richard de Guneton).

Lost Settlement.
While neither Gunton or Blundeston are mentioned at Domesday, *Dunestuna* (meaning 'farm by the coast sand-hills'), is accorded two entries. Although Suckling and Copinger both identify this with Oulton, the 1275 Hundred Rolls name it as a hamlet of Gunton next Corton. In 1086 it had 60 rateable acres of land with

GUNTON *(continued)*

woodland for 4 swine. It may have been lost to the sea or incorporated into Gunton.

Medieval Heath.

Corton Heath once covered the area in the N of the parish now taken up by the holiday theme park.

Historic House.

Gunton Hall is a modern mansion standing in the northern end of a park. It was built by Thomas Fowler who acquired the manor in 1802. Old Hall near the church was the former manor house and is a building of some interest and antiquity. Richard de Gunton was in possession of the manor in the latter part of the C13 but by 1316 the family had been replaced by the de Loudhams, and afterwards the Blomvilles. A later owner, Hewling Luson, greatly enlarged the hall in 1746 and also discovered on the estate a clay of such remarkable quality that he used it to establish a pottery. Production later moved to Lowestoft but after initial success, eventually failed.

HACHESTON *(4 miles SE of Framlingham)*

Loes Hundred. 'Haecci's farmstead' (OE) *Hacestuna* (DB). Includes the Domesday vill of Glevering.
Manors. Hacheston Manor (C11/C12 Roger Bigot). *Sub-Manors.* Glevering Hall; Canell's/Wicklows; Blomvile's.

Ancient Woodland.

Great Wood and Catt's Wood are parts of ancient woodland.

Roman Road.

A Roman road from Coddenham, c25' wide, passes SW-NE through the S of the parish on line with the old A12.

Roman Settlement & Cemetery.

A major Roman settlement was discovered here, with roadways, timber buildings, rubbish tips, hearths for metal working, pottery kilns and evidence of occupation extending from Claudius to the C4. In the area of Gallows Hill, a Roman cemetery was discovered.

Ancient Industrial Site.

A Romano-British kiln was discovered in 1964 at Bridge Farm, and later, two superimposed double-ended kilns producing cooking pots of C3-C4 type. Several ovens or small furnaces for metalworking have been excavated along with a dump of iron slag discovered in a shallow pit.

Ancient Chapel.

Five skeletons were unearthed, along with medieval pottery, in a field called Chapel Pightle, S of the church, the probable site of Wikkelows Chapel, founded in 1433 by Sir Anthony Boteller.

Site of Medieval Gallows (?)

Gallows Hill is the possible site of a gibbet on the edge of Wickham Market overlooking the Roman road.

Medieval Market & Fair.

Hickling Priory in Norfolk, which held the manor at the end of the C12, obtained the grant for a market and a "considerable" two-day fair in 1218. The fair was abolished as recently as 1872.

Deserted Medieval Settlements.

Glevering, mentioned in Domesday, is now a manor and hamlet of Hacheston. It may well have had a medieval settlement, the remains of which were destroyed during the creation of Glevering Hall Park. A large settlement is shown on Faden's 1783 map E of the river Deben and Wickham Bridge in what is now the hamlet of Lower Hacheston. This area has been decimated by the creation of the A12 Wickham Market bypass and associated slip roads and roundabouts, leaving Bridge Farm, Limetree Farm and a handful of properties.

Ancient Watermill.

Mill House occupies the site of the ancient Fulling Mill in 'fullers medowe'.

Free School.

There was a bequest by Richard Porter in 1701 for the education of twelve poor boys. The school house later fell

HACHESTON *(continued)*

into decay and in 1838 the site was disposed of; it is now a gravel pit. A new school was built in 1825.

Workhouse.
A workhouse with 14 acres of land was recorded in 1607.

Historic Houses & Ancient Moated Sites.
The Gables, N of the church, dates from the late C15; Wistaria Cottage was built c1541, and the former Queens Head, in c1600. Glevering Hall Farm, built in 1792 for Chaloner Arcedeckne, still retains part of the broad moat associated with the former hall, whilst to the N and standing in a park of some 300 acres laid out by Humphrey Repton, is the present hall built by John White in 1792. The manor connected with Glevering Hall was once owned by Leiston Abbey but came into the possession of a John Bull in the late C16. On his death, he was buried with twelve swords and "as many scabbards". Blomville was another Hacheston manor, and this was held by Campsea Ash Priory. The site of the manor house is marked by Blomvyle Hall, a white-brick mansion in Easton Lane, N of the parish. The timber-framed Queens Head public house has plasterwork in the ceiling dating from c1600. It was closed in 1962 and later became a private house. Wisteria Cottage is believed to date back to c1541.

HADLEIGH

Cosford Hundred. 'Heath clearing' (OE) *Hetlega* (DB)
Manors. Hadleigh Hall (Archbishop Lanfranc; 1541 Dean & Chapter of Canterbury). *Sub-Manors.* Plessis/ Pond Hall; Toppesfield/Toppesfield Hall; Mauser's/Hadleigh in Hadleigh; Cosford Hall.
Whilst its claim to be a royal town remains unverified (*see below*), Hadleigh has much to commend it, gaining great wealth and fame as one of the East Anglian cloth towns of the mid C14-C16; by 1568 only Ipswich and Bury were richer. It was incorporated as a borough in 1618, but was forced to surrender its proud charter during the reign of James II, and it was not regranted. The town lost 197 inhabitants to the plague in 1637.

Ancient Woodland.
Fenn's Grove is a part of ancient woodland.

Tumuli.
The 'Herst', an ancient burial mound situated N of the town near the junction of the B1070 and A1071 roads, was probably destroyed by building development. An Iron-Age round barrow 62yds in diameter and surrounded by a double ditch, which lay N of Cosford Bridge, was identified by cropmarks and excavated in 1971 when possible remains of a cremation urn were discovered.

Romano-British Site.
In 1979 a trial trench was cut through a site identified by cropmarks prior to the construction of the Hadleigh bypass (A1071) near the junction with the Whatfield road. Material from Iron-Age to C4 was unearthed. Although no buildings were identified in the limited excavated area, fragments of roof tile were found.

Roman Villa.
A Romano-British building, possibly a villa, was discovered in 1954, SE of the town, just N of the railway track. Flint foundations of two rooms and part of another were excavated by 'boys of Woolverstone LCC school' who found fragments of a hypocaust and furnace, coins, pottery and window glass. The site dated from late C2 - early C3.

Roman Road (?)
Finds in the area of the town along with evidence of long settlement throughout the Roman period *(see above)* strongly suggest an (as yet) unidentified Roman road possibly connecting Margary's 34a from Long Melford to Coddenham and Wickham Market, with that from Stratford St Mary to Coddenham and Caister by Norwich, by way of the suggestively named Stone Street (*Stanestrada*) and the ¾ mile long High Street.

Residence & Burial Site of Danish King (?)
Asser, biographer of Alfred the Great, stated that 'Headleage was once a royal town' referring to the claim that the Danish king, Guthram, resided here after becoming King of East Anglia and was subsequently buried in the

HADLEIGH *(continued)*

predescessor of St Mary's Church following his death in 889 A.D. It is conjectured that the site may possibly be marked by a beautiful C14 tomb in the S aisle, though no attempt has yet been made to verify the claim.

Site of Ancient Monastery (?)
An entry in *Index Monasticus* records a monastery in existence here in the mid C10. The evidence is based on the will of Aethelflaed 962-91 A.D. It may not have been a true monastery and may refer to the Saxon church, the remains of which were discovered in the churchyard S of St Marys Church in 1984 *(also see above)*. Alternatively, the site of Priory Farm may provide a clue; or even Friar's Hill by Friars Hall, NW of the town.

Site of Ancient Chapels.
The site of Peyton Chapel is unknown but was probably accommodated within Peyton Hall, N of the town. Another chapel, founded by Archdeacon Pykenham in 1497, stood by the almshouses in George Street, and a third, a traveller's chapel to Our Lady, stood by Toppersfield Bridge and was mentioned from 1487 to 1524.

Ancient Site (?)
The pattern of streets at Sun Court create a large and obvious semi-circular area crossed by the river Brett. An old property of C16 date within this area is called Sun Court and may, like Nayland with Wissington, suggest a site of ancient and important significance.

Medieval Bridge.
Toppersfield Bridge at the W end of town is a rare survival of a medieval 3-arch bridge dating from the C14 or even earlier. It carries the road to Layham over the river Brett. In 1591 'the Lytell Topsfeild bridge' was decayed and ready to fall down, 'yt was made new agayne by Nicholas Strutt . . .'.

Site of Gallows.
Gallows were said to have stood 'at the Hirst in a place called Hadleigh' probably on the burial mound known as 'The Herst' and 'Gallows Hill' (*see 'Tumuli'*). Mention is also made in 1305 of gallows said to have stood in Hell Street, now George Street.

Site of Pillory & Whipping Post.
A pillory (called 'Tewe') and whipping post were sited opposite the church in 1306.

Site of Mills.
A watermill for corn, with a ducking stool beside the millpond, was recorded in Hadleigh Hall Manor in 1306. At the same time the manor had a windmill for fulling cloth. Two mills are shown on Faden's map of 1783: a post mill on Mill Hill (later moved to Elmsett or Whatfield), and a smock mill which was last worked in 1905 stood N of Frog Hall.

Site of Deer Park.
A rectangular moat is shown on the 1830 tithe map as 'Park Yards'. It may have been the site of a park keeper's lodge, for a licence to create a deer park of 559 acres was granted to Helmyn Legate of Essex, Constable of Windsor Castle, in 1369 following his purchase of Plesses or Pond Hall estate ten years earlier. The deer park is shown on Saxton's map of 1576 as 'Pondhalle Parke' bounded on the N by the linear meadow and track leading to Ramsey Farm, on the S by Pond Hall Road, on the W by Pond Hall, and on the E by Ramsey Wood.

Medieval Heath & Common.
The 77 acres of Aldham Common, NE of the town in Hadleigh parish, was enclosed in1729, and Hadleigh Heath (some distance SW) in 1832. As the place-name suggests the settlement of Hadleigh was created in a 'clearing in the heath', obviously referring to this heath which must at that time have been very extensive. Faden's map shows it considerably reduced in 1783, and on enclosure it only comprised some 20 acres.

Medieval Market & Fairs.
The earliest grant of a market to the town was in 1245 and Gilbert de Kirkeby obtained a grant for a weekly market and annual fair for his manor of Toppesfield Hall in 1252.

HADLEIGH *(continued)*

Site of Martyrdom.
Dr. Rowland Taylor, a Hadleigh rector, was burned at the stake in 1555 on Aldham Common NE of the town for his Catholic teachings during the tyrannous reign of Queen Mary. The spot is still marked by a stone bearing the inscription: 'D Taylor in defending that was good at this plas left his blode'. In 1819 a memorial was erected on the site.

Free Schools.
Many of Hadleigh's charitable donations were for a long period dispensed by a group of trustees collectively known as the Grand Feoffees. The town's free school (later to be amalgamated with the National Schools) was one of their charges to which Elias Jordayn gave £100 in 1655, and Ann Beaumont bequeathed a messuage of land near Hadleigh Bridge upon trust to pay for the instruction and clothing of six poor boys. The grammar school had first been established prior to 1382 in a house in the churchyard. Here 24 free scholars were taught alongside fee paying pupils. The school was discontinued by 1840. Alabasters Elementary School was in existence separately from the grammar school in 1667.

Almshouses.
Almshouses occupied the ground floor of the Markethouse, S of the churchyard *(see below)*. Almshouses in George Street (formerly Magdalen Street), consisting of 12 houses for 24 poor people with an attached chapel, were founded by Archdeacon Pykenham and date from the C15. They were rebuilt in 1807, when two additional almshouses were added by a Dr. Good for a further four inmates. Raven Almshouses, for eight poor people endowed with lands at Raydon and Holton by John Raven in 1636, occupied Nos. 110-118 Benton Street.

Workhouse.
The old Guildhall was used as a workhouse for the poor in 1792.

Guildhall.
The Guildhall occupied the first floor of a timber-framed house originally called the Markethouse, situated S of the churchyard, and 'newly built' in 1438. It was declared a Wool Hall in 1628 when it was forbidden to sell woollen goods in any other place. The town had five guilds: Trinity, Corpus Christi, St. Johns, St. Thomas and Our Lady (1524).

Historic Houses & Ancient Moated Sites.
SW of the church is the impressive Deanery Tower, a gatehouse and the only surviving section of the palace being built by Archdeacon Pykenham in 1495 - he died before it could be completed. It is of brick, 43' high and 31' broad, flanked by panelled and embattled octagonal turrets. Toppesfield Hall, an ancient manor house situated by the churchyard, is thought to date back to 1297. A fine house in High Street, now numbers 62-66, dates from 1676 and features the motif of Sparrowe's House in Ipswich six times. At the top of Angel Street is a fine C16 red-brick barn. Pond Hall Farm (or Place Farm), 1½ miles E of town, is the ancient manor house of Helmyn Legate who, in 1371, two years after being granted permission to create a deer park, obtained a licence from Edward III to crenellate (fortify with battlements) his house. There is no clear evidence whether this was ever carried out. The Hall was later the seat of the D'Oyly family, one of whom was created a baronet in 1663. C16 Peyton Hall, 1 mile N of the town, was thought to be the seat of the Peyton family. The White Horse Inn in Stone Street, and the former Spinning Wheel Restaurant in High Street both date from the C16.

HALESWORTH

Blything Hundred. 'Haele's enclosure' (OE) *Healesuurda* (DB)
Manors. Halesworth Manor (-mid C12 Earls of Chester; C12 Thomas de Halesworth passing to the De Argentine family who held the Honor of Chester until the C15). *Sub-Manors.* Dame Margery's; Rectory Manor.
A busy town of considerable substance and already an urban settlement by 1223. Yet, surprisingly, very little is known of what is obviously an ancient history. Although a major Roman road passes through, there is little evidence from this period in the vicinity, and the area of Middle and Late Saxon settlement appears to

HALESWORTH *(continued)*

have remained within the area of the later medieval town. The de Argentein family, who held the manor here from the time of Henry II (when Reginald de Argentein was cupbearer at the coronation of the King), appear the dominating force of early Norman occupation of the town. Reginald was a direct descendant of David de Argentein who fought with William at the Battle of Hastings and, later, Sir Giles de Argentein after valiant deeds during the Crusades - he boasted that it was "an easy matter for one Christian knight to kill two Pagan dogs!" - fought beside Edward II as his bodyguard during the war with Scotland. Claude Morley, that enthusiastic and imaginative historian, thought, not unreasonably, that the family were powerful enough, and the town important enough, to have a castle, or at least a residence with major fortifications. However, his attempts to find evidence for any such building proved fruitless, though he put forward one or two less than convincing theories. Neither is there evidence for religious houses, priories, or even chapels. This suggests that the remains of many important buildings lie hidden beneath the present town. Great quantities of hemp were formerly grown locally and the manufacture of Suffolk hempen cloth gave employment to about 1,000 people in the town and neighbourhood. It was described as a 'thriving town' and 'a populous market town where much linen yarn is spun' in the C17. Until it silted up in 1761, trade was aided by the navigation of the river Blyth up to Halesworth.

Site of Tumulus.
A round barrow lay near the Roman Stone Street on the road to Bungay.

Roman Road.
The Roman Stone Street runs NE from the town towards Bungay. On the assumption that Halesworth was founded at a natural crossing of the river Blyth, the course of the Roman road S would continue on a direct line to Quay Street then, making an arc to cross the river, exit SW along what is now London Road. Its course from here is difficult to determine but probably curved SE to cross another Roman road (the present A12) perhaps via the course of the A144 - at least for the last half mile. Its final destination was probably Dunwich.

Ancient Remedial Springs.
Mineral springs which were situated near the town reputedly contained healing properties for eye inflammation.

Site of old Windmills.
Two mills are shown on Pound Hill in 1783; one was demolished before 1900 and the other followed c1905. Calvers post mill was recorded in 1788 on Mill Hill, N of the town; this was pulled down in 1942.

Medieval Market & Fair
In 1222, Richard de Argentein paid 'two palfreys' (light saddle horses, usually ridden by women), for a licence to hold a weekly market and an annual fair on the feast of St. Lukes.

Market Cross.
The removal of the old Market Cross was necessary at the beginning of the C19 after it fell into serious decay. It was said to have been similar in design to the Butter Cross in Bungay.

Free School (?)
A schoolmaster was recorded in 1700 through the bequests of Richard Parter and Thomas Neale. A new schoolroom was built in 1813.

Almshouses.
Cary Almshouses, which face the S side of the church, were founded in 1686 by William Cary. They comprised six small homes and were occupied by 14 poor widows.

Guildhall.
There were originally four guilds in the town, and the former Guildhall of St John the Baptist still stands in the Thoroughfare . Although its legacies were confiscated at the Reformation, they were restored to the Guildhall in 1585 by Elizabeth I. The building is now used for a business.

Historic Houses.
Situated near the church is Old Chantry House, the home of the Bedingfields from 1547 to 1720; Sir Robert

HALESWORTH *(continued)*

Bedingfield was Lord Mayor of London in 1701. Gothic House, with its strange Jacobean porch, and the former Old Three Tuns Inn in the Market Place, both date from 1520-40. The Old Rectory, on the site of the former manor house in Rectory Road, much restored but with fine exposed timberwork, also dates from the C16. A timber-framed C15 building in the Thoroughfare (now a wine bar) bears the arms of the de Argentein family on a finely carved wood portico. Number 6 is also timber-framed and jettied. The Elizabethan Angel Hotel, an old coaching inn, was used in the C18 for Petty Sessions for hiring servants. 'Hirings' were held in each Hundred every Michaelmas. The former Timberwheel Tea Room in Chediston Street is C16.

HARDWICK *(1 mile S of Bury St Edmunds)*

Thingoe Hundred. 'Village of the army' (OE)
Manors. Hardwick Manor (1546 Sir Thomas Darcy).
Only 115 acres in extent, Hardwick, anciently called Herdwyk, was granted by King Edmund in 945 A.D. to the cellarer of Bury Abbey, a gift confirmed by King Stephen. At the Dissolution, the Abbey estate which included Hardwick, was broken up and became the property of the Drury family of Hawstead. The remainder, which included Abbots' Lodge (or grange) and which kept the name of Hardwick, changed hands often. Probably always churchless, the parish no longer exists and has been divided between Horringer, Nowton and Bury's southern outer suburbs.

Medieval Grange & Historic House.
The site of the abbots' grange became the Elizabethan Hardwick House, partly rebuilt in 1681. The park in which it stood - "all woods . . called Hardwyckes Wood . . 50 acres in Bury St Edmunds, Nowton, Stanefield and Gt Horningsheath, granted to Sir Thomas Darcy" (1546) - was much disfigured by the erection of army huts and concrete roads during World War II. The hall's final demolition in 1925 was described as one of the greatest losses to Suffolk's domestic architecture. West Suffolk Hospital now occupies most of the site. When Hardwick Manor House was built in 1926 within the brick-walled garden of the old house and re-using much of the building material, domed cellars were discovered, almost certainly belonging to the old Abbey Grange.

HARGRAVE *(6 miles SW of Bury St Edmunds)*

Thingoe Hundred. 'Hoar grove' or 'Grove on a boundary'? (OE) *Haragraua* (DB) Morley suggests 'Hare's grave or ditch' - 'Hare' being possibly a man's nickname rather than an animal; or perhaps 'Harold's grave'.
Manors. Hargrave Manor (-1539 Abbot of St. Edmuns, Bury; 1539 Sir Thomas Kytson).

Lost Medieval Parish.
Hargrave includes Southwood (or Southwell) Park, formerly a separate parish W of the present village, but without a church. Though not listed in Domesday Book, it is named Arestedel in the *Liber Consuetudinibus S. Edmundi.*

Deer Parks.
There is documentary evidence of two deer parks here. Carter's Park, the northernmost, is likely identified by Park Meadow and Hall Lawn on the 1838 tithe map, a small wood now called Carter's Park on the present O.S. map, and a fragment of wood N of it on the parish boundary (formerly called Little Southwood Park). Great Southwood Park, mentioned in a 1761 deed: 'a mansion and 74 acres of land, lately part of Southwood Park', is remembered in Southwood Park Farm, W of the village.

Medieval Greens.
A linear green once occupied the village street from the junctions with the roads to Ousden and Chevington, terminating N of the village in a footpath leading to the church and rectory. Faden's map shows it, unnamed, and edged by properties. It was enclosed and the southern section infilled with houses. Named Hargrave Green on the 1837 OS map, its site is identified by Green Farm. Two areas of green in the SE of the parish named Little Knowle Green and Great Knowle Green (also shown on the 1837 map) are not named or shown by Faden.

HARGRAVE *(continued)*

Site of old Windmill.
A smock mill is shown standing SE of Hargrave Hall in 1783; it had gone by 1914.

Ancient Moat.
At Moat Farm, Hargrave Green, are disconnected fragments of a moat.

HARKSTEAD *(7 miles SE of Ipswich)*

Samford Hundred. 'Hereca's place' (OScand+OE) *Herchesteda* (DB)
Manors. Harkstead (1214 William de Fortibus, Earl of Albermarle). *Sub-Manors.* Buckler's Bond; Brandeston/ Brampston; Netherhall.

Ancient Woodland.
Rag Queach, Upper Grove and Broomfield Covert are parts of ancient woodland.

Ancient Settlement.
A complex series of cropmarks in the form of field systems, trackways and dense linear features provides evidence of extensive early settlement in the area of Rence Park Farm, and also S of Sparrow Hall.

Earthworks (?)
A raised platform c100' square surrounded by a stream-fed ditch is situated at the S end of Pond Wood, W of the church. Possible further earthworks lie in the meadow to the S. All may in some way relate to the Old Rectory. Faden's map of 1783 illustrates the site showing its prominence at that time.

Ancient Chapel.
In a field called 'Chapeldown', situated between Harkstead and Erwarton by 'John all Alone's', an enclosure some 875 yds. from the banks of the river Stour and E of Nether Hall is called 'Myrtle (mortal?) bones'. Together these probably identify the site of the chapel dedicated to St Clement, mentioned in Domesday and again in 1528 and 1540 when money was left for its restoration. It was apparently still in existence in 1685 when a certain Roger Andrews bequeathed his "Littel House with the Gardynge and one Pightle abutting towards the South upon St Clement's Church Yard and upon the Mill Waye towards the North."

Ancient Quay.
On the banks of the river, S of the chapel site (*see above*) and likely to have been associated with it, are the remains (in the form of a neat layer of septaria stone) of the ancient Palace Quay which once operated here.

HARLESTON *(3 miles NW of Stowmarket)*

Stow Hundred. 'Herewulf's farmstead' (OE) *Heroluestuna* (DB)
Manors. Harleston (-1538 Butley Priory).

Ancient Woodland.
Broad Border in the N of the parish is part of ancient woodland.

Martyr's Stone.
Rush Green is where Sir John Sulyard and Sir John Tyrell (*see* Gipping) are said to have burned their victims during the Marian persecutions. An ancient stone which still remains here near the roadside, marks the spot. The parish was once known as Harlestone.

Ceremonial Way.
The grove of lime trees running through the centre of the village is said to commemorate Elizabeth I's journey through the parish on her way to visit Onehouse Hall.

Medieval Greens.
The triangular Harleston Green still survives in the centre of the village, as does the small Rush Green covering the crossing with London Lane N of the hall. This was called Sheepcote Green on Faden's 1783 map.

HARTEST *(8 miles NW of Sudbury)*

Babergh Hundred. 'Wooded hill frequented by harts or stags' (OE) *Herterst* (DB)
Manors. Hartest Manor (C12/C13 Bishop of Ely).

Ancient Woodland.
Ashen Wood and Bavins Wood on the eastern parish boundary form part of ancient woodland. Overlooking the pretty village sitting snugly in the valley, they would appear to readily fit that described in the place-name.

Roman Pottery Industry.
Evidence of Roman pottery manufacture has been found in the parish.

Medieval Green.
The church overlooks the extensive Hartest Green which covered the village and from which five roads exited. It is now encroached upon by modern properties except in the NE. Cross Green, a small green named on Faden's map and now enclosed, lay on the road N of the village at a fork created by a track to The Chestnuts.

Gallows.
In the C12/C13 the Bishop of Ely claimed 'right of gallows' in the parish. The site of the gibbet is not known.

Site of old Windmill.
A post mill stood by Millhill Farm at Mile End in 1783; it was burned down c1958.

Workhouse.
A workhouse here recorded 30 inmates in 1776.

Almshouses.
Church Cottages have been known as almshouses since at least 1638.

Historic Houses & Ancient Moated Site.
Rivets Hall, an ancient moated house, once stood totally isolated on the edge of Ashen Wood NE of the village; the site still the meeting point of four tracks. Farrer, who visited the (by that time) empty hall in 1922, dated it to the early C16 but could find no records of early residents. The Bell Inn posting house dates back to the C16.

HASKETON *(1 mile NW of Woodbridge)*

Carlford Hundred. 'Hoskuldr's farmstead' (OScand) *Haschetuna* (DB)
Manors. Hasketon Hall (1201 Ernold Le Rus). *Sub-Manors.* Thorpe Hall; Rectory Manor.

Ancient Woodland.
Blunts Wood on the southern parish boundary is a fragment of ancient woodland.

Ancient Meeting Place.
A meadow below the church by the bridge provided the meeting place for Carlford Hundred in Saxon times.

Ancient Moated Sites.
A very ancient, wide and irregular oval moat lies to the W of the modern Hasketon Manor. Manor Farm House, formerly the Rectory, SE of the village, has an almost complete, square moat.

HAUGHLEY *(3 miles NNW of Stowmarket)*

Stow Hundred. 'Meadow enclosed with hawthorn hedge' (OE) *Hagele* (c1040) *Hagala* (DB)
Manors. Haughley (C12 Henry de Essex; C12 Count Thomas de Perche).
Haughley, one of the three Honors in Suffolk, held an important position from pre-Norman times until a great fire at the end of the C16 destroyed much of the village giving impetus to the rise of nearby Stowmarket. An undated rate book suggests that the parish was at one time divided into four districts: Tothill; The Street (now Old Street); New Street and The Green. The latter two remain as hamlets, whilst Tothill forms a compartitively unpopulated section between Haughley and Stowmarket by the major A14 road to the Midlands.

Motte & Bailey Castle.
Formerly known as 'Hagenet Castle', this impressive earthworks occupies an area of 7 acres and comprises a

HAUGHLEY *(continued)*

motte 210' in diameter at the base and 80' high - the largest in Suffolk. Though well disguised in trees and virtually unknown by the general public, it has been described as the county's most perfect military work. The immediate bailey to the S is rectangular, strengthened by strong ramparts and protected by a wide moat. To the W of this is another enclosure, while a third outer bailey appears to encompass and form the outline of the main village. The castle was built by Hugh de Montfort around 1100 (possibly on the site of a fortified Saxon hall owned by Goodmund in the C11) and seized by the Crown in 1163. Despite its apparent strong defences, it was taken by the Flemish forces led by Robert, Earl of Leicester in 1173 whilst under the royal custody of Ralph de Broc. It was claimed to have been burnt and so totally destroyed that it did not rise again. Its swift surrender and destruction gave rise to earlier suggestions that it was constructed only of timber, but foundations of a circular stone tower or keep have been discovered suggesting that when Edward II spent a week in Haughley in 1326 after enjoying Christmas and New Year in Bury St Edmunds, he may well have stayed at the rebuilt castle. A part of the main moat remains water-filled to provide the village duck pond.

Site of Ancient Chapel.
A wayside chapel dedicated to St John was situated on Tot Hill, SE of the village.

Ancient Gallows.
At a court held in 1475 it was ordered that the Abbot of Hales in Gloucestershire (to whom the parish of Haughley was at that time appropriated) should erect a new gallows in Luberlow Field. At the same time a William Baxteyn held lands here retained by the service of providing a ladder by which criminals hung at this gallows could mount to meet their death. This field (now Lubberlaw Field) remains today in an area known as Gallows Fields by the modern A14 road and behind a service station, restaurant and motel.

Site of old Windmill.
A post mill which stood on Haughley Green in 1783 was demolished c1896.

Medieval Market & Fair.
A market and fair were in use at Haughley in 1227 and the parish received a renewal of this grant in 1231. The great fire in the C16 brought a premature end to the former (*see above*), leaving the way clear for the development of Stow's market. (As Thorney, Stowmarket had had a market in Anglo-Saxon times, but today's Thursday market only began after Haughley's demise.) The fair was abolished in 1871.

Medieval Green.
The present modest and unnamed green in the centre of Haughley probably dates from the time the village was first created within the castle bailey. The hamlet of Haughley Green is shown with its green on Faden's map and named Hawleigh Green. It was a very large, wide and long green running S-N almost entirely on the W side of the present road to Bacton as far as Old Hall. Green Farm was its southern limit but a westerly extension either side of the road to Wetherden ended at Willow Cottages. The western boundary of the 120 acre green or common, enclosed c1854, is still clearly defined along most of its length by field boundaries and a double ditch.

Guildhall.
Haughley School was built in 1866 on land formerly occupied by four tenements called The Guildhall (later the Town House). There were four guilds here: St. John Baptist and St. James c1474, and St. Mary and St. Thomas c1521.

Historic Houses & Ancient Moated Sites.
The manor of Haughley Park was originally owned by Charles Brandon, Duke of Suffolk. After passing to the Crown it was later granted by Queen Mary to Sir John Sulyard in 1554. Sir John had been among the first to take up arms and levy men in Mary's service against supporters of Lady Jane Grey and was honoured with the position of Lord Chief Justice of England for his service. It was his son, another John, who built the hall known as Haughley Park in c1625 within a 396 acre park. Badly damaged by fire in 1961, it was immediately rebuilt. The lord of the manor of Haughley Park formerly possessed a jurisdiction of Oyer and Terminer, trying all cases in his own court, of which instances are on record as late as 1569. The Sulyards kept the manor from 1538-1811 when, by marriage, it passed to the Jerninghams. Dial Farm, SE of the church, dates from early Tudor

HAUGHLEY *(continued)*

times. The Tyrell family owned the manor of Plashwood and the old manor house was still standing in 1755. The modern house formerly had a modest park. The Old Counting House (now a restaurant) is believed to be the former counting house or bank which existed prior to the demise of the market. The Kings Arms dates from the C15-C16. At Newbell's Farm, Haughley Green, a hamlet N of the parish, a quadrangular moat, partially sub-divided, encloses a large area. Just to the E of this, Wassick's Farm has a portion of a small, square moat.

HAVERHILL

Risbridge & Hinckford (Essex) Hundreds. 'Billy-goat hill' (OE) *Hauerbella* (DB). Most claim it to be 'Hill where oats are grown' (OScand+OE) but Morley states that 'haver' meaning oats was unknown before 1300. *Manors.* Haverhill Manor called The Castle (1086-1314 the De Clare family). *Sub-Manors.* Horshams; Hellions/Helyon Haverhill.

Strategically sited beside the old Roman road at the junction of three counties; Suffolk, Essex and Cambridgeshire, and with a market going back to Anglo-Saxon times, Haverhill is a town of very ancient origin. It may well have been a Romano-British station with later Saxon fortifications but, regretfully, a devastating fire in 1665 destroyed most of the old town and its records leaving a void in our knowledge of much of the former history. Later events, more commercial than catastrophic, have also left Haverhill with a less than welcoming appearance. Heavily involved for many years in the cloth industry manufacturing checks, cottons, fustians and, in the early part of the last century, coarse cloth (drabbets) cheese cloth, towels, linen, horsehair, crinoline and umbrella silk, left its mark in drab industrial buildings. Worse was to follow when unsympathetic 1950s redevelopment for London overspill, swept away virtually everything that had survived the fire.

Ancient Woodland.

Poplar and Ladygate Woods are parts of ancient woodland situated near the southern parish boundary.

Tumulus.

'Near the town is a mound or hillock believed to be the site of a Roman station of some extent and considerable importance.' This possible round barrow which lay on the SW outskirts of town, NE of Puddle Brook Playing Fields, and has since been destroyed and built over, may well have been utilised for other purposes (*see below*).

Iron-Age Settlement.

A small Iron-Age settlement site with ditches and possible post-holes was found at Burton End, SW of the town.

Roman Road.

The High Street lies roughly on the line of a major Roman road from Cambridge to Colchester.

Roman Settlement & Cemetery (?)

Many relics of the Roman period have been discovered in the town including pottery, coins and spearheads. A Roman cemetery was discovered in 1759 between Haverhill and Withersfield when urns and a lachrymatory (a vessel in which the tears of the deceased person's mourners are supposed to have been preserved) were unearthed. The site was in an old disused lane beside the Roman road and near a rivulet 'by Haverhill Castle'.

Site of 'Castle' (?)

'A little to the west of the town are some vestiges of a castle' (White 1844). The earthwork known as 'Haverhill Castle' was situated on high ground commanding an extensive stretch of country. It stood in a strategically important position being at the crossroads of three counties and the only part of Suffolk's southern boundary which was undefended by the river Stour. The *Victoria County History* described the site thus: 'Its SE scarp and fosse were preserved until recently but now the rectangular site can only be traced by the fencing of the ground, a ditch and part of the fosse 12' deep containing water'. Later descriptions have, however, tended to confuse the 'castle' earthworks with those of the lost Castle Farm which shared its site, as with: 'An examination of the remains indicates that the earthworks are of a fortified manor house and there is no sign of a mound. The moated area is roughly oblong and much mutilated. The bleak position is now occupied by Castle Farm. But the tithe map of 1841 clearly shows part of a strong moat, with fragments of others which no doubt

HAVERHILL *(continued)*

originally joined it. The field to the NE is called Castle Arms and that to the E, The Leys, suggesting the site of fish-ponds, and even earlier descriptions point to a circular moat and a mound. The manor was anciently called Le Castell, Castell, and Castell-Hall, and there are references to a castle in 1373, 1403, and 1521. The Duke of Buckingham forfeited by attainer to the Crown "the manor called le Castell in Haverhill". Its age and purpose may forever remain conjectural for even the site itself has now gone, covered by a school playing field. A few years ago during a period of extreme drought, parchmarks were created in the E corner of the site in the form of a large semi-circle, open-sided rectangle and other miscellaneous features.

Site of Ancient Church & Chapel.
Alderton (a former hamlet) Chapel was standing near Chapel Farm, a mile N of the town, in 1624. 'Le Nether Chirche' (St. Botolph's Church of Horshams Manor?) also stood here. Two cottages on the site contain much re-used material.

Medieval Market & Fairs.
Peas Hill Market Place was the site of the town's market which was already established by the Conquest. Until 1872 two annual fairs were also held.

Site of Market Cross & Pillory.
The Market Place had an ancient Market House or Cross consisting of a chamber built on timber uprights with an outside staircase and incorporated a lock-up. The stocks stood close by. Both were removed in October 1826.

Site of old Windmill.
A windmill is mentioned in 1624 sited near the old chapel (*see above*). A post mill which lay beside the A143 road to Stradishall N of the town centre in 1783 was converted to a tower mill c1855. It was demolished in 1942.

Medieval Guildhall.
The Guildhall, near the entrance to the churchyard, was destroyed in the great fire.

Almshouses.
Almshouses for four poor people were situated in Townsend (now Queen Street) in 1624.

Workhouse.
Risbridge Union Workhouse, built 1779 for 280 paupers, was considered too small and removed to Kedington 1856.

Historic Houses & Ancient Moated Sites.
The Vicarage in Hamlet Road (built 1656) stands on the site of Cleve House the manor house of the Beaumonts, reputedly given by Henry V111 as a wedding gift to Anne of Cleves. Haverhill Hall S of the town has a square moat mostly destroyed on the E. The Queens Head survived the great fire to become the town's second oldest former coaching inn. Moon Hall has a fragment of its former moat. In Hazel Stub was a moat which has presumably now been infilled. The Manor House of Hellions, lost in the fire, stood on Market Hill in 1624. Place Farm, N of the village, was The Place (or Palace), the probable manor house of Haverhill Horsham.

HAWKEDON *(9 miles SSW of Bury St Edmunds)*

Risbridge Hundred. 'Hill frequented by hawks' (OE) *Hauokeduna* (DB). Claude Morley considers it to mean 'Hafoca's or Hawk's hill', a personal (nick)name.
Manors. Hawkedon Hall (1272 Thomas de Moleton). *Sub-Manors.* Thurstanton/Thursturston/Thurston Hall; Cresseners; Swans Hall.

Ancient Woodland.
Cresslands Wood and Thurston Park are fragments of ancient woodland.

Roman Find.
A Roman gladiator's helmet was found in the parish in 1965 and is now in the British Museum.

Ancient Mound.
A mound, standing in Hall Lane N of Thurston Hall, is 98' by 79' and 10' high with an irregular ditch on two sides.

HAWKEDON *(continued)*

Medieval Deer Park.
Thurston Park (formerly Park Wood) to the E of Thurston Hall is all that remains of Thurstruston Park, its former deer park, which existed prior to 1536. Field names suggest other former areas of the park: First Lawn, Further Lawn, Ten Acre Park and Thirteen Acre Park. It may have extended further to the S and the river Glem (note Lodge Farm in neighbouring Boxted).

Site of Gallow (?)
Gallowgate Farm stands on the boundary of St Edmundsbury and Babergh Districts, and three parishes - Hawkedon, Somerton and Boxted. It is the probable site of a medieval gibbet.

Medieval Market & Fair.
There was a grant of a market and fair to Thomas de Multon's Thurston Manor in 1280.

Medieval Cross.
In the garden of Hawkedon Hall is the base and part of the shaft of a C14-C15 village Cross; there is no record of its original site. Faden's map of 1783 appears to show the church and Hawkedon Hall standing virtually isolated on a small village green, with the main population residing on either side of the road S of the ford over the river Glem between Thurston Hall and Swan's Hall.

Historic Houses & Ancient Moated Sites.
The manor house of Hawkedon Hall, S of the church, dates from the C15. Langley's New House, ¾ mile NE of the village on the road to Rede, was built c1520 by John Langley; it has faint traces of an encircling moat. Thurston Hall (the manor of Thurstanestuna in Domesday) stands in the fork of the roads to Stansfield and Hawkedon village, within a large moat of which only the SE side remains. The Hall dates back to the late C15. Swan's Hall, a short distance further S in Thurston End near the parish boundary, is the former manor house of the Swan family, and displays a fine example of C15 timberwork.

HAWSTEAD *(4 miles S of Bury St Edmunds)*

Thingoe Hundred. 'Sloping place' or 'Place of the army' (OE) *Haldsteda* (DB)
Manors. Hawstead (-1353 Abbot of St. Edmunds, Bury; 1353 Sir John FitzEustace). *Sub-Manors.* Bokenham al Talmache; Fylets.

Ancient Woodland.
Upper and Lower Dutmoss Woods and Long Wood are parts of ancient woodland.

Gospal Oak.
An ancient and majestic oak called the Gospal Oak stood on the western parish boundary. Beneath this the clergyman used to stop to say prayers while completing the annual perambulation of the parish bounds.

Ancient Well.
An old well, situated by the W side of the road leading from Hawstead Green to Whepstead opposite Melpost, is considered to be of considerable antiquity. Enclosed by oak palings with a wooden door is an open pool with brick sides but of no great depth. It is claimed that the spring which supplies it has never run dry even in the worst of droughts. An inscription, still visible in 1784, boasted "empty me, empty the sea." The story goes that two old gaffers were conversing on this very spot, when one, whose name was Jacob, thrust his stick into the ground to emphasise a point; up welled a spring of water which ultimately came to be called Jacob's Well. The road here which is called Maltings Road (from a disused maltings) was formerly named 'Cald-well Strete'.

Medieval Deer Park.
Sir Robert Drury was granted a licence to empark his lands c1509, and the deer park called 'Great Parke' is shown on the 1616 map. 'Lytle Park' was another, smaller deer park.

Recreation.
A Camping Ground where ball games were played in medieval days adjoined the E side of the churchyard.

HAWSTEAD *(continued)*

Guildhall & Workhouse.

The Guildhall, housing the ancient Guild of St. James (c1300), was converted to a workhouse called Church House.

Almshouses.

Metcalfe Almshouses at Great Green were built in 1811 by Philip Metcalfe, replacing those founded by Sir Robert Drury in 1615 for six poor unmarried women which stood in the grounds of Hardwick House.

Medieval Green.

Faden's 1783 map does not show or name Hawstead Green which lies in the fork between Lawshall Road and Bell's Lane, S of the village; nor Bull Green at Pinford End, now enclosed and built over. Property boundaries around the junction of Bull Lane and Church Road probably trace the former shape of the latter. The map does, however, show a green in the area marked on the current OS map as Pound Green at the N end of the village where the road bends right. Infilled and developed, garden boundaries again mark the original green edge.

Historic Houses & Ancient Moated Sites.

'The uncouth figure of Hercules, removed and taken to Hardwick' was the last remnant of Hawstead Place, pulled down in 1827. It was the ancient manor house of the Fitz-Eustace family and from c1460-1610 the seat of the powerful knightly family of Drury (from whom Drury Lane in London is named). Queen Elizabeth I stayed here in 1578 when she is said to have knighted the owner on the occasion of his restoring to her a silver-handled fan which she had dropped in the moat. The house apparantly once had a cloister 45' long. Around 1610 the Drurys moved from Hawstead Place to Hardwick House. Hawstead was still complete in the 1730s but a description of the house and grounds in 1784 suggests that by this time it only comprised the N range. It reported that the moats formed a quadrangle enclosing an area 202' by 211' formerly called the Base Court and afterwards Court Yard. The house was approached by a gatehouse and a wide brick bridge of three arches spanning a moat 40' wide and faced on all its banks with bricks. Beyond the moat rose strong banks 10' above the water, and all were surrounded by a handsome terrace dominated by a stone figure of Hercules dated 1578. The terrace commanded fine views 'and befpoke a tafte fuperior to the artificial mount which in many old gardens was to be clambered up for the fake of profpect'. The house has now gone, but the fine moat, described as providing a defence between a castle and a manor house, remains, along with a stable of c1400 and an impressive series of fish-ponds running down from a spring N of the site, with another much smaller series to the S. It may well be that the history of this site goes back to Saxon times and is that referred to in the place-name as being the 'place of the army'. Hawstead Lodge with its irregular moat was shown on a map of c1616 lying within the 'Lyttle Park', a medieval deer park. A moat is all that now remains with a house to the N called Hawstead Lodge - perhaps, originally the lodge for the park. The site of the old manor house is shown on the same map as 'Hawsteede Mannor House' and situated where a public footpath now goes through the centre of a small grove due N of the church. The two irregular ponds are probably the remains of its ancient moat. Hammonds, described as a 'Gothic hall-house', was built in 1450, and Mannings Farm which dates from 1490 was dismantled in 1910 and moved to Clacton in Essex.

HAZLEWOOD *(2 miles NW of Aldburgh)*

Plomesgate Hundred. 'Hazel wood' (OE) *Haselewood* (DB)

Manors. Billesford Hall/Bilston Hall/Bilford/Bilson (1316 Clemence Titlershall).

Deserted Medieval Village.

Hazlewood was a Domesday parish comprising 1,937 acres of land including 44 acres of plantations and 200 acres called 'the flat' (now Hazelwood Marshes). It lay on the N side of the river Alde and included Barber's Point where Roman finds were made (*see* Friston). Hazlewood Hall, now a farmhouse, adjoins Hazlewood Common and, though in ruins since the beginning of the C17 when it was united ecclesiastically with Aldeburgh, there are still traces of its C13 church NE of Chapel Farm. Hazelwood - a hamlet of Aldeburgh until 1866, and a separate parish from 1866 to 1934 when it was finally divided between Aldeburgh and Friston - had 85 inhabitants in 1881 but it is not known if there was ever a nucleated village settlement here.

HELMINGHAM *(9 miles N of Ipswich)*

Bosmere & Claydon Hundred. 'The homestead of Helm's people' (OE) *Helmingheham* (DB)
Manors. Creke's Hall al Helmingham Hall al Cressy's al Joyces (1252 Geoffrey de Creke; c1509 Lionel Tollemache in whose family it has remained). *Sub-Manors.* Bockings (anciently belonging to the nuns of Campsey); Cadleys; Bromberry al Raynsbrough al Blomviles al Sulyards; Burghall/Bury Hall/Beryshall Willowes and Sidhall.

Ancient Woodland.
Round Wood, Oak Grove, and a fragment of Great Grove are parts of ancient woodland.

Site of Tumuli.
A large barrow on a hill to the NE of the rectory was flat topped and surrounded by a ditch. Another, on the Gosbeck road, just S of the junction with the B1077, was called Mill Mount. It was said in 1865 to be 'a remarkable tumulus with two very ancient stag-headed oak trees growing on it, one of which was pronounced to be a full thousand years old'. It was c66' N-S by c49' E-W and 6½' high, and probably later used for a windmill.

Romano-British Cemeteries (?)
At 'The Wilderness' which adjoins the rectory gardens, a cemetery said to contain 'several hundred' inhumations was discovered in 1864. Several trenches were excavated containing as many as 24 skeletons in each, showing signs of previous mutilation, with severed heads, etc., and apparently all male. Subsequent research suggested that the cemetery was not confined to The Wilderness but extended under the rectory stable, coachhouse and garden to the E, along a portion of the churchyard to the S, and across the moat to the N. It was said that within the recollection of many persons still living, 'two more ancient cemeteries had been met with in this parish on land belonging to Mr Tollemach, but there being no-one at the time to call attention to the matter, they passed almost unnoticed. One was on a pleasant slope facing E, on a farm about a mile from the church and must have been of much the same character as that opened at the rectory. The other on a slight rise ½ mile from the church. At both, the human remains were said to be so numerous as to require a cart for their removal'. Traces of hypocaust said to have been found at the site perhaps related to a nearby settlement for the cemetery. The *Victoria County History's* statement that 'other tumuli have been destroyed near the church yielding numerous relics' rather suggests that the above excavations may have been into burial mounds (*see above*).

Ancient Deer Park.
Helmingham Hall stands in an ancient deer park of some 375 acres. The deer are still present today.

Deserted Medieval Settlement.
Whilst there is no nucleated village of Helmingham - dominated as it is by its great hall and park which incorporates the parish church - this may not always have been so. A number of medieval house sites have been identified by field walking the ploughland on the western side of the parish, and a linear spread of pottery suggests there may once have been a small medieval settlement aligned on a street.

Historic Houses & Ancient Moated Sites.
Built by Lional Tollemache in 1512, Helmingham Hall is a fine quadrangular Tudor house surrounded by a wide and perfect moat, strongly defended and approached both by a bridge and a drawbridge, still raised each night. To the E are fish-ponds known as The Leys. The outer garden moat is thought to pre-date the house moat. The Hall, to the S of the parish - which may have replaced an earlier one situated on the site of Creke Hall (now a farmhouse) built in the C12 possibly by Geofrrey de Creke - is of four periods: c1485-8, c1750, 1800 and 1841. Of the earliest period is the plan of four ranges round an inner courtyard, with much of the S range and some of the N range. The finest surviving piece of the Tudor building is the main gateway. Elizabeth I spent five days here in 1561 as a guest of the Tollemaches - her bed is still here and a lute on which she played is one of the family heirlooms. The Tollemaches can trace their descent back to the Toelmags, who held lands at Bentley before the Conquest. Their name is said to be a corruption of the word 'tollmack' - tolling of the bell. Bocking Hall, a C16-C17 house, stands N of the moated site of the former hall, the seat of William de Bocking in the reign

HELMINGHAM *(continued)*

of Edward III (1327-77). The site was bulldozed in 1967 but fragments of the ancient moat and a scatter of Tudor brick remain. A notable discovery was made on the western side of the parish; the faint cropmark of a moated site enclosing ½ acre with associated pottery scatter. This is the probable site of Oliver's Manor. A John Oliver is recorded residing here in 1297 and a Benedict Oliver in 1327 and 1333. There are fragments of a moat at Elm Farm, partially infilled last century.

HEMINGSTONE *(5½ miles N of Ipswich)*

Bosmere & Claydon Hundred. 'Hemingr's family's farm' (OE) *Hamingestuna* (DB)
Manors. Hemingstone (C12 Rowland le Fartere; C12 Jeffrey de Apleton).

Roman Road.
The parish boundary follows a Roman road SW-NE from Coddenham, first as Clay Lane from E of Valley Farm to Coppings Farm, then as the B1078 to Hare & Hounds Corner.

Roman Building.
Building material, including a tesselated pavement and coins from 171-350 A.D., suggest a Roman building by Lower Road (B1078), E of the village.

Ancient Earthworks.
St Gregory's Church, which incorporates Saxon 'long-and-short', work stands on a platform earthworks which pre-dates it. The tower may be a C15 rebuild of one of pre-Conquest date.

Site of Chapel of Knights Hospitallers.
In 1242: 'Brother Terry de Nussa, Prior of the Hospital of Jerusalem in England, gave to Brother Luke de Manses, Simon de Odewell, and Marjery his wife, 2 carrucates of land (c240 acres) in Hemingstone, Codenham and Cleydon in Suffolk who were to find throughout their lives reasonable estover in food and drink at Hemingstone for a certain chaplain who shall celebrate divine offices for the souls of Richard, formerly Dean of Codenham and of all the faithful dead, in the chapel which is situated in a certain Messuage in Hemingstone within the said 2 carrucates.' The site of the chapel is unknown.

Medieval Green.
Olivers Green, named by Faden in 1783, stood on the SE corner of the road junction at Stonewall Farm.

Historic Houses & Ancient Moated Sites.
Hemingstone Hall is a much restored but picturesque Elizabethan house built in 1588 by William Style. A half-timbered farmhouse ½ mile NE known as Stonewall (formerly Stone Hall) was home to the Cantrells and may date from c1500. Ralph Cantrell, a Roman Catholic, is said to have protected himself and his property whilst still respecting a vow he had made never to enter a Prostestant place of worship, by erecting one of the porches in the church, known as Ralph's Hole, from where he could hear divine service without entering the church. There is also a room at the top of his house traditionally said to have been used by local Roman Catholics as a private chapel during this time. Cropmarks of a square enclosure suggest a possible moat on the N side of Church Lane near its junction with the Gosbeck road, while cropmarks of a possible 'L-shaped' moat follow the line of field boundaries and a public footpath SW of this, on the S side of the lane.

HEMLEY *(5½ miles S of Woodbridge)*

Colneis Hundred. 'Helma's clearing or meadow' (OE) *Helmelea* (DB). Includes the unidentified Domesday vill of Istevertona.
Manors. Hemley (Little known. 1584 Christopher Backler).

Medieval Riverside Industry.
Salt was an expensive commodity in the Middle Ages, costing about a guinea a bushel (8 gallons or c36 litres dry measure). Several places along the River Deben had a thriving industry extracting salt from the tidal river in salt-pans to be sent down-river to Woodbridge for refining and storing in salt houses on the quay. Salt

HEMLEY *(continued)*

cottages relating to this industry (which continued up to the C19) were recorded at Hemley in 1460.

Ancient Ferry.

Kirton Creek, which Hemley shared with Kirton, was anciently a busy customs port with ferries to Ramsholt and Shottisham on the opposite E bank of the Deben. The ferries used to beach above Hemley at a reach of the river called The Rocks (formed from septaria). The field above the cliff was known as Ferry Hempland. In the time of Elizabeth I, anyone who farmed more than 60 acres had by law to grow a crop of flax or hemp.

Lost Medieval Settlement.

A hard by the river Deben leads to the former settlement of Haspley. Cropmarks of a trackway running SW-NE with field boundaries and enclosures at the NE end, N of Hemley Hall, may relate to this lost hamlet.

HENGRAVE *(4 miles W of Bury St Edmunds)*

Thingoe Hundred. 'Hemma's family burial place' or 'Hemma's pasture or water meadow' (OE) *Hemegretham* (DB) *Hemegrede* (c1095).
Manors. Hengrave (Hengrave family held from the Abbot of St. Edmunds, Bury).

Cursus & Ancient Crop Marks.

The cursus or 'Ceremonial Way' identified by aerial photographs as running for almost a mile parallel with the river Lark from Fornham All Saints, stops short of a field in this parish which aerial photographs have shown to be full of cropmarks of pre-historic occupation in the form of ring ditches, enclosures and more complex furrows. (*see also* Fornham All Saints)

Site of Roman Settlement.

N of Hengrave Hall and the church, NW of Mill Farm on the S bank of the Lark, is the site of a Roman settlement.

Almshouses.

Four tenements comprised almshouses erected and endowed by Sir Thomas Kyson in the C16 for aged servants of the hall.

Historic House & Ancient Moated Site.

Sir Thomas de Hengrave was seated at a former Hall here in the reign of Henry III, and this family continued in residence for more than two centuries until the manor came into the possession of the Hethe family, who sold it shortly afterwards to the noble family of Stafford, Dukes of Buckenham. The present magnificent Hengrave Hall, whose gatehouse was once described as "of such singular beauty . . . that perhaps a more elegant specimen of architecture of that age can scarcely be seen", stands beside the old church whose tower could be pre-Conquest. The Hall was re-built and lavishly furnished between 1525-38 by Sir Thomas Kytson, a wealthy merchant adventurer and Sheriff of London (1533). He obtained a licence to empark 300 acres of land and create a deer park which he stocked in the same year. In 1575 Elizabeth I, the Earl of Leicester, and the entire court were entertained here. By 1712 the park had been extended to cover 500 acres. The house was reduced in size in 1775 when part of the N and NE angle were dismantled, and of the large ancient moat which once encircled the first hall on the site, only a part remains. A section of an impressive avenue running S from the hall to Hyde Wood shown on Faden's map of 1783 remains as a track called Queen Elizabeth's Walk; the map also shows another heading SE in the direction of Fornham All Saints. The Hall retains an ancient greengage tree, presumably related to that which Sir William Gage (1657-1727), a later owner, introduced from France and gave his name. During the French Revolution (1789-95), a later member of the family, Sir Thomas Gage, provided sanctuary to a sisterhood of 'Austin Nuns of Bruges'.

HENHAM *(4 miles E of Halesworth)*

Blything Hundred. 'High homestead or enclosure' (OE) *Henham* (DB).
Manors. Henham (C13 Cardo de Fressunvill/Freskenville). *Sub-Manors.* Cravens.
A hamlet of Wangford which gained civil parish status in 1866.

HENHAM *(continued)*

Ancient Woodland.

A majority of the parish (1,000 acres) comprises the woodland of Henham Park which includes many ancient oaks and areas of ancient woodland, including Tuttles Wood to the N.

Ancient Moated Site.

The first fortified manor house of the Kerdestons (*see below)* is perhaps represented by the substantial earthworks in Moatyard Covert on the northern parish boundary. They comprise an oval moat of great strength, now dry but up to 7' deep, enclosing an area c200' by 175'. There are few surface indications of the former building, but pottery sherds dating from Roman to Late Medieval provide evidence of long occupation on the site. A map of 1699 shows an unoccupied moat linked to the river.

Ancient Well.

A seat marked the site of an ancient well. The 'rest' was erected in c1740 of Georgian brick but incorporated two capitalled stone pilasters perhaps from an earlier Henham Hall. It may well be that the well had sacred associations with the death of King Anna who was slain close by in 654 A.D.

Deserted Medieval Settlements.

Henham held a strategically a very strong position in Saxon times being bounded by the Blyth to the S, tributaries of the same river on the E and N, and a rivulet running down from Westhall on the W. Though no village now exists, a former settlement may lay beneath the extensive park. The site of the lost hamlet of Middleton remains in moats and tracks in permanent pasture on the W side of the parish. W of 'The Clamps' Wood, Middleton's Tenements were mentioned in 1439. They are shown on a map of 1701 in a field called 'Great Middleton Wood' with 'Little Middleton Wood' adjoining to the E and 'Driftway Close' to the N.

Medieval Deer Park.

Henham Park embraces an earlier deer park recorded in 1538.

Medieval Commons.

Henham Common is shown and named on Faden's 1783 map lying immediately N of Henham Park, mainly to the E of the present A145 road to Beccles. Whilst not extensive, it connected with an arm of Southerton Moor which extended into the western side of the parish from Sotherton. It was enclosed in 1802.

Historic Houses.

Ralph Baynard held the manor of Henham and Wangford at Domesday. In the time of Edward I (1272-1307) they belonged to Robert, Lord Kerdeston (*see above*), and in 1440 to the de la Poles. Charles Brandon, Duke of Suffolk, built Henham Hall to a courtyard plan in the 1520s and 1530s. It was sold to the Crown in 1538 and granted to Sir Anthony Rous in 1545. It was described as having a 3-storeyed gatehouse and corner towers of brick - the remainder of the house appears to have been of timber. In 1679, in the time of Sir John Rous, High Sheriff of Suffolk, it was recorded as having 31 hearths, suggesting a massive building. It was burned down in 1773 and demolished. Its site is in the walled garden of the most recent hall, the former seat of the Earl of Stradbroke, which was built in 1793 and stood in a park of 850 acre (later extended to 1,400 acres) designed by Repton. This Hall was pulled down in 1953.

HENLEY *(4½ miles N of Ipswich)*

Bosmere & Claydon Hundred. 'At the high meadow' (OE) *Henleia* (DB). The river Finn rises in the middle of the village at Henley Watering.

Manors. Henley (C13 Bishop of Norwich; 1259 John de Weyland held as of Honor of Eye). There may have been a second manor of Henley Hall.

Ancient Woodland.

Witnesham Thicks is an area of ancient woodland. Kewland Wood appears in a will of 1694.

Roman Road.

A Roman road ran from the Gipping river crossing SW-NE forming the northern parish boundary. Its line is

HENLEY *(continued)*

roughly traced by Clay Lane (from Bell Cross to Coppings Farm), then overlaid by the present B1078 which leaves the parish at Hare & Hounds Corner.

Medieval Greens.
A driftway, now Ashbocking Road, ran NNE from Henley Watering. It formed the linear Henley Green (in the area marked Henley Square on the present OS map) and Henley Broad Green, at its junction with Clay Lane.

Workhouse.
An order for the building of a house for the poor was made in 1672, and a workhouse recorded here in 1756.

Historic Houses & Ancient Moated Sites.
Kewland Hall (formerly Rigs Hall), was a manor house. Henley Hall, seat of the Vere family for more than two centuries, was situated S of the church, its site now under a modern housing development. There is a moat at the Old Rectory SE of the village with, to the W of it, an ancient Tithe Barn with magnificent internal timberwork.

HENSTEAD with Hulver *(5½ miles SE of Beccles)*

Blything Hundred. 'Place frequented by wild birds' (OE) *Henesteda* (DB). Morley considers it 'at the high place'. So impassable was the Hundred River that its Saxon ford, then 200 yards broad, was charmingly situated in the Hundred River valley to the W of the parish at Hulver Bridge in Hulver Street, some 5 miles inland where six ways still meet. Hulver Street derives its name from the ancient provincial name for holly, cultivated here from as early as 1267. Only a handful of holly copses now remain dotted around the hamlet.
Manors. Henstead Perpounds al Poynings (1271 Sir Simon de Pierpoint). *Sub-Manors.* Blundeston, Savages and Henstead.

Ancient Woodland.
Brier Wood and Savage Wood are fragments of ancient woodland. Savage Wood marks the site of a sub-manor.

Ancient Track.
The footpath which heads N from W of Sotterley End Farm, then heads E to the church, skirting Brier Wood, is named Packway on Faden's 1783 map where it is shown leading from Sotterley Common to Henstead Green.

Site of Gallows (?)
Gibbet Tree, N of the church, suggests the site of a former parish gallows.

Medieval Green & Commons.
Faden's map shows the church on the NE edge of Henstead Green which stretched eastwards across the junction of the present B1127 and B1384 roads. Two small round commons are also shown side by side to the NE; White House Farm lay on the northern edge of Home Croft Common, and Toad Row Common just to its E is marked on the present OS map as enclosed and redeveloped. The length of the southern parish boundary as far as the Wrentham-Rushmere road was covered by Sotterley Common; its northern extent marked by Sotterley End Farm, Belgrove Farm and Sayer's Farm. The hamlet of Hulver Street is shown in 1783 mainly comprising a large square common on a NE axis named Hulver Heath, with a SE extension towards Brier Wood.

HEPWORTH *(5 miles NE of Ixworth)*

Blackbourn Hundred. 'Heppa's enclosure' or 'hedge where hips grow' (OE) *Hepworda* (DB)
Manors. Hepworth (C13 Berard de Hepeworth); Riveshall al Rushall al Reeves (C14 Sir Henry de Riveshall); North Hale (C14 Giles de Neketon). *Sub-Manors.* Master Stephens; Bretts.

Ancient Woodland.
Blue Bells Plantation (formerly Brockholes Wood) is a small part of ancient woodland.

Roman Industrial Sites.
There is evidence to suggest sites in the parish engaged in the production of Roman tile and pottery.

HEPWORTH *(continued)*

Ancient Tracks (?)
Dunhill Lane, which forms the eastern parish boundary with Thelnetham from the A143 E of Hepworth South Common, N to Beck Street NE of Springbank Farm, and Field Lane, which forms the SW boundary with Stanton from the junction with Weston Bury Lane down to the A143, are possible ancient tracks.

Medieval Commons.
Faden's 1783 map shows Hepworth North Common as a linear extension of Stanton Dale. This extension took it just into Stanton parish in the SW, and NE from Hepworth Road junction with Market Weston Road terminating at Home Farm. Hepworth Common, now marked as Hepworth South Common, lay E-W straddling the present Bury Road from W of Hepworth Road junction to E of the parish boundary with Wattisfield. The commons were enclosed in 1817 when 14 acres, known as the Poor's Allotment, were awarded to the poor of the parish in lieu of their right to cut fuel on the common.

Site of old Windmill.
A post mill is shown on Hepworth South Common in 1783. Its fate is unknown.

Historic Houses & Ancient Moated Site.
The two manors of North Hall and Reeve's Hall were held by Gilbert le Blund at Domesday. Their modern halls stand together in the N of the parish. Three sides of a square moat stand isolated S of Hepworth House.

HERRINGFLEET *(6 miles NW of Lowestoft)*

Mutford & Lothingland Hundred. 'The shallows (marshes) of Herela's people' (OE) *Herlingaflet* (DB)
Manors. Herringfleet Late Priory (C13 Roger Fitz Osbert; -1536 Priory of St Olaves). *Sub-Manors.* Loudham and Titsall's Herringfleet.

Ancient Priory.
Situated near the site of an ancient ferry over the Waveney, Herringswell Priory is a small Augustinian house founded c1216 by Roger FitzOsbert for a prior and 5 canons, and dedicated to St Olave, St Mary and St Edmund. A lane now cuts off the eastern parts of the buildings including the crossing and E end of the C13 church. This building was originally aisleless but received a S aisle of five bays c1310. The N range contained a refectory. Its undercroft of c1300 survives, surprisingly of brick. The cross-wall belongs to the time after the Dissolution when the priory was connected to a house. Also of this date (C16) belong the ruins of the N range. The priory was dissolved in 1536 and in 1546 granted with the manor to Henry Jernegan. Many of the ruins were cleared away in 1784 and the precinct wall used for repairing the road. The C13 nave is the oldest work still standing.

Ancient Ferry.
The following account comes from a manuscript of Bishop Tanner's: 'King Edward I in the 26th year of his reign (1298) sent out a writ to William de Kerdeston, Sheriff of Norfolk and Suffolk, to inquire what detriment it would be to any person for him to grant leave to Jeffery Pollerin of Yarmouth to build a bridge over the river at St Olave's Priory; and a jury being empannelled, returned that one Sireck, a fisherman, called afterwards John Atte Ferry's, began several years before to carry over passengers in his boat there, and received for his pains bread, herrings, and such like things, to the value of 20s per year'. The application was therefore rejected and the ferry continued for a further three generations until it was eventually sold out of the family to Roger de Ludham. Pressure had been building for the erection of a bridge, and now one was begun. Perhaps it was never finished for some time later, among patents of the 9th of Henry V (1422), is one for building a bridge over the water between Norfolk and Suffolk at "Seent Tholowes (St Olaves) Ferry." Again little seems to have been done until, in the reign of Henry VIII, it is generally believed Sir James Hobart built the first stone bridge. This was rebuilt in 1770 and not replaced until the iron suspension bridge of 1847.

Medieval Common.
Herringfleet Common is shown on Faden's map of 1783 extending the length of the western parish boundary through Fritton to merge with Belton Common, mainly W of Herringfleet Road, to the river Waveney marshes.

HERRINGFLEET *(continued)*

Historic Houses & Ancient Moated Sites.
The partly castellated Manor House Farm, SE of the church, was built by Henry Jernegan c1546 and was originally moated. Adjoining is one of the largest thatched barns in Suffolk finished in brick and flint chequer. Herringfleet Hall in the NE of the parish is a modern mansion enlarged in 1873 but standing beside a small oblong moated area which could possibly be the site of an earlier hall. SW of this is the Elizabethan Blocka Hall.

HERRINGSWELL *(3½ miles S of Mildenhall)*

Lackford Hundred. 'Well, Spring or Lake of the Hyrnings' (OE) *Hyrningwella* (DB)
Morley suggests the place-name refers to the western projection of the parish by a track called The Carrops. At this point, for a short way, the boundary follows the marshy course of a stream W of Fen Farm running down from the river Lark by way of Tuddenham Mill. In medieval times 'in Ecclesia de Heryngswelle' was a guild 'Sancti Ethelberti Regis' which commemorates the historic incident when the East Anglian King Aethelbeorut lay the last night before crossing the water into Mercia where he was slain in 793 A.D. - the church bears this ancient dedication to St. Ethelbert. By 1783 Faden's map was showing the whole area as a warren.
Manors. Herringswell (Abbot of St. Edmunds, Bury; 1311 Walter de Norwich). *Sub-Manors.* Blunts/Blounks al Waywashyard al Lanes.

Tumuli.
A round barrow W of the church, and a bowl barrow 98' in diameter just to the S of this, have been virtually ploughed out. Also now under the plough are: a large barrow on Kentford Heath by the parish boundary, and three just SE of Warrenhill Farm - perhaps the 'Threhowes' mentioned in a C14 document relating to Herringswell.

Site of Gallows.
The site of the ancient gibbet by the Icknield Way marked the boundary land between Freckenham and Herringswell in 1238.

Historic House & Ancient Moated Site.
The timber-framed and enlarged Herringswell Manor Farm (formerly known as Herringswell Place and as Herringswell House) once belonged to Bury Abbey. There is still a water-filled site NE of Hall Farm shown on old maps as an ancient square moat and possibly the site of the original hall.

HESSETT *(5½ miles SE of Bury St Edmunds)*

Thedwestry Hundred. 'Settlers at the boundary' (OE) *Heteseta* (DB) *Heggeset* (1225). An old Register of 1538 calls the parish Hedgesset. Morley suggests 'at the boundary' may refer to the edge of Bradfield Forest.
Manors. Hessett (-1540 Abbot of St. Edmunds, Bury).

Ancient Woodland.
Freecroft Wood, Hinderlay Wood (formerly Handyley Grove) and the larger Mellfield Wood, are all fragments of ancient woodland. Present-day greed has seen the loss of the delightful Monk Wood which lay E of Mellfield Wood.

Roman Road.
The line of a Roman road forms the western boundary from Freewood Farm N to Hicketheath Farm. It is then traced by the boundary of Chevin's Wood.

Deer Park.
The former deer park of Drinkstone Hall extended well into Hesset parish (*see* Drinkstone).

Ancient Spring.
The churchyard of St. Ethelbert is said to contain a never-failing spring which once supplied half the village with water. It was covered in 1891.

Medieval Green.
Hicket Heath is shown on Faden's map of 1783 covering a large area running S from Hickheath Farm

HESSETT *(continued)*

between Breach Wood and Tinkers Wood, partly in Rougham parish. The straight road heading almost due N is not shown on the map and appears to have been constructed some time after the heath's enclosure.

Medieval Archery Practice.
The parish butts stood on land which was sold for 3s. 4d. in 1588.

Guildhall.
The village formerly had 'a messuage called the Guildhall and four cottages used as poor-houses.'

Almshouse.
An almshouse here is said to date from 1493 by the will of Walter Nunn.

Historic Houses & Ancient Moated Sites.
Hessett Hall, the former manor house on Hicket Heath W of the village, was home of the Bacon, Walpole and Le Heup families. The Bacons were connected with Hesset from the C12 until 1653 when Lionel Bacon died without issue. It has been suggested that the reason such a small village possesses the magnificent church of St Ethelbert is due to the marriage of John Bacon to a sister of the Abbot of Bury Abbey who originally held the church. The hall, which was recorded in 1541, was destroyed by fire in the C18, but the square moat which surrounded it remains, N of Old Hall Road, with further earthworks to the S. The site is heavily overgrown with trees and shrubs and with no trace now of the old buildings. There are fragments of another oblong moat at Spring Farm now occupied by a modern house, and in a field NW of this in the SW corner of Hesset Green, is half of a wide almost square ancient moat enclosing an area 131' by 98' again with no trace of its former house. Cropmarks show part of a moat at Valley Farm (formerly Hesset Hole) on the southern parish boundary.

HEVENINGHAM *(5½ miles SW of Halesworth)*

Blything Hundred. 'The homestead belonging to Hefa's people' (OE) *Heueniggeham* (DB)
Manors. Heveningham (C12 Robert FitzWalter; Late C12 William de Heveningham. It remained in this family until 1700). *Sub-Manors.* Burton Haugh; Blaunchards.

Ancient Packway.
Dunwich Lane, an ancient packway, runs parallel with the southern parish boundary as a country road from the Roman road to the edge of Lodge Wood. Its course is lost through the wood but emerges as a footpath beyond the parish boundary and the Peasenhall Road *(see* Bramfield).

Roman Road.
The course of a Roman road running NW-SE through the parish and apparently heading for the coast at or near Aldeburgh, is traced by the road from Cratfield to Peasenhall.

Deserted Settlement.
Aerial photographs show a complex series of earthworks (since ploughed out) which have been interpreted as a 'deserted hamlet' SW of Heveningham Hall. This was probably 'cleared' prior to creating or extending the park.

Historic Houses & Ancient Moated Sites.
Standing in its great park laid out by Capability Brown which extends over 600 acres into the neighbouring parish of Huntingfield, Heveningham Hall is a spectacular mansion built for Sir Gerard Vanneck in 1778, mostly to the designs of James Wyatt. A rivulet from the river Blyth divides the park into two and provides an elongated 'lake' in front of the house. The hall has a 200' frontage and stands near the site of an earlier hall, seat of the Heveningham family which claims to trace its ancestry from Galtir Heveningham who lived in the time of King Knut. The previous hall, which was reputedly supported with oak pillars, was assessed with 32 hearths in 1674 suggesting a building of massive proportions. C16 Moat Farm, S of the village, retains a well-defined oblong moat with traces of a sub-division. A pottery scatter by the moated site of the C16 timber-framed Cocks Hall suggests occupation of the site from the late C12.

HIGHAM *(5 miles S of Hadleigh)*

Samford Hundred. 'High (or chief) homestead' (OE) *Hecham* (1050) *Heihham* (DB)
Manors. Higham Hall (1270 William de Reymes). *Sub-Manors.* Minott's/Minetts; Raven's Hall/Reymes.

Ancient Woodland.
Rowley Grove, N of the village, is a small part of ancient woodland.

Historic Houses.
The much restored Tudor House is the finest of several timber-framed houses in the village.

HIGHAM (or Higham Green) *(7 miles W of Bury St Edmunds)*

Lackford Hundred. 'High (or chief) homestead' (OE) *Hecham* (1050) *Heihham* (DB)
This former Gazeley hamlet of Higham Green became a separate ecclesiastical parish in 1861 and civil parish in 1866.

Ancient Track.
The Icknield Way forms the northern parish boundary from TL731 672 to TL749 684.

Tumulus.
A round barrow lies 400 yds. SW of Desning Lodge by the Icknield Way.

Site of Gallows (?)
Between and to the N of Gravelpit Wood and Pin Plantation, N of the A14 Newmarket road, is an area called 'Gallows Lands' on the C19 tithe map. This suggests the possible site of a former medieval gibbet.

Medieval Greens.
Three former greens are named on Faden's 1783 map. Two are shown; Lower Green to the N, covered the junction of Higham Road and Burgate Road by the War Memorial, and Upper Green to the S comprising a triangular area covering the junction of Burgate Road with a lane which eventually leads to Desning Hall. Middle Green, named but not shown, must have gone by this time. It probably comprised an area now enclosed but traced by the boundaries of a group of properties lying either side of Burgate Road. It may well be that all these greens were fragments of an even earlier single green which was much more extensive. Lower and Upper greens may have formed its northern and southern limits, with Burgate Road its eastern side and its western boundary now traced by the present curving footpath and field boundaries. Incidentally, the greens would appear to have been named according to their proximity to the Hall rather than their compass bearing - Higham Hall lies to the S of all three greens, the nearest green therefore being named Upper Green.

HINDERCLAY *(8 miles NE of Ixworth)*

Blackbourn Hundred. 'Hildr's clay' (OScand+OE) *Hilderclea* (DB)
The quality of the clay excavated in the parish has produced fine pottery since Roman times.
Manors. Hinderclay (-1540 Abbot of St. Edmunds; 1540 Edward North). *Sub-Manors.* Bartford Soham Hall.

Ancient Woodland.
Hinderclay Wood is just a tiny fragment of a once extensive stretch of ancient woodland tragically lost during the latter part of the twentieth century.

Early Iron-Age Settlement.
On the original southern edge of Hinderclay Wood, an Early Iron-Age settlement was discovered marked by a trackway, a group of hut circles and a scatter of pottery.

Site of Roman Pottery Industry.
C1-C2 Roman kilns were also found on the Early Iron-Age site (*see above*), linked with those found on Foxledge Common Wattisfield and at Rickinghall.

Ancient Well.
St Mary's Well is a perennial spring on the junction of Tuffen Lane with the road to Thelnetham church. It is

HINDERCLAY *(continued)*

said to possess healing powers especially for weak eyes.

Medieval Green.

Faden's map of 1783 shows Hinderclay Green as a large rectangular green running SW from N of the church, enclosing either side of the present road and ending in the area of the Old Rectory. Seven roads emerged from the green: four ran NNW (towards Thelnetham), one NE (Cowfen Lane), one SE (past the church), and one S (to Wattisfield). Although it has now been enclosed and redeveloped, property and field boundaries trace its former outline.

HINTLESHAM *(4½ miles NE of Hadleigh)*

Samford Hundred. 'Hyntel's homestead or enclosure' (OE) *Hintlesham* (DB)

Manors. Hintlesham (? William Denvers; early C13 William Talbot/William Pipard). *Sub-Manors.* St. Peter's/ Manor le Lyesne's; Hintlesham Priory called Veyseys.

Ancient Woodland.

Ramsey Wood and Keeble's Grove are areas of ancient woodland.

Tumulus (?)

An article on Hintlesham's history published in 1920 states that 'the chiefs of the early British encampment are buried under the old oak growing on the tumulus at the head of Brick Kiln Lane'. And further it was said that 'the oak tree still stands on a bump' and that 'Hintlesham lore has it that soldiers are buried beneath'.

Saxon Cemetery (?)

The same article speaks of finds relating to a Saxon cemetery opposite 'Hyntle Place'. This may possibly be in the area W of Birch Farm.

Earthworks (?)

The same article speaks of 'traces of a British encampment'. The old OS 6" map shows a rectilinear sided earthwork bank on the N side of Thorpes Hill in a field close by a well adjoining Belstead or (Spark) Brook. The earthworks do not continue to the SW beyond the field boundary. All the field boundaries have now gone and the earthworks would now appear to be ploughed out.

Lost Medieval Settlement (?)

According to the same article there was 'a good-sized village called Sparkford here associated with Hintlesham Priory. Foundations of houses were discovered over 60 years ago (c1860) in the '40 Acres' which belonged to the Peacocks'. The '40 Acres' has been located on the tithe map as being NE of Hintlesham Priory near the northern parish boundary.

Site of Chapel (and/or Priory?)

There is no evidence linking the farmhouse called Hintlesham Priory with any ecclesiastical building here. The name probably comes from the manor on which the house stands which anciently belonged to the Abbot of St. Edmunds in Bury, and by c1527 appears to have been held by Wix Abbey in Essex; Thomas Vesey received the manor after the Dissolution. However, the suggestion of a lost hamlet called Sparkeford being situated in the area and the mention of a Sparkeford Chapel in 1295 may relate to a lost priory on the site perhaps within the fragment of moat which survives (*see below*). A field in this location is called Chapel Field.

Historic Houses & Ancient Moated Sites.

Hintlesham Hall, now a hotel, stands in a well-wooded park of some 150 acres. The manor was anciently the lordship of the Talbots and the hall for very many years the seat of the Tymperley family for whom Thomas Timperley built the present house c1570. Evidence that they had resided in a previous hall here for some time is provided in the nearby church which contains the tomb of a John Timperley who died in 1400. The present hall has been much altered receiving a mainly Georgian exterior. The site of the Timperley's timber-framed Old Hall is N of the A1071 just E of Wolves Wood. Here is still a small fragment of the ancient moat which was shown on a map of 1595 as 'D-shaped'. An 1826 estate map shows it as a wide L-shaped(?) moat with a rectangular

HINTLESHAM *(continued)*

ditched/moated area containing buildings. Moat Farm in the S of the parish retains the majority of its square moat. A farm called Hintlesham Priory NW of the village has a possible fragment of a moat. A 1595 map of Hintlesham shows a building in the centre of an apparent rectangular moat with an entrance to the SE, in the area of Northlands, NW of Park Farm. It is marked 'Tenement Hudmans'.

HITCHAM *(7 miles NNW of Hadleigh)*

Cosford Hundred. 'Heca's home' or 'High enclosure' (OE) *Hecham* (DB)
Manors. Hitcham (-1561 Abbot of Ely; 1603 leased for life to Sir Robert Hitcham). *Sub-Manors.* Witherton al Witherton's (Barrards); Manton of Manton's; Loose Hall/Loes Manor.

Ancient Woodland.
Wood Farm in the N of the parish marks the site of the once extensive Hitcham Great Wood which has been totally destroyed. There are fragments of ancient Woodland at Home Wood (formerly Peason's Grove), Bloxhall Grove and Parker's Wood.

Roman Road.
A Roman road runs almost due N through the parish. There is no evidence on the ground until just N of Dale Farm where the road to Rattlesden traces its route to the parish boundary just S of the turning to Potash Farm.

Romano-British Settlement.
Along the trackway from Brick House Farm is evidence of a Romano-British settlement in the form of flint walls, rubbish pits and pottery of C2-C3. The farm stands beside the course of the Roman road.

Ancient Chapel.
The site of a Saxon church or chapel was discovered immediately N of Brick House Farm in 1984.

Site of Mills.
Traces of a medieval watermill exist by the river. In 1783 a postmill is recorded, but not shown on Faden's map, on the E side of the road to Stowmarket by the track and footpath which heads SE.

Site of Gallows.
A reference is made to a 'Qualmstower' in 1251 (OE *cwelm-stowa* 'place of execution') belonging to the Bishop of Ely. A 17 acre field called 'Gallowfield' was a copyhold tenement of the manor of Hitcham from at least 1612. By 1840 it was divided into two fields, Great and Little Galley Field. The site is situated at the southern end of the parish at a point where the B1115 road from Bildeston leaves the line of the Roman road by curving W to skirt these high fields before continuing again in the same NW direction.

Almshouses.
In 1663 Sir George Waldergrave gave two tenements for a residence for the poor of the parish. It was rebuilt c1818.

Workhouse.
A workhouse was in existence in 1776 when it had 30 inmates.

Guildhall.
'Old House', a superb timber-framed building adjoining the churchyard gate, was the former Guildhall and dates from c1500.

Historic Houses & Ancient Moated Sites.
Until 1562 the manor of Hitcham Hall belonged to the Bishop of Ely, and ancestors of Sir Robert Hitcham were no doubt formerly seated at the Hall. Wetherden Hall, a corruption of the surname of its first known owner, Richard Wederton or Witherton, is situated W of the village and has one of the most impressive moated sites in Suffolk; only the old servants' and outhouse range survive, occupying an entire side and probably retaining parts of both the former C15 and C17 residences. The strong moat, with the remains of another

HITCHAM *(continued)*

surrounding it, suggests an even earlier date for the site which was long the seat of the knightly family of Waldegrave. Cropmarks show a small trapizium-shaped moat to the E of the hall. Brick House Farm is part of an early Tudor mansion with, at one end, parts of two polygonal angled turrets. Evidence of the former manor house (in the form of Tudor brick) has come from the island of a square moat at Stanstead Hall, now occupied by an C18 farmhouse N of Cooks Green. Fieldwork between Cook's Green and Cross Green has found evidence of more concentrated settlement relating to this poorly-documented manor. This is N from Cross Green to Water Run, and along the Brettenham Road where fragments of four possible moats remain including those at Ennals Farm, Oak Cottage and Cross Way Farm. There are other moats: at Bloxhall to the NW, with another isolated moat SW of this in Home Wood; from the seasonally wet square moat at Oak Tree Farm near the northern parish boundary has come C13-C15 pottery - the site was recorded as Nectons in 1544 and held by a family of the same name in the C14-C15; at Loose Hall is a fragment of an asymetric moat, the site of the manor house of the Domesday vill of Losam; in Parker's Wood, NE of the village, is a rectangular moat with a causeway to the N and a scatter of C13-C14 pottery on the island; Bloxhall (Blocks Hall in 1825) has an incomplete rectangular moat c109 yds.' by 197 yds; at the site of The Hobbets, W of Hitcham Causeway, are fragments of moats shown as one small irregular moat containing a house in 1839, and a former moat at Fen Farm (formerly Bacons Manor) on the eastern parish boundary is depicted as a small, square moat situated in 'Moat Field' on an estate map - this has since been infilled and ploughed out.

HOLBROOK *(6 miles S of Ipswich)*

Samford Hundred. 'Brook in a hollow or ravine ' (OE) *Holebroc* (DB)

The parish gets its name from a brook which falls into the river Stour at Holbrook Bay near the hamlet of Lower Holbrook, a mile S of the village.

Manors. Holbrook (1240 Earl Warren).

Ancient Woodland.

Shrub Wood (now called Holbrook Park) is an extensive tract of ancient woodland to the N connected to the main parish by a narrow strip of land. A fragment to the S across the boundary in neighbouring Tattingstone still retains its ancient name. Hales Grove, just to the SE of Shrub Wood, is further ancient woodland.

Deer Park.

The ancient Shrub Wood was a former deer park.

Medieval Green.

The small Alton Green lay E of Alton Green Farm in Lower Holbrook, on the S side of the road to Harkstead.

Historic House.

The extensive lake, gardens, and one of three former fish-ponds remain of Holbrook Park, a house owned by Sir Charles Kent in 1783 and listed with 15-19 hearths in 1674; it may be that shown in 1783 lying at the N end of the village street. Park House, on the northern parish boundary, is named 'Keepers House' on the 1838 tithe. In the time of Henry III, the resident lord was Richard de Holbrook and afterwards the Daundys.

HOLLESLEY *(6 miles SW of Orford)*

Wilford Hundred. 'Hol's meadow' or 'wood clearing in a hollow' (OE) *Holeslea* (DB)

Manors. Hollesley (1269 Robert Bigot). *Sub-Manors.* Caldwell Hall.

Tumuli (?)

Two possible small barrows 2½' high lie on Lower Hollesley Common, N of Brew House.

Ancient Harbour Settlement.

Aerial photographs show a remarkable complex of small Iron-Age enclosures and ring-ditches SW of Boyton Hall Farm, near the site of Cauldwell Hall (*see below*). Hollesley once held an anchorage sheltered by a shingle spit and these enclosures must have formed the site of an ancient harbour settlement. Sometime after the C13

HOLLESLEY *(continued)*

this harbour became silted up and the land reclaimed. The site is close to another similar settlement just over the parish boundary in Boyton. (*see* Boyton)

Ancient Maritime Finds.

During the continental wars, Hollesley Bay was often visited by ships of war and in 1804 two very ancient and curious pieces of cannon were found here.

Industrial Pottery Site.

W of Poplar Farm, by a tributary called the Black Ditch, a late C13 pottery production site was excavated in 1949.

Lost Medieval Settlement.

The Domesday township of Culsley - 'a berewick of Holeslea' has long been lost. It was named Culleste in 1228.

Medieval Common.

The 800 acres of unenclosed heath known as Hollesley Heath and Lower Hollesley Common are not shown on Faden's 1783 map, but incorporated under the banner heading of Boyton Heath.

Medieval Fair.

It is recorded that in 1279 William de Stirston, bailiff of the Earl Marshall at Hollesley, moved a fair to a new site (possibly at the Holystile Crossroads) where he exacted tolls from the people without a warrent. The fair's earlier site is not known.

Site of old Windmill.

A postmill which stood NE of the road junction at Virtue's Farm in 1783 was blown down in 1881.

Site of Historic House.

A cold spring still marks the site of the remains of the manor house of Cauldwell Hall, just NE of Hollesley Young Offenders Institution. Owned by the Wingfields from the early C14, it is shown as Caulde Hall on a 1783 map.

HOLTON ST PETER *(1 mile E of Halesworth)*

Blything Hundred. 'Farmstead in a hollow' (OE) plus church dedication *Holetuna* (DB)
Manors. Holton Hall (1286 William de Vaux/Vallibus).

Roman Road.

Stone Street (A144) forms the western boundary from the junction N of Fairview Farm to the railway crossing.

Old Windmill.

The postmill which still stands S of the church dates from before 1750.

Historic House & Ancient Moated Site.

Holton Hall probably stands on the site of the manor house. It was rebuilt on the old foundations in 1883 after being partially burned down the previous year. The park extends to 100 well-wooded acres. The site of a former moat is suggested by Moat Farm in the N of the parish.

HOLTON ST MARY *(4½ miles SSE of Hadleigh)*

Samford Hundred. 'Hola's farm' (OE) plus church dedication. *Holetuna* (DB)
Manors. Holton (1258 Robert Raydon). *Sub-Manors.* Boyton's in Holton.

Medieval Green (?)

The present OS map gives the name Bacon's Green to the road junction opposite Holton Place. No green is shown or named by Faden in 1783, so it must have changed status by this time.

Workhouse.

A House of Industry was listed in 1803.

Charity School.

A Charity School for instructing all the children of the parish from 5 to 12 years old in reading, writing and

HOLTON ST MARY *(continued)*

arithmetic, and clothing them, free of charge, was established and endowed by the Rev Stephen White. A school house was erected and conveyed to trustees by Sir Francis Mannock in 1749 and the Town Pightle leased for the use of the school in 1755. The remainder of the income was used in furnishing books and rewards for the children.

HOMERSFIELD (or South Elmham St Mary) *(5 miles WSW of Bungay)*

Wangford Hundred. 'Hamar's field' (OE) *Humbresfelda* (DB)
Manors. Homersfield (-1540 Estate of the Bishop of Thetford; 1540 North family). *Sub-Manors.* Limbourne/ Lymburn called Lymborn Priories (c1160 Bungay Nunnery).

Ancient Woodland.
Thicket Wood is a small part of ancient woodland.

Romano-British Industrial Site.
A Roman industrial pottery site was discovered at Homersfield Pit. The kilns included one (excavated 1959) of C3 date, and a complete kiln containing its last firing which was unfortunately destroyed by workmen in 1962.

Ancient Earthworks.
The church of St Mary stands on an ancient platform above the Waveney. It is believed by some to have been erected upon the site of a temple to the pagan Saxon god Hamar (*see place-name)*.

Medieval Market & Fair.
The Bishop of Norwich obtained the grant of a market and fair at Homersfield in 1218. A further grant for a market and fair was made in 1226. Both were obsolete by 1874.

Deserted Medieval Settlement.
The Manor of Lymburn formerly belonged to the nuns of Bungay, and in 1569 Sir Basigburn Gaudy died 'seized of the manor'. By 1734 John Kirby observed that 'there are now few or no tenants remaining and it would scarce be known if it were not for the water mill which still retained the name Lymborn Mill'.

Medieval Common.
Limbourne Common, W of the parish by the river Waveney, is named after the small manor (*see above*).

Site of Gallows.
A gibbet stood on Gallows Hill c1550.

HONINGTON *(3 miles NW of Ixworth)*

Blackbourn Hundred. 'Honey farm' or 'Homestead of Hina's people' (OE) *Hunegetuna* (DB)
Manors. (Estates owned by Abbot of St. Edmunds, Bury, but not as a manor; 1757 Duke of Grafton).

Multi-period Settlement Site.
At Sapiston Bridge, just NE of the village on the parish boundary with Sapiston, 'huts', small pits and artefacts from a settlement site covering Neolithic, Bronze-Age, Roman and Saxon periods were discovered.

Site of Gallows.
A skeleton in a gibbet cage was found in 1936 during the construction of Honington aerodrome. W. G. Clarke's book *In Brecklands Wild* gives details of the execution and gibbeting of John Nichols for murder. Apparently John and Nathan Nichols (father and son) of Honington murdered Sarah Nichols aged 17 (their daughter/ sister) who was beaten and strangled at Thetford Lane Gate in 1794. They were executed at Bury and John's body hung in a cage at the site of the murder. The body of his son was kept in Bury and used for dissection and annatomising. The gallows stood in Gibbet Covert which was erased by the airfield. Other fields close by are named Gibbet Close and Gibbet Cover.

HOO *(4 miles SSW of Framlingham)*

Loes Hundred. 'Place at the spur of land' (OE) *Ho* (c1050) *Hou* (DB)
Manors. Hoo Hall (C13 William de Chesnet/Chesney). *Sub-Manors.* Godwins; Hoo Charsfield; Hoo Kettleburgh.
Obviously an important place in Saxon times when the entire village was embraced by one large manor of 3 caracutes (360 acres) under Ely Abbey. It must have still been very populous throughout the medieval period when manors were held by several important families (*see below*) and there were no less than five guilds here. The Domesday church includes the unusual dedication to St. Eustachius.

Ancient Woodland.
Hoo Wood, Lords Wood and Smilley Wood are parts of ancient woodland; the last two still retaining their former boundary banks and ditches.

Medieval Green & Former Settlement Site.
Hoo Green is shown in 1783 lying either side of Sandy Lane running S from the crossroads to just N of Godwin's Place. The parish now comprises only isolated farmsteads but there is evidence of former concentrated settlement around this green in the form of seven small farmhouse enclosures and two moats with exterior earthworks.

Medieval Guildhall (?)
With the five guilds of Holy Trinity, St. Mary, St. Peter, St. Andrew and St. John operating here it is likely a guildhall once existed.

Historic Houses & Ancient Moated Sites.
Godwin's Place is claimed to be one of the most ancient sites in the county, and although there is little to see of its past glories, ancient records call it the 'Great House'. The most recent hall, 'Godyns', built by John Goodwin in the C15, was demolished during the C16 by Sir Anthony Wingfield (who built himself a new hall at nearby Euston). All that now remain are three sides of a very strong moat (the W side having been infilled) on the E side of the road between the two churches of Hoo and Charsfield. From here trackways head N with possible tofts showing as crop and soil marks. The family of Godwin date back to Saxon times when (around 977 A.D.) a Godwin gave Ely a large estate here including (at Domesday) a small church dedicated to St Andrew and St Eustachius. John Godwin held the manor in 1430 and it later passed to the Wingfields. The present small farmhouse on the site was built c1620 using, it is said, some material from the old hall. At Hoo Green another large rectangular moat 23' to 30' wide and 4' deep forms a raised island 83yds by 70yds which may have been used to protect stock. Hoo Hall, now a farmhouse by the church, stands on a bold hill spur above the Deben valley (*see place-name*). The Manor of Hoo Hall has been held by some illustrious families. In the C13 it was the powerful Bigods, then Thomas de Brotherton - son of Edward I, and afterwards by the de Uffords, De Mowbrays, the Wingfields, and eventually the Dukes of Hamilton.

HOPTON or HOPTON-ON-SEA *(5 miles N of Lowestoft)*

Mutford & Lothingland Hundred. 'Place at the crescent bay' (OE) *Hopetuna* (DB)
Whilst the meaning is given by Skeat as 'Farm in a valley (or coast) recess', Claude Morley believes the name to come from the Anglo-Saxon *hop*, a circle, meaning a crescent bay. If this bay once existed here it has been eroded away as the coastline is now virtually straight. It is further S in Blything Hundred where Domesday has two entries (at present unlocated) for 'Hoppetuna' and 'Opituna'. The name Hopton-on-Sea has been in use since 1952.
Manors. Hopton (Late C11 granted to Prior and Convent of Holy Trinity, Norwich).

Medieval Common.
A rectangular common is shown by Faden in 1783 lying N of the church and village and marked by Warren Road; it is now a part of the golf course. A scatter of C13-C14 pottery has identified former settlement on the southern edge.

HOPTON *(7 miles NNE of Ixworth)*

Blackbourn Hundred. 'Farm in a valley recess' (OE) *Hopetuna* (DB).

Manors. (Estate owned by Abbot of St. Edmunds, Bury, but not as a manor; 1345 Thomas de Lovayne).

A strategically strong position forming almost an island of boulder clay surrounded by marshes and approached by the narrow neck of Weston Fen, there is no existing earthwork suggesting it as a fortified place though it appears to have been settled throughout all periods of history.

Multi-period Settlement Site.

An extensive multi-period site located S of the village unearthed material of Iron-Age, Roman, Middle-Saxon Ipswich ware, C12-C14 Medieval and a small amount of Late Medieval date showing a long period of settlement.

Site of Turbary Industry.

Hopton Turbary (peat extraction) was mentioned in 1341. The site is unknown but was likely in the area of Hopton Fen in the N of the parish.

Site of Pottery Industry.

A kiln site excavated just SW of Red House in Nethergate Street produced evidence of a Late Medieval pottery industry in the area.

Medieval Common.

Hopton Common covers an extensive area to the northern parish boundary. Immediately to its S is Hopton Fen. Faden's map of 1783 shows a large band of common and fen running along the southern bank of the Little Ouse river E from Knettishall to Redgrave comprising Hopton Common, Thelnetham Fen (lying part in Hopton parish, NE of the village), Redgrave Common and Redgrave Fen.

Site of old Windmill.

A postmill stood at Common Farm in Mill Lane in 1783. Its fate is not known.

HORHAM *(5 miles SE of Eye)*

Hoxne Hundred. 'Dirty or muddy homestead' (OE) *Horham* (c950)

Manors. Horham Comitis (1609 Peter Wood). *Sub-Manors.* Horham Jernegan's/Sherman's; Horham, Brodocks Late Copledyke; Horham, Thorpe Hall with Wotton; Buckenham/Bokenham's; Horham Late Pooley's.

Ancient Woodland.

Pedlar's Wood, a part of Devedenhall Wood (the bulk of which is in Whepstead parish), and Whitshaw Wood are fragment of ancient woodland.

Site of old Windmill.

A postmill, demolished in 1934, had been standing W of the church on the N side of the B1117 since before 1750.

Historic Houses & Ancient Moated Sites.

Sir Herbert Jernegan, who died in 1239, had his seat here, possibly on the curiously designed but very ancient moated site at Moat Farm, SW of the village. This is circular towards the N and angular towards the S. The Jernegans were of Danish stock tracing their family back to well before the Norman invasion. Two sides of a large square moat remains E of the church (on the site of the rectory?). Near the site of Cratfield Town Farm, near the western parish boundary, is a square enclosure, possibly the remains of a moat.

HORRINGER (or Horningsheath) *(2 miles WSW of Bury St Edmunds)*

Thingoe Hundred. 'Ploughed land of a man called Horning' or 'Winding stream by ploughed land' (OE) *Horningeserda* (DB)

Manors. Horningsheath Magna and Horningsheath Parva (-1546 Abbot of St. Edmunds, Bury; 1546 Sir Thomas Darcy).

Ancient Woodland.

Adkin's Wood (running S from the church), Lord Hervey's Wood, Pestle Wood (formerly Mordaboys

HORRINGER *(continued)*

Wood), and the remaining fragment of Pedler's Wood on the SW parish boundary, are all remnants of ancient woodland.

Ancient Mines.
Near Horringer Court are chalk quarries for the mining of flint, with galleries or caves to the N and small trackways with six entrances. The mine was in good condition in 1970, the passages averaging 6½' to 10' wide and 10' to 16' high arched to a point. The walls still bore evidence of candle soot deposits and the floors were well-worn. One workbench and three piles of flints remain.

Deserted Medieval Village.
There were once two parishes here; Great and Little Horringer or Horningsheath, but they were consolidated in 1548. Great Horringer has developed into the sole parish and all that remains of Little Horringer is a farm beside the moated site of the Hall. There are no remains of St Peter's Church which stood beside the hall and was demolished after the consolidation.

Medieval Greens.
Horringer Green is named and shown on Faden's map of 1783 extending S from Street Farm to just S of Horringer House on the E side of the road; its shape is still outlined by field boundaries. St Leonard's Church stands beside a village green which covers either side of the present A143 road. An unnamed linear green is shown straddling the parish boundary with Hawstead. The road N from Whepstead to Bury St Edmunds (the present B1066) ran up the middle from just S of the river Lark to Sharp's Lane. Its southern end continues for some distance as a narrow strip of green which eventually joins up with Mickley Green at Whepstead. Another small linear green lay SE of the church but it, along with the properties which lined the former link road with the church, have been swept away to create modern residential development. One of these three unnamed greens, (probably the second because of its size), was called Sheep Green and at one time held two extensive lamb fairs.

Guildhall & Workhouse.
In what was then called Horningsheath Parva, the Old Guildhall, later known as the Town House, was converted by the Marquess of Bath into four tenements for the poor in 1720. Records show repairs made to the Guildhall in 1474.

Historic Houses & Ancient Moated Sites.
The manor of Horningsheath was held by Bury Abbey who built Little Horningsheath (Horringer) Hall as a 'pleasure house'. Later home to the Gipp family, it was dismantled c1759 leaving nothing but fragments of its moat. The arms of the Abbot and Edward the Confessor were said to have been carved and painted in the 'grand chamber'. The parish includes the hamlet of Horsecroft with its water-ornamented Hall, standing on the site of the earlier hall of the Lucas family, resident here from the C16. A brass in the church commemorates Mary Lucas who died in 1616.

HOXNE *(3½ miles NE of Eye)*

Hoxne Hundred. 'Hock-shaped spur of land' or 'settlement of the Hoxa (tribe) (OE) *Eglesdune* (anciently) *Hoxne* (c950) *Hoxana* (DB). The place is on a spur of land between the Waveney and one of its tributaries, and the place-name may describe the similarity between the shape of the spur and a horse's hock.
Manors. Hoxne Manor (-1536 Bishop of Norwich; 1536 Charles Brandon). *Sub-Manors.* Hoxne Priory/Late Priory of St. Edmunds.

Ancient Woodland.
Hoxne Wood, Depperhaugh Wood and The Slades are parts of ancient woodland.

Palaeolithic Settlement.
A site of national importance dating to the Paleaolithic period was discovered in old brick-pits in the parish by John Frere in 1797. The chipped flint axes he found mark the beginnings of scientific archaeology. Further

HOXNE *(continued)*

excavations in 1970 by John Wymer found hand-axes and flakes dropped by hunter-gatherers 300,000 to 350,000 years ago.

Roman Hoard.

An exceptional hoard of Roman gold (now in the British Museum) in the form of coins and artefacts of the C4 and early C5, was discovered in a field in the parish in 1992. A follow-up excavation in the area in 1993 found 330 additional metal objects but no associated settlement - a post-hole found may have served as a marker when the treasure was probably hastily and undeterminately buried during the final days of Roman occupation. They obviously hoped to retrieve their valuables when order was re-established; it never was and the hoard remained unclaimed for 1,600 years.

Saxon Cemetery (?)

A possible Saxon cemetery site was said to have been discovered at 'Low Close' in the area of Low Street.

Site of Martyrdom of King Edmund (?)

On the death of King Offa, Edmund was crowned King of East Anglia when only fifteen years of age. Some time later a Danish army under Hinguar set on revenge for atrocities wrongly attributed to Edmund, challenged the East Anglian King to renounce his Christian faith for Paganism and share his kingdom with the Dane. Edmund refused and a great battle ensued at Snarehill near Thetford. The English were beaten and fled. The King was allegedly captured at Hoxne where a legend has developed into the circumstances (*see below*). He was said to have been tied to a tree and shot with arrows before being beheaded; the date was November 20th 870. The 'site' is marked by a modern stone cross in a field close by Goldbrook Bridge. (*see also* Bradfield St Clare).

Ancient Oak.

An ancient oak, said to be the one to which Edmund was bound fell 'by its own weight' in August 1848 and was examined. The point of an arrow was found embedded in the trunk and when cut, the tree-rings indicated an age of about one thousand years 'thereby supporting the tradition'. A section from the oak was kept for many years in Hoxne church (and is now in Hengrave Hall?).

Ancient Bridge.

Goldbrook Bridge stands on the site of the original wooden bridge under which, tradition states, Edmund hid from the Danes until betrayed by a newly wedded couple returning home who, on crossing the bridge, saw the king's spurs reflected in the water by the moonlight. Indignant at their treachery, the king is said to have put a curse on every couple who should cross the bridge on their way to the church to be married. It is said that when the present bridge was being erected in 1878, assorted spear heads, knives and stirrups, were unearthed here.

Site of St Edmund's Chapel.

A chapel composed of 'trees sawn down the middle and fixed in the ground' infilled with mud and mortar with a thatched roof, was erected on the alleged site of Edmund's death. Here his body is said to have lain for 33 years until 903 A.D. when it was taken to Beodericworth where he was canonised and the town later renamed Bury St Edmunds. The old chapel was replaced with a more permanent structure known as Hoxne Priory and situated at Cross Street.

Site of Ancient Monastery.

In his will of c950 A.D., Bishop Theodred of London and East Anglia made a gift of land to 'God's community at St Ethelbert's church at Hoxne'. Confusingly, St Ethelbert was another East Anglian king martyred in 794 A.D. Domesday records that 'in this manor is a church, the episcopal See in Suffolk before 1066'. This pre-Conquest monastery is sometimes wrongly identified with the later Hoxne Priory but more likely occupied a site by the present parish church forming part of the Bishop's Palace. In 1101 Bishop Herbert Hosinga converted it into a cell of the Benedictine Priory of Norwich for seven or eight monks. His grant included the 'Chapel of St Edmund, King and Martyr', possibly the successor to the intitial wooden chapel mentioned above. A charter of confirmation by Henry III names it as St Peter's Church. It was dissolved in 1538. Nothing remains and the site is occupied

HOXNE *(continued)*

by an Elizabethan house known as The Abbey.

Site of Ancient Chapels.

A Will of Allys Wellys (Alice Wells) in 1506 left money to be spent on tapers to be burned 'before the Image of St Edmund in the chapel at Cross Street, and 'before the image of St Edmund in the chapel in the wood'. The whereabouts of the 'chapel in the woods' was unknown until 1991 when excavations in a field called 'Chapel Piece' SE of Bungalow Farm revealed flint and rubble foundations of the former chapel. It was a simple rectangular building measuring 226'x112'. An estate map of 1757 names it Newark Chapel.

Ancient College.

A Secular College was founded some time before 1040 and dissolved around 1072.

Site of Lost Medieval Village.

Thorpe Hall, standing isolated with its three moats in the E corner of the parish, is the manor house of Harpole (Harpola 'dirty or muddy pool'). A Domesday manor and former medieval settlement it was located in well-watered pasture on a relatively elevated position, with traces of old plough and garden land and a moated area yielding medieval pottery. Ten Domesday entries comprised 27 households excluding a small manor house with 100 acres.

Ancient Mounds.

To the E of Thorpe Hall on the boundary with Horham is an earthen mound called The Mount standing in an elevated position with the land sloping away in all directions except on the W. It is c88 paces in circumference enclosed by a moat with an extension to the W 36 paces long and 18 broad. The moat is about 15-20' wide, full of water, and appears reasonably deep in places. The mound, much mutilated on the N, is about 6' high. The fact that the moat is a permanent feature and fed from both a stream and local springs suggests an early date. The meadow is called Mount Meadow on the tithe map and a few C13 pottery sherds have been found here. Another mound, named on the OS as an ancient Mill Mound lies beside the lane from Cross Street to the Hoxne to Eye road.

Site of Bishop's Palace.

Bishop Theodred referred in his will of *c*950 A.D. to his 'biscopriche at Hoxne'. A large rectangular moated site adjacent to the W side of the churchyard and now containing the vicarage, is possibly the original site where the medieval Bishop of Norwich had a palace and park possibly as early as the C10. By 1326-7 they had moved to a house further W on a site in the crook between the river Dove and the Goldbrook called Hoxne Hall which may have originally been a lodge within the park. Here, states The Chorography of Suffolk c1600, was a palace of the Bishops in Hoxne 'very fayre and gallant'. An estate map of 1619 depicts a tall four-storeyed tower gatehouse in a long range fronting the E side of a rectangular moat. The bishops resided in Hoxne until 1535 when the manor was taken by the Crown and granted to Sir Robert Southwell. The house and moat (but not the gateway) were shown on a map of 1700. The moat was filled in by 1757 and the Hall (extensively remodelled in 1830) demolished in the 1930s. The site, which lies just S of Well Plantation, is now under grass but lines of buried walls are visible from the air and vaulted brick cellars still survive below ground.

Ancient Deer Parks.

The Bishops of Norwich established a large deer park - one of two in Hoxne - which covered 500 acres either side of the parish boundary in an area now called Oakley Park. In 1275 the Bishop and his monks were prosecuted for straying into Denham while 'sporting'. In 1329 beasts were taken from the park at Hoxne to stock the King's park at Eye. A map of 'Hoxne Newe Parke' was produced in 1619 which included the moated Hoxne Hall and a lodge on Lodge Hill. A map of 1757 shows the park enlarged to the S but reduced to the N.

Medieval Greens.

The picturesque triangular green in the centre of the village remains, but Faden's 1783 map also shows a small linear green occupying the road to Wingfield (B1118) just E of the church. It is marked today by property boundaries and Green Street, at the junction with the road to Syleham (formerly known as Pig Street), may

HOXNE *(continued)*

refer to this green. A small green called Hackfield Green at the junction of five ways, now known as Heckfield Green, has been enclosed and completely redeveloped. *Hack* is the Anglo-Saxon word 'to cut, slash' and is thought by some to relate to the site of Edmund's place of execution. Reading Green was shown as a linear green running from Park Farm (Old Park) S to a footpath level with The Lodge. An area near the southern parish boundary marked South Green on the current OS map is not shown in 1783 and may have already gone by this time.

Ancient Market Town.

Hoxne had a market in Saxon times and received a grant for a market in 1227 and a fair in 1232. The market was situated on the small wedge-shaped green in the centre of the village. After the Bishop of Norwich succeeded to the estates of Theodred at the Conquest, a competitor in the form of the nearby castle of Eye presented a challenge to its continued domination. The sad story is told in Domesday Book: 'In this manor there used to be a market, and it continued after King William came. And it was a Saturday market. And William Malet made his castle at Eye. And on the same day as the market used to be held on the Bishop's manor at Hoxne, William Malet established another market at the castle at Eye. And thereby the Bishop's market has been so far spoilt that it is of little worth; and now it is set up on Fridays. But the market at Eye is held on the Saturday.' Saturday obviously being the better day, the Bishop's market quickly dwindled and eventually ceased.

Site of old Windmill.

A post mill stood N of Dairy Farm, E of the village, in 1736. Nothing is known of its later history.

Free Schools.

A school was reputedly housed in the monastery around 1536 teaching and supporting poor children of the parish. In 1761 a school was founded by the 1734 will of Charles Maynard.

Workhouse.

The Hoxne workhouse is recorded with 40 inmates in 1776.

Historic Houses & Ancient Moated Sites.

From Sir Robert Southwell the manor later passed to the Maynard family who built a mansion in Italian style called The Abbey (now Abbey Farm) on the site of the monastery (*see Ancient Monastery*); an ancient moat remains and there is another to the S. Thorpe Hall, a fine old brick house with stone dressing built c1562, has a perfect quadrangular moat, with others to the E and S. The Tudor Vicarage by the church is surrounded by the large almost perfect oblong moat which formerly surrounded the Bishop's Palace. At Chickering Hall, an asymetrical moated enclosure has an apparent outer ring of ditches, and there are fragments of a moat at Chickering Corner Farm. There is part of a small rectangular moat at Park Farm, originally the late C15 Hoxne Old Hall, which has a raised-aisled roof extended in the late C16. The house later became a lodge for the old park. C16 Redhouse Farm at South Green also retains parts of an isolated moat. At Cross Street are the apparent remains of a square-moated enclosure which continue into the field to the SE. The Leys, S of the village is an isolated system of fish-ponds (severely altered in 1984) which once supplied Oakley House, the mansion which stood ½ mile S of the village at the southern end of Oakley Park. Hoxne Place is C17, and in the village, The Swan Inn, a fine timber-framed house with ecclesiastical associations, dates back to the late C15.

HUNDON *(6 miles ENE of Haverhill)*

Risbridge Hundred. 'Huna's valley' (OE) *Hunedana* (DB)

Manors. Hundon (-C15 de Clare family; 1540 Anne of Cleeves). *Sub-Manors.* Porowe formerly called Gorreles/ Penowe Hall; Hagden Hall (a reputed manor under the College of Stoke by Clare).

Site of Roman Building.

Initial trial excavations on a site NW of the village in 1995 revealed parch marks comprising a rectangular structure c25 yds. by15½ yds., sub-divided into six rooms. Mortared flint foundations with tile and C1-C4 pottery was also revealed; perhaps the site of a Roman villa ?

HUNDON *(continued)*

Ancient Woodland.
Hundon Thicks, E of the village, and Six Acre Wood (part of Lords Wood) to the S, are ancient woodland.

Saxon Hoard.
Although no evidence remains of a Saxon origin for the church, which was burnt down and rebuilt in 1914, over 200 coins of the period were unearthed by the sexton while digging a grave in the churchyard in 1687.

Ancient Track & Former Settlement Site (?)
Aerial photographs show two trackways with adjoining field boundaries and toft plots immediately N of Babel Green. These may form part of an earlier settlement site. The village stands on rising ground along a very ancient trackway which once ran from Kentford in the N to the river crossing at Baythorne End, and on into Essex. A section of it, here called Way Bank Lane, forms part of the southern parish boundary.

Medieval Deer Parks.
A deer park is mentioned here as early as 1124. By 1509, Broxley Park had made it three adjoining parks covering an extensive area. Hundon Great Lodge stands in the middle of what was Hunden Great Park, bounded on the E side by the road which runs from Hundon Hall to Stradishall Church (B1063) and on the W by the road (now a track and lane) running from Three Ash Farm past Scotch Green to Hundon. Eastry (Easty or Estey) Park was situated on the E side of Great Park, extending a little into Stradishall parish by Gaymours Farm in the N. Its E boundary was the road from Chipley Abbey to Denston (now a track and footpath), and the S boundary, the road from Chipley Abbey to Hundon Hall. Appleacre Farm was formerly Eastry Lodge. All three parks, formerly held by Stoke Priory near Clare, were sold to Sir John Cheke in 1550.

Medieval Greens.
Faden's map shows Babel Green as a driftway, prior to the present road, lined with properties, from the junction S of the church NW to Valley Wash. There are two hamlets in the parish created from former greens. Scotch Green, a rectangular green shown but not named by Faden on the junction of Cock Lane, and a track which eventually leads to Barnardiston Hall School. Brackhall Green, a small green in the SW corner of the parish has now been built over with properties and become the hamlet of Brockley Green.

Site of old Windmill.
Mansfield's Mill, which stood on the NW edge of the village in 1783, was demolished c1928.

Free School.
The Vernon Charity was founded to educate 16 poor children and in 1753 a schoolhouse was acquired near the church.

Workhouse.
Around 1737 a workhouse was built in the parish from the bequest of James Vernon. In 1776 it was occupied by 20 inmates.

Historic Houses & Ancient Moated Sites.
During restoration of a remarkable timber-framed hall-house in the village called 'Thatchers', which dates from c1440, a large circular painting of the Agnus Dei was discovered in the chimney breast. Pinhoe Hall, S of the village, is modern but retains its ancient elongated oblong moat (now dry) and the C16 gatehouse which guarded the bridge spanning it. Near Brockley Green Farm are traces of a former moat, and there are cropmarks of a moat NE of Spring Farm shown on the 1846 tithe map as 'Thousand Acres'.

HUNSTON *(3 miles SE of Ixworth)*

Blackbourn Hundred. 'The farmstead belonging to the hunter' (OE) *Hunterstuna* (DB)
Manors. Hunston (1316 William de Langham). *Sub-Manors.* Nycols/Nicoll.

Ancient Woodland.
Hunston Wood and Hunston Grove are parts of ancient woodland.

HUNSTON *(continued)*

Ancient Earthworks.

By the country lane to Norton is a circular earthen mound overgrown by trees. Much mutilated, the mound is c26 yds. in diameter and 6' high enclosed by a wet ditch or moat c8' at its deepest and c15' wide. The moat has been destroyed on the E and NE by tipping - the E side being very vulnerable as it abutts the lane. The field boundary ditch, shown on the tithe to carry a stream which supplied the moat, has now been ploughed out. There are no signs of other earthworks connected with the site, but records and the type of disturbance on the summit confirm that the mound at one time carried a windmill, built in 1783 and some time later moved to Badwell Ash where it stood until around 1930. One oyster shell was found on the mound. The tithe and the OS maps call the site Mill Hill from its C18-C19 use, but on the far side of the lane the field is called 'Drawbridges' and an earlier map labels the earthworks 'Site of Camp'. Pevsner considered it a small motte. The manor is not mentioned until William de Langham held it in 1316.

Medieval Green.

Faden's map of 1783 appears to show a northern extension of the mighty Boten (Button) Haugh Green as the origin of the present hamlet of Hunston Green.

Historic Houses & Ancient Moated Sites.

All the detached cottages in the village go back at least to the C17; one is dated 1619. Hunston Hall stands N of the church. The site of the Old Hall, seat of the Heighams, lies SW in Hunston Grove where part of the large moat which formerly surrounded it remains. One angle of another moat 12' wide with banks 5'6" high, may have once surrounded a large area.

HUNTINGFIELD *(4 miles SW of Halesworth)*

Blything Hundred. 'Open land belonging to Hunta's people' (OE) *Huntingafelda* (DB)
Manors. Huntingfield (C12 Roger de Huntingfield). *Sub-Manors.* New Hawe/Newhall; Rectory Manor.

Ancient Woodland.

Broomgreen Covert is a part of ancient woodland.

Roman Road.

The course of a Roman road clips the S of the parish heading NW-SE and traced by the road from Cratfield for around 438 yds.

Site of Ancient Earthworks.

Beside a causeway just to the W of Huntingfield Hall, a mound seen as a circular cropmark on an aerial photograph in 1986, was shown as a probable motte c48 yds. in diameter (with a bailey)? on an earlier OS map. A medieval scatter of C12-C15 pottery sherds was found inside the ring-work plus two lead pilgrim's ampullae discovered by metal detecting.

Queen Elizabeth's Oak.

Elizabeth I, who had granted the manor to her cousin Lord Hunsdon in 1559, visited the old hall during his term there and is said to have shot and wounded a deer in the park which fled and concealed itself in a hollow oak. In 1782 the trunk was said to be 11 yds. in circumference and 7' high. Though now decrepit, this old tree still survives as 'Queen's Oak', standing beside a public footpath heading N from Bridge Street by Broomgreen Covert.

Historic Houses & Ancient Moated Sites.

For a considerable time after the Conquest the manor was the estate and seat of the Huntingfield family, one of whom founded Mendham Priory in the time of King Stephen. It then passed to the de la Poles, earls of Suffolk, who, after being granted a licence to crenellate by Edward III, built a large fortified manor house. A contemporary drawing shows the old C14 hall with castellated walls, two angle turrets and a three-storeyed gatehouse. Its great hall was built around six straight oaks which upheld the roof as they grew and upon which, in olden days, the foresters and yeomen used to hang their cross-bows and hunting poles. Elizabeth I was entertained

HUNTINGFIELD *(continued)*

here (*see above*). It was pulled down by a later owner, Sir Joshua Vanneck in 1752 after he purchased the Heveningham Hall Estate. The present hall of much more modest dimensions was built in 1700 on what appears to be the same sloping site with woods beyond as is shown in the drawing of the old fortified manor house. There is an isolated moat, now dry, SW of the village and NW of Hill Farm. An L-shaped pond in a field just E of the church may be the remains of a moat, as may extensive water-filled 'arms' at High House Farm on the southern parish boundary.

ICKLINGHAM *(3½ miles ESE of Mildenhall)*

Lackford Hundred. 'Homestead belonging to Yccel's people' (OE) *Ecclingaham* (DB)
Icklingham comprises two united parishes, All Saints and St James, each with its own church.
Manors. Icklingham Bernes Hall al Icklingham Capells (C13 Sir Ralph Berners. The manor was forfeited to the Crown when Sir James Berners was beheaded in 1388 but restored to the family in 1397). *Sub-Manors.* Icklingham St. James; Thamhill al Quaned al Quamells al Chessseners, Harling and Cutts; Sextens.

Ancient Settlement.
The district is rich in the many interesting relics of early British, Roman and Saxon settlement. Tumuli,and Palaeolithic and Neolithic impliments in considerable numbers have also been found.

Lower Palaeolithic Site.
Evidence of a settlement site of the Lower Palaeolithic period has been found in the area.

Ancient Track & Way.
The ancient Icknield Way, one of the earliest trackways remaining in England, runs from just N of Brook Farm on the A1101 road NNE by West Stow Country Park and through The King's Forest to the parish boundary just short of the B1106 Brandon road. Pilgrims Path, an ancient track, leads from the church.

Tumuli.
There is a round barrow at How Hill close to the Thetford road (A11), and one of four barrows which originally lay to the W of Queen Elizabeth Plantation remains; there is a barrow on the western edge of The King's Forest to the E of a track called Telegraph Road; ¼ mile NE of Bernersfield Farm is a group of barrows and in one, known as Mitchell's Hill, a cinary urn (now destroyed) was reported to have been found in 1923; another, known as Deadman's Grave, lies SW of Ladysmith Covert.

Roman Road.
The course of a Roman road has been identified by cropmarks running from the Roman villa site by the A1101 road (*see below*), NE through King's Forest to just W of the B1106 road to Brandon. When sectioned, it was found to be 24' wide. Suffolk Historian Norman Scarfe also suggests a conjectural Roman road heading WNW from the Icknield Way on the line of the present A1101, passing the two churches of All Saints and St James.

Site of Roman Town (?)
The site of *Combretonium* is mentioned in the *Antonine Itinerary* as lying between *Durolipons* (Cambridge) and *Venta Icenorum* (Casiter-by-Norwich). The author of *A Tour Through England* describes 'vestiges of a settlement at Icklingham which seem to have extended half a mile in length at a small distance from the river. On the W side of the ruins is a small encampment which appears to have contained about 25 acres, and is now called Kentfield. The vallum is visible all round it, except where the moorish ground has brought it to decay. Coins and fibulae have often been found here.' Several quality buildings with tiled floors and evidence of a Roman cemetery which included stone and lead coffins have been discovered. Norman Scarfe appears to make an intriguing suggestion that the Iceni, who preceded the Romans and had their main centre at Caister-by-Norwich, may have had a similar base in Suffolk, and that their name, pronounced as Ikeni, may be reflected in the name Ickingham. This would then appear to make it a likely site (as at Caister) for a possible base from which they were later ousted by the Romans.

ICKLINGHAM *(continued)*

Site of Roman Villa (?)
Partial excavations in 1877, S of the parish in a field adjoining the site of Roman kilns (*see below*), revealed part of a hypocaust containing coins of Carausius 286-93 A.D. Other occupational material unearthed, plus further building material including two lead cisterns, uncovered by ploughing in 1940, suggest this as the site of a possible villa.

Ancient Cemetery.
South of Weatherhill Farm and the site of the Roman Villa, a cemetery was discovered which, along with 'loose human bones', a stone coffin was unearthed containing a male inhumation 'about 25 years old' and another 'a man about 50'. A plain lead coffin held 'a female of about 40'.

Roman Industrial Site.
Roman kilns, found in Kiln Field in 1937 and dating from the C3, provide evidence for a Roman pottery industry.

Roman Hoards.
300-400 Roman silver coins were found in an earthen pot ploughed up in the parish in 1871, and in 1956 a hoard of Roman pewter was discovered on the edge of Berners Heath E of the Pilgrims Path.

Ancient Boundary Banks.
A section of the original parish boundary banks remain from TL783 771 (between Icklingham and Eriswell) to TL802 772 (between Icklingham and Elveden).

Site of Camp or Preceptory of Knights Templars (?)
The earthworks of an enclosure still visible today at Camp Close on Icklingham Plains W of the village have not been identified. Too low-lying for defence it may be connected with a house of the Knights Templars thought to have existed here and suggested by Temple Bridge to the S. Its importance is confirmed by the fact that (as late as 1689) it was said to have formed the separate parish of Saint Maries. C12-C14 pottery has come from the site.

Civil War Sconce (?)
To the W of Farthing Bridge, spanning the river Lark S of the village, is a slightly raised plateau 71 yds. square with a central mound 66'x39' and 2½' high. Four angle bastions 33' square and 1½' high are each surrounded by a shallow outer ditch 23' wide and 1½' deep with a further ditch 10' wide and 1' deep lying some 33' beyond. The earthworks were partially levelled after World War II and a pillbox has been erected on the S side. The four bastions would have identified this as a Civil War Sconce (fortification), but as these cannot now be confidently recognised as such, and no Civil War incidents are known to have taken place in the area, doubt has been thrown on the validity of this claim. Being low-lying by the river does not fit any alternative purpose or origin e.g. homestead moat, mill-mount or Norman fortification.

Medieval Guildhall (?)
Icklingham had three guilds: St. James (1364); Holy Cross (1366), and Rood Loft (1523), suggesting a guildhall may at one time have been sited here.

Site of Historic House.
Sextens Hall stood close by the church until the early C19. It was probably the manor house held by the Sacristan (Sexton) of the Abbey of St. Edmund. Sir John Holland, Bart., was lord here in 1625. The thatched Red Lion public house was recorded as an inn in 1694.

ICKWORTH *(4 miles SW of Bury St Edmunds)*

Thingoe Hundred. 'Icca's enclosure' (OE) *Ikewrth* (c950)
Manors. Ickworth was given by Theodred, Bishop of London, to Bury Abbey. In 1248 the de Ickworth family held the manor from the Abbot. After the Dissolution the Herveys acquired it from the Drurys through marriage.

Ancient Woodland.
Lownde Wood is a part of ancient woodland.

ICKWORTH *(continued)*

Medieval Park.
In 1254 Thomas de Ickworth had a licence to empark his lands at Ickworth.

Medieval Greens.
Ickworth Church and the site of Ickworth Hall lay beside the former Church Greene. Halbush Green and the adjoining Smiths Green were shown on Faden's 1783 map NW from Poulters Lane in an area now occupied by Hollybush Green Stud. The greens extended from Moat Farm House and are now replaced by a road.

Lost Medieval Village (?)
A survey in 1665, at the time of emparking and depopulation, shows the parish comprising a green bordered by buildings (including Ickworth Lodge), hedged fields, groves, a small open field, a church with adjoining green and the old hall. By 1750 all but the church and lodge had gone (*see below*). It has been suggested that if there had formerly been a definite village here in 1665, it was already in marked decline by that time.

Historic Houses & Ancient Moated Sites.
The old manor house of the Herveys was destroyed by fire and comprehensively demolished and robbed of its building material sometime before the end of the C17. Its foundations can still be traced by a clump of trees on the crown of a hill E of the church, on a site which archaeological evidence suggests was occupied from the C13 (the earliest buildings of timber frame). 'Hervey de Berri' was among the seventy to whom the Conqueror divided the Suffolk manors, and the Hervey family held the manor here since the early part of the C15 when they acquired the estate from the Drurys by marriage. Following the loss of the old hall, John Hervey, who was made a peer in 1703 and created Earl of Bristol in 1714, removed the village and created a new park 11 miles in circumference. It comprised some 1,800 acres, 300 of which were in the adjoining parish of Horringer. But the new hall he intended, on the site of the old hall and designed by Vanburgh, was never built. The present Ickworth House was built on a new site, planned and started in 1792 by Frederick Augustus, Fourth Earl of Bristol, but not completed until 1829. House and park are now under the National Trust. Just NW of Ivy Cottage in the S of the parish are the N and E arms of a homestead moat with no trace remaining of any building.

IKEN *(3½ miles W of Aldeburgh)*

Plomesgate Hundred. 'Ica's stream' (OE) *Ykene* (1212)
Though it is identified by Skeat as 'Ica's stream', Morley thought it 'The place of the Iceni'. The 'place' was likely to have been Yarn Hill, and he identifies the 'Ho' of 'Ycean Ho' (as it was once known) as the 'bluff jutting N into the river Alde; at the root of which bluff the church stands.' Whilst not apparently named in Domesday, Morley suggests it may be the *Udeham* (i.e. Woodham) at present unidentified and placed between Aldeburgh and Campsey.
Manors. Iken/Iken cum Framlingham. (1225 Sir William Esturmy).

Ancient Woodland.
Iken Wood, NW of the parish, is a part of ancient woodland.

Tumuli.
A round barrow just remains under the plough on Iken Heath, S of Middle Covert, while two pairs have been lost to the plough - just W of Iken Hall, and just NW of Sheepyard Covert.

Roman Industrial Site.
There is evidence of Iron Age and Roman salt workings by the river Alde estuary.

Roman Encampment & Site of Battle (?)
Yarn Hill is a small natural eminence rising out of the marshes bordering the river Alde on which there are the remains of an ancient enclosure (*see above*). A field close by near the rectory is called 'Campden Close'. Claude Morley found an iron sword at the base of the hill in the early part of the C20. This is the suggested site of a Roman encampment near which the ancient East Anglian tribe, the Iceni, are believed to have fought the Romans.

IKEN *(continued)*

Saxon Monastery (?)

Church Path from Sudbourne crosses the Priests Bridge at Northburgh (mentioned in Domesday) to the island where St Botolphs Church stands on a promontary at the head of the Alde estuary. The missionary St Botolph founded an orthodox monastery, famous throughout England, at *Icanhoe* which is generally believed to have been Iken. The *Anglo-Saxon Chronicle* states: 'In this year (King) Anna was slain and Botwolf began to build the Minster at Icanho' (possibly founded to commemorate him). Here in this isolated and atmospheric landscape it remained for 200 years from 670-870 A.D., when it was believed to have been attacked by the Danes and moved to the Roman camp at Burgh, near Woodbridge. Although Yarn Hill, at that time an island, could have been the site (large stones, possibly from a hermit's cell have been dug up on its summit), the stronger claim is for the church site where, in 1977, Stanley West found the shaft of a commemorative cross (evidence suggests it may have originally been 10' high) of about 900 A.D. embedded in the tower, and excavated a timber-framed building of probable Middle Saxon (C7) date underlying the present building. Yarn Hill may still have held a later, more permanent, chapel.

Ancient Moated Site.

S of the parish, crop-marks of an enclosure c197' square N of Wood Farm, may be those of a former moated site.

ILKETSHALL ST ANDREW *(4 miles SE of Bungay)*

Wangford Hundred. 'Ylfketill's corner of land' (OScand+OE) plus church dedication. *Ilcheteleshala* (DB) *Manors.* Ilketshall Manor includes the parishes of St. Andrew; St. John; St. Lawrence; St. Margaret; All Saints, Mettingham; St. Mary; Holy Trinity, Bungay. (C12 Ilketshall family; C14 de Norwich family). *Sub-Manors.* Wellington's; Ilketshall Bardolphs; Sherlocks; St. Andrew; Ellis's and Strattons; Lions.

Medieval Communial Commons & Green.

It has been suggested that the four Ilketshall parishes were laid out as a unit to provide for inter-commoning. The settlements were arranged in a triangular formation based on the five commons of Great, Holdens, Mill, Blacksmiths and Little with the church situated in the centre of the triangle. Great Common, a rectangular area of common land with a number of possible enclosure boundaries within, remains E of the Roman Stone Street and S of the church, lying NNW either side of Great Common Road. Faden's 1783 map names it St Andrews Common and shows a small open space at the four-way junction SE of Great Common marked Godfrey's Common on the present OS map. The same map shows a large linear common from just N of this, running either side of the road to Barsham and extending virtually to the parish boundary. Though unnamed on this map and now enclosed, the present OS map names the area Peardyke Common and Little Common. A diamond-shaped green of 15 acres in the area bordered by Manor Farm and Little Beck Farm is now cut through by Beck's Green Lane. It was shown and named Backs Green in 1783.

Site of old Windmill.

A windmill is illustrated by Faden on his 1783 map at the spot now called Mill Common. There is no record of its demise.

Historic Houses & Ancient Moated Sites.

St Andrews Hall, N of the parish, and the timber-framed Manor House at Backs Green, two miles S of the village, date from the C16. Ilketshall Hall has an ancient moat, and Corner Farm has a fragment of a small moat.

ILKETSHALL ST JOHN *(2 miles SE of Bungay)*

Roman Road.

The course of the Roman Stone Street is traced by the A144 road NW to the southern parish boundary. Its line through the parish is uncertain but it probably left in the NW corner at the point where Scotchman's Lane joins Lodge Road, heading for the Waveney river crossing.

Motte & Bailey Castle & Site of Saxon Hall (?)

The Mount, situated in a copse at Manor Farm ½ mile ENE of the church, is a conical mound some 90 yds in

ILKETSHALL ST JOHN *(continued)*

circumference and 23' high surrounded by a moat (still largely wet) and protected by a rampart. To the S is a horse-shoe bailey with an enclosing ditch which joins with that around the motte on the western side. Although now the remains of a conventional, well-preserved motte and bailey castle, probably built in the late C11 or early C12 by one of the Ilketshall family who were recorded here between the C12-C15 (pottery sherds on and around the site confirm occupation at least between the C13-C14), the site may have an even earlier origin as this, and the three other Ilketshall parishes, were anciently called Ulfketil's Hall from one of the Saxon Earls of East Anglia who had a seat here. Whilst no excavation work has been carried out here in an attempt to find evidence of earlier occupation, this may well have been the site of his residence, later adapted by the Normans. The local church has a possible Saxon round tower.

ILKETSHALL ST LAWRENCE *(3 miles SE of Bungay)*

Roman Road.

The Roman Stone Street (now the A144) heads NW bisecting the parish from the junction with Hog Lane in the S to just N of the junction with Mole Lane on the northern boundary.

Ancient Enclosure.

The church stands within an ancient enclosure of uncertain date. Although it is situated beside the Roman Stone Street there is no evidence to support a Roman date for the site.

Ancient Track.

The Packway, an ancient track, runs as a public footpath from Mill Houses on the Roman Stone Street (A144), NE over the parish boundary to Beck's Green Lane.

Medieval Green.

The square St Lawrence Green, bordered by Green Farm and shown on Faden's 1783 map, still remains.

Historic House & Ancient Moated Sites.

St Lawrence's Hall Farm stands on the site of the medieval residence of the Bardolphs, a C14 knightly family and long time lords of the manor. Moat Farm, situated in the S of the parish, has the remains of a moat, and Kings Fene, further S, has parts of a moat supplied from the stream which provides the southern parish boundary.

ILKETSHALL ST MARGARET *(3 miles SE of Bungay)*

Ancient Woodland.

Spring Wood is a fragment of ancient woodland.

Roman Pottery Industry.

A Roman kiln was discovered in the parish.

Workhouse.

The parish had a small workhouse with six inmates recorded in 1776.

Ancient Moated Sites.

There are two sides of a rectangular moat at Charity Farm, NW of the village; a complete oblong moat at Brook Hall, SE of the village; two corners of a square moat at St Margaret's Hall, and one arm of a moat at Rookery Farm, on the southern tip of the parish. The isolated Tithe Farm is old and timber-framed with oak beams, some of which are 'so roughly hewn that the pattern of the tree from which they were laboriously hacked . . is plainly to be distinguished'.

INGHAM *(4 miles N of Bury St Edmunds)*

Blackbourn Hundred. 'Inga's homestead' (OE) *Ingham* (DB). It has recently been suggested that the first element of the name may refer to a member of the ancient Germanic tribe called the *Inguiones.*

Manors. Ingham (-1540 Abbot of St. Edmunds, Bury; 1540 Sir Nicholas Bacon).

INGHAM *(continued)*

Ancient Woodland.

The Folly (formerly Foremans Folly) and, just to the N of it, The Severals, are fragments of ancient woodland.

Tumulus.

The Seven Hills 'barrows' on the parish boundary by the W side of the road to Thetford may only be natural undulations with just one barrow formerly existing here, that visible on an aerial photo of 1977.

Romano-British Cemetery.

In 1873, during the construction of the railway between Bury and Thetford, a Romano-British Cemetery was discovered in a field known as Cow Path Breck, N of the village.

Roman Road.

A Roman Road which passed ESE-WNW through the parish on a line just N of the church, is nowhere evident on the ground, although a footpath leaving the A134 road S of the church runs WNW on a virtual parallel line.

Ancient Road.

The Icknield Way Path (A134) forms the eastern parish boundary.

Ancient Track.

The 'Cow-path' was an ancient trackway which led from Ingham to Elveden where there was also a Romano-British settlement.

IPSWICH

'Gip's (harbour)'? (OE) *Gipeswic* (c975)

Although the town stands on the river Gipping which only takes the name Orwell from the spot where it becomes tidal (Stoke Bridge), all the experts appear to agree that the first element 'Gip' is, in fact, a personal name, i.e. 'a harbour belonging to a man called Gip'. The river rises, not in the village of Gipping to which it gives name, but in the adjacent hamlet of Mendlesham Green; the origins of Orwell are less certain. Whilst ancient tradition speaks of a one-time Port of Orwell, there is no evidence to support this. The Anglo-Saxon *oran wella* means 'well beside the brink'. At an Ipswich inquisition taken on 5 June 1340 it was stated that the port of Erewell "takes its originall and name from a certain fountaine called Erewell which is in the towne of Rattlesden (the river Rat joining the Gipping at Stowmarket) and floweth by a river through the middest Burrough aforesaid to the Port aforesaid". This fountain almost certainly refers to "a spring which rises in a meadow called Orwell meadow to the north of Rattlesden church", though the Rattlesden River itself originates from a moat at Brooke Hall in the neighbouring village of Felsham.

Ipswich includes the parishes of St. Clement; St. Helen; St. Lawrence; St. Margaret; St. Mary-at-Elms; St. Mary-at-Quay; St. Mary-le-Tower; St. Mary Stoke; St. Matthew; St. Nicholas; St. Peter; St. Stephen; and parts of Belstead, Bramford, Rushmere, Westerfield and Whitton-cum-Thurlston. In 1066 there were two 'wicks' (hamlets) called Wykes Bishop and Wykes Ufford, owned by Edward the Confessor's wife, Edith, and her brother, Earl Gyrth. The latter was later known as Grenewic in Carlford Hundred - Greenwich Farm, a place of some importance and identified as the former Hogs Island.

Historic Town.

Whilst the town itself does not make its appearance before Saxon times, it has been confidently claimed from the most recent excavations that it may well be the earliest post-Roman town in England. This is not hard to believe when one looks at the position of its ancient harbour on the north bank of the river Orwell, some twelve miles from the open sea with direct access to mainland Europe, with whom it appears to have been trading since the late C6. It has even been suggested that it might have been the largest known early trading community in NW Europe. The Middle Saxon town covered about 125 acres and was a thriving commercial and industrial centre long before Dunwich, Thetford or Norwich. It was known for its pottery, commonly called 'Ipswich ware', which was made between c625 and 850 A.D. and distributed over East Anglia and as far as Kent and Yorkshire from kilns discovered in the Carr Street area. By 964 A.D. the town was already minting coins of King Edgar, and

IPSWICH *(continued)*

later, Edward the Confessor's Queen Edith had a grange here and her brother, Earl Gyrth, another with the townsmen paying them a royal rent of honey and fifteen pounds in cash. Ipswich was sacked by the Danes in 991 A.D., and again by Thurkell the Tall in 1010. Six years later Cnut sailed up the Orwell to successfully secure Thurkill's hold on East Anglia. Despite the fact that they were only 'passing through', it appears that these insurgants so destroyed the town that, after the Conquest the Normans found the town, which had only a short time before been thriving and prosperous, in a very sorry state. Domesday makes clear how dire conditions were: 'In the time of King Edward (the Confessor) there were 538 burgesses (the most in England) who paid custom to the king, and they had forty acres of land. But now there are 110 burgesses who pay custom, and 100 poor burgessses who can pay no more than one penny a head to the king's geld. Thus, upon the whole, they had forty acres of land, and 328 houses now empty, and which, in the time of King Edward, scotted to the king's geld.' Whatever the cause, their new masters were obviously so unimpressed that they concentrated their major bases elsewhere in East Anglia, at rival towns like Norwich, where they built a great castle and cathedral, and Colchester, where they erected the largest and one of the earliest castle keeps in Britain. The town eventually made its comeback built on the strength of its maritime and commercial potential. Already a royal town before the Conquest, Ipswich received its royal borough charter from King John in 1190. Its salt industry flourished from Norman times to Elizabeth I, with salt pans on the Orwell and great salthouses along the quay, and the town became a great shipbuilding centre, (one of eight English towns with records of shipbuilding going back to a very early date - a king's galley was built by Philip Harneys and Thomas Alyred in 1295). The Halifax and Nova Scotia yards built ships for Edward I for his conflicts with the Scots. The largest ships built here were the famous Orwell, of 1,350 tons and launched in the presence of nearly 30,000 people in 1821, and the William Fairlie, 1,348 tons. By 1524, Ipswich had reached the zenith of its importance, becoming the sixth wealthiest provincial town in England. From this position it should have achieved true greatness, for its most famous son, Cardinal Wolsey, Chancellor to Henry VIII and the second most powerful man in the country, was about to turn Ipswich and Oxford into major university cities. Oxford he did, yet barely had the first bricks been mortared for his Ipswich College in June 1528, when he fell from power and died a broken man two years later. His college died with him and so did the fortunes of the town for the next two centuries. Sir James Thornhill, the artist, on a visit to the town in 1711 during the height of its depression, wrote in his journal of 'a river without water, streets without names and a town without people'. The lack of good Georgian buildings in the town highlights this period of the town's history; the quality of the Victorian houses signal its resurgence during the industrial revolution when 39 warships were built in one Ipswich shipyard alone between 1804 and 1813. Ambitious and forward-looking planners, realising the need for larger ships and their restricted facilities to provide them, created the new wet dock in 1837, the largest in the country at the time and the key to the port's revival.

Ancient Settlements.

The earliest settlement in the area appears to be on the NW outskirts where signs of Palaeolithic man were discovered in an old brickfield off Dales Road. In the same area traces were found of a rough wind-screen used by early Stone Age men for protection against the elements while they shaped their flint axes and arrow heads in an area with little natural cover. At Bramford Road by the river Gipping, long blades and leaf-shaped spearheads in worked flint of the Earlier Upper Palaeolithic period were washed into the low lying gravels, and other finds of the period were made E of the town in Foxhall Road. Two Bronze-Age round-houses have been identified in Lovetofts Drive on the Whitehouse Estate, and a Bronze-Age settlement discovered on the site of the former Ipswich Airport between Gainsborough and Nacton roads in 1998.

Tumulus.

Bronze-Age Beaker pottery was found in a round barrow on Fox's Heath S of Ransomes Industrial Park. 118' in diameter and c2' high it has now been lost under the Nacton interchange of the Ipswich southern bypass.

Iron-Age Find.

In the late 1960s during residential development in the light sandy soils of the Belstead area of the town, six decorative gold torcs were unearthed by a digger driver dating from the C1. B.C. The find, claimed at the time to be the 'richest Iron-Age hoard yet found in England', is now in the British Museum.

IPSWICH *(continued)*

Roman Villa.

In 1854 a Roman villa was discovered at Castle* Hill, Whitton, NW of the town - once a separate parish but now a suburb of Ipswich. (*see Whitton-cum-Thurlston*). * The name 'castle' refers to this site.

Roman Cemetery.

In the northern part of Dales Road brickyard valley, a Roman cemetery was discovered which had been in use for over two hundred years.

Roman Road (?)

John Kirby's C18 map marks a Peddars Way running NW-SE across the southern edge of Christchurch Park. Its position and direction suggest that it may well have been part of the known Roman road (probably from Coddenham and the Gipping river crossing at Starnford) which ran to the Roman fort at Walton (Felixstowe) via Stratton Hall. This Ipswich section was re-named Anglesea Road in the C19.

Ancient Roads.

During excavation work for sewer laying in Westgate Street c1884, a corduroy road was unearthed. It had been laid across a marshy area and comprised logs secured to each other by wooden pegs. Animal bones and deer antlers were retrieved in soil beneath the road along with pottery sherds suggesting a possible Saxon date.

Anglo-Saxon Cemetery.

The first settlement in the area developed across on the west bank of the river Gipping some distance from the town centre. Here a large Anglo-Saxon pagan cemetery of 500-600 A.D. was excavated between the Hadleigh and Handford roads.

Saxon Town.

Excavations, most of which have taken place during the post-war development of the town, have revealed Ipswich's ancient Saxon boundaries and pushed back the date of its foundation to the late C6 or early C7, making it perhaps the earliest post-Roman town in England. The area of the Middle and Late Saxon town has been established as lying between Upper Brook Street and Upper Orwell Street (TM1660 4450); off Foundation Street (TM1660 4430, TM1650 4440, TM1650 4430); off Shire Hall Yard (including Medieval defences) (TM1660 4420); at the corner of Foundation Street and Smart Street (TM1650 4420); off Star Lane (TM1630 4410); between Turret Lane and Star Lane (TM1640 4400); off Greyfriars Road (TM1640 4410) and off Foundry Road (including Medieval defences) (TM1680 4430).

Ancient Battles.

Due to its vulnerability to invasion from northern Europe via the Orwell, Ipswich found itself the initial target for enthusiastic Scandinavians during the troubled years before the Conquest. The first recorded conflict involved King Alfred's fleet who entered the lower reaches of the Orwell and Stour to defeat a Danish raiding party off Stourmouth in 885 A.D. In 991 A.D. the town was sacked by the Danes under Olaf who arrived in the Orwell with 93 ships, and again by Thurkell the Tall in 1010. Six years later it was the turn of Cnut (Kanute) who, having failed to take London, sailed up the Orwell to secure Thurkill's hold on East Anglia. Even after the Conquest, Sweyn of Denmark entered the Orwell in 1069 to attack Ipswich, but he was defeated outside the town by the more militarily competent Norman forces under the barons Roger Bigod, Robert Malet and Ralph Wader.

Ancient Defensive Banks.

The town's first defences were raised in the early C10., and excavations have shown the ditch to be c20' wide and 5' deep. There is evidence to show the earthen banks had been broken down during the pre-Conquest invasions and not repaired or renewed until 1204 in the reign of King John. Then an 8' bank was erected and a 10' deep ditch cut 'by the aide of the county and off the county of Cambridge', suggesting outside help with the cost, a not unusual arrangement in those times. Not long ago the bank could still be seen in Old Foundry Road, where large post-holes may have represented a former timber revettment. In 1352 the town obtained a licence from the king to strengthen and crenellate the town with a stone wall (similar to Norwich), but for whatever

IPSWICH *(continued)*

reason this was never implemented. Further plans to fortify the town as late as 1642 again came to nothing. The line of the medieval wall can still be traced in names like Tower Ramparts and St Mary le Tower Church - on the site of the northern fortification where wall towers stood.

Town Gates.

In the ramparts which encompassed Ipswich were four main gates giving access to the medieval town and called by their location: Northgate, Southgate, Eastgate and Westgate. The Westgate (also known as St Matthew's or Bar Gate) was the most important - guarding the approaches from London and Norwich - and stood near the junction of Westgate and Crown Street; the Northgate (or St Margaret's Gate) stood at the point where Tower Ramparts meets Northgate Street. The Westgate was pulled down in 1780 and Northgate in 1794. When the site of the former was excavated during major re-development of this part of Ipswich in 1967, it was shown to have been constructed of large flints and erratic boulders with ashlar quoins; the plinth dated the original gate probably to the C13. It was rebuilt shortly after 1446 and its upper storey used as a town gaol. We also read of a fifth, Losegate, which stood on the bank of the Orwell, at a spot where there was once a ford. Speede's plan of the town in 1610 shows the precise locality, stretching across the river some way beyond the Old Stoke Water Mill, between the ground occupied by the churches of St Peter and St Mary-at-the-Quay. It is possible, however, that Losegate may refer to, and be a derivatory of sluice-gate.

Ancient Meeting Place.

The old Saxon meeting place for the half hundred of Ipswich was the 'Thingstead' on St Margaret's Plain, just outside the old walls of the town a little NE of the North Gate.

Sites of Ancient Fords & Bridges.

Gusford, the Domesday *Gutthuluesforda,* was a district on the SW borough boundary where a ford crossed Belstead Brook - in Anglo-Saxon times called 'Theofford' or 'Thetford', 'the ford of the people or tribe'. There has been a bridge at Stoke - the point where the river Gipping coming in through the town from Stowmarket becomes the tidal river Orwell and flows SE to the sea - since at least 970 A.D., when the first, no doubt of wood, became the earliest known in Suffolk. Transport using the bridge in 1495 had to pay a toll towards its upkeep. It was re-built, again in timber, in 1559. In the mid C17 its maintenance had probably lapsed for its use was only permitted when the ford was impassable. Reconstructions both in stone and cast-iron have followed. Handford Bridge crossed Pottaford and was described in 1352. At one time it was known as Five Arches Bridge and shown on Saxton's map of 1575 when two arms of the river must have been bridged together, probably by two bridges with a linking causeway. Friars Bridge, set up on the approach from the town marshes, was shown on maps from 1575 to 1783, when it was named either side of the Gipping but no actual bridge shown.

Wayside Crosses.

Wayside crosses are known to have stood at exits to the town. One stood 'In the way from Russhme (Rushmere) Halle onto Humberdowney (Humberducy) Lane', another was described as 'the Crosse that stante be Robt Andrewes in the vicinity of Stoke Hill Wood' (elsewhere said to belong to the prior of St Peters), a third 'that stante in the highway between Yippiswich and Russhme'; a fourth 'that stante in Whytton Streete', and one 'by the highway that goeth from Ipswich unto Tuddenham'. The grant of a piece of common soil in St Margaret's Parish 'opposite to a certain place in which there was formerly a certain cross', may also refer to the latter. These wayside crosses were also known as Stoneing or Sanctuary crosses and regarded as places of sanctuary which robbers and villains invariably respected providing, of course, the cross could first be reached! A Stoneing Cross is placed on Ogilby's map of 1674 in Stoneing Cross Street a little to the left of the Handford Bridgeway.

Ancient Mint.

The town had a mint established in the late Saxon period (925 A.D.) which was still operating in the late C12/ early C13. Coins produced here include those of Eadgar (954-975); Harold I (1035-1040); Henry I (1100-1135) and John (1199-1216). The site of the mint is not known.

IPSWICH *(continued)*

Site of Norman Castle.

There is undisputed evidence for a castle at Ipswich in the C12; the only uncertainty being where it stood and what form it took. 'The Normans erected a pile or castle here which Hugh Bigod defended for a while against Stephen, the usurping King of England, but surrendered it in the end. This fort is quite gone, so that there remains not so much as the ruins thereof . . .'. 'This earl Bigot, in King Stephen's time, had a castle at Ipswich, which the King besieged and at last tooke (1153), butt at this day there is noe mention where it should stand'. These old descriptions seem to sum up the history of Ipswich castle quite well. Despite the town's favourable location, the poor state of the town at Domesday and the Normans apparent disregard for its importance at the time suggests that the fortification was not one of any magnitude and may even have been totally of timber construction. Yet it was to play its part in English history, for Stephen's son Eustace, successor to the English throne, caught a fever whilst assisting his father and died in camp shortly after the stronghold fell, thus paving the way for the new Plantagenet dynasty. There have been a number of suggestions as to its site but most fall outside the town's fortifications. A site near St. Stephens Church was called The Mount, but Keith Wade has noticed a realignment in the old Saxon street pattern at a point where Elm Street curves around some unknown and now lost obstruction. The position and shape of this obstruction may identify the castle motte. This realignment was preserved throughout the Norman period (and remarkably mostly remains today).

Site of Saxon Grange & Bishop's Palace.

Within the bounds of 'Gipes Wic' - the dwelling of Gipi - were two 'Wicks', one either side of the river. In the reign of Edward the Confessor, the wick (or grange) on the W bank belonged to his queen, Edith, and that on the E bank to her brother, Earl Gyrth. In Holywell Park the remains a large quadrilateral moat of about 6 acres connected to a linear series of ponds (the holy wells referred to in the name) mark the site of the outlying grange belonging to Queen Edith in 1066. The manor was later granted by Richard I to John Oxenford, Bishop of Norwich, who had a palace or manor house here, and possibly a chapel dedicated to St Mary. In 1535 it passed to the Crown. Earl Gyrth's 'Wick' is remembered in Greenwich.

The Ancient Market Place.

The town had a market in Saxon times and the grant of a daily market after 1200. Ipswich still retains the basic outline of its old Saxon streets, and the Cornhill has been the market place and heart of the old town probably since its origin. The first known building here was St Mildred's Chapel, probably founded c700 A.D. on the site of the present Victorian Town Hall. Alongside was a possible hall of the Wuffingas, the ancient royal family of East Anglia. The latter was later replaced by the old Guildhall called Town or Moot Hall, and the Toll House or Hall of Pleas stood close by in the time of Richard II. An open timber octagonal Market Cross was erected c1628, and along with the large timber Shambles or Flesh Market - brought here from Ulverston Hall and re-erected in 1583 - formed three sides of an oblong market. Both were demolished in 1792, the former replaced by a Market Cross known as Daundy's Cross which carried the arms of this notable family, and the latter with the Rotunda. The Moot Hall and Hall of Pleas were pulled down in 1812 and replaced by a new Town Hall which in turn was replaced by the present hall erected in 1868.

Site of Saxon Minster (?)

St Peter's Church, in St Peter's Street, is believed by some to stand on the site of an ancient Saxon Minster. It is here that Cardinal Wolsey chose to build his great college (*see Site of College*).

Ancient Priories.

The town probably had three Saxon churches and Domesday records a further eleven. The town had five priories, several hospitals, guilds and other religious fraternities. The priories, founded in the C12 and C13., were large and richly endowed. Two belonged to the Black Canons, and the other three to Black, Grey and White friars. Between 1390 and 1515 several religious houses in various parts of the kingdom were dissolved and their revenues settled on different colleges in Oxford and Cambridge. In 1525, by licence of Henry VIII and the Pope, Cardinal Wolsey dissolved about thirty religious houses for the founding and endowing of his colleges at Oxford and Ipswich. The site of the Augustinian Priory of Holy Trinity was on the N side of the town

IPSWICH *(continued)*

where Christchurch Mansion now stands. Holy Trinity Church dates back to Domesday, but the priory, founded in 1172 by Norman, son of Aelfnoth, was destroyed by fire shortly after its completion. John de Oxford, Bishop of Norwich, rebuilt the priory in 1194. Initially it had eight canons including the prior but this was later raised to 20. Numerous Suffolk churches were appropriated towards its maintenance and it was a considerably richer foundation than its sister monastery of St Peter and St Paul. Dissolved in 1536, its only remains are part of its precinct wall, which form the northern boundary of St Margaret's churchyard, and a continuation northwards along Bolton Lane. The Augustinian Priory of St Peter and St Paul stood close to St Peter's Church in St Peters Street at the S end of town. Although little is known of its history, it was probably founded by Roger de Rheims c1135. Early in the C13 a dependent cell was founded at Letheringham, and although it appears to have had a considerable income in 1291, this was not maintained. It was suppressed by Wolsey towards his college in 1528 and its buildings occupied for a short time by staff there. They have now totally disappeared. The Church of St Peter and St Paul initially served as the chapel for the College to which it was connected. A Franciscan Monastery was founded in 1290 by Sir Robert Tiptot of Nettlestead and Una his wife, NE of St Nicholas Church on the W side of town. Unfortunately they were not well connected or regarded and suffered accordingly. Lord Wentworth of Nettlestead, hereditary patron, wrote to Cromwell that "the warden and brethren live there in great necessity, for the inhabitants were extending their charity to the poor and impotent instead of to 'such an idle nest of drones'". He complained that they were selling the jewels of their house and, as he was their 'founder in blood', he sent for the warden who stated that they had been compelled to sell something, for during a twelvemonth they had only gathered £5 and could not continue in that house three months longer. There were no lands, only the bare site, with a garden or two enclosed. Lord Wentworth then called to mind how this order was 'neither stock nor griffe which the Heavenly Father had planted, but merely a hypocritical weed planted by that sturdy Nembrot, the Bishop of Rome'. All that now remains is a short piece of wall recovered from a garden in Friars Street during redevelopment of the area and removed and incorporated into the Greyfriars Concourse. The Dominican or Blackfriars Priory was in School Street, near Foundation Street, on the E side of town. It was founded in 1263 by Henry III and dedicated to St Mary. The priory soon began to flourish and the premises covered a large area. In 1348 the town bailiffs granted the Black Friars a plot of land 103' long S of their lands for which the friars were to pay 6d a year rent, and to keep up the town wall opposite the plot, and also the two great gates, N and S of their court; and through these gates the community were to be allowed to pass whenever any mishap fell on the town, or other necessity required. On the dissolution the whole was sold to William Aubyn, one of the king's sergeants-at-arms. In 1569, the buildings were purchased by the Corporation and converted into an almshouse and grammar school - the latter having been previously incorporated in Wolsey's College. The buildings were pulled down in 1852 and now only part of the E wall of the refectory 120' by 24' with seven arches remains. The land of the Carmelite or White Friars Priory extended from St Stephens Lane to Queen Street on the S side of the Buttermarket, a site now occupied by the Buttermarket Shopping Centre. It was founded in 1278 by Sir Thomas de Loundham and visited by Henry VI in 1452. Dissolved in 1538, there are no remains.

Ancient Hospitals.

The lepers' hospital of St Mary Magdalene founded c1150 was annexed to St James c1380. It was mentioned in 1520, escaped suppression under Henry VIII, and was last mentioned in 1606. There are no remains. It stood at the junction of Fore Street and Back Hamlet and in the C14 was supported by a yearly fair. Another lepers' hospital, St Leonards, stood outside the town in St Peter's Parish near the old church of St Augustine. It was probably only slenderly endowed, relying mainly on the alms of travellers, yet it survived suppression and was still there in 1606. St John's Hospital, mentioned in 1340, stood in St Matthews Parish.

Ancient Shrine.

The most important of the town's chapels was the Chapel of Our Lady. This stood near the old West Gate on the corner of what is now Lady Lane and St Matthews Street. It contained the shrine of Our Lady of Ipswich and was first mentioned in 1297. Wolsey later ordered that an annual procession be made to this chapel by the dean and

IPSWICH *(continued)*

his college in Ipswich on September 8th, this being the Nativity of the Virgin Mary, the titular saint of the town. At the Reformation in 1535 the statue was removed at night along with that of Our Lady of Walsingham, taken to London and publicly burnt in Chelsea by order of Sir Thomas Cromwell.

Ancient 'Miraculous' Cross.

Upon the site of (or in the close proximity of) a house known as the 'Gold Rood' in St Mary Stoke parish formerly stood a famous miraculous Cross or Rood. The Cross is remembered in Golden Rood Lane.

Ancient Chapels.

There were at least four other chapels in the town. St Mildreds Chapel (sometimes listed with the churches) stood on the Cornhill; All Saints Chapel stood in St Matthews Parish probably next to St Johns Hospital and was mentioned c1340; St Edmund de Pountenay's Chapel, founded before 1290, was impropriated to the Priory of St Peter and St Paul. It is thought to have stood a little behind 15 Lower Brook Street, on the S side of Rosemary Lane and alongside the rectory which occupied the corner site, its churchyard extended to Foundation Street; and St John's Chapel, in Caldewell, also mentioned in 1291 - this was probably in the area of present-day Cauldwell Hall Road, E of the town. Another ancient chapel, St. Alburt's (Aethelbeorth's) mentioned in a will of John Squier 'Clerk of St Albright's Chapel near Ipswich c1518', stood just S of the junction of Bramford and Sproughton Roads. 'Albrihtestou' a berewick (or outlying or sub-manor) of Bramford, was granted by William II to Butley Abbey in 1094. Its chapel was first mentioned in 1354. A late C15 preambulation of the boundary or Franchise of Ipswich refers to 'the river meadows under Bordesowe (Boss) Hall, and so forth into a highway that cometh from Ipswich to St. Albrytys Chapel into the way that goeth to Sproughton...' Aethelbeorht, a former king of East Anglia, died in 794. The site is now believed to be covered by either the railway or later housing or industrial development.

Site of College.

Born in the town in 1475, the son of a wealthy and respected merchant (not a butcher as is commonly claimed), Thomas Wolsey rose to become Lord Chancellor to Henry VIII in 1515. From his position as the second most powerful man in the kingdom he planned a college of secular canons in his home town which would outshine all other similar foundations in England. Having obtained a licence from the Pope and King in 1524 he suppressed a number of the smaller monasteries in East Anglia - Snape, Dodnash, Wykes, Felixstowe, Rumburgh, Montjoy, Bromhill, Blythburgh, Horkesley and Tiptree, as well as the priories of St Peters and Trinity in Ipswich - to provide endowments; the corporation offering the property which Richard Felaw had bequeathed to them for the support of a free school and hospital. His magnificent foundation was to comprise a dean, sub-dean, 12 fellows, 8 singing men, 8 choristers, 12 bedesmen, a grammar-school master and two assistants, and 50 'grammar children', and the buildings of the dissolved Augustinian Priory of St Peter and St Paul were to provide provisional accommodation for the college whilst work proceeded. Wolsey, who initially intended this collegiate acadamy as a nursery for his new college at Oxford, saw John Holte, titular Bishop of Lydda, lay the first stone on 15th July 1528, from whence work proceeded apace. Then in the Autumn of 1529 came Wolsey's downfall and the college, although struggling on for several months, was brought to an untimely end. Wolsey never recovered and within a year had died a broken man. The King seized the endowments and appropriated the considerable amount of building material which had been accumulated, and the incomplete buildings fell quickly into ruin and disappeared, leaving only one minor Tudor gateway. It still stands today, isolated in the heart of dockland; drab and virtually forgotten; one man's dreams for a permanent memorial to himself and his town denied even the peace of the dead by the traffic roar from a newly created ring road. The tower of St Peter's Church (which had provided the college chapel) was also destroyed at Wolsey's fall from power and receives a mention in Shakespeare by one who is defending Wolsey in a speech to Queen Catherine:

'He was most princely; ever witness for him
Those twin tower of learning that he raised in You,
Ipswich and Oxford! one of which fell with him,
Unwilling to outlive the good that he did.'

IPSWICH *(continued)*

Ancient Deer Park.

Christchurch Park, a public park of c28 ha. situated near the centre of Ipswich, was anciently a deer park belonging to the adjacent Domesday priory of Holy Trinity.

Martyrs' Memorial.

A memorial in Christchurch Park commemorates the Prostestant martyrs burned at the stake in Ipswich during the Marian persecutions. These included the first, Robert Sammuell, who met his death in 1555 within two years of Mary's accession, and a year later two Ipswich women, Joan Trunchfield, a shoemaker's wife, and Agnes, wife of Robert Potten an Ipswich brewer of St Mary Elms, who were burned upon Cornhill.

Site of Ancient Gallows.

The town's gallows stood on Rushmere Heath.

Site of old Windmills.

A postmill stood in the area of Alexandra Park in 1674. Two mills stood on Town Marshes around 1733, both gone by 1812. Two mills were recorded on Stoke Hill, one in 1736, the other 1764. The first was moved to Earl Stonham in 1849, the other demolished in 1887. A postmill which stood on Bishops Hill in 1736 was later moved to Offton. A tower mill on North Hill Road in 1783 was gone by 1886, but the postmill recorded in Bell Vue Road in 1764 was still standing in 1873. In the first half of the C19 there were seventeen windmills in Ipswich and two watermills at Handford and Stoke.

Site of Racecourse.

A residential area in SE Ipswich still known as 'The Racecourse' is the site of two oval racecourses on the heath near Nacton Corner. They are marked and named 'The Courses' on Bowen's map of 1755 and known as the 'New Race Ground' in 1751. The smaller course to the NW is probably that which survived as the 'Race Ground' and is shown in fine detail on Faden's map of 1783. Ipswich Races, as they were known, drew noblemen to the town from far afield in the C18 and early C19. Despite being covered by C20 housing, the property boundaries still trace the outline of the course over much of its length. Flat races ceased in 1883, and steeple-chasing as recently as 1902.

Almshouse & Workhouse.

A fine group of almshouses, originally known as 'The Foundation' (from where the street in which they stand takes its name), were founded in 1552 by Henry Tooley, a wealthy merchant. The site formerly occupied by the Dominican Priory was purchased in 1569 for Christs Hospital 'for poor people' but it became mainly a 'workhouse' for 'idle vagabonds and sturdy beggars' of the town to which William Smart added several endowments.

Historic Houses & Ancient Moated Sites.

The site of the ancient Brook Hall may have been located during reconstruction of the Valley Road/Norwich Road junction when evidence of a high status C11-C13 building was discovered. Pykenham's Gateway in Northgate Street was the entrance to a mansion built of Suffolk brick c1471 by William Pykeneham, Archdeacon of Suffolk and Dean of Stoke by Clare College; the inner entrance is of wood. The Ancient House (sometimes known as Sparrow's House) is said to have been built by George Copping for Robert Sparrowe late in the C16. It was rebuilt in the C17 when the exterior walls were covered with remarkable pargetting - the best example of this Suffolk speciality in the county. Christchurch Mansion was built between 1548 and 1551 by Edmund Withipoll on the site of the Augustinian Priory of Holy Trinity, some of the stonework being re-used in its construction. Later owners were the Devereuxs in 1642 and the Fonnereaus in 1732. To save it from demolition in 1892 it was purchased by F. T. Cobbold, MP, who presented it to the town along with a generous endowment to create a museum and art gallery. Despite often over-enthusiastic redevelopment there are still a number of C15 and C16 houses remaining in the town - many well disguised by modern facades. The ancient moat of the former Boss Hall in Sproughton Road has now been filled in. The original hall obtained the name Boss from Edward de Bordeshaw who resided here in the reign of Henry III and excavations show that its moat had been constructed in the C14, sealing C13 occupation beside the river Gipping. Traces of septaria walls survived until recent times. A later hall was built on the site in the reign of James I. Among the old hotels and

IPSWICH *(continued)*

public houses of Ipswich, the Great White Horse is probably the most famous. The present building was a former coaching inn but a 'Whit Hors Inn' stood on the site as early as 1518. Charles Dickens made the inn famous by featuring it in 'Pickwick Papers' and Lord Nelson and Lady Hamilton stayed here in 1800. The yard of the Golden Fleece practiced the popular pastime of bull-baiting as late as 1805. The Golden Lion in the Cornhill was a C16 coaching inn. The Neptune Inn in Fore Street has the date '1639' painted on the front but this may refer to the date of its transferance from a private house for the building is likely to be at least a century earlier. The former Half Moon with its fine carved corner-post is situated in Foundation Street and dates from at least 1522 when it was left to the Corporation in the will of Richard Oake. It was later said to have been the residence of that great town benefactor Henry Tooley who died in 1551. The Old Bell stood on the corner of Vernon Street and Bell Lane and is known to have been in existence in 1639. The Sun Inn, now a shop at the bottom end of St. Stephens Lane, is Tudor in origin as is the former Coach and Horses which hides behind a Georgian and Victorian facade. The Black Horse in St. Matthews was a private house until after 1689. The Swan in King Street predates 1664 when it paid out 40s. per annum to buy coals for the poor of the parish to be distributed on St. Thomas's Day. The Woolpack, which dated from the middle of the C16, was originally a timber inn which stood beside a long wool warehouse which ran from the corner of St. Margaret's Churchyard to the entrance to Christchurch Park. This was in the days when the Fonnereau family lived at the hall and before any of the surrounding streets had been built. A toll-gate then stood just below the Woolpack and almost opposite the entrance to Christchurch Park. Here farmers coming into town payed tolls for their gigs and carts. When this toll-gate disappeared so did most of the Woolpack's trade. It was rebuilt in brick and became one of the earliest brick-built inns in Ipswich. The Griffin Inn (pulled down in 1842) stood partly on the site of the former Crown and Anchor Hotel (now part of Debenhams). When the town's first Playhouse collapsed in 1728, another was built in the Griffin's yard. Dogs Head Street gained its name from the curiously named Dogs Head in The Pot Inn. An ancient map of 1674 names the street 'Dogs Head in The Pot Lane'.

IXWORTH *(6½ miles NE of Bury St Edmunds)*

Blackbourn Hundred. 'Gicsa's enclosure' (OE) *Gyxeweorde* (c1025) *Giswortha* (DB)
Manors. Ixworth (-C13 Le Blund/Blunt family; C13 William Criketot).

Roman Fort & Civilian Settlement.
A large Roman fort and civilian settlement dating from the C1 was partially excavated prior to work on the A143 Ixworth bypass in 1985.

Roman Road.
The length of Ixworth High Street is on the line of a Roman road.

Site of Roman (?) & Medieval Bridge.
Black earth and sherds from a pipeline trench in 1951, along with a wooden post and, 4 yds further along, evidence of a second post on the same side of the road and 15 yds towards the river Black Bourn, suggest the possibility that these may be the remains of Roman bridge timbers. An iron ring and Samian pottery have also been found here. The present bridge over the Black Bourn was erected in the C19, but there is record of an earlier bridge in the 1533 will of Hewe Baker who left the sum of 40s. 'to making of one bridge of lyme and stone at the mylle of Ixworth'.

Roman Villa.
The foundations of the hypocaust of a probable Roman bath house were discovered SE of the village in 1834. Excavations in 1849 and 1948 revealed a considerable apsidal building dating from C1-2 A.D. with a range of rooms (one with a large quantity of painted plaster) and another pillared hypocaust and furnace house. There was evidence of destruction and a well contained much Roman debris.

Saxon Settlement.
There is evidence for early Saxon occupation of the ruins of the Roman villa (*see above*), along with three 'hut' sites to the SE.

IXWORTH *(continued)*

Ancient Vineyard.

There is an entry in Domesday Book for a vineyard of three arpents (c3.75 acres) at Ixworth. A working vineyard exists today at Wyken Hall, just E of the parish.

Site of Priory.

An Augustinian Priory dedicated to the Virgin Mary was founded close by the parish church by Gilbert le Blunt c1170. The buildings were destroyed in a civil riot some years afterwards and rebuilt by the founder's son on a new site close by. Though never very wealthy, it was of considerable importance in local affairs. By 1492 it had a prior and 14 canons in residence, 16 in 1526 and 18 at the time of its dissolution in 1537. It was then granted to Richard Codington and his wife Elizabeth in exchange for the manor of Nonsuche in Surrey; their canoped tomb lies in the present church. Parts of the monastic buildings are embedded in Ixworth Abbey, a C17-C18 house which now stands on the site. The early C13 Prior's House retains its vaulted basement complete, and in front of the main entrance to the house are the massive exposed foundations - discovered in 1835 - of parts of the original cruciform priory church with a central tower and aisled nave. When it was destroyed, the leads from the roofs were melted down in a furnace; these remains, comprising several hundredweight, together with two pigs of lead bearing the royal stamp of Henry VIII, were also discovered.

Medieval Common.

A large area of common named Ixworth Heath is shown on Faden's 1783 map W of Abbey Farm, lying between Heath Farm and the northern parish boundary; its former site is now bisected by Heath Road. Now enclosed it formerly continued W into Troston Common, and also S either side of the Thetford Road, across the river, narrowing to end just short of the village centre.

Ancient Mills.

The watermill on the Blackbourn NW of the village dates back at least to the early C16 and no doubt occupies the site of earlier ones. A windmill, shown in 1783 standing by Crown Lane E of the village, was gone by 1882.

Medieval Market & Fairs.

Excavations have shown that the parish was a thriving market centre in the Roman period. The priory was granted a market and two fairs by Richard II in 1384. Street names in a survey of 1625 indicate the original site of the market at the junction of Stow Lane with High Street - the portion nearest High Street known as Old Street/Old Market. By this date, however, it had been repositioned to a site opposite the Pickeral Inn.

Medieval Cross.

A Stone Cross was situated at Townsend in Stow Lane in 1533. The pedistal remains in the grounds of Cross House on Stowlangtoft Road.

Medieval Guildhall & Workhouse.

The Guildhall, situated E of the churchyard, dated from 1476 and held the guilds of St. John Baptist, Corpus Christi, St. Peter and St. Thomas of Canterbury. It became the Town House in 1625 when it was divided into several dwellings to house six poor women and seven men. In 1709 it formed a workhouse. The Rectory now occupies the site.

Historic Houses.

The ancient Pickerel Inn is mentioned in a will of 1533, and there is a timber-framed house in the village street with fine pargetting. Theobalds Restaurant is housed in a building which dates from the C16 and Priory Farm is a possible hall-house.

IXWORTH THORPE *(1½ miles NW of Ixworth)*

Blackbourne Hundred. 'Ixworth's secondary settlement' (OE+ON) *Torp* (DB) *Ixeworth Thorp* (1305). The village was a manor of Ixworth Priory under William le Blund in the C11/C12 which, at the Dissolution, passed with Ixworth to Richard and Elizabeth Codington. It was first mentioned in 1280 as Thorp de Ixworth and in 1327 called Ixeworthethorp.

IXWORTH THORPE *(continued)*

Ancient Woodland.
Oak Grove, SW of the hamlet, is a part of ancient woodland.

Medieval Green.
A small triangular green, named Thorp Green in 1783, was situated at the junction of Brand Lane and Ixworth Road. Properties are shown lining its northern and eastern sides; of these only Lynton House remains. The green has now been enclosed.

Deserted Settlement.
Although its name suggests that this was only a dependent settlement of the neighbouring parish of Ixworth (sometimes called Thorpe-by-Ixworth) with no church recorded here at Domesday, it must have obtained one very soon after as its little thatched church of All Saints has a Norman doorway. The church stands alone on a hill, but fieldwalking has revealed evidence of an early settlement of late Saxon-early Norman date close by on the far side of the Thetford road. Later Medieval settlement has also been found around the now enclosed greens near the site of the manor house on the Honington parish boundary.

Historic Houses & Ancient Moated Sites.
An irregular oblong moat (now dry) by Lynton House, may have been the site of the ancient manor house held in the 1280s by William de Pakenham, described as the chief lord of the vill of Thorpe and successor to the Blund family founders of nearby Ixworth Priory. Manor House Farm is the probable site of its successor, the former manor house of the Croft family. Fieldwalking has revealed a scatter of Medieval pottery in a field named 'Old Moat' on a map of 1769, and in a field on the same map called 'Thorpe Hall', a dark soil mark was noticed which yielded Medieval pottery sherds, lava quern fragments and burnt flints. Another moat shown near Holms Wood has left no trace.

KEDINGTON *(3 miles ENE of Haverhill)*

Risbridge Hundred. 'Farmstead of a man called Cydda' (OE) *Kydington* (1043-5) *Kidituna* (DB)
Manors. Kedington (C12 Richard FitzGilbert). *Sub-Manors.* Cotton/Cotton Hall; Palmer's Manor or Tenement.

Ancient Woodland.
Jolly's Wood near the SE parish boundary, and a section of woodland by the river Stour, are fragments of ancient woodland.

Ancient Cursus (?)
W of Hall Farm, N of the church and E of the river Stour, parallel ditches seen in cropmarks may identify an ancient ceremonial way. The ditches are c65' apart and run E-W / ENE-WSW with an indistinct terminal(?) at the W end. c164 yds. long, the E end may extend to and beyond the field boundary. The N ditch is on the same alignment as the field boundary shown on the 1842 tithe map. Nothing has been found by fieldwalking the route.

Ancient Ditch System.
1977 aerial photographs revealed an arc of ditches interrupted by a series of causeways which appear to defend, or define, a small promontory formed by a meander of the river Stour. A scatter of worked flints was discovered just outside the enclosure.

Sites of Ancient Mounds (?)
There is circumstantial evidence for a mound in a field near Baythorne Lodge called Home Pasture, and another S of Great Wilsey Farm and a tributary of the Stour.

Ancient Tracks.
A section of Way Bank Lane, a track which runs SW from the Brockley Green to Hundon road, forms a part of the eastern parish boundary with Stoke-by-Clare. It is shown and named on Faden's map of 1783 and may date

KEDINGTON *(continued)*

back at least to Saxon times.

Site of Roman Villa (?)

In a previously undisturbed field near the river Stour, NW of Cotton Hall, pottery and evidence of flint wall foundations, box and roof tiles, and occupation and destruction levels were discovered when first ploughed in 1977-8. It may be the site of a Roman villa.

Roman Building.

Beneath the floor of the nave and N aisle of the church of St Peter and St Paul are the remains of a Roman building with a section of mosaic paving discovered during C19 restoration.

Anglo-Saxon Cross.

An Anglo-Saxon stone Cross of c900 A.D., now incorporated into the E gable, previously stood E of the church gate.

Medieval Greens.

An area near the southern parish boundary is named Calford Green on the present OS map with, just to the S, Woodland Green. Neither are named or shown on Faden's 1783 map and both may already have gone by this time. The road which now leads S from the village to the area (the present B1061) appears to be shown terminating near Ruse Farm on this earlier map. Faden also makes no mention of an elevated area now named Danes Common, W of the village.

Site of old Windmill.

A tower mill occupied a site now covered by the grounds of Risbridge Hospital in 1783. It was demolished in 1945.

Historic Houses & Ancient Moated Sites.

Kedington Hall, situated on the N side of the churchyard and the seat of the Barnardistons for several centuries, was pulled down in 1785 after the family line terminated in 1745. Flourishing in a direct line for nearly thirty generations it was one of Suffolk's most important families with many of its members holding high office. The outline of the moat, some walling of the former garden, and a fine avenue of trees remain. The nickname 'Roundhead' was given to Sir Samuel Barnardiston in 1641 by Queen Henrietta Maria, who, observing him during a procession of London apprentices who 'wore the hair of the head cut round', cried out, "See what a handsome round-head is there." The name thus became a byword in English history. Ketton House is an ancient building and provides the village with its local pronunciation, 'Ketton'. Eagle's Farm near Calford Green, has C17 chimneys and there are remains of a moat close by at Eastcotts. On the site of Little Wilsey Farm, close to the parish boundary, was another moat recently infilled.

KELSALE *(1½ miles N of Saxmundham)*

Hoxne Hundred. 'Celi's corner of land' (OE) *Keleshala* (DB). Incorporates the smaller parish of Carlton *(see Carlton)* and is now known as Kelsale-cum-Carlton.

Manors. Kelsale (1270 Roger le Bigot).

Ancient Woodland.

Lonely Wood (formerly Brushwood), which occupies the N bank of the Gull Stream near the western parish boundary, is a part of ancient woodland.

Medieval Packway.

A packway is shown and named on Faden's 1783 map running NW from the village. Part remains as a track and footpath leading off the present A12 past Hall Farm. The old route has been lost beyond the end of a small wooded area where the present footpath turns right towards Kelsale Hall. It originally curved W to meet the Kelsale-Sibton road at the point where it turns sharp left. Its likely route from here is traced by a footpath heading N from the bend, and it can be picked up again at Sibton Green, N of Sibton. The packway, with its likely associations with the Bigod family, probably connected that which ran

KELSALE *(continued)*

from Walton(Felixstowe) to Dunwich, with that heading N to Bungay.

Site of Chapel.
Flint and mortar foundations have been unearthed on the site of a medieval chapel marked on the 1840 tithe map, W of Rubblestone Farm.

Medieval Deer Park.
The Bigods created a deer park to the N of Kelsale Hall. Its extent is drawn on a map of 1616 by John Middleton and one stretch of the original boundary earthwork can be seen - marked 'Pond Bay' on the OS map - 300 yds S of Kelsale Lodge (presumably the park-keeper's lodge). Park Gate Farm now marks the eastern edge of the park.

Medieval Greens.
Several greens are shown and named on Faden's map of 1783. North Green is shown as rectangular, S of North Green Farm, running NW-SE. East Green was a large inverted L-shaped green SE of Eastgreen Crossing, shown bordered on all sides by properties; it was enclosed in 1854. Callow Green lay S of the link road between the present A12 and B1121, S of Dorley's Corner - the area is now called Curlew Green; and the small triangular Hams Green stood at the junction of the Kelsale-Sibton road with a track leading to Lonely Farm. Carlton Green is situated close to the southern parish boundary with Saxmundham.

Ancient Market.
The Bigods inherited a market here at Domesday which had formerly been granted by Edward the Confessor. It was short lived, however, for the year after he came to the throne, Edward I - in what would appear to be retaliatary action for being crossed by the family - granted Saxmundham, only a mile away, a market and fair which soon eclipsed that at Kelsale. The site beside the guildhall is suggestive of that occupied by the former market place.

Site of old Windmill.
The post mill which stood on Dorley's Corner in 1764 was dismantled in 1923. Another mill is shown W of Carlton Rookery in 1783 - its fate unknown.

Guildhall.
The Guildhall, a timber-framed house 200 yds. SW of the church, probably predates 1439 when we find that a 'Guild of St John the Baptist' was in existence in Kelsale. After providing for other needs in the parish it was converted into a school and residence for the master in 1870.

Free School.
A school, possibly held in the church, was mentioned in the Town Lands Trustees accounts in 1573. Around 1765 a Free School was endowed for the education of ten plus poor children. By 1818 the Grammar School was providing free education for 85 boys.

Almshouse.
The Guildhall was used as an almshouse for the poor c1614.

Workhouse.
A workhouse is recorded with 40 inmates in 1776. This role was later taken over by the Guildhall which was let to the parish for 14 years from 1825.

Historic Houses.
Kelsale Lodge, of ancient origin, has an old Tudor barn still bearing the terracotta lions of the Bigod and Molbray families. An ancient moat lies in The Garden Wood just NW of the modern Kelsale Hall. The early C16 Manor House, N of the church, has parts of an oblong moat which formerly enclosed a large area; sometimes known as Church Farm, the house was enlarged in 1906. There are other moats: at Denny's Farm - producing C13 pottery scatter; at Maple Farm, and another, just to the N of Town Farm, where there are two sides producing C13 and C14 pottery bounding a field near the parish boundary.

KENTFORD *(4½ miles E of Newmarket)*

Risbridge Hundred. 'Ford over the river Kennet' (OE) *Cheneteforde* (C11)
Manors. Kennet and Kentford al Kennett al Kentford (C13 Roger Bigot).

Lower Palaeolithic Site.
A major settlement site of the Lower Palaeolithic Period was situated in the parish.

Tumuli.
A round barrow c35 yds. in diameter beside the Icknield Way (B1506), E of the village, unearthed an inhumation grave. Two other round barrows (since destroyed) lay NE of the village.

Prehistoric Way & Roman Road.
The Icknield Way, one of the earliest prehistoric tracks in England, carries the Roman road from its crossing of the river Kennett WSW-ENE through the parish; its line is disected by the crossing of the present major A14 road.

Ancient Ford & Site of old Bridge.
The prehistoric Icknield Way (B1506) fords the river Kennet just W of the street and church, giving the parish its Saxon place-name. Earthworks roughly parallel with the road and 11-22 yds. into the field, in the form of a linear depression 6½'-10' wide with small raised banks on either side c6½' wide and 1½' high, are recorded as 'Piers of Old Kentford Bridge' on an earlier OS map. In 1934, the *Suffolk Chronicle and Mercury* showed a photograph of a massive overgrown masonry buttress beside the river and present bridge, describing it as Roman.

Medieval Heath.
Kentford Heath is shown on Faden's 1783 map covering the entire eastern half of this small parish. It is now confined to the N, extending into Herringswell.

Guildhall.
'A piece of ground, copyhold of the manor of Kennett-cum-Kentford, on part of which a messuage formerly stood, called the Guildhall.'

Historic Houses.
The Bell Inn, better known as Kentford Bell, is an ancient timber-framed building on the old Bury to Newmarket road. The Cock public house is also some four hundred years old.

KENTON *(2½ miles NNE of Debenham)*

Loes Hundred. 'Farm on the hill-ridge', 'Royal manor' or 'Cena's homestead' (OE) *Chenetuna* (DB). Morley is confident that the place-name is evident in the long ridge of the western hill running parallel with the river from Kenton Lodge to the church.
Manors. Kenton (C13 Sir Peter Braunch; C13 Ivo de Kenton). *Sub-Manors.* Sudden Hall.

Royal Manor.
In Saxon times the East Anglian kings occasionally held their court at nearby Debenham and this may have been their adjacent royal manor (*see place-name*).

Ancient Track.
A small length of the ancient Waddlegoose Lane, running from Debenham to Earl Soham, forms a part of the southern parish boundary and may date back at least to Saxon times.

Medieval Chapel.
In 1524 John Garneys - whose knightly brass is housed in the church - founded a chapel in Kenton. It survived for only twenty-two years until 1546 when it was demolished.

Historic Houses & Ancient Moated Sites.
The red-brick manor house of Kenton Hall was built in the C15/C16 by the Garneys family who resided in the village for some 400 years until 1685. It occupies one of a series of moated islands; two small square ones enclosed by a much wider one. It was badly damaged by fire in 1919 and only a small part of what was a very

KENTON *(continued)*

large mansion remains. The site was occupied in the C13 and C14 by the Kentons who resided in what must have been a fortified manor house on one of the two island sites. Margery de Kenton held the manor in 1346 by service of one knight's fee of Evade Clavering, the widow of Sir Thomas de Ufford. Sudden Hall, a farmhouse SE of the village, still retains two sides of a square moat. The former manor house of Sudden Hall seated a family of the same name during the reign of Edward I. At Moat Farm W of the village an ancient, circular moat surrounds the house, and another, roughly oblong in plan, encloses this and a large area of land. There is a fragment of a moat at the vicarage - one side with its two angles.

KERSEY *(2 miles NW of Hadleigh)*

Cosford Hundred. 'Assembly Island' (OE) *Caeresige* (c995) *Careseia* (DB). Though many authorities give the meaning 'Island where cress grows', Morley feels the place-name relates directly with Cosford Hundred. The village stands in an elevated position running down to the valley of the river Brett. The river has now taken its name from Brettenham but it was originally called Cors giving rise to Cosford Hundred and the lost Domesday township of Corsfield which lay in the neighbouring Babergh Hundred. Cosford Hall in Hadleigh may well be the site of the later Hundred Court since it immediately flanks the stream, but an earlier and original Cosford Hall is shown on early OS maps as that island in the Brett which gave name to both Kersey (Corsey) and the Hundred. Here too Kirby names Cosford Bridge. Kersey later became one of the thriving west Suffolk centres for the cloth industry.

Manors. Kersey (C13 Hubert de Roylli). *Sub-Manors.* Sampson's Hall; Priory Manor.

Site of Henge (?)

A single ring ditch 23 yds in diameter with opposed causeway, identified by aerial photographs W of Rushes Farm, may represent the site of a possible henge.

Ancient Chapel & Priory.

Priory Farm is situated on the top of the hill on the opposite side of the valley from the church. On a site here about 1215, Thomas de Burgh founded a chapel known as the Chapel of the Good Rood of Rest as a hospital or free chapel. This was converted into a priory for Augustinian canons dedicated to St Mary and St Anthony by his widow, Nesta de Cokefield, some four years later and endowed with the tithes of Kersey and Lindsey. It was already in financial difficulty by 1347, and in 1444 Lord Powys, who had acquired the patronage, obtained permission for its dissolution, granting the site to what later became King's College, Cambridge. What little is left of the buildings stand in the grounds of the farm. These comprise one major fragment of the C13 cruciform church, the S chapel or aisle of the chancel - now converted into a barn. Much of the SE pillar of the central church tower still stands, and the W range of the cloister (the converted hospital) is now incorporated inside the farmhouse which, although now brickfronted, appears to embody the remains of a C14 aisled hall - perhaps the Prior's lodging.

Medieval Greens.

Wicker Street Green is shown as a long, narrow green on Faden's map of 1783. Though enclosed and replaced by the road SW to Boxford, most of the properties which originally lined it remain today. Withermarsh Green, further NE, ran NE from the junction near Manor Farm to Harts Farm at Kersey Uplands - the area now called William's Green on the present OS map. The area around Kersey Uplands was called Leaves Green. The small triangular green on the junction NW of Uplands Farm was called Quoits Green in 1783. The outline of the large green called Kersey Tye, although enclosed, can still be roughly discerned. A wedge-shaped green called Nokes Tye is still partially defined by field boundaries near the eastern parish boundary. It ran from the present modern development S of the church, NE, bordered by Oaks Tye Farm and Noaks Tye Farm.

Medieval Market & Fair.

A grant for a market in Kersey was obtained by Philip Basset in 1252, and a grant for a fair in 1618.

Water Mill.

The C17/C18 mill complex was reported to be in a bad state of repair in the 1960s.

KERSEY *(continued)*

Guildhall (?)

The fact that the parish supported the three guilds of Holy Ghost, Our Lady and St. Peter (1445) makes it likely that a Guildhall once existed in the village.

Workhouse.

A workhouse is recorded here with 30 inmates in 1776.

Historic Houses.

The Manor House of Sampsons Hall on the Boxford road, demolished in 1824, preserved the name of its owner, Sampson of Harkstead, who, during the Peasants' Revolt of 1381, led a group of rebels in the Ipswich area. The Little Manor is a timber-framed C14-C15 former hall-house with N and S cross-wings. It is now divided into two cottages known as Woodbine Cottage. Kedges End is a C17 former wool merchant's home later occupied by a horse doctor - still indicated by horsetails hanging from the eaves (1980). The timber-framed Bell Inn dates from the C15 and the former Quills Restaurant (now a private house), from the C16.

KESGRAVE *(3 miles NE of Ipswich)*

Carlford Hundred. 'Ketill's grave' (OE) *Gressegraua* (DB) *Kersigrave* (1231). Several give the meaning as 'ditch where cress grows', but Morley considers it a personal name connected with one of the burial mounds in the parish.

Manors. Kesgrave/Tuddenham's in Kesgrave (C14 Sir John de Holbroke).

Faden's map of 1783 shows Kesgrave with just a church and an inn, standing on opposite sides of a crossroads and surrounded by open heathland. Today the parish has been completely redeveloped as a dormitary suburb for neighbouring Ipswich.

Tumuli.

There are several burial mounds situated in the parish: a round, bowl-shaped mound c16' in diameter of which no trace remains; a bowl-shaped mound 33' in diameter which has been ploughed out; a pillow-shaped mound c16' long and 10' wide also now ploughed out; a probable bowl-barrow at Dobb's Corner 49' in diameter much damaged by rabbits; two overlapping Bronze-Age round barrows SW of Dobb's Corner; and in the N of the parish are three barrows W of the school. There is documentary evidence of barrows previously located in Kesgrave Wood which were destroyed in 1852 while constructing a driveway between the lodges to Kesgrave Hall when 'a considerable quantity of urn fragments (evidently Roman) were found, some nearly perfect and containing human bones'.

Mound.

A mound at a crossroads in the parish known as 'Dobb's Grave' was found to contain the skeleton of John Dobbs, a young shepherd, who hanged himself; a stake had been driven through his heart. It was anciently the custom (last observed in 1823) to bury suicides at crossroads in this manner.

Historic House.

The Bell Inn, itself dating back to Tudor times, stands on the site of a Rest House provided by Butley Priory who held the church here from 1180 until the Dissolution.

KESSINGLAND *(5 miles SSW of Lowestoft)*

Mutford & Lothingland Hundred. 'Cultivated land belonging to Casa's people' (OE) *Kessingalanda* (DB). Includes the Domesday vills of Kislea and Rodenhala (part of which is in Pakefield).

Manors. Kessingland Stapleton's (1251 Roger de Montalt). *Sub-Manors.* Kessingland Itchinghams/ Echinghams; Kessingland and Kingstons; Rothenhall (1419 John de Rothenhall owns as of Honor of Chester).

Ancient Settlement Site.

Near Cliff Farm in the N of the parish, evidence of Mesolithic, Roman and Medieval settlement has been found along with a cobbled surface which extends into the pasture field.

KESSINGLAND *(continued)*

Site of Nunnery (?)

In the reign of Edward III the local church had been appropriated 'to the Nuns of St Clare in the Minories of London' who retained it until the Dissolution. After passing through several hands it was purchased by William Whiston, Vicar of Lowestoft and Kessingland, and settled by him on the vicarage at Kessingland. The church, while it belonged to the nuns, was considerably larger than the present building. However, after losing its income from that source after the Dissolution, it fell into decay and services discontinued until the church was rebuilt on a reduced scale in 1694. Near the site of the old vicarage, often referred to as The Nunnery and burned down in 1833, stood a flint wall about 40 yds long with an ancient buttressed house which supposedly formed part of a monastery relating to the nuns.

Medieval Common.

The roundabout at the southern end of the Kessingland bypass on the present A12, along with a housing development, occupy the former Kessingland Common, shown on Faden's 1783 map. Runhill Heath is also shown on the map covering the N of the parish in the area of Heath Farm and extending into Gisleham. Heathland is also shown covering a continual strip of coastal edge from the village S to Covehithe.

Medieval Market & Fair.

Kessingland, anciently a place of considerable importance, had a weekly market granted to Roger de Montalt in 1251 and an annual fair obsolete by 1891.

Site of old Windmill.

A windmill is shown E of Dam Lane and NW of Nutgrove Wood in 1783. Its history and fate are unknown.

Historic House & Ancient Moated Site.

A fragment of a moat remains at Moat Farm. Stapleton Manor House, which stood W of the churchyard, was demolished around 1823.

KETTLEBASTON *(7 miles NNW of Hadleigh)*

Cosford Hundred. 'Ketilbjorn's farmstead' (OScand+OE) *Kitelbeornastuna* (DB). Always shown as Kettlebarston until William White omitted the 'r' in his 1844 directory.

Manors. Domesday shows the entire township represented by the manor of Manetuna (C12 Godwin Kettlebarston enfeoffed to Robert Peche). In 1445 Henry VI granted the manor of Kettlebarston, along with that of Nedging, to William de la Pole, Duke of Suffolk to hold by the service of carrying a golden sceptre surmounted by a dove at the coronation of the king, and a sceptre of ivory with a golden dove upon it, at the queen's coronation.

Roman Road.

A length of Roman road (Margary 34a) is aligned from the ford over the river Brett near Wagger Farm and joins a known stretch ENE through Bildeston High Street. It is not evident on the ground.

Site of Medieval Chapel.

Chapel Farm on the parish boundary with Hitcham is the site of a chapel founded by John Jerveys in 1435 and dedicated to St Thomas.

Historic House & Ancient Moated Site.

The extensively modernised C17 Kettlebaston Hall, immediately W of the church, stands on the site of an earlier hall. It still has the SW and NW arms of its 328' x 295' moat. There are remains of a moat at High House Farm in the N of the parish.

KETTLEBURGH *(2½ miles SSW of Framlingham)*

Loes Hundred. 'Ketil's hill' or 'Hill by a narrow valley' (OScand or OE+OE or OScand) *Ketelbiria* (DB)
Manors. Kettleburgh (-C13 Crown property; C13 Sir William Charles). *Sub-Manors.* Kentons.

Medieval Greens.

Now enclosed and called Easton Green, Faden's 1783 map names it Kettleburgh Green and shows it as a good

KETTLEBURGH *(continued)*

sized green roughly rectangular running SW-NE from E of the church with the drive to the hall leading off from mid-way along the NW side. The present lane running S and SE from School Hill is of later date and cuts across the original site. The map also shows a Kettleburgh Common just N of the church in a crook of the road bordered by The Old Rectory. It appears to have been very small, as it is today.

Medieval Market & Fair.
Permission to hold a market and fair were granted to Sir William Charles in 1265.

Site of Watermill.
A watermill, situated by the Deben in the S of the parish, was in existence in 1637.

Site of Ducking Stool.
An area known as Great Cockstool in 1747 possibly refers to the former site of a ducking or cucking stool, an instrument comprising a chair fastened to the end of a pivital beam and suspended over water - in this case probably the Deben - and used as a punishment for errant (mainly)women.

Historic Houses or Ancient Moated Sites.
The moated site of Kettleburgh New Hall, SE of the church, was the seat of the Stebbing and Pennyng families. It was built by the Stebbings c1527. At Domesday this was the main manor of Earl Alan of Richmond, and the site of the earlier manor house, Kettleburgh Old Hall, marked by a large, almost square (88 yds x 84 yds) well-preserved (but mostly dry) moat, lies immediately NW of the church. Foundations of the hall built by Sir William Charles in 1261 were still in existence in 1908. Rookery Farm, near the SE parish boundary, has disconnected ponds and medieval pottery including C13 rims from a possible moated site.

KIRKLEY *(1 mile SSW and now forming a part of South Lowestoft)*

Mutford & Lothingland Hundred. 'Clearing near or belonging to a church' (OScand+OE) *Kirkelea* (DB)
Manors. Kirkley al Kirkley Fastolf's/Kirkley Hall (1271 Alan de Wymundhale; 1378 Hugh Fastolf).

Lost Medieval Port.
Kirkley Ham is reputedly the site of an ancient haven and link waterway of the river Waveney with the sea. It had silted up and disappeared by the the map of 1777. An Elizabethan cup in the church, dated 1567, is inscribed 'for the towne of Kyrkley', signifying how this haven gave Kirkley its former medieval status being first mentioned as a port in 1322. The church too is a rebuild of a much larger mother church (the tower of which remains) with origins dating back before Domesday. However, the growth of Lowestoft saw the town decay and Faden's 1783 map shows only Kirkely Heath, an extensive area of heathland. Kirkley was abolished as a civil parish in 1907 and merged with Lowestoft; the heath used for the urban expansion of what is now known as South Lowestoft.

Medieval Market & Fair.
A licence was granted for a market and fair to Alan de Wymundhale in 1271.

KIRTON *(6 miles S of Woodbridge)*

Colneis Hundred. 'Farmstead with a church' (OScand+OE) *Kirketuna* (DB)
Again we have the rare occurrence of a parish which anciently held a Norse church, though the earliest parts of the present building only date from the C14 and C15. Kirton includes the former Domesday vills of Guthestuna and Struestuna creating the three small hamlets of Guston, Croxton and Strewston.
Manors. There were two Kirton manors: 1 (C14 Walter de Stratton); 2 (C15 Thomas Sampson).

Lost Medieval Settlements & Port.
Strewston, Croxton and the port of Guston were the more important places here on the banks of the river Deben till the C16, with Kirton itself merely 'the settlement by the church'. They have now all gone but their sites are still evident in earthworks showing enclosures, features, trackways and interlaced field systems. Croxton is remembered in the name of several local families. Beside the river Deben lies Kirton Creek, 'a queer place, lost and remote with a brooding silence' as W.G. Arnott so aptly describes it. But it was not always thus, for this was

KIRTON *(continued)*

the site of the ancient port of Guston, already operating at Domesday when it was called Guthestuna, a limb of the extensive port of Goseford which extended all along the S bank of the Deben from the estuary. All trace has now gone but once it was a busy customs port with ferries belonging to Walton Manor plying from the 'Stone' to Ramsholt and Shottisham on the northern bank. Sluice Farm is thought to have once been the old Ferry House. The ferry ceased in the middle of the C19 and the small hard which can be seen today only dates from the 1880s when it was built to carry bricks produced in the nearby brickyard.

Medieval Market & Fair.
Croxton obtained a grant for a market and fair in 1270.

Medieval Green.
Kirton Green is shown by Faden in 1783 as a triangular green on a fork in the road NW of the church.

KNETTISHALL *(8 miles NNE of Ixworth)*

Blackbourn Hundred. 'Knotte's shelter' (OE) *Gnedeshalla* (DB). The place-name may apply instead to a very pestilent biting gnat still prevalent over all the Brecklands of Norfolk and Suffolk.
Manors. Knettishall (1248 Hugh de Shardilow said to have enfeoffed Nicholas de St. Edmunds; 1316 Eleanor de Gnateshall). *Sub-Manors.* Stanton; Salthouse.

Tumuli.
Barrows lie on Hut Hill in the Knettishall Heath Country Park, and in Brickkiln Covert, E of Norwich Lane. There is another of Bronze-Age date in a rectangular enclosure on Nick's Hill, discovered in 1926, and documentary evidence of a fourth on the western boundary near New American Lodge.

Bronze-Age Cemetery.
A Bronze-Age cemetery was discovered in gravel pits on Stonehill in the S of the parish.

Roman Roads.
The Peddars Way adjusts its line to cross the Little Ouse river forming the western parish boundary. Another road heads NE through the parish as a minor road from TL969 792 to the Rushford-Hopton road.

Earthwork.
An undefined circular earthwork lies to the N of Heath Covert.

Deserted Medieval Village.
All Saints Church (with Norman origins), disused many years ago and now in complete ruin, is all that remains of what is now a deserted village. A field opposite named Camping Ground suggests the site for former medieval ball games. The medieval lords of the main Knettishall Manor appear, without exception, to have resided in East Harling across the border in Norfolk and been buried in the church of that parish.

KNODISHALL-CUM-BUXLOE *(4 miles SE of Saxmundham)*

Blything Hundred. 'Cnott's shelter or corner of land' (OE) Buxloe - Hlaw 'an artificial mound' or 'a mound with buried treasure' *Cnotesheala* (DB)
Manors. Knodishall (Anciently held by Jenney family until c1765).

Tumuli.
One large and eight small barrows lie in two rows running E-W at Knodishall Common just SW of the village. One, trenched c1860, showed evidence of Iron Age or Saxon date.

Roman Settlement.
There was a large Roman settlement in the parish considered by many the still unlocated town of *Sitomagus* which lay on the *Iter IX*, a road listed on the *Antonine Itinerary* of Roman roads in the county.

Ancient Tracks.
Ancient tracks form the majority of the western parish boundary from just N of Friston Church.

KNODISHALL *(continued)*

Lost Medieval Village.
Buxlow, once a separate parish, was first mentioned in the Feet of Fines for 1247 when the Leiston abbot sued a man "in Buckyslowe". Its earthworks would appear to lie W of the ruined base of the round towered Buxlow Church at Knodishall Green where paths still converge. However, in what are surely errors, Bowen's map of 1753 shows a symbol for 'church or chapel in ruins' as being just N of Friston church and Faden's map thirty years later also marks 'Buxlow' immediately N of Friston with what appears to be a faint cross and with woods to the E (Grove Wood?), yet shows Buxlow Forest N of Knoddishall Green (since destroyed for the construction of a World War II airfield). Buxlowe had 30 inhabitants in 1381 but by 1603 the church was probably disused; the parson of Buxlowe-cum-Knoddishall serving 'one church only', and an observer in the middle of that century claiming the church to be "decayed and ruinated tyme out of minde". Its name was superceded by that of Knoddishall Green at the time of the Civil War and consolidated with Knodishall in 1721.

Medieval Market & Fair.
Coldfair Green was the likely site of a fair and a former market, mentioned at Knodishall in the C17.

Medieval Green.
Knoddishall Green is shown on Faden's 1783 map in the NW corner of the parish as a widened roadway on which stood the old Buxloe Church. Coldfair Green is shown covering the junction of the present B1069 Friston-Leiston road with that going NW to Knodishall Church. Though retaining the name, it has now been completely redeveloped with new homes. A small fraction to the S is retained as Knodishall Common.

Site of old Windmill.
A windmill stood E of the church and Church Farm in 1783.

Historic Houses & Ancient Moated Site.
The knightly family of Jenney was resident in the parish at Knoddishall Hall from the beginning of the C15 (maybe earlier) until the middle of the C18. The church contains the brasses to John Jenney (1460) and his wife Margaret. The present hall is a farmhouse on the site of the old hall destroyed by fire in the 1860s. Red House Farm, formerly known as 'Ghosts Hole', is a fine Elizabethan house dated 1678. A rectangular moated site with buildings within was shown on the 1927 OS map at Little Moor Farm on the S edge of the former Friston Moor (Common), on the western parish boundary.

LACKFORD *(8 miles NW of Bury St Edmunds)*

Thingoe Hundred. Probably a corruption of 'ford over the river Lark' (OE) *Lecforda* (DB).
This great Domesday manor of 600 acres with two water mills gave its name to Lackford Hundred. Whilst it is true that the parish is actually listed in Thingoe, the river crossing lies exactly astride the hundred boundaries of Lackford, Thingoe and Blackbourn.
Manors. Lackford (Abbot of St. Edmunds; 1203 Benedict de Blakenham).

Multi-period Settlement Site.
Major sites dating from the Early Mesolithic period (pre-6500 BC) through Iron-Age, Roman (C2-C4), early Saxon and Saxo-Norman have been located in the areas of Home Heath, Hall Heath and Brook Farm.

Ancient Track, Ford & Roman Road.
The prehistoric Icknield Way passes through the parish from the Cavenham-Risby road NE to the ford across the river Lark (just to the E of the A1101 bridge) which relates to the place-name. It also provides the route of the Roman road between Tuddenham, Higham and Icklingham (Margary route 33).

Tumuli.
A round barrow lies W of Cuckoo Hill. There was originally a second, opened in 1869 to reveal a pair of cremations. Some way SE of these, aerial photographs have identified another.

Roman Settlement & Pagan Temple.
Morley noted that the *Camborico* or *Camborito* of the *Antonine Itinerary* means 'crooked ford' which aptly

LACKFORD *(continued)*

describes where the ancient Icknield Way changes direction to cross the Lark, which bends here on the borders of Lackford, Cavenham and Icklingham parishes. A large Roman settlement dating from C1-C3 contained a Roman pagan temple or shrine built in timber and clay from which probably came the 'Cavenham Crowns', three bronze headdresses worn as part of a ceremony; the two sheet bronze 'crowns' have adjustable fastenings to allow them to fit different sized heads.

Anglo-Saxon Cemeteries.
Beside the Roman settlement, a C6 Anglo-Saxon cemetery of at least 1,000 cremations in globular urns, accompanied by numerous brooches, combs and personal objects, showed that villagers were cremated until their C7 conversion. On 'Gravel Pit Hill' (tithe map) is an "ancient cemetery" partially excavated by Prigg in 1867. Its location is described as "between Lackford and Cavenham on the W side of the high road connecting the two places, standing on Off Hand Farm" (Field Barn on tithe, now Bunkers Barn). "..in front of this the ground is broken from having been dug into for gravel at sundry times". He describes the discovery of 2 'urns' and remains of a funeral pyre. The site could be prehistoric but more probably Saxon.

Site of Gallows (?)
The site of a gallows is suggested by Gibbet Hill on the 1842 tithe map. The field lies on high ground and is a likely position for a gallows, overlooking as it does the point where three hundreds meet. No trace of a mound or actual site is now evident.

Medieval Green.
Lackford Green, S of Lackford Bridge, would appear to have been a triangular green within the area outlined by a footpath and the Icknield Way running NE, and the present A1101 running NW and meeting the Way at Brook Farm; Manor Farm would have stood on the southern edge. The whole area has been enclosed and developed, and although named on Faden's 1783 map, it is not shown, suggesting it may already have gone by this time.

LAKENHEATH *(5 miles N of Mildenhall)*

Lackford Hundred. 'Hithe of the stream dwellers' (OE) *Lacingahithe* (945) *Lakingahethe* (DB). 'Heath' comes from the Anglo-Saxon *Hyth* meaning 'a landing place for boats'. These active waters (*see below*) later partially dried out to become the fens of today.
Manors. Lakenheath (1541 Granted to Dean and Chapter of Ely). *Sub-Manors.* Undley Hall; Radmere/ Redmere al Rodmere.

Ancient Great Lake.
An interesting but controversial suggestion has been made to provide an answer to the puzzle over the northern parish boundary - the county boundary with Norfolk - which fails to follow the line of the Little Ouse River for its whole length. The boundary is said to have been set out by the order of Abbot Brithnoth c974 A.D. at a time when a large area of Lakenheath parish was covered by a now extinct lake. An area of land just to the NW of this extinct lake is called Redmere Fen, probably derived from the Old English word *Hreod* meaning reed, hence Reed Mere. Examination of the surface of the land showed shell-marl covering an area of 2,200 acres which would have made it the largest lake in England after Windermere. It probably came into existence 500-100B.C. and, being shallow, its margins were subject to drying out in Summer. In 1327 a licence to amortice the manor of Undley Hall to the Prior and convent of Ely included a fishery in Wyndelee Mere.

Neolithic Settlement.
An area covering 140 yds x 120 yds at Maid's Cross Hill has provided considerable indications of a large Neolithic settlement including 'necked beaker' pottery.

Iron-Age & Multi-period Settlement.
A settlement discovered in Sahara Field on Lakenheath Airbase included pits, hearths and occupational material of an Early Iron-Age farmstead. The extensive pottery scatter over ½ mile identified an area of multi-period settlement.

LAKENHEATH *(continued)*

Tumuli

Maid's Cross Hill is a barrow reconstructed after ploughing. At Undley, a mound visible as earthworks is a Bronze-Age barrow. Two beakers now in the British Museum (and one in the Cambridge Museum which may also have come from here) are recorded as being from 'Undley Barrow, Lakenheath'. The location of this barrow is unknown but is reputed to be Undley Ringwork.

Romano-British Settlement.

A Roman settlement site was found at Caudle Head on the southern parish boundary at the edge of Lakenheath Airfield. Groups of post-holes, Iron-Age pits, hearths and C1-C2 finds were unearthed plus an enclosing boundary ditch with traces of palisading which may be of Saxon date showing extended settlement.

Roman Building (?)

Fired clay, wall plaster, bricks and debris of Roman date was reported in 1950-54 on Undley Common. Later ploughing uncovered a burial.

Roman Pottery Industry.

Five Romano-British kilns were discovered in the area of Sandy Drove track and excavated in 1974.

Coin Hoard.

A hoard of C1 coins found on a 'Roman field' in the parish were declared Treasure Trove in 1959.

Metal Working Industry.

A quantity of bronze (casting?) waste was found in the N end of a field near Sharpe's Corner.

Fishing Industry.

Five fisheries were listed in the parish at Domesday (*see 'Ancient Great Lake'*)

Extensive Anglo-Saxon Cemetery.

Prior to redevelopment work on Lakenheath Airbase, a known Anglo-Saxon cemetery site extending into Rearing Field was partially excavated in 1997. Over 150 graves were discovered and international attention was created when one was found to contain a Saxon warrior buried with his horse.

Ancient Earthworks.

In a field just NE of Undley Hall Farm, some 1½ miles SW of the village, is a circular earthwork of uncertain purpose. It is 132' in diameter with an entrance on the S. The N edge is eroded by ploughing. Romano-British ware and C2 terra sigillata have been found in the upper silting of the surrounding ditch together with domestic rubbish.

Ancient Tracks.

There are remains of an ancient track called Pilgrims Walk near the top of Maids Cross Hill. A number of drove trackways along which were driven herds of cattle and flocks of sheep in prehistoric times remain in the form of tracks and footpaths. They include: Millmarsh, Broadwater, Sandy, Eldon, Common, Highbridge Gravel, Docking, Whitefen, Nothfen, Calledge, Cawseyhorn and Smeeth Droves.

Deserted Medieval Village.

The present hamlet of Undley, ½ mile W of the town and now barely above the fen level, was formerly a Domesday island called *Lundale* which was two furlongs long and two furlongs broad with two fisheries and a glebeless church, gone by 1254.

Ancient Gallows.

A gibbet was situated at Undley.

Medieval Cross.

The remains of a Medieval Cross in the form of a stone base complete with a socket for the shaft lies on the S side of Maid's Cross Hill, a modern mound 'reconstructed from the barrow material when the area was first ploughed.' A loop in the road here points to its antiquity.

LAKENHEATH *(continued)*

Medieval Market & Fair.

There had been an early market here but the Abbot of Bury considered that 'Laking' infringed his privileges (despite being over 12 miles from his market in Bury). The dispute was carried to the King's Court where in 1201 it was settled in favour of the abbott who sent in his bailiffs with 600 armed men to suppress the market by force. It was terminated, but in 1309 the Prior of Ely obtained a new grant for a market and fair.

Site of old Windmill.

A windmill stood on the W side of Maids Cross Way near its junction with Cemetery Road in 1783.

LANGHAM *(3 miles E of Ixworth)*

Blackbourn Hundred. 'Long homestead or enclosure' (OE) *Langham* (DB). As the parish is now square in shape, the place-name probably refers to the original manor embracing the hall and the area between Castle Ditches and the river Blackbourne's tributary stream.

Manors. Langham (C11-1264 Le Blund family; 1264 William de Criketot; C14 Sir William de Langham).

Ancient Woodland.

Langham Thicks on the western parish boundary is part of ancient woodland.

Anglo-Saxon Cemetery.

A small Anglo-Saxon cemetery lies in the walled gardens north of Langham Hall.

Earthworks.

To the E of the church and moated site of the old hall *(see below)*, a mound at the end of a long strip of land running between deep ditches, rises 6' to 8'. It may have at one time been the site of a medieval mill for documents describe a lane called 'Le Myllhill' and a 'Millway' heading towards it from the ford on Langham road.

Deserted Medieval Settlement.

'Castle Ditches', which no doubt take the name from the moated site of the former fortified manor house, are applied to the large area of pasture E of the church but may have originally identified the land to the S, between church and flood plain. The *Victoria County History* describes Castle Ditches as earthworks of bumps and hollow-ways, gone by the middle C19, which may have formed the outline of the original village settlement.

Medieval Common.

A Langham Common is shown and named as a square area on the SE corner of Langham Thicks on Faden's 1783 map. A track named Common Lane now leads to the site.

Medieval Market.

A grant for a market in Langham was obtained in 1225 by the Le Blund family and renewed in 1256.

Historic Houses & Ancient Moated Site.

A moated earthworks lies in an overgrown copse just SE of the church in Langham Park. The moat has three impressively broad sides up to 24' wide but only an 8' wide water ditch appears to defend the S side. The site, however, abutts the flood plain of a tributary of the river Blackbourne which in early times would have provided its own protection. A Walsham-le-Willows Field Book refers to a small plot as 'of the Hellimott', and in 1695 as 'of The Hellimott at Langham'. The name likely refers to this earthworks which represents the site of the fortified manor house of the le Blunds and Cricketots dating back to at least 1264. Sir Patrick Blake built the present hall on a new elevated site in 1760. There are the remains of another possible moat at Stock Hill.

LAVENHAM *(6 m NNE of Sudbury)*

Babergh Hundred. 'Lafa's valley and homestead' (OE) *Lauenham* (DB)

Manors. Lavenham (The De Vere family held the manor from Domesday; 1604 Sir Thomas Skinner).

By 1525 Lavenham, an obscure village in the Early Middle Ages, had raised itself - as one of the main East Anglian centres for the thriving cloth industry - to rank as the 20th most wealthy town in England. Four guilds were established to regulate this industry. In 1330 Edward 111 gave a special charter authorising his tenents in

LAVENHAM *(continued)*

Lavenham to pass free of tolls throughout England, and an idea of the importance of the town during the C14-C16 was provided in 1397 when the Crown demanded loans from seventy of the chief towns in the country. Lavenham paid the sum of £20 - the same amount as Derby and Plymouth! Later, after the decline of its blue cloth trade, the town turned to weaving horse-hair, an industry which the womenfolk carried on in their own homes. Lavenham was badly hit by outbreaks of plague and smallpox: 27 died in 1699, 180 in 1712 and 282 in 1713. In a further outbreak in 1778, over 500 contracted the disease.

Roman Road.

School Farm Lane traces the course of a Roman road forming part of the southern parish boundary from TL912 471 to Washmere Green. For a short way from here it is marked by the field boundary.

Roman Building.

Basil Brown recorded that information was given him in 1948-9 by a lady resident of a Roman tessellated pavement believed to lie beneath the lawn in the vicinity of Grove House, sited between Lady Street and Barn Street. A Roman bath or crypt was said to have been discovered in the garden of Grove House as well as an underground passage from Barn Street towards the Guildhall. The remains were described in 1897 as discovered 'some years ago' and 'what seemed to be a Roman bath of considerable size was reburied after attracting many visitors.'

Roman Settlement.

'From time to time' coins, pottery and other signs of Roman occupation have been found in all parts of the town.

Roman Hoard.

A hoard of Roman coins dating from M. Antonius 30 B.C. to Trojan 98-117 A.D. was found by a labourer in a ploughed field in the parish.

Roman Pottery Industry (?)

Near Lavenham Hall was the site of 'ovens which some people think are Roman, or made of Roman tiles, but which are probably Medieval pottery ovens.' The site was also described as 'the remains of a building said to be a Roman pottery. The works remaining are made of Roman tiles with brick floors.' The site is now flattened and incorporated into the adjoining field.

Ancient Mound.

From the Earthwork Reconnaissance Survey conducted in 1994/5, a low circular mound of uncertain purpose was located in pasture near Lavenham Park Farm, c39'-c42' in diameter and only c6" high.

Site of Ancient Vineyard.

A vineyard of one arpent (1¼ acres) was recorded in Lavenham at Domesday.

Medieval Deer Park.

The de Veres, Earls of Oxford, had a deer park covering the whole northern part of the parish. It was disparked in the C17 to make Lavenham Park Farm, but much of the park boundary still survives as an earthwork.

Site of Gallows (?)

Hangman's Lane off the present A141 Brent Eleigh road is suggestive of the site of a medieval gibbet.

Stocks & Whipping Post.

The town's stocks and whipping post stood close to Bridewell in 1689.

Site of Medieval Archery Practice (?)

In 1717 Frances Causton and Rev. William Moore gave two cottages and 2½ acres of land in Lavenham called Butt Field, let at £4 10s per annum for the distribution of bread on Ash Wednesday and Christmas Day in Monks Eleigh. This Buttfield on the junction of the roads to Long Melford and Sudbury is suggestive of the meadow where archery practice once took place.

LAVENHAM *(continued)*

Medieval Crosses.

The Market Cross is said to be a former ecclesiastical Wayside Cross, built in 1501, and replacing one of timber in the C16 or C17. The shaft is of a rounded form, surmounted by a ball and set in a massive socket rising from three steps, beneath which is a plinth of masonry. Another stone Cross stands in the churchyard.

Market Place & Cross.

The Market Place was formed in the C13. Bull-baiting took place here every November 5th until stopped by Rev. Buck in 1792. The 'sport' continued on Washmere Green until 1842.

Medieval Market & Fairs.

In 1248 Robert de Vere, Earl of Oxford, obtained a grant for a weekly market and fair in Lavenham, and another was obtained by his son, Robert, in 1290 for an annual Whitsun 2-day fair. In 1330 Robert made allowance for his tenants to pass toll-free throughout all England; a dispensation confirmed by Elizabeth I in 1585. A famous horse fair which continued into the C20 was held on Shrove Tuesday. The market was discontinued in the latter part of the C18.

Site of old Windmill.

Mill House, N of the town, site of a post mill in 1783, was replaced by a tower mill in 1830, demolished 1921.

Medieval Guildhalls.

There were four Guilds in the town: Holy Trinity, St. Peter and Our Lady (1524), and Corpus Christi (1529). The Guildhall, the original hall of Corpus Christi, on the S side of the market place dates from c1500 and is considered one of the finest timber-framed buildings of its type in the country. In the celler, Dr. Rowland Taylor, the Hadleigh martyr, is said to have been imprisoned for the few days before he was burned on Aldham Common. The Hall is now in the hands of The National Trust. At the foot of Lady Street is another former Guildhall, the C15 timber-framed hall house of Our Lady and known as the Wool Hall. The Guildhall of Holy Trinity in Prentice Street was demolished in 1879, and the Guildhall of St. Peters in High Street, pulled down in 1896.

Medieval Grammar School.

A Free Grammar School which had been founded in the reign of Edward VI ((1547-53) was endowed by Richard Peacock in 1647 for the education of five poor children. It occupied the Old Grammar School in Barn Street, a late C15 merchant's house which had previously been an open hall. The landscape painter, John Constable, and the agricultural journalist, Arthur Young, were both pupils here.

Almshouses.

Upwards of thirty cottages in and near Church Street were used as almshouses for poor people to live rent-free on the endowments partly provided by William Lummas in 1573.

House of Correction & Workhouse.

The Guildhall of Corpus Christi was used as a House of Correction in 1689. Closed in 1787 it was re-opened as a workhouse replacing another which was recorded with 80 inmates in 1776.

Historic Houses & Ancient Moated Sites.

A visit to Lavenham, one of the best preserved small towns in the country, is like a step back in time. The site of the great hall of John de Vere, the13th Earl of Oxford, is marked by a large wooded moat near the top of Park Road, NW of the town. Lavenham Hall, N of the church, was his bailiff's house and a rectangular moat lying just over half a mile from the church (completely dry and covered by a plantation) probably marks the site of the hunting lodge situated at the southern edge of the deer park and marked on a map of 1580 as Lavenham Parke Lodge. The De Vere House in Water Street is C15. Other fine timber-frame buildings in addition to those already mentioned include: The Swan Inn, which incorporates an adjoining Wool Hall in its extension and has parts dating back to the C14; The Angel Hotel, first licenced in 1420, has a C16 plaster ceiling but painting of an even earlier period has been exposed; Shilling Old Grange, where Jane Taylor penned her famous nursery rhyme 'Twinkle, Twinkle, Little Star'; The 'Priory' in Water Street, built in 1536; The Old Grammar School (*see above*); The Barn in Barn Street; the much-photographed C14/C15 Crooked House; the C15 Woolstaplers

LAVENHAM *(continued)*

Hall; Little Hall - a fine open hall of 1450 with a late C14 service crossing; the C15 Great House (now a restaurant), and Tickle Manor (now a tearoom), built in 1532 by the son of a priest and later owned by the eccentric Tickle family. Many more of the town's houses were built at the time of Lavenham's greatest wealth and are fine architectural examples of the period. Among its wealth of timber-framed shops and private houses are over 220 listed buildings.

LAWSHALL *(6 miles S of Bury St Edmunds)*

Babergh Hundred. 'Dwelling by the lake' (OE) *Lawessela* (DB). Suffix is not hall or hale but *sele* meaning dwelling place. Morley suggests that this original place was beside the stream near Coldham Hall where geological surveys show that tracts of alluvium lie E and W of Warbanks (*see below*) which may well have been lakes 2,000 years ago. With the dense timber on either flank on the flat heavy boulder clay, and the ramparts of Warbanks, this would make a notable military post.

Manors. Lawshall (-1535 St. Benedicts of Ramsey; c1535 John Rither).

Ancient Woodland.

Frithy (formerly Frith) Wood is part of ancient woodland.

Ancient Defensive Ditches.

The Warbanks, on the eastern parish boundary extending into Cockfield and Shimpling, are of very ancient origin. They comprise long ramparts and ditches crossed by a Roman road running between Alpheton and Bradfield Combust, just N of Thorn Corner. Formerly a single defensive system they are now in three parts, the Lawshall section being the most prominent. A small bronze bust of a woman was found within the earthworks.

Pottery Industry.

Evidence of an extensive medieval pottery production site lies close by the church.

Medieval Greens.

Henningfeld Greene is depicted on a map of 1611 and Faden's map of 1783 names it Hinyfields Green. Partly enclosed in the C19, it takes its name from the Hanningfield family, manorial lords in the C14. It covered an area between the two forked roads to the church and Donkey Lane NW, and to Shimpling and Lawshall Green SE. Lawshall Green, shown and named in 1783, was rectangular and lay almost N-S by Drake Memorial Well, SE of Hanningfield Green. Harts Green, shown as a small triangular green on the same map, is still shown on the OS map as Donkey's Lane. Herberts Green, another small triangular green, is now covered by a development NW of the village and E of the road, and is named Harrow Green on the current OS.

Site of Gallows.

The Abbot of St. Edmunds claimed 'right of gallows' in Lawshall. It is possible that, as this right was also claimed by the lords of the neighbouring parishes of Shimpling and Hartest, this duty was shared by one gibbet, situated in the area of Ashen Wood where the three parishes meet.

Workhouse.

A workhouse is recorded here with 20 inmates in 1776.

Historic Houses, (former Monastery ?) & Ancient Moated Sites.

In 1578 Elizabeth I dined at Lawshall Hall near the church (formerly Manor House). Whilst mainly of Tudor brick, its origins are ancient with walls 6' thick in places. Tradition states it was a monastery in pre-Reformation times - it is known that Ramsey Abbey acquired the manor in 1022 - and to have had communication with Coldham Hall in the adjoining parish of Stanningfield by means of subterranean vaulted passages (although the distance involved makes this very unlikely). It still retains evidence of its former moat and there are six other moated sites in the parish. Rowney Farm, S of Butler's Hall, has the remains of a large but mutilated moat; Coopers Farm has two sides of a small square moat; Barfords Farm, N of Harts Green, has an oblong moat with traces of another towards the S; New House Farm, N of Shimpling Street village, has the greater part of a small square moat, and Trees Farm, Hibb's Green, has fragments of an irregular moat. SW of the

LAWSHALL *(continued)*

Rectory, at the junction of Hartest Lane and Golden Lane, is a perfect square moat with extensions suggesting a formerly more extensive moat, and fragments of a moat remain at Green Farm, Lawshall Green. At Hanningfield Green a length of moat is shown on the W side of Hanningfields Farm on the 1842 tithe map (since infilled). This is the site of the manor house of 'Henrfeildes' Manor recorded on a map of 1611. An Alicia de Hanigfeld is mentioned in 1327.

LAXFIELD *(6 miles NE of Framlingham)*

Hoxne Hundred. 'Leaxa's clearing' (OE) *Laxefelda* (DB)

Manors. Laxfield (-1536 Leiston Abbey; 1536 Charles Brandon). *Sub-Manors.* Studhagh/Stodhagh; Laxfield Rectory; Wathersdale; Burt's/Bourt's Hall.

Laxfield appears to have been of some importance during medieval times. It also has the dubious distinction of being the birthplace of the notorius William Dowsing (died 1679). He was appointed by Cromwell to oversee the demolition of church ornaments in Suffolk, a task which he appears to have carried out with some enthusiasm.

Ancient Woodland.

Laxfield Wood, on the southern parish boundary, is a part of ancient woodland.

Ancient Track & Site of Gallows (?)

Deadmans Grave Lane, an ancient track, forms part of the northern parish boundary. At its western end where it joins the B1116 Fressingfield to Laxfield road, three parish boundaries meet (Laxfield, Stradbroke & Fressingfield). Here human remains were discovered suggesting that it was the site of a former gibbet.

Site of Martyrdom.

After imprisonment for his faith in Eye and Norwich, John Noyes, a local shoemaker, was burned at the stake here in the parish on 22 September 1557.

Medieval Green.

Faden's map of 1783 shows Baniers Green as a widening of the road E of Corner Farm, NE of the village. It is now lost but the area is called Banyard's Green Hamlet. Owl Green on the southern parish boundary is named on the same map, but not shown. A small area, now enclosed and developed on the N side of the country lane running E from the B1116 road and named Owl's Green on the present OS map, may trace its former outline.

Medieval Market & Fairs.

Richard de Swinesthorp obtained the grant for a market on his manor of Studhagh in 1226. There were also two annual fairs here in 1472, abolished by 1872. The Market Place stood in front of the Royal Oak Inn.

Site of old Windmills.

A post mill stood in Winks Lane in 1783 and another stood S of the Framlingham Road on the SW edge of the village in 1736. The latter was pulled down c1941, but the fate of the former mill is unknown.

Free School.

In 1718 John Smith left his manor of Stadhaugh and all his freehold land in Laxfield in trust so that the first year's rents could provide for the building of a school for twenty poor boys of the parish to read, write and cast accounts, and for eight of them to be apprenticed out to some good handicraft trade.

Guildhall.

The fine and much restored timber-framed Guildhall dates from c1519.

Workhouse.

The workhouse had 30 inmates in 1776.

Historic Houses & Ancient Moated Sites.

The Royal Oak inn dates from the C15/C16. Moat Farm, NE of the village, has a fragment of an irregular moat with another just NW of this at Stadhaugh Manor Farm. The latter still retains its Saxon name meaning '*(Stede)* farmstead in a *(healh)* sheltered position'. Boats Hall (a corruption of its 1240 lord, Hugh Burt -

LAXFIELD *(continued)*

hence Burt's Hall), W of Ubberstone White Horse, has a nearly square moat; the moat at Yewtree Farm, ½ mile NE of the village, can still be traced; Hall Farm, W of Well's Corner, has a small, square moat, and at Well's Corner itself, three sides of a rectangular moat at Elms Farm have produced C13-C15 pottery. There is a moat at Aldridge's Farm on the NW parish boundary, triangular in design; and Dowsing Farm, birthplace of William Dowsing - that desecrator of church furnishings - is 'green moated and idyllic'. Limetree Farm has three sides of a square moat; Cratfield Lodge, fragments of three sides of a moat astride the parish boundary; a complete, square moat with two dry sides and two wet lies south of Banyard's Green where C14 sherds have been found, and the ancient St Jacob's Hall also appears to have part of a narrow rectangular moat.

LAYHAM *(1½ miles S of Hadleigh)*

Cosford Hundred. 'Sheltered enclosure' (OE) *Hligham* (c995) *Leiham* (DB)
Manors. Layham Hall/Netherbury Hall (C13 Hugh de Despenser). *Sub-Manors.* Overbury Hall.

Ancient Woodland.
Coram Street, Layham Grove and Valley Farm Wood are all parts of ancient woodland.

Ancient Chapel.
St Mary's Chapel was founded by Sir Robert de Layham in 1247. Its site is unknown.

Ancient Watermills.
There was a water corn and fulling mill in existence in 1722. The earliest date recorded for Layham Mill is 1531 but it is believed a watermill has occupied the site since Domesday. The present building was orginally 5-storeyed but was partially destroyed by fire in 1904.

Medieval Green.
Now represented by a lane, farm and barn, Pope's Green must have been long gone by Faden's 1783 map.

Historic Houses & Ancient Moated Site.
The manor house of Overbury Hall, built c1520, was the former seat of the D'Oyly family. Moat Hall, built in 1844, stands SW of the village on the site of the former hall, a fragment of whose moat still remains. The Queens Head public house dates from the C15/C16.

LEAVENHEATH *(1 mile NW of Nayland)*

Leavenheath, meaning 'Leofwines heath', is a parish ecclesiastically created on 13 January 1863 from parts of Stoke by Nayland, Wissington, Assington, Nayland and Polstead. It has been a civil parish since 1952.

Ancient Woodland.
Spouses Grove, W of the village, and Leadenhall Wood to the N, are fragments of ancient woodland.

Medieval Heath.
The area of the modern parish was once 'Leaden Heath' shown on Faden's 1783 map as a broad open space. Its northern boundary is marked by the present A134 road where it bears W; its western limits by Leaven (formerly Leaden) Hall, Leadenhall Wood and the modern development known as The Green; its southern limits by a footpath running virtually E-W, parallel with and S of High Road, and its eastern side extending along Plough Lane (formerly Bull Street). It is bisected N-S by the present A134 road.

LEISTON

Blything Hundred. 'Leofstan's farm' (OE) *Leistuna* (DB)
Manors. Leiston (C12 Ranulph de Glanville). *Sub-Manors.* Bade Hall/Wade Hall.

Ancient Woodland.
Buckles Wood is a part of ancient woodland.

Ancient Chapel.
Upon an eminence above the marshes to the SW of the sea-sluice at Minsmere Haven are the fragments of a

LEISTON *(continued)*

small stone house known as Sizewell Chapel, all that remains of the original Leiston Abbey, founded in 1182 for Premonstratensian Canons and dedicated to St Mary by the Lord Chief Justice, Sir Ranulf Glanville. The chapel stood on a damp, windswept and totally unwholesome site (the area has since been drained). Although Robert de Ufford, Earl of Suffolk, rebuilt the abbey in 1363 on a safer and more convenient site some two miles further inland (*see below*), in 1531 John Greene became a consecrated hermit after resigning as Abbot of the new Leiston Abbey and lived here at the Chapel of St. Mary. Maybe this is the same chapel referred to in an entry on a certificate compiled by commissioners for Henry VIII in 1547/8 which included a reference to a Free Chapel in Leiston parish, built for the ease of the people "on the sea banckes, where the inhabitants be alwayes ready to kepe watche and worck for the defence and saftie of the same towne and countrye." Unfortunately the remains of the chapel building were desecrated by the insertion of a defence pill-box during the second world war.

Abbey.

Leiston Abbey was refounded by Robert de Ufford, Earl of Suffolk, after the marshy situation and growing risk of flooding to the orginal site had led to a move further inland in 1363 (*see above*). The new abbey - on the present site and re-using much of the old material transported from Sizewell - had a short life. In 1382 it was burned to the ground in a fire. What remains today as the most considerable monastic ruins in Suffolk are from the abbey which was rebuilt from the fire, again using fragments of the previous building. The church was 168' long with a central tower, aisled nave, transepts, and chancel with aisles or side chapels. The chancel, with the frame of the great E window, is mainly complete; the N chapel has been re-roofed and is in use; little is left of the crossing tower and what does remain incorporates earlier fragments re-used from the C12 and C13 abbey. The walls of the transept rise almost to their original height; the nave is very ruinous and its S aisle and W end now form part of the house. On the S side of the church stand the ruins of the monastic buildings which surrounded the cloisters - the brick walls and octagonal stair turret are part of a porch added in the C16. This was never a great institution - the number of canons in residence never exceeding 20 - and it was dissolved with the lesser monasteries in 1536 when the last abbot received a pension of £20 and the canons were turned out penniless. The site was granted to Charles Brandon, Duke of Suffolk, the following year and then allowed to fall into ruin.

Deserted Medieval Village.

Sizewell, 'Sisa's well or spring' (OE) *Syreswell* (1240), was formerly a parish with a church or chapel of St Nicholas, 'down' by 1735 (Kirby). A well remains at Sizewell Hall (now in Aldringham-cum-Thorpe) right on the cliff. Sizewell had a market, but this may have been short-lived as one was granted to Leiston only 75 years later (*see below*). Interestingly, it is recorded as having 40 taxpayers in 1524 compared with Leiston's 33. Its demise was swift, however, for by 1674 it was shown to have only six inhabited houses. The former parish, now merely a hamlet of Leiston, is best known today for providing the site for two nuclear power stations.

Site of Smuggling.

Sizewell Gap was a favourite place for landing contraband and was used extensively by the notorious Hadleigh Gang.

Turbary.

The confirmation and charters of Henry II and Richard I of 1186 and 1189 granted the Manor of Leiston 'with its turbary' to Leiston Abbey. The Cellarer's accounts of 1320-1 record the cost of making 61,000 blocks of peat with the bread, beer and other drinks to improve the 'work-rate' of the labourers. Two areas are pinpointed by John Ridgard as the possible site; one between Nursery Covert and Dunwich Forest, and the other E of this and NE of Grimseys. The latter site looks the more likely of the two. Flooded peat cuttings have also been identified by Ridgard a little further N at Minsmere (*see* Theberton).

Medieval Green.

Tyler's Green was named and shown on Faden's 1783 map W of the Abbey and N of Gypsy Lodge.

Quaker Burial Ground.

Land was purchased in 1670 and a Quaker Meeting House built c1713. The area was planted with trees in 1786 and a new house built in 1861.

LEISTON *(continued)*

Medieval Market.
Sizewell had a market grant in 1237 and the Abbot of Leiston Abbey obtained a market and fair in Leiston in 1312. The tolls on St. Andrew's Fair (called 'Cold Fair') were 13s. 4d. in the C18. It was disused by 1844.

Site of old Windmill.
A monastic mill, standing near the Abbey before 1608, was not demolished until c1870.

Historic Houses.
Leiston Hall dates from the C17 and The White Horse Hotel from the C18.

LETHERINGHAM *(3½ miles SW of Framlingham)*

Loes Hundred. 'Homestead belonging to Leodhere's people' (OE) *Letheringaham* (DB)
Manors. Letheringham (1195 William de Glanville; c1309 William de Bovile).

Ancient Woodland.
Cutler's/Cutters/Curtis's Grove and the remaining fragment of Old Park are ancient woodland.

Roman Road.
The course of a Roman road curves W-E through the parish just N of Potsford Brook, forming the parish boundary from Prospect Farm to Potsford Wood.

Ancient Ford.
The Roman road forded a tributary of the river Deben at the Domesday *Potsforda*, a point where the present road bridge carries the B1078 over what is now Potsford Brook.

Ancient Track.
The Drift, a green lane running from The Lodge to the river, exhibits hedge species which date it to well over 400 years old.

Priory.
A small Augustinian Priory, founded c1200 by John de Bovile as a cell to St Peter's Priory in Ipswich, never had more than three or four canons in residence at any one time. The Priory Church was in a ruinous condition by 1780. In the will of Thomas de Wingfield of Letheringham Hall, dated 1378, he requested that his body be interred under the lower step of the high altar. The Priory was dissolved in 1536. All that now remains - except for the two Norman W bays of the priory church now incorporated in the church of St Mary (restored in 1789) and odd bits of stone and masonry in the churchyard - is the late C15 brick gatehouse and part of the precinct wall. Domestic buildings which stood on the N side of the church were mostly destroyed in a fire of 1610. It had been thought that the priory church had always been the parish church but the discovery of burials near the Old Hall to the E of the park suggest the site of a former parish church demolished in the C17.

Medieval Deer Park.
The old deer park belonging to Letheringham Old Hall, shown on a map of 1576, is remembered in Letheringham Lodge (the park lodge), Old Park Farm, Park Farm, Park Corner and Park Road. It was disparked in 1712 and covered with plantation. Only a fragment remains of what was until the latter part of this century an extensive area of Old Park Wood.

Civil War Skirmish.
During the Civil War Letheringham Abbey was attacked. A number of skeletons unearthed from shallow graves near the Mill and Old Hall in 1842 and 1873 suggest the scene of a skirmish in the vicinity.

Watermill.
The watermill situated near Letheringham Hall was built in c1730.

Almshouses.
Adjoining the E side of the churchyard is a long, early C17, brick range now used as farm buildings. These were almshouses built by Sir Robert Naunton for his 'decayed servants' and mentioned in his will

LETHERINGHAM *(continued)*

of 1635: 'I doe give towards the mayntenance of seaven poore woemen that are inhabite in myne AlmesHouse built by mee at Leatheringham.'

Historic Fortified House & Ancient Moated Site.

All that remains of the Old Hall, former residence of the de Boviles, Wingfields and Nauntons, and pulled down about 1770, is the farmhouse now known as Letheringham Hall which comprises the main block rebuilt c1790 (both wings having been demolished). It was built by Sir Robert Naunton, Secretary of State to James I in the late C17 after the converted priory building adjacent to the church had been burned down c1610. In 1674 it was recorded as having 37 hearths making it at that time one of the largest mansions in the county. The present hall stands within the ancient moat which is large and defensive with remains of flint, stone, and brick walls on inner and outer banks and what appear to be corner bastion tower bases. There is a suggestion of an earthen bank on the outer side of the moat to the N, and beyond, a possible outer court enclosed by another moated area. An early description of the Old Hall said that it was moated with inner and outer walls, gatehouse, towers and courtyard and that the moat was linked by a sluice to the river Deben. It has also been suggested that slight mounds in the S and SE corners of this outer area are tower bases probably constructed for the purpose of look-out towers during or prior to the Civil War siege when the Hall and nearby Letheringham Abbey were attacked. The moated Letheringham Lodge, 1¼ miles SE of the village, is a late C15 building which incorporates timbers from the old Shire Hall at Wickham Market. It has been suggested that the lodge may have served as a banqueting house rather than a hunting lodge. The Initials 'EW' over the door no doubt stand for Elizabeth Wingfield, formerly Elizabeth Drury, who married Sir Thomas Wingfield of Letheringham Hall in 1601. Another moat surrounds a small oblong island S of the village.

LEVINGTON *(7 miles SE of Ipswich)*

Colneis Hundred. 'Leofa's farmstead' (OE) *Leuentona* (DB). Levington includes the Domesday vills of Stratton (*see Stratton Hall*), Struston, Cuverdeston and Gutheston. *Manors.* Burnavilles (1233 Hugh de Burgh).

Claude Morley points to the comparative density of population in Colneis Hundred at this time when the dearth of timber upon its light soil and the presence of the Orwell and Deben estuaries on either side resulted in the development of a number of small but active hamlets.

Tumuli.

Eight burial mounds on Levington Heath line the parish boundary on the N side of the Felixstowe road.

Roman Road (?)

It is likely that the course of the Roman road to Walton Castle passed through the N of the parish to Stratton Hall (a name which means 'paved road' and probably refers to it), possibly on the line of the old Felixstowe road - the present A1156 to Trimley.

Coin Hoard.

A hoard of Roman coins were discovered in the parish.

Site of Ancient Ship.

Levington Creek, one of the largest along the river Orwell, extends to a wharf near the church. Here, the remains of a vessel, apparently a Viking ship, were found embedded in the mud. It was thought to have been one of a fleet of Danish vessels which raided Ipswich in 991 A.D.

Mound.

A long mound, slightly wedge-shaped and aligned cE-W with a surrounding ditch, situated at the edge of Home Wood on the N bank of the Orwell, was excavated 1954 but nothing was found.

Medieval Heath.

Only a fraction of Levington Heath remains. Faden's 1783 map shows it extending from the northern part of the parish well into Bucklesham.

LEVINGTON *(continued)*

Lost Medieval Village (?)
Dunham Bridge is given by Kirby as the name of a village or hamlet 'extraparochial as 'tis said' of this Hundred. Morley suggests that it may have spanned Levington Creek and given birth to the present Downham Reach on the Orwell.

Fertiliser Industry.
In 1718 in a farmer's yard in Levington the first coprolite was dug from the ground. Edmund Edwards, spreading a field with manure from his yard, required a load or two to finish the work and included some of the soil that lay nearby, though it looked to him no better than sand. Observing that the resultant crops were at their best in the area in which this soil had been laid he was encouraged to use more the next season and his success led to others doing likewise. It was discovered that this farmer's soil had contained coprolite, a crag or shell containing fossilised animal dung, in which the area was rich. So began a lucrative fertiliser industry, the coprolite being dug out from all along the estuary and thousands of tons shipped annually from the Debenside quays to all parts of the kingdom. The industry, remembered in Coprolite Street in Ipswich, continued well into the C19.

Site of old Windmill.
A post mill stood on the heath in 1783.

Almshouses.
In 1654 Sir Robert Hitcham founded six red-brick almshouses ½ mile N of the village for poor single women, three from Nacton and three from Levington.

LIDGATE *(7 miles SE of Newmarket)*

Risbridge Hundred. 'Place at the swing or clapper-gate' (OE) *Litgata* (DB). *Hlidgeate* from the Anglo-Saxon *hlid* meaning hinged lid of a box. Claude Morley hypothesises that if we take the castle here to have originally been a fort *(see below)*, built (by King Anna?) to repel a hostile force's outflanking movement along the southern side of the Devil's Dyke into Suffolk; to any such tactic this fort would present a 'side bar'. Although not marked as such on any map, it has been suggested that the brook following the river Kennett was once called The Lydd, a common Celtic river-name found in at least four English counties.
Manors. Lidgate (c1115 Maurice de Windsor).

Roman Villa.
The complete plan of a corridor-villa was discovered by aerial photography. It consisted of a main range with two side wings, and sub-divided into more than 20 rooms with indications of at least one phase of rebuilding. There also appears to have been a small earlier building partially covered by the SE wing. Just to the S was a large buttressed barn for the owner's grain. Both buildings lie within a ditched polygonal enclosure. The site has not been excavated.

Ancient Tracks.
Poundhouse Plantation traces an ancient track N from the Newmarket road forming part of the eastern parish boundary, whilst Bury Lane which runs to Genesis Green in Wickhambrook forms parts of the northern boundary W from Rookery Farm. The parish boundary forms a rectangular diversion at a point where Lady's Lane forks N to provide the parish boundary between Wickhambrook and Ousden, running parallel to Lord's Lane. All these lanes may, in some way, relate to the field names (*see below*).

Former Ecclesiastical Buildings (?)
There is evidence that the village was formerly larger and more important, stretching towards Wickhambrook. In addition to its castle and market, field names such as Bishopshall, Bishops Hall Gate and Bishops Hall Meadow point to lost ecclesiastical buildings.

Former Medieval Market & Market Place.
An ancient sunken green lane runs SE from the B1063 road and the river Kennet crossing to the site of a former triangular area called 'Tinkers Close' just in front of the church and castle. This is the probable site of the

LIDGATE *(continued)*

medieval weekly market, no doubt instigated by the Hasting family who resided here between the C13 and C15, although no record of a grant exists. The lane now makes a right-angled turn to avoid a deep scarp, probably formed by chalk quarrying after the lane had gone out of use.

Motte & Bailey Castle.

Locally known as 'King John's Castle', the extensive earthworks to the N of the village comprise a Norman motte and bailey castle which appears to have been later adapted to a fortified manor house. Standing on a fine elevated site it has a (now) rectangular motte with a part of its earthen rampart remaining and is surrounded by a deep moat of enormous strength with an entrance on the S. There are three baileys, the principal of which is to the S and is now occupied by the church and churchyard. The church dates from the C13 and may replace an earlier Saxon or Norman building reputedly sited at 'Church Hole'. The ditch which surrounded it remains on the N and W but has been destroyed on the S. To the N of the motte is a narrow rectangular bailey partly enclosed by a moat, and a large curving pond to the E protected a third bailey (or courtyard) of a much later date in which some farm buildings stand. Some ivy-clad fragments of flint walls occupy the main bailey E of the church and may now form the only remains of the castle precincts - stone being taken away over the years to repair the local roads. The outer bailey contains the earthworks of possible Burgate Plots - manorial records referring to 'burgesses' and 'burgate tenure' some at least at, or in 'le baille'. Below the castle by the road is a small sheet of water called Bailey Pond. The manor was given at the Conquest to Reynold sans Nase (so named from losing his nose during the battle), but the castle may have been built by William de Waterville who next held the manor, or more likely Maurice de Windsor (who held in the early C12), or even Ralph de Hastings (whose family were the major residents here from the late C12. It was probably John Hastings, Earl of Pembroke, who converted the earthworks into a fortified manor house around 1376 when he inherited the manor. His successors were the Jermyns. It was the poet John de Lydgate, a learned monk of Bury, born in the village, who suggested a pre-Norman origin for the earthworks (*see place-name*), i.e. 870 A.D, though earthworks were often automatically attributed to the Danes in early times:

"Born in a village which is called Lydgate,
By olde time a famous castel towne,
In Danes time it was beate down:
Time what St Edmund martir maid and King was slain."

Medieval Deer Park.

A documented deer park, probably Cropley Park, shown on Bowan's map of 1755 and Faden's map of 1783, had largely gone by 1836 when only Park House and its driveway was shown. By 1958 this too had gone.

Historic House.

Amongst several old houses in the village street, the remarkable Suffolk House dates from the C14, and has a gabled end decorated in ornate brickwork. It was the birthplace of the celebrated writer and poet John Lydgate (1375-1451), a monk of Bury, and one of the founders of English literature. An uninscribed brass in the church is said to mark his burial place though it was more likely to have been in Bury Abbey. The house also contains a mysterious hiding place. The old Star public house is said to have an underground passage leading to adjacent cottages.

LINDSEY *(4½ miles NW of Hadleigh)*

Cosford Hundred. 'Island in the marshes of a man called Lelli' (OE) *Lealeseia* (c1095) *Lelleseye* (1263)
Manors. Lillesey/Lindsey/Lindsey Hall (C13/C14 William de Montchensey). *Sub-Manors.* Beaumonds Hall/Beaumonts.

There was an important cloth manufacturing industry in the parish in the C14-C15. A cloth called Lindsey-Woolsey, a light woven material for women's clothing, was produced here.

Ancient Woodland.

Howe Wood is part of ancient woodland.

LINDSEY *(continued)*

Motte & Bailey Castle.
Situated in the S of the parish and covering 5 acres, the site known as 'The Mounts' and 'Lelesey Castle', was probably already a fortified site when the Normans arrived and adapted it for their own purposes. The low mound, now only 12' high, rises from the southern end of a large bailey enclosed by a massive ditch and bank. The earthworks sit astride a stream which was probably used to fill the moat. The marshy ground gave considerable protection but little warning of attack; this was said to have been overcome by the erection of a wooden look-out tower some 'seven times twenty feet high' - a Norman foot being the equivalent of our 9": this would have made it 105' high! Perhaps they meant seven plus twenty, which would have made it more realistically over 20' high. The arrangement of the earthworks is complicated and suggests three interconnecting sites. The Norman castle was mentioned in the C12 and probably built by one of the powerful de Cokefeld family - likely Adam de Cokefeld in the time of King Stephen. The lords later abandoned this very inconvenient and inhospitable fortification and moved to the drier land in the adjoining meadow where they built a new fortified manor house; perhaps as early as 1204 when it is known that Thomas de Burgh (husband of Nesta de Cockfield) obtained a licence to fortify his house at 'Leleshay'.

Ancient Chapel.
At Chapel Farm near Rose Green is a single cell thatched building of flint, brick and stone c30' by 16'with two Early English lancet windows on each side wall and a plain S door. An E window was later inserted and the W doorway is of early Tudor brick. There is a late C13 piscina in the S wall. The chapel was built c1250 possibly for the monks of St. Edmunds and anciently attached to the old manor house and castle which stood close by *(see above)*. Patrons included Henry de Segrave (1302) and the Monte Caniso family (1318-39).

Medieval Greens & Common.
Rose Green was named but not shown on Faden's 1783 map. It lay on the crossroads W of the chapel and is still named on the present OS map. Strangers Green is shown as an inverted triangular green running down from Lindsey Hall to the Lindsey-Kersey road. The 93 acre Sheepden Common was enclosed in 1845.

Medieval Market & Fair.
Although there is no record of a grant, a market was known to have been held on the site called 'Market Field' between the former manor house and the ancient chapel. Here was also an annual summer fair for pedlary.

Medieval Guildhall.
A Guildhall existed here which housed St. Peter's Guild (1362).

Historic Houses.
A manorial bank adjacent to Lindsey Chapel marks the site of the ancient manor house, probably built by Thomas de Bure and later owned by Godfrey de Bellomonte who had a grant of free warren here in 1296. An old farmhouse bears the date 1695.

LINSTEAD MAGNA *(4½ miles WSW of Halesworth)*

Blything Hundred. 'Place where flax is grown' (OE) *Linestede* (DB). Linstead Magna and Linstead Parva were one parish through medieval times.
Manors. Linstead Magna (1316 William de Huntingfield).

Deserted Medieval Village.
A parish with a few scattered farms and no village. The church, at the end of a lane in a very isolated position surrounded by fields, has now gone, and the old manor house now marked only by a series of moats. There were formerly five farmsteads centred on the church and village green. Ditched enclosures adjoin Wood Farm and Park Lane, and suggestive field names like Park Meadow, Ladies Green and Spring Field show the area of the hunting ground of the former Hall, in the hands of the manorial lords Sibton Abbey; Linstead Farm was possibly their hunting lodge. Uluric's flourishing Domesday vill was crossed by a maze of lanes linking 16 households at its peak in the C16, but by 1881 only four households were left, the population moving to the

LINSTEAD MAGNA *(continued)*

sheltered valleys of neighbouring Cratfield and Linstead Parva. The church, still in use in 1881, was part ruined by 1908 and the site along with the gravestones ploughed out in 1965, apparently without protest.

Historic House & Ancient Moated Site.

At Linstead Hall is a complicated system of moats and ponds around the site of the ancient manor house of the Huntingfields. They comprise an oblong moat (equally divided) near the SE angle, with another smaller moat. The timber-framed Linstead Farm dates from the C16.

LINSTEAD PARVA or Linstead Chapel or Lower Linstead *(4½ miles W of Halesworth)*

Manors. Linstead Parva (1313 William de Huntingfield). *Sub-Manors.* Hovells (?)

Deserted Settlement.

At Collipy's Green, permanent pasture shows earthworks of green, ditches and house platforms of an abandoned settlement along the present B1123 road.

Medieval Green.

The linear Linstead Green, now enclosed, is shown on Faden's map of 1783 covering the 4-way junction to Metfield, Rumburgh, Chediston and Huntingfield, extending along the Metfield road to the junction with Christmas Lane as a linear green bordered by the road and the parish boundary, and S along Huntingfield Road to the parish boundary where it joins Cookley Green in place of the present road. Linstead Green is made up of three former medieval greens: Collipy's, Blacksmith's and Morrell Haugh.

Historic Houses & Grange.

Chapel Farm, W of the church is a timber-framed raised aisled hall. Abbey Farm, at Morrellhaugh Green, is the site of a Grange of Sibton Abbey which enclosed 75 acres of arable land in 1325 - much as today.

LITTLE BEALINGS *(3 miles SW of Woodbridge)*

See Great Bealings.
Manors. Little Bealings (C13 Henry de Playford; 1334 absorbed by Seckford Manor).

Ancient Multi-period Settlement Sites & Cemetery.

Top soil stripping on Playford Heath in connection with gravel quarrying in 1987 revealed an Iron-Age farm site with evidence for a group of huts overlaying a Late Bronze-Age cemetery containing c25 burials. Mesolithic, Bronze-Age, Iron-Age, Roman and Pagan Saxon material was found in the surrounding area of the site pointing to multi-period settlement here.

Roman Hoard.

A hoard of 500 C3-C4 Roman coins was discovered in the parish.

Historic House.

The Grove, E of the church, is a fine Elizabethan house.

LITTLE BLAKENHAM or Blakenham Parva *(4 miles NW of Ipswich)*

See Great Blakenham.
Manors. Blakenham Parva (1220 Thomas de Ardern).

Medieval Common.

Blakenham Common is named on Faden's map of 1783 in the area between the present B1113 road and the river Gipping.

Site of Historic House.

The manor of Lovetofts was named after John de Lovetot 'who had a grant of free warren here in 1277'. He died in 1295. The manor is now only represented by Lovestofts Farm which stands on the SW parish boundary with Flowton. Near the site stood Lovestofts Hall, the manor house and ancient seat of the Tibetot family, still shown on maps up to 1955.

LITTLE BRADLEY or Bradley Parva *(5½ miles NE of Haverhill)*

See Great Bradley.

Manors. Bradley/Overhall al Harveys (1281 Jourden Witherfield). *Sub-Manors.* Netherhall al Norley Mote.

Ancient Woodland.

Doley Wood, NE of the village, is a fragment of ancient woodland.

Deserted Medieval Village.

The site of a deserted medieval settlement here is suggested by earthworks NE of the church, together with others SE of the church and Hall Farm in the form of crofts, house platforms, roads, ponds and a possible leat system in the southernmost meadow, along with sherds of medieval pottery.

Historic Houses & Ancient Moated Sites.

A moated enclosure with a mound or house platform near Hall Farm E of the church, located during a field survey in 1985, may be the site of the original Hall, perhaps occupied by the Le Hunte family who were in possession until 1703. It was formerly approached by a fine avenue, now mostly destroyed. There is a curious moat at Norley Moat House, 1½ miles to the E; oblong in shape with one corner convex and one concave. The site probably represents that of the former manor house of Norley Mote.

LITTLE CORNARD or Cornard Parva *(2½ miles SSE of Sudbury)*

See Great Cornard.

Manors. Little Cornard (1333 John Somersham). *Sub-Manors.* Cawston/Caxtons; Peacocks Hall; Serles Manor; Catcheleigh, Appulgarys, Folybroke and Caneworth Manors - subsidiary manors to Caxtons.

Ancient Woodland.

Fitch's and Mumford's Woods in the E of the parish, and Appletree Wood in the S, are ancient woodland.

Roman Tile Production Site.

Roman tile kilns were discovered in 1953 between the railway and the river Stour W of Stock's Farm Cottages.

Ancient Track.

An ancient way connected the present B1508 road with Workhouse Green. It remains in the form of a track with substantial ditches and banks, in parts forming the parish boundary. In the hedge are 16 species - between 7 and 11 species in each 30 yds length - suggesting that the way dates back between 700 and 1100 years.

Site of Ancient Battle (?)

On the parish boundary with Great Cornard, at a place called 'Dane's Hole' near Killingdown (Chilling) Hill by Sharpfight (Shalford - Shelving ford) Meadow, a battle is said to have taken place between the Angles and the Danes. Swords and ancient armour are said to have been found here.

Medieval Green.

Workhouse Green, now a hamlet in the S of the parish, is not shown as a green in 1783 and may already have gone by this time.

Deserted Medieval Village (?)

There is no longer a village settlement in the parish, only a scatter of farmsteads. However, Dr Jessup in his account of the Black Death in East Anglia in the C14 refers to the fact that in one of the two manors in this parish 21 families were 'absolutely obliterated' in the course of 6 months. Caxtons, anciently belonging to the de Grays, was one and Peacocks, formerly held by the Cranes and Newmans, whose manor house lies near the church, the other. The latter manor would probably have formed the original village settlement by the church probably destroyed by this pestilance.

Workhouse.

A workhouse, situated at Workhouse Green, is recorded as having 14 inmates in 1776.

LITTLE FINBOROUGH or Finborough Parva *(2½ miles SW of Stowmarket)*

See Great Finborough. Little Finborough is not a part of Finborough but in the manor of Bricett and was appropriated to Bricett Priory.
Manors. Finborough Parva (C13 Hugh de Cantelupe).

Site of Anglo-Saxon Cemetery (?)
An Anglo-Saxon cemetery site is thought to be situated in Finborough but may be in the adjoining parish of Great Finborough.

Ancient Moated Site.
Remains of a moat appear to surround Little Finborough Hall, linked by a path to the church to the N and by a former drove road to Bowl Road and Moat Farm in Combs parish.

LITTLE GLEMHAM or Glemham Parva *(7½ miles NE of Woodbridge)*

See Great Glemham. Includes the Domesday vill of Beversham.
Manors. Glemham Parva (C13 Sir William de Kerdeston). *Sub-Manors.* Beversham Manor; Over Pistrie/ Petistre-cum-Armigers.

Ancient Woodland.
Great Wood is a part of ancient woodland.

Tudor Hoard.
A hoard of Tudor coins is said to have been discovered in the parish.

Medieval Deer Park.
Glemham Hall's medieval park covers some 376 acres and includes oak trees which are claimed to rank among the finest in the county. The park is mentioned in c1560 and the deer in 1598. It was landscaped by Repton about 1803 and William White stated that it still held 100 head of pure bred old English black deer in 1885.

Moated Earthwork.
A circular water-filled moat, 131' in diameter externally and 66' internally, is situated on the southern edge of Little Glemham Park by the remains of a track bordered by old oak pollards leading E from the main A12 road to St Andrew's Church. The central island is in the form of a slightly raised platform with a central depression.

Historic Houses & Ancient Moated Sites.
The red-brick Glemham Hall was built c1715-25. Nothing remains of the original hall (which had 15-19 hearths in 1674) except some Elizabethan panelling in an upper room. This estate was held by the eminent military family of Glemham, one of whom, probably Sir Henry Glemham, was the hall's original builder. Sir Thomas Glemham fought as a Royalist in the Civil War. He was Governor of York and defended Carlisle against the Parliamentarians. Later imprisoned, he was exiled to Holland where he died in 1649. His body was returned to be buried in the church here. W of the village on the parish boundary the right angle of a broad square moat remains at Moat Farm, formerly the Manor House of Pistree Hall. On the site of Little Glemham Manor, a rectangular moat enclosing buildings is shown on the estate map of 1720. The site is now under grass but slight undulations show its former position. A survey of 1592 stated that the 'scite of the said Mannor Howse ys seated upon a pece of ground inclosed . . . containing by estimation 1 acre and a half'. It also mentions a fish-pond. A dramatic gatehouse, shown in a painting of c1600, was still standing in 1720. On the eastern boundary, just W of the river Alde, a small copse is enclosed by a square ditch or very narrow moat.

LITTLE LIVERMERE or Livermere Parva *(4 miles NW of Ixworth)*

Blackbourn Hundred. 'Mere of yellow-iris' (OE) *Litla Livermera* (DB) *Lyuermere Parua* (1327)
Livermere Magna and Livermere Parva were already separate parishes by Domesday. Their prefixes are really a misnomer for they comprised virtually the same area - 1500 acres and 1400 acres, but were in different hundreds,

LITTLE LIVERMERE *(continued)*

the line of demarkation bisecting the lake.

Manors. Livermere Parva al Morieles/Muryelle (1200 William de Windevill; c1240 Henry de Livermere).

Tumuli.

Although nothing remains on the ground, there is documentary evidence for nine round barrows in the area of Brand Spinney, S of Spinney Road.

Ancient Tracks.

The Icknield Way Path (now the A134) forms the northern section of the western parish boundary, and a track known as Green Lane - metalled in its northern and southern sections - forms the eastern parish boundary.

Deserted Medieval Village.

The larger part of this wedge-shaped parish was depopulated to form with Great Livermere a large landscaped park and lake (*see* Great Livermere). All that now remains are two isolated farms - Park Farm and Heath Farm - and the ruined church of St Peter. Aerial photographs clearly show the earthworks of the house platforms and main street of the original village running NW of Park Farm. A variety of documentary sources enable us to trace the emparking of Little Livermere and the resulting decline in population.

LITTLE SAXHAM or Saxham Parva *(4 miles W of Bury St Edmunds)*

See Great Saxham.

Manors. Saxham Hall Parva/Graces (-1484 Abbot of St. Edmunds, Bury; 1484 Thomas Darcy). *Sub-Manors.* Geddyngs/Topesfields; Large's.

Ancient Woodland.

Dairy Wood, Twist Wood and Larner's Wood are parts of ancient woodland.

Medieval Deer Park.

A deer park, shown and named as 'The Parke' on a map of 1638, stretched from the Bury road S - the southern end later incorporated into Ickworth Park.

Site of Gallows (?)

The site of a possible gibbet is suggested on the 1840 tithe map by fields named 'Higher Blood Hill' and 'Lower Blood Hill', and 'Hangings Field' which adjoins the Barrow to Bury road. 'Black Plantation' lies 219 yds. N of the latter. All bar Higher Blood Field adjoin the 'Precession Waye' (1638) along the parish boundary.

Medieval Green.

Heath Green is shown as a large green on Faden's 1783 map forming an arc from N of Warren Lodge, curving NW to follow the line of the road which heads N to meet the present A14. Several properties are shown lining the southern edge of the green and the road to Honeyhill Farm.

Historic House & Ancient Moated Sites.

E of the church and Croft's Place, the foundations and ancient moats of Little Saxham Hall remain in the middle of a field. The moats which encircled the site appear of a very elaborate plan - the hall apppearing to have stood on a piece of land situated between two quadrangles, both of which were three parts surrounded by water. The eastern portion has gone, but on the western side the moats join forming a lake containing a small island, possibly the site of an even older hall. It has even been suggested that these were originally Saxon earthworks. The foundations are of a fortified hall with gatehouse and drawbridge built by Sir Thomas Lucas in 1516. Sir Thomas was later sent to the Tower of London for 'speaking scandalous words of the Lord Cardinal (Wolsey)'. The Hall was visited by James I and Charles II while the seat of the Crofts. It was pulled down 1771-3 by Richard (Lord) Crofts, a particular favourite of Charles II who came here on at least four occasions (on the second, in 1668, Samuel Pepys was present). Another ancient moat lies S of the church on the road to Chevington.

LITTLE STONHAM or Stonham Parva or Stonham Jerningham *(6 miles ENE of Stowmarket)*

See Earl Stonham. The Jerningham family were anciently manorial lords here for many years and during this period the parish was named after them.
Manors. Stonham Parva/Stonham Jernegans (1239 Sir Hubert Jernegan). *Sub-Manors.* Flude Hall/Flede Hall cum Waltham Hall/Walham Hall.

Roman Road.
The old Roman road from Colchester to Caister-by-Norwich (here the busy A140 Ipswich to Norwich road) passes due N through the parish. The eastern parish boundary follows its course from Angel Hill to the top of Paines Hill and then runs parallel with it to just S of The Rosery.

Former Medieval Settlement Site (?)
In long established pasture adjacent to the A140, near its junction with the A1120, are the earthwork of possible house platforms fronting the roadway but raised above the road which has worn a considerable gully. Some small apple trees suggest that one or more of the properties may have existed until quite recently. A second scarp in the W facing slope c45 yds W of and parallel to the road are probably more property boundaries.

Historic Houses & Ancient Moated Sites.
The Clock House, ¾ mile N of the village, is of early C14 date and retains its original crown post truss. It has early Tudor circular chimneys with fleur-de-lis decoration. A small cottage is all that remains of Westwood Hall. It has been suggested that what appears to be fragments of a complicated moat system involving four separate enclosures may, in fact, be the remains of 2 E-W canals forming part of an Anglo-Dutch style water garden, contemporary with the date of the house which has the initials 'B.G.' and '1650' on a carved wooden pediment over the door. The initials refer to Barnaby Gibson 1597-1657. Waltham Hall, which represents one of the two manor houses of Waltham with Fleet Manor in the N of the parish, may at one time have been moated; the manor house of Fleet, known as Flede Hall, has now gone but stood on the deserted wooded site W of Clockhouse Lane. In 1481 the Rev. John Beale bequeathed in trust his tenement called the Pie, with a piece of ground called Caxtrelis or Catisset, and a yard called Ide's Yard, to feoffees, that out of the rents thereof they should keep the premises in repair, and lay out the remainder in repairing the highways of Little Stonham. This is the Magpie Inn (formerly Pye Inn), probably dating from 1481, which retains a rare, though much restored survival, its old sign set on a wooden frame spanning the Roman Pye Road for the repair and maintenance of which a part of its revenues were no doubt alloted. Little Stonham Hall, near the church, (now Hall Farm) has the remains of a complex moat, and Read Hall, a former manor house and original C15 hall-house (with additions of 1601), is partly moated.

LITTLE THURLOW or Thurlow Parva *(4½ miles NE of Haverhill)*

See Great Thurlow.
Manors. Thurlow Parva (-1536 Abbot of St. Edmunds, Bury; 1536 Henry Turner).

Ancient Woodland.
Park Grove, Park Tuft and Wadgell's Wood (partly in Great Thurlow parish) are all sections of ancient woodland.

Ancient Mound.
A mound, 85' in diameter and 1½' to 2' high, called 'Mill Mound' on the OS map, lies by the road to Great Bradley N of the Almshouses. Although it once held a smock mill (shown on the enclosure map c1846), it may be of more ancient origin.

Site of House of Knights Templars (?)
Temple End Stream flows E-W through the parish. By its bank is Temple (now Low Farm), Temple End, and Temple End Farm, with Temple End Plantation NW and Temple Wood to the S (sadly now lost). All are suggestive of a house of the Knights Templars located here, though no documentary evidence supports this. Yet the area appeared important enough to form the hamlet of Saint Maries as late as 1689.

LITTLE THURLOW *(continued)*

Site of Ancient Chapel (?)
A chapel dedicated to St Petronilla was mentioned in 1461, but the site is unknown.

Medieval Green.
Pound Green was a long, narrow green running N-S from near the junction of the road to the church. It was probably named after the village pound which no doubt once occupied it.

Site of old Windmill.
A post mill stood on the existing mill mound beside the B 1061 road N of the village in 1736. Its fate is unknown.

Almshouses.
The Soames Almshouses were endowed by Sir Stephen Soames in 1618. They stand on a small knoll to the N of the village. In his will he declared that they should provide habitation for eight poor unmarried persons, men and women, 64 years of age and over, and who should have been resident in the parish for 24 years. He ordered that the ninth room in the middle of the almshouses should be occupied by a person who should read prayers to the rest. He also willed that his executors should purchase a weekly rent-charge of £30 to provide weekly payments of 14d to each of the nine almspeople, and to supply them with eight loads of good faggots yearly, and with a gown each every two years.

Town House.
A Town House was established in 1693 by Josiah Houghton for the use of the poor.

Free School.
The parish's great benefactor, Sir Stephen Soames, also built and endowed a free Grammar School for 8-12 boys in 1614. He stipulated that they should be taught by a master and usher in 'English and Latin, writing and ciphering'. The fine School House (disused by 1891) still stands at the junction with Temple End Road.

Historic Houses & Ancient Moated Sites.
Little Thurlow Hall, W of the church, was built in 1847. Beside it are parts of a large quadrangular moat marking the site of the former Elizabethan Hall built by Sir Stephen Soame, Lord Mayor of London. There is a magnificent monument to him in the church dated 1619. Charles II stayed here and the bowling green on which he is said to have played, remains, as does a wood engraved with a crown said to have been recovered from the moat. To the N of the site are two fish-ponds (remaining from a series of five shown on the tithe map of 1846) connected with the former hall which was destroyed by fire in 1809. In a small isolated spinney NW of the hall is a small square moated site known as 'The Island'.

LITTLE WALDINGFIELD or Waldingfield Parva *(4½ miles NE of Sudbury)*

See Great Waldingfield.
Manors. Woodhall al Waldingfield Parva (1267 Adam de Cokefield had grant of free warren). *Sub-Manors.* Netherhall; Holbrook Hall; Luns Hall.

Ancient Woodland.
Long Wood and Walding Wood which both lie near the eastern parish boundary are parts of ancient woodland.

Ancient Priory (?)
The Priory is an ancient house opposite the church with a C14 crypt. It is reputed to be (and listed as such on the 1st series OS map) part of a Benedictine Priory founded c1114. However, there appears no documentary evidence for this and it has since been suggested that the crypt may well be the remains of a chapel in what was once the manor house. This may also account for the remarkable timber work in the attic and the fine fireplaces.

Medieval Green.
Humble Green lay on a bend in the road NE of the village and is marked on the present OS map. Faden names but fails to show it in 1783, suggesting it had already gone by this time.

LITTLE WALDINGFIELD *(continued)*

Site of old Windmill.
A post mill which stood near Waldingfield Bridge on the B1115 road pre-dated 1693.

Almshouses.
In 1608 Isaac Appleton left four tenements adjoining the churchyard for the residence of poor parishioners. Recognisable from its imposing chimney stack, it was sometime used as a pesthouse.

Historic House & Ancient Moated Sites.
The Manor House of Nether Hall, NW of Humble Grove, retains a portion of a square moat. A moat 263' square, now showing as a crop-mark in an arable field E of the village, was probably the 'moat and land within being sometime the cyte of the manor of Woodhall' (alias Waldingfield Parva Manor) mentioned in a will of 1580. The site was shown in Park Wood on the tithe map of 1841, and the hall probably pre-dated 1544. Just to the SE of Holbrook Hall (built in 1883) is the site of the former Tudor hall it replaced which was destroyed by fire in the 1870s. The Priory, opposte the church, may represent another ancient manor house (*see above*).

LITTLE WENHAM or Wenham Parva *(6½ miles SW of Ipswich)*

See Great Wenham.
Manors. Wenham Parva (1270 Sir John de Vallibus). *Sub-Manors.* Vaux, Germans/Jermyns; Stodhaught; Caltham.

Ancient Woodland.
Wenham Thicks is a remaining fragment of ancient woodland.

Medieval Green.
Faden shows Kings Green as a wedge-shaped widening of the road from Wenham Grange E to a track and footpath going N to join the Chattisham road just W of Charity Farm. The southern side of the road was wooded.

Fortified Manor House & Ancient Moated Sites.
Little Wenham Hall, situated near the church, was built c1270-80 (White suggests an earlier date of 1260) probably for the Lord of the manor Sir John de Vallibus and inherited by his sister Petronilla of Nerford in 1287. Always known locally as 'The Castle', it is of great historical importance, firstly as the earliest known use of Flemish brick in the country (and the best preserved), and secondly, although fortified, it is a domestic hall not a castle keep - one of the earliest fortified manor houses. L-shaped with a spiral staircase leading to a first floor entrance and the great hall and richly vaulted chapel, it has always stood alone. The only part of the original house which is missing is probably the garderobe; a C16 wing added to the SW angle was later pulled down. The stair turret rises considerably above the other roofs to act as a look-out and all the parapets are seriously castellated with narrow arrow-loops. The hall later passed to the Holbrooks, then to the Debenhams. A daughter of this family married Sir Thomas de Brewse c1440. John Brewse, last of the famiy, sold the hall to Joseph Thurston and it was a Thomas Thurston who was last to live here, parting with the estate in 1765. The site which includes Little Wenham Hall Farm (built c1700) and a barn with massive walls (built 1569 and supposed at one time to have been a chapel) is partly enclosed by a large L-shaped moat. The probable moated site of Kings Green Cottages is shown in crop-marks as a square enclosure S of Wenham Road and W of Wenham Thicks.

LITTLE WHELNETHAM or Welnetham Parva *(2½ miles SSE of Bury St Edmunds)*

See Great Whelnetham.
Manors. Welnetham Parva (c1280 Thomas de Weyland; c1499 annexed to Welnetham Magna).

Roman Road.
A former Roman road passes almost due N through the parish, first roughly on the line of the minor road which forks from the A134 Bury-Sudbury road at the public house to the point where this road turns right, then unseen on the ground until Linkwood Road traces its course from the junction with the Whelnetham to Bradfield

LITTLE WHELNETHAM *(continued)*

St George road past the parish boundary lying half way along the western edge of Rushbrooke Wood.

Ancient Priory & Chapel.

The house of Crutched or Crossed Friars was founded in 1273 as a cell of the main house of the Order situated near the Tower of London *(see below)*. Cloisters formerly linked the priory to the Chapel of St. Thomas the Martyr. Six friars' cells were removed c1939 due to their 'worm-eaten condition'. The Order had another cell in Linton, Cambridgeshire, sometimes known as Barham Priory.

Ancient Saxon Watch-Tower (?)

Although thought to be the foundations of the bi-apsidal chancel of an earlier Saxon church on the site, Alec Clifton-Taylor suggested that the remains of a circular flint building in the churchyard E of St Mary's Church may be those of a Saxon watch tower.

Medieval Green.

Faden's map of 1783 shows a small unnamed wedge-shaped green half way along the eastern side of the lane connecting the roads from Little Whelnetham to Bradfield George and Bradfield St Clare, N of the reservoir and the disused railway. It has now been enclosed and occupied by a small development of houses.

Historic House & Ancient Moated Site.

Chapel Hill Farm, on the W side of the A134 Bury-Sudbury road, belonged to the friars and incorporates some remains of the priory (*see above*). They comprise an angle buttress and some flint wall to the E, and more flint walling in the E wall of the farmhouse. The rest of the house dates from after the Dissolution when it was granted to Anthony Rous. 500 yds NE of the church on the site of the old rectory, two sides of a small square moat lie S of the ancient Parsonage Lane which connects the village with the Roman Linkwood Road.

LITTLE WRATTING or Wratting Parva *(2 miles NE of Haverhill)*

See Great Wratting.

Manors. Little Wratting/Capell's (C11/C12 De Clare family; 1316 Alberio de Capel). *Sub-Manors.* Blunts Hall; Wilsey Hall.

Ancient Earthworks.

The diminutive church stands on an earthen platform on the hillside and there is evidence that the churchyard was once circular - part of the curved enclosure bank being visible near the roadside. The nave of the present church is possibly Saxon which would suggest the earthworks are of this date or even earlier.

Historic House & Ancient Moated Sites.

The late Georgian Blunts Hall on the crossroads, stands on the site of the former manor house shown on Faden's map of 1783 and the tithe map as an L-shaped moat. It was a sub-manor of Little Wratting from at least 1380. The site of its former park lies to the W where a track from the Haverhill road ends abruptly in the middle of a field. One mile NE of Haverhill, Great Wilsey's Farm, with its remarkably well-preserved rectangular moat, is another former manor house site. The site of the rectory also has the remains of a moat.

LONG MELFORD *(3 miles NW of Sudbury)*

Babergh Hundred. 'Ford by a mill' (OE) *Melaforda* (DB). 'Long' prefixed the name some time after 1327.
Manors. Melford (-1545 Abbot of St. Edmunds, Bury; 1545 Sir William Cordell; c1600 Savage family).
Sub-Manors. Monks Melford/Melford Monachorum (1199 granted to Hospital of St. Saviours); Lutons Manor; Woolhouse, Woodfoule & Blakes Manor (reputed manors of Kentwell); Cranevyles al Crainaviles; Kentwell (De Kentwell family from mid-C13); Melford Rectory.

Ancient Woodland.

The extensive Lineage Wood, and the more modest Spelthorn Wood, are ancient woodland, as are fragments of groves known as Oak, Kiln, Cold, Ashen and Doghouse.

LONG MELFORD *(continued)*

Mound.

Remains of a mound (now lost to the new Melford bypass?) just to the W of a track known as Roydon Drift on the N side of the stream, may have been a round barrow but more likely an earthwork feature connected with the former Melford Hall park.

Roman Road.

The Roman road from the Midlands to the Coast via Coddenham crosses at Mill Ford and then Melford Green where its line can still be detected as a hump in the grass. Excavations on the present A134 at the southern end of the street revealed the ancient road running SSW-NNE. It was 21'6" wide and consisted of alternate layers of hard-packed gravel and cement nearly 3' thick. It was flanked by ditches 6' wide which had been infilled and reduced. C1-C2 material confirmed the road as contemporary with the settlement. Another Roman road forked ENE from Hall Street, its course probably represented by Bull Lane.

Belgic-Roman Settlement.

One of the largest known Belgic-Roman settlements lay beside the Roman road covering virtually the entire one mile length of the W side of Melford Street. Numerous signs of occupation particularly along the Hall Street section include burials, pottery and coins covering the period of Vespasian 69-79 A.D. and Hadrian 117-138 A.D.

Ancient Fords.

There were two ancient fords across the Chad Brook on the course of the Roman road. One by the site of the mill at the northern end of the street (sadly removed in the 1950s.) relates to the place-name, and the other by Ford Hall in the hamlet of Bridge Street on the northern parish boundary.

Roman Villas.

Two Roman villas have been discovered here. In 1958 between Listen Lane and the old railway track , a sewerage trench cut through part of a tessellated pavement indicating a possible bath house and other fragmentary floors containing C1 Belgic and C2 Roman pottery - there was also a ditch. Another, identified from aerial photographs NE of Rodbridge House, comprised a rectangular building with wings, with a possible second small rectangular building nearby. A small section was excavated prior to the construction of the bypass, and a dense surface scatter of tile, large flints and C1-C3 pottery show up in the ploughed field.

Medieval Deer Parks.

In the C12 Abbot Samson of Bury Abbey created a deer park out of a wood called Elmesete in the N of the parish. Here the earthen banks and hedgerow outline are still visible today and form part of the parish boundary. According to the monk Jocelin he made a number of parks which he filled with deer and kept a huntsman and hounds. When he entertained visiting dignitaries he would sit for a while with his monks in a glade under the trees watching the hounds in pursuit. By 1386, although still called Great Wood, it was yielding £2 per annum from its 260 acres in grazing rent but only 8s worth of wood in the form of faggots. It remained until the Dissolution after which it became one of the earliest landscaped parks. The licence to empark was granted to Lord Savage in 1613 and it allowed full rights of chase and warren around the 340 acres of Melford Hall. An area of woodland immediately to the N of Bull Lane marks the site of Little Park, the smaller of the abbot's two deer parks in Melford, mentioned in 1386 and named 'Little Parke' on a map of 1580.

Ancient Spring.

A petrifying spring was said to exist on Cranmer Green.

Ancient Chapels.

Melford Place replaced the ancient residence of the Martyn family, one of whom was Sheriff of London in 1559 and Lord Mayor in 1567. The old house incorporated the Chapel of St James which had been built by Lawrence Martyn some time after his father's death in 1428. When Melford Place was rebuilt in the C18 it retained this old chapel and, when the house was destroyed by fire in 1967, the chapel fortunately survived to now be incorporated in the latest house on the site. Another chapel is mentioned in c1580 '. . . near the pond in the park where there was a little chappel, I think of St. Anne'. This site can be identified as being NW of Kentwell Hall (with which it

LONG MELFORD *(continued)*

was no doubt associated) by the fish-ponds on the northern edge of Pond Plantation. A will of 1531 mentions particularly the 'Vestment and decorations in this private chapel'.

Medieval Greens.

Long Melford Green remains much as it has done for centuries, bordered by Melford Hall, church and hospital. Faden's 1783 map shows a chain of triangular greens running E from Rodbridge Corner. Cox Green was shown on the N side of the road by Hospital Farm and Stalag Tye was opposite Potters Farm. There was also a square-shaped green called Cuckoo Tye by Cuckoo Tye Farm marked on the present OS map.

Medieval Market & Fairs.

Abbot Samson obtained a grant from King John for a weekly market and annual fairs on the green. This was confirmed and extended by Henry III in 1235 and ratified by Edward III in 1330. Chapel Green was also called the Old Market.

Medieval Crosses & Conduit.

The C16 brick conduit on the green was built by Sir William Cordell to provide water to Melford Hall from the spring it enclosed. Near it is the base of the medieval C13 Market Cross. Churchwarden's accounts for 1556 give details of its repair: 'for carrying the stonys for the grete crosse on the grene XIId" Its final destruction was probably in 1642 when mobs of Roundhead Puritans occupied and plundered Melford Hall and Rectory. A Churchyard Cross which stood on the S side of Holy Trinity Church was destroyed in 1548.

Site of old Windmill.

A post mill was standing on Windmill Hill near Windmill Farm on the A1092 before 1758. It had gone by 1887.

Hospital & Almshouse.

The 'Hospital of the Holy and Undivided Trinity' standing by the delightful green near Holy Trinity Church, was founded by Sir William Cordell in 1573 'for twelve poor men and a warden and two lay sisters to wait upon them'. It was endowed from lands and tithes of the Hospital of St Saviour in Bury which had been granted to him by Queen Mary in 1553. Everything did not always run smoothly here as John Hills, Governor from 1632-49, found. Countess Rivers, then patron, wrote to him: 'Many complaints have come to me of Yor house, both by yor selfe and most of the Brethren, as in tipling and wenching . . .' He was required to reform these abuses in himself and his brethren with a terse final warning: 'See you faile not'. The hospital was rebuilt in 1847.

Workhouse.

A workhouse was recorded here in 1776 with 150 inmates.

Historic Houses, Grange & Ancient Moated Sites.

North of the village and green, an avenue of pollarded limes ¾ mile long planted in 1678 leads to Kentwell *(Kanewella)* Hall, from the AS. *Cenan wella* - 'Cenan's well' - the well lies just S of the hall. The present hall standing within its picturesque moat was built just prior to 1563 by Sir William Clopton replacing an earlier hall called Lutons which the family had occupied since 1383 and which stood on another moated site close by (in or near a wood called Pond Plantation). Interestingly, the moat of the present hall predates even the moat of Lutons and must go back at least to the C13 when it was in the ownership of the Abbots of Bury (*see Medieval Deer Park above*). This wide moat, crossed by two bridges, surrounds the hall and there are remains of a much larger outer moat which is now only partly complete. An original timber-framed barn, known as the Moat House, is thought to date from the earlier site. The Elizabethan Melford Hall, seat of the Parker family and now under the National Trust, stands to the E of the green. Until the C18 'the moat (then filled with water) continued round on the N side where there was a gateway with a bridge over the N moat'. It was anciently one of the granges of the Abbot of Bury and granted after the Dissolution to Sir William Cordell who built the present hall. Here in August 1578 he entertained Elizabeth I; her first call on her progress

LONG MELFORD *(continued)*

through Suffolk. A member of the Royal suite wrote of the visit: 'As I hearde there were 200 young gentlemen cladde alle in whyte velwet, and 300 of the graver sorte apparrelled in blacke velwet coates and with faire chaines, alle redy at one instante and plaice, with 1,500 servying men all on horsebacke well and bravelie mountyd to receive the Queene's Highnesse into Suffolke . .' The hall is much altered for, during the second world war, it was occupied by the military who accidentally burnt down the N wing. Parsonage Hall, W of Cranmore Hills, was formerly Melford Rectory Manor. A terrier of 1613 states that the site of the Rectory contains an area 'wherein there is a 12-room manor house . . . inclosed with a moate.' The remains of the oblong moat lie close to the E bank of the river Glem from which one narrow channel supplies it with water while another carries the overflow back to the river. The rough site of the old Melford Place on Chapel Green and belonging to the Martyn family, is shown on a map by Amyce drawn in 1580 (*see Ancient Chapels*). The family, many among them wealthy cloth merchants, resided here for 400 years until 1815. Other old houses in the village include the C15 (or earlier) Cadge's House; the beautifully timbered Bull Hotel which became a coaching inn in 1580 but as a former wool-merchants house dates back much further; quaint Brooke House (bearing the date 1610 but probably much older); the Tudor timber-framed Old House and The Limes. The Black Lion Hotel is a C17 coaching inn, and a pottery is now housed in the C15 Posting House. In the hamlet of Bridge Street, Ford Hall retains a mutilated moat, and The Rose & Crown is an old inn.

LOUND *(5½ miles NNW of Lowestoft)*

Mutford & Lothingland Hundred. 'Small wood or grove' (OScand) *Lunda* (DB). Morley suggests it as probably sacred; a grove where all the Norsemen of the neighbourhood assembled to pay homage to their gods in the days before Christianity.

Manors. Lound (1316 Sir Robert de Blundeston). *Sub-Manors.* Stalham's in Lound.

Ancient Woodland.

The fragment of Great Wood on the southern boundary is all that remains of the ancient woodland from where the parish possibly obtained its Domesday name.

Neolithic Settlement.

In 1939 Rainbird Clarke reported that 'over the whole area converted into reservoirs, but especially in that sector N of Bunkers Hill, stone implements were recovered from the surface of the sand under about 6'-7' of peat . . . . at least 18 flint and 2 stone axes, with numerous flint flakes, etc.'

Site of Roman Building (?)

One brick and one flint wall were unearthed in ploughsoil off Church Lane adjacent to a rectilinear field system, trackway and possible ring ditch observed in aerial photographs. Coins and pottery sherds found on the site date from Constantine I (317-320 and 335-337 A.D.) and Theodora (337-340 A.D.).

Site of Ancient Battle (?)

Near the mill dam at Bunker's Hill in the latter part of the C18 several pieces of ancient armour and coins were found. SE of this is an area called Bloodman's Corner, E of a track running N from Jay Lane, four leaf-shaped and one barbed and tanged arrowheads were discovered. This evidence all suggests the site of a possible Saxon-Danish battle.

Earthworks.

On the N side of Jay Lane (just S of the site of the arrowheads - *see above*) Early Medieval and one possible Middle Saxon pottery sherd were found 'from a ploughed down rectangular structure'.

Medieval Greens.

To the NE of the church the small Lound Green is now partially infilled and marked Cuckoo Green on the present OS map. A small triangular green lay between East Wood and Earth Lane SW of the church called West Heath on Faden's 1783 map.

LOUND *(continued)*

Site of old Windmill.
A post mill which stood at Mill House by Yarmouth Road in 1736 was replaced by the present tower mill in 1837. The mill was last worked in 1939.

LOWESTOFT

Mutford & Lothingland Hundred. 'Ludwig's knoll' (OScand) *Lothu Wistoft* (DB) *Lothewistoft* (1212). Claude Morley suggested the knoll may have applied to the rounded prominence of the Old Town cliff near the lighthouse.
Manors. Lowestoft (Formed part of the large possessions of the FitzOsberts at Domesday and it passed from them by marriage to the Jernegans).
The original settlement of Lowestoft was confined to the northern side of Lake Lothing which divided it from the extensive Kirkley Heath to the S. The town, which formerly comprised one narrow street (High Street) about 1½ miles in length with a few smaller streets and lanes (known locally as scores) branching off, saw its population rise from 2,332 in 1801 to 13,620 within 70 years and its boundaries continued ever southwards. Incorporating the former township of Kirkley, which had grown up on the heathland, a dense urban sprawl was created S of the water and now known as South Lowestoft. Before the fishing industry's decline, Lowestoft ranked next to Yarmouth as the most important fishing station on the east coast. The town had been a centre for fishing since the Middle Ages and probably even from Roman times when the first ancient settlement was washed away by the sea. The town's population suffered severe losses during the various plagues; that of 1603 accounting for 316 deaths, and 280 persons were buried in the parish in the space of five months in 1663. Over 140 houses were burned down in 1644 in one of several serious fires.

Ancient Woodland.
Foxburrow Wood on the northern outskirts of the town is a part of ancient woodland.

Roman Fishing Industry.
It is likely that Lowestoft has been a fishing station from as early as Roman times for, in 1534, it was said that the remains of a block-house was visible, left high and dry at an exceptionally low tide about four furlongs E of the present beach.

Roman Road.
The Oulton Road (A12), running virtually N through the western side of the borough, is thought to be on the line of the old Roman Road to Burgh Castle. It was recorded in the early C17 as 'Stangate', a name which implies a Roman origin.

Site of Beacon & Gallows (?)
Just S of Belle View Park, E of the town, remains in the form of a heap of flint stones may have been the site of a beacon and/or gibbet as suggested by the names Gallows Score and Beacon Hill.

Ancient Manorial Boundary Ditch.
Marked by a public footpath running from the point where the B1074 road heading E, turns sharply S, to just W of the church by the Yarmouth Road, a ditch is thought to be part of the former ancient parish boundary and the surviving boundary ditch of the Manor of Akethorpe. Hedge dating in 1993 suggests an age for the ditch of c400-450 years. Magdalene College acquired the manor c1460. Situated between Lowestoft and Corton, it was never a township and disappeared sometime after 1478, probably lost to the sea.

Ancient Lighthouse.
Lowestoft had two lighthouses; one is the earliest (on shore) recorded in England. The Upper Light stands on the edge of the cliff to the N of the town. A circular tower, built in 1676 of brick and stone, it stood 40' high and was 20' in diameter. It was rebuilt taller in 1873. The timber Lower Light on the W side of the harbour which dated from 1609, was rebuilt in cast-iron in 1866.

LOWESTOFT *(continued)*

Civil War Conflict.

Often at odds with its powerful neighbour Yarmouth, usually in disputes and 'incidents' over fishing rights, open warfare developed in 1643 during the Civil War when the town was fitting out vessels for Charles I. Not surprisingly, Yarmouth supported the Parliamentarian cause. Yarmouth eventually emerged triumphant and a year later Oliver Cromwell was marching into Lowestoft at the head of a 1,000-strong cavalry to set up his headquarters at the Swan Inn.

Sea Battle.

One of the bloodiest sea battles in the wars with the Dutch took place 30 miles off Lowestoft on 3 June 1665. In an engagement which lasted from three in the morning till seven in the evening a Dutch fleet consisting of 102 man-of-war with 17 yachts and fire-ships was completely routed by the English fleet of 114 man-of-war and 28 fire-ships commanded by the Duke of York. The Dutch lost 32 ships sunk, burnt or captured, and it is claimed 6,000 of their men lost their lives or were taken prisoner. The English, in contrast, lost but two ships with 600 men killed or wounded.

Medieval Chapel.

Prior to the Reformation the town had two chapels. Good Cross Chapel, which stood at the S end of town, was said to have been destroyed by the sea. The other, in the centre of High Street, being in a ruinous condition was taken down and rebuilt in 1698.

Medieval Market & Fairs.

Henry IV granted William de la Pole, Earl of Suffolk, 'one market and two fairs below the village of Lowestoft' in 1308, which shows the extent of the town's later growth south. Originally held 'beneath the cliff' it was removed to the area of High Street now called Old Market. In 1698, when the Corn Cross was erected, it was moved again to the present Market Place almost central to the street - the present inn marking the site of the market-house.

Ancient Crosses.

The Corn Cross, erected in 1698, is now the old Town Hall. Until the completion of St Peter's Chapel in 1833, part had for some time been used as a chapel-of-ease The Church or Wayside Cross formerly stood in the churchyard of St Margarets 'to remind the passenger of the vicinity of death and implore the pius tribute of a prayer for the repose of those who were here interred'.

Napoleonic Forts.

During the threat from Napoleon in 1815, Lowestoft was protected by three fortifications: one at the N and one at the S ends of the town and a third near the Ness. Each were mounted with cannons.

Site of old Windmills.

Gunton Mill, dating from at least 1650, was still standing near the junction of Corton Road and Yarmouth Road in 1751. A tower mill which stood in Church Road in 1751 was demolished c1899, and another mill was shown standing in 1736 in the area of Gunton Cliff.

Free School.

The grammar school was founded by Thomas Annott. The foundation maintained 'one honest and sufficient person, learned in the art and knowledge of grammar and the Latin tongue and other things incident and necessary belonging to the said art, who was to instruct forty boys born in Lowestoft'. Any shortfall was to be made up from boys in the half hundreds of Mutford and Lothingland. The school was initially housed in Town Close adjoining the churchyard, but when this became ruinous in 1674, the town chamber above the Corn Cross was fitted out as a school room. A new school house was built in 1788 on the E side of High Street.

Historic Houses.

Severe fires in the C17 accounted for most of the town's old houses, and those that remain are mainly in the area of High Street. South Flint House (now converted into flats) stands on the corner of Wilde's Score and dates from 1586, and 54 Mariners Street has the date 1521 cut into a beam. The Royal Falcon Hotel, also in High Street, dates from 1551.

MARKET WESTON *(7 miles NNE of Ixworth)*

Blackbourn Hundred. 'Farmstead or village west of another' (OE) *Westuna* (DB). Possibly to the west of Thelnetham (?)
Manors. Weston (1225 Robert Hovel).

Roman Pottery Industry.
The find of a Romano-British kiln in 1965 near Hillside Farm, ½ mile SE of the village, shows a pottery industry in the parish at that time.

Medieval Market & Fair.
Sir Robert Hovell secured a grant for a market and fair in 1263 which later prefixed Weston's place-name. A later Robert Hovell was charged with taking a toll of 'whatever bushells of corn came to the market of Weston'.

Medieval Greens.
Weston Green is shown on Faden's map of 1783 covering the area of the present village and up towards the church. Further E the linear High Green developed along the Thelnetham road terminating around Wards Farm, beyond the parish boundary.

Historic House & Ancient Moated Sites.
Near the site of the old manor house of Weston Hall SE of the village are two sides of a large rectangular moat. The Hall, ancient seat of the Bokenham family, stood within a triangular-shaped park marked now by roads from the village heading NE towards the church and ESE towards Thelnetham, and a footpath which runs NW past Home Covert connecting them. The Hall was demolished c1854. Fragments of moats remain at The Lodge.

MARLESFORD *(5 miles SSE of Framlingham)*

Loes Hundred. 'Maerl's ford' (OScand?+OE) *Merlesforda* (DB).
Manors. Marlesford (1236 Jordan de Sackville).

Ancient Ford.
The parish obtains its place-name from an ancient ford. Morley speculated that this ford through the river Ore on the great highway between Beccles and Ipswich (Yarmouth did not then exist) was much deeper then than now.

Medieval Green.
Marlesford Common, shown on the 1st Ed. OS map of 1837 and Faden's map of 1783 where it was called Marlesford Green, ran N from Keeper's Lane as an elongated triangle to the junction with the road to Parham. After enclosure in 1877 it was replaced by New Road. The old open space is still remembered in Common Farm.

MARTLESHAM *(2 miles SSW of Woodbridge)*

Carlford Hundred. 'Homestead by a woodland clearing frequented by martens' (OE) *Merlesham* (DB) *Martlesham* (1254). Includes the Domesday vills of Barkestone and Preiston.
Manors. Martlesham Hall (1316 Richard Brewse). *Sub-Manors.* Scots; Hethe's.

Ancient Woodland.
Lumber Wood, S of the church, is a part of ancient woodland.

Tumuli.
There is a group of eight Bronze-Age barrows on Martlesham Heath. Another lies just S of the A1214 road E of the roundabout, and more are sited by the Police headquarters.

Roman Pottery Industry.
Roman pottery kilns have been discovered in the parish.

MARTLESHAM *(continued)*

Ancient Saxon Settlement.

It appears likely that the first settlement in the area was on the S bank of Martlesham Creek where the isolated church and hall now stand. It is known that the hall site is an early one (*see Historic House*), and the place-name meaning (*see above*) would certainly apply at this spot, a clearing with a maze of footpaths by the creek between the ancient woodland of Sluice Wood and Lumber Wood. Across the creek was the ancient royal vill of Kingston where evidence of earlier occupation in the area of Creek Nursery has been found by field walking (*see* Woodbridge). In the area of Preiston (the Domesday vill of *Prestetuna)*, an early Saxon settlement site has been located; the presence of sherds of Ipswich ware indicating a C9 foundation date. Later, the present main settlement grew up beside the turnpike road from Ipswich to Yarmouth. There are several references to *Barchestuna,* another manor here of 1 carucate (120 acres), and known in 1346 as Barkestone.

Ancient Beacon.

In the C15 a Commissioner of Beacons was appointed. He levied 'beaconage' for watching and maintenance, as well as for the horsemen or 'hobblers' who were to speed inland with news of invasion. Dotted about the countryside are a number of 'Beacon Hills', many marking the sites of these beacons. Beacon Hill in the N of the parish is one of these sites. It must have been here in 1460 when the road was called 'Beacon Waye'.

Medieval Bridge.

The first stone bridge to replace the ancient ford across the river Fynn at Seck-ford was erected in 1444.

Relic of Sea Battle (?)

The Red Lion inn (*see below*) has as its sign a figurehead in the form of a red lion. This is said to have been taken from the wreck of a Dutch ship cast ashore after the Battle of Sole Bay in 1672. (*see* Easton Bavents). It has also been suggested that it is a figurehead taken from a wreck off Benacre c1740.

Medieval Heath.

Faden's map of 1783 shows an extensive swathe of ancient heathland called Martlesham Heath stretching SW from the village and on through Foxhall parish where it is known as Foxhall Heath. Large sections still remain today though continually under threat from the urban sprawl of Ipswich and its satellite developments.

Historic House.

Martlesham Hall, in an isolated position near the church, stands on the site of the former home of Sir John Verdun who was seated here in 1328. The timber-framed Red Lion Inn, at the foot of the hill beside the old Ipswich road, dates back to Tudor times

MELLIS *(3½ miles W of Eye)*

Hartismere Hundred. 'A (water)mill or mills' (OE) *Melles* (DB)

Manors. Mellis (C12 Sir Robert de Sackville). *Sub-Manors.* St. John (C13/C14 Master of Templars claimed view of frankpledge); Lancaster al Werts/Pountneys; Heigham Hall/Barringtons.

Pre-Historic Settlement Site.

A Neolithic settlement site was discovered in 1955 during pipe-laying on the S facing slope of a field NW of the bridged ford. It included a hut site 15' in diameter with a central, sunken, circular hearth containing three large burnt stones at the base and filled with black earth, flints and Iron-Age pottery sherds. A ditch ran from the S side of the hut site.

Ancient Way.

Furze Way, an ancient track which runs SE from Burgate to Thornham Magna, enters the parish as Stonebridge Lane and continues to Mellis Green. S of the Green to the parish boundary it takes the name Cowpasture Lane.

Ancient Well.

There is an ancient well protected by a fence and wooden canopy on Mellis Green.

MELLIS *(continued)*

Mound.
An earthen mound in the centre of Mellis Green, NW of Potash Farm, which is thought to be a mill mound, may have earlier origins.

Medieval Green.
Bordered by great ditches, Mellis Green, one of the largest greens in Suffolk, covers an area of c1,400 acres and stretches nearly two miles. It was administrated by the Court Leet in the Middle Ages and by the Hundred Court in the C19.

Commandry of Knights Hospitallers.
The 'Master Militas of the Templars' claimed both frankpledge and assize here in 1285 when they held the Manor of St John. Following the suppression of the Order in 1312 it was converted to a Commandry of the Knights Hospitallers and after the Dissolution their manor was granted to Sir Thomas Cheney. The site is unknown but Chapel Farm just S of the parish boundary in Thornham Parva, approached by an ancient track from the village known as Cowpasture Lane, may give a hint.

Site of old Windmill.
A post mill stood on Mellis Green in 1783. It was pulled down c1898.

Town House.
A town house is recorded at Mellis in 1614.

Historic Houses & Ancient Moated Sites.
Pountney Hall on the western parish boundary, now only a farmhouse, was the manor house and longtime seat of the Clarkes who had a large park here. Elm Tree Farm is of early C16 date and Mellis Hall had an extensive series of moats, one of which seems to have enclosed three distinct areas; what now remains is the main rectangular moat. There is a large and perfectly preserved quadrangular moat at the Rectory, and there are also moated sites beside Mellis Green at Hall Farm, and at Potash Farm.

MELTON *(1 mile NE of Woodbridge)*

Wilford Hundred. Probably 'farm by the sandbank' (OScand+OE) *Meltune* (c1050) *Meltuna* (DB). Though there is considerable debate over the meaning of the place-name, Morley suggests it thus and points to the sandbank along the water-course 'as apparent today (1950) as it was when the Vikings sailed up the Deben to harry the land a thousand years ago'.
Manors. Melton Manor/Melton with Ufford (Prior and Convent of Ely).

Roman Tile Industry.
A Roman kiln, found near the church in 1846, pointed to a tile production site here.

Medieval Bridge.
The ford at Wilford was first crossed by a stone bridge sometime in the C14 and rebuilt in 1539. It was still called Wilford Bridge on Saxton's map of 1575.

Medieval Gaol.
Melton held the gaol for the Liberty of St Etheldreda (known as Friars Dene) where a Francis Noone of Martlesham Hall was confined before being burned on Hasketon Heath in 1558. Situated on the road S of the post office, it was c80' by 40' with walls 3' thick and two-storeyed - red-brick with timber-frame above. Documentation shows that the bailiff of the Liberty had his gaol in Melton in the C13. Dutch prisoners were kept here after the naval battle of Sole Bay in 1665. The frame stood until 1963.

House of Industry.
Holding upwards of 250 inmates in 1765, Melton's House of Industry was disincorporated and purchased by the County to be reopened for pauper lunatics in 1829. By 1911, 943 inmates were held in what was now called St. Audrey's mental hospital, one of the first asylums in which modern therapeutic methods were employed.

MENDHAM *(8 miles SW of Bungay)*

Hoxne Hundred. 'Mynda's homestead or village' (OE) *Myndham* (c950) *Mendham* (DB)
Manors. Mendham Hall (-C14 Abbot of St. Edmunds, Bury; C14 Mendham Priory). *Sub-Manors.* Mendham Priory; Mendham Kingshall; Walsham Hall; Oakinhill Hall (reputed); Thorpe Hall; Shotford Hall.

Site of Monastery & Ancient Minster (?)
'In the place called Hurst or Bruninghurst, being then a woody isle on the Suffolk side of the river Waveney', stood one of the two Clunic monasteries of Suffolk founded in the reign of King Stephen (c1145) by William, son of Roger de Huntingfield as a cell to Castle Acre in Norfolk and dedicated to St Mary. A 'minster' may already have existed here before the Conquest for in his will Bishop Theodred of London c945-951 A.D. refers to 'the minster at 'Myndham' and also gave to 'the community at Mendham Church' the estates of Scotford (Shotford in Norfolk) and Mydicaham (Mettingham). Dissolved in 1536 it was given to the short-lived Benedictine Abbey of Bisham in Berkshire and afterwards passed to Richard Friston and his wife Ann. It was described in 1804: 'The buildings form a quadrangle of about 70' each way, the N side of which is formed by the church which, while the priory was inhabited by the Rants family (first half of C18), was kept neat and clean, but upon them leaving, the building was in part demolished and the remainder converted into a malthouse. The (Mid-C14?) church appears to have been 120' long and 30' wide. The E side of the quadrangle is partly formed by a possible refectory now begun to fall into ruin. The entrance is through an elegant semi-circular arched doorway prufusely ornamented with sculptured foliage'. When the ruins were demolished in 1943 some fine Norman arcading was removed to Mendham Place and most of the stone carried away for cottages in nearby Metfield.

Medieval Chapel.
Shotford Chapel, founded by Oliver de Ingham in 1347, once stood in All Saints Churchyard.

Site of Gallows (?)
Because of its size, legend has it that 'Hulk's Grave', at the fork of Mill Lane with the country lane to Whittingham in Fressingfield on the SW parish boundary, was the grave of a giant. The site - gradually eroded by the road and now virtually disappeared - is situated on the boundary of 3 parishes: Withersdale, Mendham and Weybread, and was believed to at one time held a gibbet and be the place of execution.

Workhouse.
A workhouse is recorded here with 20 inmates in 1776.

Historic Houses & Ancient Moated Sites.
Middleton Hall has a C17 frontage but goes back at least to the C15. It was named after a C14 manorial lord. The manor house of Walsham Hall has a staircase of c1650, a time when the leading Parliamentarian Hobarts lived there. Moat Farm has massive chimney stacks, a Tudor hall and two arms of an ancient square moat. Oakhill Farm, W of Weston House, retains three parts of an oblong moat. Remains of another moat lie at Highfields (formerly Bryants Farm), N of Metfield Road; the N side only survives, with adjacent fish-pond. (For Thorpe Hall and its moat *see* Withersdale)

MENDLESHAM *(7 miles NNE of Stowmarket)*

Hartismere Hundred. 'Myndel's homestead or village' (OE) *Mundlesham* (DB). Includes the hamlet of Mendlesham Green.
Manors. Mendlesham (C12 Manasser/Mansey de Danmartin). *Sub-Manors.* Winchesters; Cordeboef's/ Freetent, Corbornes; Busshes/Buces al Busse's; Flede Hall/Fledd's Hall/Walkames.
The village was formerly a small market town and still retains evidence of its more important and prosperous medieval past in Front Street and Old Market Street.

River Source.
A footpath heads E from The Cedars, situated on the road N from the hamlet of Mendlesham Green to Mendlesham. Nearly half way towards The Tan Office another turns N towards Grove Farm. At the end of the field on the left is the source of the river Gipping which runs W, through the parish of Gipping, to whom it gives name, and

MENDLESHAM *(continued)*

on via Stowmarket (where it is joined by the Rat from Rattlesden) to Ipswich. Here, at Stoke Bridge, its waters become tidal and it changes name to Orwell, flowing out into the North Sea at Felixstowe.

Roman Road.
The Coddenham to Caister-by-Norwich Roman road (A140) forms the entire eastern parish boundary.

Romano-British Settlement Sites.
Extensive field-walking in recent times has revealed around 15 Romano-British sites mostly isolated and relating to the Roman road. One covered some two acres and may have formed a settlement of several households.

Seat of a former King of East Anglia (?)
Camden considered that Dagobert, one of the East Anglian Saxon kings resided here, and that a 1235-6 grant of land *'in parochia Sancti Edalberti'* suggests that the church's first dedication was to King Aethelbeorht. Late in the C17 an ancient silver crown weighing c60 ounces and thought to have possibly belonged to him was found, and in 1758 a gold concave ring with an inscription in Runic characters was also unearthed here.

Ancient Tracks.
Old Hundred Lane, dating back at least to Saxon times, forms the ancient parish boundary with Gipping, Stowupland, Earl Stonham and Stonham Parva, and the Hundred boundary between Hartismere and Stow. The Lane remains intact from SW of Redhouse Farm, Cotton to N of Whitehouse Farm, Middlewood Green; then as a field boundary heading ENE to the road; it is then lost until the lane commences again in its most impressive form from NW of Waltham Hall to the A140. The parish still retains a number of old tracks in the form of green lanes including Whiteups, Hobbies, Eldens, Potters and Babbs.

Ancient Stone.
Travelling preachers were said to have read from the bible to the townspeople whilst standing on the 'eratic' (a great stone probably deposited here after the Ice-Age) which still stands in Old Market Street.

Ancient Chapel
Botetourt Chapel, founded here in 1310 by Sir John de Botetourt, was dissolved c1461. Its exact site is unknown but a Chantry Corner remains NW of the village on the road to Cotton.

Medieval Strip Fields.
Red House Farm, N of Cay Hill in the hamlet of Mendlesham Green, stands at the apex of a 90 acre medieval open field called Mounteneys Field which retains remnants of the former medieval system of cultivation.

Medieval Deer Park.
The curving road from the sharp left-hand bend near Poplar Farm to Chantry Corner, NW of the village, traces the western boundary of a former medieval deer park possibly belonging to Winchesters Manor.

Medieval Green.
Mendlesham Green, a hamlet of Mendlesham, takes its name from the triangular medieval green shown on Faden's 1783 map. It extended SSE from Willow Farm, bordered by Fir Tree Farm and The Cedars - the present road S was constructed following enclosure - to the road junction; W along the road through the village bordered by Cherry Tree Farm (one of the five green edge properties and where the wide green boundary ditch is still evident) to Green Farm, and NNE back to Willow Farm. The present rectangular piece of ground under cultivation (formerly allotments) only comprised the central section of the original green enclosed in 1828 and dug up in 1831 to provide potatoes for the poor of the parish. Tan Office Green lay E of Mendlesham Green.

Site of Gallows (?)
Cay Hill at Mendlesham Green, is the alleged site of a former medieval gibbet.

Roads.
R. Blome writing in *Britannia* in 1673 complains that 'all the roads leading into it (Mendlesham) are full of slaughs, that there is little resort to it, especially in winter.' The Turnpike Road (the A140 Ipswich to Norwich road) was said in 1711 to be 'so very ruinous deep and full of holes that the same are become dangerous for any

MENDLESHAM *(continued)*

person or persons, coaches and waggons that pass these ways.' A toll was inaugurated to supply funds for repairs. Tollgate Cottage, built to collect these tolls from passing travellers, collapsed in 1981.

Martyr's Monument.

The large eratic in Old Market Street provides a memorial to the Mendlesham Martyrs, 28 local people who suffered for their Protestant faith during the Marion persecutions. Some were imprisoned, some - including five children - 'beggered' and compelled to be vagabonds, four were burned at Bury and one at Norwich.

Medieval Market & Fair.

The first grant of a market to 'Menelshol' was in 1238. Later, in 1281, Hugh Fitz Otho obtaining a grant for a Tuesday market and October fair here; both were obsolite by 1891. The Market Place remains though partially encroached upon by later development.

Quaker Settlement.

Tan Office Lane leads to a C17 Quaker settlement. The main house, 'Duncans', was left in trust by Robert Duncan in 1673 that the Trustees "shall permit and suffer, without gift or reward, the people called Quakers to inter the dead bodies of their friends, children and servants and all other sober people that shall at any time desire to bury, or be buried there; and to and for no other use or uses whatsoever, except to feed it with horses or beasts from time to time." A Quaker Chapel was attached to the N side and the burial ground and leather tanning ponds are close by. The thatched Perkins Farm, on the junction of a green lane formerly called Purketen Lane which leads to the A140 road, is another C17 Quaker property.

Site of old Windmills.

Lings Mill stood at Cay Hill in Mendlesham Green in 1783. It was demolished c1918 and the site now marked by Mill House. A smock mill stood on the NW edge of the village before 1781.

Free School.

The 1473 will of Robert Cake gave rents of land and property to be applied to educate children in a free school founded in 1491. A free Grammar School was founded here by Peter Duck in 1618 and Three schoolmasters/ tutors are recorded. A school house is mentioned in 1674 and the school survived until the end of the C18.

Workhouse.

A workhouse is recorded in Mendlesham with 30 inmates in 1776. In the C19, 12 tenements were occupied rent free by the poor. One woman remembered the Mendlesham Almshouses where the old women had their feet tied up in rags because they could not afford shoes.

Historic Houses & Ancient Moated Sites.

A comprehensive survey of Mendlesham by a local farmer has identified a number of moated sites in the parish. Mendlesham Hall with its fine timber work at the junction of Hill Farm Road and Wash Lane is C16 and almost surrounded by a large rectangular moat. Boyland Hall is said to have been built by Richard Garneys in 1571. Elizabethan wall paintings have been discovered at Elms Farm. White House Farm near the northern parish boundary retains one side of its moat. Oak Farm in Oak Farm Lane is Elizabethan. Ashes Farm, which was probably associated with Coerdeboefs Manor, has a C15 central section (formerly an open hall) and two C16 cross-wings. It lies within a complex series of fragmentary ditches and ponds which may at one time have formed a rectangular moat; pottery from the site covers a long period of settlement from C11-C16. Moatyards, by the source of the river Gipping, is the probable site of Winchesters Manor. One elongated pond survives - possibly once part of the W side of a moat. When a moated mound here was levelled in 1959, two C14 Bronze seal matrices were recovered, one decorated with an Ascension scene, the other with a lion rampant. Poplar Farm, NW of the village, has portions of two adjoining square moats, and Moat Farm a little further along the road is C15 and was endowed by Henry Jessop in 1516 to provide a schoolmaster for the parish. Medieval pottery was recovered from the moated site at Old Farm. Church Farm (Knyvett House) on the possible site of 'Knyvetts' Manor House - the capital manor of Mendlesham - has a large trapezoidal moat on the E side of the churchyard, with a possible second to the N and a fish-pond and hollow way to the S.

MENDLESHAM *(continued)*

Pond Field is a probable moated site associated with Garlonds and Cutlers Tenement belonging to Winchester Manor. All that survives is an elongated pond which may have formed the W side and pottery sherds covering C11-C15. E of Potters Farm are two sides of a square moat by the parish boundary. Mendlesham Lodge (Lodge Farm) has half a rectangular moat with other water ditches. Church Pightle retains one side of a large square moat with a C13 pottery scatter. Tan Office has the remains of a possible moat in the form of a large ditch to the W with a fragment of the N side and a subsidiary enclosure for farm buildings to the N. This is the probable site of Reyners and Maggs Tenement. The moat was once possibly centrally divided with the entrance to the S formerly cobbled. Pottery sherds date from the C13 and there is evidence of possible brick kilns at the northern end of the site. E of the village, Buces, one of the four Mendlesham manors, has one side of its rectangular moat (once sub-divided?), along with a mound 118'x98' and 6½' above water level (a possible mill mound or dovecot?). The eastern arm of a large square moat survives at Wicks Farm, Backhouse Field, along with C13-C14 pottery. Evidence of other moats in the form of soil marks show on sites identified on the C19 tithe map as Eldens (small, square, C13-C14 pottery), Berrys Meadow (square ditched enclosure, C12-C17 pottery), Pond Meadow (small rectangular, C13-C14 pottery); Great Missips (square ditched enclosure with Medieval pottery); Barn Missips (small rectangular, C13 pottery); Great Whitups (possible ditched enclosure?, C13-C14 pottery) and Home Farm (rectangular, mostly infilled with two ponds surviving).

METFIELD *(8 miles SSW of Bungay)*

Hoxne Hundred. 'Place cleared in the forest to make meadowland' (OE) *Medefeld* (1214).
Until the 1327 Subsidy Metfield had been regarded as a mere hamlet of Mendham and centuries later in 1764 Kirby stated that "Metfield is sometimes called a Chapel of Mendham of which parish it was a part in the time of Edward the Confessor and Bishop Aylmer".
Manors. Metfield/Metfield Jermy (c1325 Sir John Jermy).

Ancient Stone.
In the churchyard stands an 'eratic', a stone probably carried here by water and glaciers at the end of the Ice-Age.

Ancient Track.
A short length of the NW parish boundary is traced by Honeypot Lane.

Mound.
There is no evidence that the mound surrounded by a water-filled ditch situated on the deserted green and known as Mill Mound pre-dates the C17-C18 pottery found on the site.

Medieval Green.
Two sections of green are shown on Faden's 1783 map. The first, unnamed, surrounded the church and has now been infiltrated by residential development, whilst the 41 acre Metfield Common lay mostly to the S of the present B1123 road, SE of the village, and is partly enclosed - footpaths and field boundaries still trace its extent. It is named on the present OS map.

Medieval Archery Practice.
A medieval bill of 1551 for 'Makyinge ye butts', suggests that a field in the parish was used for medieval archery practice.

Site of old Windmill.
A post mill stood E of Willows Farm in 1783.

School.
A schoolhouse was in existence in 1590.

Town House/Workhouse.
A Town House was occupied by 'poor persons' of the village in 1692 . The village workhouse which may have superseded it was recorded as having 30 inmates in 1776.

METFIELD *(continued)*

Medieval Guildhall.
A Guildhall is recorded in Metfield in 1556. This may have later become the Town House and/or workhouse.

Historic Houses & Ancient Moated Sites.
The parish has several moated sites. Metfield Hall (now a farmhouse rebuilt c1838), SW of Metfield Common, stands on the site of the Old Hall destroyed by fire. It still retains the strong oblong moat, the NW corner of which is exceptionally broad. Old Vicarage Farm has fragments of the moat which surrounded the Rectory. Close to this (and a possible dower house) Yew Tree Farm has a small trapezoid moat from which has come C14-C15 pottery. The Chestnuts has part of a moat abutting the Fressingfield road. Oak Farm has parts of a rectangular moat with C14 pottery. The rectangular moat survives along with a C14-C15 pottery scatter on the site of Fox's Farm, though the NW corner has been infilled. Remains of a roughly rectangular moat with water-filled ditches at Docking Hall has produced C13-C14 pottery. The site of a small rectangular moat at Tithe Farm has been infilled and ploughed out with C12?-C14 pottery being found on the site. Rookery Farm has three water-filled sides of a rectangular moat. There are the remains, in the form of a N arm, of a small rectangular? moat at Oakhill from which has come C14-C15 pottery. One arm survives of a moat at Valley Farm with C14-C16 pottery, and a moated site shown on the 1825 OS map as 'Homestall' has since been ploughed out.

METTINGHAM *(2 miles E of Bungay)*

Wangford Hundred. 'The village belonging to Maete's family' (OE) *Metingaham* (DB)
Manors. Mettingham Castle cum Bungay Soca (C13 Sir John de Norwich).

Roman Road.
A short section of the Roman Stone Street forms part of the western parish boundary, running from NW of Grove Farm as a track, crossing the B1062 road and the river Waveney at Wainford to enter Norfolk.

Site of Roman Watch Tower (?)
With the objective of protecting the river Waveney crossing at Wainford, a Roman watch tower may have been sited at the point where the Roman road is evident on the ground in the form of a track coming from Grove Farm to the B1062 road which is here called Watch House Hill.

Medieval Castle.
The first fortified earthworks were probably erected in the late C13 when the Manor of Mettingham was held by Sir John de Norwich. In 1342 Edward III granted a later Sir John, Governor of Angouleme, a licence to crenellate (fortify) his dwelling house, and it is the ruins of this building we see today, 1 mile S of the village. The site, which covers some five acres, is protected by a series of moats of roughly rectangular shape, the smallest and widest of which probably enclosed the earlier Norman castle. This was rebuilt on a larger, more impressive scale in the moated area immediately adjoining on the N, as a fortified manor house rather than a castle. What remains is the three-storeyed gatehouse guarded by a barbican of which some of the walls remain. To the E and W extend part of the outer walls; the earthen ramparts exist W of the northern enclosure and along part of the E side of the southern enclosure wherein now stands a modern house.

Medieval Green.
The extensive, roughly rectangular Mettingham Green is shown on Faden's map of 1783 running NW from the Castle to Grove Farm. New Road now cuts off the northern section which has been enclosed and occupied by Carlton House. This road and those defining the western extent of the former green, namely Annis Hill (except the northern section to the present B1062) and Lodge Road, are later additions.

Site of Medieval College.
A college was founded in 1350 by Sir John de Norwich at Raveningham for a master and eight canons, and dedicated to St Mary. It was transferred to Norton Subcourse in 1387 and finally settled at Mettingham Castle in 1394. Here it remained until the Dissolution. It was a fairly wealthy institution and consisted of a master and nine chaplains who were endowed with the castle for their residence and the manors of Mettingham, Bungay

METTINGHAM *(continued)*

Soke and several others in Suffolk and Norfolk. The college supported and educated fourteen boys. The collegiate buildings were erected in the small moated site where the first Norman castle originally stood and where some fragments of the walls still stand. Following the closure of the college we find a William Mills accused of teaching a school without a licence in 1597.

Former Settlement (?)
Aerial photographs of earthworks, mainly ditches, W and N of The Valley House in Benstead Marshes S of the river Waveney in the N of the parish, include a possible square moat with an internal bank, and a group of rectangular and rectilinear enclosures along a winding trackway (?)

Workhouse.
A workhouse is recorded with 12 inmates in 1776.

Historic House & Ancient Moated Site.
C17 Mettingham Hall, ¼ mile SE, stands on an earlier site which retains a T-shaped fragment of its ancient moat.

MICKFIELD *(3 miles WSW of Debenham)*

Bosmere & Claydon Hundred. 'At the broad clearing' (OE) *Mucelfelda* (DB)
Manors. Mickfield (C12 Roger de Hoo). *Sub-Manors.* Hammonds; Flede Hall (the manor house sited in Stonham Parva parish); Wolney Hall (the manor house sited in Creeting St. Mary parish).

Roman Road.
A short section of the western parish boundary follows the course of the Colchester - Caister Roman road.

Historic Houses & Ancient Moated Sites.
Mickfield Hall, N of the village, was the home of Nicholas Garneye who lies buried in the chancel of the local church. It stands on a very ancient site which retains an oval-shaped moat with an entrance to the S. Two sides of a small square moat remain at Greenwood's Farm (originally Greenweeds Hall), and Reads Hall (now a farmhouse) has two sides of a rectangular moat which appears to have been originally sub-divided. Three arms of a square moat at Pooley's Farm abutt the road, and three sides of a moat show on aerial photographs near White House where C13 pottery has been found.

MIDDLETON-CUM-FORDLEY *(4 miles NNE of Saxmundham)*

Blything Hundred. 'Middle farmstead' (OE) *Mideltuna* (DB). Middleton was situated along an ancient Packway (*see below*) and its place-name doubtless refers to it being the middle township along this route between Dunwich and Kelsale.
Manors. Middleton with Fordley (c1269 William de Croketot). *Sub-Manors.* Chickering; Austins; Brent Fen (1294 Robert Swillington had grant of free warren).

Ancient Track.
An ancient packway probably dating back at least to Saxon times has been identified running from Kelsale to Dunwich. This packway was in general use throughout the period of Dunwich's affluence.

Mound.
A circular mound c98' in diameter is shown on the OS map in the 1950s at TM4121 6740 adjoining a field boundary (since removed) which bends slightly to avoid it (?) The date and origin of the earthwork are unknown.

Medieval Common.
Middleton Moor, from the Anglo-Saxon term *'mor'* meaning waste or common land. The common lies at a crossroads on the present B1122 road W of the village.

Deserted Medieval Village.
Fordley, which occupies nearly half the total area, was once a separate parish with the larger population of the two. It now forms one of the four Middleton manors. Its Saxon name means 'meadow beside the ford' - the ford

MIDDLETON-CUM-FORDLEY *(continued)*

in question doubtless being Wrackford Run which, in 1900, was 'unbridged and a most delightfully wild, lonely and romantic spot, gay with burgeoning wild flowers and sunshine'. Fordley Church stood to the S of Middleton's and shared the same churchyard. In 1620 complaint was made to the Bishop of Norwich that when the services of the two did not exactly coincide, the bells of one disturbed the congregation of the other. The Bishop directed that in future the same minister should serve both churches and provide services alternately. The problem was finally resolved in 1659 when the benefices were united, and Fordley abandoned and left to decay. No trace of it now survives.

Medieval Market & Fair.
Middleton obtained the grant for a market and fair in 1270.

Site of old Windmill.
A post mill, dismantled before 1914, was standing in 1783.

Historic Houses & Ancient Moated Sites.
Timber-framed Fordley Hall, 1¼ miles NE of the village, is a much-restored Tudor building with a Late C17 frontage. Bordering the medieval green known as Middleton Moor, Moor Farmhouse was probably built by Thomas Pynnowe c1600.

MILDEN *(4 miles SSE of Lavenham)*

Babergh Hundred. 'The place of Melda's family' (OE) *Mellinga* (DB) *Meldinges* (c1130)
The village was anciently known as Melding, and in the C18, Milding.
Manors. Milden Manor al Wellshall (C13 Sir Peter de Melding). *Sub-Manors.* Burrs/Bowers.

Ancient Woodland.
Hazel Wood, Hall Wood (part in Little Waldingfield parish), Bulls Wood, and Bull's Cross Wood (part in Groton and Edwardstone parishes), are all sections of ancient woodland.

Motte & Bailey Castle.
Foxburrow Hill near Milden Hall, SW of the village, is a small Norman motte with what may be the remains of a bailey. The earthworks have been much mutilated (particularly the 'bailey' to the N) for gravel/sand extraction. The circular mound is now c12' high and was surrounded by a moat. The castle was probably built as an adulterite fortress by William de Melding in the C12 during the turbulent reign of King Stephen, and short-lived.

Medieval Green.
Milding Green is shown on Faden's 1783 map as a narrow linear green lying either side of the road S of Powney Street, some distance SW of the church. It commenced from a pound (now Pound Farm) and ended at Lower Farm, just N of Bull Cross Wood.

Historic Houses & Ancient Moated Sites.
On the site of the former manor house, the present Milden (Milding) Hall, one mile W of the church and now a farmhouse, was rebuilt in the early C18 when the seat of the Canham family. There is a complete rectangular moat at Moat Farm (formerly Bowery Farm), the earlier residence of James Alington, lord of the manor of Burrs or Bowers, who died in 1626; his remarkably preserved effigy adorns a tomb in the local church. Part of a dry moat remains at the Rectory and there is another moat in Church Road E of Rashbrooks Farm. Wells Hall, ½ mile SE of the village on the parish boundary, is C16 and once the seat of the Shoreham family. It has a good brick gatehouse, a wide, almost complete, square moat (partly in Brent Eleigh) and a fish-pond.

MILDENHALL

Lackford Hundred. 'Mild(burh)a's shelter' or 'The middle valley' (OE) *Mildenhale* (c1050) *Mitdedehalla* (DB). Morley puts forward the first meaning and identifies Mildburha as Saint Milburga, grand-niece of King Anna of East Anglia and niece of King Wulfhere of Mercia. With King Anna nearby at Freckenham and Clovesho being identified with Mildenhall (*see below*), 'what more likely than that a Mercian princess should found and

MILDENHALL *(continued)*

inhabit as its first Mother Superior some monastery at 'Mild(burh)a's shelter' beside the river Lark?'
Manors. Mildenhall (Abbot of St. Edmunds, Bury; 1259 Richard de Clare). *Sub-Manors.* Aspalls.
This the largest parish in Suffolk comprising 16,700 acres, part of which is fenland, and part light sandy soil, has encouraged very early settlement with a remarkable number of pre-historic sites being discovered, along with those of both Roman and Saxon periods. The town's heyday was before the Old Fen Sea dried up. The whole jutted westward into this sea at the three islands of Holme-Eye, Little-Eye, and Kine-Eye, and as late as 1065 there were three fisheries in the huge manor of some 1,500 acres given to Bury Abbey by Edward the Confessor. A great fire in 1507 is said to have destroyed 37 houses and many outbuildings within the space of two hours.

Tumuli.
A possible round barrow lies in Mildenhall Woods, S of the present A11 road. The Three Hills are a group of bowl-shaped barrows lying at Warren Hill to the N of the road to Bury St Edmunds. They are 70' in diameter and 9' high and said at one time to have been surrounded by ditches. They were opened in 1875 when the internments were found to be inhuman and orientated; many iron implements were unearthed.

Lower Palaeolithic Sites.
The surrounding area of the above tumuli has proved to be a settlement site of the Lower Palaeolithic period and one of the most prolific in Britain for finding flint hand-axes. A Lower Palaeolithic lakeside settlement site of national importance was discovered in the C19 at High Lodge on the eastern parish boundary.

Mesolithic Settlement Site.
At King's Site, Wilde Street, NE of Beck Row, a Mesolithic settlement and tool production site produced several thousand flint artefacts. At Phillips I Site, Bronze-Age settlement material was unearthed.

Neolithic Settlement Site.
At Hurst Fen, ½ mile N of St Helena Farm, debris of a Neolithic farmstead of about 3500 B.C. was found covering an area of 180 yds by 90 yds. Some of the small hollows may have been post-holes for buildings.

Late Bronze-Age Site.
On the S edge of Mildenhall Fenn, ½ mile W of Weston Ditch, are the remains of a major Late Bronze-Age site. W of the hamlet of West Row, on the edge of the fenland S of the speedway stadium, a prehistoric site was excavated c1989. A Bronze-Age 'house' in the form of a circle of post-holes c16' in diameter, with a porch, was discovered - the first to be recorded in Suffolk.

Site of Roman Building.
At Thistley Green in the hamlet of West Row, a 2-roomed Roman building was discovered in the winter of 1942, along with a hypocaust, pottery of C4, and evidence of huts as well as brickwork and oyster shells.

Site of Roman Hoard.
Ploughing in a field a short distance from the above site in 1942, unearthed what has become nationally known as the 'Midlenhall Treasure' - a hoard of 34 pieces of C4 Roman silver tableware; the largest object being the great dish c2' in diameter depicting Bacchus's triumph over Hercules. Now on permanent display in the British Museum.

Roman Metal Working Site.
At Hollywell Drove, Beck Row, a C1-C4 metalworking and pottery site was discovered along with a concentration of Bronze and Iron Age pottery.

Saxon Settlement & Meeting Place of the Anglo-Saxon Council.
The site of Cloveshos ('cloven' hoof), the Meeting Place of the Anglo-Saxon Church Council, was thought to be in the parish. It had been known that these councils were held at a place called Clovesho in the years 747, 800, 803, 822 and 824 A.D. Morley describes the site as being two hills upon the N bank of the river Lark divided by a huge chalk-pit probably from where the Romans had shipped material for their known embankment of the Old Fen Sea. The western 'hoh' is now represented by Judes Ferry Inn and the eastern by Bargate Farm. He

MILDENHALL *(continued)*

suggested that Godmundesley, 'Godmund's meadow' was the site of an important *witena gemot* - supreme Council of the Nation - of the Mercians in 747 A.D. This political council, he sumises, was held alongside and in conjunction with Clovesho at the spot called by the clipt name of "Mondes" on the river Lark's N bank between Clovesho and Wamhill Hall, facing Worlington church.

Anglo-Saxon Cemetery.

An Anglo-Saxon cemetery, discovered near the Lower Palaeolithic Site at Warren Hill, was excavated in 1875-6.

Mound.

A roughly circular artificial mound with a semi-circular ditch c164' in diameter surmounted by a C19 (?) brick and flint gazebo, stands in the garden on the W side of Bargate House. The date and purpose are unknown and while it might have originated as a modern garden feature, Claude Morley identified the site as 'Clovesho' (*see above*) in 1923 when the surrounding gulley was labelled 'Moat'.

Medieval Pottery Production Site.

Eldon Lane, Holywell Row, is the probable site of a C13-C14 pottery industry.

Turbary.

An area marked 'Turffe Pits lately digg'd' on a map of 1616 is probably at The Delph in the NE corner of the parish.

Medieval Greens.

Faden's 1783 map showed several small greens in the parish at that time: Cake Street, E of Holywell Row in the hamlet of Beck Row had a small square green on the N side of the street, with another of similar proportions in Holywell Row itself. N of this in Beck Row a linear green extended from the junction with the road to Stock Corner, NE, all the way to Wilde Street - marked Wilde Street Green for its whole length in 1783 - terminating at the Peterfen Drove and Littleyfield Drove fork. Another linear green lay on the N side of the road and followed it W and SW - the road running W and then NW to Littleport (A1101) appears a later addition. There was another unnamed green at West Row in the area N of Elm Tree Farm. This can be traced by the road network, a track going NE and Mildenhall airfield on the E. The present OS map marks Thistley Green to the W.

Ancient Watermills.

There was a watermill in the manor given by Edward the Confessor to Bury Abbey in 1065 'that the monks might eat wheaten and not as they did before, barley-bread'. Three watermills were listed in 1341.

Medieval Colleges.

There were two colleges of priests mentioned in 1380. The sites are unknown.

Medieval Hospital.

St George's Hospital was mentioned in 1480.

Medieval Market.

The town's first grant for a market was in 1219 but this may not have been implimented. Another was granted in 1412. Its late date has much to do with the restrictions placed by the abbots at Bury who considered it might compete with their own.

Market Cross.

The Market Cross of hexagonal timber stands in the Market Place. It has been much restored and dates from the reign of Henry V.

Medieval Guildhall (?)

It is likely that a Guildhall once existed here as the parish operated six guilds: Corpus Christi (1450); Great Guild of Trinity and St. John Baptist (1464); St. Mary, St. James, St. Thomas the Martyr, and Blessed Trinity(1533).

Almshouses

The almshouses near the church were founded by Sir Thomas Hanmer in 1723 for four poor widows.

Historic Houses & Ancient Moated Sites.

Near the church is the site of the Manor House, built in the reign of Elizabeth I and added to by Sir Henry North.

MILDENHALL *(continued)*

It was afterwards the seat of the Hanmer and Bunbury families. Wamil Hall, 1 mile W of the town, is an early Elizabethan house, formerly the seat of the Warners who were lords of the manor and descended from the Swedish Royal family. The Hall was partly destroyed by fire in 1898 and restored. Asphall Hall, two miles NW, has three sides of a rectangular moat. The Bell Hotel dates from the C17 and Cobbles Restaurant in the Market Place to the C16.

MONEWDEN *(5½ miles SW of Framlingham)*

Loes Hundred. 'Deep wooded valley with bare crest' (OE) *Munegadena* (DB). The place-name describes the deep valley through which runs a tributary of the river Deben.
Manors. Monewden with Sulyards (1259 John Weyland).

Ancient Woodland.
Tabies Wood, NW of the village on the parish boundary, is a part of ancient woodland.

Medieval Deer Park.
There is documentary evidence of a deer park here in the C13 to the NW near the church.

Medieval Green.
The small triangular Monewden Green, which ran W from the church and widening to Green Farm, was enclosed in 1832.

Historic Houses & Ancient Moated Sites.
The early C18 Monewden Hall on the northern parish boundary replaced the old C16 hall, residence of William Reve. He died in 1595 and is commemorated in St Mary's Church. Cherry Tree Farmhouse is a timber-framed house of c1600, and Red House, ¾ mile SW of the village, dates from 1592. NW of the village is a dry but impressive quadrangular moat with rounded corners on the site of Folly Farm (c1710). It is thought that this moated site was the park-keeper's lodge set in the medieval deer park. The farmhouse was demolished in the 1950s. The Office (now Beechwood), NE of the village, has fragments of a possible rectangular moat covering an area 246' by 131'. However, 'The Office' could refer to a Tan Office and the moat fragments may, in fact, be a series of tanning ponds. Rookery Farm in the S of the parish beside the Otley road, was built in 1593 and both house and farm (extending to 90 acres) remain much as they were in a survey of 1656, preserving field boundaries and a unique collection of plants in two permanent pastures; these include the rare Fritillary - the only place in Suffolk where this plant now grows.

MONKS ELEIGH *(6 miles NW of Hadleigh)*

Babergh Hundred. 'Illa's clearing in the wood' (OE) *Munegadena* (DB) *Monekesillegh* (1304). Illa was most likely a monk as the manor was given to the monks of Canterbury by Brithnoth, Earl of Essex, who lost his life in 991 A.D. fighting the Danes in the Battle of Maldon. After the Dissolution it was given to the Dean and Chapter of Canterbury.
Manors. Monks Eleigh (-1534 St. Paul's, London; 1534 Sir William Waldegrave held probably as lessee of Prior of Holy Trinity, Canterbury). *Sub-Manors.* Boyton al Boyden Hall.

Ancient Woodland.
The site of the ancient Manna Wood lay just E of Manna Wood Farm at Stackyard Green.

Roman Road.
In the hamlet of Monks Eleigh Tye, a short section of lane W from Tye Farm traces the course of a minor Roman road. The road, which continued ENE from Tye Farm through cultivated fields to cross the river Brett by a ford near Wagger Farm, is not here evident on the ground.

Site of Roman Building (?)
A quantity of tile and fragments of hypocaust of Roman date were recovered from a field W of the church. Unfortunately the site appears to have been built over in 1983.

MONKS ELEIGH *(continued)*

Ancient Track.
Nova Scotia Lane forms the northern parish boundary.

Medieval Green.
Two triangular greens are shown on Faden's 1783 map: Swingleton Green covered the present Swingleton Hill and Back Lane road junction just E of Scripcross Bridge and is shown bordered on all sides by properties. Stackyard Green - unnamed in 1783 but marked as such on the present OS - covered the Dulls Lane fork at Manna Wood Farm. The map also shows a small square green at Monks Eleigh Tye (calling it Brent Eleigh Tye) at a point where the road to the village turns SW. The green was bordered by Tye Farm and Hawkins Farm. The present green by the church where the village pump stands is not shown as such in 1783.

Mills.
The Mill, a former watermill, lies at the E end of the village. Two post mills stood in the village towards the end of the C18. One occuped an isolated position at Clay Hill and the other stood N of the church where a pond still marks the site.

Medieval Market & Fair.
Monks Eleigh received the grant for a market and fair in 1259.

Medieval Guildhall.
A C15 timber-framed house in the high street is named 'The Guildhall'.

Workhouse.
A workhouse is recorded with 15 inmates in 1776.

Historic Houses & Ancient Moated Sites.
The Mill at the E end of the village is part C15. Highlands Hall is a former hall-house dating from 1594, and Monks Eleigh Hall is from c1650. Among several fine old properties at Swingleton Green - the hamlet lying along the southern bank of the river Brett - The Fenn is C16 with an early Georgian front. The moat at the C15 Manor Farm consists of two sides of an oblong enclosure with a ditch extending E for 300'. The irregular rectangular moat at Tye Farm abutts the Roman road. The area ESE of this is apparently featureless but cropmarks still trace field boundaries, trackway and a sub-square enclosure or moat (?) that were partially surviving in 1958.

MONK SOHAM *(3 miles NE of Debenham)*

Hoxne Hundred. 'Homestead by a pool (with early possession by monks)' (OE) *Saham* (DB). The parish formerly belonged to the monks of Bury by gift of Alfric, Bishop of East Anglia.
Manors. Monks Soham (-1545 Abbot of St. Edmunds, Bury; 1545 Anthony Rous). *Sub-Manors.* Blomvile's/ Woodcroft Hall.

Ancient Track.
The ancient Waddlegoose Lane forms a short section of the southern parish boundary.

Medieval Greens.
Faden shows Soham Green as triangular and situated in the crook of the road from Bedfield to Kenton; Green Farm stood on its eastern edge. Hungers Green remains on the northern parish boundary by a footpath N of Church Farm, but its SW extension towards Monk Soham Hall has gone.

Guildhall.
Records trace the Guildhall back to the C15 when 'A messuage called the Guild Hall was occupied by poor persons put in by the overseers of the poor'. In 1534 John Mayewe made bequests to the Guildhall and Church Steeple.

Poorhouse.
A poorhouse was in existence in the parish in 1792.

MONK SOHAM *(continued)*

Historic Houses & Ancient Moated Sites.

The late C16 Monk Soham Hall near the church, still with a fragment of its former encircling moat, and Blomvilles or Woodcroft Hall in the S of the parish, also with detached fragments of a possible former moat, are both ancient manor houses. At Hill Farm, S of Monk Soham Green, are remains of three moated enclosures adjoining one another, and there are remains of two oblong moats at The Firs to the N of Monk Soham Green, to the S of which are remains of other moats partly enclosing two rectangular areas.

MOULTON *(4 miles E of Newmarket)*

Risbridge Hundred. 'Mula's farmstead' (OE) *Muletuna* (DB)
Manors. Moulton/Stonehall Manor (1316 William de Beauchamp). *Sub-Manors.* French Hall.

Ancient Way.

The ancient Icknield Way (B1506) forms the northern parish boundary and also the county boundary with Cambridgeshire.

Mound.

Within the grounds of Moulton Manor, SW of Dalham Road, a circular mound c15' high was excavated in 1850. Nothing was found and although it could be a garden feature, it has been suggested as the site of a watch tower since, upon digging the outer line of the trench, evidence of a stone wall was found around the mound. The site lies just W of the Kennett and a short distance S of the Icknield Way's crossing of this river at Kentford.

Medieval Bridge.

A rare C15 packhorse bridge survives at the N end of the village. It formerly spanned the river Kennett, here now little more than a stream and re-routed in recent times to better preserve the bridge. Built of flint and stone with four pointed arches, it is very narrow and the parapets have been kept low to allow goods carried by mules and pack-horses to overhang the bridge. A short distance away is a flint footbridge of similar design and date.

Site of Chapel.

A Rectory Chapel is mentioned by Morley who stated that the site was known.

Shrunken Town (?)

A large area of earthworks on the open meadows, bordered by The Street to the W, the Kennett to the E, playing fields and the green to the N and Church Road to the S, comprise banks, mounds, hollows, ditches and small enclosures. This may once have formed part of a larger Medieval settlement here - even a town - for Moulton had a market and possesses an impressively large church capable of holding some 500 worshippers.

Ancient Folly.

On Folly Heath are the remains of an ancient pyramidal building said to have been built by one of the Earls of Oxford and seen from a distance of some 20 miles.

Medieval Market.

John de Agreaus of French Hall Manor obtained a grant for a market in 1298. However, there appears to have been one here since 1227 - perhaps unlicensed.

Historic House.

Moulton Manor was built to replace White Hall, burned down in 1921. Whereas White Hall, or Stonehall, stood in front of the mound *(see 'Mound' above)*, Moulton Manor was erected behind it.

MUTFORD *(5 miles ESE of Beccles)*

Mutford Hundred. 'Ford (across the Hundred River) where moots were held' (*see below*) (OE) *Mutford* (DB)
Manors. Mutford (C12 Balderic de Bosco/Bois; c1204 Stephen de Longchamp). *Sub-Manors.* Soca Bectun; Soca Franchevile; Soca Luvel.

A parish of sufficient importance in Saxon days to give name to and provide the assembly site for the Hundred. When Balderic de Bosco/Bois obtained the manor he was also granted moiety of the Hundred of Mutford, the

MUTFORD *(continued)*

patronage of the church, the Hundred Court, wreck of sea, view of frankpledge with privilege to erect gallows and tumbrill.

Ancient Wodland.

Mutford Big Wood and Little Wood are part of ancient woodland.

Ancient Meeting Place.

Four footpaths meet at a footbridge over the Hundred River S of Marsh Lane Farm, the possible site of the ancient ford which formed the meeting place of the Hundred in Saxon times (*see above*).

Site of Gallows.

Lord of the Manor, Balderic de Bois, was granted the priviledge to erect a gallows in his manor of Mutford in the C12. A field close by the ford (*see above*) is called 'Hanging Piece', and the road beside it, 'The Haggifer' (hanging ford).

Ancient Site.

In March 1870 a gamekeeper, digging for a lost ferret in a small natural hollow on the SW side of Mutford Wood close by the road which runs from Carlton Colville to Mutford village, came upon some large stones of a perculiar shape. When the stones were raised they were found to be between 3' and 7' in length of natural sandstone and had been embedded on end about 3' into the soil. The group of stones were set in a semi-circle over a length of 17½' giving the appearance of a small scale Druidal erection. In the loam above the soil were sherds of medieval? date, animal bones (some burned), plus a few oyster shells.

Medieval Common.

Mutford Common, now enclosed, is shown in 1783 covering most of the area outlined by Hulver Road, Mutfield Little Wood, a footpath SE of Hulver Road to Mutford Hall, and field boundaries NE from Great Horns Hill Wood to Chapel Road. In the area of Marsh Lane Farm, near the SW end of Hulver Road, was another small area of common called Sheep Heath, now developed.

Workhouse.

A small workhouse is recorded here with 10 inmates in 1776.

Historic Houses & Ancient Moated Sites.

Mutford Hall, SW of the church and now a farmhouse, dates from 1607 and was formerly the seat of the Hemgrave and Jernegan families. Ash Farmhouse, ½ mile NW, is Elizabethan.

NACTON *(3 miles SE of Ipswich)*

Colneis Hundred. 'Nakki's farmstead' (OScand+OE) *Nachetuna* (DB). Nacton Includes the Domesday vills of Kembroke, Alesbourne and Purdis Farm (formerly Parnels, a medieval corruption of Petronille).
Manors. Brokes Hall al Cowhaugh al Cow Hall (C13 Richard de Holbroke). *Sub-Manors.* Sholond/Sholland Hall/Lame Manor; Purdies/Purdews; St. Peters (-1527 St. Peters, Ipswich).

Ancient Woodland.

The extensive Bridge Wood is part of ancient woodland.

Neolithic Settlement Site.

A site in the parish, prolific in Neolithic implements, pyramidal cores and thousands of flint flakes, and listed by the *Victoria County History*, has not been identified.

Bronze-Age Settlement Site.

A Bronze-Age settlement site was discovered on the crest of a hill at the southern end of Bridge Wood on the N bank of the river Orwell.

Roman Road.

The known Roman road which ran from its Orwell crossing at Downham(?) to the Roman shore fort at Walton doubtless passed through the parish, its course as yet unidentified.

NACTON *(continued)*

Tumuli & Scene of Battle (?)
In woods in the area of Seven Hills thirteen round barrows line the parish boundary for ¼ mile just N of Orwell railway station. The area is called Knights Heath and tradition states they may contain the bodies of the dead from Earl Ulfketel's battle with the Danes thought to have been fought near Ipswich in 1010 when they attacked the town. Another round barrow lies in Porters Covert.

Ancient Priory.
Only fragments remain of the Augustinian Priory of Alnesbourn, one of the smallest in Suffolk. They comprise some septaria walling in the barn of Priory Farm which stands on the site of the chapel, and some old material in the farmhouse which occupies the site of the priory itself. It was probably founded by Alberte de Neville c1200 as an independent house, and dedicated to the Blessed Virgin Mary. The priory, which had 12 canons in 1291, continued until 1452 when it became a cell of Woodbridge Priory. It was already in ruins by c1514.

Site of Chapel.
A chapel dedicated to St. Petronille stood in the other small manor of Purdies (Purdis) Farm, mentioned by Kirby in the C18. It may have been a wayside chapel beside the old Roman road which led to their fort at Walton (Felixstowe). It has now gone along with the church which probably stood in the area of the present Purdis Farm and Hall.

Medieval Common.
Nacton Heath lay between the heath of John Rous in the N and the road leading from Ipswich to the church of St Petronille to the S. It was mostly enclosed in 1810.

Deer Park.
Shown on Faden's map of 1783 (but not Bowen's of 1755), Orwell deer park was thought to have been laid out sometime before 1764 by Francis Vernon, Earl of Shipbrook.

Lost Settlements.
The parish included the Domesday vills of Kembroke, Alnesbourn and Purdis Farm. There is also some account of three churches in the parish: Hallowtree, St Petronille and Bixley. The Fastolf family were patrons and probable lords from 1310. Two miles SE of Ipswich, in what was once the ancient parish of Hallowtree, the little manor of Alvesbourn is traceable to Saxon times when its name was derived from the local owner, Aelfes. At Domesday it was in the hands of the Norman Ivo Taillebois and its area of some ¾ mile by ½ mile contained a mill, 200 acres of arable land and later a priory (*see above*). Even in 1764 John Kirby was proclaiming that 'the parish was much fuller of inhabitants formerly than it is at present for now there are not more houses upon it, than formerly there were churches!' Other lost settlements such as Merton, Neckmere and Britolston were recorded in an area of open common called Cawdwell Heath which stretched from Brightwell to Walton and was not enclosed until 1805.

Recreation.
One December night in 1803 the first recorded steeplechase was run over the four miles between Ipswich Barracks and Nacton Church, the cavalry officers wearing nightshirts over their uniforms and nightcaps on their head.

Workhouse.
The Woodbridge Union Workhouse was built in 1756. In 1765 troops dispelled rioters who were set on pulling the building down. In 1841 it is recorded as holding 187 inmates. The workhouse was closed down in 1900.

Historic House.
Broke Hall, which adjoins Orwell Park - where the house of the celebrated Admiral Vernon, captor of Porto Bello, once stood - was for many generations the seat of the Broke family. The Hall, originally the manor house of Cow Haugh, was built in 1526 by Sir Richard Broke, Lord Chief Baron in the reign of Henry VIII, and rebuilt and considerably enlarged by Philip Bowes Broke in 1767. Admiral Sir Philip Bowes Vere Broke was created a Baronet in 1813 after distinguishing himself as captain of the 'Shannon' in the famous engagement with the United States frigate 'Chesapeake' during the American War of Independence.

NAUGHTON *(5 miles N of Hadleigh)*

Cosford Hundred. 'Nagli's (?) farmstead' (OScand+OE) *Nawelton* (c1150). Morley suggests 'at the orchard farm'. Not a parish at Domesday when it was likely all forested and a part of Whatfield. It was united with Nedging in 1934 to form Nedging-with-Naughton.
Manors. Naughton (1316 Thomas de Cokefield).

Medieval Green.
The church stands beside a small triangular medieval green.

Historic Houses & Ancient Moated Sites
C17 Naughton Hall by the church is surrounded by an irregular rectangular moat with entrance in the SE adjacent to Naughton Green. Brickhouse Farm is Tudor in origin. Old (Manor) House is a C15 timber-framed building. Fidget's Farm, SW of the church, has an irregular square moat in good condition. Fragments of moats remain at Naughton Manor, the C18 rectory (2 sides), Pigeon Hall (filled in 1983?), and in the churchyard.

NAYLAND *(9 miles SE of Sudbury)*

Babergh Hundred. 'Place at the Island' (OE) *Eilanda* (c1150) *Neiland* (1227)
Manors. Nayland (C13 Robert de Bure, Earl of Essex).
Nayland is now little more than a large village but it was once a thriving small town, its wealth deriving from its flourishing cloth-making industry in the 15th and 16th centuries. Trade declined in the C17 and with it the town.

Roman Pottery Industry.
A Roman pottery production site was discovered in the parish.

Ancient Earthworks.
The river Stour which runs through the village forms the county boundary between Suffolk and Essex. A loop in this river encloses a large area of land on the E of the village and a curved moat at the southern end forms a D-shaped island of a piece of high ground called Court Knoll, just S of the church. This was probably the earliest settlement and a likely meeting place of the Babergh Hundred Court. The area was the Norman centre of the large Domesday lordship of Eiland, which included the parishes of Wissington, Stoke, and the Horkesleys on the Essex side. Although the site is now under the plough, a faint rampart separated from an outer ditch by a berm can still be detected, as can a circular mound in the NE corner with traces of a surrounding ditch. A building constructed of Roman tile and Kentish rag in the N part of the enclosure was excavated by Major Dick in 1924. Two photos of this excavation clearly show coursed stonework with occasional tile, and a scatter was visible in the ditch E of the mound in 1960. Doubt has been expressed whether this was in fact a Roman building or a later Norman construction - possibly a ringwork, motte and bailey castle or fortified manor house, erected within an earlier camp and possibly re-using some Roman tile.

Medieval Market & Fair.
Hubert de Burgh obtained a grant for a weekly market in 1227 and an annual fair. The market was obsolite by 1844 and the fair by 1891.

Village Stocks.
The village stocks, erected in 1569, were last used in 1855.

Workhouse.
A workhouse with 40 inmates is recorded in 1776.

Historic House & Ancient Moated Site.
The Mansion House was anciently situated in pasture ground called 'The Courts'. Alston Court, a former aisled hall-house built c1450 and possible successor to Court Knoll, was the home of a wealthy wool-stapler. The old Queen's Head Inn dates from the late C14.

NEDGING TYE *(4 miles N of Hadleigh)*

Cosford Hundred. 'Place of Hnydda's family' (OE) Later affixed by 'Tye' meaning 'common pasture'. *Niedinga* (DB). Nedging joined with Naughton in 1934 to become Nedging-with-Naughton.
Manors. Nedging (-1538 Abbot of St. Etheldreda, Ely, leased to various persons; 1538 Charles Brandon).

Ancient Woodland.
Glebe Town Grove and Tyrell's Grove are parts of ancient woodland.

Ancient Oak.
An ancient oak stood in the grounds of Nedging Hall for well over 500 years. It was, supposedly, the largest in England (1844).

Roman Road & Ancient Track.
Needham Lane forms the northern parish boundary with Wattisham and traces the line of a Roman road to Coddenham.

Medieval Greens.
The 'Tye' of Nedging Tye comes from the green shown on Faden's 1783 map covering the road junctions from Redhouse Farm NW of the village to Blue Gates in the SE. This has been enclosed and overlaid with roads. The linear Green Street Green ran along the northern side of Wallow Lane, E of the village.

NEEDHAM MARKET *(3 miles SE of Stowmarket)*

Bosmere & Claydon Hundred. 'Home of refuge' or 'Poor homestead' (OE) *Nedham* (C13) *Nedeham Markett* (1511). Although not mentioned directly in Domesday, Needham was created along the major road in one corner of his manor of Barking by the Bishop of Ely. Morley believed it to be the *Manwick* mentioned three times in Domesday - a contraction of Monkwick i.e. Monks' Village.
Once merely a hamlet of Barking, its Tabernacle of St. Thomas Martyr (in existence in 1460) being merely a chapel-of-ease to the mother church at Barking, Needham's greater potential standing as it did by the river Gipping and on a busy main trunk road with a link to the ancient Roman road from Colchester to Caister-by-Norwich, led to it enjoying subsequent expansion at Barking's expense. The town's principle trade of wool-combing (weaving and wool-combing sheds existed in Church Street, Hawks Mill Street and in the High Street) was destroyed when it suffered badly from the plague in 1663-5, barriers being erected at either end of town to stop the spread. At the time the town was described as deserted with grass growing in the streets, and the resultant poverty led to a comment by Thomas Fuller in 1662 that 'They are said to be on the highway to Needham who haste to poverty'. Needham separated from Barking to gain civil parish status as recently as 1901.

Early Settlement.
Evidence of a ring ditch (probably of Early Bronze-Age date and mostly destroyed by the railway line) and of Anglo-Saxon buildings, suggest a settlement at Needham by the 6th century.

Ancient Mere.
Bosmere, an ancient 9 acre lake in the grounds of Bosmere Hall just E of the town, is connected with the river Gipping and gives its name to the Saxon Hundred.

Ancient Mill Site.
Hawksmill Street leads to the river Gipping where a water mill has occupied the site since Domesday.

Medieval Way.
The Canser or Causeway, a wide hedge-enclosed pathway about 1½ miles in length, leads to Barking Church and was formerly used as a route for hand-drawn coffins - Needham church being only a chapel-of-rest to the mother church at Barking and without a graveyard of its own *(see also* Barking*)*.

Plague Mounds (?) & Houses.
An ill-defined mound 115' in diameter and 3½' high lies on the W side of the present B1113 road and NW of the Lion Inn and the first turning to Barking. The town was badly hit by the plague between 1663-1665 and the

NEEDHAM MARKET *(continued)*

town isolated. Barriers were erected either end of the High Street to keep visitors out (and the affected inhabitants in) to contain the spread. Tradition says that the dead were buried in a field near the Lion Inn and also in one near the Chain Bridges on the Stowmarket Road. The mound, which was cut through in 1981, proved to be natural. A pottery sherd of Medieval date and two fragments of human bone were recovered. The modern Chainhouse Road, off Barking Road, is named after the barrier once sited nearby. Charity Houses in Bridge Street were used as sickhouses with convalescence taken in the 'airing houses' at nearby Darmsden.

Recreation.
Camping Land, where a medieval type of football was played, was in existence in 1476.

Site of old Windmill.
A smock mill which stood at The Pightle in 1764 was pulled down c1880.

Medieval Market & Fair.
Barking had a market and fair in 1226 which was moved to the more strategically-placed Needham some time before 1511 by which time 'Market' had been added. This may have been some time between 1480-1500 when the chapel of 1251 was rebuilt on part of the market place as a church independent of Barking, The outbreak of plague saw the closing of this market and despite efforts to revive it - the latest being in 1838 - the close proximity of Stowmarket (4 miles) has ensured successful resistance to the plan. There was also an annual October fair.

Free Grammar School.
Timber-framed 2 and 4 High Street (more recently occupied by Lloyds Bank) was built and endowed by the will of Sir Francis Theobald of Barking Hall in 1632 as a Free Grammar School using the materials from the dismantled Guildhall at Barking - further evidence of the transfer of power. The trustees were directed to appoint a graduate from Cambridge University to be master and to teach the youth of Needham, Barking and Darmsden the first principles of grammar and perfect them in reading and writing. The school, which had 30-40 attending in 1892 with accommodation for 20 boarders, closed in 1909.

Almshouses.
The origin of the almshouses just past the entrance to the Causeway is unknown. The Tudor building, repaired and refronted in 1836, consists of four ground rooms and four first-floor rooms for eight poor women. The deeds date from 1784.

Quaker Settlement.
Needham Market was an important centre for Quakers for several generations, and behind the post office is a building with attached graveyard dating from 1704, which provided their Meeting House.

Historic Houses.
In a town with several fine houses, the heavily-timbered Ancient House in Hawk's Mill Street dates from 1380. It was owned by John Flegg, a wealthy clothier, in 1476. The former Bull Inn has a finely carved corner post of 1485, and The Limes, built c1500, is timber-framed behind a Georgian red-brick casing of 1771. It was formerly a Boule House, an inn for pilgrims on their way to Bury Abbey. Tudor House in High Street is another C15 building, as is the Barclays Bank premises on the corner of Barratts Lane. Samuel Alexander established one of the earliest private banks here in 1744. The Swan inn, externally of C18/C19, has C16 origins. Buildings dating from the 1400s are believed to have formerly housed the Kings Head public house. The old Lion public house stands on the parish boundary with Barking.

NETTLESTEAD *(6 miles NE of Ipswich)*

Bosmere & Claydon Hundred. 'Place where nettles grow' (OE) *Netlestedam* (DB) *Netlestede* (1215). Includes the Domesday vill of Tunstall.
Manors. Nettlestead (1171 John de Dreux; C13 Robert de Tibetot).

Medieval Deer Park.
Saxton's map of 1575 marks a deer park at Nettlestead, still remembered in the farmhouse and former hall

NETTLESTEAD *(continued)*

known as Nettlestead Chace - 'Chace' being an obsolete form of 'Chase' or deer park.

Medieval Greens.
The church and hall are shown on Faden's 1783 map standing on the edge of a small green. Newman's Green is named but not shown and may already have gone by this time. It was probably situated in the angle of the road S from Baylham Stone and E of High Hall Farm.

Historic Houses.
Nettlestead Chace (formerly Nettlestead Hall) - the greater part of which was pulled down at the beginning of the C19 leaving what is now a farmhouse - was a former aisled hall-house and the residence of the Wentworth family from 1450 to c1645. Their arms remain in the spandrels of the arch of the old mid-Tudor gateway, a portion of which remains. The timber-framed Grange is C16 and High Hall is the remaining part of an Elizabethan manor house ½ mile NW of the village.

NEWBOURNE *(7 miles SE of Ipswich)*

Carlford Hundred. 'New stream' i.e. Stream which has changed course. (OE) *Neubrunna* (DB). The parish takes its name from the stream (or bourn) running S from the church through the marshes to Kirton Creek. Newbourne, which includes the Domesday vill of Haspley to the E, is partly encircled by a number of ancient springs, particularly to the N, while crag pits here contain at least 20' of marine deposits.
Manors. Newbourn cum Martlesham (C13 Richard de Brewse). *Sub-Manors.* Haspley with Newbourn (anciently devised to Priory of Woodbridge).

Historic Houses.
Newbourn Hall is a Tudor hall-house with the Purpett coat of arms in plaster on one of the walls. It appears to have been originally built around a courtyard. The main building, which was enlarged c1612, dates from c1500, but the door leading to the private chapel is considered C14. The hall was anciently the seat of Sir Richard Broke, Knight. The Fox public house is believed to date from the C16.

NEWMARKET

Lackford Hundred. 'New market town' (L) *novum forum* (1200) *Novum Mercatum* (1219) *la Newmarket* (1418).
Newmarket, which comprises the two parishes of St Mary's and All Saints, developed at neighbouring Exning's expense from the C13 through its position on one of the oldest routeways in England . Four hundred years later it had lured the court of James I to hold their tournaments in tilting, hawking and harrying the bustard on its famous heaths; and first recorded horse race organised in 1619. With continued royal patronage through succeeding monarchs the town became the centre of English horse-racing and breeding. In 1683 the greater part of the old town was consumed by fire.

Ancient Way.
Palace Street has been identified as forming a part of the ancient trackway known as the Icknield Way. A will of John Withall, who died in 1524, left 20s to be spent in the 'reparation of the way called Hiklingsway leading from the tenement called the Rame in Newmarket towards the Church of All Saints.'

Ancient Dyke.
The great linear earthwork of Devil's Dyke crosses the racecourse NW-SE just beyond the SW parish and county boundary in Cambridgeshire.

Roman Finds.
In 1764 a number of Roman coins of Trajan, Faustina and Maximianus Herculius were found near the heath.

Medieval Market & Fairs.
Tradition asserts that Exning's market, dating from c1200, moved out of the village due to a pestilence

NEWMARKET *(continued)*

and that this new site developed into present-day Newmarket, though it was more likely due to Newmarket's more strategic position on the major highway. The town also held two annual fairs.

Site of Royal Palace.

James I built a lavish palace here c1608 known as the King's House on the site of the Griffin Inn (mentioned in a will of 1439). He used this house when taking part in 'the pleasures of the chase', and here conferred 99 knighthoods. Charles I used it when hunting, racing and coursing in the area; a time when he was painted by Rubens. It was destroyed by the Parliamentarians in the Civil War and its timber-framed remains rediscovered during 1995 excavations. The site lies between the Black Horse Inn and the Jockey Club on the W side of Sun Lane. At the Restoration, Charles II built a new red-brick Palace House Mansion on the site designed by Sir Christopher Wren, and it was from this time that the town became a recognised racing centre. James II often came here as the Duke of York, and William III is said to have 'raced all day and gambled all night'. The mansion was replaced in 1863 by a Non-Conformist chapel.

Site of Cock-pits.

Newmarket appears to have been as important as London for cock-fighting in the C18, and John Chapman's plan of the town in 1787 shows a cock-pit near the top of the street where Jane's fashion shop now stands. Another existed in the cellars of the Bushel Inn in the Rookery Precinct.

Site of old Windmills.

before 1669 a post mill was standing near what is now the junction of the A1304 and B1061 roads, S of the town. In 1780, Langley's smock mill stood on the S side of the B1103 road, S of the present hospital, on land now occupied by a school. It was disused by 1885.

Civil War Incident.

During the time of the Civil War all racing was banned in the Royalist town of Newmarket. The Kings Arms, now lost along with its site, was the venue for a confrontation between a group of Royalist colonials invited there for 'present entertainment' and a troop of Cromwell's men under the command of a Captain Pickering. A pitched battle insued, but despite killing one of the troop, the royalists were overpowered and taken prisoner.

Historic Houses.

The Bushel inn belongs to the period when King Charles II held court and went racing in the town. He no doubt visited it and may have even owned it for he owned several taverns in the town. He was also an ardent fan of the cock-fighting which took place here; traces of the cock-pit remain in the cellar. The original White Hart Inn, Newmarket's leading coaching inn, was destroyed by fire in 1683. Its replacement was destroyed by a Nazi bomb and a new public house built on the same site. The Rutland Arms occupies the site of The Ram pulled down in the latter part of the C18. A passage is said to run beneath the Rutland Arms which once connected the Palace with Nell Gwynn's house.

NEWTON *(3 miles E of Sudbury)*

Babergh Hundred. 'New farmstead or village' (OE) *Niwetuna* (DB)

Manors. Newton Hall (-1285 Abbot of St. Edmunds, Bury; 1285 John de Morse). *Sub-Manors.* Sayham al Siam/Saxham Hall; Botelers al Butlers/Buxtons.

Ancient Woodland.

Lord's Wood on the southern parish boundary and Alstrop Wood and High Wood in the north are ancient woodland.

Roman Road.

The road SSE from Great Waldingfield towards Newton is Roman and, from the drive to New Barn to the junction with the A134, provides a part of the Newton western parish boundary. The line of the road and the boundary continue in the same direction beyond the junction with the A134 as field boundaries to just N of Newton Leys.

Mound.

Hawk Hill, an oval mound shown and marked 'mound' on the C19 OS map, lies on the track which formerly

NEWTON *(continued)*

connected Trott's House by the A1071 with Newton Hall, S of the church. Its origin and purpose are unknown.

Medieval Green.

Faden's 1783 map shows the 40 acre rectangular Newton Green. It remains today partly used as a golf course. Sacker's Green, shown as a small green to the SW on the parish boundary with Little Cornard, has been enclosed.

Medieval Stocks & Pound.

The village stocks and pound are said to have been situated on the green.

Medieval Market & Fair.

Newton received a grant for a market and fair in 1257.

Workhouse.

A workhouse with 24 inmates is recorded in 1776.

Historic Houses & Ancient Moated Site.

Now mostly of C18 date, Newton Hall retains its original timber-framing. Roger's Farm, ¾ mile NE of the village, is of c1600 with remains of a medieval garderobe and traces of an ancient encircling moat. It retains interesting wall paintings of 1623 depicting biblical subjects. Botelers occupies the site of the former manor house, and close by in the church which they are thought to have built, is the impressive C15 tomb of Margaret Boteler. The C16 Saracens Head public house, situated on the green, was listed as an inn 1600-1649.

NORTH COVE *(3 miles E of Beccles)*

Wangford Hundred. 'Place of shelter' (OE) *Cove* (1204). 'North' appears a recent addition (to distinguish it from South Cove) as it was called simply Cove or Cove-by-Beccles till at least the mid C14. Even Cove was not its Domesday name for the earliest settlement was centred on the ancient earthworks at Wade or Wathe Hall (*see below*). Suckling considers this to be the Domesday *Hatheburgfelda* - 'clearing by the war-fort', which, if so, takes the site back at least to Saxon times.

Manors. Wathe/Wade Hall/Woodhall (C12 Robert Watheby of Cumberland; 1239 Jernegan family). *Sub-Manors.* Cove's al Jerningham al Worlingham.

Lost Medieval Village.

North Cove incorporates the lost parish of Little Worlingham (Worlingham Parva or Worlingham St. Peter) which comprised only 114 acres. Its church was last mentioned in 1492, but was rediscovered during construction of the Beccles bypass when 20 burials were unearthed and footings revealed to show it had a round tower and a combined nave and chancel. Pottery covered the period from Saxon Thetford Ware to C15.

Medieval Green.

Faden's map of 1783 appears to show North Cove Green occupying the fork made by the joining (N of North Cove Hall) of the present lane running N from Beccles Road with another, now gone, from just W of the church.

Historic Houses & Ancient Moated Sites.

Wade Hall (*see above*), now a farmhouse, is situated in the north of the parish with an ancient track (Wadehall Old Dam) continuing N to the river Waveney at Six Mile Corner. It stands near an ancient circular entrenchment in the midst of the marshes, 'a mound surrounded by a moat at the back of the present house' (1901). This is the moated site of the ancient Wathe Hall. The manor belonged to Robert de Watheby during the reign of Henry II, and Hugh Jernegan gained it around 1200 by marrying Watheby's daughter. The earlier building was probably a fortified manor house and its castellated appearance probably accounts for the area between the hall site and the Waveney being called Castle Marshes and the mill by the river, Castle Mill. North Cove Hall, red-brick and standing in its own park W of the village and NE of the church, is another ancient house. S of the church and immediately E of the site of the now demolished Barker's Farm, two arms of a probable moat with a third side indicated by a field boundary were recognised from aerial photographs.

NORTON *(7 miles ENE of Bury St. Edmunds)*

Blackbourn Hundred. 'Farmstead or village north of another' (OE) *Nortuna* (DB)
Manors. Norton (-1316 Owned by the Crown; 1316 John de Pakenham). *Sub-Manors.* Harding; Little Haugh.

Ancient Woodland & Medieval Deer Park.
The extensive remains of Norton Wood are ancient woodland and also provided part of the medieval deer park of the abbots of Bury who had their grange just E of here at Elmswell Hall.

Tumulus (?)
In the hamlet of Stanton Street, in the grounds of the suggestively named Little Haugh Hall which stands on the site of the former manor house, is a probable ancient burial mound. Its steep sides and the presence of brick and rubble on the summit are indicative of its later adaption to a prospect mound within the garden design of the present C18 house. William White states intriguingly in his history of the county that 'Henry VIII was induced by a credulous kind of avarice to dig for gold (not personally I assume!) at Little Haugh Hall - no doubt on this site - but was disappointed in his search'.

Roman Road & Ancient Way (?)
The A1088 which passes NNW through the parish, is thought by many to follow the course of a Roman road to Ixworth where it joins another known Roman road coming in from Pakenham. It may also have been part of the ancient Peddars Way, the line of which could have taken it through the parish.

Site of Roman Building (?)
A concentration of building material and pottery sherds near the church suggest a Roman building once stood here.

Ancient Mound.
There is now little to identify the original purpose of the moated earthworks known as the Mount, but it has almost certainly been pulled down from N to S to partially infill the moat on the S and enable the field on this side to be 'squared off' for easier cultivation. The field names of 'Mill Hill', 'Upper Miller's Field' and 'Middle Miller's Field' confirm the earthwork's later use for a windmill, but the fact that the mound was moated does not suggest that this was its orginal function; the OS map supports this opinion. Sherds of Iron Age pottery found by the site may not be contemporary, but the course of the ancient Peddars Way could possibly have taken it close to the site which is situated just beyond the edge of the former Button Haugh Green.

Ancient Track.
An ancient trackway connected Bury Abbey with the Abbot's Grange at Elmswell. Its route passed through Norton and its course can still be traced in Norton Wood.

Medieval Greens.
The massive Button Hoo or Boten Haugh Green extended from Great Ashfield and Elmswell into the NE of the parish as far as Manor Farm (where it was called Little Green) and Harding's Farm. Norton Heath is shown on Faden's map of 1783 on the W side of the present A1088 Ixworth Road bordered on the N by Hawe's Lane, on the E by the straight road W of Street Farm and to the W by the Blackbourn river. It continued S to the parish boundary. All have been enclosed.

Medieval Market & Fair.
Norton had the grant for a market in 1241 and a fair in 1254.

Historic Houses & Ancient Moated Sites.
Norton Hall, E of the village, has three parts of its ancient moat. Harding's Farm still showed the substantial irregular moat of the former Harding's Manor House (c109 yds. across NW-SE) on the 1958 OS map. By 1979 only a small internal pond remained, the rest infilled or built over. Little Haugh Hall, another former manor site, also retains parts of its moat.

NOWTON *(2 miles S of Bury St. Edmunds)*

Thingoe & Blackbourn Hundred. 'Farm for cattle' (OE+Oscand) or 'New homestead or village' *Newetune* (c950) *Neotuna* (DB)
Manors. Nowton (Abbot of St. Edmunds, Bury; 1203 Benedict de Blakenham as tenant of the Abbey).

Medieval Greens.
Low Green is shown on Faden's 1783 map near Nowton Lodge Farm. High Green is not shown on the map and may already have gone by this time. It lay to the W of the church and hall and is now bordered by the C19 almshouses.

Deserted Medieval Village.
Nowton appears to have been drained of population by its great neighbour Bury, and although now incorporating the small parish of Hardwick and the hamlet of Horsecroft, comprises little more than the church, hall, C19 almshouses and the extensive Nowton Court (early Victorian 'Tudor') with its park. It had 180 inhabitants in 1881.

Historic House & Ancient Moated Site.
The manor house of Nowton Hall, seat of the Payne family, dates from at least 1595 and is still partly surrounded by an ancient rectangular moat and remnants of a great park.

OAKLEY (formerly Oakley Magna and Oakley Parva) *(3 miles NNE of Eye)*

Hartismere Hundred. 'Wood or clearing where oak trees grow' (OE) *Acle* (DB)
Manors. Oakley/Hoo Hall (C13 Goscelin de Lodne/Hoo family). *Sub-Manors.* Beauchamps/Woodhall.

Roman Road.
The Roman road from Coddenham to Caister-by-Norwich (now the A140) forms the western parish boundary with Stuston from Warren Hills to Scole Bridge, where it crossed the river Waverley into Norfolk.

Roman Settlement.
The recent creation of the Scole-Stuston by-pass on the A143 revealed the outskirts of the Roman town which underlay Scole on the Norfolk bank of the river Waveney, on the Oakley parish boundary. It shows two phases of occupation; a domestic phase, followed by a period of agricultural use. The area was always prone to flooding and consequently unsuitable for ploughing, therefore the Roman period was discovered sealed beneath a layer of silt leaving undisturbed remains of buildings in the form of post-holes, a cobbled roadway, and a later timber causeway dated to the C5-C7. Four wells were also found.

Site of Roman Building (?)
In a meadow SE of Scole Bridge and NE of Scole Plantation, Claude Morley observed oblong mortared foundations, 60 yds S of the river edge and barely 10' above the water level. The remains standing 18" above the surrounding pasture were thought by him to be the N wall of the lost church of Little Oakley, but this church is now considered to have been on the opposite side of the road to the present Oakley Church. In 1977 a slight aggar, visible in water meadows immediately E of the embankment on the Suffolk side of Scole Bridge, produced a thin scatter of Roman pottery including Samian ware, tile and red tesserae, plus a scatter of metal work. In 1986 a mortar and flint block was observed 61 yds. from the Waveney (in the same area as Morley's discovery) plus a few sherds of Roman pottery which suggested this as the possible site of a Roman building which once stood a similar distance E of the important Roman road to *Venta Icenorum*.

Site of Saxon Bridge (?)
On the parish boundary E of Birdwalk Plantation, rectangular block-fired clay and stones found under tree roots on the bank of the river Dove were thought to be the remains of an old bridge. Basil Brown attributed it to a Late Saxon date and considered that there must in ancient time have been a road or major trackway in the vicinity. The OS Ist series map shows a track called Little Carr running parallel with the river before crossing here by 'New Bridge'. This bridge has now gone.

Lost Medieval Village.
Oakley once comprised two parishes, Great and Little Oakley, but they were consolidated as far back as 1449 and

OAKLEY *(continued)*

the latter along with its church of St. Andrew (or St. Peter?) has been lost. The site of the old Oakley village has been suggested as N of Little Oakley Church which stood on the E side of the road opposite St Nicholas Church. A Mr. West described levelling the old medieval village with its central street in the 1940s 'for American military needs'. 'Plague pits' said to have been found in the vicinity in the 1950s may have been the graves from Little Oakley Church.

Medieval Deer Park.
A former deer park of the Bishops of Norwich was mapped by William Stokes in 1619 and in existence as 'New Park' by 1326-7. Enlarged before 1757 and again in the C19 (encompassing c500 acres in 1855), it is now disparked although its outline still survives. *(see also* Hoxne).

Medieval Green.
Faden's 1783 map shows a large unnamed green on the western parish boundary mainly E of the Roman road. It can be traced today by a footpath which runs from this road S past Scole Plantation to the present B1118 and S and W of this road back to the A140 enclosing a rectangular area which extends into Brome parish.

Site of Mills.
In 1736 a post mill stood 'by the watermill' on the river Dove at a point where three footpaths meet. It was moved to Bedingfield in 1828.

Historic Houses & Ancient Moated Sites.
The site of an ancient moat 150'x90' now comprises a low rectangular platform with a low external bank on the N side with an adjacent fish-pond, in permanent pasture at the W end of the village street. The Grove may be the site of the house of Sir Robert Bucton who built the tower of St Nicholas Church. Capon's Farm was moated.

OCCOLD *(2 miles SE of Eye)*

Hartismere Hundred. 'Oak copse' (OE) *Acholt* (DB)
Manors. Occold/Occold Hall (C12 Eye Priory; 1536 Charles Brandon). *Sub-Manors.* Benningham.

Site of Ancient Chapel.
Cropmarks of a trackway continuing from the end of the existing track running past Benningham Grange in Benningham hamlet - one of the two Occold manors - lead to Chapelfield, the site of an ancient chapel. It appears to have been out of use as a chapel by 1291 - 'Ocolt with the Chapel of Beningham is assessed at 17 pounds 6 shillings and 8 pence in 1254 and at 20 pounds in 1291 when "anciently required to find curate to preach in the now extinct chapel at Benningham" '. There are no remains.

Medieval Green.
The small linear Nutmeg Green lay on the W side of the present B1077 road to Rishangles where Occold Hall stands, bordered on the W by an ancient moat. Although gone by 1783, there was a green in the hamlet of Benningham south of the hall. Its position is marked by a track called Benningham Green and by Green Farm.

Historic Houses & Ancient Moated Sites.
To the N of Occold Hall a quadrangular moat surrounds a plantation, and there is a small, square moat fed from a stream from the W at High House Farm S of the parish on Dublin Road. At Benningham Hall, Benningham Green, a hamlet 1¼ miles to the E, is a strong quadrangular moat, and there is another moat at The Grove which, situated at the end of Bullshall Road, suggests it was formerly known as Bulls Hall.

OFFTON *(7½ miles NW of Ipswich)*

Bosmere & Claydon Hundred. 'Offa's farmstead' (OE) *Offetuna* (DB). Absorbed the hamlet of Little Bricett or Bricett Parva before 1535.
Manors. Offton Castle (C13 William Talbot). Little Bricett (1227 John de Wachesham; 1227-1538 Lionel Tollemache and family). *Sub-Manors.* Offton Monks.

OFFTON *(continued)*

Ancient Woodland.

Middle Wood, just NW of the church, is a part of ancient woodland.

Pre-Conquest Fortification & Later Norman Motte & Bailey Castle.

At Castle Farm, S of the church, are the earthworks of Offton Castle on an impressive site commanding the country between the rivers Brett and Gipping. Its origins are believed to go back to pre-Norman times when it was first known as *Pileberga* (Anglo-Saxon for 'stockaded castle') and occupied by either King Offa of Mercia (755-796 A.D.), or King Offa of Essex - depending on which king afterwards gave his name to the village. William de Ambli converted the old Saxon fortification into a Norman castle in 1150 during the reign of King Stephen. The earthworks comprise a rectangular mound - its shape probably an even later conversion for use as a manor house - surrounded by a moat about 35' in breadth still containing water. On the S side is evidence of an embanked enclosure, probably a bailey contemporary with the C12 castle.

Lost Medieval Village.

1½ miles W is the hamlet of Little Bricett or Parva Bricett, formerly a separate parish but annexed to Offton in 1503. It had a church which was appropriated to Thetford Priory by Robert de Rheims and provided the manorial church for Talmage or Tollemache Hall. This church has long since been destroyed but its site was still visible until ploughing during the last war. A spread of medieval pottery covering an acre some 100 yds. to the W of the hall, and a similar distance E, suggest the site of the former village.

Medieval Green.

Faden showed the small Kelly Green in 1783, S of the castle, lying either side of Offton Road, its site now marked by Caley Green Farm.

Historic Houses & Ancient Moated Sites.

Talmage or Tollemache Hall was one of the two former manor houses, and is now a farmhouse. 'The principal portion of this edifice, once very extensive, was taken down in the early part of this century (C19). It was surrounded by a moat, traces of which still exist' (1858). It takes its name from the ancient Tollemaches, one of whom, Hugh Talmach, held the manor in c1227. It continued to be held by the family until 1538 and was later the seat of the Kemps and D'Autreys. Maskell's Hall, NW of the village, retains two arms of its square moat.

OLD NEWTON with Dagworth *(3 miles NE of Stowmarket)*

Stow Hundred. 'New farmstead' (OE) *Neweton* (1196). Dagworth: 'Daecca's soil' *Dagaworda* (DB) *Manors.* Old Newton (1161 Sir Robert de Mounteney). *Sub-Manors.* Nether Hall al Barrards; Dagworth and Sorrells in Dagworth (C13 Walter de Dagworth).

Site of Roman Cemetery.

Roman cremation burial urns were found at the bottom of a narrow shaft by workmen raising stone in a low lying meadow near Boards Farm on the southern parish boundary in c1875.

Ancient Track.

Hundred Lane forms a part of the northern parish boundary and ancient Hundred boundary between Hartismere and Stow, running from the junction with Swilltub Lane E to just beyond a track to Cotton Hall where field boundaries going S outline the parish boundary's eastern limits. Haugh Lane, which crosses and recrosses the railway track, forms part of the western parish boundary.

Site of Battle (?)

'The Battle of Stonebridge', fought in 870 A.D. between the Saxons and Danes, is traditionally said to have taken place in the valley S of Stonebridge Lane where a ford crosses the young river Gipping - here now merely a stream dividing the parishes of Old Newton and Stowupland (*see also* Stowupland).

Site of Ancient Chapel.

Dagworth is the known site of a Domesday church or chapel, half-owned by Breme or Bremere, a freeman killed at the Battle of Hastings. The 'Chapel of St. Margaret at Dagworth' was mentioned in 1485 (but may be confused

OLD NEWTON *(continued)*

with Darsham in this record), and shown 'in ruins' on Bowen's map of 1753. There were petitions in both 1502 and 1511 calling for help with maintenance and repair. 'Its foundations were still traceable' in 1844 but by 1992 nothing remained, although, at the position marked 'X' on the OS map, a thick patch of nettles may pinpoint buried foundations. The site is immediately SE of Dagworth Hall between the embanked footpath and the stream; the area above the valley to the E is called Chapel Hill.

Deserted Medieval Settlement.
All that remains of the original settlement of Dagworth - now merely a hamlet of Old Newton - comprise little more than Dagworth Hall, a much reduced Tudor farmhouse beside an ancient ford over the young river Gipping.

Medieval Greens.
There are two greens in the parish on Faden's 1783 map. Otertons Green is named S of the church but not shown - it may already have gone by this time, and a roughly rectangular green is shown but not named near the northern parish boundary by Ward Green Farm, and named as such on the current OS map.

Medieval Gallows.
In the C13 Walter de Dagworth claimed right of gallows, free warren and assize of bread and beer.

Site of old Windmill.
A post mill stood on Mill Hill in 1783. Its fate is unknown.

Medieval Guildhall.
Documents speak of repairs to the foundations of the Guildhall in 1462.

Historic Houses & Ancient Moated Sites.
Ancient Newton Hall, ¾ mile SE of the village, retains a part of its original moat. In the C16 the then owner, Margaret, Countess of Salisbury, was accused of 'communicating items of a seditious nature'; although 70 years of age, she was executed without trial. There are other moats at Pooley's Farm (3 sides), and at Rookery Farm just N of the village, where 2 moated enclosures adjoin; the larger S moat has lost its NE angle, and the northern one, its eastern side; a stream supplies water from the W. The site of pre-Tudor Nether Hall - a moated enclosure just N of the church - was shown tree-covered on the 1839 tithe map and named 'Moat & Plantation'. C13 pottery sherds have been recovered from the site which was bulldozed flat in 1967. Another rectangular moated site was visible on a 1971 aerial photograph just NE of Yew Tree Cottage near the northern parish boundary. It is marked 'Moat Pightle' on the 1839 tithe map when the enclosure itself was not shown and had probably already gone by this date. Another rectangular enclosure shown on the same photograph at Mayhew's Farm (but not shown on the tithe map) suggests that the remaining water-filled arm was once part of another moat. Dagworth Hall, a farmhouse of c1912, has Tudor origins.

ONEHOUSE *(1 mile NW of Stowmarket)*

Stow Hundred. 'Single or isolated dwelling' (OE) *Anuhus* (DB)
Manors. Onehouse (1270 Henry de Caldecotes). *Sub-Manors.* Caldecotes.

Ancient Woodland.
Northfield Wood is a part of ancient woodland.

Medieval Market & Fair.
Henry de Caldecote obtained a grant for a market and fair in 1270.

Workhouse.
The Stow Union Workhouse was built as a House of Industry in 1778. By 1821 it had 235 inmates. Stow Lodge Hospital, which includes the building, now occupies the site.

Historic House & Ancient Moated Site.
The place-name refers to the original manor house here. It was the seat and estate of Bartholomew de Burghersh who was one of the 12 barons into whose care the Prince of Wales was committed at the Battle of Cressy in the

ONEHOUSE *(continued)*

reign of Edward III. He died at Onehouse in 1396 without male issue. The solitary situation of his residence probably gave rise to the name of the parish which was covered in woodland except for a narrow strip which ascended from the valley to the Old Hall. The site is now marked by three fragments of the ancient moat within which stands the present Hall, formerly the residence of the Pettiward family. Elizabeth I in one of her progresses through the county is said to have breakfasted here. Onehouse Rectory dates from the C16.

ORFORD *(5 miles SSW of Aldeburgh)*

Plomesgate Hundred. 'Estuary by the peninsula' (OScand) or 'Ford at the seashore' *Oreford* (1164). A narrow strip of land between two waters i.e. the Kings and Lantern (or Lapthorn) Marshes between the sea to the SE and the river Ore to the NW.

Manors. Orford (c1184 Robert de Valoines; 1316 William de Cleidon).

Orford was sacked by the Danes in 870 A.D. and at Domesday merely a hamlet of neighbouring Sudbourne. Even today when roles have been reversed, Orford's great church is officially merely a chapelry to the mother church there. The Normans developed Orford into a medieval port of some importance. Granted a Charter in 1256, it sent three ships and 62 men to the seige of Calais in 1359. Later it became a borough governed by a mayor and returned two members of parliament until 1832 when it was disfranchised - though the corporation continued until 1886. Yet by the end of the C16 it was already said to be 'lying in the greatest ruin and decay'. The cause of this was the continual extension of the shingle bar which eventually made the harbour inaccessible to large vessels, leaving the town to decay and become little more than a village and small quay with an oyster fishery. The town and river Alde are now separated from the sea by a narrow peninsula known as Orfordness and Lantern Marshes. Great quantities of building material are turned up by the plough in fields to the W and S of the castle - some of which still carry street names - showing the considerable extent of the former town in which the castle was centrally situated. Along with the church, it remains defiant as a lasting monument to Orford's former glory.

Ancient River Walls and Sea Defences.

Unfortunately, no historic records survive of the original creation of Suffolk's river walls or other sea defences. It is believed none were created, at least in any permanent way, until the Normans came. However, a record exists for Orford marshes which were 'inned' in 1169 for the protection of the castle.

Norman Castle.

Orford castle was built on the direct orders of Henry II, presumably to house a garrison to nullify the increasing power of the Bigods in East Anglia. Alnoth, chief engineer and keeper of the King's Houses, carried out the work between 1165 and 1167. Bartholomew Granville, Sheriff of Norfolk and Suffolk, was appointed constable and it was he who drained the marshes opposite the castle on the other side of the river Ore, still known as the 'King's Marshes'. Norden's illustrations of c1600 show that the castle buildings were very extensive with an outer gatehouse and curtain walls, but the keep, though remarkably complete, is today the only section of the fortress still remaining. It has eighteen sides externally, but is circular within. 63' high to the battlements with 3 large angle turrets rising a further 20', the walls, constructed of local septaria with freestone ashlar for the corner stones, are enormously thick (some 20' at the base). The entrance is by a modern C19 staircase which has been built on the outside to replace the forebuildings. The keep has 3 floors connected by a spiral staircase of 200 steps and contains a great chamber and a chapel which is almost complete with ten round Norman arches. The keep stands on an irregular mound surrounded by a double ditch but the remains of the bailey have been largely destroyed by digging for sand. Between the ditches was an embattled wall some 40' high, a fragment of which remained into the last century. The initial test came with the arrival of forces from Flanders in 1173 led by the Earl of Leicester, but these apparently managed to bypass the castle, whose revolutionary design was never really put to the test.

Ancient Priories.

The site of the priory of Austin Friars, founded c1295 by Robert de Hewell and built in 1299, is bounded by Quay

ORFORD *(continued)*

Street and Bridge Street. Further land acquired in 1337 enabled the friars to enlarge their rather cramped quarters. Some of the buildings were destroyed by lightning in 1363. After the Dissolution the buildings were dismantled and now only part of the precinct walls remain, together with some unrecognisable fragments incorporated in the houses which stand on the site which was granted to Robert Lord in 1544. There was also a Benedictine Nunnery here, founded by Ralph de Albini.

Site of Medieval Hospitals.

It is suggested that St. Leonard's Hospital 'stood near Sudbourne Park' on the northern parish boundary. Possibly for lepers, it was founded c1267 and mentioned in 1320. It is recorded as being dissolved c1350. A female skeleton, 2 Tudor bricks and C11-C14 pottery was found E of the Hall in 1956 very close to the site of 'The Hospital', a group of buildings shown on Norden's Survey of Orford in 1600-1. St. John the Baptist Hospital was mentioned in 1390 and dissolved c1500. There are no remains and its site is unknown but may have been associated with the chapel mentioned below.

Site of Ancient Chapels.

A chapel attached to St. Leonard's Hospital was still in use in 1586, its site thought to be near Sudbourne Park. St. John's Chapel, mentioned in 1500, stood on the land still called St. John's Chapel Field, N of the church and E of Ferry Road. The Chapel House was still in existence in 1546. Within the church itself was Our Lady Chapel, mentioned in 1384 and endowed with lands of Chantry Farm.

Site of Mound (?)

A decorated semi-circular bronze padlock has been found on the site where Norden on his 1600-1 map shows a possible mound by the present B1084 immediately N of the village.

Oyster Industry.

Orford has long been known for its oysters. Evidence of the industry still remains in oyster beds by the quay, and in a group of rectangular estuarine oyster beds on the N side of Stony Ditch on the S side of the river E of Stonyditch Point.

Site of Ancient Tide Mill.

Well-preserved heavy oak timbers were discovered in wet soil during the construction of a sewer S of Chantry Farm on Chantry Marshes in 1954, and similar timbers were visible below water in a nearby dyke. These are no doubt surviving sections of what John Norden's c1600 map illustrated with the representation of a water-wheel and channel and the words 'here stode a water mill now decaid'. It is thought to date back to the C12.

Medieval Green.

Beacon Green is mentioned in the 1591 will of James Coe.

Site of Gallows.

Norden's map of 1600-1 marks 'The Gallows' by the junction of five ways at Millfield Cottages NW of the village. Although shown further N than the mound (*see above*), it is possible that an error in siting could mean that the mound, gallows and find are connected. Ananias Appleton's map of 1588 also illustrates a gallows but shows it just W of the castle possibly in the area of Broom Covert on the western parish boundary.

Medieval Stocks.

The stocks which stood near the White Hart inn were removed in 1873 and are now housed in the church.

Medieval Market & Fairs.

Encroachment has reduced Market Hill to half its former size. It is the site of the medieval market established here before 1154 along with two fairs. A further grant was awarded in 1256. It had lost much of its importance by 1679 when it was described as a small market for butter, cheese and meat, and was finally abolished in 1891, some 18 years after the fair.

Old Windmills.

The building of a mill in Orford was recorded as early as 1163 and there is reference to two mills being lost

ORFORD *(continued)*

c1318. A windmill stood on land called The Harp in 1637. In 1736 a post mill stood near Millfield Cottages N of the village, possibly on the ancient mound (*see above*). It was demolished in 1913.

Beacon & Lighthouses.
The 1591 will of James Coe refers to a Beacon Green and a beacon is shown on an early map. Situated at Orfordness, this beacon was lit as a warning to shipping between 1603-1704. It was replaced in 1661 by two lighthouses, the High Light and the Low Light. One of the lights was elevated in 1709 and after the Low Light was washed away in 1724, both were replaced in brick in 1739. The Low Light was discontinued in 1888 and in ruins by 1925. The High Lighthouse, rebuilt again in 1792, remains.

Almshouses.
Robert Bence's will of 1611 provided for six or more almshouses to be made from four small tenements in Bridge Street to provide for six aged widows/widowers.

Workhouse.
A workhouse is recorded in Orford with 20 inmates in 1776.

Historic Houses & Ancient Moated Sites.
The C15 Kings Head was used by smugglers, and the former quayside inn The Jolly Sailors dates back to the C16. The former White Hart has C14 foundations and the Crown & Castle Hotel was built in the C17. The Town Hall was built by the Marquis of Hertford in 1779, and rebuilt in 1903. He also built the Assembly House five years earlier.

OTLEY *(6 miles NW of Woodbridge)*

Carlford Hundred. 'Otta's woodland clearing' (OE) *Otelega* (DB)
Manors. Overhall (1250 Henry de Hastings). *Sub-Manors.* Netherhall (C12 Adam de Otteley).

Roman Road.
The B1078 road and a section of the southern parish boundary follow the course of a Roman road across the southern part of the parish. The road is lost under cultivated fields from just after Otley College, and prior to the junction with the B1079 road at Otley Bottom, eastwards. A section was cut revealing a gravel-made road only 14' wide and 18" thick with ditches 25' apart. A couple of early Roman pottery sherds were found on the surface.

Motte & Bailey Castle.
The Mount, or sometimes misnamed Otley Barrow (probably in error for Otley Bottom, its situation), is a small motte castle with traces of two enclosures, situated on the southern side of the Lark valley, ¼ mile S of the church. It stands beside the course of a Roman road, and close to (and utilising) the entrance to the 'gull' which at one time may have been a navigable river. It is suggested that the earthworks may originally have been a fort to protect an important ford here. What remains is a reasonably well-preserved circular mound c20' high with a flat top surrounded by a much damaged moat. To the immediate NE are indications of an extensive bailey enclosed by ditches with the gull forming the NE side. There is another curvilinear enclosure to the S which was undoubtedly a later addition. The earliest ownership can probably be traced to the C12 when its first Norman owner may have been Adam de Otteley.

Former Medieval Settlement Sites.
The main settlement of Otley now extends along the Cretingham road from the junction with the B1079 towards Otley Green, but there is evidence of former nucleated settlement around the church. 'A moated enclosure adjoining the churchyard of Otley on the NNE side, with the entrance near the church, is surrounded by a trench (moat) averaging 8' deep.' (1911) Earthworks, ponds and ditches adjoin the NE corner of the churchyard where finds of medieval pottery were made 'some years ago'. Also to the E of the church 'in the 3-acre hay meadow to the NE of the house (High House on the eastern parish boundary) are several medieval house platforms and hollow ways. These adjoin and are to the SE of an ancient (arm of a) moat.' This settlement is no doubt

OTLEY *(continued)*

from the early days when the Lark was navigable from Martlesham Creek through Bealings, Grundisburgh, Clopton and Burgh to its head-waters here in Otley.

Medieval Green.

Faden names Otley Green NE of the village, but its form is not clear on his 1783 map. It covered 25 acres and was enclosed in 1809.

Historic Houses & Ancient Moated Sites.

Otley Hall, home of the Gosnold family, dates from c1454 when its owner was John Gosnold, but occupation of the adjoining double-moated site of an earlier manor house goes back to the reign of Richard I. In an area predominantly Parliamentarian in support, the Gosnolds, who appear to have lived here about 260 years, suffered much for their Royalist sympathies during the Civil War. The front portion of the present house with its gatehouse and drawbridge has been destroyed but it is still partially surrounded by a broad moat. The hall has some of the best woodwork in Suffolk with linen-fold panelling in several of the rooms, and is described by Pevsner as one of the county's most interesting C15 houses. Most of the credit for this must go to John's son, Robert (1470-1555), who did extensive work on the house during his occupation. Fish-ponds lie to the SW. Moat Farm, E of the village, is C15, its extensive fragments of moat so disconnected it is difficult to trace their original course. There is a narrow but complete moat W of the village at Wood Farm, and remnants of a moated enclosure adjoin the NE side of the churchyard with an entrance near the church. It was surrounded by a trench averaging 8' deep and marks the site of the original manor house. Timber-framed Otley High House on the eastern parish boundary is also moated. Its unusual plan has been little altered since it was first built c1500. To the N of this are the remains (one water-filled arm) of another possible rectangular moat. Cropmarks of a square moat with two adjacent (fish)?-ponds and an outer ditched enclosure, S of the B1078 and W of the Agricultural College, are shown with a house in 1723, going out of repair in 1807, and gone by 1905. The site was named Charity Farm.

OULTON *(2 miles W of Lowestoft)*

Mutford & Lothingland Hundred. 'Old farmstead' or 'Ali's farmstead' (OE or OScand+OE) *Aleton* (1203)
Only formed as a separate parish in the C13 after, as Norman Scarfe suggests, the prosperous Ali extended his estate *Aleton* by 'acquiring' a major part of Flixton.

Manors. Oulton/Oulton High House (1280 Edmund Bacun). *Sub-Manors.* Fastolf's, Fastolf Hall, Oulton Hall/Tenement, Rolfe's, Houghton Hall (c1445 John Fastolf).

The old village of Oulton has now been enveloped by the massive residential sprawl of Oulton Broad leaving just the church and rectory. Oulton itself is now limited to the N of the parish, virtually again a part of Flixton.

Roman Road.

The eastern parish boundary lies just to the W of, and follows the line of the present Oulton Road (A12) which is thought to be on the course of the Roman road to Gorleston with a branch to the Roman fort at Burgh Castle.

Ancient Track.

A small section (Frost's Alley Score in neighbouring Lowestoft) remains of an ancient track traceable from Oulton to Lowestoft.

Ancient Earthworks (?)

Claude Morley wrote of the remains of an unrecorded earthworks - probably (he thought) that of a Saxon fort - which 'crowned the extreme summit of a hoh, running S to near the W end of Oulton Broad, here some fifty yards wide, and there abruptly falling away on every side but the N. The excavation is 23 paces E and W by about the same distance at right angles whence upon the W side extends a smaller and continuous one of 11 paces E and W by a dozen at right angles'. A circuit from the church by public footpath encompasses this 'hoh'.

Medieval Common.

Oulton Common, N of the church, was shown and named on Faden's 1783 map. It is outlined by roads and

OULTON *(continued)*

named Camps Heath on the current OS map. The map shows another area of unnamed common NW of Mutford Bridge on the N bank of Lake Lothing and extending W. This is now mainly under an extensive residential development forming a part of the Lowestoft outer suburbs.

Medieval Market & Fair.
The grant for a market and fair was obtained in 1307.

Site of old Windmill.
In 1736 a tower mill called Ladymill stood NW of the present swing bridge to the W of the A1117 road in what is now Oulton Broad. It was demolished in 1932.

Workhouse.
The Mutford and Lothingland House of Industry was built 1765 and enlarged 1836. In 1841 it held 141 paupers.

Historic House.
Oulton High House (now called Manor House), near the junction of the present A1117 and B1074 roads, was formerly the seat of the Hobarts and dates from the late C16. It replaced the manor house of the Fastolfs which may have been sited near St Michael's Church in the S of the parish where several members of the family are buried. The brass effigies of John Fastolf, who died in 1445, his wife, Katherine (1478), and an unnamed priest - probably another member of the family - were stolen from the church in the mid C19.

OUSDEN *(7 miles SE of Newmarket)*

Risbridge Hundred. 'Owl's valley' (OE) *Uuesdana* (DB). Morley, however, considered that it translated to a personal name i.e. 'Ufe's valley'.
Manors. Ousden/Newhall (C13 William de Criketot).

Ancient Woodland.
Littly Wood, just S of the village, and Glumpsey Wood on the northern parish boundary are ancient woodland.

Ancient Tracks.
The southern parish boundary follows the course of the ancient Bury Lane running into Genesis Green, Wickhambrook. Another old lane runs NE from the last marking part of the eastern boundary to Lady's Green.

Medieval Market & Fair.
Sir William de Criketot obtained the grant for a market and fair here in 1253.

Historic Houses & Ancient Moated Sites.
All that remains of the old Ousden Hall, built by the Moseleys in the early years of the C17, is the porch at the N end. The house, former seat of the Praed family, was demolished in 1955 after being used as a P.O.W. camp for Germans and Italians in World War II. A 1924 copy of an earlier estate map shows a U-shaped moat to the S of the house - the E arm running alongside the churchyard - plus two fish-ponds. Glebe Farm, on the SE parish boundary, still retains the major part of its irregular moat.

PAKEFIELD *(Now a part of South Lowestoft)*

Mutford & Lothingland Hundred. 'Pacca's clearing' (OE) *Paggefella* (DB)
Manors. Pakefield Pyes/Drayton ([no dates] John Pye and by John Drayton; 1378 Hugh Fastolf). Includes the Domesday vill of Rothenhall (*Rodenhala*).

Lost Domesday Vill & Medieval Village.
The Rothenhall mentioned in Pakefield - John de Rothenhale (1236), Peter son of Leofweald de Rothenhall (1311-16), and William son of Saeweald Rothenhall of Pakefield (1421) - is believed to refer to the Domesday vill of Rodenhala, probably a hamlet to the E of Pakefield and now lost to the sea. Pakefield originally had two churches, St Margaret and All Saints, and when the former fell victim to the waves in the first half of the C14, the latter was adapted to take its parishioners. This involved building a northern extension with its own altar, etc.

PAKEFIELD *(continued)*

and erecting a solid wall between the two. It is possible that the old church of St Margaret served the lost hamlet of Rothenhall. In 1743 the parishes were officially united and the dividing wall dismantled. Pakefield, which was 'a pretty large fishing town' according to Kirby at this time, continued to be eroded by the relentless North Sea. Between 1824 and 1844, 70 acres of coastline was washed away and the same amount again by 1902. By 1916, houses, the Green, boating sheds, yawl sheds, The Cliff Hotel, The Ship Inn, The Lord Nelson, The Oddfellows Arms and the Fishermans Shelter had all been washed away. By 1932, 90 houses had disappeared over the cliff. What remains has been divided between Gisleham and Carlton Colville parishes, and Lowestoft which had earlier (1907) enveloped Pakefield's neighbour Kirkely - itself an important medieval port - in the remorseless march of its southern outer suburbs.

Ravine.
A ravine in the cliff here is called 'Crazy Mary's Hole', a favourite haunt for 'lovesick maidens'.

Medieval Green.
Pakefield Green, shown on Faden's 1783 map lying W of the church, has been lost to Lowestoft residential development.

Medieval Stocks.
The village stocks, which no doubt at one time stood on Pakefield Green, are preserved in the churchyard.

Site of old Windmill.
A post mill is shown standing W of the church in 1783. It was pulled down in 1000.

Almshouses.
Almshouses in the village accommodated 20 poor persons in 1674.

Historic House & Ancient Moated Site.
Pakefield Hall, just W of the beach and N of the holiday camp, is an Elizabethan house rebuilt in 1849. It still retains its long rectangular moat.

PAKENHAM *(5 miles NE of Bury St Edmunds)*

Thedwastry Hundred. 'Pacca's homestead or village' (OE) *Pakenham* (c950) *Pachenham* (DB)
Manors. Pakenham Hall (-1545 Abbot of St. Edmunds, Bury; 1545 Robert Spring). *Sub-Manors.* Newhall al Malkinshall al Beaumonts; Netherhall al Ladies Hall al Richards Hall (C13 vested in John de Pakenham, steward to Bishop of Ely); Red Castle.

Ancient Woodland.
Pakenham Wood is a section of ancient woodland.

Ancient Lake Dwellings.
Barton Mere (*see* Great Barton).

Neolithic Settlement.
Excavations on the Roman Camp N of Pakenham windmill, in advance of the new bypass, revealed a group of small pits yielding worked flints and pottery sherds of Neolithic period.

Early Bronze Age Barrow, Roman Cremations & Anglo-Saxon Site.
Excavations, carried out at Grimstone End 1½ miles NE of the village in 1953 as a result of aerial photographs, revealed a barrow covering Late Neolithic pottery and containing eight Roman cremations inserted at a later date. This was overlaid by an Anglo-Saxon settlement site.

Roman Road.
The Roman Peddars Way bisects the parish SSW-NNE from just N of Millfields. Another (lesser) Roman road, runs SE from Puttockshill on the NW parish boundary, to a former ford at Fulmer Bridge near the site of the Roman fort. A coin of Trajan was found on its course. From here it is identified in cropmarks on aerial photographs just S of Baileypool Bridge.

PAKENHAM *(continued)*

Roman Fort.

A Roman Fort at Mickle Mere, between the mill stream and the Grimstone End road, comprising a parallelogram enclosed by three ditches and built to command the ford where the Peddars Way crosses the river Blackbourne, was noted from aerial photographs and excavated prior to the construction of the Ixworth bypass. Other roads and features visible, post-date the fort and are part of the Roman settlement. The site was densely populated until at least the middle of the C4 and shows no evidence of earlier or later settlement to the Roman period.

Roman Settlement & Cemetery.

A Roman Settlement which developed in connection with the nearby fort *(see above)* lay N of the Thieves Lane-Cutter's Lane junction, NE of the windmill and S of Mickle Mere. It stretched N to the Southern end of the present village where (in 1950) a Roman wall 9'6" long made of rammed chalky clay was discovered. In 1810, near the windmill, workmen discovered 'a square place full of pots set in rows, a great many of them of a dark colour, several of which had covers. Unfortunately, none were preserved but they were likely Roman. A farmer ploughing nearby in 1952 advised Basil Brown that he had found substantial wall footings at a depth of 3'. These were eventually destroyed. Other cemetery sites have been located to the E, and to the N at Bridge Farm where in 1906 four skeletons were found at a depth of 4-5'. All were young males and reported 'lying at all angles'. Another was found in the 1940s, and another in 1948, whilst other (human)? bones were unearthed here in 1959. These finds all go to show the extent and length of the settlement.

Roman Villa & Early Saxon Settlement.

In a field on the Great Livermere Road, near Redcastle Farm to the N of the village, a circular mosaic in a surround of red tesserae (since destroyed by cattle) was uncovered in an apse in 1776. It was excavated in 1953 when half the building of a Roman villa was exposed. It had short wings and an apsidal central room with the remains of a tessellated floor and pottery indicating occupation from mid C2 to C4. Painted wall plaster and window glass was also found. There were indications of early Saxon settlement within a few hundred yards of the villa. Aerial photos have shown possible buildings associated with the villa on the W side of the road.

Roman Industrial Pottery Site.

At Grimstone End, 1½ miles NE of the village, a brick-floored Roman kiln with a complex system of draught flues and furnaces was found in 1955. More recently, two or three kilns of the common Suffolk 'pedistal' type, along with two large floored kilns making colour-coated wares have been recorded. During quarrying operations in 1960, an unusually small kiln was discovered.

Ancient Earthworks.

The Domesday Church of St. Mary is said to stand on a fortified site which predates it.

Medieval Common.

Faden's 1783 map shows Pakenham Common extending N from Pakenham Wood mainly on the E side of Bull Road, narrowing and sweeping W to be bounded on the N by the manor house of Maulkin's Hall (shown as Moking Hall).

Medieval Market & Fair.

A market and fair may have been granted to Pakenham in 1256.

Mills.

Pakenham is unique in Britain in having both a working watermill and windmill. Domesday Book records a watermill on the site of the present building which is late C18 and follows one of Tudor date. The tower mill close by (built 1810) stands on the site of an earlier windmill shown on a map of 1783.

Almshouses.

Almshouses were built here in 1674.

Medieval Guildhall.

Charity Cottages were known as The Workhouse or The Guildhall in 1647. It is possible that they were converted into the almshouses in 1674 (*see above*).

PAKENHAM *(continued)*

Historic Houses & Ancient Moated Sites.

Newe House, E of the village, was built c1622 by Robert Bright. His family's former home, which they held for several generations from about 1545, was the manor house of Nether Hall, S of the village. A sketch of that period shows it surrounded by parkland and even then a very old building. It was almost entirely rebuilt in late Victorian times. Barton Mere takes its name from the ancient lake which sits astride the Pakenham and Great Barton parish boundaries; it was formerly the home of a branch of the ancient L'Estrange family. Just N of Old Hall, now a farmhouse, is the site of Pakenham Hall which belonged to the Spring family in the C16-C17 - Sir William Spring was listed as having 24 hearths in 1674, which identified it as a large mansion. The hall is depicted on Faden's map of 1783 with a triple-gabled frontage and an avenue to the W. It was demolished between 1804-1810 and the site is now under cultivation, but fragments of its former moat (and fish-ponds?) remain. In the SE of the parish, an L-shaped pond to the E of the present house is probably the remains of the moat of the manor house of Bemans or Beaumonts - an Abel Beman was concerned with land in Pakenham in 1380-1; the hall was shown on the 1904 OS map. Old moats remain at Maulkin's Hall manor house, NE of Pakenham Street (rhombic-shaped and complete except for part of the southern side), and at Redcastle Farm, on the NW parish boundary (square, the western side almost levelled).

PALGRAVE *(5 miles NNW of Eye)*

Hartismere Hundred. Several suggestions as to the place-name meaning include 'Grove where poles are obtained', 'grave enclosed with palings' and 'Pal's (Saxon god) sacrificial trench'. (OE) *Palegrave* (962) *Palegraua* (DB)
Manors. Palgrave (962-1554 Abbot of St. Edmunds, Bury; 1554 Sir Thomas Cornwallis). *Sub-Manors.* Fenhouse.

Site of Ancient Chapel.

St. John's Farm, on the western parish boundary, is the site of the Chapel of St John the Baptist mentioned at Domesday, in the taxation of 1256, and in a will of 1433. There was a small landscaped park here, now disparked but retaining field names Large Park and Little Park. Lands belonging to the chapel and lying in Botesdale were granted to Francis Boldero and Robert Parker in 1545, and a Charity Certificate of 1546 states that this was a free chapel whose founder was unknown; the incumbent at that time being Henry Cornwallis - 'It is no parish church, but a chapel now decayed, half a mile from the parish church'. The lordship anciently belonged to Bury Abbey, and the chapel, subordinate to that monastery, was served by five secular priests. Dismantled in the C16, the N and S walls of the yard were located in 1721.

Medieval Green.

The triangular green in front of the church, shown on Faden's map of 1783 with seven roads emanating from it like spokes of a wheel, remains today.

Free School.

The date of the foundation of the Free Grammar School here is not known but three schoolmasters/tutors are recorded between 1585 and 1794. It was closed in 1822 and later became the Girl Servants School.

Guildhall & Workhouse.

The Town Estate includes "a messuage called the Guild Hall, now used as a parish workhouse". As a workhouse it housed 30 inmates in 1776.

PARHAM *(2½ miles SSE of Framlingham)*

Plomesgate Hundred. Possibly 'Barred-in enclosure' or 'Meadow where pears grow' (OE) *Perreham* (DB)
Manors. Parham Hall (C12 Ralph de Collevill). *Sub-Manors.* Hickling Hall (c1185 Robert de Valoines gave manor to Hickling Priory, Norfolk).

Ancient Woodland.

Parham Wood, NW of the village, and Kilderbee's Grove on the northern parish boundary are parts of ancient woodland. Queen Mary's Wood which lies on the NE parish boundary has historical interest if tradition is to be

PARHAM *(continued)*

believed. Following the death of Edward VI, Mary Tudor left Framlingham Castle on 31st July 1553 and headed for London to claim the throne (accompanied, it is said, by 40,000 men - probably more than ten times the actual figure!). The route they are said to have taken went S through this wood and along the eastern parish boundary to meet the major highway to London at Stratford St Andrew. Unfortunately, only two isolated sections of this wood remain -Queen Mary's Covert and Queen Mary's Plantation - and what remains of the track (still known as Bloody Mary's Ride) now ends just past Oak Farm.

Ancient Burial Site.
In 1734 a male skeleton, an urn, and a spearhead were said to have been found in a gravel pit here 'belonging to some Danish chieftain'. The site of the gravel pit is in a field called Fryar's Close, SE of Parham Wood, and the finds were more likely Saxon.

Medieval Greens.
The parish is shown on Faden's 1783 map to have had several greens. Northern Green, roughly rectangular, lay NW-SE across a kink in the road N of the village; its limits are marked by Home Farm, Green Farm, North Green Farm and footpaths. Further S, the present area called Mill Green was named Cutlers Green but not shown - it may have gone by this time. Further S still, the hamlet of Silverlace Green was named and shown. Morley suggests the name may have come from a corruption of the medieval monkish *silva luce* meaning 'sacred grove'.

Medieval Fair.
A fair was held on Hallowmas Day in 1618.

Stocks.
The village stocks are preserved in the roofing of the churchyard lychgate.

Site of Castle (?) and Fortified Manor House.
Across fields, ½ mile SE of the village and enclosed by double moats, the inner one still wet and of great strength, the romantic Old Moat Hall incorporates what remains of the Tudor Hall of Sir Christopher Willoughby, built between 1498 and 1527. More interesting still is what stood on this impressive site prior to that. Evidence suggests three former major buildings. The oldest comprised the substantial earthworks of a possible castle erected by Gilbert de Colville in the C12 (or Theabold de Valoines after 1208) with outer and inner moats. The ancient outer moat has earthwork banks to the NW, SW and the NE where there are remains of substantial fish-ponds and signs of outbuildings, and the inner probably being originally less symmetrical than now. The buildings within may well have been of timber. The next period saw the construction of the fortified manor house by the de Uffords (probably William, second Earl of Suffolk, who died in 1382) in flint and sandstone and still to be seen in parts of the present hall, the walls of the moat, and the dressed stone fragments built into the walls of the outbuildings; the moat was probably squared off at this time and the fish-ponds built. The last period saw the construction of the mainly Tudor hall of the Willoughby's with a courtyard, the foundations of which lie immediately under the present lawns. The fine old gateway to the hall was inscribed with the arms of the Uffords and Willoughbys.

Historic Houses.
For two and a half centuries the Warner family occupied Parham House (built c1630), the only remains of which are the two pillars standing in a field about a mile from the village. Parham (New) Hall, rebuilt in 1852, stands on the site of Ducking Hall, with its associations with the Suffolk poet George Crabbe. Church Farmhouse was built in the C15.

PEASENHALL *(7 miles SSW of Halesworth)*

Blything Hundred. 'Sheltered land where peas grow' (OE) *Pesehala* (DB). The plural Anglo-Saxon *pisan* for peas became 'pesen' in medieval English and 'peasen' in the C16.
Manors. Peasenhall (1267 Roger Bigot, Earl of Norfolk; 1302 Nicholas de Segrave). *Sub-Manors.* Jurdis Manor; Falesham Hall.

PEASENHALL *(continued)*

Roman Roads.
The modern A1120 Badingham Road lies on the course of a Roman road bisecting the parish from Boundary Farm in an ENE direction. The present road has deviated from the line of the old road where it approaches and passes through the village. Another Roman road heads NW - SE (?) from the first at a junction near the church in the centre of the village (probably a little SW of the present road junction). The course can be traced by the present road NW from the fork by The Vicarage to the parish boundary beyond High House Farm, but the Rendham Road SE from the junction is not on the line of the Roman road except, perhaps, for the section from Corner Farm S to the parish boundary. This road may have terminated at Aldeburgh where all evidence of possible Roman occupation has long since been swept away by the sea.

Site of Major Roman Settlement (?)
The parish's (and possibly Sibton's) important position on the junction of two main Roman roads, suggests that this could once have been the site of a major Roman settlement - possibly *Sitomagus*.

Earthwork.
An earthwork of undetermined origin lies immediately SW of Snow's Hall, N of the parish.

Medieval Green.
Faden's map of 1783 shows a very long linear green running N from the river Yox to the junction with Dunwich Lane. This green has gone and been replaced by Halesworth Road.

Recreation.
Camping Close of two acres recorded in 1487 abutting Peasenhall Street to the S, suggests the site of a Camping field where a form of medeival football was played.

Historic Houses..
Wool Hall (or New Inn), NE of the Angel Inn, is a small timber-framed hall house of C15/C16 date. The Ancient House, NW of the church, has C16 linenfold panelling behind an Early C18 facade.

PETTAUGH *(10 miles N of Ipswich)*

Thredling Hundred. 'Peota's shelter or enclosure' (OE) *Petehaga* (DB). The place-name aptly describes the low-lying land near the church beside the Deben's effluent which traverses the Roman road.
Manors. Pettaugh Hall (C15 Henry Lancaster). *Sub-Manors.* Abbot's Hall (1310 Abbot of Leiston); Woodwards.

Roman Road.
The Roman Stone Street enters the parish on the line of Debenham Road NE of Walnutree Cottage. Beyond here, Ipswich Way roughly traces its course for a short way before entering the village. The line of the road is picked up again beyond the village by the present A1120 road and runs to the parish boundary at Boundary Cottages.

Ancient Tracks.
Pettaugh Lane provides a length of the Saxon Hundred boundary between Bosmere and Claydon from E of New Hall to the Roman Stone Street. Winston Head Lane provides a short section of the western parish boundary, and the ancient boundary between Thredling and Claydon Hundreds.

Site of old Windmill.
In 1783 a post mill stood at the staggered crossroads where the Roman Stone Street from Coddenham crosses the A1120. It was rebuilt in 1865 and finally dismantled as recently as 1957.

Workhouse.
Pettaugh had a workhouse with 15 inmates in 1776.

Historic Houses & Ancient Moated Sites.
Pettaugh Hall which lies S of the church was the seat of the Fastolf family c1524-c1670. NW of the church

PETTAUGH *(continued)*

stands the C16 Ancient House. There are moats at Moat Grove, W of the village (mutilated and now in no definite form), Laffitt's Hall, E of the village (3 sides of a small square), and Abbot's Hall, S of the last (originally rectangular - the W arm only now surviving), with possible fish-ponds to the E.

PETTISTREE *(4 miles NNE of Woodbridge)*

Wilford Hundred. 'Peohtred's tree' (OE) *Petrestre* (1253). Pettistree was only represented by its manor at Domesday - the vill of Bing which included the hamlet of Loudham ('Hluda's village'). It did not obtain an overall parish name until the C13. It also has no hall in its name. The church is dedicated to St Peter & St Paul and Morley suggests the place-name means 'Peter's Tree' - probably an old oak which stood by (or preceded) the church, under which the Black Dominican Friars preached soon after their introduction to England in 1221. Page locates Longburgh (the Domesday *Laneburc* and *Laneburgh*) here, but although its name suggests a place of considerable size, it is unlikely that it represented the missing original parish name as it only comprised 36 rateable acres and had no church.

Manors. Bing Hall (1253 Roger de Huntingfield). *Sub-Manors.* Daveler's al Bacons (Late C13 Bartholomew Davillers); Loudham Hall (1356-1543 Blennerhasset family).

Ancient Woodland.

Part of Ufford Thicks comes within the parish and is a section of ancient woodland.

Roman Tile Industry.

A Roman tile kiln was discovered on Byng Hall estate in 1846, apparently left in complete working order. Several hundred tiles, some unbaked, were unearthed.

Medieval Green.

Various lengths of water to the S which were once thought to have formed a square and to have extended eastwards for additional strength to the principle site of Pettistree Lodge, are now considered boundary ditches connected with the ancient green which lay SW of the church and was partially enclosed by 1840.

Deserted Medieval Villages.

Pettistree comprised the Domesday vills of Bing, Loudham and Caresfelda, two of which developed into townships of their own. Bing (or Byng) is situated NE of the present A12 near the Pettistree/Ufford parish boundary. Taking its name from the Byng Brook, the manor appears to have been in existence by the C9 and developed on either bank by a ford, now Byng Bridge. It was recorded with a population of 76 at Domesday and was said to have been a 'large town in Edward's reign' when Joan of Huntingfield, who then held the manor, claimed the right to hold a weekly market (1286). Later Byng church and water mill were given to found Ash Abbey in neighbouring Campsea. The former parish is remembered today in a farm called Byng Hall, Byng Hall Road, Byng Lane and Byng Bridge. The other Domesday vill which developed its own identity was Loudham to the E, centred around its hall, park and church. The hall was the seat of the Ludhams and Blenherhaysetts. The park was shown to be very extensive on Faden's 1783 map and any existing settlement here may have been removed in its creation. The church with 60 acres of glebe was mentioned in Domesday and in 1591, but appears to have been lost by 1603. It stood to the W of the hall. The only original house of Loudham hamlet which remains today is the C17 Sandpit Cottage.

Medieval Market.

In 1253 Roger de Huntingfield obtained the grant from Henry III for a market in Bing. Joan of Huntingfield had this grant renewed by Edward I in 1286.

Historic Houses & Ancient Moated Sites.

Loudham Hall, an Elizabethan manor house 3 miles NE of Woodbridge, was rebuilt by Charles Wood after 1730 but has now been demolished. Pettistree Lodge, I mile S of Wickham Market, stands within the remaining half of an ancient oval moat. The family of Wyard long resided here in Pettistree. Park Farm was attached to the nunnery at Campsey (*see* Campsey Ash).

PLAYFORD *(4 miles NE of Ipswich)*

Carlford Hundred. 'A ford of play (or even battle)' (OE) *Plegeforda* (DB). The ford in question was probably situated where the road N through the village crosses the river Fynn just E of the ancient site at Playford Hall. *Manors.* Playford/Playford Hall with Michelis (C12 Richard de Playford). *Sub-Manors.* Meer/Mere Hall; Lees.

Ancient Woodland.

Lux Wood, S of the village, is a small part of ancient woodland.

Site of Ancient Battle (?)

The 'Battle of Finnesburn' was fought when Danes falling back from Thetford in 1005 encountered the Saxon army. Playford lays claim to the site by the river Finn, but "For five long days the battle's sound was heard by Finburghe's earth-raised mound." gives the better claim to Finborough (*see* Great Finborough).

Site of Medieval Archery Practice (?)

Butts Road - 'Butt' in this instance referring to an archery target - which heads N from the western end of the village, marks the probable site of a meadow in which archery practice took place.

Historic House & Ancient Moated Site.

Playford Hall is an interesting Tudor mansion and former seat of the Fleton family (1546-1719), one of whom assassinated the Duke of Buckingham in 1659. When Sir Henry Felton owned in 1674 it was recorded as having 25 hearths. It was probably built by Sir Anthony Felton who died in 1613. It was also home to Thomas Clarkson (1761-1846) who played an equal part with the more famous William Wilberforce in the abolition of the slave trade. The Hall originally enclosed three sides of a courtyard but one wing and the chapel have been destroyed. There are two large fish-ponds to the SE and its strong square moat with a bridge and brick rivetting of late C16 and C18 date originally enclosed an earlier hall, home of the eminent knight, Sir George Felbrigg, whose splendid brass effigy of 1400 adorns the church, and whose family held the manor from late C14 to early C15.

POLSTEAD *(4½ miles SW of Hadleigh)*

Babergh Hundred. 'Place by the pool' (OE) *Polesteda* (DB). The parish no doubt gained its ancient name from the the village pond, a great expanse of water opposite the church by the road junction.
Manors. Polstead (C12 Henry de Essex). *Sub-Manors.* Sprotts; Casteles; Newstead/Newstead Hall.

Ancient Woodland.

There are several fragments of ancient woodland in the parish: Millfield Wood, N of the village in the hamlet of Polstead Heath; Stack Wood, between Polstead Heath and Hadleigh Heath; Whinnyfield Wood, Marsh Wood, and Stoney Grove, N of Bower House Tye; Bushy Park Wood, W of the village; Hightrees Farm, N of Whitestreet Green; Broom Hill, S of Whitestreet Green, and Howe and Haugh Field, E of Watson's Corner and W of Polstead Heath.

Medieval Deer Park.

Hall and church lie within a former 100 acre deer park W of the village which perhaps emparked an earlier settlement.

Ancient Gospel Oak.

The remains of an oak tree known as the 'Gospel Oak' is reputed to be over 1,300 years old and the 'oldest in England' - a claim often repeated. It stands in Polstead Park between the church and the hall and has a girth of 35'. It is said to mark the spot where missionaries stood and preached to the Saxons. A Gospel Oak Service was initially held around the tree every August, and from 1954, at Polstead Hall.

Ancient Chapel.

A chapel dedicated to Our Lady was mentioned in 1401.

Medieval Heaths & Greens.

Faden's map of 1783 shows Evans Heath and Hadleigh Heath running from Whinneyfield Wood NE to the road junction. It is now cut by the A1071 road going N and a new enclosure road heading NE called Evan's Heath. Polstead Heath to the S beyond Stack Wood has been completely built over but retains the name. Mock Beggar Green was a small green now called Bower House Tye. Wich Green was at Watson's Corner. Whitestreet Green, a narrow roadside green situated NW of the village, has been completely redeveloped and become a hamlet of

POLSTEAD *(continued)*

the same name. Salvetree Green, a tiny green bordered by Tills Farm, has probably been lost to the present A1071. Polstead Green stood E of the church on the road to Hill Farm.

Medieval Fair.

A Toy Fair held on Polstead Green every 16 June from 1759 was abolished in 1872.

Workhouse.

A workhouse with 30 inmates is recorded at Polstead in 1776.

Historic Houses & Ancient Moated Sites.

Polstead Hall, W of the church (altered and re-fronted c1816), is timber-framed and C16. Polstead Rectory is late C15 and Street Farm is a C16 farmhouse by the green. Bower House Farm lies at the W end of Bower House Tye (Mock Beggar Green in 1783) and retains a fragment of the E arm of its former moat. 'Bowre House' was leased by Richard Bocking, an ashburner, who died in 1540; the 1840 tithe map shows 'moat' as a pond but also shows an L-shaped pond to the S of the farmstead. The C15 Corders House, incorporating ships timbers in its construction, was home to William Corder executed for the murder of Maria Marten in the Red Barn in 1827.

POSLINGFORD or Poslingford-with-Chipley *(2 miles NE of Clare)*

Risbridge Hundred. 'The enclosure of Postle's (Poslingas) family' (OE) *Poslingeorda* (DB) *Poselingwrtha* (1195). Includes Chipley hamlet. It appears that down to 1327 it was called Poslingworth; its change probably refers to the crossing at the southern end of the village (where Chilton Chapel stands) of the Clare Brook by the road from Clare to Bury, although this is in the hamlet of Wentford which already represents the ford.
Manors. Poslingford Hall (-C12 Baynard family; 1275 Gilbert de Clare or Robert FitzWalter [disputed]).
Sub-Manors. Overhall; Netherhall.

Ancient Woodland.

A fragment of Hollybud Wood (formerly Arlibut Wood) on the northern parish boundary (the major part of which is in Denston parish), Shadowbush and Long Wood, also in the N of the parish, and King's Wood in the E, are all parts of ancient woodland. The extensive Chipley Wood, another section of ancient woodland situated N of Chipley Abbey, has now been lost to irresponsible 'prairie' farming, and lax government protection.

Ancient Track.

A footpath which enters the parish at TL784 476, passing New House Farm and heading N past Long Wood, traces the Hundred boundary between Risbridge and Babergh.

Ancient Priory.

1½ miles NW of the village in the hamlet of Chipley is a farmhouse known as Chipley Abbey. It stands on the site of the Priory of the Blessed Virgin Mary, a small Augustinian house founded before 1235 and only recorded with a Prior and two canons in 1343. The buildings were in a ruinous state by 1455 when the income had fallen to about £10. About 1468 the Bishop of Norwich gave permission for the priory to be annexed to the college at Stoke-by-Clare. The farmhouse incorporates a fragment of the W range of the monastic buildings which had been used as a cow-shed before their demolition in 1818. The priory church is said to have also been demolished at this time and some of the carved stones transported to the rectory garden. The 'very curious brick foundations of unknown significance' discovered in 1952 a field to the W may belong to a former dovecot connected with the priory.

Deserted Medieval Village.

In 1428 Chipley with its priory was listed as a parish with under 10 households. The priory church may have at one time incorporated (or provided) the parish church.

Medieval Fair.

From 1231 and throughout the Middle Ages in the hamlet of Wentford in the S of the parish on the road to Clare, an important fair was held annually in a field adjoining Wentford Chapel *(see Clare)*

Medieval Green.

Gosland Green, named but not shown on Faden's map of 1783, is remembered in Gosland Green Cottage.

POSLINGFORD *(continued)*

Almshouses.

The Church and Poor's Estate comprised land and two cottages, purchased in 1675, for the repair of the church and relief of the poor. The Poor's Cottage, which was in three tenements for the residence of poor persons of the parish, was burned down in 1870 and only two rebuilt.

Historic House & Ancient Moated Site

Replacing the old Manor House which they had demolished, New House, E of the church, was the home of the Goldings, a family formerly of great local importance. Sir Thomas Golding was Sheriff of Essex and Hertford in 1561 and 1569. Chipley Abbey is partly surrounded by its moat and two of the old fish-ponds remain.

PRESTON *(2 miles NE of Lavenham)*

Babergh Hundred. 'Farmstead of priests' (OE) *Prestetona* (DB)

Manors. Preston Hall/Church Hall (1155 Aubrey de Vere, Earl of Oxford). *Sub-Manors.* Swifts; Maisters; Mortimers; Priory (1219 Thomas de Mendham granted manor to Prior of Holy Trinity, Ipswich).

Medieval Green.

The current OS map names Rooksey Green on the NW parish boundary by Rookwood Lane (named after a wood which still survived in 1783). No green is named or shown on Faden's 1783 map and it may well have already gone by this time. Property boundaries now shown on the N side of the lane may well trace its former outline.

Workhouse.

A workhouse is recorded here with 16 inmates in 1776.

Historic Houses & Ancient Moated Sites.

Rushbrook Farm, overlaying the boundaries of Brettenham and Thorpe, was itself a separate 'vill' at Domesday. The manor house of Preston Hall retains fragments of a moat and was probably built (c1575) on the site of an earlier hall. It was the seat of the antiquarian Robert Ryece in the early C17, and formerly held by the de Veres, Earls of Oxford. There are two curved arms of a moat at Manor Farm, W of the village, on the site of Maisters (or Maysters) Manor. It was given by Gilbert de Kentwelle to the Preceptory of the Knights of St John at Battisford prior to 1234. At the Reformation it was granted to Andrew Judde who also obtained Priory Manor at the same time. This latter manor was held in the C13 by the Mendham and Walsham families (probably as under-tenants of the de Veres). It was granted by Thomas de Mendham to Holy Trinity Priory in Ipswich before 1331 from whence it took its name; as did Priory Farm which retains a single E-W arm (and possible remains of a S arm) of its former elongated rectangular moat. Mortimer's Farm represents Mortimers Manor which took its name from Sir William Mortimer who died in 1297.

RAMSHOLT *(5 miles SE of Woodbridge)*

Wilford Hundred. "Ram's or raven's (or Raven's [personal]) copse' (OE) *Ramesholt* (DB). Includes the Domesday vill of Peiton (Peyton).

Manors. Ramsholt (1307 Fee held by Roger Bigot). *Sub-Manors.* Peyton Hall (1135 De Peyton family; Late C14 John de Vere).

Ancient Settlement.

Evidence in the form of cropmarks seen on aerial photographs of complex and interconnecting trackways, field systems, ditches, and dark patches of extensive ancient settlement are seen N, NW and SE of the church. Sherds of Iron Age, Roman and Saxon pottery have been found over the area.

Ancient Quay & Ferry.

Fishing smacks once used the dock here which was built to ship coprolite, a fossilised animal dung which was dug up along the shores of the Deben and Orwell and used as fertiliser. A former oystery went out of use at the end of the C19. The present Ramsholt Arms was formerly the ferry-house for an ancient ferry which sailed between the quay and Kirton on the opposite shore of the river Deben.

RAMSHOLT *(continued)*

Saxon Watch tower (?)

It is thought that the ancient round tower of All Saints Church which overlooks the River Deben from its lonely, lofty site, may have originally been used as a Late Anglo-Saxon watch tower keeping an eye out for possible Danish raids.

Anglo-Saxon Settlement.

The Anglo-Saxon settlement of *Peituna* (OE Paega's Farm) recorded in Domesday is now represented by a small Jacobean house called Peyton Hall some distance SE of the church (*see below*).

Deserted Medieval Village.

Between the Ramsholt Arms and the church, a narrow valley of a tributary stream originally sheltered the main Medieval settlement. This appears to have gradually drifted away when the dock traffic dried up and the ferry ceased operation. Ramsholt still had 138 inhabitants in 1881, but now comprises only church, inn, four farms and a cottage.

Historic House & Ancient Moated Site.

The Old Hall, ancient seat of the Peytons, once stood on the site of the present farmhouse of Peyton Hall. In the C13 the family assumed the name Ufford and went on to become one of the most powerful and influential in Suffolk. The outline of the ancient hall's once strong moat remains, although most of the N side has been destroyed during construction of driveways and farm buildings; marshes protect the site from the W which may never have been moated. The meadow to the E may at one time have been a park and cut stone and brick fragments litter fields around the site.

RATTLESDEN *(5 miles W of Stowmarket)*

Thedwestry Hundred. 'Ratel's or Hraetel's valley' (OE) 'Hrethel, the king of the Geats and brother of Swerting, has left his name in Rattlesden in Suffolk'. (Haigh) *Ratesdana. Ratlesdena* (DB)

Manors. Rattlesden Hall (Abbot of St. Etheldreda, Ely). *Sub-Manors.* Woodhall; Rattlesden Castle/Thurmodes; Clopton Hall; Stanham's/Stonham's.

Lost Ancient Woodland.

Rattlesden has suffered dramatic loss of virtually all its once quite extensive ancient woodland. Field boundaries still show the extent of Rattlesden Wood (shown by Faden's in 1783) and Micklewood which covered a large area S of Louse Lane between Hightown Green (*see below*) and the parallel course of the Roman road; Birds Wood (one of the remaining fragments of the former Clopton Groves) on the northern parish boundary; and Howe Wood, S of Edgar's Farm, were felled in 1963.

Ancient River Source.

There is C14 testimony that the great river Orwell - formed from Stoke Bridge in Ipswich where the Gipping meets the tidal salt waters and runs to the sea - gets its name from a spring called Or-well in this parish. From this spring rises the river Rat which joins the Gipping at Stowmarket and flows on to Ipswich. It would appear the whole length from Rattlesden to the sea was once navigable with the (now dry) valley here being once a broad river, for the Bury monk John Lydgate describes how stone was carried here by sea and river from Normandy for the great Abbey at Bury.

'A newe cherche de dyde edefye
Ston brought from Kane out of Normandye
By the Se, and set upon the strande
At Ratylsdene, and carried forth be lande'

Roman Road.

A length of Roman Road enters the parish at Pie Hatch Farm, forming the eastern parish boundary and heading N traced by the country road to Buxhall. When this road bears right, the Roman road continues straight on outlined by field boundaries which formerly marked the course of Mitchery Lane (formerly Misery Lane). The

RATTLESDEN *(continued)*

lane itself appears just E of Manor Farm, continuing N to Walnut Tree Farm - the great drainage ditch of the old Roman road surviving like a length of moat all along its eastern side. From here the course (which from just S of the farm ceases to provide the parish boundary) is carried by Baby Lane the short distance to Poystreet Green, (formerly Posford Green) where the Roman road, drained by great ditches on either side, forded the stream. It then takes the line of a footpath heading across fields towards the church in Rattlesden village. Its course from here is lost until picked up again either by a footpath SW of Francis Farm going NW to the parish boundary SW of Corner Farm, or traced by the road from Corner Farm to Woolpit passing E of Abbey Farm. When sectioned, despite its impressive ditches, the road was found to have been only 15' wide.

Medieval Greens.

On Faden's map of 1783, Poy Street Green is shown as a tiny triangular green on a four-way junction S of the village and apparently on the line of the Roman road *(see above)*. Hightown Green is shown as a wide swathe of green lined with properties running S from Kettles Farm beyond the parish boundary by Fengate Farm and terminating at the country lane in neighbouring Brettenham between The Poplars and Potash Farm. It has been overlayed by the road to Brettenham as far as Burnthouse Farm, and from here by a public footpath to the parish boundary. S of Louse Lane, between the green and the parallel course of the Roman road, lay Rattlesden Wood, unfortunately now completely lost and replaced by arable fields. Clopton Green Farm on the northern parish boundary stands on the southern edge of Clopton Green. It originally extended either side of the Woolpit road.

Medieval Stocks.

The village stocks were probably situated in Top Street by the Almshouses. There was an account for repairing the stocks (7s. 6d.) in 1783.

Site of old Windmills.

W of Hill House Farm a disused tower mill stands beside the site of a smock mill shown standing in 1783. It was pulled down c1900.

Guildhall.

A late C16 map shows "a cottage near the Churchyard called Gildehaule". There were three Guilds in the parish: St. John Baptist and St. Trinity were likely held in the Guildhall; a third, St Margaret, was thought to have been sited some two miles from the church at Hightown Green in a dwelling house called St. Margaret's Priory.

Workhouse.

A workhouse with 26 inmates was situated in a thatched building NE of the Five Bells Inn. Accounts date from 1741. It was closed and sold in 1838.

Historic Houses & Ancient Moated Sites.

Friars Hall, in the village, is a delightful example of a small medieval house. Clopton Hall, NE of the village and built in 1681, stands on a very early settlement site and has the wet NE corner remains of a probable moat, with a series of three fish-ponds to the S (said to have been dug by the monks) created from natural springs. The original house is believed to be the guest house which belonged to the Abbot who held the manor until 1517; it was emparked in 1204. The manor house of Wood Hall, E of the village on the parish boundary, has a large rectangular moat some 120 yds. by 87½ yds, partly dry with the S arm filled in. The Old Moot House is a hall house and former meeting house of c1430. Edgard's Farm, S of the village, has the remains of a sub-rectangular moat. The N arm of a moat survives at Hollybush Farm, SW of Homestead Plantation, with a continuation and possible fish-pond to the N. There are possible remains of a moat on the W side of the road between Kettles Farm and Brook Farm, just SE of Homestead Plantation; remnants of another isolated, moated site on the country lane between Hollybush Farm and Mill House on the western parish boundary; also at Fengate Farm on the southern parish boundary; just W of Fenn Farm, close by, and another (now lost) S of Louse Lane and W of the course of Mitchery (Misery) Lane.

The former leper hospital of St. Petronella, Bury St. Edmunds from an old print.

The West Gate, Ipswich in 1769 from an engraving.

St. Gregory's Church, Sudbury, with College founded by Simon, Archbishop of Canterbury, in 1375.

Sudbury Grammar School in 1700.

(Above) Thomas Wolsey's College of St. Mary at Ipswich from an old print showing Wolsey, The Bishop of Lydda and possibly Thomas Cromwell.

(Below) The Market Cross & Moot Hall, Ipswich from an old print.

Flemish brick was used for the first time in building Little Wenham Castle in the mid C13, one of the earliest fortified manor houses in the country.

The scant remains of the Bigods' manor house of Walton Old Hall (c1291), photographed in the 1950s. Edward III is thought to have stayed here several nights in 1339 before embarking for France.

Livermere Hall, demolished 1923, from an old print.

Brightwell Hall, demolished 1750, from an old print. The church is shown in the top left-hand corner.

A romanticised print of Oakley Park, former seat of Sir Edward Kerrison. The mansion, which stood in Hoxne parish, was described as having 'a gallery, 80 feet long, supported by eight Italian marble columns of unrivalled beauty.'

Assington Hall which was burned down in 1957. Oliver Cromwell lodged here during the Civil War as a guest of the Parliamentarian Gurden family.

The Lowestoft High Light originally built in 1676, from an old print.

The magnificent Flixton Hall, built in Elizabethan style by Sir Nicholas Tasburgh in 1615. Despite being sympathetically rebuilt after a fire of 1846, one of Suffolk's finest buildings was scandalously pulled down in 1950.

On a moated site occupied by the Abbots of Bury Abbey in the C13, Rushbrook Hall, pictured here in the 1950s, entertained the entourage of Elizabeth I 'in great splendour'. The mansion was destroyed by fire during its demolition in 1961.

This three-arched Tudor bridge still spans the moat of the lost palace of Charles Brandon and Mary Tudor at Westhorpe. Mary was the sister of Henry VIII and one time Queen of France.

RAYDON *(3½ miles SSE of Hadleigh)*

Samford Hundred. 'Hill abounding in rye' (OE) *Rienduna* (DB). Rye bread was the staple food in Suffolk in Saxon times. The parish is comprised of two villages, Upper and Lower Street.
Manors. Raydon/Raydon Hall (1258 Robert de Raydon). *Sub-Manors.* Mark's/Merks; Sulveyes/Sullies/Martyns/Sulveges.

Ancient Woodland.
Raydon Great Wood on the northern parish boundary is one of the largest sections of ancient woodland still in existence in Suffolk. It is bisected by the old disused railway track, now a public walk. Long Wood and Squire's Grove, just to the NE, are also ancient remnants.

Site of Tumulus (?)
The suggestively named Barrow Hill rises above the valley of a tributary stream of the river Brett, W of the village.

Priory (?)
A priory of Cluniac monks is said to have been founded in the village during the time of Henry II and continued until the Dissolution. Nothing is known of this priory and Priory Farm, on the western parish boundary with Shelley, may have obtained its name from the fact that, after being in the hands of the Hasting family, Raydon Manor along with neighbouring Shelley was appropriated to Battle Abbey.

Mills.
Before 1783 a 'timber-built' windmill stood just S of the watermill by the river Brett which provides the western parish boundary.

Medieval Market & Fair.
Robert de Raydon had the grant of a market and fair here in 1310. In 1364 the grant was made to Helmingus Legett.

Guildhall (?)
The 1559 will of Robert Wapull of Raydon left 20 shillings "towards making the well at Guildhall when the township beginneth to make it."

Historic House.
Spider Hall at the foot of Barrow Hill in Nether Raydon is C16 with a six-bay thatched barn.

REDE *(7 miles SSW of Bury St Edmunds)*

Thingoe Hundred. 'Place at the reed bed or clearing' (OE) *Reoda* (DB). Morley considers it a personal name - 'Reade's (or Red's) place'. Either way, the earliest settlement was not likely near the church in the E of the parish, but at the ancient moated site of Rede Hall on the northern parish boundary by a distant tributary of the Chadd Brook. This would probably satisfy both place-name criteria.
Manors. Rede Hall (1200 John de Beauchamp). *Sub-Manors.* Picard al Pickard's al Cresseners.

Ancient Woodland.
Francis Wood, and the group of Great, Brush and Bromagefield Woods, on or near the western parish boundary, are all part of ancient woodland.

Site of Mound & Gallows (?)
A Mound called Mount Plantation, shown with a wet ditch on the 1839 tithe map, lay on the SE parish boundary between Mount Field and Mill Field. The latter field name suggests that the mound was sometime used for a windmill, but it may have had earlier origins and purpose. Its siting near Scoles Gate on the junction of three parishes - Rede, Hawkedon and Brockley - also make it a likely site to have held a gibbet.

Medieval Greens.
Reed Green, SW of the church, is shown and named on Faden's map of 1783 as rectangular with a southern extension running down to the stream SW of Pykards Hall. There was formerly a green near Rede Hall.

REDE *(continued)*

Historic Houses & Ancient Moated Sites.
The ancient site of Rede Hall, now a farmhouse on the northern parish boundary, is surrounded by an almost complete rectangular moat (the W side partially filled in). To the S the farm buildings are partly enclosed by a fragmentary outer moat. The complex lies to the N side of a former green and the house is shown surrounded by a small park in 1838. Remains of a moat are shown around Pykards Hall on the 1838 tithe map. This is the site of the manor of Picard (or Pickard's or Cressener's). A John Pykard had the grant of free warren here in 1305, a Nicholas Pykard was the holder in 1346 and Walter Cressener in 1428. The Plough public house dates from the C16.

REDGRAVE *(8 miles WNW of Eye)*

Hartismere Hundred. 'Reedy pit (or ditch)' or 'Red grove' (OE) *Redgrafe* (C11). Claude Morley feels more inclined to 'Red grave' implying some ancient conflict possibly connected with the three Saxon cinerary urns found in the parish (*see below*).
Manors. Redgrave (-1544 Abbot of St. Edmunds, Bury; 1544 Sir Nicholas Bacon).

River Sources.
The rivers Little Ouse and Waveney form the northern parish boundary with South Lopham and the county boundary with Norfolk. In the swampy fens at Lopham Gate, just over the boundary, a most unique situation arose when two copious springs, rising only nine yards apart, proceeded to run in opposite direction - westwards to create (with another spring-head which rises in Wattisfield) the Little Ouse, and eastwards giving birth to the Waveney which reaches the sea at Great Yarmouth.

Iron Age Settlement.
Two hut sites and occupational material were revealed when an Iron Age settlement was discovered covering fields either side of Beer Lane during pipeline excavations in 1959.

Tumulus.
A burial mound shown at Gallows Hill on the 1837 OS map near the western parish boundary, has since been lost to quarrying and is now woodland. In 1858 a Mr. J. Warren met an old man whose father had occupied land on Moneypot Hill on which stood a large mound of earth. In removing it 60-70 years before, a large number of pots were found and are now displayed in the museums at Bury and Norwich. Perhaps this the burial mound on Gallows Hill.

Roman Pottery Industry.
There was an extensive Roman pottery industry in neighbouring Hinderclay and Wattisfield, and kiln sites dating from late C1 to early C2 were found in this parish, W of the village and E of Cowfen Lane.

Ancient Way.
A Deed of 1410 shows 'Ikelyngge Weye', an ancient route running N-S through the parish (from Waters Farm to Little Grange?).

Site of Gallows (?)
Gallows Hill suggests that a gibbet was once sited on Redgrave Common, probably on the burial mound *(see above)*.

Medieval Deer Park.
Redgrave Park, a former deer park of about 200 acres enclosed by oak palings, is shown on Saxton's old map of 1575.

Medieval Green & Common.
Redgrave Green, shown on Faden's 1783 map, covered an area either side of the present B1113 from where the road bears NW, to the junction with Church Road. It survives, though partly now enclosed and developed. As today, development was round the green-edge in 1783 with the church still isolated to the E of the village. Some 386 acres of Redgrave Common was enclosed in 1818.

REDGRAVE *(continued)*

Medieval Archery Practice.

Butts Plantation, near the southern parish boundary, is suggestive of the site of a field used in medeival times for archery practice.

Medieval Market & Fair.

Redgrave obtained the grant for a market and fair in 1219 when the Bury Abbots held the manor. This grant was confirmed in 1227.

Site of old Windmill.

A post mill which stood on Gallows Hill in 1783 was demolished c1903.

Free School.

A licence to erect a Free Grammar School was granted in 1560. One schoolteacher was recorded between 1650 and 1699. There was an endowment to educate three poor children in 1686.

Workhouse.

Redgrave workhouse is recorded with 30 inmates in 1776.

Site of Historic House.

Redgrave Hall, built in 1545, remodelled in 1763 and mostly pulled down in 1950 (the rest since), stood on the ancient site of the original Hall and its deer park, built in stone in 1211 by Abbot Sampson as a hunting lodge for the abbots of Bury. The large serpentine lake covering 46 acres still remains. Sir Nicholas Bacon, Lord Keeper to Elizabeth I, made Redgrave Hall his seat, and his descendant, another Sir Nicholas, was created the chief baronet of England by James I in 1611. Sir Edmund Bacon, who held the Hall in 1644, was said to be one of the wealthiest men in Suffolk at that time. About the close of the C17 it was sold to Sir John Holt, Lord Chief Justice of the King's Bench. The Half Moon public house in Half Moon Lane was said in an article to be 'centuries old'. It is believed at one time to have been a bakery and brewed its own beer.

REDISHAM *(5 miles SW of Beccles)*

Wangford Hundred. 'Read's village or homestead' (OE) *Redesham* (DB)

Manors. Redisham Hall (1206 Hugh de Berry).

Ancient Woodland.

Gorse Thick, NW of the village, is ancient woodland.

Site of Motte (?)

Marked as 'Castle Mound' on the 1958 OS map and listed as a fort or defensive work by the *Victoria County History*, but elsewhere 'Mill Mount', the ditched earthworks in the SW corner of the parish was irresponsibly flattened and ploughed out by the local farmer in 1983. It was described in 1950 as a circular mound about 9' high surrounded by a moat with an outer rampart. It may have been a small adulturine motte erected in the time of King Stephen and later adapted as the base for a windmill from where it took its name.

Earthworks.

A large platform in a pasture field W of Church Farm may be the site of Redisham Hall. It was mentioned on an Indenture of Settlement in 1765 when Susan Knights referred to her farm 'distinguished by the Mound of Reddisham Hall' (*see Below*).

Deserted Medieval Village (?)

There is evidence in the form of shallow gulleys, low banks and mounds in unploughed pasture of previous settlement from Church Farm all along the road W to the Ilketshall parish boundary. Redisham originally comprised two villages, Redisham Magna or Great Redisham (the manor was known at the Conquest as Up-Redisham) and Redisham Parva or Little Redisham, and these earthworks suggest evidence of shrinkage of the former towards the present isolated settlement by the parish boundary. Redisham Parva has now been incorporated in neighbouring Ringsfield to the north. Nothing remains of this village - probably lost through emparking - except the ruins of All Saints Church (disused by 1450) in the park of Little Redisham Hall.

REDLINGFIELD *(3½ mles SE of Eye)*

Hartismere Hundred. 'Readel's family's clearing' (OE) *Radinghefelda* (DB) *Radlingefeld* (1166)
Manors. Redlingfield (1120 Prioress of the Benedictine Nunnery (*see below*) claimed view of frankpledge and assize of bread and beer; 1536 Edmund Bedingfield).

Ancient Woodland.
Little Wood, S of the village, is a part of ancient woodland.

Ancient Track.
Hundred Lane forms part of the western parish boundary and the hundred boundary between Hoxne and Hartismere.

Nunnery.
A C14 rectangular 2-storeyed barn of flint 54' by 15' with buttresses and fragments of windows, forms part of the buildings (possibly a guest house or infirmary) of the small Benedictine nunnery, founded in 1120 by Manasses, Count of Guisnes, and Emma his wife, daughter of William de Arras, lord of the manor of Redlingfield. The building shows sign of much rebuilding and rebuttressing. Though the foundation charter stipulated that there should be 13 nuns in the convent, the house was always poorly endowed and this number never appears to have been attained. At a visitation in 1427, the prioress, Isabel Hermyte, was compelled to resign and was banished to Wix nunnery after having admitted numerous offences including that she had 'laid violent hands on Agnes Brakle on St Luke's Day' and that she had 'been alone with Thomas Langelond, the bailiff, in private and suspicious places such as a small hall with windows closed and *sub beggerowes*'! On several other occasions bishops complained of the irreguar conduct of the inmates. Amazingly the priory made it to the Reformation in 1536 when it was dissolved and granted to Edmund Bedingfeld. If it had a conventional church it has completely disappeared (the nuns had use of the parish church so it may never have had one of its own), but its chapel is now the small, towerless parish church of St Andrew, and Redlingfield Hall, now a farmhouse, contains some remains of the nunnery buildings and possibly stands on the site of the refectory. A fragment of the moat which enclosed the nunnery remains along with 3 large fish-ponds to the W at The Leys.

Medieval Green.
Redlingfield Green remains as shown on Faden's 1783 map as a small square green lying E of the village and Green Farm.

Stocks.
The church tower held the village stocks in the C15/C16.

RENDHAM *(4½ miles E of Framlingham)*

Plomesgate Hundred. 'Cleared homestead' or 'Homestead by a hill' (OE) *Rimdham/Rindham* (DB)
Manors. Rendham (1316 John de Bruisiard/Bruseyard). *Sub-Manors.* Barmes/Barnes.

Ancient Settlement Site (?)
Aerial photographs show cropmarks W of Upper Grove Farm near the northern parish boundary. These comprise a ring-ditch c66' in diameter with a causeway facing NE adjoining a larger enclosure or ring-ditch further E in the same field c88' in diameter with a causeway facing S. There are also faint cropmarks of another possible ring-ditch c26'-33' in diameter in the NE portion of the enclosure which may be of a circular hut.

Roman Find.
In 1907 the 12" high bronze head of the Emperor Claudius (41-54 A.D.) was found by 'a youth named Arthur Godball' in mud on the banks of the river Alde which forms the SW parish boundary just below the village. It is thought to have been hacked off the full statue in the Temple of Claudius and looted during the burning of Colchester in 61 A.D. by Boudicca's followers in the Iceni uprising against Roman atrocities, and abandoned in their later retreat. It is now in the British Museum.

Medieval Feature.
On the N bank of the river Alde, S of the road to Bruisyard at the W end of the village, a palisade comprising

RENDHAM *(continued)*

pointed stakes 6" square and round stakes with planks between, was discovered in 1967 on a site with a concentration of C13-C14 pottery sherds. Its purpose is not known but the remains may have formed part of a timber bridge.

Medieval Green.
Rendham Green was shown on Faden's 1783 map as a very small triangular green in the fork of the country roads N of the church and Rendham Court Farm.

Free School.
In 1704 a Free School was founded here by the will of Thomas Neal, supported by rents from lands in Bramfield.

Historic House & Ancient Moated Site.
The Manse was built in red brick c1750. Parts of a small moat remain adjoining the S side of the B1119 road and very close to the eastern parish boundary. A C19 map marks the site 'Poor House'.

RENDLESHAM *(5 miles NE of Woodbridge)*

Loes Hundred. 'Rendel's homestead' (OE) *mansio Rendili* (c730 A.D.). Skeat considers Rendlesham 'very old' relative to normal Saxon place-names and almost certainly already in existence by King Redweald's reign (593-617 A.D.) (*see below*).
Manors. Naunton Hall (C13 Henry de Naunton). *Sub-Manors.* Colvilles; Bavents/Bavents Hall; Caketons.

Ancient Woodland.
Whitmore Wood, between the old US airfield and the A1152 road, is part of ancient woodland.

Tumuli.
How (or Haugh) Hill, named 'Hoo Hill' on the OS map, SE of High House Farm, was described in 1972 as being a broad low mound 66' in diameter and 1' high, but now appears to have gone. There is a drawing by Davy of a Saxon urn said to have been unearthed here and now in the British Museum, but Bruce Mitford considers the urn's location at Hoo Hill Piece further to the E. Another round barrow on the eastern edge of Cottage Wood, SE of Ash Lodge, 82' in diameter and 6½' high, was identified in 1983 as Bronze Age.

Ancient Track & Way.
An ancient track known as Rogues Lane which runs E from Ash Road by Rogueslane Belt to the former Ash Green (now Barnes Grove), provides part of the the northern parish boundary with Campsey Ash. Friday Street, now comprising a footpath track across the heath, was a former medieval highway and is marked and named on Faden's map of 1783.

Site of Seat of Saxon Royal House (?)
According to Bede, the seat of the East Anglian Royal House of the Wuffingas *mansio Rendili* was at Rendlesham. Redweald, King of the East Angles, kept court here and embraced Christianity; afterwards, persuaded by his wife, he is said to have had altars in the church for the worship of both Christ and Woden. Sudhelm, another East Anglian king, was afterwards baptised here by Cedda, Archbishop of York. A little further S is the site of the Sutton Hoo tumuli with the world famous Saxon ship burial believed to have once contained Redwald's body, and, adjoining this site, an extensive Saxon cemetery (*see* Sutton). An ancient gold or silver crown weighing about sixty ounces and supposed to have belonged to one of the East Anglian kings was found in the parish in 1690. It was apparently sold and melted down. Several sites for Redwald's timber 'palace' have been suggested: Field names on an 1828 map of Rendlesham include 'Great Woodenhall', 'Great Hall Wall', 'Middle Hall Wall', etc., plus Hall Walls Wood lying to the N of the parish, and Woodenhall Grove (now Bush Covert), all of which, as Norman Scarfe states, just seem too good to be true. The church has an extraordinarily early dedication to the C7 St. Gregory (as at Sudbury), which may again point to a location close by. Pottery finds SW and NW of the church have confirmed early settlement here (*see below*). At Thistly Belt, about halfway between Rendlesham Hall and the Campsea Ash road, a ring of trees defined by a shallow ditch, with another shallow ditch dividing it from E to W may also suggest the possible site.

RENDLESHAM *(continued)*

Medieval Industrial Sites.
Evidence of industrial activity in the form of hop and hemp fields, and lime burning and brick making kilns has been found in the parish.

Deserted Medieval Village.
The siting of the Saxon royal seat here suggests a considerable population in those days, and the subsequent granting of a market, fair and free warren suggests that there was also an active village settlement in medieval times. Fieldwalking has confirmed that this settlement was always likely to have been in the area of the present church. A fairly dense scatter of Roman, Saxon and Medieval pottery was found in the SW of the field adjacent to the church, and in a field to the NW of the church a wide scatter of Roman, Saxon (including early Saxon handmade pottery) and Medieval sherds have been discovered. Yet apart from the new development relating to the abandoned American Airbase of Bentwater, there are now only six isloated properties in the parish.

Medieval Green.
The area between the church and Naunton Hall marks a former green.

Recreation.
Camp Field, next to the water tower, probably identifies a former meadow used for medieval ball games.

Medieval Market & Fair.
A market and fair was granted to Hugh Fitz-Otho by Edward I (1272-1307), and free warren by his successor Edward II to Hugh de Naunton.

Historic Houses.
The site of the old hall known as 'Rendlesham White House' (previously Naunton Hall), the main of four Rendlesham manors (which also included Colvyles, Bavents and Caketons), lies to the E of Rendlesham Hall Farm. It was situated in an extensive park of some 300 acres later landscaped by Humphry Repton. It is shown on Faden's map of 1783 but not on Bowen's of 1755. The house was burned down in 1830 leaving 'some ruins including a tower and the front entrance doorway'. A new hall was erected on the site between 1868-71 by William Burn, Fifth Lord of Rendlesham 'in Jacobean style', but this suffered the same fate being badly damaged by a fire in 1898 and rebuilt again in red brick. After being requisitioned by the army in 1939, it was left in such a bad state after the war that in 1949 it had to be pulled down. Two elaborate lodge houses survive from the earlier hall: the Woodbridge Lodge - all flying buttresses, and the Ivy Lodge in mock Norman, both dating from c1790. A farmhouse called Naunton Hall, N of the church, represents the early C17 house built by the Spencer family who acquired the Manor of Naunton Hall in 1556. High House Farm retains part of the former C17 house.

REYDON *(2 miles NNW of Southwold)*

Blything Hundred. 'Rye hill' (OE) *Rienduna* (DB)
Manors. Reydon (c1205 Sir Hugh de Cressy; c1276 William de Valence, Earl of Pembroke). *Sub-Manors.* Reydon Blevilis; Reydon Wingfields/Reydon Ugghall.

Tumuli (?)
Three mounds thought to be Bronze Age round barrows situated near Reydon Grove Farm and S of Smear Lane may, in fact, be clearance mounds from Twelve Acre Pit immediately to the E.

Roman Industrial Site.
Roman building material found in the plantation at Reydon Smear along with a scatter of pottery along the eastern boundary of the wood are marked as Roman brick kilns on the 1982 OS map. It is also possible that they are evidence of tile kilns, or the remains of a salt working site similar to that at Blythburgh which was originally also identified as a tile kiln site.

Site of Ancient Quay & Watermill.
At one time fishing vessels and small coastal craft used to ascend the river Blyth as far as this parish and

REYDON *(continued)*

Wolsey's Creek (formerly Woods-End Creek) where there was a watermill and where vestiges of a wharf remain. This probably fell into decay in the reign of Henry III in consequence of the rising prosperity of Southwold - said to have been at that time only a hamlet of Reydon. On the same rivulet is Wolsey Bridge which was converted into a sluice for draining the marshes by Sir John Rous in 1747. The bridge was stated by Gardner to have been built at the expense of Cardinal Wolsey who, as a boy, is said to have helped his father drive cattle from the Reydon Marshes to Ipswich. Whether this story is true depends on your viewpoint over his father's occupation as a common butcher or wealthy merchant.

Site of Ancient Chapel.
The Chapel of St. Margaret de Rissemere, mentioned in a grant to Wangford Priory of c1200, is said to have stood at Rissemere (the hamlet of Reydon Smear?) 1 mile E of Reydon Church. Nothing is known of its history and there are no remains.

Medieval Shrine.
In 1472 pilgrimages were made to an image of St. Remigius, perhaps connected with the chapel (*see above*).

Medieval Park.
Reydon was described by historian Thomas Gardner in 1754 as enjoying 'a market and a park, there being some lands still retaining the appellation of the market close with high, low and middle park pieces and park lane'.

Medieval Common.
Reydon Common is shown on Faden's map of 1783 covering an extensive area E and S of the church and joining Cove Common to the N.

Medieval Market & Fair.
Reydon received the grant for a market and fair in 1310.

Shrunken Medieval Settlement.
Apart from the church, old hall site and a scattering of isolated farmsteads, there is little to show that Reydon was once a place of some importance. Yet in medieval times it had a market and St Margarets was the 'mother church' of Southwold. It later decayed through the 'late' development of Southwold and its fishing industry. Reydon's church was subsequently eclipsed by the magnificent effigy built in the town in the second half of the C15, and today Reydon has ironically become the site for Southwold's residential overspill.

Medieval College.
A College is said to have been founded here by Sir John Wingfield and granted to the Bishop of Norwich. It was dedicated to St. Mary, St. John Baptist and St. Andrew.

Historic House.
The former Reydon Hall which stood in its own park and was the seat of the Ewen family, was taken down in 1684 by Oliver Dave and a new hall, considerably altered in 1860, erected on a different site.

RICKINGHALL INFERIOR *(8 miles NE of Ixworth)*

Blackbourn Hundred. 'Sheltered corner of land of Rica's people' (OE) *Rikingahala* (DB). The place-name refers to the sheltered nook which lies in the valley on the E bank of a tributary of the river Waveney in the NE corner of the parish.
Manors. Rickinghall Inferior al Westhall (-1544 Abbot of St. Edmunds; 1544 Sir Nicholas Bacon).

Ancient Woodland.
Calke Wood in the NW of the parish, and the extensive Westhall Wood in the S, are ancient woodland.

Iron Age Settlement.
A settlement site dating from c300-150 B.C., with signs of a rectangular hut, was discovered W of Broom Hills.

Multi-Period Industrial & Settlement Sites.
A multi-period site was excavated by Basil Brown SE of Broom Hills in 1964-8 when the discovery of over 1,000

RICKINGHALL INFERIOR *(continued)*

Mesolithic and Neolithic worked flints provided evidence of a flint industry here. The excavations suggested that the site was once a Neolithic causeway camp measuring c98 yds. by 175 yds, but due to the fact that 109 sherds of C5-C6 pagan Saxon pottery sherds and many Saxon metal objects were also found here, Basil Brown thought that a pagan Saxon manor house had been imposed upon the Neolithic camp. Unfortunately the great local archaeologist - immortalised for his discovery of the Sutton Hoo ship burial; considered the greatest discovery in British archaeological history - became ill on the site which was then abandoned. He never excavated again. Calke Wood, NW of the parish, revealed another multi-period settlement site. It consisted of an area of hollows many of which contained features. The area was encompassed within an earthwork - possibly Medieval field boundaries - and had been used extensively as a source of pottery clay throughout the settlement periods and into modern times. All periods were represented here - Mesolithic, Neolithic, Bronze Age, Iron Age, Roman, Saxon, Medieval and Post-Medieval.

Medieval Greens.

Allwood Green, not mentioned at Domesday when it was probably all virgin forest, became Suffolk's largest green providing common grazing for the five parishes across whose boundaries it lay - Gislingham (E), Finningham (SE), Walsham-le-Willows (SW), and the two Rickinghalls, Inferior (NW) and Superior (NE). A licence 'to close a waye leading from Merssh to Aldewodegrene' in 1332 confirms its orginal name of Aldwood. Despite its immense size, it was enclosed under the 'Enclosure of Commons Act' of 1818 and nothing remains. Snape Green was shown on Faden's 1783 map as a strip green on the junction of a road which once ran from the point on Snape Hill, E of Snape Plantation, where a drive now heads N past Snape Farm.

Site of old Windmill.

A post mill which stood on the S side of Mill House in 1783 was down c1885.

Historic Houses & Ancient Moated Site.

There are indications of a moat in front of Hill House, NW of the church, with ponds and infilled ponds surrounding the building. The house is referred to as Mansion House in 1819. Broom Hills on the northern parish boundary was a manor house and former dower house of Redgrave Hall. In the hamlet of West Street, old building foundations and a flint-lined well were thought by Basil Brown to have possibly been the site of West Hall Manor, a major manor of Rickinghall belonging to the Abbey at Bury. Nearby is the farmhouse called West Hall and the ancient Westhall Wood. The Bell Hotel dates from the 1600s.

RICKINGHALL SUPERIOR *(8 miles NE of Ixworth)*

Hartismere Hundred. The Hundred boundary between Blackbourn and Hartismere runs NE-SW down the middle of the southern end of Rickinghall Street dividing the parishes of Inferior (NW) and Superior (SE). The northern end of the street is entirely in Superior where the boundary is provided to the NW by the stream. *Manors.* Facon's Hall (C13 Talbots of Hintlesham). *Sub-Manors.* St. Johns/Fitz Johns (1428 Bishop of Chichester); Crowe's Hall.

Iron Age Site.

Two Bronze Age circular pits excavated at Cooks Field in Gardenhouse Lane produced worked flints and pottery sherds.

Roman Industrial Site.

A large Roman pottery site situated S of the street and extending over Gardenhouse Field and Pound Field was excavated by Basil Brown in 1946.

Roman & Saxon Site.

In the hamlet of Candle Street, S of the church, a Roman site of the C3-C4, and a Saxon hut site of C7-C8 were discovered.

Ancient Way.

The ancient road known as Pake Way (the present B1113) leads from Allwood Green to Rickinghall passing to

RICKINGHALL SUPERIOR *(continued)*

the E of Falcon's Hall. It has now been bisected by the new A143 bypass.

Medieval Green.
The massive Allwood Green which covered parts of five parishes formerly covered the southern corner of the parish (*see* Rickinghall Inferior). Sugland Green, a small square green is shown on Faden's 1783 map by Suggenhall Farm in Church Lane.

Medieval Market.
Although there is no record of a grant, in 1679 Rickinghall Superior is referred to as 'a little market town with a good market on Thursday'.

Guildhall.
A charter dated 1521 speaks of 'one acre of land with house built thereon called "The Guildhalle" in Rickinghall Superior'. On another charter of later date this "Gyldehall" is said to lie in a field eastwards of the churchyard.

Historic House & Ancient Moated Multi-period Site.
Excavations by the archaeologist Basil Brown in 1961-64 at the moated site of Falcons (formerly Facons) Hall, revealed it as a multi-period settlement site with Neolithic flints, Roman pottery sherds and sherds of Middle Saxon Ipswich Ware, and Medieval. Portions of the rectangular moat survive and revealed the remains of at least two buildings thought to have been former manor houses. The earliest was constructed of clay and timber with C14-C15 pottery, and to the E was a further wing of a separate building of early brick and flint with C16-C18 pottery. There were many C13 sherds also found suggesting the possibility of an even earlier building. The name Facon's Hall probably refers to Walter Fawkonn, son of John of Eye, the owner in 1327. An ancient way traced by the present B1113 road passes E of the site (*see above*).

RINGSFIELD *(2½ miles SSW of Beccles)*

Wangford Hundred. 'Hring's clearing' (ON + OE) *Ringesfelda* (DB). Annexed to Ringsfield from 1450, the decayed hamlet of Redisham Parva was absorbed into Ringsfield in 1627.
Manors. Ringsfield (1314 Garneys family; absorbed by Redisham Hall Manor); Redisham Hall Manor (1206 Hugh de Berry; 1420 Garney family). *Sub-Manors.* Redisham Parva.

Ancient Woodland.
The Great Wood, The Briary, and The Bottle and Glass Wood, in the W of the parish, are all parts of ancient woodland.

Site of Deserted Medieval Village.
Aerial photographs show traces of the vanished settlement of Little Redisham (Redisham Parva) in Redisham Hall park where there is still a fragment of the wall of its church of St James, in ruins by 1613 and shown as such on Faden's map of 1783. Once a separate parish it was consolidated with Ringsfield some time ago (*see above*).

Medieval Green.
Ringsfield Common, a large wide linear green, is shown by Faden following the line of Redisham Road N from the junction of footpaths, past Pound Farm to the road crossing. It then went NE following the present Cromwell Road, N from Cromwell Road crossing on the line of a public track to Ringsfield Road and terminating N of Barnaby Farm, probably where the road turns sharp right and left and a track goes W to Lodge Farm.

Historic House.
An impressive monument to Nicholas Garnys (1592) in the churchyard of Ringsfield Church says that he "builded Redisham Hall" (demolished 1820). A new house was built on another site by John Garden in 1823.

RINGSHALL *(4½ miles S of Stowmarket)*

Bosmere & Claydon Hundred. 'Hring's sheltered corner of land' (ON + OE) *Ringeshala* (DB). The place-name describes the site of the hall and church which occupy a sheltered position in the valley on a bend in the stream. *Manors.* Ringshall (c1523 John Blyant). *Sub-Manors.* Charles Hall; Rawlins; Rockell's/Willisham and Rockells.

Ancient Woodland.
Muckinger Wood to the E, and Ten Wood (part of which has been lost to the airfield), are sections of ancient woodland. Charles Hall Wood, SW of Charles Hall and still shown on the 1959 OS map, was de-forested at the time the road from Moat Farm to Ringshall Church was re-aligned further N to facilitate the expansion of the airfield; it is still outlined in field boundaries.

Roman Road.
The course of a Roman road (Margary 34a Bridge Street - Coddenham) passes ESE-WNW under the runway of Wattisham Airfield and then on the line of a service road as an extension of Needham Lane and forming part of the southern parish boundary.

Ancient Earthworks.
The church is thought to stand on an earlier fortified site - perhaps Hring's sheltered home (*see above*).

Site of Ancient Chapels.
There was formerly a free chapel here, built in 1174, and belonging to the Prior and Convent of Norwich. Endowed with 'thirty two acres of land, and two parts of all tithe, corn and hay of the ancient demesne' it was granted along with the manor to the chapel of St. Edmund at Hoxne in 1294 and served by a special chaplain until the dissolution of Hoxne Priory. The *Gentleman's Magazine* described it as the 'Chapel in Ruins' in 1823. Some remains are said to have been incorporated in Chapel Farm to the W. Box Tree Farm, also lost with the road re-alignment (*see above*), was built c1300 as a timber-framed chapel and converted to a 2-storey building in the C16. It received a brick front in 1903.

Medieval Green.
Ringshall Green is named but not shown by Faden in the area of Ringshall Stocks.

Medieval Market.
Thomas Charles, Lord of the Manor of Charles Hall, obtained the grant for a market in Ringshall in 1270.

Historic Houses & Ancient Moated Sites.
Chapel Farm, a Georgian farmhouse, sits within the ancient irregularly-round moat which previously encompassed the Manor House of the Rockwells. It was inherited by Sir Thomas Gresham who came here in 1565 to arrange for the preparation of timber from adjacent Battisford for the building of his Royal Exchange in London. Ringshall Grange, S of the church and the former Rectory, retains the major part of its rhomboidal moat, and there are moats at Moat Farm near the western parish boundary, and at Burnthouse Barn N of Chestnut Farm; both have three parts of a square intact. Ringshall Hall, by the church, stands on the site of the old hall demolished towards the end of the C18. A farmhouse on the northern parish boundary stands on the site of the manor house of Charles Hall and carries the name; in 1270 Thomas Charles was in possession.

RISBY *(4 miles NW of Bury St Edmunds)*

Thingoe Hundred. 'Farmstead in brushwood' (ON) *Ringeshala* (DB)
Manors. Risby al Risby Sextens al Westley (-c1539 Abbot of St. Edmunds, Bury; c1539 Sir Thomas Kytson). *Sub-Manors.* Charmans; Coldhall.

Ancient Woodland.
Hyde Wood on the eastern parish boundary, and Oak Pin and Old Broom N of the village, are ancient woodland.

Ancient Linear Earthwork.
Black Ditches, a linear earthwork of bank and ditch, and a possible ancient boundary, runs NNW-SSE through

RISBY *(continued)*

Risby Poor's Heath, and is traceable on the ground for 1½ miles in three sections from the northern parish boundary. The ditch on the W side is filled in and there are slight indications of a second ditch (*see* Cavenham).

Tumuli.

There are several round barrows in the parish. One at Barrow Bottom beside the main Newmarket Road was cut through by road works in 1771 when several inhumation burials, an urned cremation and two iron spears were found, followed three years later, by a full skeleton; roadworks in 1975 finally destroyed the barrow. The remainder were on Risby Poor's Heath N of the village. One opened in 1820 by Sir Thomas Gage had finds dating from Bronze Age to Saxon; it was ploughed flat in 1977. Another 98' in diameter and 3' high had an empty Iron Age pot and was destroyed on the SW side by the Risby-Cavenham road. This is also now under the plough, as is another, in the intriguingly-named Highwayman's Vineyard, levelled by ploughing in 1977. One of two round barrows on 'Long Heath Field' was 56' in diameter but has been completely levelled; the other, 38' in diameter and 1½' high remains under grass recently replanted with young trees. In the NE corner of the Heath, a barrow 50' in diameter and 5' high was bulldozed flat in 1981; another 60' in diameter and 3' high is no longer visible in the ploughed field. A low mound 131' in diameter and under one foot high S of Twenty Acre Hill may be the remains of another round barrow.

Medieval Green.

The two small triangular greens remain as shown on Faden's 1783 map on the road junctions in the village W of the church.

Guildhall (?)

A Guildhall may have originally been sited in Risby as four guilds, including Holy Trinity, were formed here.

RISHANGLES *(4 miles S of Eye)*

Hartismere Hundred. 'Brushwood slope' (OE) *Risangra* (DB) *Ryshangles* (1327). It is said that rushes formerly grew here in great profusion which no doubt accounts for the strange-sounding Anglo-Saxon name 'a hill-side wood, near which brushwood or rushes grow.'

Manors. Rishangles (C12 Sir Robert Sackville held of Honor of Eye; 1302 Bryan de Hickling vested in Redingfield Nunnery).

Medieval Green.

The 1783 map shows Rishangles Green covering the junction near Common Farm, S of the church on the present B1077 road.

Site of old Windmill.

A composite mill called Wright's Mill was burnt down in 1903. It had stood on the W side of the B1077 road at The Homestead since before 1783.

Historic Houses & Ancient Moated Sites.

Woodhouse Farm, N of the church, has a rectangular moat, and there are the remains of a square moat (one arm and a fragment of another, probably with enclosures) at Barnaby's Farm, S of the parish. Buck's Hall, on the southern boundary, retains 2 sides of a rectangular moat.

ROUGHAM *(3½ miles SE of Bury St Edmunds)*

Thedwestry Hundred. 'Homestead on rough ground' (OE) *Ruhham* (DB). Probably all rough heathland in Saxon times and given to Bury Abbey by Earl Ulfketel at the Conquest.

Manors. Rougham Hall (-1539 Abbot of St. Edmunds; 1539 John Drury). *Sub-Manors.* Elde al Oldhall al Old Haugh and Lehoo; Lawneys; Kings Hall; Chavents; Lee Hoo; Sudburyes al Drurye's; Netherhall.

Ancient Woodland.

Kiln Grove and Elderstub Wood SW of the parish, Tinker's Wood at Kingshall Green to the S, and Cherin's Wood on the eastern parish boundary, are all parts of ancient woodland.

ROUGHAM *(continued)*

Roman Road.

The course of the ancient Peddars Way, a former Roman road, runs SSW-NNE to provide the parish boundary with Rushbrook along Eastlow Road. Its line is completely lost beyond the tumulus - probably by the creation of Rougham Park - but is taken up (though not evident on the ground) by the parish boundary from the Thurston to Battlies Green road NE to the northern parish boundary, immediately S of Thurston village.

Roman Tumuli.

In Eldo (Oldhaugh) Manor, a 'Grange of the Abbot' (Kirby), N of Newhall Covert, Eastlow Hill, a group of four Roman barrows, stood at the intersection of the Rougham Green road with the old Roman route now taken by the road from Little Whelnetham. Two of the three which have been destroyed were 50' in diameter and contained cist burials, glassware and early C2 terra sigillata. The larger barrow, still surviving and over 20' high, was opened in 1844. In a brick vault within, a lead coffin raised on a platform contained a single male skeleton. The absence of finds suggests a Christian burial. There is a mound, marked and named as such on the OS map, on the N side of the road from Thurston to Battlies Green. This may be another round barrow.

Roman Villa (?)

SW of Lake Farm, and a short distance from Eastlow Hill, the remains of a Roman building with white stucco flooring was found in the 1840s. Surface finds of tile tesserae and painted wall plaster have confirmed the position of one or more buildings.

Medieval Heath & Greens.

An extensive heath is shown covering a large area of the parish on Faden's map of 1783. It was called Blowthorn Heath and extended from beyond the NW boundary, S to the area of Blackthorpe where a small area which survived enclosure in 1815 is still called Rougham Heath. Just beyond this NW extension into neighbouring Great Barton is Cattishall (perhaps the site of another of Ulfketel's halls). Now enclosed, the triangular Rougham Green (shown on the same map) ran NE from Eastlow Farm following the line of Moat Lane. The E side is marked by a footpath called Oak Lane, and the S side by a curving field boundary behind Rougham Green Farm. The large Kingshall Green ran S from Kingshall Farm on the line of the present road, to the parish boundary where it connected with Bradfield Green. The Rougham enclosure map also shows a field named Bromley Green. Although not shown by Faden its position is now marked by Broom Plantation.

Site of old Windmill.

A post mill stood on Mill Heath in 1698. It was disused by 1882.

Free School.

In 1720 Edmund Sparke, one of a noble family of benefactors, bequeathed certain estates here for the foundation of a free school and willed that the scholars should include four from neighbouring Thurston. A year later Thomas Sparke made provision for schooling eight children of Rougham and Bradfield St George as well as weekly bread distribution among the poor of the parish.

Medieval Grange.

The manor of Elde or Old Hall belonged to the Abbot of St. Edmunds in Bury and held a Grange. They also held Lawneys Manor and had property in the manors of Kings Hall and Chavents. The site of Old Hall was N of the church in the area of the 'nursery' on the S side of the present A14 road. The public footpath from the church, still bordered by an avenue of old trees, marks the line of the formal approach to the Hall.

Historic Houses & Ancient Moated Sites.

The building which replaced the grange (*see above*) was the hall probably erected by Sir Jeffrey Burwell, a great benefactor of the parish, in the early C16. North of the Hall is the park of the building which probably replaced this, Rougham Hall, built c1834 'with battlements and towers' but itself derelict by 1961. There is a large impressive trapezoid moat at Moat Farm, Rougham Green, and the remains of another (one wet arm) just SW of this on the site of The Chantry (formerly the Rectory) and shown on the enclosure map of 1815 as a rectangular trapezoid. There is a large strong rectangular moat, perfectly preserved, at Rougham Place to the NE and just S

ROUGHAM *(continued)*

of the main A14 road. Rougham Place is now a farmhouse but the original house was H-shaped and shown within the moated area on the 1815 map. The house was erected by Sir Robert Davers after 1684, but prior to this (until 1640) the manor was held by the Drury family who no doubt had an even earlier house on the site. There is evidence of former enclosures and associated features covering the whole field S of the farmhouse. Lawney's Farm, mentioned in a will of William Drury in 1450, is now mostly of C17 date but still retains the N and W arms of a rectangular moat. Chevin's Wood, on the eastern parish boundary, is the site of a very old circular moat which formerly surrounded the manor house of 'Chavents' (recorded 1271-1420). Part of the moat was still showing in 1958 but has now gone; C13 pottery has been found on the site. C16 Rookery House which stands beside the major A14 road to Bury and the Midlands has been converted to Ravenwood Hall Hotel.

RUMBURGH *(4 miles NNW of Halesworth)*

Blything Hundred. 'Wide stronghold' or 'Strongold made of tree trunks' (OE) *Romburch* (c1050) *Ramburc* (DB) *Manors.* Rumburgh (1286 Sir John de Vallibus; given at an unknown date to Rumburgh Priory).

Ancient Fort (?)

Whether 'wide', used as a 'moot' or meeting place for the Saxon Council, or made of tree trunks (which it inevitably would have been), the place-name confidently points to a major 'stronghold' here. The only possible site in the parish evident on the ground is that of the moated priory (*see below*). It has been suggested that this was previously a Roman encampment which formed a garrison to defend the Roman Stone Street they had constructed nearby, though it is still some way to the W of this road. The Saxon place-name would then have been taken from this site which they recolonised, perhaps using it for council meetings and later establishing the priory here within the moat. Another possible site is the suggestively-named 14 acre 'close' called 'Warpullocks' mentioned in 1758 and again in 1826 as part of Town Estate lands.

Ancient Track.

An ancient packway, now a public footpath, heads N for Bungay from Banks' Lane (which forms a part of the eastern parish boundary for a short way) to The Street, then N from opposite Moat Farm to the parish boundary W of the remains of Rumburgh (also known as Tinker's) Wood. The Way then turns NE passing N of the wood.

Priory.

Rumburgh Priory, one of the most interesting of the smaller religious houses of Suffolk, was founded about 1065 by Ethelmar, Bishop of Elmham and Thurstan, and Abbot of St Benet at Holme as a Benedictine Priory dedicated to St Michael and St Felix. At Domesday it had 12 monks in residence. In the early C12, Stephen, Earl of Brittany, made it a cell of the great Abbey of St Mary at York, the abbots of which thereafter appointed the priors until its suppression in 1528. It was then assigned to Cardinal Wolsey's collegiate foundation at Ipswich. A survey of the site was made soon after this which stated that 'there ys a seynt in the churche of Rumburgh called Seynt Bory (Bury), to which there is moche offeryng uppon Michelmass-day of money and cheses.' Measurements of the buildings were given from which it has been possible to reconstruct their plan. The Norman priory church is a long aisleless building with an unfinished oblong C13 W tower and a C15 S porch. Nothing remains of the monastic buildings which stood to the N - the site of the refectory is occupied now by the C17 timber-framed Abbey Farmhouse. The precinct was surrounded by a rectangular moat, part of which remains. A gatehouse stood on the western side, and there are traces of other enclosures. After the Dissolution, and despite strong protests from York, Cardinal Wolsey (who had taken possession of the priory) refused to return valuables which the Abbot of York had deposited here.

Medieval Common.

Although the 100 acre Rumburgh Common, shown and named on Faden's 1783 map, was enclosed in 1851, its limits can still be easily identified. The new straight road heading SW from opposite Rumburgh Place Farm at the top of Nunn's Hill defines its southern limit. From here it headed N, its boundary outlined by the rear property boundaries W of Mill Road and E of New Road (created following enclosure). The northern boundary is marked by the curving road leading into The Street.

RUMBURGH *(continued)*

Recreation.

It is thought possible that Rumburgh Common was used as a Camping (form of medieval football) ground.

Historic Houses & Ancient Moated Sites.

Moat Farm, E of Rumburgh Common, retains the northern side and a fragment of the southern side of its medieval moat. There is also a moat and traces of other enclosures at the Priory (*see above*).

RUSHBROOKE *(3 miles SE of Bury St Edmunds)*

Thedwestry Hundred. 'Rushy' brook' (OE) *Ryscebroc* (DB). Morley considers the place-name to come from a limb of the river Lark, here called Black Water, which would have been broadly marshy in early times.

Manors. Rushbrook (1180 Scotland de Rushbrooke held of the Abbot of St. Edmunds, Bury).

Ancient Woodland.

The extensive Rushbrooke Wood (formerly Link Wood and mostly in Bradfield parish), is part of ancient woodland.

Roman Road.

The Roman road from Long Melford to Pakenham (Margary 33a) follows the line of the existing Linkwood Road and Eastlowhill Road (the latter forming the eastern parish boundary with Rougham) SSW-NNE through the parish.

Medieval Chapel (?)

A diary of a Henry Machyn, giving an account of the funeral of Sir Thomas Jermyn in 1552, suggests that Sir Thomas had maintained a chapel of 'syngyng men' at Rushbrook. This would support the theory of collegiate priests existing in the parish. A Field Book compiled by Sir Jermyn Davers in 1730 lists a Chanters (Chaintus) Close. The unusual design of the interior of St. Nicholas church (the aisle being divided into three distinct sections) suggest that the chapel may have been sited in the church.

Site of Medieval Park.

Fragments of Rushbrooke Hall's great park survive SW of the hall's moated site, in Polsespond Wood, Great and Little Spinney and North Hill Covert. Also in former lodges at Park Farm in the SW, and on the eastern corner of Little Spinney in the NW.

Deserted Medieval Village.

In pasture opposite the church, hollow ways and house platforms mark the site of the original village by the former Green. It would appear to have been demolished as recently as 1938 when the estate and village were purchased by Lord Rothschild who created a 'new' village of mock Tudor houses the following year; the farm buildings also date from this time. Fieldwalking in 1979 by Polsespond Wood, NW of the church, also discovered 'fairly well preserved ditches and banks with traces of a moat (?) and various humps and bumps' S of the Rushbrooke Estate (a later 1955-63 phase of house-building).

Medieval Green.

Shown but unnamed on Faden's map of 1783, Rushbrooke Green was a small square green situated in the area of Home Farm and infilled with houses on the 1839 tithe map. A green-edge ditch on the S side of the SE extension running towards the church partly survives as an earthwork in parkland. Home Farm was formerly known as Green Farm.

Medieval Pump House.

In the centre of homes that form the modern village on the Rushbrooke Estate stands a small octagonal brick pump house of c1600 (?) Its position originally formed the centre of Rushbrooke Green *(see above)*.

Almshouses.

There were formerly two almshouses here. One 'for three poor women and one poor man' was rebuilt by Thomas, Lord Jermyn, Privy Counciller and Comptroller of the Household to Charles I, who endowed it in 1700. The other comprised four tenements erected by Sir Jermyn Davers about 1724, but unendowed.

RUSHBROOKE *(continued)*

Historic House & Ancient Moated Site.

Rushbrooke Hall was described as being a large Tudor mansion forming three sides of a square with polygonal turrets at each corner and standing in an extensive wooded park of 150 acres skirted on the W by the river which supplied the deep moat and a lake of seven acres. The ancient moat from which the E and W sides of the house rose sheer out of the water was 35' wide in places and lined with dressed stone. The site went back to at least the C13 when it was held by the Abbey at Bury - Rushbrooke Lane, now part country road, part public footpath, originally ran direct from the site to the South Gate at Bury. After the Dissolution it was granted by Henry VIII to the Jermyns who probably built the most recent hall. The family had held the manor from c1230 to 1703, and during the period they resided here (c1550-1683), they rose to considerable eminence. Sir Robert twice entertained the entourage of Elizabeth I here in great splendour: in 1578 ' Sir Robert Jermyn, of Roesbroke, feasted the French ambassadors two several times, with which charges and courtesie they stood marvellously contented'. Tragically, the great mansion came to an ignominious end, being destroyed by fire during its demolition in 1961 - a period which became known for its insensitivity towards anything old and resistant to change. The moated island is now overgrown with trees though the line of the main range of buildings can still be detected and the cellars still exist, though now filled in.

RUSHFORD *(4 miles SE of Thetford)*

Blackbourn & Guiltcross (Norfolk) Hundreds. 'Enclosure where rushes grow' (OE) *Rissewrth* (c1060) *Rusceuuorda* (DB)

Once in Suffolk, along with its neighbour Thetford, then partly in Suffolk and partly in Norfolk, the parish which lies either side of the Little Ouse river (providing the county boundary) has now become a part of Norfolk with the Suffolk portion annexed to Euston. The church and college are in the former, and Rushford Hall in Suffolk. There is now no indication of any village settlement S of the river which housed 26 of the 169 inhabitants in Blackbourn Hundred in 1881.

RUSHMERE *(6 miles ESE of Beccles)*

Mutford & Lothingland Hundred. 'Rushy mere' (OE) *Ryscemara* (DB). Suckling says that 'Rushmere Hall occupied a low situation in the meadows at the south of the village' (between the Hundred River and the main road from Wrentham).

Manors. Rushmere (1263 Thomas de Latimer).

Medieval Green.

Hanners Green was a small square green SE of the church on a country road just N of The Hollies Farm and now marked by Hanner's Green Pit.

Historic House.

Rushmere Hall is a former Elizabethan house of c1600, reduced to a farmhouse (1846).

RUSHMERE ST ANDREW *(2 miles NE of Ipswich)*

Carlford Hundred. 'Rushy mere' plus church dedication (OE) *Ryscemara* (DB). Includes the Domesday vill of Bixley. As White explains 'From Bixley Decoy Ponds a rivulet flows eastward to the Deben, and has near it some poor marsh land. These ponds or meres which anciently abounded in rushes gave name to the parish'. Although Bixley is in Rushmere, Bixley Decoy is just to the S of the parish boundary in Nacton parish. However, they remain N of the Hundred boundary in Carlford, whilst Nacton lies in the adjoining Hundred of Colneis.

Manors. Rushmere/Rushmere Hall (1203 William de Freney). *Sub-Manors.* Bixley.

Site of Gallows.

The urban sprawl of Ipswich which threatens to envelop the parish is held at bay by Rushmere Heath. Here once stood one of the major Ipswich gibbets beside which, in 1763, a woman was burned to death for murdering her husband.

RUSHMERE ST ANDREW *(continued)*

Lost Medieval Village.
There is documentary evidence of an ancient settlement at Bixley, a Domesday 'vill' with a church dedicated to St Petronville. It was probably located in the area formerly occupied by Bixley Hall, Bixley Farm and Bixley Lane, and now by Bixley Heath nature reserve and the huge residential development of Brook Hall; or perhaps centred on a field named 'Bixley' on the Rushmere St Andrew tithe map of 1840. Topsoil stripping to the N of the former site of Linnets Farm, N of the Foxhall Road, revealed an area of probable medieval settlement with pits, ditches and C13-C14 pottery.

Medieval Heath.
The larger portion of the great Rushmere Heath remains much as it did on Faden's 1783 map with only small encroachments of condensed residential housing development. It forms a break in the eastward suburban sprawl of Ipswich.

SANTON DOWNHAM (formerly Downham) *(2 miles NE of Brandon)*

Lackford Hundred. 'Enclosure on a hill' (Downham) 'on sandy soil' (Santon) (OE) *Dunham* (DB). Originally known as Downham, the parish later incorporated the hamlet of Santon.
Manors. Downham (-1538 Ixworth Priory; 1538 Richard Codington). *Sub-Manors.* Downham al Monks Hall; Marsier al Mercies.
In 1668 a violent sandstorm blew sand from the hills of Lakenheath some five miles away threatening to envelop the whole parish. Some roads were blocked to a depth of 8'-9'. It buried and destroyed several houses and cottages and so choked the river that it virtually destroyed the navigation.

Palaeolithic Settlement Site.
At White's Pit, Warren Wood near the eastern parish boundary, a settlement site of Palaeolothic period was found.

Flint Mine.
In Taflin's Quarry, a working chalk pit on the outskirts of Brandon on the western parish boundary, galleries were discovered 'with antler pick marks on them'. These marks are now thought to have been made by iron picks during more recent (up to C19) gun flint production.

Iron Age Settlement.
An Early Iron Age farmstead was discovered and excavated in 1935 just SW of High Lodge House in Downham Highlodge Warren. It was marked by pits and hearths containing pottery.

Tumuli.
A round barrow lies W of the parish and S of the Little Ouse river, 59' in diameter and 3½' high, and another mound* still further E is 98' in diameter and may also be the remains of a barrow. A very slight barrow lies on the S side of the river almost opposite Santon church, and a round barrow lies under grass SW of Little Lodge Farm, again just S of the river but in the E of the parish; this is 88' in diameter and 5' high. S of Woodcock Cottage is a round barrow 105' in diameter and 3½' high and there is documentary evidence of a further two in the area. A roughly circular mound which looks artificial may be the remains of a barrow further S within Downham Highlodge Warren.

Earthworks.
A long low mound c87 yds by 65' to the E of the above* has not been identified. Just N of the tumulus on the S side of the river opposite Santon church, is an earthwork in the coniferous plantation c153 yds. long by 131' wide with an entrance on three sides. Lying adjacent to a series of banks and enclosures it may be for livestock.

Deserted Medieval Village (?)
It is supposed that a village settlement S of the river, belonging to Santon went with the isolated and disused church of All Saints and the moated site (of Santon House?) on the northern bank of the Little Ouse in Norfolk. The church appears to have been rebuilt from a larger one in 1628 and virtually rebuilt again in the C19.

SAPISTON *(3 miles NW of Ixworth)*

Blackbourn Hundred. 'Sap's Farmstead' (OE) *Sapestuna* (DB)
Manors. Sapiston (1326 John de Brydwelle). *Sub-Manors.* Sapiston Grange (C11/C12 Gilbert le Blund; -1538 Ixworth Priory).

Ancient Woodland.
Great Grove (formerly Sapiston Grove) NE of the village is part of ancient woodland.

Former Course of Ancient Road.
A road, said to be the conjectured course of Peddars Way prior to 1671, was described as running SSW from America Lodge on the NW corner of Coney Weston parish, entering Bardwell and running along the edge of Fakenham Wood as Wood Lane to provide the western parish boundary. From the SE corner of the wood it headed S through Sapiston passing through Sapiston Grove (now Great Grove) and leaving the parish E of Lanket's Grove. Apparently the road was abandoned, and eventually disappeared after being blocked by an Act of Parliament in that year.

Medieval Heath.
The northern part of the parish is shown covered by Bardwell Heath and bisected by Heath Road on Faden's map.

Deserted Medieval Village.
Lumps and bumps in grassland N of Sapiston church may represent the remains of a deserted village. If this is so it must predate 1758 and probably 1667 when maps showed most of the houses in the parish to be located (as they still are) along what is now Heath Road, very few of which survive. The church site looks ripe for settlement being situated by the mill and the ford over the river Blackbourn, and in the loop of an ancient track (Clay Lane) from the Bardwell Road to Honington village. There are also disused pit workings to the immediate SE. The monks of Ixworth Priory may have removed the settlement to create their grange (*see below*).

Mills.
A watermill, now disused, probably occupies the site of an earlier mill owned by the monks from the nearby grange. A post mill stood NE of the church in 1736, again possibly on the site of one formerly run by the monks.

Site of Medieval Grange.
The Grange stands on the site of a former grange belonging to the monks from Ixworth Priory who held the sub-manor of Sapiston Grange.

SAXMUNDHAM *(7 miles NW of Aldeburgh)*

Plomesgate Hundred. 'Saxmund's homestead' (OE) *Sasmundeham* (DB)
Manors. Hurts/Hurtz/Hurt's Hall (1336 Sir John de Wingfield). *Sub-Manors.* Murkets/Saxmundham Market; Swan's.

Ancient Woodland.
A stretch of ancient woodland called Great Wood once occupied the area S of the B1119 Leiston road and E of Hurts Hall. This has long since been lost.

Ancient Chapel.
The short-lived Swan Chantry Chapel, founded in 1308 by Robert Swan, Lord of Swan's Manor, was dissolved sometime after 1385. Its site is not known but Old Parsonage House has been rebuilt and called The Chantry.

Medieval Market & Fairs.
Edward I appears to have granted John de Ramseye Saxmundham's market and fair in 1272 to spite the Bigods who had one just down the road at Kelsale, but who had offended him - not their first or their last confrontation with a succession of Medieval English kings. Edward II confirmed the grant in 1310 and also one for a fair on a seven acre site at the request of Thomas de Verley. In 1679, Saxmundham was described as a 'little market town' with 'pretty full market on Thursdays'.

SAXMUNDHAM *(continued)*

Town House & Workhouse.

The Town House originated from c1657, and a Workhouse is recorded with 60 inmates in 1776.

Historic Houses.

Hurts, the main manor of Saxmundham, is now represented by Hurts Hall, standing in its own 250 acre park S of the town. It is an 1893 rebuild in Elizabethan style by Charles Long of the former manor house which stood on the site and was completely destroyed by fire in 1890. The manor was the lordship and seat of Thomas de Verley who probably built the first hall on the site some time around 1281. After later being the possession of the nunnery at Marham in Norfolk, it was granted at the Dissolution to Sir Nichols Hare. One of his successors built the predecessor to the present hall about 1650. The Bell Hotel in the centre of town is a former posting house and excise office.

SAXTEAD *(2 miles NW of Framlingham)*

Hoxne Hundred. Probably 'Seaxa's place' (OE) *Saxsteda* (DB). The parish evolved from a mere berewick (sub-manor) of Framlingham.

Manors. Saxstead in Saxstead (1275 Roger Bigot; 1316 Priory of Ely).

Roman Road.

The Roman road (Margary 34b) running from Coddenham to Peasenhall passes SW-NE through the southern section of the parish. Its course is traced by the present A1120 as it enters the parish but this road then makes a diversion N through the village and that of neighbouring Dennington before rejoining the line of the old road. The only evidence on the ground is the SE boundary of the field immediately NE of Wood Hall which traces its route to the parish boundary. Two sections were dug across the course of the old road SW of the hall in 1972. These revealed a gravel road with flanking ditches 3' wide and 21' apart, and pottery sherds which dated from the C3 to the C4.

Ancient Track.

Hollow Lane forms the northern parish and district boundary. It runs SW of the Monk Soham road in its original form as a hollow way, and NE now upgraded as the road to Tannington.

Ecclesiastical (?) Burial.

Workmen digging a drain behind the Volunteer Inn (now The Old Mill Inn) on the green discovered a human skeleton, wooden coffin, a coin of Henry VI (1422-1461), and a gold ring bearing emblems of The Trinity, a figure of the Virgin Mary and the inscription *de bon coeur* - 'of good heart'.

Medieval Green.

Lying either side of the roads to Yoxford and to Framlingham, Saxtead Green remains much as it did on Faden's map of 1783. Another, tiny green is shown but not named to the W of World's End Farm; the present OS map marking the spot Saxtead Little Green.

Village Stocks.

The old village stocks and whipping post, probably originally set up on Saxtead Green, are preserved in the church porch.

Old Windmill.

The first reference to a mill in the parish was in 1309. The present postmill, the finest surviving in Suffolk and still in full working order, stands beside Saxtead Green. It is not known when it was built but the earliest reference dates from 1706.

Ancient Moated Sites.

Strangely, although the surrounding parishes have a wealth of fine ancient moated sites, Saxtead officially has none. However, Boyce's Farm may have the remains of a moat, and there appears to be fragments of a small moated site on the S side of the A1120 road immediately past the turning to Monk Soham. The ancient Saxtead Green is bordered by two lengths of wide wet ditches in the SW of the parish.

SEMER *(3 miles NW of Hadleigh)*

Cosford Hundred. 'Lake or marsh-pool' (OE) *Seamera* (DB). The parish takes its name from the mere which still lies immediately S of the church. It was obviously of more considerable extent and importance in Anglo-Saxon times and the parish was known as Semere until after 1764.
Manors. Semer (-1542 Abbot of St. Edmunds, Bury; 1542 Sir Clement Heigham).

Ancient Woodland.
Semer Wood, near the western parish boundary, is a part of ancient woodland.

Ancient Mere.
Semer Mere, S of the church, gives the parish its ancient Saxon name. It is fed by the river Brett and this tranquil river valley is a likely spot for early settlement.

Ancient Settlement.
The parish is one of scattered farms mainly in the E with church and hall site isolated by the ancient mere. The only modest concentration is in the hamlet of Ash Green on the eastern parish boundary. However, cropmarks of numerous ring ditches and enclosures have been observed throughout the parish providing strong evidence of populous early settlement, with the largest concentrations N of Semer Bridge and in the area of Highfields in the N, with others near the western boundary, and in the SE corner.

Medieval Green.
A small triangular green on the southern parish boundary is shown on Faden's 1783 map bordered by the present road to Lindsey and Drakestone Farm. It was named Greeston Green but the present OS map marks the area (which has now been enclosed and developed) Drakestone Green. Another unnamed triangular green was shown immediately N of Sayers Farm extending as a widening of the present A1141 Hadleigh to Monks Eleigh road, W across the Lindsey parish boundary.

Ancient Mill.
A water mill, operated by a tributary of the river Brett, was already a feature of Ash Green *(Asce)* by the time of Domesday.

Smuggling.
The village is known to have contained a 'safe' warehouse used to store contraband tea by the notorious local band of smugglers known as the 'Hadleigh Gang'.

Workhouse.
The Cosford Union Workhouse was built in 1780 as a House of Industry to accommodate up to 500 inmates. In the event it held less than 200.

Historic House.
Semer Manor (called 'the Hall' in 1783) occupies the site of the former manor house just W of the church, appropriated to the use of the cellarer of Bury Abbey.

SHADINGFIELD *(4½ miles S of Beccles)*

Wangford Hundred. Morley considers it 'Thieves' or pirates' clearing' (OE) *Scadenafella* (DB). In 1276 it was called 'Shatenefeud' meaning the Devil's own clearing. There is no evidence as from where these descriptions may have arisen.
Manors. Brosyard with Verdons (1306 John de Bruisyard held of the Crown). *Sub-Manors.* Francis or Cuddons.

Ancient Woodland.
Great Wood and Titsal Wood, W of the church, are substantial remains of ancient woodland.

Medieval Common.
Shadingfield Common is shown and named on Faden's map of 1783. Its NW boundary is marked by West End Farm; the NE, a V-shaped track to Fox Farm; S to Lodge Farm, and W along a public footpath by Park Farm and

SHADINGFIELD *(continued)*

then N back to West End Farm. The western boundary is now ploughed out. Two moated sites lie in the NW corner. The common was enclosed in 1806 under an Act of 1804, at which time it was said to total 90 acres. Part of the common appears to have been turned into a C19 park for Shadingfield Place (now Park Farm).

Ancient Fair.

In 1257 the Bocland family obtained the grant for a fair and free warren here.

Site of old Windmill.

A post mill stood in the NE corner of Shadingfield Common in 1764. It was pulled down c1905.

Historic Houses & Ancient Moated Sites.

Hall Farm, on the eastern parish boundary, stands near the site of Shadingfield Hall which Copinger described in 1911 as being 'a red-brick building of c1540 originally surrounded by a moat some remains of which still exist. Within the moat was a wall about 8' high pierced with squints for the discharge of arrows.' The hall was the residence of the Cuddon family and was demolished when the new hall (a large white brick mansion) was built in 1814. One arm of the moat - which may have enclosed the earliest C13 Brocland Hall - remains today with the site of the Tudor hall presumably S of this. West End Farm, NE of the village at the NW end of the former Shadingfield Common, has a complete rectangular moat except for the S arm. To the E of this, C16 Moat Farm has three parts of a large quadrangular moat with, close to its external bank on the NE, another small one enclosing an island which may formerly have held a dovecot. There are probable remains of a fish-pond to the immediate W of the SW angle. C13 pottery is said to have come from a 'homestead' moat on the southern parish boundary SE of the church. Remains of a small rectangular moat (now U-shaped) is on the W side of the A145 road at Shadingfield House N of the church.

SHELLAND *(4 miles WNW of Stowmarket)*

Stow Hundred. 'Land on a slope' (OE) *Sellanda* (DB). Originally Shelf-land, i.e. sloping-plateau which well describes its position sloping down from the plateau of Shelland Green to Buxhall Fen by the river Gipping. *Manors.* Shelland (1300 Sir Ingebranch de Belet). *Sub-Manors.* Rockylls.

Ancient Woodland.

Shelland Wood on the northern parish boundary is remains of ancient woodland.

Medieval Green.

Shelland Green runs from the Woolpit to Stowmarket road as a wide linear green to the church and on as a strip green to Harleston Green and village.

Historic House & Ancient Moated Sites.

Rockylls Hall, on the NW side of Shelland Green, was originally surrounded by a broad and deep rectangular moat of which only the long southern wet arm survives with signs of a sub-division. Built c1500, the house once belonged to the Drury and Gresham families. In 1934 it was gutted by fire and largely rebuilt. It takes its name from the C12 tenant William de la Rokele, lord of Rockels Manor in Ringshall. New Farm, in the S corner of the green, retains two sides of an irregular moat. Shelland Hall stands beyond the SW boundary in Rattlesden parish.

SHELLEY *(3 miles SE of Hadleigh)*

Samford Hundred. 'Clearing on a slope' (OE) *Sceueleia* (DB). The clearing contained the hall site and this upland plateau ran down to the W bank of the river Brett. The parish was once merely a berewick of Bergholt. *Manors.* Shelley (1272 Robert de Tateshall held of the barony of Tibenham, Norfolk).

Ancient Woodland.

Snakes Wood on the southern parish boundary is part of ancient woodland.

Medieval Market & Fair.

Shelley received the grant for a market and fair in 1227.

SHELLEY *(continued)*

Historic Houses & Ancient Moated Sites.
Standing beside the strong, part brick-revetted square moat of an even earlier hall - the home of John de Appleby in 1316 during the reign of Edward II - Shelley Hall, SW of the church, retains an important fragment of the beautiful Tudor manor house built by Sir Philip Tylney in 1520. His great-grandson entertained Elizabeth I here in 1561 and Edmund Tylney was Master of the Revels in the Royal Household between 1579 and 1608. The house still exhibits the arms of the Tylneys with the motto in Norman-French translating as 'Hope gives me strength'. Shelley Priory Farm, in the W of the parish, once belonged to Butley Priory from where it gained its suggestive name. It was formerly called Burnt House Farm.

SHIMPLING *(4½ miles WNW of Lavenham)*

Babergh Hundred. 'The settlement of Scimpel's people' (OE) *Simplinga* (DB). The parish was at one time called Shimplingthorne (Shymplyngthorn 1442), the 'thorn' or 'thorpe' being added perhaps to represent either the roadside hamlet of Shimpling Street to where all the major settlement had by this time moved (presumably from an original church and hall site by the Chad Brook), or another hamlet, thorpe or 'thorn' still perpetuated in Thorne Court (the old rectory) and Thorn Corner on the NE parish boundary, and the moated site of Shimpling Thorne by Alpheton Hall Wood on the eastern parish boundary.
Manors. Shimpling (1303 Robert FitzWalter). *Sub-Manors.* Chadacre/Chadacre Hall, Giffords & Boxteds; Rowheads/Rowshedges.

Ancient Woodland.
Aveley Wood (formerly Harbridge Grove), S of the church, is a small section of ancient woodland.

Site of Roman Building (?)
'Several years ago' (previous to 1992) a local builder described how he had discovered 'a mosaic floor' in a contractor's trench during extension work at Shimpling Hall. This was not reported by the farmer at the time and he has since 'sold up'.

Sites of Ancient Mounds (?)
The site of a possible mound of undetermined age and function is suggested by the field name 'Howe Field' at the western end of the parish, W of Gifford's Farm, and by the names 'How Field' (N of this in Hartest parish) and 'Howe Field' (S in Stanstead parish). Situated at the junction of four parishes (the above plus Boxted) suggests a possible meeting place for the local Saxon council. Mount Farm, SW of the church, was originally known as 'The Mount' which may suggest that another ancient mound once stood here.

Medieval Green.
A triangular green, shown but unnamed by Faden's in 1783, lay in the extreme W of the parish at the junction of the road leading from the church with that heading NW to Hartest and bordered by Gifford's Farm.

Site of Gallows.
Lord of the Manor, Robert FitzWalter held 'right of gallows' in Shimpling. It would appear that this gibbet stood on the mound in the extreme W of the parish in the area of Howe Field (*see above*).

Site of old Windmills.
Two mills stood in the parish in 1783: a post mill on Mill Hill (moved c1875) and a mill E of Kiln Grove and the road from Shimpling to Lawshall. A smock mill dated 1792 which stood in The Street was demolished in 1935.

Fainting House.
The Fainting House stood in the churchyard and was for the use of swooning ladies who found long and powerful sermons too great a strain. It was equiped with a fire for added comfort.

Historic House & Ancient Moated Sites.
Shimpling Hall, on high ground near the church, dates from c1475. Chadacre Hall, by the Chad Brook NW of the parish, was the seat of the Plampin family when shown on Faden's map. The present hall, situated in a 95 acre park, was erected in 1834 by Thomas Halifax. It was opened as Chadacre Agricultural Institute in 1921 and

SHIMPLING *(continued)*

closed in 1988. The manor of Chadacre (or Chadacre Hall) was anciently held by the de la Lee, and de Harleston families. There are moats on the site of the former Rectory on the parish boundary W of Alpheton Hall Wood (trapezoid); the site of Shimpling Thorne, N of Shimpling Park Farm; at Shimpling Street (rectangular, dry and isolated); Hunt's Moat, NW of Alpheton village (small, square and dry with traces of foundations); and at Mount Farm (The Mount), where there are water-filled fragments of a possible curved moat.

SHIPMEADOW *(3 miles E of Bungay)*

Wangford Hundred. 'Meadow for sheep' (OE) *Scipmedu* (DB). 'Ship' was the ancient local pronounciation of 'sheep' - hence this name being applied to public houses situated well inland.
Manors. Shipmeadow (1240 Walyter de Shipmeadow).

Medieval Green.
A small round green is shown but not named on the southern parish boundary on Faden's 1783 map. It was bordered on the S by Rookery Farm and on the E by Clarke's Lane. The OS calls the area Shipmeadow Common.

Workhouse.
The Shipmeadow House of Industry, built on an 'E' plan and in existence in 1765, was employed in spinning for Norwich manufacturers. It later became the Wangford Union Workhouse and held 250 inmates in 1831. Later still it was described as a Pest House.

SHOTLEY *(9 miles SE of Ipswich)*

Samford Hundred. 'Clearing of huts' or 'clearing where shooting takes place' (OE) *Scoteleia* (DB)
Manors. Shotley Hall/Kirketon (C12 John de Visdelou/Vicedeliew; 1286 Guy de Visdelieu claimed 'wreck of the sea', 'view of frankpledge' and other manorial franchises). *Sub-Manors.* Overhall with Netherhall; Thirkleton/Thorkleton al Shecke.
In much the same way as Kirton, the parish of Shotley was originally made up of several hamlets. Heading S from Chelmondiston you came first to Colton or Calweton Creek, then Thurkelton (probably taking its name from Thurkytel who was to distinguish himself by fleeing from the Danes in 1010 A.D.), Kirketon or Shotley (in the area of Shotely Hall - site of Shotley Hall or Kirkton Manor), Thorpeston (the beach opposite Sleighton Hill), and Fishbane (on the road to Shotley Gate near Shotley Marshes). Kirketon or Shotley, the main village, absorbed the other settlements only some 150 years ago and became Shotley, mainly to avoid confusion with Kirton. Strangely none of the names of the previous hamlets (with the exception of Colton) appear to have survived.

Ancient Woodland.
Oldhall Grove in the centre of the parish, is part of ancient woodland.

Ancient Settlement & Roman Road (?)
Aerial photographs have identified numerous crop marks suggesting ring ditches, field boundaries, enclosures, tracks and the possible line of a minor (Roman?) road.

Site of Ancient Naval Battle.
In 885 A.D. the invading Danes met King Alfred's fleet at Stourmouth, off Bloody Point in the Orwell estuary. Despite losing 19 ships, they later sailed up the river ravaging Ipswich and the surrounding countryside.

Site of Ancient Chapel.
A chapel was founded here c1430 by Nicholas Fikkett. Its site and history are unknown.

Medieval Common.
Cowton Common on Faden's map of 1783 lay inland from Colton Creek in Colton, one of the Domesday vills. It is named Shotley Common on the present OS map.

Medieval Market & Fair.
In 1303, William de Visdelieu had the grant for a market and fair here.

SHOTLEY *(continued)*

Old Windmill.
An open-trestle post mill is shown in Shotley on an old print dated 1730.

Historic Fortifications.
Two Martello Towers - forts erected around 1812 as defence against a possible invasion by Napoleon - remain within the confines of the former Royal Naval Training Establishment, HMS Ganges, at Shotley Gate. The bottom ring is still intact on one, while the other still has the bottom and second tier intact. A later earthwork battery mounted with 14 heavy guns defended the entrance to what is known as Harwich Harbour.

Medieval Ferry House.
The Bristol Arms public house at Shotley Gate was formerly the ferry house for the ferry to Harwich.

Historic Houses & Ancient Moated Site.
Modern buildings occupy the ancient moated site of Old Hall, S of the church, beside Oldhall Road and just N of Oldhall Grove. The rectangular moat, now dry, abutts the road. Shotley Hall, just to the NW, has early C16 origins. The Rectory by the main road to Ipswich was built in 1697, with later additions.

SHOTTISHAM *(4½ miles SE of Woodbridge)*

Wilford Hundred. 'Scot's homestead' (OE) *Scotesham* (DB)
Manors. Shottisham Hall (1288 John de Vallibus). *Sub-Manors.* Talvies/Talvas.

Barrow Cemetery & Prehistoric Settlement Site (?)
A spectacular group of round ditches seen as crop marks in aerial photographs suggest a barrow cemetery or even the hut sites of a major prehistoric settlement just N of the church. The elevated church may itself stand on Roman or Iron Age earthworks connected with the site.

Medieval Watermill.
A lease dated c1650 states that a property at Shottisham Sluice was let together with the 'millhouse, floodgates, waterwheel, millstones, woodwork and ironwork.'

Medieval Common.
Shottisham Poor's Common covered a large area in the S of the parish. All that remains is a fragment on the E side of Tom's Wood on the southern boundary, a short distance E of Shottisham Hall.

Historic Houses.
A building adjoining the W side of Church Lane is marked 'Site of the Manor of Shotsham' on a map of the parish in 1631. Bussock Barn, N of the parish, is the site of Bussock House. Wood Hall, now a hotel and conference centre, dates from 1566.

SIBTON *(5 miles NW of Saxmundham)*

Blything Hundred. 'Sibba's farmstead' (OE) *Sibbetuna* (DB). Includes Domesday vill of Wrabetuna (Rapton).
Manors. Sibton (C11/C12 Robert FitzWalter; c1149 Sibton Abbey). *Sub-Manors.* Sibton Hall.

Ancient Woodland.
Hencoup Wood, Coe Wood and Spring Wood, in the S of the parish, and Big Wood and Kendall's Wood in the N, are all parts of ancient woodland.

Roman Road.
The modern A1120 road overlays a Roman road but deviates from it passing through the village of Peasenhall. Here it crosses another running NNW-SSE (diverted slightly to cross the river Yox by a ford) through part of Sibton. The curving line of the old road may possibly be picked up again by the present road from Sibton church to the parish boundary at Park Farm, Hemp Green.

Site of Roman Settlement (?)
It has been conjectured that Peasenhall, where the actual crossing of the Roman roads appears to be centred, or

SIBTON *(continued)*

Sibton, beside the crossing and close to the river and the ford, may be the site of the Roman town of *Sitomagus* mentioned in the Roman road map of Britain. The name Sibton could have retained elements from the Roman.

Ancient Ways.

A public footpath follows the course of a medieval Way known as The Packway running N from Sibton Green to Walpole, and the course of the ancient Dunwich Lane. This is described in an old ballad as the route taken back to the refuge of his castle at Bungay by the notorious medieval baron Hugh Bigod whilst fleeing the army of King Henry II. It forms the northern parish boundary as a public footpath from the water tower on Peasenhall Road opposite Lodge Wood to a copse just W of Earlsway Farm.

Abbey.

Sibton is the only Cistercian abbey in Suffolk. It was founded in 1149 by William de Cheney and dedicated to St Mary. Colonised by Cistercian monks from Warden Abbey in Bedfordshire, it was richly endowed with the income from no less than 25 Suffolk parishes. Little is known of its history and it does not appear to have been dissolved in the usual way. The last abbot was a nominee of the Duke of Norfolk to whom he sold the whole abbey and its possessions in 1536 bringing it to an end as a religious house. The transaction was confirmed by an Act of Parliament in 1539 and the abbot and all the monks received pensions from the duke. The ruins which lie on the N bank of the river Yox are under private ownership and very overgrown and neglected (though some recent efforts have been made to clear the site). They comprise the S wall of the aisle N of the cloister and, S of the cloister, remains of the refectory within which is a large blank Norman arch. The font remains, square and possibly Norman, and W of the refectory are some ruins of the kitchen. 'Stone coffins' were discovered in 1832.

Site of Medieval Hospital.

St Nicholas Hospital stood near the entrance gates to the abbey. It was founded in 1190 by a Sibton abbot, its income dependent on the abbey. In 1264, Simon, Bishop of Norwich, appropriated it to the church of Cransford for the better support of the inmates. The hospital fell into disuse and disrepair in the C16. The site was once marked by 'flint walling - probably remains of hospital' and slighly to the E of this 'tile and flint scatter'.

Ancient Chapel.

Dedicated to God and St. Nicholas, this ancient chapel was situated within Hamon's House in the village in 1201 and served by its own chaplain. However, the household of Hamon were still expected to attend the mother church on major church festivals.

Medieval Greens.

In 1520 the Sibton Abbey Cartularies list 60 acres called Courte Grene Close in Sibton. It is not known to which of the following identified greens (if any) it refers. It may refer to Sibton Great Green which Faden's map shows lying over the eastern parish boundary with Yoxford. It covered the two forks, E and W and the road N to Bramfield. It was bordered by Green Farm and Kendall's Wood on the S, and North Green Farm on the N. To the W it linked with the linear Sibton Little Green which was bordered by South Green Farm and terminated at High House Farm. The course of another large curving linear green is traced by the present Halesworth Road which replaced it from the crossroads on the southern edge of Lodge Wood, S to the 'T'-junction by the river Yox. Hemp Green, named on the present OS map, appears only as a widening of the Yoxford road (A1120) in 1783.

Deserted Medieval Village (?)

Rapton, the *Wrabetuna* of Domesday Book (where it was listed with a church), was granted to Sibton Abbey in the C12 after which time any village settlement may have been destroyed to create the North and South granges. There is evidence of early enclosure especially round the North Grange. Although there is no documentary evidence as to its exact location, a whole field in the area of South Grange (now a farmhouse) is covered with the extensive pattern of lumps, hollows and ponds of a possible hamlet. The present Rotten End was previously called Rapton End and White House known as Rapton Hall. A Wrabeton Strete is also recorded in 1493.

Old Windmill.

Suffolk's oldest datable windmill (1668) has been converted into a house near Abbey Farmhouse SW of the church.

SIBTON *(continued)*

Medieval Moated Granges.
The existence of a grange owned by the Abbey is referred to as early as 1201. The Abbey owned at least five granges in Suffolk in 1325 of which North Grange and South Grange were in Sibton. North Grange Farm lies beside the Halesworth Road. To the S of it, two sides remain of an isolated and overgrown wet moat which could possibly identify the site of the original North Grange. Roads enclosing a virtual rectangular area S of the church may outline the original extent of South Grange the moated site of which lies on its southern boundary.

Historic Houses & Ancient Moated Sites.
Sibton Abbey, W of the Abbey ruins near Poys Street, is a house built from the ruins of the abbey by John Scrivener in 1610. In 1783 a 'great house' is shown N of the Yoxford road at Hemp Green. This had gone by 1837 presumably replaced by Sibton Park further N 'built in 1827' and standing in a park of 1000 acres including gardens and a lake. This park had been reduced to 200 acres by 1912. Apart from the sites relating to North Grange and South Grange (*see above*), there are moated sites at Hill Farm, N of Sibton Park, and at High House Farm, on the edge of the former Sibton Green (where two arms and part of a third survive of a former rectangular moat).

SNAPE *(3 miles SE of Saxmundham)*

Plomesgate Hundred. 'Boggy piece of land' (OE) or 'poor pasture' (OScand) *Snapes* (DB). Includes the Domesday vill of Becclinga.
Manors. Snape (c1099 William Martel gave the manor to St. John at Colchester for the foundation of Snape Priory [which did not occur until 1155]; 1524 Cardinal Wolsey). *Sub-Manors.* Courtlets/Cantlets; Bekling (1408 Michael de la Pole); Tastards; Rysing; Scotts; Snape Hall.

Ancient Ford.
There is considerable doubt over the origin of the place-name. Although the church (still with traces of Norman work) and hall are situated on heathland, if the meaning is to be believed the original settlement may have been in the hamlet of Gromford. 'Grom' is a variant of the Anglo-Saxon *grim* meaning 'fierce'. The ford is that at Snape Watering which carried Farnham Road across the river Fromus (a tributary of the Alde) running S from Saxmundham and not bridged until 1918. Hence we have 'fierce ford' suggesting the river was somewhat deeper and swifter in those days. Named 'Thelford' on Faden's 1783 map, i.e. 'plank ford'.

Roman Industrial Site.
At Sandy Point on the river Alde, a baked clay scatter in reddish silt, coarse-ware sherds and a burnt clay feature exposed by tidal erosion, are probably remains of a Roman salt working site.

Course of Roman Road (?)
Aldeburgh was a Roman station or fort, but all evidence has now been swept away by the North Sea. The road heading SE from Peasenhall (which has nowhere been confidently identified on the ground), would most likely have passed through Snape, and it is therefore a strong possibility that the modern A1094 entering the parish as Farnham Road, crossing the ancient Gromford at Snape Watering, passing the Anglo-Saxon cemetery site (*see below*), and heading E to leave Snape for Aldeburgh N of Firs Farm, may overlay this ancient road.

Tumulus.
In 1828 at Black Cottages, at the junction of five ways SE of Rookery Farm, a Nathen Licence is said to have built a small windmill on a mound called Round Hill and to have cut into the side to facilitate a shed, at which time 'curious old earthenware and coloured glass, bits of corroded iron and a large number of bones' were found. In 1868 it was said that this barrow 'was higher than the other Snape barrows' (*see below*).

Anglo-Saxon Cemetery & Ship Burial.
At Church Common the road from the church to Aldeburgh bisects a large Anglo-Saxon inhumation and

SNAPE *(continued)*

cremation cemetery. At least six round barrows lay either side of the road. Three were excavated between 1840 and 1863, but not before two carriages-full of 'Londoners' had taken their fill around 1820. Several stood near the Priory, one of which revealed a Saxon ship burial, only the second to be found - the first was at the now world famous Sutton Hoo. When opened, athough it had been robbed, the remains were found of a clinker-built long boat c47' long with a beam of about 10'. It had been placed in a 60' trench dug in the centre of a flat cremation urn field and a scrapped up mound built up over it. Though there was no sign of a body, some reddish hair was found (perhaps from a shaggy cloak) together with a Saxon gold ring which was dated c635-50 A.D. and vessel fragments suggesting a wealthy (but not royal) status. Seasonal excavations are continuing on this extensive site and one grave has uncovered a body buried in a small dug-out boat only 10' long. It was accompanied by an iron knife, a belt with an iron buckle, and a pair of drinking horns.

Priory.
To the W of Snape Bridge is the site of a priory founded for black cannons by William Martel, Albreda his wife, and Jeffrey their son, in 1155, and dedicated to the Blessed Virgin Mary. It was endowed with the manor of Snape including the benefit of wrecks of the sea from Thorp to Orfordness. Intended for 12 monks it is doubtful if this number was ever attained and it remained dependent on more powerful institutions. It was given as a cell to the Benedictine Priory of St John in Colchester but following complaints against the abbot at Colchester by the Countess of Suffolk claiming that he had not been keeping to his obligations to provide sufficient numbers at Snape, it regained its independence c1443. William de la Pole refounded the priory in the reign of Henry VI and it became, for a short period in 1509, a cell to Butley Priory before becoming one of the East Anglian religious houses suppressed by Cardinal Wolsey in 1527 to provide revenue for his Ipswich College. A fine C13 barn plus some slight remains are to be seen incorporated in the outbuildings of The Abbey, a modern farmhouse on the site. In 1842 many of the foundations were dug up and some skeletons, coins and tiles were found. There are cropmarks of a large subrectangular feature in the same field and to the E of the site.

Ancient Bridge.
The ancient hump-backed bridge (now replaced) probably dated from the C15, itself replacing an even earlier one. According to W.G. Arnott, in his *Alde Estuary,* an ancient map of the world at the Vatican in Rome names only two places in England: Walsingham and Snape Bridge perhaps (he suggests) marking the course of a Pilgrim's Way.

Medieval Commons.
Faden's 1783 map shows a large area of common in the hamlet of Gromford, on the E side of the river Fromus, heading S from Saxmundham to join the river Alde, and the W side of Gromford Lane. Named Caldwell Green, Cordial Green and Cundle Green as well as Wet Common, it extended from Abbey Farm in the S to the ford in the N, with an extension E to the church. From here it was joined by Church Common which extended E roughly bordered by the present A1094 Aldeburgh road and a footpath as far as the Priory. Snape Common in the S of the parish covers a large area E of Snape Bridge; its northern limit was the street running E from the inn, and its southern, the river.

Medieval Fair.
A fair was held annually in 1618 on August 15 and 'Our First Lady in Harvest'.

Mills.
The manor had a watermill and rabbit warren in 1520. A windmill dated 1668 remained in the parish until 1933.

Workhouse.
A workhouse here held 20 inmates in 1776.

Historic Houses.
The C15 Crown Inn was used by smugglers and the Golden Key dates from the C17.

SOMERLEYTON *(5 miles NW of Lowestoft)*

Mutford & Lothingland Hundred. 'Sumarlici's homestead' (OE) Morley suggests an old Danish invader's farm named by Saxons 'Summer pirate's farm' (OScand+OE) *Sumerledetuna* (DB). Somerleyton was known throughout the Middle Ages by the more attractive name of Somerley.
Manors. Somerleyton (1239 Peter FitzOsbert).

Site of Bronze Age Hoard.
A Late Bronge Age metal hoard, discovered in the parish in 1926, included axes, sword blades, etc.

Lost Settlement.
Within this Danish parish was a hamlet called Manthorp from where the De Manthorpe family - traceable with gaps from 1189 to 1745 - took their name. Before 1190 Wilhelmus de Manthorp held socage in Somerleyton and, about 1280, John de Manthorpe was granted land in Ashby in Manthorp showing that the hamlet lay on the N edge of Somerleyton abutting upon Ashby parish exactly where Faden's 1783 map names 'Manthorp Green'. Manthorp was last mentioned in 1321.

Medieval Common.
Faden's 1783 map shows an extensive semi-circular common enclosing the present village W of the church from the lane running S from the northern end of Station Road, clockwise to the Old Rectory. Manthorp Green stands to the E of Somerleyton Hall bordered by Green Farm.

Medieval Fair.
In 1792 an annual fair for toys held annually every 31 July was recorded.

Site of old Windmill.
A post mill is shown standing SW of Mill Farm in 1783. It had gone by 1880.

Workhouse.
A very small workhouse with only three inmates is recorded in 1776.

Historic Houses
A branch of the Jernegan family held the manor and were seated in Somerleyton for thirteen generations until the reign of James I. The present Somerleyton Hall was begun in 1844 by Sir Morton Peto and is now one of the finest modern mansions in East Anglia. It still contains a C17 core with Queen Anne additions and parts date back to Elizabethan times. The gardens were laid out c1610 after an earlier rebuild and Faden's map of 1783 shows heavy tree-lined avenues to the S of the house. There was also a deer park of 300 acres and maze. During the Civil War the village of Somerleyton was staunchly Royalist and, suspecting that its then owner Sir John Wentworth was himself sympathetic to the cause, Cromwell's troops came and encamped at the hall for several days in 1642. In 1649 Cromwell's son-in-law made the hall his temporary headquarters. A wing of Park Farmhouse dates back to the C15. The Old Rectory is shown N of the church on Bowen's map of 1755. A new rectory was built in 1773 which is shown by Faden as 'Great House on the site of the Old Rectory'.

SOMERSHAM *(5½ miles NW of Ipswich)*

Bosmere & Claydon Hundred. 'Summer enclosure' (OE) *Sumersham* (DB). Possibly an outlying tract of forest where swine-herds were sent with their stock just for the duration of the warmer summer months.
Manors. Somersham (1198 Geoffrey de Amerley). *Sub-Manors.* Woodhouse.

Ancient Woodland.
Somersham Park in the SE of the parish is ancient woodland.

Ancient Chapel.
According to old wills, a chapel once existed in Somersham street but its site and history are unknown.

Medieval Green.
Kelly Green is shown as a small green lying either side of the road to Elmsett on a map of 1783. Now enclosed, Caley Green Farm, Hill Farm and Grove Farm which stood around its edge, trace its former extent.

SOMERTON *(7 miles NE of Clare)*

Babergh Hundred. 'Summer farm' or 'Sumarlici's homestead' (OE) *Sumerledetuna* (DB)
Manors. Somerton (C12 Richard Neville). *Sub-Manors.* Hores.

Site of Roman Pottery Industry (?)
Possible Late C1 Roman pottery kilns were destroyed creating an artificial pond NW of Somerton Hall.

Medieval Market & Fair.
A grant for a market and fair was granted to 'Sumertone' in 1225. The fair was recorded as a Toy Fair in 1759.

SOTHERTON *(4 miles ENE of Halesworth)*

Blything Hundred. Southern farmstead' (OE) *Sudretuna* (DB)
Manors. Sotherton (1226 Sir Hugh de Burgh, Earl of Kent).

Deserted Medieval Village (?)
Beresford considers there was once a village settlement here since deserted. Although short lived, it had a market in 1226 (*see below*) which would suggest a notable settlement in medieval times, probably around the church where there are ponds NW of Church Farm and a track which once connected the present A145 road with the B1124. Nothing is visible on aerial photographs of the parish which is bordered on the S by Blyford and Henham, neither of which have a village settlement, although Henham's may have been lost under emparkment (*see* Henham).

Medieval Market.
Sotherton had the grant of a market in 1226 to Sir Hugh de Burgh, which appears to have been abandoned within three years in favour of neighbouring Westhall.

Medieval Common.
The extent of Sotherton Moor, a common enclosed under an Act of 1802, is shown by Faden in 1783 and mapped by Isaac Johnson in 1794. It was a large arrow-shaped section of moor through which passed King's Lane. The 1783 map shows it, edged by isolated dwellings. These can probably be identified as Southerton Hall and Moor Farm in the N and Valley Farm in the E. The western limit was Blyford Wood.

Historic Houses
Sotherton Hall is a C16 timber-framed building. Church Farm is another building of similar period.

SOTTERLEY *(5 miles SSE of Beccles)*

Wangford Hundred. 'Saetere's meadow or clearing' (OE) *Soterlega* (DB). Morley considers the place-name to be taken from the pagan Saxon god Saetere. This reasoning also leads him to place the unlocated Domesday vill of Croscroft - 'the croft beside the cross' - in this parish.
Manors. Sotterley (C13 Edmund de Sotterley held as of the Honor of Chester*; 1275 Roger de Sotterely claimed view of frankpledge and assize of bread and beer). *The Manor of Sotterley was held of the Honor of Chester by service of one armed horseman to attend the Earl of Chester into Wales for 40 days at his own cost during times of war (1314).

Ancient Woodland.
Southwell Lane Wood (described in a manuscript as 'one of the best wooded estates in Suffolk') and Ashley Wood, in the S of the parish, are sections of ancient woodland.

Deserted Medieval Village (?)
Another Suffolk parish which Beresford lists under lost medieval villages. There is no evidence for a settlement here and the church stands in isolation by the hall as it may always have done. Any village settlement (or remains of an already abandoned settlement) would probably have been destroyed when much of the parish including hall and church was emparked by Sotterley Hall in 1744. (*see below*).

SOTTERLEY *(continued)*

Medieval Green & Common.

Sotterley Green is shown on Faden's 1783 map as linear extensions running W and S from the SW side Sotterley Park. The western arm extended along the line of the present Sotterley Road to a point where it turns NW, whilst the southern arm ran either side of the stream past Lower Green Farm to where the present lane turns E to the War Memorial and the stream SW. The great Sotterley Common extended SE from the park into Henstead and Wrentham parishes. Its southern limit is marked by Waterloo Road, but in Wrentham it then turned S to terminate by the road at Moat Farm and White Horse Farm. An eastern arm extended all the way to Savage Wood on Wrentham's eastern boundary. The Common has been mostly enclosed and intercrossed by roads.

Site of old Windmill.

A post mill stood N of Mill Farm in Hulver Street in 1736. It was gone by 1914.

Workhouse.

A workhouse is recorded here with 14 inmates in 1776.

Historic Houses.

Sotterley Hall was formerly the seat of the Playters who held the manor as early as the reign of Edward II (1307-1327); one was created a baronet in 1623. In 1674 the hall was listed as having 20-29 hearths (very large). In 1744 they sold the estate to Barne Miles who built the present house on the site of the old one and created a 489 acre park out of existing woodland and farmland (perhaps emparking a medieval village?). The church contains several ancient monuments to the Playter family including one to Sir Thomas Playter, his two wives and 22 children. Right against the northern parish boundary an incomplete H-shaped building has been identified by aerial photographs with a 'consolidated substance made up of small stones, etc.' seen on the ground in a field immediately NE of Valley Farm.

SOUTH COVE *(3½ miles N of Southwold)*

Blything Hundred. 'South cove' (OE) *Soua* (DB)

Manors. South Cove with North Hales (1307 John de Cove); Polfreys or Blueflorycove (nothing known).

Ancient Mound.

Now under the plough but clearly visible, a mound 187' in diameter and c6½' high, surrounded by a ditch 52'* wide fading out on the W side, overlooks to the W what remains of a suggested ancient dock and quay dug out of the E side of the river entering at Easton Broad - much wider and deeper in earlier times. (*see* Frostenden). The site has suffered from erosion of the light soil which has caused lychets to develop and the area of the mound is covered in marine shells and tile. It may have Danish origins, but its purpose has yet to be established. The mound was trenched in 1951 by Peter Woodard who found what he thought were foundations of a palisade wall with evidence of burning and the remains of timber within the wall. Aerial photographs have shown that the surrounding moat was oval with an E-W axis. *Soil erosion has made the original width of the moat indistinct.

Lost Medieval Settlement (?)

The parish which comprises two manors, South Cove or North Hales and Polfreys or Blueflory Cove, now only consists of four isloated farmsteads and a church sited beside the war memorial on the present B1127, at a point where two other minor country roads converge. One comes from Cove Bottom to the SSW, and the other an extension of Gypsey Lane from the W. Other lanes, Hitcham's to the NW and Golden Square, now appear to serve no purpose. Except for Brick Kiln Farm and Red House Farm, the few isolated properties shown bordering Cove Common (*see below*) have now gone.

Medieval Common.

Faden's map of 1783 shows Cove Common running S from the road S of Brick Kiln Farm to join Reydon Common.

Medieval Fair.

In the early C14, Lord of the Manor John de Cove and his wife Eve obtained free warren in South Cove and the

SOUTH COVE *(continued)*

privilege of holding a fair here.

Guild or Common House.

In 1482 the Guild of St. Gregory had met in the church, but a document of 1485 records that a 'Common house (was) to be built for the guilds and others to hold "potations".

SOUTH ELMHAM *(Comprising 9 parishes)*

Wangford Hundred. 'Enclosure near the elm tree' (OE) *Almeham* (DB). Morley suggests, not unreasonably, that the generally accepted place-name is far too general for such a large and unique district comprising some 9,000 acres, and relates it instead to a grant from the East Anglian King (and recent convert) Sigebert to our earliest Bishop, i.e. 'alm'(the gift (land) enclosure) rather than 'elm'. The Saxon *AElmesse* meaning 'our alms' and 'alms-giving' abbreviated to Aelmes-ham, thence Elmham, prefixed by the church dedication. St Nicholas was united with All Saints after its church went into ruin some 350 years ago.

Manors. The Liberty, Manor or Township of South Elmham (-1535 See of Norwich; 1535 granted to Sir Edward North). *Sub-Manors.* New Hall; Kings Hall.

The fact that South Elmham 'district' includes nine parishes each prefixed by its saint - including Homesfield (South Elmham St Mary) - forming a sub-division (ferthing) of Wangford Hundred and with a possible Saxon 'minster' at St Cross, makes this ecclesiastical centre one of great importance. It may well be that the group of churches within the South Elmhams formed their own religious centre. Yet in truth its significance cannot yet be fully understood. In neighbouring Norfolk, North Elmham again has a 'minster'.

The isolation of these scattered farming communities which may have operated a common grazing system could not have been helped by the transport problems, for the narrow, twisting lanes which connected them were said in the C18 to be 'unsafe for travelling and practically impassable for several months of the year'.

Brick Industry.

350,000 'Breketylls' (bricks) were being made in South Elmham Manor in 1464 and sent to Hoxne.

SOUTH ELMHAM ALL SAINTS & ST NICHOLAS *(5 miles SW of Bungay)*

Deserted Medieval Settlement.

Beresford considers in his *Lost Villages of England* that there has been migration from the isolated church and moated manor house to the green.

Medieval Green & Common.

Faden's map names a triangular area S of the site of the lost church, St Nicholas Green; it is now enclosed and partially built over. All Saints Common near the NE parish boundary, however, remains virtually unchanged today from that shown in 1783.

Historic Houses & Ancient Moated Sites.

The Elms is an ancient moated house dating from the C14. A rectangular moated site 128 yds by 82 yds adjoins the NE side of All Saints churchyard. The OS map marks it 'Church Farm on site of Manor House' and Barker states that Church Farm 'stands on the site of the moated Grange once occupied by a branch of the Throgmorton family.' Immediately SW of the churchyard another rectangular moat, originally 87 yds by 55 yds, has been levelled and ploughed. It was shown unoccupied on the 1841 tithe map and thought to be the former site of the Rectory. Pottery sherds gathered from the site cover a period from C13-C17. Beside Meen's Farm, S of the church, are two sides of a moat with a possible outer yard and some evidence of C12 occupation. Immediately W of the site of St Nicholas Church is a small rectangular moat, and there are two moats by All Saints Common; one, of trapezoid shape on the E side, and another now flattened and ploughed but its rectangular shape still discernable with a scatter of C14-C16 pottery. There is evidence for another possible moat near Chestnuts Farm where a substantial scatter of C14-C15 pottery (with some C13?) was found S of a long infilled pond which may have at one time formed part of a small moat.

SOUTH ELMHAM ST CROSS (or ST GEORGE alias SANCROFT) *(5 miles SW of Bungay)*

Wangford Hundred. 'Sandy enclosure' (OE) *Sancroft* (1254). The parish is sometimes named from a family who held the manor here.

Sub-Manors. St. Cross/St. George (C13 Sancroft family).

Iron Age/Roman Industrial Site.

Parish Field, on the W side of New Road and S of Greshaw Farm, has revealed quantities of iron slag and Iron Age/Roman C1-C2 pottery sherds suggesting an iron-working site here.

Ancient Minster(?) & Former Roman Camp (?)

Lying isolated in a copse ½ mile SSW of the site of the Bishop's Palace at South Elmham Hall, this strong moated site, although called the 'Minster', has defied positive identification. When the East Anglian Bishopric founded by Felix (at Dunwich?) c630, was divided between Dunwich and 'Elmham' c670, it may have related to North Elmham in Norfolk where Saxon ruins do survive, or here at South Elmham (or even initially South Elmham and later North Elmham). The 'minster' here has proved a mystery in purpose, date and plan. Assigned to the C7, C10, mid C11 (Saxon) or late C11 (Norman), excavations revealing part of a C10 coffin lid built into the flint foundations. While not conclusive, this did suggest a date no earler than this. Its curious plan consists of an apse (not preserved but excavated) nearly as wide as the nave which is short, wide and aisleless with a square apartment of the same width as the nave at the W end. This may have been a porch, portcullis, or more likely the substructure of a tower (as at North Elmham). Finds on the site have been surprisingly sparse. The building, which was 101' long with flint walls still standing to c15', occupies a moated outworks comprising a strong moat and ramparts which in all probability pre-dates it and may have been the site of the place-name (*see* All Saints). Accounts speak of 'urns with burned bones and ashes' being ploughed up frequently in the area around the site, but these have not been verified. It has been suggested that it was possibly intitially built in wood on an existing Roman camp by Bertgils Boniface c652-670 A.D. and later rebuilt in flint and stone (c1050) by Bishop Ailmer as one of two sees of the Bishops of East Anglia - the other being *Dunwic* (Dunwich).

Site of Bishop's Palace.

South Elmham Hall occupies the site of the Bishop's Palace. It was part of the estate of William, Bishop of Thetford, at Domesday, and Bishop Walter Suffield (1244-1257) is said to have resided at Elmham when hunting. Bishop Roger Skerning died at his manor house of South Elmham in 1278 and Bishop Henry Despenser (1370-1406) had a licence to crenellate his manor house here in 1387. The site comprises a large quadrangular moat, 33' wide, enclosing about 3 acres. The E entrance is flanked by two stubs of masonry remaining from an original gatehouse. A massive flint and mortar wall is incorporated into the N side of some farm buildings and the S side of a barn in the NE quarter of the site. Against the W side of the moat and close to another bridge, a ruined flint building is called the 'chapel' though this may in fact be merely the remains of secondary lodgings - the C13-C14 core remodelled in the C16. The present hall contains the mortared flint core of the original palace with stonework in the form of arched doorways - not earlier than C13 and more likely C14. The house was externally remodelled by Lord North in the C16, after it had been granted to him - possibly in a ruinous state - following the Dissolution. The hall is now a working farm.

Site of Medieval Deer Park.

Sir John Tasburgh's Flixton Hall deer park, 'new in 1611' (*see* Flixton), extended S into South Elmham parish bounded by Park Road.

Deserted Medieval Settlements.

The church and hall stand isolated and a scatter of medieval pottery from around the perimeter of Greshaw Green shows that from the C13-C16 this provided the dominant feature and probably the major settlement site. The northern edge of the parish shows a number of deserted medieval sites of the same period mainly along Park Road, the former southern edge of Flixton park. The deserted green-side crofts continue to St James where they date mainly from C14-C16.

Medieval Green.

The extensive Greshaw Green was named Grazer Green on Faden's map of 1783 when it was shown as extending

SOUTH ELMHAM ST CROSS *(continued)*

from just N of Home Farm (S of the church), SSE along the line of New Road and Common Road to Hemplands Farm in the neighbouring parish of St James; a footpath here marks its southern extent. It provided common pasture for all the South Elmham parishes - at that time the domain of the Bishops of Norwich - and was the dominant feature of the medieval landscape here, covering a large portion of the parish. The green was enclosed 1853-4.

Ancient Moated Sites.

Three sides remain of a rectangular moat at Moats Hall, W of the church, formerly the site of the rectory; and at College Farm, N of the village, are two sides of a square moat.

SOUTH ELMHAM ST JAMES *(6 miles NW of Halesworth)*

Sub-Manors. Rawlings (C15 Bishop of Norwich).

Medieval Deer Park.

Part of the parish, called 'St James' Park', was anciently in the possession of the Bishops of Norwich who occasionally resided here in the C12 and C13. They had a deer park bounded on the NE by St James Lane, on the SE by the boundary with Chediston, and on the SW by the boundary with Metfield. The NW boundary may be marked by the dog-leg in St James Lane. It was disparked c1566 and is remembered in Park Farm and Park Farm Cottages.

Medieval Green.

The great Greshaw Green extended S into the parish (*see* St Cross).

Historic Houses & Ancient Moated Sites.

C13-C14 pottery has been found on the site of a rectangular moat (now infilled) which may have been a lodge of the Bishop of Norwich's deer park. Three arms drawn on the OS map of 1953 may refer to a former rectangular moat close by the church at Church Farm. The site of St James Town Farm was probably moated. The farm was demolished in 1946 and the site now shows as a cropmark with Medieval and Post Medieval pottery scatter, with further C13-C14 pottery scatters just SE and NE of the site.

Site of Pottery Industry (?)

A possible C16 pottery kiln site lies SE of the church and E of Rookery Lane.

SOUTH ELMHAM ST MARGARET *(5 miles SSW of Bungay)*

Deserted Settlement.

Earthworks in the form of hollows and possible house platforms lie in pasture, bounded by a rectangular extension to the S of the parish immediately E of the site of the Bishop's Palace at South Elmham Hall, and NE of the Minster.

Medieval Green.

A Margarets Green, named and shown by Faden, survives as a small green with a mill mound in the corner.

Historic Houses & Ancient Moated Sites.

A large irregular oval moat between the church and the green marks the ancient site of the Old Rectory. Another, roughly rectangular, on the edge of St Margaret's Green, enclosed a timber-framed house burned down 'within living memory' (1986). The site has revealed C15-C16 pottery. The infilled remains of a moated enclosure of approximately ¼ acre lies in pasture on the E side of the green adjoining Rookery Farm.

SOUTH ELMHAM ST MICHAEL *(4 miles S of Bungay)*

Ancient Way.

A packway heading N to Bungay forms a part of the southern parish boundary passing to the NE of what remains of Rumburgh Wood. It is then traced in field boundaries as it heads NW parallel with the eastern parish boundary to the Ilketshall St Margaret road, W of Boundary Farm.

SOUTH ELMHAM ST MICHAEL *(continued)*

Coin Hoard.
A hoard of C13-C14 coins was discovered in the parish.

Medieval Green.
St Michaels Green is shown on Faden's map of 1783 as a long green running SE from the church on the line of the present road to Ilketshall St Margaret. Its limits can still be defined by Green Farm and Home Farm.

Site of old Windmill.
A post mill stood NW of the church on the W side of the road to St. Peter in 1799. It was demolished in 1955.

Historic Houses & Ancient Moated Sites.
There are three sides of a shallow square moat beside St Michaels Green just to the W of the church. It may mark the site of the former manor house. Boundary Farm, on the SE parish boundary with Ilketshall St Margaret, dates from the early C16.

SOUTH ELMHAM ST PETER *(3 miles S of Bungay)*

Deserted Medieval Village (?)
Crofts and tofts indicated by soil marks in Church Meadow, N of the church, may indicate the remains of a lost medieval settlement in this tiny parish.

Historic House & Ancient Moated Sites.
St Peter's Hall, home to the Tasburgh family who lived here until 1615, probably dates from the C15 but incorporates C15 to C17 material from the ruins of St Nicholas Church and Flixton Abbey (including flushwork emblems and monograms). The three-light windows are Gothic and the large fireplace and ceilings, c1500. It stands on a strong moated site of which two arms remain with a northern extension.

SOUTHOLT *(5 miles SE of Eye)*

Hoxne Hundred. 'South copse' (OE) *Sudbolda* (DB). Anciently considered a hamlet of Worlingworth.
Manors. Southolt (1263 William de Bovile gave to St. John's Abbey, Colchester; 1545 Anthony Rous).

Medieval Greens & Commons.
Southolt Green was the linear Church Green running along the N side of the road to Worlingworth, gradually widening into the large triangular Worlingworth Green. Now enclosed, it is remembered in Big Green and Green Farm. In 1963 Southolt had two existing commons; Great Common, covering 14.25 acres, and Little Green of some 1.25 acres.

Historic Houses & Ancient Moated Sites.
Southolt Hall, NE of the village, still has part of a strong irregular moat, and The Lodge (formerly Paradise Farm) in the village itself, has three sides of a square moat. There are fragments of other small moats opposite Moore's Farm on the N side of the road, and immediately W.

SOUTHWOLD

Blything Hundred. 'South forest' (OE) *Sudwolda* (DB). The parish was once known as 'Southwood'.
Manors. Southwold (1259 Abbot of St. Edmunds and Richard de Clare exchanged this manor with that of Mildenhall; 1338 portion annexed to Wangford Priory).
The present town stands on a treeless knoll, its ancient forest, like that of Dunwich, now beneath the waves; though it may still have existed at the Domesday Survey. Southwold is nearly an island with the North Sea on its eastern side, Buss Creek on the N and Blyth haven to the S. The town developed later than its east coast rivals like Orford, Dunwich and Blythburgh - at one time it was little more than a hamlet of Reydon (only 9 were recorded here in 1086) - but in time it surpassed them in trade and commerce. This was greatly assisted by a

SOUTHWOLD *(continued)*

strong fishing industry (particularly in herring) centred on Buss Creek (busses being the name given to fishing vessels). However, its influence was ended abruptly when, on the night of April 25 1659, a great fire, fanned by a violent wind, consumed virtually all the public buildings and 238 houses; 300 families were made homeless. The results are still evident in the mainly Georgian and Victorian architecture and the open greens of South, North, East, St James's, Bartholomew, Barnaby, and St Edmund's.

Site of Ancient Encampment (?)

'An ancient encampment once existed at Eye Cliff. Local tradition says it was occupied by the Danes.' If it did, the fort and cliff have long been lost to the sea which has encroached over one mile since Domesday. It would probably have been situated S of the town guarding the entrance to the river Blyth.

Medieval Town Defences (?)

A C16 map, prior to the great fire, shows the 'island' of Southwold with bridge, windmill, gallows, various buildings, a street layout and an angular, seaward-facing defensive wall.

Site of Ancient Chapel.

The first chapel here was probably built in the time of King John (1199-1216) by the prior and monks of Thetford. After some 200 years this chapel was destroyed by fire and replaced by the present parish church considered, until 1751, only a parochial chapel under the parent church at Reydon. In Southwold's churchyard lies that celebrated antiquarian Thomas Gardner and his two wives Honour and Virtue. On his gravestone is inscribed, 'Between Honour and Virtue, here doth lie, The remains of Old Antiquity'.

Ancient Naval Finds.

A digger cleaning part of Buss Creek c1990 lifted a number of timbers from two different ships; one possibly a merchantman, the other a much finer vessel. Radio carbon dating from one of the timbers produced a date of 970-1155 A.D. The Battle of Sole Bay was fought off the coast here in 1672 (*see* Easton Bavents) and, following an incident in 1993 when fishermen snagged their nets and brought up cannon balls, local marine archaeologist Stuart Bacon, diving at the spot, recovered an 11' bronze demi-culverin cannon dated 1530 located within a 'cave' below a 10' high mound of conglomerate'. It is believed that this is the wreck of the Royal James, a 1,426 ton ship of 104 guns, built just prior to the battle. In 1995 a second gun was raised.

Site of Fortified Manor House (?)

In 1259 Richard de Clare obtained the manor of Southwold from Simon, Abbot of Bury Abbey, and in the following year obtained a licence to fortify his house at Southwold. 'Tradition says this castle stood on the site of, or near, "Hill House", formerly the Codsons House'. A house at Skilman's Hill now called "Castle Keep" is claimed to be the location and site of the original castellated manor house. Despite a claim by Claude Morley that pieces of dressed stone had been discovered in a garden in the area, there is nothing to substantiate this or other claims for a fortified house here and it may be that, whilst it is known that a licence was granted, the work was never actually carried out.

Site of Historic Fort (?)

A map of 1588 shows a large moated fort of a triangular plan with large quadrangular corner bastions and known as Fort Sussex(?) situated in the area of the present Boating Lake, just N of the town. It is suggested, however, that it may have been planned as a precaution against the Spanish Armada but never built, though, intriguingly, the N side of the site and the parish boundary both follow a sharp angular course which traces part of the fort plan.

Ancient River Crossing.

Mights Bridge forms the river crossing of the Blyth at the entrance to Southwold. This is the site of a former drawbridge shown on maps of 1575, 1610, 1755 and 1783. The construction date is unknown but bridges have been recorded here from as early as 1227.

Site of Salt Working & Fishing Industry.

'There is now little trace of the salt works or the wind pump at the head of Salt Creek which supplied brine,

SOUTHWOLD *(continued)*

though the salt works cottage still exists as does the salt in the walls of the new buildings on the site.' This site is identified as being on Town Marshes W of Gun Hill. The salt industry which operated until c1900 was probably closely related with the fishing industry for Southwold was the designated centre of the Free British Fishery in 1750. Salt production and/or storage is recorded in the town prior to 1509 when William Godell willed 'houses with all the salt in them' to Southwold. A linear series of ponds to the S, shown on the 1976 OS map, may be salt pans.

Historic Cannons.
The six old Elizabethan cannons which stand on Gun Hill - some bearing the Tudor Rose and Crown - are said to have been captured at Culloden in 1746 by the Duke of Cumberland and presented when he visited the town on his way back to London after the victory. These seige guns, known as Culverins, required fourteen horses to draw each one.

Medieval Gallows.
A C16 map shows a gibbet on the outskirts of town.

Site of old Windmills.
A post mill with an open trestle and known as White or Tower Mill stood S of the church on Southwold Common before 1723. Close by, Black or Great Mill was recorded in 1798; this mill was demolished in 1894.

Medieval Greens & Commons.
The open spaces of South, North, East, St James's, Bartholomew, Barnaby, and St Edmund's Greens are said to have been formed as a result of the great fire of 1659, but local C18 historian Thomas Gardner considered many of these may have already been in place prior to this. On Southwold Common in 1546, 'every poor man pays for his Cowgate (grazing) 1s. 8d. each year'.

Whipping Post.
A whipping post stood on the green outside the church.

Medieval Market & Fairs.
The town still retains its ancient market which was granted to the Abbot in 1222 and renewed along with that for an annual fair in 1227. A grant for a second fair was obtained in 1490. The Market Place and Market Hall were destroyed in the fire of 1659.

Medieval Market Cross.
The original medieval Market Cross was 'taken down in 1809 and sold for the sum of £39'. It stood where the pump now stands and was described as having "an open circular form supporting, by wooden pillars, a large room above which was reached by outside steps; a doom-shaped roof covered with lead, in the centre an ornamental iron spindle having on its point a gilt copper vane pierced with the date 1661."

Site of Medieval Guildhall.
The old medieval Guildhall which stood in front of the church was taken down in 1815 and a more 'commodius building' erected in its stead. It originally housed the Guilds of St. Margaret and St. Mary (c1459).

Workhouse & Hospital.
A workhouse built on lands of Town Farm in 1738 was pulled down in 1774 and replaced by a hospital for smallpox victims.

Historic Houses.
Sutherland House in High Street was the Royal Residence and Headquarters of the Duke of York (later James II) from 1666 to 1672. The town lost most of its old buildings in the great fire of 1659 but retains a number of old inns and former inns: The Red Lion (1672); The Swan Hotel [formerly The Kings Head] (1743); The Southwold Arms [formerly The Green Man] (1765); The Harbour Inn (1766); The White Lion (1656); The Crown (1766); The Victoria (1765) and The Two Brewers (1766). The Black Shore Inn was said to be a haunt for smugglers in the C18.

SPEXHALL *(2 miles NW of Halesworth)*

Blything Hundred. 'Woodpecker's shelter' or 'Valley with brushwood' (OE) *Specteshale* (1197). Includes the Domesday vill of Stone Street. The parish is bounded on the N by Grub Lane. Copinger recalled that he was told that a 'bower' was excavated at both angles of its eastern junction with the Roman road around 1910 - the possible site of the place-name ?

Manors. Spexhall (1288 John de Vallibus). *Sub-Manors.* Banyards; Burghard's Manor; Rivet(?)

Roman Road.

The modern A144 road follows the course of the Roman Stone Street (Margary 36) running NNW-SSE through the parish. The northern end, from School Farm to Rose Farm, and the southern end, from the railway crossing by Fairstead Cottages, forming the parish boundaries with Holton.

Ancient Tracks.

A lane running from Millpost Crossing (the railway crossing) N to Deadman's Grave, forms a part of the eastern parish boundary. A length of Wash Lane N from the Wisset Road, forms a part of the western boundary.

Site of Medieval Archery Practice (?)

Butt's Road which forms the eastern parish boundary, suggests the site of a meadow close by where archery practice took place in medieval times.

Medieval Gallows (?)

Deadmans Grave, E of the Roman Stone Street, may be the site of a former gibbet.

Historic Houses & Ancient Moated Sites.

Spexhall Hall, ¾ mile N of the church, has parts of three sides of a large rectangular moat. Spexhall Manor, a timber-framed manor house ½ mile S of the church, has the water-filled N and W arms (and the remains of the S arm?) of a possible moat. The house was refronted and enlarged in 1888. Spexhall Grove Farm retains a moat and earthworks in permanent pasture. NE of Grove Farm, near the northern parish boundary, Spexhall Wood has fragments of two sides of a moat, now bulldozed and cultivated.

SPROUGHTON *(2 miles NW of Ipswich)*

Samford Hundred. 'Sprow's farmstead' (OE) *Sproeston* (DB)

Manors. Sproughton Manor called Lovedays (1286 Roger Loveday holds of Honor of Lancaster). *Sub-Manors.* Dangeville's; Bordeshaw/Bradshaw/Bosford Hall al Boss Hall; Necton's/Netton's; Northwood's.

Ancient Woodland.

Burstall Long Wood in the NW corner of the parish, and Hazel Wood in the NE corner, are sections of ancient woodland.

Roman Road.

With one slight deviation, the B1113 follows the course of the Roman road N through the parish from the junction with Pigeon's Lane to Grindle Lane.

Ancient Tracks.

Grindle Lane, running W from just N of Hope Farm on the B1113 Roman road, forms the parish and ancient Hundred boundary. Pigeon's Lane, which crosses Swan Hill, forms part of the southern parish boundary.

Historic House.

The Rectory near the church is Elizabethan.

STANNINGFIELD *(5 miles SE of Bury St Edmunds)*

Thedwestry Hundred. 'Stony clearing' (OE) *Stanfelda* (DB)

Manors. Stanningfield Hall (C12 Robert FitzWalter). *Sub-Manors.* Coldwell Hall; Saxies.

Roman Road.

The modern A134 follows part of the Roman road N between Long Melford and Pakenham from just E of Shrub

STANNINGFIELD *(continued)*

Farm to TL891 556, the line of the eastern parish boundary with Cockfield.

Roman Pottery Industry.
Tile and pottery wasters which were discovered just W of the church, indicate the presence of kilns here, working in the C3-C4.

Medieval Greens.
Faden's map of 1783 shows Stanningfield Green lying across the junction now marked by Hoggard's Green; it has now been completely built-over. Moor Green ran N from Moor Green Farm and the junction with Old Lane.

Historic Houses & Ancient Moated Sites.
Coldham Hall, some distance from the church, has a medieval quadrangular earthwork to the rear (presumably an infilled moat). Old maps show twin gatehouses at the entrance to the driveway (in Lawshall parish) and an avenue of trees lining the driveway to the NW. The Hall is an interesting Elizabethan mansion built in 1575 by Robert Rokewode. He married a daughter of Sir William Drury of Hawstead, and was the father of Ambrose Rokewode, executed at Tyburn in 1605 for his involvement in the Gunpowder Plot. The Rokewodes were Roman Catholics and when in 1578 Edward Rokewode entertained Elizabeth I at Euston, she had him imprisoned and fined on discovering he was a 'papist'. The Rokewode family were to stay in possession of the manor for over 500 years. A complex earthworks in a wood called The Queech, W of the church, surveyed in 2000, may form the remains of the moated site of a lodge connected with the family. C12-C17 pottery had previously been found near by. Only fish-ponds and traces of the moat remain from Stanningfield Hall which stood near the church. Barfields has the remains of a rectangular moat, and a fine square moat with a spur to the SW by Gt Saxes Farm appears to have been infilled during the 1980s. Another rectangular moat with a possible entrance on the N stood 547 yds SE of the church within a field called 'Moat Field' on the C19 tithe map.

STANSFIELD *(5 miles NE of Clare)*

Risbridge Hundred. 'Stan's clearing' or 'Stone fields' (OE) *Stanesfelda* (DB)
Manors. Stansfield (-1302 de Clare family; 1302 Sir Thomas de Grey). *Sub-Manors.* Gatesburies/Gatesbye's; Priditon.

Ancient Woodland.
Black Wood, N of the parish, and Price Wood in the SE are fragments of ancient woodland.

Medieval Green.
The ancient Purton Green Farm in the centre of this elongated parish stands on the edge of the medieval Purton Green which runs as a linear green down to the stream. The site of the small Acton End Green, situated on the southern parish boundary and shown on Faden's map of1783, is marked on the present OS map as the hamlet of Assington Green.

Site of old Windmill.
A mill which stood by Mill House in 1783 was replaced by a tower mill in 1840. This mill, though disused, still survives.

Historic Houses & Ancient Moated Sites.
Three sides of a sub-rectangular moat remain at Purton Green Farm, ½ mile N of the village in the SW corner of the green. The N side is occupied by the late C13 timber-framed and aisled Purton Hall of two bays with a third two-storey bay. The upper bay of the hall was rebuilt and narrowed as a parlour with a chimney in the mid to late C16. The walls of the lower bay were rebuilt possibly in the early C16. The Old Rectory near the church has parts going back to the late C15. Elm Hall, S of the village, is a partly moated timber-framed house dating from the C15 and C16. The amazingly impressive series of six large 'fish-ponds' N of Cordell Hall (formerly Cardwell Hole) are, in fact, modern.

STANSTEAD *(6 miles NW of Sudbury)*

Babergh Hundred. 'Stony place' (OE) *Stanesteda* (DB). The place-name refers to glacial gravels which comprise the southern part of the parish. Here the main nucleated settlement is bounded on the E and W by two rivulets.
Manors. Stanstead/Over Hall (1219 Osbert de Wachesham). *Sub-Manors.* Netherhall; Woodhouse.

Ancient Woodland.

The extensive Stanstead Great Wood, Bar and Calves Wood, and Scotchford Wood in the S of the parish, and Woodhouse Wood just NE of the village, are all part of ancient woodland.

Medieval Green.

The small triangular green which fronts the church is shown on Faden's 1783 map as little more than a widening of the road.

Roman Villa.

Two walls of a Roman villa were discovered in the parish in 1993. They comprised flint and mortar footings, 2' wide and 7 coarses high, forming the SE corner of a room measuring at least 23' by 19½'. Fragments of hypocaust, flooring, tesserae and wall plaster were also found.

Site of old Windmill.

A post mill, blown down c1939, had been standing S of the Hall since around 1799.

Historic House & Ancient Moated Site.

Stanstead Hall, S of the church, was built c1620, but a pond nearby may be the remains of a moat on the site of the old rectory rather than the earlier manor house of Stanstead Hall, which old maps show to have been situated N of the church. The hall was home to the Wachesham family. Sir Gerard de Wachesham was Sheriff of Norfolk and Suffolk in 1290. Oaklands is an attractive timber-framed house in the village.

STANTON (All Saints & St John the Baptist) *(3 miles NE of Ixworth)*

Blackbourn Hundred. 'Stony village or homestead' (OE) *Stantuna* (DB)
Manors. Stanton All Saints (-1539 Abbot of St. Edmunds; 1539 Sir Thomas Jermyn). *Sub-Manors.* Stanton St. John, Michfields & Badwells (C14 Edmund de Stanton; 1533 absorbed by All Saints).
Formerly two parishes each with its own church. St John appears to have developed beside a Roman road from Ixworth (known N of the parish as Knab Lane), and All Saints as a separate (later?) development to the SE along the old Bury Road. Although Faden's 1783 map names the parish St John Stanton, already the main development is shown along the Bury Road at All Saints. Today, St John's church is in ruins, whilst the parish of All Saints continues to develop and expand.

Ancient Woodland.

Kiln Wood, High Wood and Wykes Wood (formerly Great Wood) are all parts of ancient woodland.

Ancient Tracks.

South of the village street, The Grundle - a gull formed as a result of melting ice at the end of the last Ice Age - was utilized in earlier times as a sunken way and remains today as a public footpath. It continues SE in the direction of Badwell Ash as Packloose Lane. Posters Lane forms a part of the southern parish boundary with Bardwell. Field Lane forms the NE boundary with Hepworth.

Roman Roads.

Field boundaries trace the course of the Roman Peddars Way from N of the Roman villa site at Stanton Chare, crossing the road from Sapiston to Barningham to the W of Slate Hall, and continuing NNW; the route also forms a part of the parish boundary with Bardwell. Another Roman road passes NNE through the N of the parish heading from Ixworth to Knettishall where it crosses into Norfolk. It is nowhere evident on the ground but must have passed close by the Roman villa (*see below*).

Roman Villa.

In 1933 at Stanton Chare, NW of the village, a Roman villa was uncovered and partially excavated between 1935-9. It revealed a wing c300' long consisting of a double apsidal building joined to a bath block by a

STANTON *(continued)*

corridor. The interior of what appears to have been a large estate building included wall painting and window glass. Evidence suggests an original wooden aisled building of pre-130 A.D. which had later been converted and extended. Coins dating from Nero to Honorius shows occupation until at least the end of the C4. The villa appears to have stood unusually close to the junction of two Roman roads *(see above)*.

Saxon Hundred Court.
Morley considered that 'there is a good deal of indirect evidence to show Stanton as a centre of jurisdictive activity early in or immediately preceding Saxon times', suggesting the Blackbourn Hundred Court met here.

Ancient Chapel.
A chapel owned by the monks from Bury Abbey existed near Stanton Hall in the Middle Ages.

Ancient Shrine.
A shrine, dedicated to a saint called St. Parnell (a medieval corruption of Petronille) and said to have been once held in All Saints Church, was the subject of medieval pilgrimage.

Medieval Greens & Commons.
The SE part of Bardwell Heath extended into Stanton, tapering down either side of the Barningham road and called Stanton Dale on Faden's 1783 map; Dale Road traces its western boundary. Chare Lane marks the site of Stanton Chare, an elongated leaf-shaped green or common which extended from St John's Street (the B1111 road), W to Lower Chare Farm; the Roman villa site stood SW of the green. Upthorpe Common, shown on the same map, was later used as a World War II airfield and is now an industrial estate. Faden shows a roughly square unnamed green adjoining Kiln Wood, on the junction of Wyken Road and Posters Lane, with another, tiny square green, just E, on the junction by Dovehouse Wood.

Deserted Medieval Settlement.
Upthorpe, a hamlet of Stanton to the SE, is shown on Faden's map of 1783 with many properties not only around the fringe of Upthorpe Green but by the network of roads connecting it to the main village of All Saints. All signs of this settlement have been destroyed by the construction of the airfield and later industrial development. Its name 'thorpe' suggests that it was always a secondary settlement of Stanton.

Site of old Windmill.
A smock mill which stood on the W side of the Diss to Bury Road (A143) between Glassfield Road and Bardwell Road in 1764 was demolished c1939.

Fairs.
Stanton had an annual Toy Fair in 1759 and a Pedlery Fair in 1792, abandoned in 1891. The Cock Inn also held Hiring fairs c1784.

Guildhall (?)
Although there is no record of a Guildhall here, there were three guilds operating in Stanton: Guild of St. John (1475), Guild of All Saints (1472), and Guild of Jesus (no date).

Town House.
In 1799 the Town House was occupied rent free by the poor.

Historic House.
The existing Cock Inn and Rose & Crown are likely to be the two inns mentioned in the C17. The old thatched bakery in the village street which dated back to the C16 was destroyed by fire in 1975.

STERNFIELD *(1½ miles S of Saxmundham)*

Plomesgate Hundred. 'Open ground of a man called Sterne' (OE) *Sternesfelda* (DB)
Manors. Mandeville's (C12 William Gulafre). *Sub-Manors.* Virlies/Glanville's.

Site of Ancient Mound.
SE of the village, on the N side of Kiln Lane, a 'U'-shaped ditch with an entrance facing the lane is named Mill

STERNFIELD *(continued)*

Mount on the OS map. No mound remains and none has been recorded on maps from 1753 onwards, so the earthworks is likely to date back at least to medieval times.

Ancient Tracks (?)

Back Lane and Sloe Lane, running E from Farnham Road, form a part of the southern parish boundary, the latter joining a track running NNW past Rudley's Grove to Kiln Lane which in turn forms a part of the eastern parish boundary. Both are likely to have an ancient origin.

Fortified House & Ancient Moated Sites.

When Michael de la Pole took possession of the sub-manor here he was granted a licence to fortify his mansion in Sternfield. Its site is unknown but may relate to the earthworks (*see above*) or one of the other moated sites which remain in the parish. Parts of a rectangular moat remain ENE of the church and just SW of Hill Farm, and cropmarks have revealed the site of a possible trapezoid moat SW of this and N of the B1121 road.

STOKE ASH *(3½ miles SW of Eye)*

Hartismere Hundred. 'Settlement by the ash tree' (OE) *Stoches* (DB). Morley tells us that 'here doubtless stood some notable ash tree. In the days of Saxon paganism, it would have been as celebrated for pilgrimages as was later St Edmund's shrine at Bury. All the Gothic peoples venerated the Great Ash called Ygg-drasill; "its branches", says the Prose Edda, "extend over the whole universe and its stem bears up the earth; beneath the root, which stretches to the land of the Giants, is Mimir's well wherein all wisdom is concealed"'.

Manors. Stoke Hall (-1536 Eye Priory; 1536 Edmund Bedingfield). *Sub-Manors.* Stoke Ash with Thorpe; Woodhall.

Roman Road.

The A140 Ipswich to Norwich road follows the line of the old Roman road from Coddenham to Caister by Norwich N through the parish from the junction with Mill Lane on the southern boundary to just W of Westwick Farm on the northern boundary. The western parish boundary follows the same line N from The White Horse Inn. A trial excavation of the old road (at Coddenham) has dated it to 70 A.D.

Roman Settlement & Cemetery.

There may have been an important settlement near The White Horse Inn beside the Roman road, where many finds of good quality pottery sherds have been made. Sepulchral urns were discovered on the E side of the road just N of the church, and in 1851, the Right Hon. Lord Henniker exhibited a British cinerary urn found on the N side of the rivulet below the church along with fragments of other vessels, one containing bones of a young skeleton, probably female. Other finds of a similar nature have been made in the same area at different times. To date there is insufficient evidence to confirm Rainbird Clarke's suggestion of a Roman posting station here.

Medieval Green & Site of Gallows (?)

Stoke Bowling Green is shown by Faden in 1783 at the junction of The Street and Deadman's Lane. The latter suggests the site of a gallows possibly sited where four parishes meet - Stoke Ash, Thwaite, Thorndon and Wetheringsett

Site of old Windmill.

A mill stood on the corner of Mill Lane beside the road to Norwich (A140) in 1764. It was burned down in 1883.

Historic Houses & Ancient Moated Sites.

The C17 White Horse Inn is of ancient origin - the petty sessions were held here monthy until the latter part of the C19 when they were transferred to Eye. The Rectory dates back to 1600, and Gardiner's Hall in the N of the parish, to 1666. Colsey Wood, on the southern parish boundary has a sub-rectangular moat in a good state of preservation. Wood Hall, on the western boundary, is the most ancient and important site in the parish. It is named in a Fine of 1310 as "the manor of Wodehalle" and the remains of a trapezoid moat which at one time probably surrounded the former manor house survives along with evidence of an outer moat some 100 yds in length. The manor was owned in the C13 by the de Geradvile family and a century later by the Poleys. The present house dates from the mid-C16 or earlier. A small, wide, sub-square moat is shown at the southern end of The Street on the C19 tithe map and named Darleys Garden.

STOKE BY CLARE *(5 miles ESE of Haverhill)*

Risbridge Hundred. 'Outlying farmstead or hamlet (of Clare)' (OE) *Stoches* (DB). Includes the Domesday vill of Boyton, now represented by Boyton End where an aerial photograph has shown the site of an unrecorded church (perhaps St. Augustine). 'Stoke' appears to have been used in Suffolk, like 'thorpe' to denote a hamlet or secondary settlement.
Manors. Stoke Ho (-1124 de Clare family who then endowed the Priory with the manor). *Sub-Manors.* Elbury/Erbury (-1553 de Clare family).

Ancient Woodland.
Lord's Wood on the northern parish boundary is the remains of ancient woodland.

Ring Ditches & Ancient Ritual Structure.
Listed by English Heritage S of the A1092 and Chapel Street Farm.

Ancient Track.
Way Bank Lane, named on Faden's map of 1783, forms a part of the NW parish boundary.

Ancient Priory & College
Against the S side of the green by the church, the grounds of the College incorporate minor parts of a Benedictine Priory. This was founded c1090 by Geoffrey de Clare at Clare Castle as a cell to the great abbey of Bec in Normandy, and transferred here in 1124. Little is known of its history, but it gained its independence from the abbey in 1395. About 1415 Edmund Mortimer, Earl of March, having augmented its revenues, obtained the king's permission to change the institution to a college of secular priests or canons dedicated to St John. The college consisted of a dean, six canons, eight priests, four clerks and six choristers. Many of its charters and documents have been preserved. The college - which gave accommodation and asylum to many leading reformers, hiding many in cavities within the thick walls and in chimney places, during the reign of Queen Mary - successfully withstood an attempt by Cardinal Wolsey to appropriate it for his college at Ipswich in 1526, and it was not dissolved until 1548. The last dean was Matthew Parker who attended Anne Boleyn on the scaffold and who later became Archbishop of Canterbury under Elizabeth I. The remains consist of the E parts of the Norman nave (made two-storeyed by the college), the transepts (which were used for domestic purposes), and the cloistered E wall of the dormitory.

Medieval Green.
Properties at the northern end of the village are still attractively arrayed round the medieval green which was shown, but unnamed, on Faden's map of 1783. This may be the Fulling Mill Green (now Mill Green) recorded in 1660.

Medieval Fair.
A fair for pedlary, operating c1618, was described as nearly disused in 1891.

Mills.
A Fulling Mill stood on the green in 1660 (*see above*), and a deed of 1693 contains a reference to 'Moore Mill' which may have been sited by Moor Hall (*see below*). A windmill stood on the E side of Blacksmiths Hill, N of the village, in 1783; its fate is not known.

Almshouse.
In 1526 Richard Brown directed an almshouse comprising three cottages to be erected at Stoke for six poor people. It was demolished in 1959.

Workhouse.
A workhouse in Upper Green housed 23 inmates in 1776.

Historic Houses & Ancient Moated Sites.
Hill Farm in the hamlet of Boyton End, 1½ miles NW of the village, is an unaltered early C17 building. Moor Hall originates from 1140 with additions c1240 and alterations in the C18. Deeds dated 1710 refer to 'hop grounds' called Moores.

STOKE BY NAYLAND *(2 miles NE of Nayland)*

Babergh Hundred. 'Outlying farmstead or hamlet (of Nayland)' (OE) *Stoc* (c970)

Manors. Tendring Hall al Stoke by Nayland (1282 William de Tendring); (Copinger noted another manor here owned by Geoffrey le Scrope in 1343). *Sub-Manors.* Gifford's Hall; Levenhay al Netherhall; Scotland Hall; Withermarsh; Capel; Chamberlains; Causers, Peachams or Shardelowes; Dounes; Stoke Rectory. The East Anglian cloth industry saw the parish expand and thrive throughout the C16 and C17, attaining an adult population of 900 by 1603.

Ancient Woodland.

Mark Wood and Hazel Grove on the northern parish boundary are sections of ancient woodland.

Ancient Settlement.

Cropmarks of over forty ring ditches plus field systems, tracks and enclosures have been recognised in the parish from aerial photographs, showing dense and very early occupation of the area.

Tumulus.

A long barrow has been identified by cropmarks on the line of a path which runs NE from the Nayland to Stoke by Nayland road (B1087) to Tendring Hall Farm, SE of the village.

Site of Saxon Monastery (?)

Stoke Priory, a mansion built in 1829 *(see below)* and situated a mile N of the church, is so named from its supposed connection with a monastery which is said to have existed, possibly on this site, before the Conquest. Many donations are said to have been made to it by Earl Aelfgar and his family who would appear to have been its founders. It was destroyed before 950 A.D.

Ancient Chapels.

Opposite the gatehouse of Gifford's Hall (*see below*) are the scant remains, in the form of the surround of a W window, of the Chapel of St Nicholas, built (supposedly) by a Richard Constable in 1216. This building of flint consisted of nave and chancel with a flat E end. There was a free chapel dedicated to Our Lady in the parish known as 'Stoke Chapel', but nothing is known of its history or site apart from the fact that it acquired ½ acre of land for its own cemetery in 1429.

Medieval Greens.

Withermarsh Green is shown on Faden's map of 1783 as a square green with a long tree-lined avenue to Giffords Hall. It also shows a small common called Sawyers or Sayers Tye which commemorates the Sayer family who held the C14 farmstead site here. It is now occupied by the plant nursery and paddock of Sawyers Farm. Another apparent green is shown on the SE corner of Higham Marshes.

Deserted Medieval Settlement.

The considerable manor of Withermers 'four furlongs broad by eight in length' comprised some 500 acres with its own church dedicated to St Edmund the Martyr. It is now represented by the hamlet of Withermarsh Green, NE of the parish and the river Box. The place-name means 'wether' or' young ram's marsh'.

Medieval Market & Fair.

William de Tendring obtained the grant for a market and fair here in 1303.

Medieval Recreation.

The Overseers Book shows the letting of Camping Close which was the probable site of a camping ground where medieval ball games were played.

Mills.

A watermill known as Stoke Mill dates from 1760 but there is evidence of earlier mills on the site. In 1783 a windmill stood by a track called Londs Lane, NE of Weylands Farm.

Hospital.

In 1618 Lady Anne Windsor founded a hospital here for four poor women and endowed it from her manor of Higham.

STOKE BY NAYLAND *(continued)*

Almshouses.
In 1675 five tenements in or near the churchyard provided almshouses for the poor at the bequest of Thomas Purslowe.

Workhouse.
The Old Workhouse in Back Street built in 1619 was formerly a Guildhall. A new Workhouse was recorded with 40 inmates in 1776.

Ancient Guildhall.
The C16 timber-framed Guildhall stands in its picturesque and much photographed position beside the lovely church of St Mary. Here the Guilds of St. Mary, St. Thomas and Holy Trinity met from 1524 to carry on their business. In 1691 a bucket and pulley was ordered for the common well which stood nearby.

Historic Houses.
The present Gifford's Hall, 2 miles NE of the village, was built by the Mannock family c1459; the superb roof over the great hall dates from 1480-1500. This family held the manor from 1428 to the 1880s. The Giffords were lords in the late C13, and the old banquetting hall and buttery (and possibly the kitchen) remain from their original manor house. Stoke Priory stands on the site of a Tudor house. Street House is mid-C16 and incorporates a late C14 open hall. The C15 Scotland Place, an open-hall house in the small hamlet of Scotland Street, is named from John de Scotland who owned this sub-manor in 1334. Thorington Hall, in the hamlet of Thorington Street, is a timber-framed house of c1600, later much enlarged and restored. In The Grove to the N of Tendring Hall Farm is the site of Tendring Hall, built in 1784 by Sir John Soane for the Rowley family. A landscaped park of c110 hectares. was designed for the hall c1791 by Humphrey Repton. The hall was demolished in 1955. It stood on the site of an earlier one built by Sir John Williams (d.1743) - Sir John's 'fine seat' is referred to in 1735. Sawyers Farm still retains the medieval detached kitchen dating from c1400 which became a service range for a new hall built in the 1590s. Nothing remains of this hall, and the kitchen has now been linked to the present farmhouse. The Maltings comprise three timber cottages built c1482 by Sir Roding. The Crown Inn dates from c1530 and is probably that listed as an alehouse or tippling house in the Overseers Book of 1689. The Black Horse is an old beamed public house and the former Rose Inn in the hamlet of Thorington Street dates back to the C16.

STONHAM ASPALL *(6 miles E of Stowmarket)*

Bosmere & Claydon Hundred. 'Stone enclosure' (OE) *Stanham* (DB). Disected by the Roman road to *Venta Icenorum* (A140), the original Stonham was divided into three parishes before the C14, each taking its name from the manorial family. Called Stonham Lambert after its rare church dedication (only one other in England) until 1292, this became known as Stonham Aspall from the lord of the manor Roger Aspale or Haspele. The 'stone enclosure' of the place-name may refer to a Roman building, perhaps the bath house discovered here (*see below*).

Manors. Stonham Aspall al Stonham Antegan (1275 Peter de Nereford; 1312 Roger de Aspal). *Sub-Manors.* Stonham Aspal called Broughton, Manor de Broughton's, Hall al Easke Stonham al Stonham Antigayne al Stonham Edmunds al Broughtons (C15 Robert Stonham; 1601 Sir Robert Broughton).

Romano-British Bath House.
The robbed remains of two rooms each 10' by 8' were discovered in 1962 during the cutting of a sewerage trench W of the church and just S of the A1120 Stowmarket to Yoxford road. The site is only a short distance E from Pains Hill on the Roman road (A140). Excavated over the following three years, it was identified as a Roman bath house originally consisting of a cold room with a plunge bath attached, and an apsidal heated room. In the last phase of development the roles of the two rooms were reversed, and a plunge bath and water tank added. The building appears to have been half-timbered on stone footings with a tiled roof, glazed windows and painted walls. The hypocaust pillars had survived but not the floor above. It dates from the C3 with alterations taking place in the late C3 and early C4.

STONHAM ASPALL *(continued)*

Roman Road.

The western parish boundary follows the course of the road from Coddenham to the Roman town of *Venta Icenorum* just S of Norwich. To the S at Pains Hill it lies on the present A140, but where this deviated slightly to the left, the boundary continues in a straight line (probably following the true course of the ancient road).

Ancient Track.

Winston Head Lane forms the eastern parish boundary with Winston and Pettaugh, and also follows the line of the Hundred boundary between Stow and Thredling.

Medieval Green.

Stonham Green, a wide linear green which was named and shown on Faden's map of 1783, tapered down from the junction with the present A1120 road as it crossed the parish boundary with Crowfield. It was named Broad Green in the C16. It has now been replaced by the Crowfield road. A strip green called Northern Green on the same map ran SSE from just N of Dove Farm House to the point where the road bends SW. It has been replaced by a road and the area now named Mill Green. A third green is shown in the C16 called Hazel Green. It ran W from Colmans (Red House Farm) to Futters and is now marked by a pond and the point where a footpath turns S. Its western and southern limits are also still marked by ponds.

Medieval Recreation.

Camping Lands situated near the church probably identify the site where medieval ball games were played.

Site of old Windmills.

A windmill which stood SW of the church was first mentioned in 1452. Another at La Roode near the western parish boundary was pulled down in 1640.

Town House.

A Town House was in existence in 1600 situated in the SE corner of the churchyard. It was physically removed (with rollers) to East End Road in 1873.

Free School.

A School, free to all the boys of this parish and neighbouring Pettaugh, was founded by Rev, John Metcalf in 1612. It stood on the site opposite the green which, until recent years, was occupied by a garage.

Historic Houses & Ancient Moated Sites.

Broughton Hall, modernised in the C16 and C17, is a moated house near the SE corner of the churchyard. It stands on the site of an earlier hall and was formerly the seat of a branch of the Wingfield family. The moat was curved suggesting great antiquity. A possible fish-pond remains to the E. Mowness Hall dates from the late C15 or early C16, and East End Manor, 1¼ miles E of the village, is a C15 timber-framed building still retaining a large part of its moat. Lewis's Farm to the E of the village had a small square moat which was infilled by 1973 leaving no trace. A small rectangular moat is shown on the C19 tithe map SE of the church, with a possible causeway on the S side. It was named 'moat & orchard' on the apportionment and the field to the S, 'Moat Field' but it has now been mostly filled in. The site produced pottery sherds of C13-C14 date. Also dating back to the C14, and each still bearing the name of the family who built it, are Symondes, situated next to the Ten Bells Inn (of c1500), and Elseys In The Field. Impaugh Farm is another house of ancient origin.

STOVEN *(5 miles NE of Halesworth)*

Blything Hundred. 'Place at the tree stump' (OE or O/Scand) *Stouone* (DB). A very early settlement site for, as Morley informs us: 'In 603(A.D.) Pope Gregory ordered English churches to be erected upon the sites of former Saxon pagan temples. These Saxons were tree-worshippers which takes the place-name Stoven (the early Stovin meaning a broad tree-stool whence the trunk had been cut) back to pre-Christian days.'

Manors. Stoven (1219 Sir Hugh de Jernegan holds of Roger Bigit; 1316 Robert de Biskele/Bixley).

Ancient Woodland.

The extensive Stoven Wood to the W of the parish is ancient woodland.

STOVEN *(continued)*

Medieval Greens.
Stoven had three greens: Stoven Green (now Church Green to the S on the junction of the Brampton to Frostenden road with that to Sotterley), and Middle Green both remain, but Further Green, shown on Faden's 1783 map and now marked by North Green Farm, has been lost. Confusingly, the present OS map names Further Green Farm at Middle Green.

Town House & Workhouse.
The cottage known as the Town House, in existence since before 1674, was taken down in 1882. In 1776 this may have provided the workhouse where six inmates were recorded.

Historic Houses & Ancient Moated Site.
North Green Farmhouse one mile NW of the village dates from the C16, and Church Farm opposite Church Green retains a large part of its square moat.

STOWLANGTOFT *(6½ miles ENE of Bury St Edmunds)*

Blackbourn Hundred. 'Place of assembly or holy place' (OE) *Stou* (DB) *Stowelangetot* (C13) The name is a corruption of Stowe Langetot. The Langetot family held the manor in the C12 and early C13.
Manors. Stowlangtoft (1206 Richard de Langetot; C13 Sir Nicholas Peche). *Sub-Manors.* Colvyles.

Ancient Woodland.
Stocking's Wood and Nine Acre Wood in the S of the parish are parts of ancient woodland.

Roman Road.
The present A1088 road, passing through the parish from the A14 junction NW to Ixworth, forms the parish boundary for a short section N of Stanton Street. It may (apart from a loop from Stowlangtoft Spinney to Bridge Farm) follow the line of a Roman road (Margary 330). It runs through known Roman sites both N (Roman building) and S (Grimstone End settlement) of its course at Stow Lane. Ditches of uncertain date cross N of Bull Road crossroads.

Coin Hoard.
In 1764 a total of 12,420 Roman coins were found 'in a pot in a field' in the parish.

Ancient Earthwork Camp.
The church stands within an oblong double-trenched camp with clearly defined ramparts on the eastern and northern sides of the churchyard (those to the S have been destroyed by the road). On the E side the inner moat is 3' deep and 15' wide, and the outer one a similar depth but only 10' wide. On the N the moat is a similar depth but only 8' wide. A spearhead and coins have been found here. This may well have been the original 'place of assembly' or 'holy place' which created the place-name.

Site of Pottery Industry.
Kiln Lane, Kiln Plantation and Kiln Farm in the N of the parish point to the site of a probable medieval pottery industry in the area.

Medieval Green.
Faden's 1783 map shows a green either side of Kiln Lane opposite the hall.

Medieval Cross.
There is record of a payment of 20s in 1530 for a 'Cross to stand at Fitzjohn's'. This was possibly a wayside cross placed by the present A1088 Ixworth road.

Almshouses.
Almshouses were built in the C18 to accommodate four poor widows. The founder is not known.

Historic Houses & Ancient Moated Sites.
Stowlangtoft Hall was preceded by an earlier manor house on a different site to the S called Stow Hall, built in 1625. It was the residence of Sir Simon D'Ewes, one of the most learned antiquarians of the C17. It was

STOWLANGTOFT *(continued)*

probably pulled down prior to 1783 and partly rebuilt in 1792. It was finally burned down prior to 1859 when the present hall was built on a new site. There are likely to have been previous halls on the old site where ownership can be traced back to 1206 when Richard de Langford held the manor and was resident here. A moat, now dry, survives in Round Grove, 765 yds SE of the church. It is rectangular, some 79' by 66' with a break in the SW corner which may be original. The island is lower than the surrounding land and there are traces of an external bank on the N and E. A small square moat is shown on the 1824 OS map N of the church. It averaged 10' wide except on the W where it attained a width of 30'. The W side only now survives. Coins (possibly Roman) and a spur were found near the site in 1845. Both these moats may mark sites of earlier manor houses.

STOWMARKET

Stow Hundred. 'Meeting place' (OE) *Stou* (DB) 'Market' had been added to the name of Stowe by 1253, and a John "de Stowe Market" was mentioned in Patent Rolls of 1299.

The place was earlier a royal manor called 'Thorney', a name which shows that the original settlement was on an island - or more likely, peninsula - in the river Gipping. Morley suggests that it probably came from the pagan Saxon god of rain, Thunor. He it was who was said to have been 'born out of the water, to have filled the rivers and poured the milk of the cloud cows upon the thirsty earth'. The present church stands on an ancient site (perhaps once used to worship this pagan god). Thorney comprised three Domesday estates: *Ciltuna*, still represented by Chilton Hall (a former hamlet now incorporated into the town and used for residential expansion); *Torpe* or Thorpe, a still unlocated hamlet held in 1065 by Gutumund of Haughley - which may suggest it lay to the NW of the present town (in the area of Tot Hill?) - and the now totally lost *Torstuna* or Thurston. The Hundred Court for Stow Hundred was held in the town.

Manors. Thorney (at Domesday); Stowmarket al Abbot's Hall (C12-1538 Abbot of St. Osyth, Essex; 1538 Sir Thomas Darcy). *Sub-Manors.* Columbine Hall al Tjorney Columbers; Thorney Hall; Thorney Campsey; Thorney Kebles (may be the same as Campsey); Clements; Cardons; Thorney Lizon's al Liesnes; Thorney Mumpliers with Braziers.

An ancient chronicle declared, at the time the Conqueror took over the manor from Edward the Confessor, that "the productions of the land were more numerous, the stock larger, the whole population richer and more comfortably circumstanced in this hundred and in Suffolk in the years 1066 and 1086 than in any of the Midland or Western Counties." In 1348-9, following the Black Death, Flemish and Dutch merchants settled in East Anglia and the town became a centre for the woollen industry. At the beginning of the C17 the Stow cloth trade was flourishing but although still being termed a 'borough' up to 1683, Stowmarket had begun a steady decline until, in 1793, the Gipping was made navigable to Ipswich, returning industrial and commercial wealth to the town. Later the railways which superceded the barge traffic would continue this expansion. Sadly, being for so long a centre of industry has taken its toll on the town's important antiquity which is now little in evidence.

Site of Roman Pottery Industry (?)

A Roman pottery industry is thought to have operated on the site of Chilton Hall, NW of the town, where a pottery kiln was found in 1970.

Ancient Moot.

Stow gives its name to the Hundred and was the meeting place of the Hundred Court. The site is no longer identifiable.

Ancient Camp (?)

Danescroft, on Finborough Road, is the reputed site of a Danish camp used whilst attacking the area c870 A.D.

Site of Ancient Hall.

Thorney was the chief manor of Stowmarket and Thorney Hall a sub-manor. The hall was said to have been the residence of the King's bailiff from the Conquest to the reign of Henry I. Its site was in the area of Creeting Road and its remains were converted into maltings in 1912 (not the maltings in Station Road). Faden's map of 1783

STOWMARKET *(continued)*

shows an avenue to the hall NW of Stowupland Road. It was part of the royal manor of Thorney and had its own church or chapel (*see below*). The manor was granted to the Abbot of St Osythe, Essex, by Henry II. He had free warren in Stowmarket in 1268.

Ancient Chapels.

St Mary's Church or chapel, one of two recorded here at Domesday was rebuilt in 1473-8 by four freemen 'on their own land near the cemetery of the mother church' because the mother church could 'no longer take the whole of the parish'. It was demolished c1546 and the main church took over the dedication at the expense of St. Paul. Another chapel to Our Lady in Stowe and recorded in 1524 is thought to have formerly stood in a field still called Chapel Field on Tot Hill.

Site of Ancient Mill.

The mill mentioned here at Domesday was probably that which adjoined the bridge at Combs Ford. It later passed by Royal warrant to the Abbey of St Osyth.

Site of Ancient Grange.

Abbot's Hall, an early C18 house, stood on the site of Stow Hall, a grange of the Abbots of St Osyth. A late medieval barn, formerly 160' long and once part of the grange, has been incorporated into the Museum of East Anglian Life which occupies the site. On an island in the lake (perhaps a former fish-pond) is a summer house.

Medieval Market & Fair.

Thorney Manor was one of only nine places mentioned in Domesday as having a market, and Richard de Amundeville obtained a grant for a market and fair for Thorney Hall Manor in 1338. It was probably held originally around the church or in Stowupland Street. The Abbot of St. Osyth held a fair on his manor in the same year. This took place on the Camping Land opposite Abbot's or Stow Hall (in the area of the present museum). Coins of various reigns have been found here, including those of Edward I, the period when the fair was first established.

Medieval Recreation.

Camping Land opposite Abbot's or Stow Hall identifies the possible site where medieval ball games were played.

Smallpox Hospital.

A serious outbreak of smallpox broke out in 1678 when 51 soldiers quartered in the town died. The site of their mass grave is known as Soldiers Hill. An isolation hospital built to tend smallpox victims gave name to Sick House Lane.

Former Guildhall.

There were four Guilds operating in the town: Our Lady, St. Margaret, St. Peter and St. John (1450) and frequent mention is made in records of a former Guildhall here. Its earliest listing is 1460 and in 1619 it was partly used as a school house and partly as a poor house. It may have been situated in the churchyard of St Peter and St Mary's Church where massive foundations have been found, though these more likely relate to the second church which once shared the site.

Workhouse.

A workhouse is recorded with 85 inmates in 1776.

Historic Houses & Ancient Moated Sites.

Edgar's Farmhouse, Combs Lane, dates back to the 1340s and is a timber-framed aisled hall of two bays originally open to the roof, with a third bay of two-storeys at the lower end. There is a crown-post roof and the whole forms a part of the Museum of East Anglian Life. There are fragments of a much damaged irregular rectangular moat at Chilton Hall Farm. Another moat, square and standing in the SW corner of a larger square outer moat, lay N of the C16 Cedars Hotel, in the flood plain S of the river Gipping. Excavations revealed evidence of two clay-floored buildings within the moated area, one with a hearth. Pottery dated the site to the C13. The only remaining house of interest in the town itself is the former Rose Inn (now a solicitors) which dates from 1461. It reputedly once held prisoners being transported to Bury and Ipswich gaols.

STOWUPLAND *(1 mile NE of Stowmarket)*

Stow Hundred. 'Stow on the plateau' (OE). Although known for hundreds of years as Ultim, Upland or Upland of Stow, Stowupland is comprised not only of Thorney, which it shares with its near neighbour, but other independent former Saxon estates including Roweham, held by Saxo in 1065 (which Vincent Redstone thinks is represented by Saxham Street), and Columbers, a manor represented by Columbine Hall.
Manors. Always incorporated in the manorial system of Stowmarket.

Iron Age Settement.
In a southern projection of the parish S of Sheepcote Hall, excavations over four years on the site of a new residential housing development have unearthed evidence of an Iron Age settlement including roundhouses dating to between 200 B.C. and 43 A.D. (the date of the Roman invasion), at the centre of a patchwork of agricultural fields. Finds included pottery and querns for grinding corn and a number of fences and ditches providing animal pens and drainage leading down towards the river Gipping.

Roman Villa.
A small Roman villa, probably built around 120 A.D., was discovered on the crest of a hill within its own farming estate of rectangular fields leading down to the river during the same archaeological excavations (*see above*).

Roman Site.
Although numerous finds from what appears to be an affluent, but mainly timber, Roman farmstead were made in the area of Park Farm, surrounding field names Great and Little Castle Field and Great and Little Bovells (the de Bovells were lords of the manor here) are suggestive of a former more substantial, as yet unlocated, earthwork.

Ancient Track.
Old Hundred Lane, N of the hamlet of Saxham Street, forms the extreme northern parish boundary with Mendlesham and the ancient hundred boundary between Stow and Hartismere.

Ancient Chapel.
Stowupland was without a church until 1843 but it would appear that a chapel known as St John the Baptist Chapel in Thorney once existed here. The parish included the manor of Thorney, held by the nuns of Campsea, the church of which had the same dedication. After the Dissolution the manor passed to Thomas, Duke of Norfolk.

Site of Ancient Battle.
'The Battle of Stonebridge' in 870 A.D. fought between the Saxons and Danes is traditionally said to have taken place 'at the foot of Columbine Hall Wood, in a valley through whose meadows the river creeps along' near Stonebridge, S of Stonebridge Lane. In 1844 Hollingworth wrote in his *History of Stowmarket* that 'for many years (in Pit Meadow) the bones of men and horses in great abundance have been found and relics of this ancient warfare lie in heaps 4' to 5' below the surface and are circumscribed as if collected in shallow pits. Bones of horses and men, broken and entire, are intermingled with spurs without rowells, bits of sword-blades 2" or 3" broad, pieces of the heads of spears, scraps of armour, horses' shoes of great breadth and made to cover nearly the whole hoof, nails and rivets. There has been about ½ acre of this meadow disturbed for gravel upon which these remains rest and they have been found in every part; at present the ground is more abundant with them, and they increase. Recently the remains of an ancient stone road appeared below; the ford of the rivulet Gipping near them is called Stone Bridge. Some lines of entrenchment exist about Columbine Hall, immediately above the field of conflict'. In 1900 the owner of the hall referred to bones, weapons and a silver armlet which had been unearthed when the meadow was ploughed. No recent work has been carried out to confirm or deny these assertions.

Medieval Green.
One of the largest remaining medieval greens in the county, Thorney Green, still occupies a 'T' shaped area extending from Poole's Farm NE to Green Farm and SE to the present A1120 road.

Workhouse.
A workhouse is recorded here with 20 inmates in 1776.

STOWUPLAND *(continued)*

Historic Houses & Ancient Moated Sites.

Columbine Hall, itself an ancient house ¾ mile NW of the church and bordering the NE side of Thorney Green, stands on the fortified moated site of an even earlier manor house. The moat is large and trapezoidal in shape with two adjacent ponds. It is at its widest on the W and N sides which are wet and has access via a causeway to the S. The hall is sited in the NW corner of an island of 0.8 acres, with W and N walls rising sheer out of the water. Constructed on mortared flint up to the first floor level, it has a jettied, timber-framed upper storey. In the middle of the W wall, a blocked entrance indicates the site of a possible earlier gatehouse with access across a wooden bridge. The present house dates from the late C14 or c1400. The site takes its name from the Manor of Thorney Columbers held in the C13 and C14 by the Columbers or Columbiers family of Nether Stowey in Somerset. The Hotots were under-tenants in the C14 and C15, an heiress of whom married James Tyrell (d.c1539). Later owners included the Gardiners, Sir Robert Carey, the Earl of Monmouth (though not a resident), the Poleys and the Gipps. In a meadow called Park Hill can still be seen the overgrown trenches which, according to tradition, were dug by the Danes when encamped against the place *(see battle site)*. Crown Farm has two sides of a square moat with spur, and three sides of a possible moat are shown as still surviving on the tithe map at Gipping Farm. There is evidence of former moats at Green Farm and Poole's Farm which both border the ancient green.

STRADBROKE *(9½ miles NW of Framlingham)*

Hoxne Hundred. 'Place by a brook which one can easily stride or straddle' (OE) *Stetebroc* and *Statebroc* (DB) 'Strad' would be suggestive of a paved (Roman) road, but Morley states that the 'r' was not added until it was written as Stradbrok in the 1327 subsidies.

Manors. Stradbroke with Stubcroft (C11 Ernald Rufus (le Rus) held of Honor of Eye; 1280 Richard de Brewse).
Sub-Manors. Shelton Hall; Hyllys/Hills, Drawsword's and Denneys; Woottons; Wotton's/Thorpe Hall with Wotton's; Barleugh/Buslaugh Hall.

Ancient Mound - Site of Battle (?)

At Battlesea Green are the remains of an earthen mound. Now named Mill Mound it likely once held a windmill (though one is not shown on Faden's 1783 map so it is therefore likely to be earlier in origin) but further suggestive names of Battlesea Hill and Rattlerow (?Battlehlaw - 'a burial mound') suggest the possible site of some ancient conflict here beside the Strad Brook.

Chapels.

In the manor of Scheltons, John de Schelton had an ancient chapel in use between 1306 and 1455. The remnants of an C18 Roman Catholic chapel are incorporated in the upper storey of a C17 farmhouse called The Rookery (formerly Battlesea Hall). The house was owned by the Catholic Fox family and sold by them to the Henniker-Majors of Thornham Magna. The medieval retable in Thornham Parva church is thought to have come from this private chapel.

Medieval Greens.

The former Battlesea Green on the NW parish boundary extending into Wingfield, was shown as such on Faden's map of 1783. It was probably a part of the 132 acres enclosed under a Private Act of 1811 which included a SE extension called Rattlerow Green. The 1837 OS 1st Ed. shows the green reduced to a triangular portion in Wingfield parish. The northern arm extension to the parish boundary (divided by North Lane) probably traced the limits of the former Pixey Green which, along with Barley Green - which extended from NE of the church, SE either side of the present B1117 as far as Barley Bridge - were enclosed around 1814. Wootten Green, marked and named (Wotting) by Faden, lay either side of the present B1118 road which runs ENE-WSW to the S of the village; this has also now been enclosed. Ashfield Green is remembered in the name of a three-way road junction, E of the village.

Medieval Market.

Stradbroke had the grant of a market in 1225, and fairs to Sir Richard de Brewse in 1309 for cattle and pedlary, and hiring of servants, which continued until 1872.

STRADBROKE *(continued)*

Site of old Windmills.

The mill which stood at Barley Green c1704 was demolished in 1940. The following year the old mill which had stood at Skinners Green since 1688 was also pulled down.

Former Guildhall.

Bishop Grosseteste was born in Stradbroke in 1168, reputedly in the Town House, a timber-framed building which stood on the T-junction in the village, just SW of the church. He became Bishop of Lincoln and died in 1253 at Buckden Abbey. The Town House was called St. Anne's Guildhall in 1463.

Free School.

According to an old document, a Free School, endowed by Michael Wentworth for the education of five poor children, was 'kept in the chamber of the Guildhall' which he had given to the parish in 1587. Twelve additional children were educated here in 1667 from the Warner Charity provided in the will of Mary Warner.

Workhouse.

A workhouse with 40 inmates is recorded in 1776.

Historic Houses & Ancient Moated Sites.

The Rookery (formerly Battlesea Hall) has a series of isolated rectangles beside the NW parish boundary on the W side of Battlesea Green. While these may be parts of an C18 ornamental canal, a slightly wider ditch at the N end (E side) may be part of a small original moat incorporated into the system. Stradbroke Hall near the church has a very large rectangular moat, partly sub-divided, and behind the S side of the village street are portions of three sides of a moat on the site of the Rectory, with another series of rectangular moats (or more likely fish-ponds) SE by Home Farm (formerly Boyton Trust Farm). Broadway Hall (formerly Whitbread's Farm) near the eastern boundary, retains a small but complete trapezoidal moat. At Wootten Green on the southern parish boundary a small, square enclosure (a probable moat) has been bulldozed and ploughed flat. Fragments of what was once a large rectangular moat remain on a site now occupied by Cheney Farm at the southern end of the former Pixey Green, SW of Ebdens Corner; further S, Red House has the western arm of a possible rectangular moat. The Queens Head in Queen Street, recorded in 1650, probably dates from the C16.

STRADISHALL *(5½ miles NW of Clare)*

Risbridge Hundred. 'Dwelling on the (paved) road' (OE) *Stratesella* (DB). Includes the Domesday vill of Farley. *Manors.* Stradishall (-C15 de Clare family). *Sub-Manors.* Cockrell's al Fosters; Shardelowes.

Tumuli.

A group of burial mounds called 'Edmund's Hills' lie by the B1063 road, S of the village.

Roman Road (?)

'Strade' is suggestive of a Roman road possibly on the line of the A143 which bisects the parish WSW-ENE.

Deer Park.

The boundaries of one of three medieval deer parks mentioned in 1509 as covering parts of Hundon and Stradishall parishes are marked by the road running WSW by Three Ash Farm, and the road running S from Stradishall Church. Hundon Great Lodge, situated between the two roads in Hundon parish, served as lodge for two of the parks. Tradition suggests Elizabeth I may have stayed here whilst hunting in the area.

Medieval Green.

A small green called Three Ashes was situated on the SW parish boundary by a road junction. It is now marked by Three Ashes Farm.

Site of old Windmill.

A post mill which is shown NW of Howes Farm in 1783 was demolished in 1884.

Almshouse.

In 1584 a double cottage next to Mansion House was provided under the Hoult's Charity for two poor men and

STRADISHALL *(continued)*

women plus £3 per annum for their benefit. The building fell down in 1813.

Workhouse.
The workhouse built by John Vernon in 1737 was converted to a Wesleyan Chapel in 1843. It held 16 inmates in 1776.

Medieval Guildhall.
Repairs are recorded to the Guildhall in 1474.

Historic Houses & Ancient Moated Sites.
Moat Farm on the corner of Farley Green has a trapezoidal moat, and earthworks on the eastern parish boundary W of Denston Hall, may be the remains of a moat. A building is shown within the enclosure on a 1778 estate map but this had gone by the 1839 tithe when the site was named Old House Yard. The Weavers, a former Town House, dates from the C16/C17.

STRATFORD ST ANDREW *(3½ miles SW of Saxmundham)*

Plomesgate Hundred. Strate Forda - 'Ford where a Roman road crossed the river' plus church dedication (OE) *Straffort* (DB)
Manors. Stratford (-1535 Ranulph de Glanville gave to Butley Priory; 1535 Charles Brandon). *Sub-Manors.* Griston; Arnigers.

Ancient Woodland.
Great Glemham Wood on the western parish boundary, and the sparse remains of Denney Grove to the N of it are remnants of ancient woodland.

Roman Road.
A Roman road forded the river Alde at a point where the present A12 crosses Stratford Bridge (*see above*).

Fair.
In 1759 Stratford is recorded as holding a Toy Fair on 11 June.

STRATFORD ST MARY *(11 miles SW of Ipswich)*

Samford Hundred. 'Ford where a Roman road crossed the river' plus church dedication (OE) *Stratfort* (DB)
Manors. Stratford Hall (C12 Hubert de Munchensy; 1316 John de Stratford). *Sub-Manors.* Vesey's/Bonhall Payses; Overhall; Spanbies/Spanbies-Sulyard.

Neolithic Henge Monument (?)
A ringed bank some 89' in diameter with a ditch 12' wide and a 9' wide entrance was thought to have been surrounded by a circular timbered 'sanctuary' and been a possible Neolithic henge monument - though many scholars would disagree. The field in which the crop mark lies, S of Kings Wood, is named Mount Field on the C19 tithe map. Evidence in the form of an internal cruciform feature showing as a crop mark in dry summer suggest the earthwork once held a post mill.

Cursus & Ring Ditches.
The SE and NW corners survive (from the creation of the A12 Stratford bypass) from a large rectangle approx 240 yds by 109 yds lying on a NW-SE axis SW of the church. Close by are two pairs of ring ditches. The group lie some distance S of the 'henge' earthworks with which they may be associated (*see above*).

Roman Road.
As its name implies - and like Stratford St Andrew in NE Suffolk - the Roman road from Colchester forded the river (in this case the Stour) here to enter Suffolk at a point where the present A12 crosses Stratford Bridge.

Roman Settlement.
Although no finds have been made within the enclosure to firmly date it, the site of the Roman settlement of *Ad Ansam* on the Antonine Itinerary has been suggested as having stood on Gun Hill overlooking

STRATFORD ST MARY *(continued)*

the Stour a quarter of a mile SW of the village. Here the Roman Inter IX road enters Suffolk and probably forked to Hadleigh and Bildeston. The name comes from the Latin *ansa* meaning handle or loop - presumably a description of a bend in the river at this point, traced by the sharp bend in Dedham Gun Hill.

Medieval Market & Fair.
William de la Pole was granted a market and fair here in 1384, plus a special charter for a court leet.

Watermill.
A watermill has existed on the same site in The Street since 1619. The last building shown on the OS map of 1843 was used for the manufacture of macoroni and was known as 'Macaroni Mill'. The business closed in 1890.

Medieval Gallows.
A Gallows Field is shown situated opposite 'The Gables' and the church on a map of 1821.

Free School.
A Free School was founded in 1588 by the bequest of Lettice Dykes for the education of two poor children. Robert Clarke's bequest in 1731 was for ten poor children and it had 40 by 1818.

Historic Houses & Ancient Moated Sites.
Priesthouse, W of the church, is a C15 timber-framed house; Corner House is dated 1596; Weavers House is early C16, and Brook Farm, ½ mile NW of the church was built c1500. The Kings Arms is a former coaching inn and The Swan posting house dates from the C16 - George II is said to have stayed here in 1736. The Blackhorse Inn is associated with the highwayman Matthew Keys who is said to have left his watch, sword and pistol in lieu of payment for his bill.

STRATTON HALL *(7 miles SE of Ipswich)*

Colneis Hundred. 'Farmstead on a Roman road' (OE) *Strattuna* (DB). Stratton Hall was extra-parochial and anciently a separate parish; it is now a part of Trimley.
Manors. Stratton Hall cum Seabridge (pre-C15 Sir Olliver de Stratton; 1421 John Shardlowe).

Ancient Woodland.
Stratton Hall Wood is part of ancient woodland.

Roman Road.
As its name implies, a Roman road - the exact line of which has still to be identified - ran through the parish from Downham Bridge to the Roman fort at Walton (Felixstowe).

Ancient Track.
Near Stratton Hall, 'The Pack Field' indicates the line taken by 'Earl Bigod's Way', the old packway which ran between the earl's castles at Walton and Framlingham. Sections are still marked by footpaths on the O.S. map.

Deserted Medieval Village.
The parish, which now comprises merely Stratton Hall Farm on the site of the former manor house, was once a major medieval manor listed at Domesday as having a total of 17½ freeman, 2 villeins and 11 borders working land held by Robert Malet and Roger Bigot, plus a church and a mill. C13-C14 pottery finds from fieldwalking in 1989 has pinpointed the possible site of the medieval settlement, and ploughing has revealed the site of the former church of St Peter situated near the head of Levington Creek.

Ancient Chapel & Lazer House.
'The ruins of Stratton Chapel, now overgrown with trees and bushes, are still to be seen in the middle of the first field going from Levington to Trimley, called Chapel Field. Here was formerly a Lazer House endowed with a 'moiety of the tithes of Stratton.' (1764). 'All traces of this church were removed about 60 or 70 years ago, and the stones taken to Trinity *(Trimley?)* to build a barn, which I believe is now demolished.' (1902). 'The foundations of the church can still be seen.' (1908). The site of St Peters Church or Chapel lies isolated by the parish

STRATTON HALL *(continued)*

boundary near the head of Levington Creek where remains are still turned up by the plough. Near Levington Hall five skeletons were unearthed while cutting a trench, and a further two unearthed c1970. These may come from the cemetery of the church or leper hospital.

STUSTON *(3 miles N of Eye)*

Hartismere Hundred. 'Stut's farmstead' (OE) *Stutestuna* (DB)
Manors. Faucons al Fakons/Falcons (-1544 Flixton Priory; 1544 Sir Thomas Cornwallis). *Sub-Manors.* Beziller/Boylands; Beauchamps; Hugh/Hoo Margaret's al Stuston Hall.

Bronze Age Pottery Industry.
In 1955 on Stuston Common, in a large pit some 8-9' in diameter, archaeologist Basil Brown found an oval hearth some 2' across and 6" deep of Early Bronze Age date and probably used for making pottery. Two sherds of Beaker pottery were found.

Roman Roads
The Roman road to *Venta Icenorum* (A140 Ipswich-Norwich) runs SW-NE to form the eastern parish boundary. At Scole Bridge where it crossed into Norfolk 'original blocks of paving stone' were found in the river Waveney sometime before 1889. The road at this point was 21' wide, constructed of packed flints and ditched on the W side. Another Roman road 18' wide, cambered and constructed of compacted gravel, has been discovered, 9" below the surface, running N-S across Stuston Common.

Roman Camp (?) and Wharf.
Aerial photographs have revealed what may have been a temporary Roman marching camp on the southern side of the river crossing into Norfolk. Adjacent to the road found 9" below the surface (*see above*), evidence of buildings and 13 piles of a Roman wharf were discovered along with portions of leather sandals preserved in the silt and a large quantity of pottery.

Roman Building.
Flint foundations of a building 11'6" square were found on Stuston Common some 18" below the suface, 70' W of the N-S Roman Road described above. It had a central flint hearth and occupation debris; coins found on the site dated from C1-C3.

Earthworks.
Rectangular earthwork were revealed by cropmarks, ditched on the W side where it abutts Stuston Common. An enclosure is shown here on the 1st edition OS map. The site revealed a scatter of mainly C13-C14 pottery.

Medieval Common.
Stuston Common, shown on Faden's 1783 map, remains, part of which is now used as a golf course.

Historic Houses & Ancient Moated Sites.
Stuston Hall, built by Richard Nix, Bishop of Norwich in the C16, lies NE of the church. Close by is the broad moat surrounding the site of the earlier hall, former seat of the knightly family of Castleton. To the S and severed by a road are fragments of a double moat. Lily Farm, E of the church and W of the A140, has the possible incomplete remains of a small sub-rectangular moat of which only the E and SE portions survive.

STUTTON *(7½ miles S of Ipswich)*

Samford Hundred. 'Village or farmstead infested with horse-flies' (OE+OE) *Stuttuna* (DB). Includes the Domesday vill of Alfiddestuna.
Manors. Stutton Hall (1265 Reginald de Paveley). *Sub-Manors.* Creeping Hall; Argents; Crowe Hall; Alton Hall; Rectory of Stutton (C13 Henry, son of Nicholas, Rector of Stutton, claimed 'wreck of sea', 'view of frankpledge', and 'assize of bead and beer' in Stutton).

Ancient Woodland
Argent Manor Wood, N of the village, is a part of ancient woodland.

STUTTON *(continued)*

Tumuli.

The parish contains three ploughed-out barrows.

Multi-period Settlement.

Ring ditches located by aerial photography and many stray finds of Neolithic, Mesolithic, Roman and Saxon date point to former concentrated early settlement in the area. There were six notable manors here at Domesday; one, centred on Alton Hall - thought to represent the large Domesday manor and settlement of Alcildeston is now mostly covered by the Alton Reservoir, although a necessarily superficial survey of the site prior to flooding failed to find evidence of early pottery.

Salt Industry.

Saltmaking in pans at the waterside flourished here for many centuries, probably even from Roman times.

Historic Houses & Ancient Moated Sites.

Standing in its own park of 130 acres, Stutton Hall is a timber-framed manor house rebuilt in brick in 1892. It is thought to have been originally built for Sir Edmund Jermy in 1553 and retains an interesting gateway. The manor house of Crowe Hall, built c1605 by the Latimers, was extended in the late C17. It was formerly the seat of the Smyth family; Crepping Hall to the W, former manor house of the Wingfields, still retains its C16 barn. Stutton House was originally built as the Rectory in 1710.

SUDBOURNE *(1 mile N of Orford)*

Plomesgate Hundred. 'South stream' (OE) *Sutborne* (970) *Sutburna* (DB). Includes the Domesday vill of Nordberia.

Manors. The manor of Sutborne (Sudbourne) which was granted to Aethelweald, Bishop of Winchester in 970 A.D. subsequently became the headquarters of St. Etheldreda's Liberty comprising 5½ Hundreds. (-1550 Abbot of St. Etheldreda, Ely; 1555 Bishop of Norwich).

Ancient Woodland

Watling Wood, W of the church, and Sudbourne Great Wood (including Captain's Wood) to the N, are parts of ancient woodland.

Ancient Settlement.

A complex of small Iron Age enclosures is evident on aerial photographs at Valley Farm in the centre of the parish. There is also evidence of Roman and Early Saxon settlement. The parish of Orford was originally included within its boundary - Sudbourne Church still being the mother church of Orford.

Roman Salt Industry.

A site known as 'Red Hill' probably comprises the remains of Roman salt workings.

Coin Hoard.

When Sudbourne Church was restored in 1884, over 2,600 silver pennies were discovered under the floor of the N chapel. They covered the reigns of Kings John, Henry II and Henry III, and William the Lion of Scotland.

Workhouse.

The local workhouse which was recorded with 30 inmates in 1776, was still in existence and occupied by paupers in 1840.

Site of Historic House.

Sudbourne Hall (now demolished) was a rebuilding by James Wyatt c1784, enlarged by Sir Richard Wallace. It stood in a park covering 500 acres. It replaced an earlier hall which had been burned down. This had been built for Sir Michael Stanhope (died 1619), Groom of the Chamber to Elizabeth I and James I. It is shown on Norden's map c1600 as an H-shaped courtyard plan building and called Chapmans or Sudburn House. It was the home of Viscount Hereford in 1674 when it was recorded as having 36 hearths showing it to be one of the largest mansions in the county. Church Farm House dates from the C17.

SUDBURY

Babergh Hundred. 'Southern fortified settlement' (OE) *Suthbyrig* (c995) *Sutberia* (DB). Now incorporates the former parish of Ballingdon.

Ancient Origins.

Sudbury is of very ancient origins. 'It was anciently called South-Burgh, as Norwich is said to have been called North-Burgh' wrote Kirby in 1784. Its position led to it being a place of considerable importance throughout at least the 300 years between 570 and 870 A.D., and finds indicate a high status settlement as far back as the Iron Age. It later became an important industrial centre, with the English wool trade probably being first established here by two Flemings who came to England in the time of Edward III (1327-77). It was subsequently a major weaving centre, and later still silk-working was introduced and continues to this day. The river Stour was formerly navigable for barges as far as Sudbury - the Stour Navigation Company being set up in 1705 - and by the C19 thousands of tons of merchandise were being carried by water yearly, taking local products to the seaports at Manningtree and Mistley for transportation to London by sailing barge and bringing back coal and fertilisers. Although the Company continued until 1935, the railway had reached Sudbury by 1849 and gradually took over this previously waterborne traffic. Remnants of this trade remain in the form of a preserved lighter berthed in the Quay Basin, and part of the granary warehouse (now converted to a theatre). This building once served as the town's first power station - a cable being taken from the station and linked from house to house and back again (much in the form of Christmas tree lights). It was said that 'if someone removed a bulb in the market place, the whole town went out'.

Saxon Royal Town & Ancient Market.

The Anglo-Saxon Chronicle recorded that Aelfhun, Bishop of Suffolk, died at 'Suthburgh' in 797 A.D. The town was already an urban centre by the late Saxon period and had a Royal Mint established in the reign of King Ethelred II (978-1016) which continued until the C12. Many coins inscribed *Sudby* have been found from time to time including those of Etheldred, Cnut (1016-1035), Edward the Confessor (1042-1066), William I (1066-1087), William II (1083-1100), Henry I (1100-1136) and Stephen (1135-1139). It has been suggested that this mint may possibly have been situated at the fork between the A134 and the B1508, E of the town centre on a site now built over. Sudbury formed part of the estate of Earl Morchar which was forfeited at the Conquest, by which time it already had a market, and claimed borough status.

Ancient Defences.

Sudbury's name means 'southern fortified settlement', and a section of the town defences comprising three parallel ditches was revealed in 1992 at Mill Lane School. Excavations here showed that they had been dug in the Late Saxon - Early Medieval period and refilled by the late C12-early C13. The area of the original town is defined on the W side by 'Mill Stream', on the N and E sides by the defensive ditches - now traced by the surviving curving street pattern formed by Friars Street, Burkitts Lane and Croft Road (with a secondary settlement surrounding the C15 church of St Peter) - and to the S by a defensive ditch backfilled by the C13. After the early Roman period there was a gap of 700-800 years before this part of the town was re-occupied.

Site of Augustine Priory.

There are scant and re-used remains of the Blackfriar's Dominican Priory in Friars Street. It was founded by Baldwin de Shimpling and Chabil, his wife, sometime before 1247. The priory, which was fairly wealthy, initially covered five acres and there is a record of it having been twice extended. The conventional church became a popular burial place for important local dignitaries. In 1380 the priory was granted a piece of land in 'Babyngdonhall' (Ballingdon Hall) containing a spring for the creation of an aqueduct, but so fierce was the opposition of the townspeople that it took five years to secure, and even then their labourers had to be provided with royal protection while they carried out the work. The monastic buildings were pulled down in 1821 by Sir James Marriot who removed the best of the material to Twinstead. The sole remains are a half-timbered archway and doorway, probably from the gatehouse, now incorporated in an hotel.

Site of College

Simon de Sudbury, Archbishop of Canterbury in 1375, was a native of the town. During his period in office he

SUDBURY *(continued)*

crowned Richard II and was made Lord High Chancellor in 1380. His family name was Theobald, his father being Nigel Theobald, a leading Suffolk wool merchant. Simon built the chancel of St Gregory's in 1365. This is the mother-church of Sudbury and stands on the site of an earlier Saxon church of c780 A.D., on which design it is reputedly based - 'About the year 970 (A.D.) Atheric gave one moiety of a hospital he had founded to St Gregorys in Sudby'. In 1375, on the spot where his father's house stood, Simon founded and endowed (with his brother John) a secular college for a warden and five canons. Further buildings were erected to the W of the churchyard where the former Union Workhouse (built c1820) stands. Simon was later beheaded on Tower Hill by Wat Tyler's rebels - it is said that eight blows of the axe were necessary - and his head borne on a pole round the city before being exhibited over London Bridge. It was returned to Sudbury where the macabre object complete with shrivelled ears was placed on view in the vestry of his church where it still remains. His body lies under an altar tomb in Canterbury Cathedrel. At the Dissolution, the college became vested in the Crown and granted to Sir Thomas Paston. Nothing remains on the site, which covered about 3 acres, except some cellars. The last remains of the buildings were pulled down in 1836. A modern archway in the wall opposite the tower is surmounted by the Archbishop's coat of arms carved in stone. The college continued as a Grammar School on a new site.

Chapel & Site of Priory or Grange.

A chapel founded c1115 by the Saxon, Wulfric, master of the Mint to Henry I, became a cell to the abbot and convent of Westminster Abbey who founded near it a subordinate priory of Benedictine monks. The priory could never have been more than a grange and no typical monastic buildings appear ever to have been erected. The Priory House was pulled down in 1779 but an annual service continued in the chapel until c1830. This chapel remains, a late C14 or early C15 single celled structure, used for many years as a barn. It stands in St. Bartholomew's Lane about ½ mile outside the town on the E side of the road to Long Melford.

Ancient Hospitals & Chapels

A Preceptory of Knights Hospitallers was founded near Ballingdon Bridge, not far from Baldwin de Shimpling's priory; it was endowed with tolls from the bridge, fifteen houses in the town and many rents. There are no remains. Christs Hospital & Chapel were founded about 1200 by Amicia, Countess of Clare, and mentioned in 1277. Another chapel, the Free Chapel of St. Sepulchre, was given by William FitzRobert, Earl of Gloucester, (who died in 1183) to Stoke College and this grant was confirmed by his daughter, Amicia, Countess of Clare, in 1206. In 1383, Richard II granted it to Peter Harmodesworth. The chapel's exact site was discovered in 1826 during house building 'at the upper end of, and fronting Sepulchre Street to the S; the W end abutting upon Gregory Street.' One of the buttresses of the chapel, 4' in height, was found '23' N of the roadside surrounded by many skeletons.' St Leonard Leper's Hospital, situated on the N side of Melford Road and SW of St Bartholomews Chapel by St Bartholomews Lane, was founded by John Colneys or Colness, its first warden, in 1272. It was stipulated that there were always to be three lepers in residence and that after Colney's death one would be chosen warden and the other two were to obey. It was further stated that when one of them died, resigned or were expelled, the survivors were to choose his successor within six months. Although poorly endowed, the hospital survived the suppression and several references are made to the 'hospital called Colnes.' 'The little house at Colnes' was rebuilt in 1619. In 1822 the building was let in rooms to 15 poor people and in 1867 the net income of Colney's charity was applied towards the support of St Leonard's Cottage Hospital.

Ancient Water Meadows

The water meadows - the oldest recorded in East Anglia - were first mentioned by name in the latter part of the C12 although they probably pre-date the Norman Conquest. In 1252 Richard de Clare, Earl of Gloucester & Hereford, gave the area of Portmans Croft and King's Marsh to the Burgesses of Sudbury for 'forty shillings of silver' to be paid at the Feast of St Michael each year. Now managed for the Freemen of Sudbury by trustees, the common lands are a designated Local Nature Reserve.

Mills.

A water mill, recorded in Domesday, stood on the site of the present Mill Hotel. It was marked 'The Mill House' and 'The Mill Hill' in 1714 on Brewer's map of the town. The present mill on the site dates from 1820. The

SUDBURY *(continued)*

industrial history of the area is reflected in the fact that this was one of four water mills between Sudbury and nearby Long Melford. An open-trestle post mill stood on the E side of the road to Lavenham and Stowmarket (B1115) on the NE outskirts of the town before 1614 and was also shown on a plan of 1714.

Medieval Bridge.

A bridge was known to have spanned the river Stour in the suburb of Ballingdon at the beginning of the C13 - Amicia, Countess of Clare, endowing the hospital of St John with tolls from this bridge c1200. The bridge, 'formerly of stone', was swept away by a great flood on November 4th 1520 but rebuilt the following year. On September 8th 1594, this too suffered the same fate. Stone piers and wooden piles were still visible in 1892.

Medieval Gallows.

In his will of 1588 Martin Cole left his wife a place called Gallows Hill. This likely site of the town's former gibbet is unknown.

Guildhall

The old timber-framed C15 Guildhall stands in Friars Street.

Historic Houses & Ancient Moated Sites.

The most impressive of several old medieval houses in the town is Salter's Hall, in Gainsborough Street, dating from c1450. Beside it is the C15 timber-framed Chantry House. Old Moot Hall is also C15, though not the original Moot Hall which was situated at the western end of Market Hill. The Bull Inn in Church Street was built in 1540 and the Ship & Star Inn is also C16. It is said that Dr. Rowland Taylor, the martyr, stayed a night in the custody of the sheriff at The Anchor ((formerly The White Hart) in Friars Street while on his tragic way back from London to Hadleigh where he was burned at the stake on Aldham Common in 1555. At Woodhall Farm, 1 mile N of the town and E of the site of St Bartholomews Chapel, a rectangular moat encloses an area 200'x150', the presumed site of a medieval manor house. By 1991 its overgrown and mutilated remains formed part of an industrial estate.

SUTTON *(3 miles SE of Woodbridge)*

Wilford Hundred. 'South farmstead' (OE) *Suthtuna* (DB). Includes the Domesday vills of Udeham and Stokerlanda.

Manors. Sutton Hall (1316 de Glanville family). *Sub-Manors.* Stokeland; Wood Hall or Udeham (1481 Wingfield family); Fenn Hall; Pistries/Pettistree; Osmonds

Ancient Settlement.

During the 1984 Sutton Hoo excavations (*see below*) the team also unearthed Neolithic pottery and excavated Bronze Age ditches showing a long period of settlement on the site extending from Neolithic to Saxon period.

Tumuli.

Three round barrows lie NW of Bussock Woods on the eastern parish boundary. A supposed Neolithic long barrow on the edge of woodland by Sutton Common picnic site near the northern parish boundary may, in fact, be part of a rabbit warren. A circular mound on Sutton Heath, close to the above, c4' high with a slight ditch on the E side may be another rabbit warren mound and post-medieval.

Roman Cemetery (?)

A hoard of Roman coins along with urns and other material was found in the area of Sutton Hall suggesting the site of a Roman cemetery.

Sutton Hoo Tumuli - Site of Royal Saxon Cemetery.

In the N of the parish the remains of at least fifteen barrows, situated on the crest of a sandy heath escarpment 100' above the river Deben at Sutton Hoo, are now confidently identified as the cemetery of the East Anglian Royal House of the Wuffingas from adjoining Rendlesham - the site of their palace has yet to be located. Three barrows were excavated in 1938. One, Mound 2: 100' in diameter and 7' high, unearthed an 18' boat. The real find, however, took place the following year when local archaeologist Basil Brown excavated the largest of the

SUTTON *(continued)*

group, now named Mound 1. It had orginally measured 120' by 70' and 12' high but had been reduced by robbers who, in the C16-C17, sank a shallow pit in the top of the mound in search of loot. Brown discovered the outline of a clinker-built seagoing rowing boat 86' long with provision for 38 oarsmen and a gabled cabin. There was no body but the ship must have formed a cenotaph, and the contents of the burial (now in the British Museum) which included the famous Sutton Hoo helmet and buckle have been described as 'the most brilliant treasure ever found on British soil', and date the site to the mid C7. Mound 3 is 85' in diameter and 6'6" high (excavated 1938, artifacts and bones found); Mound 4 is 60' in diameter and 3' high [1975](excavated 1938, artefacts and bones found); Mound 5 is 80' in diameter with little left and the original height unknown (partially excavated 1970 revealed grave with silhouette of a crouched inhumation, with other inhumations discovered beyond the barrow); Mound 6: 70' in diameter, 3' high; Mound 7: 100' in diameter, 6' high; Mound 8: 60' in diameter, 3' high; Mound 9: 70' in diameter, 4' high; Mound 10: 90' in diameter, 6' high; Mound 11: 60' in diameter, 2'6" high; Mound 12: 70' in diameter, 1'6" high; Mound 13: 55' in diameter, 1' high; Mound 14: 60' in diameter, 1' high; and Mound 15: 50' in diameter, 1' high. Another (unnumbered) has been identified 59' in diameter and 2½' high on the N side merging to ground level on the S. Martin Carver's 1984 excavations claim to have identified up to 19 barrows and exposed a 'common' burial site adjoining the royal cemetery. He also excavated a number of 'sandmen' - the solitary soil stain remains of burials both Pagan and Christian. The National Trust have now acquired Sutton Hoo and developed it as a major centre open to the public.

Earthwork

A small circular 'camp' of slight elevation may be traced in Bussock Wood with indications of a moat on the SE side which is also visible on the N.

Salt Industry.

Some salt cottages recorded at Sutton in 1406 suggest a salt working site by the river Deben.

Medieval Quay.

The derelict quay at Methersgate was an important landing place for the manor of Campsea in the Middle Ages for shipping coprolite (fossilised animal dung dug up along the Deben shore and used as a fertiliser) and for storing hemp.

Site of Gallows (?)

'Gallows Walk' and 'Gallows Corner' on the 1844 tithe map suggest the site of a former medieval gibbet.

Deserted Medieval Settlements.

Fieldwalking on a site marked on William Haiward's map of Sutton in 1629 as the 'Manor of Sutton' and showing four buildings, was rewarded with a scatter of pottery extending over the whole field, covering handmade, Ipswich Ware, Thetford Ware and a thin scatter of Roman. Metal detector finds included brooches, buckles and coins of mainly C16-C17 date. 'Sutton halle' is mentioned in 1452, but the present hall lies about a mile to the S and is a C19 building (but on a farmstead site existing in 1629). Sutton Hall manor was acquired by the Ferneley family in 1541; the family also held Woodhall, another Sutton manor. Haiward called Sutton a 'town' - 'a description and platte of the town of Sutton' - and there is documentary evidence of around thirty houses with their buildings which are now lost. This included the Domesday vill of Stockerlanda held by Gilbert de Colville - later the Manor of Stockerland, now represented by Ferry Farm in the N of the parish; also the 'site of ye maner of Fenhall' with a history recorded from the C14 (the manor house thought to have been demolished c1596). Another (later) settlement developed on the former green behind Stonner Point, the manorial landing place of Woodhall Stonner. The quay here was in frequent use until the early C19.

Ancient Ferry.

Guston Stone Ferry, an ancient ferry rented by William Redgrave - a wealthy Woodbridge merchant - in 1464, operated to Sutton Mill Fleet (now known as Shottisham Sluice).

Historic Houses

Wood Hall stands on the probable site of the Domesday vill of 'Udeham', which had a mill and was held by

SUTTON *(continued)*

Gilbert, Bishop of Evreux. It was named Woodeham in 1203 and Woodhall in 1482. Haiward's map shows it as E-shaped Jacobean of two-storeys with straight gables and mullioned windows, surrounded by a ditch or moat. Pettistree Hall, where a rectangular moat surrounding 'Pistrehall' is shown on Haiward's 1629 map, was the manor house of the Manor of Petristres (mentioned in 1456) and called Woodhall Pistrees in 1494. The site of the old hall, described as a 'fine old mansion in the Elizabethan style', is now occupied by a farmhouse called Pettistree Hall. In the C14 ships belonging to the Port of Goseford came under the jurisdiction of the Liberty of St Etheldreda and all returns of shipping were made to the Bailiff of the Liberty who, at a later date (1422) was William Pettistree of Pettistree Hall.

SWEFFLING *(3 miles W of Saxmundham)*

Plomesgate hundred. 'The place of Sweftel's family' (OE) *Sueflinga* (DB) *Sueftlinges* (c1150)
Manors. Sweffling, Sparkes al Leighs (1316 William de Dalizone). *Sub-Manors.* Derneford Hall; Sweffling Campsey cum Snape Campsey.

Earthworks.
In Castle Hill Field, E of Whitehouse Farm on the eastern parish boundary, a low mound situated in marshy ground was reported to have produced Roman finds in 1909. However excavations c1950 discovered only a rammed chalk floor.

Medieval Chapel.
The Independent Congregationalists group was formed and built a chapel here in 1650. It was removed to Rendham in 1750.

Site of old Windmills.
Three post mills standing together and all with roundhouses operated in the parish in the late C18. Girlings Mill, dated 1775, stood by Sweffling Grange until dismantled in 1935; Middle Mill (just to the NW) and High Mill (just to the NE) were both shown in 1783. Middle Mill was dismantled some time after 1899, and High Mill in 1911.

Ancient Ford & Historic House.
Dernford Hall, named on Faden's 1783 map, occupies a site which may well have been one of some importance in earlier times, for a short distance to the N, five footpaths meet at a footbridge over the young river Alde, obviously the site of the ancient Dern ford.

SWILLAND *(5 miles NNE of Ipswich)*

Bosmere & Claydon Hundred. 'Land where pigs were kept' (OE) *Suinlanda* (DB). Includes the Domesday vill of Newton. Claude Morley informs us that an ancient Deed mentions a wood in Swilland called Morsehaye (the wood of a Saxon called Mor); maybe the wood in which the swine were kept and to which the place-name (*see above*) refers.
Manors. Swilland (1270 Hugh de Babington). *Sub-Manors.* Newton Hall.

Roman Road.
The modern B1078 follows the course of a Roman road from Coddenham and forms the short northern parish boundary past Little Moat Farm.

Poor House.
A Poor House which stood in the village was taken down in 1808.

Historic Houses & Ancient Moated Sites.
Moat Farm, on the northern parish boundary, has the remains (in the form of one wet arm) of its rectangular moat. N of the church and (Swilland) Hall Farm, soilmarks may represent field boundaries or the moat of an earlier hall. Newton Hall, owned successively by the Reydon, Tuddenham, Bedingfield and Armiger families, lies 1¼ miles SE of the church.

SYLEHAM *(3½ miles NW of Stradbroke)*

Hoxne Hundred. 'Enclosure by a miry place' (OE) *Seilam* (DB). The enclosure referred to in the place-name is occupied by the church (*see below*).

Manors. Syleham Comitis (1275 Roger de Clifford). *Sub-Manors.* Syleham, Monks Hall/Tylney's/Syleham Hall; Esham.

Ancient Causeway.

Syleham Church stands on a sandy hillock by the Waveney surrounded by marshes. A raised causeway a quarter mile long is its only connection to the road. A similar causeway on the other side of the river in Norfolk (exactly opposite to this) runs from the river back to the main road passing through Brockdish. The river was formerly spanned by a wooden bridge and an extract from an old town book for 1657 belonging to Brockdish reads: 'Laid out 17/- for the Brockdish part of Syleham Bridge leading over the river to Syleham Church.'

Site of submission to Henry II (?)

The church with its round tower and Saxon long and short work stands in a marsh beside the Waveney, accessible only by its quarter mile causeway (*see above*). The isolated and eerie atmosphere of this site could not have been improved by the *ignus fatui*, locally known as the Syleham Lights - a gas which, when it escapes from the ground, spontaneously ignites. Here (it is confidently suggested) is the site where, in 1174, the rebellious Earl Hugh Bigod swore submission to Henry II. The king had encamped at Syleham in July 1174 with 500 carpenters to prepare siege engines for the reduction of the walls of the Earl's castle at Bungay during one of the many confrontations between this notorious family and their current monarch. The evidence of where they started to undermine the walls - before Bigod paid a heavy fine to save his fortress - is still visible today.

Ancient Cross.

Syleham Cross may have been erected to commemorate Earl Bigod's submission to Henry II *(see above)*. 'There used to be a Cross standing in the road just opposite the entrance to the path leading to the church'. A large new commemorative wooden cross has now been erected on the site.

Site of Ancient Mill & Toll Bridge.

Syleham Mill stands beside the bridge over the river Waveney dividing Suffolk from Norfolk. Rebuilt in the mid-C16, it probably stands on the site of a Saxon watermill given to the Cluniac Priory of Thetford c1094 along with a church, fisheries, etc., and listed in the Domesday Survey. Following the Dissolution, it was purchased along with the (toll?) bridge. In 1976/7, when the river level dropped 18" below normal, 'piles of an ancient river crossing in a rotten condition' were exposed. The former water mill was converted from a corn mill to a weaving mill in 1839 'for the manufacture of linen drabbets and ready-made clothing.' The top portion was burned down in the 1920s and replaced with a factory building.

Ancient Chapel.

An ancient chapel once stood in Esham, a former hamlet of Syleham, SE of Syleham Hall. This hamlet is now known as Earsham Street and a part of Wingfield parish (*see* Wingfield).

Turbary.

An extract from the *Inquisition of Ninths 134 - Silh'm* reads 'Tithes of hay and turbary worth 13s 4d per annum'. The turbary's location is unknown but was probably centred either side of the church and causeway.

Medieval Green.

Syleham Green is shown on Faden's 1783 map occupying the whole area of the village and exited by four roads. Now enclosed and built over, the area retains its C19 name Great Green. A small triangular-shaped green known as Syleham Little Green stood at the southern end of Green Lane and was bordered on the S by Red House Farm.

Historic Houses & Ancient Moated Sites.

Monks Hall, SW of the church by the river Waveney, is Tudor and of much interest. Syleham Hall on the eastern parish boundary still has part of its ancient moat. W of the last, small fragments of a moat remain at Whitehouse Farm.

TANNINGTON *(4 miles NW of Framlingham)*

Hoxne Hundred. 'Tat's son's farmstead' (OE) *Tatintuna* (DB). The spelling of the parish name had been 'Tat' since Anglo-Saxon times. The change to 'Tann' took place some time after 1540. The church's dedication to St Ethelbert would suggest that Tannington is a very early Saxon settlement site.
Manors. Tannington/Braiseworth's (1316 William Runeton/Rungeton). *Sub-Manors.* Osberne's.

Site of Earthworks.
Nothing now remains of an earthwork called Fiddler's Hill located E of Tannington Lodge at TM2610 6760. A description of 1908 tells of a hill surrounded by a deep moat, except at the entrance on the southern side towards the road. 'No written account of this hill can be found. It was (or is) said to be haunted by someone murdered or drowned in the moat from where music is supposed to be heard. The moat is so deep in places that no bottom can be found.' Robert Fisk, born in 1752, told in 1836 of a fixed mill on the hill owned by a fiddler. A Mr. Dunthorpe also described the site in 1836. 'The hill is 12' higher than the field and 33 yards in diameter at the base. The moat is 11 yards wide and not so deep as tradition claims.' Although he did not think it could possibly have been a mill mound, a will of 1554 refers to 'Mill Mount' rather than 'Fiddler's Hill' - and the tithe map, likewise. The hill was partially excavated with no major finds and the moat found to be c6' deep.

Medieval Green.
Tannington Green, NNE of the church and shown on Faden's 1783 map, ran N mainly to the W of the straight new road which has replaced it. Tannington Hall lay on its western side and The Chestnuts and The Woodlands formed its southern and northern extent.

Guildhall (?)
Faden's map of 1783 names a building illustrated on the west edge of Tannington Green, 'Guild Hall', the property of a J. Dade. The Dades formerly had a seat and estate in Tannington and this building would appear to be Tannington Hall.

Historic Houses & Ancient Moated Sites.
The parish has six moated sites. Braiseworth Hall, SE of the church, has a series of moats contained within one large oblong moat; the latter strengthened by a rampart on its inner margin which remains round one third of the whole cincture providing a stronger defensive arrangement. It indicates that the earlier hall on the site was a fortified manor house. William Runeton held the manor in 1316 followed by Peter de Briseworth, who certainly resided here and was outlawed in 1367. Tannington Lodge has a large impressive rectangular moat; a long narrow moat forms (with the W side of the main moat) the E side of an approach or drift called Tovells Entry on the tithe map; another long narrow moat forms the W side. Outbuildings N of the site are called Drift Buildings. Fields SW of the moated site called Osborne Meadow and Hither Osborne confirm this to be the manor house of the small manor of Osbernes held at one time by Robert Osberne. Tannington Hall has a large rectangular moat with spurs which originally surrounded an earlier hall, isolated from the church on the edge of Tannington Green. To the N of this another rectangular moat formerly surrounded The Hoplands, but this has now been bulldozed flat. The Chestnuts, NE of the village, has the northern fragment of a small moat; and Wood Farm, near the southern parish boundary, has two square enclosures isolated and now largely filled in.

TATTINGSTONE *(5 miles SSW of Ipswich)*

Samford Hundred. 'Tat's (Tata's) farmstead' (OE) *Tatistuna* (DB) *Tatingeston* (1219)
Manors. Tattingstone (C12 William de Holbroke).

Ancient Woodland.
Woodley Wood on the eastern parish boundary is part of ancient woodland.

Ancient Settlement.
Many of the field systems, trackways and enclosures seen as cropmarks on aerial photographs (and suggestive of very early settlement in the area) may have survived the flooding of the valley to create the Alton

TATTINGSTONE *(continued)*

Reservoir. According to map references they appear to lie mainly on the E bank, NW of Birchwood House.

Chapel.

St Margaret's Free Chapel, founded by (William?) de Holbrook, stood S of Coxhall Road and NE of the church on what is now the northern bank of the Alton Reservoir, and was mentioned in 1434, and in 1471 when owned by the Earl of Oxford. Floor tile fragments have been found in the area of Little and Great Chapel Fields.

Workhouse.

The Samford Hundred House of Industry was built in 1765 with accommodation for 500 paupers. It was later renamed St. Mary's Hospital.

Historic Houses & Ancient Moated Sites.

In the park of Tattingstone Place, rebuilt by Thomas White c1764, is an irregular quadrangular moat of an earlier Place (or Palace) belonging to the Beaumonts. In the C18, Roger White built Tattingstone Wonder, three small cottages for his farm workers, the side facing Tattingstone Place disguised to look like a church. Tattingstone Hall stood E of the church and dated from C16-C19. It had a rectangular moat with outer yard and fish-pond. When the hall was demolished prior to being submerged beneath the Alton Reservoir, a limited excavation of the site was carried out. It was found that the moat island had been raised and leveled with crag sands before construction work on the hall. The discovery of a single medieval sherd (C13-C14) from below this sand suggests that the moat may have surrounded a medieval hall though no sign of this earlier building was found.

THEBERTON *(2 miles NE of Leiston)*

Blything Hundred. 'Theodbeorht's farmstead' (OE) *Thewardetuna* (DB) *Tiberton* (1178)
Manors. Theberton (1200 Roger Bigot).

Ancient Woodland.

Buckles Wood, on the SE parish boundary and running into Leiston parish, is part of ancient woodland.

Tumuli.

Sherds of an Early Bronze Age cinerary urn were found 'in a mound' in the garden of Theberton Old Rectory sometime before 1962. It was said to be 33' in diameter and 5' high and mutilated by having a path cut through it and landscaped with holly bushes. In the southern corner of Greenhouse Plantation is a mound 25' in diameter which may be a barrow or perhaps only a C18-C19 landscaping feature.

Turbary.

Extract from *Inquisitions of Ninth of 1341 - Theberton*: 'item, tithes of turbary valued at 16s 4d.' John Ridgard states that 'Theberton Bogs are unquestionably flooded peat cuttings dating back, in charter material, to at least the 12th century.' The site is presumably that defined on the 1783 map as Theberton Common.

Site of old Bridge.

A bridge named Ton Bridge is shown crossing the Minsmere old river at Eastbridge on Faden's map. Its construction date is unknown but it is also shown on Bowen's (1755), Blome's (1673) and Saxton's (1575). A bridge still exists here crossing the old river and 'new cut'. Eastbridge was an ancient causeway whose earlier name of Earl's Ford is commemorated, though totally corrupted, in the present 'Eels Foot Inn'.

Site of former Gallows (?)

'Hangman's', the name of a bridleway leading over Saunders' Hill, N of the Minsemere River, is suggestive of a medieval gibbet being at one time erected here.

Site of old Windmills.

A post mill and tower mill stood together near Rattla Corner before 1756. The tower mill was dismantled c1923.

Historic Houses & Ancient Moated Sites.

Theberton Hall was built in 1792 by George Doughty, but the 100 acre park and grounds called Theberton Park were in existence in the C16, no doubt supporting an earlier hall. Fragments of a moat remain at Moat Farm.

THELNETHAM *(3 miles NW of Botesdale)*
Blackbourn Hundred. 'Water meadows/enclosure frequented by swans near a plank bridge' or 'Wita's plank-home' (OE) *Telneteham, Telnetteham, Thelneteham and Teolftham* (DB). Wita probably lived on an islet approachable only by a wooden plank bridge. As Morley states, the various spellings in Domesday for this parish renders the name obscure and he provides the latter meaning (though without much conviction). The only section of the place-name on which all agree is the 'plank bridge'.
Manors. Thelnetham (-C13 Peter de Brettenham). *Sub-Manors.* Cressy; Eye Thelnetham; Rectory of Thelnetham.

Ancient Woodland.
Brockley Wood on the southern parish boundary, and a fragment of Black Horse Wood to the N, are ancient woodland.

Ancient Track.
Dunhill Lane follows the western edge of Brockley Wood NW to form the western parish boundary with Hepworth.

Site of Ancient Earthwork.
Basil Brown found worked flints on the site of a ploughed-out mound NE of Kay's Farm.

Ancient Cross.
Part of the plinth and a foot of the shaft of the medieval preaching cross known as the 'Trappetes Cross' stood at the crossroads N of Cross Green Farm. It was moved to the orchard of Evergreen Oak Inn in 1951. The cross was erected by John Cole in accordance with his will of 1527 which said: 'I will have a new crosse made accordinge to Trappettes Crosse at the Hawelanesende and sett upp at Short Groves ende, where the gospell ys sayde upon Ascension Even, for which I assigne Xs.' Shortgrove Lane runs from Hopton village to a junction with Gypsy Lane in Thelnetham, and then along the parish boundary to Weathercock Farm. It is likely his cross was erected at the high point (TM001 779) near the junction of Shortgrove Lane and the former Gypsy Lane and Market Lane heading SSW to the Market Weston Road.

Medieval Brick-making Industry.
A brick-making kiln of medieval date was discovered at Sandfield Farm near the southern parish boundary.

Medieval Greens.
The southern half of Cross Green, marked and named by Faden, was enclosed under an award of 1821 - the northern half was probably already private property by then. Hedge Green was also named and shown by Faden. A roughly triangular piece, described as 'parcel of Hedge Green Common', was enclosed in 1821, but its original shape is not exactly clear. The Slade, a linear green, ran from Lodge Farm in a SW direction on the line of the present road joining (and carrying on beyond High Green) Market Weston and terminating just SW of Martin's Nest; its long SW side followed the parish boundary. Another linear green ran between Dunhill Lane (which forms the western parish boundary) and Ord's Grove and Blackhorse Wood to the N and Brockley Wood to the S; its eastern edge traced by a N-S footpath near the site of Thelnetham Hall. Faden appears to call it Weston Pindle on his 1783 map.

Site of old Mill.
Thelnetham Mill, a post mill which had stood on Thelnetham Fen since well before 1780 was transferred to Diss in 1818 to be replaced by a new mill built the next year for William Button. This mill ceased working in 1924.

Medieval Guildhall (?)
There may at one time have been a guildhall which housed the three guilds known to have existed in the parish: St. John Baptist (1464), St. Peter (1519) and St. Nicholas (C15/C16).

Historic Houses & Ancient Moated Sites.
There are the remains of two sides of a rectangular moat (now dry) just NW of Lodge Farm. Basil Brown examined the site and found fragments of possible C13 pottery. Hall Yards (in Hall Field) is the site of a ploughed -out moat from where C14-C16 pottery sherds, brick roof tiles and building debris have been found. The large moated site also produced an iron arrow head.

THORINGTON *(4 miles SE of Halesworth)*

Blything Hundred. 'Thorn-tree enclosure or farmstead' or 'Thuri's farmstead' (OE) *Toretuna* (DB)
Manors. Thorington/Thorington Wimples with Wenhaston Wimples Ufford Westons (1247 Geoffrey de Wymples). *Sub-Manors.* Thorington Hall al Sowters.

Ancient Woodland.
Big Wood and Common Wood on the eastern parish boundary, and Holly Hills Wood to the N of these, are sections of ancient woodland.

Roman Road
Cropmarks of a linear feature running NNE from the present A12 road across Thorington Park, would suggest that the A12 from Rush's Spring, SW, is a Roman road and projects NE to Wenhaston. The line of the cropmark is shown as an existing road by Faden on his map of 1783. Stone House Farm to the NE, and a track heading from here to Hazels Lane, may trace its original route NE from the park. The A12 was probably rerouted to the E and off the line of the Roman road when Thorington Park was created.

Romano-British Settlement
SW of Thorington Hall Farm, a small area was excavated in 1978 across the parish boundary. It produced a scatter of Iron Age and Roman pottery and tile, slots, post holes and a rubbish layer suggesting a small settlement.

Roman Industrial Site
East of the above, at Park Farm Quarry, Dovehouse Park, a possible Roman industrial oven was revealed during gravel diggings in 1991. A pit had baked clay bricks - possibly the remains of a C1-C2 pottery kiln. Its location was a dog-leg in the line of the Roman road. The site also unearthed some Iron Age sherds and worked flint scrappers and flakes.

Medieval Iron Working Site.
Pottery and slag finds at Brook Farm on the northern parish boundary, have identified a medieval ironworking site.

Earthwork
An earthwork of undetermined date lies in permanent pasture W of The Forge and N of Thorington Road. The tithe map names the site 'Sparham'.

Historic Houses & Ancient Moated Site.
Thorington Hall was the seat of the Bence family in the C17. It was rebuilt in white brick in 1820 and stood in a park of nearly 200 acres. The Hall was demolished in 1949. There is a square, isolated moat at Walnut Tree Farm on the western parish boundary.

THORNDON (or Thorndon All Saints) *(3 miles SW of Eye)*

Hartismere Hundred. 'Hill where thorn-trees grow' (OE) *Tornduna* (DB)
Manors. Thorndon (1320 Granted in dower to Isabel, Queen of England; 1337 Robert de Ufford). *Sub-Manors.* Godrich's Thorp al Claxton Hall al Colston Hall al Lampets; Hesteley Hall; Thorndon Parva.
The river Dove passes through the parish to connect with the Waveney. It is likely that in earlier times it was considerably wider and deeper and probably navigable to Stanewell (*see below*).

Ancient Woodland.
A tiny fragment of Lounde's Wood remains E of Rose Cottage and Hall Road. A sizeable section of what was anciently called Lowing Wood survived until recent times.

Hoards & Ancient Settlement Site.
A Late Bronze Age hoard comprising axes, decorated spearheads, hammers and knives was dug up in a gravel pit in the parish in 1811. Another, comprising similar artefacts, found in a field on the Thorndon/Rishangles parish boundary in the mid-1970s, was thought to have been dredged from a ditch and deposited there.

Roman Brick & Tile Industry.
Brick kilns of Roman date were referred to in 1591.

THORNDON *(continued)*

Anglo-Saxon Settlement.

The site of the former Hestley Green has yielded archaeological evidence of early settlements. An Anglo-Saxon settlement/cemetery in the area of White House Farm is suggested by an old undated newspaper article which stated that 'weapons, brooches, beads, etc. have been found at White House Farm' and 'Some Saxon remains discovered in the parish *not long since* were shown at the Rectory.' 'Some very interesting remains consisting of fine bronze fibulae, portions of iron and bronze weapons, upwards of thirty beads made of rich blue glass, amber and various coloured clays, now in the possession of the rector, were dug up by some men when draining a field in the occupation of Mr Robert Kerry of White House Farm in the hamlet of Hestley' (White 1885).

Ancient Bridge (?)

Upright wooden posts and horizontally-laid brushwood were exposed by bank erosion alongside the E bank of the river Dove on the parish boundary with Braiseworth and Eye, just N of Catbridge. Further erosion later destroyed this bridge or track/platform.

Medieval Deer Park.

A deer park was in existence by 1288 when it is recorded as having been 'broken into and deer stolen'. Known as Rishangles Park, it lay to the E of Hestley Green and is now represented by Rishangles Lodge. It belonged to Edmund, Earl of Cornwall, as a part of the Manor of Thorndon which in turn belonged to the Honor of Eye. John le Parker who had custody of the park of Rishangles died c1307. It was later owned by the Uffords and then the de la Poles, Earls of Suffolk, who leased it to the Grimston family in the 1420s. The Brandons, later Dukes of Suffolk, held it in 1520, but in 1538 it passed to the Crown and was presumably disparked as it was not included in a list of parks for 1560 or on Saxton's map of Suffolk in 1575.

Medieval Greens.

Faden's 1783 map shows a triangular green straddling the Dove near the northern parish boundary, just S of Braiseworth Old Hall Farm. Called Standwell Green it is remembered in the name of the hamlet to the S. The name comes from the Saxon *Stanewell* (stony mere) referring to the point where the Dove splays out into a small pool now called Thorndon Pool. Thorndon Green is shown as a linear green running W from the church to the road junction. Several croft sites which once lay on the green edge produced scatters of Early Medieval and Medieval pottery. A large L-shaped green called Hazely or Hesteley Green ran SSE from Hestley Hall following the line of the road that replaced it to Green Farm and then ENE to the B1077 just S of Rishangles Green.

Site of old Windmill.

A post mill with roundhouse stood W of the church and N of the Street in 1797. It was dismantled in 1924.

Historic Houses & Ancient Moated Sites.

There are eight moated sites in the parish. Rishangles Lodge has parts of a square moat with outlying ponds. This was the lodge of the deer park and also the country house of Edward Grimston *(see above)*, citizen and mercer of London who died in 1478 and was buried in Thorndon Church. 153 yds to the N a small moat encloses an irregular oval island c52' by 33'. In a hilltop position with a wet ditch and low mound it is called 'Mount' with 'Dove House Piece' to the N and 'Dove House Meadow' to the S. Just to the NW of the lodge, in the NW corner of what was Rishangles Park, a wet moat lies in a valley, isolated, unoccupied and surrounded by a wet drainage ditch or watercourse on the N,W and S sides. This could be the fish-pond of about ½ acre 'in the park near the gate towards Thorndon' for which Edward Grimston received a licence in 1479. Moat Farm, situated at the S end of Hestley Green and originally a hall house, retains a small rectangular moat, the E side of which remains wet. To the S are the possible remains of fish-ponds. Hestley Hall at the N end of the Green is an ancient site containing the mansion of the Bishop family in the C17. It has three moated areas, to the E of which is a small moated island known as 'The Mount', possibly a dovecot. The manor was held by Robert de Ufford and later, in the mid-C14, by the de la Poles . Lampits Farm (formerly Colston Hall) on the western edge of Hestley Green has a complicated system of disconnected moats - one circular but irregular - which seem to have protected four separate areas, and Shorts Farm to the N of this has a series of rectangular enclosures. There are two square enclosures in the street associated with the C15 Old Rectory with later rebuilding and extensions, and at Thorndon Hall, to the SE beside the B1077 road, parts of a trapezoid moat remain.

THORNHAM MAGNA *(3½ miles SW of Eye)*

Hartismere Hundred. 'Homestead where thorn-trees grow' (OE) *Magna* - Great *Thornham* (DB). Known, for no reason that is apparent, as Thornham Pilcok in the *Nonarum* of 1340, its name. along with neighbouring Thornham Parva and Thorndon, suggest the district was anciently covered with brambly undergrowth rather than wooded.

Manors. Thornham Hall al Briseworth's (C14 William de Briseworth). *Sub-Manors.* Thornham; Hemenhall/ Hemenhales.

Multi-period Settlement.

Recent (and ongoing) archaeoligical investigations on the Henniker Estate have revealed evidence for settlement in the area over all periods from 2,500 B.C.

Roman Road.

The eastern parish boundary is formed by the A140 which lies on the course of the Roman road from Coddenham to Caister-by-Norwich (*Venta Icenorum*).

Earthworks.

An undetermined earthwork lies just SW of the church and Corner House.

Site of old Windmill.

The foundations of a late C17 postmill lie by a footpath running ENE from the village to the A140. It was first mapped in 1675, ceased work c1940, and burned down in 1959.

Historic Houses.

Thornham Hall, which dated from the C15/C16, was burned down in 1954 and the present house (which occupies the 300/400 acre park of the former) is the residence of the Henniker-Major family. The Four Horseshoes inn is of ancient origin.

THORNHAM PARVA *(3½ miles SW of Eye)*

Hartismere Hundred. 'Homestead or village where thorn-trees grow' (OE) *Parva* - Little *Thornham* (DB)
Manors. Woodhouse (C14 Richard de Chirche).

Roman Road.

The Roman Road from Coddenham to Caister-by-Norwich (now the A140) forms the eastern parish boundary with Braiseworth.

Ancient (boundary?) Ditch.

Grimm's Ditch, in the form of a sunken lane S of Thornham Parva churchyard, continues across the A140 Roman road *(see* Braiseworth). The field is named 'Grimsditch' on the 1843 tithe map and the earthwork is recorded in medieval times as *'in campo qui vocatur Grimisdich'* (temp Henry III; Harleian MS 52A49). It may have provided a boundary ditch - perhaps dividing the ancient British Trinovantes and Iceni tribes.

Ancient Way.

Furze Way, an ancient track, passes NW-SE through the N of Thornham Parva and forms a short section of the northern parish boundary with Thornham Magna. At the point it enters the parish it is called Cowpasture Lane. It may be connected in some way with the ancient Grimm's Ditch (*see above*) which roughly continues its line E of the Roman road (A140).

Ancient Hermitage & Chapel.

In the 1220s a monk called Vitalis established a hermitage here, and a chapel dedicated to St. Edburga was built in the area of Chapel Farm on the NW parish boundary by the ancient Furze Way (Cowpasture Lane).

Ancient Moated Site.

In Lady Henniker Wood (formerly Moathouse Wood) W of the village of Thornham Parva, a polygonal moat may represent the site of an even earlier Thornham Hall.

THORPE MORIEUX *(9 miles SSE of Bury St Edmunds)*

Cosford Hundred. Thorpe - 'Outlying hamlet' or 'secondary settlement' (OScand) *Thorp* (DB). The ancient seat of the Morieux family, but their name was not officially suffixed to the village until after 1327 (Sir Thomas Morreux was High Sheriff of Suffolk in 1355).
Manors. Thorpe Morieux (1200 Roger de Muryeus; 1418 Sir John L'Estrange). *Sub-Manors.* Gorget's/Gorges; Throgton al Thruton al Castell's (1289 Bartholomew de Castello).

Ancient Woodland
Thorpe Wood and Great Hastings Wood in the N of the parish are parts of ancient woodland.

Brick Making Industry.
Kiln Field, S of Brick Kiln Cottages and to the E of Manor Farm, are suggestive of a former brick-making industry in the area.

Ancient Boundary Stone.
An ancient triangular boundary stone remains by the Felsham road where three parishes (Thorpe, Cockfield and Felsham) and three hundreds (Babergh, Thedwestry and Cosford) meet. On it is inscribed 'This parts the bounds of three Hundreds and three Towns.'

Medieval Green.
A rectangular green called Thorpe Green lay beside Green Farm on Green Road.

Whipping Post.
The low signpost at the corner in the village incorporates the former medieval whipping post.

Historic Houses & Ancient Moated Sites.
The heavy clay lands of Thorpe Morieux have been intensively farmed causing the severe destruction of the archaeological evidence in the parish. Although there are possibly seven moated sites here, in no instance has more than a fragment survived the plough. There are signs of a possible former moat at Thorpe Morieux Hall, S of the church, the seat of the Risby family (1550-1780); the Hall is believed to date from c1525. Now only a farmhouse, it is a fine Tudor building with a two-storeyed Elizabethan porch. Moat Farm on Bury Road has a detached fragment of a square moat. The farm has been rebuilt but its former 'Tudor bricks' have been re-used in outbuildings. The dry W and S arms survive of a moat measuring c109 yds by 66 yds, formerly with two straight and two curved sides, beside Manor Farm, the probable site of the former manor house; there is now no trace of a building within the enclosure. Only a fraction of the dry NE arm remains of the moat at Maltings Farm, now mutilated by tipping. Again there is no evidence of a former building in the enclosure which is now occupied by modern outbuildings. There are flimsy remains of a moat NE of Valley Farm on the N side of Green Road. This is the site of the former Water Hall of which nothing is known; all buildings have been demolished and a bungalow erected on the site. A moat at Underwood Farm has been completely destroyed and modern buildings erected on the site; it was probably sub-rectangular and two arms remained in 1958. At Green Farm, Thorpe Green, moat-like features may be medieval, or perhaps later drainage ditches.

THRANDESTON *(3 miles NW of Eye)*

Hartismere Hundred. 'Thrandr's farmstead' (OScand+OE) *Thrandeston* (c1035) *Thrandestuna* (DB)
Manors. Thrandeston Woodhall (1234 John de Dagworth). *Sub-Manors.* Welholme's; Maveson's; Goddold's/Goshold's/Goswoald's; Ampners.

Roman Road.
The Roman road from Coddenham to Caister-by-Norwich (now the A140) forms part of the eastern parish boundary with Eye.

Medieval Greens.
Great Green, a large rectangular green shown and named on Faden's 1783 map, has been enclosed. It lay S of the Old Bury Road, its southern extent probably marked by Abbey Farm and its SW edge by Pond Farm. The smaller rectangular Little Green lay just to the SW, and just NW of the church.

THRANDESTON *(continued)*

Fair.

A fair for sheep and toys in 1759 also provided the site for the Court of Pie-poudre.

Historic Houses & Ancient Moated Sites.

The present Goswold Hall, SE of the village, probably dates from the C16. The larger part of the ancient moat which surrounded the former hall still survives and is crossed by a brick bridge. It forms part of the Goswold Hall estate - perhaps at first Godesweald . i.e. 'God's wood hall' (Morley) - given by William the Conqueror to Walter le Bowyer (the Bowman). Church Farm, home of the Goate family, dates back at least to the C17 but is probably much older; it has two sides remaining of a medieval moat, and portions of a very damaged moat remain at Maltings Farm, near the eastern parish boundary.

THURSTON *(5 miles E of Bury St Edmunds)*

Thedwestry Hundred. 'Thur's or Thor's farmstead' (OScand+OE) *Thurstuna* (DB)

Manors. Thurston (-1539 Abbot of St. Edmunds, Bury; 1539 Crown property). *Sub-Manors.* Netherhall/ Netherplace (C13 John de Pakenham - forms part of the Manor of Netherhall, Pakenham).

Bronze Age Cremation Site.

Near Black Plantation (now renamed Skeleton Plantation) two Bronze Age cinerary urns were found sometime before 1870 accompanied by a large quantity of calcinated bone.

Roman Road.

A length of Roman road (Margary 33a) one mile 230 yds long heads NNE from the parish boundary through a large housing estate and is traced on the ground by Mill Lane which runs to the northern parish boundary. The road, in the form of an agger with ditch on either side and Romano-British pottery sherds, was discovered while digging house foundations on the estate in 1957. When sectioned it was found to have a width of 17'.

Site of Hundred Meeting Place.

Located near the railway station between Thurston and Pakenham villages (and mentioned in 1899) is a small eminence called Thedwastre Hill. This hill gives its name to the hundred and was the probable meeting place or moot of the Thedwastre Hundred in Saxon times. The name should not carry the 'y' (*see place-name*); the old spelling is Thedwardestre and in one case Thedwardistree. It means Theodward's tree, an oak which obviously provided the focal point for the Hundred Court on Thedwastree Hill, an area of open heathland.

Ancient Track.

A short length of track known as Packway Lane forms a part of the northern parish boundary.

Unidentified Remains (?)

In 1955 Basil Brown marked a site in a field to the N of St Peters Church (calculated as TL9297 6542) 'Remains struck by plough', but did not enlarge on the discovery and no other reference to this find has been found.

Lost Medieval Settlement (?)

Thurston has suffered intensive modern residential estate development which contrasts sharply with Faden's 1783 map which shows the parish covered by common and green. Although on the map there is hardly a sign of habitation and its church, though centrally situated, stands in total isolation, the heathland is criss-crossed by a network of roads and tracks which suggests a concentration of population at some earlier period of its history.

Medieval Green.

As stated above, Faden's map shows that much of the parish was covered by Thurston Heath or Common with an isolated church and few signs of settlement. Parts, lying NE of Thurston Road, are now known as Thurston Planche and Stockhold Green. The Heath also covered the area of Thurston Grange in the NW, and the site of the former Pernal Green is marked by a lane to the S still named Purnal Lane. Its name also survives on the 1840 tithe map in three fields which, in conjunction with a map of 1698, have been used to approximately determine its position. A memorandum of the same year relating to Nether Hall talks of 'Purnell Close or Field

THURSTON *(continued)*

which was thrice called Purnell Green which was believed to have been a common.' Much of the area NE of the church and E of Beighton (Beyton) Brook was covered by the extensive Thurston Green. Its northern extent is traced by the road from the village E to Norton; eastern, by Packway Lane; southern, by Birds Road and a footpath to Grove Farm; and an irregular western boundary running E of the church, and touched in part by Green Farm. The area is now enclosed and called Great Green.

Site of old Windmill.
A post mill stood SE of Mill Farm by Mill Lane in 1750. It survived until c1953 when it was demolished.

Medieval Guildhall (?)
There were three guilds in Thurston - Guild of St. John Baptist; Guild of St. Peter, and Guild of St. Margaret de Grenende (1490) - suggesting that a Guildhall may have once been sited here.

Historic Houses & Ancient Moated Sites.
Nether Hall belonged to the Bright family for several generations from c1545. The possible location of Old Netherhall, burned down and replaced on a new site by the present hall, may be at the point where Meadow Lane, heading N from the village, ends abruptly. The earlier hall may have gone by 1448 and its site may go back to at least 1200 when people called 'De Aula' are referred to in the Kalendar of Abbot Samson and again in the Assize Roll of 1249. The manor probably belonged to the Abbey at Bury, then to the de Pakenham family from whom it reverted to the Abbey in 1393. The Crown granted it to the Bacons in 1544. The site is mentioned in two wills of 1448 and 1503: 'The field called Eldhalle by the way leading to the meadow called Altone Medewe.' Documentary evidence places Alton Meadow around the N end of Meadow Lane and the Old Hall was probably sited in this area.

THWAITE *(5 miles SSW of Eye)*

Hartismere Hundred. 'A forest clearing' (OScand) *Theyt* (1228). Interestingly, although the 'h' is dropped in its pronunciation, it was spelt Theyt without the 'w' in 1228. A Norwegian word showing that this was one of the earliest Viking settlements in Suffolk, Morley conjectures its development thus: 'We may date it (Thwaite) roughly at 890 (A.D.); the earliest recorded Norse attack on East Anglia occurred in 839; and its position, so far inland and actually abutting upon the Roman road to Norwich, shows not only the completeness of their 870 conquest - or the good terms already then established with the Saxons - but is also one of our best illustrations of the broad forests obviously still clothing High Suffolk'.
Manors. Thwaite (1316 Abbot of St. Edmunds; 1557 Anne of Cleeves).

Roman Road.
The A140 Roman road heads through the parish from Brockford Street in the S to Mill Lane which forms the northern parish boundary.

Earthwork.
Just to the W of Brockford Street and the Roman road from Coddenham to Caister-by-Norwich, three sides of a possible rectangular enclosure have been identified by cropmarks. A small scatter of Roman pottery found 219 yds to the NE may or may not be associated with the site but the earthwork is likely to be earlier than the field patterns within which it lies skewed.

Ancient Site (?)
The tiny St George's Church stands on what may be an ancient moated site. Though rebuilt it still retains a single slit lancet of c1200.

Ancient Chapel (?)
Manuscripts suggest the possible site of an ancient chapel in the parish, though this may refer to the church.

Medieval Fairs.
Sir George Reeve had the franchise for two fairs per year (in June and November) in Thwaite in 1671; one for cattle, the other for toys. The fairs were still operating in 1891 but by then both were for cattle.

THWAITE *(continued)*

Historic Houses & Ancient Moated Sites.

There are several moated sites in the parish. Thwaite Hall - dismantled and removed to America - leaves behind its quadrangular moat. It is shown approached by a tree-lined avenue on Faden's map of 1783. A deep gull carrying a stream past Brockford Hall may have at one time been utilised to create a moat around the property. All that now remains is the wide SE arm. A small square unoccupied moat with a causeway to the N lies opposite Willow Farm on the W side of the A140 Ipswich-Norwich road; the E side has been mutilated by tipping. There is another small square moat at Thwaite Lodge Farm with enclosures. The church which has a C12 lancet window shows evidence of being on a possible moated site; a deep ditch remains on the W and S sides. This moat or ditch may at one time also have enclosed the adjoining Grange. The arm from a set of (Saxon ?) hand-held scales was unearthed close by. The Bucks Head, a former coaching inn, stands beside the A140 Roman road and Ipswich to Norwich turnpike road. The timber-framed High House just beyond the turning to Wickham Skeith was formerly The Cock Inn whilst, at the bottom of the hill, Low House (now lost) was the former Queens Head.

TIMWORTH *(3½ miles N of Bury St Edmunds)*

Thedwestry Hundred. 'Tima's enclosure' (OE) *Timeworda* (DB)
Manors. Timworth (-1539 Abbot of St. Edmunds; 1541 Anthony Cockett).

Ancient Woodland.

The extensive Timworth Thicks on the NE parish boundary is a stretch of ancient woodland.

Deserted Medieval Village (?)

Although the parish consists of an isolated church and hall, but no village, there is evidence that a village did once exist around the church. At least 14 buildings are shown on Faden's map of 1783, of which the only survivals are those to the SE of the present crossroads. Those shown along the S boundary may actually be off the N edge of Timworth Green. Scatters of sherds cover Iron Age, Roman, Saxon, Medieval and Post-Medieval periods. Population reached a peak of 241 in 1851 but had dropped to 56 by 1981 - virtually back to its Domesday figure.

Medieval Greens.

Timworth Green survives as a small triangular green with a new central pond. It was shown as open space but not named on Faden's map of 1783 and development to the SE of the pond appears to encroach on the former green. Buildings originally lined both the N side (which appears further N than the present road) and the S side which probably included the present Timworth Farm.

TOSTOCK *(7 miles E of Bury St Edmunds)*

Thedwestry Hundred. 'Outlying farmstead or hamlet by the look-out place' (OE) *Totestoc* (DB)
Manors. Tostock (Abbbot of St. Edmunds; C13 John de Manston). *Sub-Manors.* Tostock Hall/Berdwells/Little Hall.

Ancient Woodland.

Cindron Hills (Bridge Farm Wood) on the southern parish boundary is part of ancient woodland.

Medieval Greens.

The surviving Tostock Green, E of the old rectory, is not shown specifically as such by Faden, but the map does show small greens N of Tostock House in the area now called Tostock Leys, and on the western edge of the parish on the N side of Woodend Green Farm, traced by field edges on the S side of the country lane.

Medieval Guildhall (?)

The parish may at one time have had a guildhall as three guilds: St. John (1487), St. Peter and St. Andrew (1507) once carried on business here.

Historic Houses & Ancient Moated Sites.

The manor belonged to Brithulf, son of Leoman the Saxon, at the Conquest, and Norman Scarfe suggests that

TOSTOCK *(continued)*

Tostock Old Hall, seat of William Berdewell in 1445, may occupy the original settlement site of the parish whose oldest spelling Totestoc could be interpreted 'the dairy farm with the look-out'; the church stands above where the land rises to a spur. Tostock House is late C16, early C17. It was re-faced in brick and flint in the C18. The Gardeners Arms public house has a fireplace of c1640.

TRIMLEY ST MARTIN *(8 miles ESE of Ipswich)*

Colneis Hundred. 'Trymma's meadow' or 'Island or clearing of the tree-cross' (OE) plus church dedication *Tremelaia* (DB). Includes the Domesday vills of Alston, Grimston Hall, Morston, Norton, Plumgeard, Thorpe and Turstanestuna. Norman Scarfe suggests the latter meaning as a site hallowed by a very early cross; since the two Trimley churches of St. Mary and St. Martin share the same churchyard, the cross was probably sited here. *Manors.* Grimston Hall with Morston Manor (C13 Geoffrey de Bellemonte). *Sub-Manors.* Martson/Moston Hall; Capel/Capel Hall.

Ancient Settlement.
Cropmarks of ring ditches and field systems suggest dense early settlement of the area.

Roman Road.
A Roman road is known to have led from a crossing of the river Orwell (probably at Downham Reach) to the Saxon Shore fort at Walton (Felixstowe). Although its exact course is unknown, it certainly passed through Trimley parish and is perhaps traced by Trimley High Street. Along its route possibly lay the hamlets of Wykes Bishop, Greenwich Farm, Warren House, Hallowtree and Alnesborne, and through the parishes of Nacton, Levington, Stratton Hall, Trimley and Alteston (near Marston Hall, where the road was known as Alteston Street) to meet the coast at Coleness, once the most easterly point in England.

Romano-British Settlement.
In response to a network of cropmarks recorded from aerial photographs, a prehistoric and Roman settlement site was discovered during fieldwalking below Sleighdon Hill and Thorpe Common.

Industrial Site.
A Late Iron Age/Early Roman salt working site was discovered in the parish with evidence of another operating from Norman times to Elizabeth I, near Cuttings Grove at Leiston, a lost Trimley hamlet on Trimley Marshes.

Ancient Packway.
The line of Earl Bygott's Path or Bygottsway, a medieval packway which ran from Walton Castle to the Bigods' fortresses at Framlingham and Bungay, passes through the parish N and S of the present A12 road.

Lost Medieval Settlements.
Here along the Trimley shore between the rivers Orwell and Deben was once extensive settlement - one of the most populous districts in the county with many villages and hamlets crammed into a few square miles. The former settlements here which can be traced back to Domesday estates are: Grimston-with-Thorpe (*Grimestuna* and *Torp*) on the Orwell slope known as Sleighton Hill, a gravelly cliff which descends to the waters of the river Orwell, and where, along its beach known as Thorpston, the lord of the manor claimed right of wreck; Morston (*Morestuna*) which merged with Grimston sometime before 1370 and is now represented by Morston Hall, an C18 house on the Orwell slope; Norton (*Nortuna)*, shown to have later merged with Candlet in St Mary's parish; *Maistana,* which lay in Lower Walton, and Capel Hall, which lay by the waters of Kings Fleet.

Medieval Common.
Trimley Heath, shown on Faden's 1783 map, covered much of the NW of the parish: from Falkenham Road in Kirton just S of Kirton Church, to the junction with Back Lane; SW to the area of the present school in Kirton Road; on a line S along this road, through the modern residential development; probably NW along the line of the old A12 road and SW along Thorpe Lane and NW traced by a footpath passing N of Woodruff Grove. It possibly then continued NNE marked by a present track and minor road which runs from the present dual-carriageway and leads to Morston Hall. It was enclosed in 1804 and 1808.

TRIMLEY ST MARTIN *(continued)*

Site of old Windmill.

A post mill with roundhouse stood in Mill Lane to the N of the village in 1783. It was not demolished until after 1918.

Historic Houses & Ancient Moated Sites.

The Domesday vill of Grimston-with-thorpe is represented by Grimstone Hall, now a farmhouse. It was the home of the Elizabethan explorer Thomas Cavendish, who in 1588 became only the second Englishman to sail round the world, plundering several towns on the South American coast of their treasures as he went. Three years on, flushed with success, he set sail from Plymouth with a larger force to repeat the adventure but this time became detached from the group in the night and was never heard of again. Capel Hall, over in the E of the parish, belonged to the Hobarts in the C16 and later the Edgars.

TRIMLEY ST MARY *(8 miles ESE of Ipswich)*

Colneis Hundred. 'Trymma's woodland clearing' plus church dedication (OE) *Tremelaia* (DB). Includes the Domesday vills of Candlet and Leofstan.
Manors. Trimley St. Mary/Candelent/Candlett/Fourthe (-1362 Bigot family). *Sub-Manors.* Blofield Manor; Alteston (1292 Godfrey de Bellemonte granted free warren).

Ancient Woodland.

Painters Wood and the adjoining Salters Wood are sections of ancient woodland.

Ancient Settlement.

Post holes were found when an Iron Age/Early Roman settlement was excavated in 1998.

Roman Road.

The lost hamlet of Micklegate means 'Great Road or Way' and refers to the Roman road which once ran from Coddenham, via the outskirts of Ipswich to the Saxon Shore fort at Walton (Felixstowe).

Roman Tile Industry

A field known as 'Kiln Field' is reported to have yielded Roman tiles.

Salt Working Industry

There is evidence of three salt working sites in the parish. The 'Old Salt Works', S of Salter's Wood and shown on the OS map as a roughly rectangular ditched earthwork, produced only one fragment of C13 pottery from a trial excavation c1960. Another two sites have been identified on Trimley Marshes, W of Christmasyards Wood and just SW of Garden Wood.

Lost Medieval Settlements

As has already been stated for Trimley St Martin, here along the Trimley shore between the rivers Orwell and Deben, was once extensive settlement - one of the most populous districts in the county. The former settlements in this parish which can be traced back to Domesday estates are: Blowfield, at the head of Walton Creek; Candlet (*Candelenta*) on the Deben slope and represented by Candlet Farm (Morley suggests the name is Latin and means 'white heat' and that it perhaps describes a small beacon which stood over the Kings Fleet in Roman times); and Alston (*Alteinestuna*). The Domesday vill of Alston, Alteston or Attempstone had a church dedicated to John the Baptist, which apparently survived until at least 1460. It was marked on Faden's map as 'old chapel now down' and its site said to lie 1½ miles W of Grimston Hall where in 1720 'bones are often ploughed up on the Alston Hall Farm'. This is one of only two villages in the county known to have been obliterated solely by the 'Black Death'. The area is marked by Thorpe Common and Thorpe Lane.

Historic Houses & Ancient Moated Sites.

Blofield Hall (now demolished) was still shown on the 1975 OS map sited in a rounded enclosure. Blofield was a sub-manor of Trimley in c1292 and owned by John Blofeld in 1362. Documentary evidence suggests a manor house had probably occupied the site since the C14. The last hall was described in the 1950s as being C17 in date, and on two floors. Candlet Farm may have at one time been moated. The site has yielded C13-C17 pottery.

TROSTON *(6½ miles NNE of Bury St Edmunds)*

Blackbourn Hundred. 'Throstr's family's farm' (OScand) *Trostuna* (DB)
Manors. Troston (-1536 Abbot of St. Edmunds; c1536 Thomas Bacon). *Sub-Manors.* Rougtownes (1495 William Felton).

Ancient Woodland.
Troston Heath in the N of the parish is ancient woodland.

Bronze Age Cemetery.
A Bronze Age cemetery was discovered in the parish.

Tumuli.
Tumuli in the parish may well have been associated with the Norse settlers (*see above*). Black Hill Barrow on Troston Heath is c115' in diameter and 10' high with no sign of a ditch. Another, 55 yds. SW of Black Hill has a spread mound and measures c98' in diameter by 3' high. There was a third on the heath (now lost) described in 1936 as being 35 paces in diameter and 5' high; it had probably been destroyed by 1950. On the S side of the road in the village itself and E of the previous group, Troston Mount is 3' high and c115' in diameter.

Ancient Trackway.
Basil Brown noted on his 6" OS map in 1951, 'Some evidence obtained that helps to confirm ancient trackway.' He was referring to a track which sets out from Ixworth Thorpe as Brand Lane, becomes the metalled road passing Honington Airfield and the tumulus of Troston Mount, been cut across and destroyed by the runway, and reappears as a track to the parish northern boundary beyond Rymer Farm. For its whole length - apart from a section along the road from the junction with Heath Road and passing the Airfield buildings - it forms the NE parish boundary.

Site of Gallows (?)
The field adjoining the Troston Mount tumulus is named 'Gibbet Pightle' suggesting a gibbet at one time stood on the mound.

Medieval Hospital.
There was supposedly formerly a hospital in the parish for the sick monks from the Abbey at Bury. Its site and history are unknown.

Medieval Common.
Troston Common is shown as a rectangular area adjoining Ixworth Heath on Faden's map of 1783. Its northern extent is marked by Kiln Grove; its western by Common Lane; eastern by field boundaries, and southern by the parish boundary comprising the field boundary, two fields S of the road.

Historic House & Ancient Moated Site.
The manor house of Troston Hall which lies to the SE of the village is a much restored timber-framed Elizabethan house. Two distinct ditched arms lie to the N along the southern edge of Church Lane and Common Lane. The C19 tithe map shows them as irregular shaped linear areas of water - the possible remains of a moat.

TUDDENHAM ST MARTIN *(2½ miles NE of Ipswich)*

Carlford Hundred. 'Tudda's homestead' (OE) plus church dedication *Todenham* (DB)
Manors. Tuddenham/Loudham Hall (1293 Robert de Westerfield; c1310 John de Tuddenham). *Sub-Manors.* St. Bartholomews/Bertilmemes.

The parish is sited in the lovely green and fertile Fynn Valley. The river, now little more than a stream, is thought to have been some 5' higher in Saxon times.

Roman Settlement.
Evidence of a Roman settlement site was discovered in the parish.

TUDDENHAM ST MARTIN *(continued)*

Coin Hoard.

A hoard of Roman coins was unearthed in the parish no doubt connected with the above settlement. The 114 coins covered the period from Constantinius II (337-361A.D.) to Honorius II (393-423 A.D).

Earthworks (?)

J.Wodderspoon in his *Memoirs of Ipswich* (1850) speaks of "Earthworks, apparently the remains of . . . defence . . . on the road to Tuddenham, about half a mile from the town . . ."

Site of old Windmill.

A post mill stood W of the church by Westerfield Lane before 1782. It was demolished c1901.

Historic Houses & Ancient Moated Sites.

Tuddenham Hall, ¼ mile N of the church, is a modernised early C17 house and the former seat of the Minters. Fountains Inn dates from the C16.

TUDDENHAM ST MARY *(3 miles SSE of Mildenhall)*

Lackford Hundred. 'Tuda's homestead' (OE) plus church dedication *Todenham* (DB)

Manors. Tuddenham cum Badgecrofts al Hengraves al Shardelowes (1236 Eborard de Trumpington). *Sub-Manors.* Banstead/Bensteads; Netherhall.

This early Saxon township, mentioned in a charter of 854 A.D., occupied a peninsula between the (then) half mile broad river Lark on the N and Herringswell Fen to the S.

Tumuli.

Two possible ploughed-out round barrows, S of Mitchel Head, were seen in the spring of 1981 as two chalky circles with a surrounding dark ring. One was about 30 yds in diameter and the other smaller. Nothing remained visible on aerial photographs in 1986.

Ancient Roads.

The ancient Icknield Way, later used by the Romans (Margary 333), forms the southern parish boundary with Higham. Another ancient road which connected the Abbeys of Ely and Bury St. Edmunds also crossed the parish.

Saxon Cemetery.

E of the Higham Road, ½ mile S of the church, a Saxon cemetery was discovered in a gravel pit. Finds included one inhumation burial of a warrior with iron sword, shield boss and knife.

Medieval Cross.

A Cross which once stood on the village green was removed in 1934.

Site of old Windmill.

A smock mill stood at the junction of Tuddenham Road and Herringswell Road NW of Mill Farm in 1783. It was disused by 1901.

Grange.

Sibton Abbey had a Grange here for sheep husbandry in the C12/C13.

Medieval Guildhall (?)

There were four guilds operating in Tuddenham: St. Anne (1480), Trinity Guild, Guild of Our Lady and St. John Baptist (1490), suggesting a guildhall may have once been sited here.

Free School.

A Free Grammar School was founded by John Cockerton in 1723. The school house was rebuilt in 1846.

Historic Houses.

The Manor House with frontage to Mill Stream is C17 in date. The manor house of Netherhall was built c1640.

TUNSTALL *(7 miles NE of Woodbridge)*

Plomesgate Hundred. 'Site of farmstead' (OE) *Tunestal* (DB). Includes the Domesday vill of Dunningworth. *Manors.* Tunstall (c1272 Sir Thomas de Weyland). *Sub-Manors.* Baynard's/Banyards.

Tumuli.

A bowl barrow lies in Tunstall Forest ¾ of a mile S of Heath Cottages. It is sited on the crest of a spur with traces of an encircling ditch and an outer concentric bank c66' in diameter and 3½' high. N of Heath Cottages is another bowl barrow c46' in diameter with a surrounding ditch c1' deep. There are traces of an outer bank and the mound is 4' high from the bottom of the ditch. A scatter of burnt flints were discovered over the mound. A barrow may be represented by a small mound SE of Heath Cottages, deep into Tunstall Forest. It is c34' in diameter and under 1½' high. In a sub-circular barrow some 49' by 5' high on the edge of Blaxhall Heath, clipped by a track on its western edge and heavily overgrown, a Roman urn containing ashes, two coins and a piece of a sword, 3" long, were found in 1834.

Site of Ancient Ford.

Evidence that the river Alde was anciently forded at Snape Bridge is provided by the local pronunciation of "Dunnifers" to the hamlet and former township of Dunningworth which is sited here. Kirby refers to a Dunnifer Fair which points to an original Dunnanford, 'the ford of Dunn'.

Deserted Medieval Village.

The former parish of Dunningworth (*Duniworda* in Domesday - 'property of Dunn's family'), near to (and sometimes known as) Snape Bridge on the northern parish boundary of Tunstall, is now only represented by Dunningworth Hall. Its northern boundary was the river Alde, and its southern may have been Rimple Hill where there is still a boundary mound. Dunningworth formerly had a church dedicated to St Mary. It was still in use in 1561 but seems to have fallen into decay soon after this. Its site is represented by Chapel Field, SW of the hall on the edge of Tunstall Forest, where several skeletons were discovered in 1841. Kirby's map of 1736 shows it with a tower, situated in a field by the Blaxhall road not far from Dunningworth Hall. Faden appears to name the site 'Abbey Ruins' in 1783. Dunningworth was ecclesiastically joined to Tunstall in the late C16.

Medieval Fair.

Dunningworth Fair was a large horse fair held at Snape Bridge.

Historic House.

Gabis Farm is a timber-framed Elizabethan house opposite the church.

UBBESTON *(6½ miles SW of Halesworth)*

Blything Hundred. 'Ubbi's farmstead' (OScand+OE) *Upbestuna* (DB). Morley considers it a late (c1020) Danish settlement.

Manors. Ubbeston (1286 Robert de Ubbeston).

Ancient Woodland

Ubbeston Wood, N of the church, is ancient woodland.

Roman Encampment (?)

The church stands beside the Roman road near Ubbeston Wood on the N bank of a 40' hoh thought by many to be a Roman encampment. To date no evidence has been found to prove this claim.

Roman Road.

The Roman Road from Weybread to Peasenhall (Margary 35) bisects the parish NW-SE. Its course follows the existing road SE from the parish boundary but is lost where it crosses the Blyth valley. Beyond the hall a footpath runs parallel (slightly NE) to the course of the old road to the SE parish boundary.

Ancient Track.

The line of a former packway used by the Bigods to link their castles at Walton and Bungay (which branched NE via Huntingfield Hall from another heading E and represented by Dunwich Lane in the neighbouring parish

UBBESTON *(continued)*

of Heveningham) may be represented by the road heading ENE from the church and passing Packway Farm.

Deserted & Relocated Settlement.
The village settlement in the Blyth valley appears to have been abandoned in favour of linear settlement along the B1117 road at Ubbeston Green, leaving the church and hall isolated. At Domesday there appears to have been two manors and two churches here.

Medieval Green.
A tiny triangular green, at the junction of the B1117 road near Green Farm with one heading N to the church, is marked Ubbeston Green on Faden's 1783 map. The green has now been infilled with properties and become a small hamlet named Ubbeston Green.

Historic Houses & Ancient Moated Sites.
Ubbeston Hall, now an C18 farmhouse, was the former residence of the Sones family, and the Kemps in the C17. There are monuments to the two families in the church. Two sides of a square moat remain at Grove Farm on the western parish boundary. A probable moat, represented by an enclosure - the N and E sides and N corners visible as hollows in a ploughed field - adjoins the N side of the churchyard. The site has a scatter of C12-C13 pottery. Pottery datable to the same period was found on a small square enclosure SE of the church which may be a former moated site.

UFFORD *(2½ miles NNE of Woodbridge)*

Wilford Hundred. 'Uffa's enclosure' or 'Uffa's ford' (OE) *Uffeworda* (DB). Includes the Domesday vill of Sogenhoe.
Manors. Ufford (C13 John de Peyton; 1298 de Ufford family). *Sub-Manors.* Sogenhoe; Ufford Sutton; Otleys; Kettleburgh Ufford.
The name Ufford is generally ascribed to the first of the Uffa (or Wuffa) dynasty. This royal East Anglian family may well have set up their initial home here at 'Uffa's enclosure' before establishing their royal manor of Kyson in Kingston ('King's town') by the Deben (*see* Woodbridge), and their royal burial ground across the river at Sutton Hoo (*see* Sutton). Taylor stated 'The name Wuffa, King of the East Angles, may perhaps be found at Ufford in Suffolk' (*see below*).

Ancient Woodland
Round Grove, adjacent to the A12 Woodbridge bypass, and Ufford Thicks on the northern parish boundary, are parts of ancient woodland.

Metal-working Site.
On the eastern parish boundary by the Ufford Road, metal detector finds in 1995 of 'bronze slag fragments (found over most of the site)' plus 'silver slag fragments' and 'copper ore pieces' were suggestive of a Roman metal-working site. Two Late Iron Age coins were also discovered here.

Mounds.
Two low earthen mounds each c64'-82' in diameter and c1½' high lie to the E of Grove Farm and immediately to the N of the grounds of St Audrey's Hospital.

Site of Saxon (Wuffa's) Settlement (?)
In 1939 R. W. Maitland wrote: 'In the name of Ufford we have a definite connection with Uffa (or Wuffa); and on the rising ground in front of Ufford Place (now gone leaving only parkland and nursery S and N of The Avenue) considerable remains of a Saxon settlement were found about a hundred years ago which Mr. Reginald Smith of the British Museum assigns to the latter part of the sixth century. Wuffa reigned c550-586 A.D.'

Ancient Ford (?)
Claude Morley considers Uffa gave his name to a ford here - providing the parish place-name -possibly at a point where Bridge Road now spans the Deben SE of the church.

UFFORD *(continued)*

Ancient Chapels.

Sogenhoe Chapel was founded c1291 by Robert de Ufford and remained in being under the instigation of the Ufford and Willoughby families until 1527. A Terrier dated 26 October 1613 describes the site of Sogenhoe Chapel as 'a piece of land lyinge in the Chappell field wheron it is supposed a chappell hadd once stode . . .' The Rector paid 70s. per annum for the site in 1732/4 and Bowen's map of 1755 shows it in ruins. Traces are said to have remained of the ancient religious house at a farmhouse (Grove Farm) in 1937. The site of Chapel Field is to the N of the loop in the B1438 road where it joins the A12. The land is now used as nurseries. Another chapel sited in Ufford was attached to the manor of Otley.

Stocks & Whipping Post.

Close by the churchyard gate stands the medieval village stocks and whipping post.

Hospital & Almshouses.

In 1690 Rev. Thomas Wood left monies in his will for repairs to the hospital he had built in Ufford and for four men from Wickham Market to have places here. The red brick cottages were still in existence as almshouses in 1894.

Historic Houses & Ancient Moated Sites.

Bowen's map of 1755 and Faden's of 1783 shows 'The Castle' adjoining the W side of the ruined Sogenhoe chapel. 'On the W of the site of Sogenhoe Chapel is a piece of land in the form of a rectangular parallelogram containing about an acre and a half; there still appears a ditch or moat surrounding it, on which piece of land it is said there stood a castle (anciently the seat of the de Uffords, Earls of Suffolk) but we do not hear of any ruins being dug up there, so this may only be conjecture.' - Kirby 1763. 'In this parish are the remains of the moat of a castle' (Parker 1855). The first of this knightly family of de Ufford certainly held the Manor of Sogenhoe - Robert de Ufford died seized of it in 1298 - and may well have had a fortified manor house here. It is interesting that the field so described does exist, but it is N and not W of the chapel site and shows no sign of having been moated or built upon. However there is a field W of the chapel called Sogenhams which may reward investigation. It lies N of Grove Farm (a late C17 farmhouse formerly known as Ufford Hall) 'upon the 3rd field from the E end of the road between Ufford and Bredfield village'. The manor house of the Otleys and Lambs is probably that described as an alternative site for the Ufford's 'castle', being 'in a field called Office meadow, adjoining a farmhouse belonging to the Mills Trust (of Framlingham) about 2 furlongs N of the church. In a dry summer, marks of the old foundations may be traced there.' However, this site is located in the adjoining Manor of Otley. Park House, in Lower Street, retains an early C16 wing.

UGGESHALL *(5½ miles ENE of Halesworth)*

Blything Hundred. 'Uggi's corner of land' (OE) or 'Uggi's sheltered valley' (OScand) *Uggiceheala* (DB)
Manors. Uggeshall (1275 Roger FitzOsbert).

Ancient Salt Industry.

The river Wang forms the southern parish boundary and Domesday Book lists a 'salthouse' here, showing there was still a tidal connection with the coast at Easton Bavents at that time.

Ancient Track.

The ancient Green Lane which runs to Frostenden Church provides the northern parish boundary.

Medieval Greens.

A Golds Green is named but not detailed on Faden's 1783 map. It stood opposite the entrance drive to Uggeshall Hall. The extensive Frostenden Clag Common lay along the eastern parish boundary, partly in Ubbeston. Primrose Lane now shows its position and the ancient Green Lane its northern limits.

Site of old Windmill.

A post mill which stood on Uggeshall Hill in 1736 was demolished in 1923.

Historic House.

Uggeshall Hall may stand on Uggi's ancient Saxon or Danish site. The present hall dates from Tudor times.

WALBERSWICK *(1½ miles SSW of Southwold)*

Blything Hundred. 'Walbert's dwelling or dairy farm' or 'Walhberht's creek' (OE) *Walberdeswike* (1199). The Hundred Rolls of 1275 first spelled this township *Walberdeswyk,* a name which represent *Wealhbeorhteswic*, a Saxon name, plus *wic* 'a creek'. Here the Dunwich River formerly reached the sea and, according to the old ditty, "To Dunwich, Soul (Southwold) and Walberswick, we pass in at a lousy Creek".

Manors. Always attached to Blythburgh and shared the same manorial lords.

From modest beginnings when its little Domesday thatched church - a mere chapely of Blythburgh, its wealthy neighbour - stood on the borders of the marsh, Walberswick later developed into a considerable port at Blythburgh's expense (*see* Blythburgh). This resurgance can be recognised in the ruins of its later majestic church. The encroachment of the sea, and the depression of the fishing industry following the Reformation, finally brought about its decay. In 1451 it had 13 barques trading to Iceland, Ferro and the North Seas, and 22 fishing boats employed off the coast. The town suffered four great fires, (before) 1583, in 1633, 1683 and 1749. Its great church of St Andrew was rebuilt by the parishioners between 1473-1493 but, although repaired (after being sacked by the Puritains) and continuing until 1696, by 1625 Walberswick was already said to be 'one of the poorest townes in England'. The diminishing population, unable to maintain it further, took down most of the building, save the SW corner which they reserved for services, leaving the rest to decay.

Tumuli.

There are two round barrows near Tinker's Walk: one, situated ½ a mile W of Eastwoodlodge Farm, is 72' in diameter and 3½' high (in 1992); the other, 123' in diameter and c2' high, stands beside the D1307 road which clips the NW edge.

Earthworks.

On the southern parish boundary with Dunwich, by the causeway through Westwood Marshes E of Fen Hill and N of Dunwich Forest, a faint earthworks known as Stonehill Mount, Castle Heath, lies in woodland S of a stream near Stonehill Bridge. It has been suggested as a camp used during the siege of Dunwich by the Earl of Leicester in 1173. Another suggestion has come from Peter Warner of Homerton College, Cambridge, who has investigated the site and feels this may well have been a small motte and bailey castle belonging to William de Criketot, importantly sited beside the (Roman)? road from Dunwich to Caister and positioned to defend Blythburgh and the local ports situated on the coast.

Medieval Dock

In Oldtown Marshes by Dunwich River, a pottery scatter covering Medieval and Post-Medieval periods identifies the site of the old port. Apparently, timbers from the old town 'dock' (part of the 'quay'?) survive and can still be seen at very low tide. 'Walberswick Old Church' and 'Walberswick Old Quay' are marked in approximately this position at the head of Horse Reach on a 1753 map which is a copy of Ralph Agas's 1587 map of Dunwich.

Lime Kiln.

A lime kiln is mapped at South Gayfer Quay, Walberswick (possibly just in Southwold parish). In 1630 Thomas Rannales of Walberswick is listed as a lime burner.

Medieval Common.

The extensive Walberswick Common, shown and named in Faden's map in 1783, remains, although the village has developed and extended N and S along the main road. Towards the end of the C16 Sir Robert Broke became lord of all the Blythburgh manors and was soon in conflict with the town. In 1612 he seized 1,400 acres of the common land and fens and then, in 1632, the quay. Despite a ruling by the courts demanding the return of lands and quay to the people, Sir Robert contested this by putting in men and dogs to drive away 'trespassers'.

Lost Medieval Village.

Stonehill Mount (*see above*) is thought to stand on the site of the now lost village of Hethern which, in 1463, was down to two houses. It was previously the manor of Cliffs or Cleaves, then called Hethern. Listed under

WALBERSWICK *(continued)*

Blythburgh Hundred and thought to be somewhere in these bounds, the long-lost estate called Warle (*Wael-leah* in Domesday meaning weir or fish-trap meadow), was held by William de Wonchensey in 1275. Running as it does to the banks of the river Blyth, Henham would provide the ideal description for the place-name.

Medieval Gallows (?)

Hangman's Cross in Deadman's Covert on the western parish boundary, suggests that this may be the site of a former gibbet.

Medieval Cross.

An account of 1470 states: 'Paid for makyng the Cross - 5 nobilys and 40d.' It stood at the road junction W of the church.

Almshouse.

An almshouse was founded in Walberswick in 1522 by T. W. Odiorn with further endowments by T. A. Richardson in 1572.

Historic House.

The Bell Inn is said to date from the C15/C16.

WALDRINGFIELD *(4 miles S of Woodbridge)*

Carlford Hundred. 'Clearing belonging to Waldhere's family' (OE) *Waldringfeld* (c950) *Waldringafelda* (DB) *Manors.* Waldringfield al Waldringfield Hilton (1305 Sir Robert Hilton). *Sub-Manors.* Rivershall (1316 Richard Bruce).

Tumuli

Soil marks of six round barrows were recognised in 1962 on Waldringfield Heath, S of Heath Farm. One, which had been much levelled by 1949, measured 45' in diameter in 1959. Three others measured 45', 44', and 28' in diameter.

Early Settlements.

There appears to have been two manors and two settlement sites in the parish. Rivershall Manor, represented by Rivers Hall on the opposite bank to the medieval Methersgate Quay, was probably the Waldhere's original settlement on the heath by the Deben ('Waldhere's family's clearing' *see above*). In 1305 Sir Robert Hilton was patron of the living in the more important Waldringfield-with-Hilton. This settlement further S which centred around the church and old rectory appears to have been abandoned in favour of a return to the river bank by the Maybush Inn, from where it has now spread W along the street. Domesday records a *Minima Waldringafelda* or Lesser Waldringfield which probably refers to the earlier and depopulated heathland settlement.

Industrial Site.

The move back to the river (*see above*) was probably triggered by the coprolite and Portland cement industries which began here. The fossilised animal dung was found in great quantities along the river and used as a fertiliser, whilst the mixture of chalk and mud from the river bank produced a commercial cement. The medieval Methersgate Quay on the opposite bank of the Deben was created and flourished on the strength of this coprolite trade.

Historic Houses & Ancient Moated Sites.

Rivers Hall, N of the church and at one time residence of the Bruce, Curson, Jermy and Wingfield families was purchased by Thomas Essington in 1662. He later sold it to Sir Samuel Barnardiston. A Chilton Hall, named on Faden's 1783 map, is possibly the site (but a misspelling) of the original manor house of Hilton Hall. Although shown further N on the map it may refer to the site of the present White Hall, S of the church. The Maybush Inn (formerly The Cliff Inn) has been licensed since c1745.

WALPOLE *(2½ miles SSW of Halesworth)*

Blything Hundred. 'The Britons' pool' (OE) *Walepola* (DB). Claude Morley suggests this meeting of the river Blyth with four streams running in four directions at the bottom of the valley was the *weala pol* - 'the Briton's pool', an area then of broad marshes where the *weala* (Britons), or foreigners (to the Saxons), had their settlement. The present church - doubtless erected upon earlier Saxon foundations - stands upon a hoh above the 'pool'.
Manors. Walpole (1288 John de Vallibus). *Sub-Manors.* Chickering (C13 William de Royng).

Saxon 'Causeway'.
At the W end of the village, substantial timbers, dating from the Middle to Late Saxon period, have been identified close to the river Blyth, possibly from a causeway leading to Walpole Bridge which now carries the B1117 road over the river.

Ancient Tracks.
Packway Farm is situated near the junction of two ancient routes now traced by public footpaths. Dunwich Lane, an ancient way from Walton (Felixstowe) to Dunwich, heads WSW-ENE from the Roman road towards Bramfield Castle and forms the southern parish boundary. 'The Packway' heads N from Sibton Green, via the pool known as Packway Water and Old Greenway Farm, towards Bungay. Another ancient way, Earl's Way, enters the parish S of Holly Tree Farm, crosses Walpole Lane, and continues N past Walpole Hatch Farm to join Halesworth Road before crossing the river Blyth at Walpole Bridge. Sites along these medieval routes are mentioned in an ancient ballad describing the flight of that notorious baron Hugh Bigod from the forces of Henry II in the C12.

Chapel.
The timber-framed Congregational Chapel or 'Old Meeting House' claims to be one of the oldest in existence in the country. It was founded as a chapel for the Independents in 1646.

Site of old Windmill.
A post mill which stood just S of Walpole Old Hall in 1736 was blown down in 1919.

Workhouse.
A small workhouse is recorded here with six inmates in 1776.

Historic Houses & Ancient Moated Sites.
The Elms, SW of the chapel, dates from 1613 and has some original pargeting. Walpole Old Hall, N of the village, is Tudor in origin. Fragments of a moated enclosure survive at Packway Farm adjacent to the parish boundary. There is evidence of earthworks and part of a moat in permanent pasture S of Hill Farm (renamed Walpole Hatch Farm), E of the village.

WALSHAM LE WILLOWS *(5 miles E of Ixworth)*

Blackbourn Hundred. 'Walh's homestead' (OE) *Wal(e)sam* (DB). 'Le Willows' - in this sense meaning 'beside the willow trees' - was added much later; in fact not in use until after the Dissolution. Whereas Walpole (*see above*) suggests the home of a band of Britons (foreigners to the Saxons), Walsham refers to a single Briton.
Manors. Walsham (-C13 le Blunt family; C13 William Criketot). *Sub-Manors.* Church House/Easthouse/Esthouse (1307 John de Walsham, subsequently passing to Ixworth Priory); High Hall al Wydecattes/Walsham Overhall.

Ancient Tracks.
A track running NE from Botany Farm to Finningham Road is part of Hundred Lane which not only forms a part of the eastern parish boundary, but also the ancient Hundred boundary between Blackbourn and Hartismere. West Street forms a part of the former 'Thetford Way', a packway which led to Botesdale Market and in existence in 1577.

Mound.
Much damaged traces of a mound with part of a surrounding ditch lie in the SW corner of a field W of Long

WALSHAM LE WILLOWS *(continued)*

Plantation. Its early use as a mill mound is inferred by a 1695 survey which names the site West Mill Mount and West Myll Waye, but it is not known if the earthworks has an earlier origin.

Monastic Country Retreat.

The Vicarage, also known as The Priory, is an ancient house with carved shields and an inscription 'SWR RICHARD ALDRIH CHANV'. This probably refers to Richard Gotts, prior of nearby Ixworth in 1504. This was the manor house of Walsham Churchhouse which belonged to the priory at Ixworth, and was used as a residence for the priests who officiated in Walsham Church.

Medieval Green.

Alwood Green, also known as Hallowed Green, is shown lying across five parishes on Faden's map of 1783 - Walsham, Rickinghall Superior and Inferior, Gislingham and Finningham. It was enclosed under an Act of 1818, though not implimented until two years later. The Walsham section was bordered on the W by the road passing Town Farm (which subsequently gained much of the land), and on the N,E and S by the parish boundary. Hall Green occupied the site of Sumner Road, and Cranmer Green appears to have been enclosed by the C15.

Medieval Recreation.

On the NW corner of the main crossroads in the village, to the W of Summer Road on Camping Close, is a site known as The Game Place. This was an open-air theatre described in a 1577 survey as 'a place compassed round with a fayre banke cast up on a good height and houseinge many great trees called populars growinge about the same banke, in the myddeste a fayre round place of earth made of purpose for the use of stage playes'. Although these places may have at one time been quite common, they usually comprised a mere open space not a major construction such as this. The fact that the site was called Camping Close suggests that it was also used for the medieval ball game at the same time as (or prior to) the theatre.

Mills.

Walsham Mill stands on the site of mills dating back around 400 years. A post mill called Crowland Mill shown standing by a path running due S from The White House in 1783, was still there in 1884.

Medieval Cross.

The parishes of Walsham, Stanton and Badwell converge at a junction of trackways in an area known in 1695 as High Cross. Here, it is beleived, stood a Medieval Cross.

Medieval Guildhall.

There were three guilds operating in Walsham: St. Trinity (1446), St. John Baptist (1446) and St. Catherine (1521). The 1577 Fieldbook describes Walsham 'Guyld Hall' and places it in the area now occupied by Elmside Farm residential development. A 1990 site survey recorded it as a ditched enclosure in a meadow.

Town House.

The C17 Town House was divided into four for the occupancy of the poor of the parish.

Workhouse.

The Guildhall (*see above*) was later used as a workhouse and recorded 20 inmates in 1776

Historic Houses & Ancient Moated Sites.

Once the Walsham manor of Wyldcattes, when it was held by the de Walsham family (c1293-1351), C16 High Hall, NE of Cranmer Green and Finningham Road, retains parts of its quadrangular moat, the N and E sides now infilled. A Field Book of 1577 may identify another moat on Cranmer Green (now under the plough) but at that time 'in the messuage with yard and croft held by John Jessup'. Crowland Hall, in the hamlet of Crownland to the SE, retains two sides of its former square moat. It was originally called Crownland, a manor forfeited to the Crown in 1514. The two sides of a square moat at Old Hall on Finningham Road, shown in the 1950s on the OS map, have now gone. This was probably home to the Hunt family. The Laurels dates from the C17.

WALTON *(10 miles SE of Ipswich)*

Colneis Hundred. 'Settlement of the Romano-British people' (OE) *Waletuna* (DB). Includes the Domesday vills of Maistana and Oxelanda. Walton was abolished as a civil parish in 1914.
Manors. Walton (-1524 Bigots[Bigods], Brotherton and Howard families, Earls & Dukes of Norfolk).
Sub-Manors. Caldecote Manor; Langeston.

Ancient Ports & Havens.
Portus Adurni, the name of the Roman fort *(see below)*, suggests that this, or Colness (from which came the name of the Hundred) may have been the river Deben's name prior to Saxon times. In these early days Walton and Felixstowe were indistinguishable and the whole area centred on the Roman Fort called *Burgh*. The fort had three approaches - Wadgate, Micklesgate and Burghgate, plus the later vills of Gulper and Langer. The Saxons found the old abandoned fort provided a defended, walled home for the Britons and named it *weala tun* which later became Walton. It was the most important place on the peninsula and main limb of the ancient port of Goseford (Goseford Haven was still being mentioned as late as 1554). Further N, Stambak, a very early haven where Felixstowe Ferry now stands, appears to have silted up and been gone by the C13. The port of Harewell (Orwell) was mentioned in 1285 and likely applied to a district rather than a town or settlement. It lay between two inlets, Wadgate, and the wider Colness River by an area of water which anciently cut off Landguard (then Langerston) from the mainland making it an island (an area of water now reclaimed for Felixstowe Port). Wadgate, which ran up into the land by what is now the Ordnance Hotel, was a coastal haven where ships could lay up when the sea was rough. The Manor of Walton extended over the greater part of Felixstowe parish and was considered a manor of great extent and importance at the time of Domesday when it was held by Roger Bigot. It provided a landing place for the Earl of Leicester and his Flemish army in 1173 when they were received by Hugh Bigot. Queen Isabella and Prince Edward along with their French supporters also landed at Walton to expel Edward II from the English throne in 1326. Changing fortunes have seen Felixstowe, still only a village in the mid-1800s, come to more recent prominence as first a seaside resort and then a major international port, leaving the fading Walton to become merely its suburb.

Roman Fort.
Kirby stated in 1740 "He that shall look for this castle within the bounds of Walton strictly taken, will never find it; but on a high cliff in Felixstowe at a distance of about a mile from the mouth of Woodbridge river, and two miles from Orwell Haven". This fort - one of a number under the command of the Count of the Saxon Shore built along the east coast by the Romans to defend this outpost of their empire against foreign insurgances - stood on high cliffs above the North Sea, about 1 mile S of the Deben estuary. It was first recorded in 1613, and like Burgh Castle near Great Yarmouth, was rectangular in plan with bastions and an entrance on the E. Erosion led to the collapse of the site into the sea. A letter in 1722 described the walls as being '. . .turned with an angle and composed of pebble and Roman bricks in 3 courses, all round footsteps of buildings, and several large pieces of wall cast down upon the Strands by seas undermined ye cliff all which have Roman brick. At low water mark very much of the like is visible at some distance in the sea. There are two entire pillars with walls. The cliff is 100' high.' In 1740 its western foundations were still in place some 187 yds in length - local people were said to call the ruins 'Stone-works'. Although an exceptionally low tide in the 1950s exposed some masonry blocks, the last remains were seen in 1933. It now lies some 225 yds offshore at a point three-eighths of a mile S of the golf club house.

Roman Cemetery.
On the present edge of the cliff is the last remnants of the Roman cemetery site associated with the fort and coins have been found ranging from Severus Alexander 222-35 A.D. to Honorius 395-423 A.D.

Roman Road.
A section of the Roman road which ran from Coddenham to the Roman fort (probably via a ferry at Downham Reach just outside Ipswich) was exposed in 1916 during the construction of Brackenbury Barracks, and another section some 80 yds long revealed in 1935 along Cliff Road between Church Road and St George's Road.

WALTON *(continued)*

Hundred Meeting Place.
This may have been at 'The Mount' SE of Kembroke, 'Holm Hill' in Kingsfleet, or a now lost site at Cole Ness.

Site of Saxon Monastery (?)
Again, as for St. Fursey at Burgh Castle, near Gt. Yarmouth, the Roman fort here may have provided a protected sanctuary for St. Felix to install his East Anglian see; this has also been confidently claimed by Dunwich but as both Roman sites are now under the sea, final proof lies buried with them.

Site of Felixstowe Priory.
Felixstowe was anciently part of the parish of Walton and did not receive its present name until the Priory of Black Monks dedicated to St Felix was founded here by Roger Bigod, Earl of Norfolk, who gave it as a cell to the Benedictine Cathedral Priory of St Andrew at Rochester about 1105. He endowed it with lands taken out of his Manor of Walton and it afterwards became the manor of Felixstowe Priory. Little is known of its history, and it only maintained a prior and two monks at the time it was suppressed by Cardinal Wolsey in 1528, and the income appropriated towards the foundation of his Ipswich College. It originally stood on the cliff by Walton Castle but due to erosion by the sea was moved 1½ miles inland to a meadow behind Walton Church in the C13. The church accounts mention ruins still standing in 1734, some 200 years after its suppression. The site is still called Abbey Meadow and used to contain a building called the Abbey Barn which incorporated in its structure old wooden beams from the priory; this was destroyed by fire in 1911. Excavations on the site found no evidence of a church and it was concluded that the parish church of St Mary was used by the priory.

Site of Norman Castle.
Within the confines of the Roman fort the Normans built a castle in much the same way as they had at Burgh Castle, except that in this case it was built by the powerful Bigods, Earls of Norfolk, and was no doubt on a much grander scale. However, it failed to survive attack by the army of Henry II in 1174 (after Bigod had joined the rebel forces of the Earl of Leicester) and was destroyed on the king's orders two years later. Its demolition was said to have been so complete that 'to prevent it ever rising again, the stones of it were carried into all parts of Felixstow, Walton and Trimley and footpaths pathed with them, on both sides of the road'.

Ancient Trackways.
It has been calculated that the sites of the Priory, Walton Old Hall, Old Felixstowe Church and Walton Castle lie in a straight line roughly equidistant from one another at just over ½ mile intervals. Trackways, some of them of considerable age, originally linked these sites. Earl's Path (or Bygott's Way) is part of an ancient packway which linked the Bigod castles of Walton (Felixstowe) and Framlingham. It can be identified in the parish running from Gulphers Road by the golf links SW to pass under the A14 dual-carriageway at Trimley.

Medieval Ferry.
Walton Ferry ran from the Ferry Boat Inn to the steps near the naval yard at Harwich from the C15 to the C19. In the C13 the Bigods claimed rights of groundage, wreck, fishing and ferriage in an attempt to control the bitterly contested river trade.

Medieval Market & Fairs.
Roger Bigod obtained the grant for a market and fairs here in 1288. All were long obsolite by 1844.

Market Cross.
Near the church was once an ancient Market Cross, a small hexagonal building constructed of oak, on the site of the market set up by Roger Bigod. It was taken down c1853 after being used for some time as a lock-up.

Site of Walton Old Hall.
A house, long known by the name of Old Hall, was supposed to have been erected as the manor house of Walton by the Bigods about 1291 following the destruction of their castle, and called 'Stone Room'. In this house Edward III lodged several nights in 1339 before setting sail for France, during which time he confirmed the charter granted to Ipswich. It was ruinous by 1514 when it was known as 'Corte House', and in the early part of the C19 the ruins of this extensive mansion were still standing about 73' in length, 32' in breadth

WALTON *(continued)*

and varying from 6 to 24' in height. In 1881 the skeleton of a window 24' high was blown down and by 1932 all that remained was an irregular mass of overgrown masonry in the corner of the ground of the Felixstowe Cricket Club behind a building used by the local tennis club. The site is now the Felixstowe School Sports Ground and is situated between Links Avenue and the Orwell Hotel.

Tudor Fort.

Langer Fort, now known as Landguard Fort, situated near Landguard Point on the southern tip and within a Nature Reserve, was built to guard Harwich Harbour. It was first mentioned 1540-5, but there may well have been a fort of some description on the site much earlier. Its name derives from a vast ridge which lay out to sea called Langerston or Langer-stone which defended the haven and was used by fishermen to dry their nets. It has had rebuilds; the first in 1624 when it was described as having four bastions called the King's, Queen's, Warwick's and Holland's, each mounting fifteen large guns. It was rebuilt again in 1717-20, and the present fort dates from 1875. Its military history is hardly memorable. In 1667 the Dutch fleet succeeded in landing 3,000 men at the foot of the cliff and made a small-arms attack on the fort. They were forced to withdraw in disarray when an English ship lying off-shore fired at the beach showering the invaders with pebbles !

WANGFORD *(3 miles SW of Brandon)*

Lackford Hundred. 'Ford that could be crossed with a wagon' (OE) *Wamforda* (DB) *Wainford* (1197)
Modifications to the landscape made by the great sand-inundation of 1668 (and perhaps others) have removed any signs of a former ford here. There is little doubt, however, that at one time Wangford Fen extended much further W and across the road leading to Brandon. The church has a rare dedication to St. Denis.
Manors. Wangford/Wangford Grange (C13 Philip de Ikeworth). *Sub-Manors.* Hakbeck/Hagbeche; Flemmings; Crepping.

Tumuli.

There is documentary evidence of Bronze Age barrows on Wangford Warren 'rifled by the intensely ignorant tenant and the relic destroyed as being of no account' (1878). One of them, a mile due NW of the church, was locally called Oat Hill. They may have been lost under Lakenheath Airfield. A low oval mound SE of Shakers Lodge in Wangford Woods, 16' long, 10' wide and c1½' high, discovered after tree felling, may be a pillow mound. A nearby plantation, marked Pole Hill Slip on a 1905 map, suggests the name of the earthwork.

Romano-British Settlement

'Near Wangford is a regular sandy track where bones of men and animals, fragments of Roman pottery, broken querns, pieces of metal and coins and other relics have been frequently found, and about 1 mile from the village several Saxon urns have been dug up.' So wrote Basil Brown, probably referring to an area of dark soil 35yds by 40yds he partially excavated in the 1950s. Mixed Roman and Iron-Age settlement levels were found featuring artefacts. A C4 rectangular 'hut' 8' by 12' had daub walls and possible floor level with signs of burning and a mass of charred hulled barley, pits and an area of chalk and clay 7' by 6' with pot boilers and Iron-Age sherds.

Earthworks & Saxon Cemetery (?)

Roman, Ipswich and Thetford ware pottery along with quantities of Saxon metal artefacts were found in earthen banks to the W and NE of the church. The banks may have been built as a barrier to rabbits from the adjoining 'warren', and the finds associated with the large Saxon cemetery discovered on Lakenheath Airfield.

Site of Former Grange.

A rectilinear earthwork with internal sub-divisions is visible on an aerial photograph E of the church and road junction. It appears as an enclosure with single banks on the NW and SW sides and probably double banks on the SE and NE sides. Faden shows two buildings at this location in 1783 marked 'Grange', with a road or track passing the site to the N. To the NE of this it shows a very large area of water named 'fish-pond'. This is probably the mere called Puthawk Mere now identified by a low area on the edge of Wangford Wood. The Grange was

WANGFORD nr. Brandon *(continued)*

mentioned in 1291 as belonging to the Cistercian Abbey at Warden in Bedfordshire and used during the C12 and C13 for sheep husbandry. It was variously known as Livermere Grange or Elmermere Grange, and fields nearby were recorded in 1251 as Lyvermerefield and Almermerefield. The Grange was dissolved in 1537 and leased to the Crown.

Deserted Medieval Village.
Though probably never heavily populated, there was a settlement near the church which has now completely disappeared with the exception of Wangford Farm. Properties are shown around a possible green area on Faden's 1783 map and the parish had a population of 56 in 1881. Most of the parish, once covered by a massive rabbit warren, lies under the great conifer forest of Wangford Wood or, as in the case of this possible village settlement, beneath Lakenheath Airfield.

Medieval Green (?)
Though not naming it as such, Faden's 1783 map traces what was perhaps an oval green lying S of the church, edged on the W by scattered properties and on the S by Wangford Farm.

Former Guildhall.
A deed connected with the manor dated 1632 speaks of 'all that messuage or tenement sometimes Tollers, with the house and yards belonging, and the barne and ground adjoining thereto called the Guildhall.' A much earlier one in Latin describes a messuage as 'jac int messagium voc le Guyld hall, ex parte austr.'

Historic House.
Wangford Hall, S of the church and now represented by Wangford Farm, was the seat of Lord Chief Justice Wright in the reign of James II. It was built in the 1680s.

WANGFORD *(3½ miles NW of Southwold)*

Blything Hundred. 'Ford by the river Wang ' (OE) *Wankeforda* (DB)
Manors. Wangford (c1160-1540 Wangford Priory; 1540 Thomas, Duke of Norfolk).

Ancient Ford.
Wang is a Saxon word for 'an open field', suggesting that the river crossing was by an open field. A possible site is where a road leaves the A12 heading E and crosses the river to Hill Farm through the extensive Wangford Common - the 'open field' of the place name? A more likely site for the former ford, however, is where four roads join the present A12 trunk road to cross the river Wang in the village just SW of the church.

Site of Priory.
Adjoining the S side of the parish church, on what is now called the Abbey Lands, a small Cluniac monastery with a prior and three monks was founded before 1160 as a cell to Thetford Priory. Its founder, Dondo Asini, a steward of the king's household, dedicated it to St Mary or to St Peter and St Paul. All Cluniac houses were considered alien during the wars with France and as such Wangford was taken into the hands of the Crown. In 1327 Edward II restored their possessions and control and it continued until the Dissolution when it was assigned to Thomas, Duke of Norfolk. Nothing remains of the Norman building above ground since an arcade of 6 bays was removed from the E end of the N aisle over 100 years ago. The Cloister adjoins the S wall of the church. Human remains were found on the site in 1961.

Medieval Greens.
Barnaby Green, shown on Faden's 1783 map, lay immediately to the S of the present A12 road on either side of the road to Elms Farm. Wangford Green was an open common E of Henham Park, enclosed in 1817.

Site of old Windmill.
A post mill stood by Wolsey's Creek in 1736. It was demolished c1917.

Medieval Guildhall.
It is possible a guildhall once stood in the village where four guilds are known to have existed: St. Peter, St. George (1458), Guild of the Virgin (1460) and St. John Baptist (c1468).

WANTISDEN *(7 miles ENE of Woodbridge)*

Plomesgate Hundred. 'Want's valley' (OE) *Wantesdena* (DB)
Manors. Wantisden Hall (C13 Sir Thomas Weyland; 1406 Butley Priory).

Ancient Woodland.
Dogger's Grove on the northern parish boundary is a fragment of ancient woodland.

Earthwork.
Cumberland Mount in Staverton Park, locally called 'Caesar's Camp' and 'Cromwell's Mount', is a horseshoe-shaped earthwork comprising a single bank and ditch approx. 300' x 220' with an entrance to the S. Beyond this to the S, SE and SW were once, apparently, defensive banks. During excavations in 1910 finds of C12-C13 pottery sherds proved fairly conclusively that the site was of medieval date. It has been suggested that it may have formed a 'camp' during the Peasants Revolt of 1381 when 'a mob headed by John de Batisford marched through Woodbridge, attacked and laid waste the house of Fraunceys at Melton, and then divided into two parties, one remaining to ransack the ruins, the other led by William Bernard of Copdock marched to the house of John Staverton at Eyke, which they plundered carrying away goods to the value of 100 shillings.' Or perhaps it is the site of the old Staverton Hall itself. Less colourfully, perhaps, it may have been a compound for deer - even where they were culled, as it is suggested that Staverton comes from the AS. *Stearfa*, meaning 'slaughter'. Evidence of traces of a small wooden building within the enclosure may have identified a herdsman's hut. The deer park dates from the period of the pottery finds.

Ancient Deer Park
For details of Staverton Park, a part of which lies within this parish (*see* Eyke).

Deserted Medieval Village (?)
There is no settlement at Wantisden. The church, the abandoned moated site of the original hall and the present Wantisden Hall, stand in curiously isolated positions approached only by lanes and footpaths across fields. Extensive fieldwalking to the E and S of the church has failed to find any deserted nucleated village site, so it must be assumed that if one existed it lies immediately to the W of the church and is now lost under the massive runway and buildings of the former Bentwaters Airbase

Medieval Grange (?) & Ancient Moated Sites.
Old Yards marks the site of the original manor house of Wantisden Hall formerly surrounded by a moat 6' deep, divided into two parts, one rectangular, the other semicircular. The site was known in the mid C19 as 'The Bow and Arrow Place'. Local tradition places its destruction in 1381 during the Peasants Revolt. The massive moat has now been converted to part of a reservoir. The first house on the later site dated from 1550 and was built by Richard, son of Sir Anthony Wingfield. 'It was a large house with diapered brick E and W gable ends'. Sculptured stones were dug up near the site in 1837 and 1852, 'some representing the heads of prelates', while stones with C14 mouldings were found in the 1960s. These finds coupled with the fact that Butley Abbey held the manor and monks from there entertained Mary Tudor, Queen of France, in the deer park with 'fun and games' in 1528, suggests the original hall may have been a monastic grange.

WASHBROOK (formerly Belstead Magna) *(3½ miles SW of Ipswich)*

Samford Hundred. 'Stream for washing (sheep or clothes)' (OE) *Wasebroc* (DB)
Manors. Great Belstead/Washbrook Amer/Hamer/Amor Hall (1214 William de Fortibus, 7th Earl of Albemarle; C14 Abbey of Albemarle in Normandy; c1371-1538 Dartford Nunnery, Kent; 1538 Sir Percival Hart).

Roman Road.
Apart from a kink in the road N of Amor Hall, The Street and Swan Hill trace a length of the Colchester to Coddenham Roman road (Margary 3c) partially forming the parish boundary with Copdock.

Deserted Settlement.
Evidence in the form of eight tenements shown lining the street on a 1595 map in the area of Washbrook Church in the hamlet of Washbrook Green, shows that this was the likely original village settlement of the

WASHBROOK *(continued)*

parish. This area was later deserted in favour of a new settlement which would grow up straddling the busy Roman road.

Lost Settlement & Site of Ancient Church or Chapel.
'Within the bounds of this parish there was formerly a hamlet with a church (or chapel) called Felchurch, a sub-manor to Amor Hall Manor. It was appropriated to the Abbey of Albermarle and upon the dissolution of the alien priories given to the nunnery at Dartford. In 1540 it was granted to Sir Percival Hart with the rectory and advowson of the vicarage of Washbrook. The vicarage of Felchurch was instituted in 1301, 1314 and 1338. It was mentioned in 1254, 1291 (when mention was also made of a mill), 1340 (when four wool-assessors were recorded here) and in 1535.' Kirby stated in 1764 that he had been informed that 'in a field bordering on the road leading from Sproughton to Copdock Water, about 40 rods on this side of the water, next Sproughton, the ruins of a church if they are not now, were not long since visible.' The field to the E of this is known as Chapel or Chapel Yard and is called 'Chapel' on the 1837 tithe. A terrier of 1635 describes 'The Chappell Yarde' as containing 3 rods and abutting glebe lands to N and S; this is the southernmost dog-leg of a now enlarged field where human bones have been found.

Historic Houses & Ancient Moated Sites.
Birch House Farm on the SW parish boundary retains a small quadrangular moat, and there is a larger one at Colesgreen Farm - two sides of an elongated rectangular moat.

WATTISFIELD *(6 miles ENE of Ixworth)*

Blackbourn Hundred. 'Wastel's clearing' (OE) *Watlesfelda* (DB). Called 'Watlesfeld' until at least 1340, and Watesfield in 1783.
Manors. Wattisfield (-1538 Abbot of St. Edmunds; 1544 Sir Ambrose Jermyn). *Sub-Manors.* Gyffords and Hallymotte (1287 Sir William Gifford).

Early Settlement Sites & Roman(?) Road.
Large black patches evident in a field W of Peartree Farm and Walsham Road were thought by Basil Brown to be possible hut sites. With finds including Mesolithic and Neolithic flints, and pottery sherds from Iron-Age to Early Medieval, Brown considered that this had been a settlement site since prehistoric times. In 1955 he rediscovered 3 circular huts(?) E of Honeypot Farm, sites previously reported in 1941, and discovered two more which he excavated. He failed to date any finds. Close to the Foxledge Roman kiln site *(see below)* he excavated a rough rectangular enclosure some 300' square covering a Roman hearth but with a hut inside containing Early Iron-Age pottery. Saxon finds were also made on this multi-period site. On cutting a trench across the southern end of Wranglands field, a cambered metalled road c20' wide was revealed *(see below)*.

Roman Pottery Industry.
Investigations undertaken since 1934 on the edge of Calke Wood and the former Foxledge Common have revealed a series of some 24 irregular pits on the clay deposits - perhaps kilns or for clay extraction. They date from C1-C2. A kiln found just S of the road bounding the S edge of the wood was removed to Wattisfield Pottery for preservation (where it can still be seen). Other Roman pottery kilns have been found NW of Wattisfield Pottery, SE of the church, near Clipper Cottage, and E of Kilnyard Barn, suggesting a major pottery industry in continuous production throughout the Roman period from C1-C4.

Medieval Pottery Industry.
Remains of two clamp kilns producing Medieval ware were discovered by Basil Brown on the slope down to the Grundle, just NW of Grundle Farm.

Ancient Way.
A stretch of road known as Wattisfield Causeway was incorporated into the main road. In 1628 the will of Sir Nicholas Bacon left £33 6s. 8d. for the purchase of land, the rent from which to be applied to the repair of this Causeway.

WATTISFIELD *(continued)*

Medieval Strip Fields.

The remains of possible medieval strip fields have been recognised on the E side of Honeypot Lane.

Medieval Monastic Fish-ponds.

Halymotes is a sub-manor of Wattisfield. It means 'the holy moats or ponds' and occupies sites of monastic fish- ponds. It would appear to occupy land between Wattisfield and Walsham from the site of a former green called Hell Green to the present Fishpond Farm and Fishpond Barn across the Walsham parish boundary. The Abbot of St. Edmunds, Bury, held the main manor here until 1538.

Medieval Greens.

Two adjoining greens were shown on Faden's 1783 map: Hall Green occupied the grounds now taken up by Southview, S of the village, and the larger Hell Green continued to the S and extended W to Red House Farm.

Site of Gallows (?)

Wattisfield's Church Register contains the following entry: "Ano. dom. 1582. Ano. Elyzabeth 24. Thomas Parken was executed upon a gibbet on Millhill, in Watersfild (near Wattisfield Potteries), the 24 day of March, for the murder (in Croftes Wood) of his wife, and was hanged up in Iornes." A residence called The Croft stands on the hill between church and hall and eastwards from this in earlier days stretched a wood which may well have been the 'Croft's Wood'. Gibbeting in chains, following execution, remained a common practice in England till the beginning of the C19. The body was bound round with hoops of iron, and hung up by a loop of iron over the head. It often hung twelve months or more, and as the flesh around them rotted, the bones often fell to the ground and were collected and buried by the victim's friends and family.

Site of old Windmill.

A post mill which stood on the edge of Wattisfield Pottery in 1783 was demolished in 1914.

Old Meeting House.

Built in 1706, the Old Meeting House was pulled down to make way for a new building in 1876.

Historic Houses & Ancient Moated Sites.

A site near Grundle Farm by Honeypot Lane, excavated by Basil Brown in 1945 and 1955, was identified as probably being part of the Wattisfield manorial site of Gyffords and Halymote. A 20' wide metalled road was found running E-W, with 6' wide and 4-5' deep ditches on either side. The road was made of chalk and marl with pieces of pottery rammed into the clay base. Along with a small rectangular building 6' by 10' were indications of a moat and remains of buildings leading from the site to Grundle Farm. Near Pear Tree Farm (built on early foundations) a medieval well exists. Basil Brown recognised a possible ploughed-out moat in 1956 near Peartree Farm, later confirmed in cropmarks by aerial photographs. Indications of a moat at Moat House he thought represented the site of old Wattisfield Hall just SE of the present hall. This C16 timber-framed hall was believed to have been the home of Charles Brandon before he moved to Westhorpe to build the palace for himself and Mary Tudor, sister to Henry VIII. Squirrels Hall, built c1840, stands on the site of the former hall of the same name. The C16 Black Swan Inn, closed in 1969, was reputedly a haunt for highwaymen operating on the Bury to Diss road. Turpins Free House & Carvery opened in 1986 on the former site.

WATTISHAM *(6 miles SW of Needham Market)*

Cosford Hundred. 'Waet's homestead' (OE) *Wecesham* (DB)

Manors. Wattisham Hall (C13 Osbert de Wachesham).

Ancient Woodland.

Devil's Wood (formerly Dead Man's Wood), W of the village, is a part of ancient woodland.

Roman Road.

From Needham Lane a length of Roman road (now ploughed out) runs to the edge of Wattisham Airfield as a public footpath following the parish boundary. The road originally crossed the river Gipping probably at Sharmford to join the road to Caister by Norwich (A140).

WATTISHAM *(continued)*

Ancient Chapel.

Loose Chapel was mentioned in 1110 when given to Bricett. Loose Hall lies just beyond the northern parish boundary and a chapel is marked on the OS 1st edition map by the modern castellated house called The Castle.

Medieval Green.

In the hamlet of Wattisham Stone, S of Devil's Wood, a small green is shown and named 'Green' on Faden's 1783 map, now replaced by a section of the road running WSW from the church.

Historic Houses & Ancient Moated Sites.

Ancient as the present Wattisham Hall may be, it stands on a site which is much earlier still. Along with other farm buildings, the hall is enclosed within a circular moat 44' wide and 82 yds in diameter with another manorial moat cut at a later period enclosing another large irregular quadrangular area; this includes the church and churchyard in its NW corner and contains the remains of fish-ponds. This moat averages 12' wide with banks 3' high. This obviously ancient fortified site long predates the medieval buildings within. The original fortified hall on the site was the residence of the knightly family of de Wachesham from at least the late C12 when Giles de Wachesham held 30 acres here. The Castle is a castellated Gothic farmhouse of c1770.

WENHASTON *(3 miles ESE of Halesworth)*

Blything Hundred. 'Wenheard's farmstead' (OE) *Wenadestuna* (DB). Includes the Domesday vill of Mells. *Manors.* Wenhaston (1271 John de Vallibus; 1312 John de Norwich; 1375 Mettingham College). *Sub-Manors.* Wenhaston Grange; Mells Manor.

A C14 reference to 'Wenhavestun' suggested (at that time) the river Blyth was still navigable to Wenhaston.

Ancient Woodland.

Mells Wood in Mells hamlet is ancient woodland.

Roman Settlement.

There was a large Roman settlement here, initially located E of Wenhaston Black Heath as a surface scatter of pottery sherds and artefacts over three fields.

Ancient Chapels.

The remains of the Norman chapel of St. Margarets stands boldly atop a hoh over the former mill at the river crossing in the hamlet of Mells, about 1½ miles SE of the village on the S bank of the Blyth. It is about 50' long, constructed of flint rubble and consisted of a nave and apsed chancel. The nave walls and the narrow chancel arch remain - the latter with ivy-clad walls c8' high - in a farmyard of Old Chapel Farm. It is thought to have been built by Ebrandus de Mells about 1104 and held by Sibton Abbey. It was in use until 1465 after which it was abandoned and allowed to fall into decay, with no sign of any subsequent restoration. In Bartholomew Lane, near Wenhaston Old Hall and the Bramfield stream, stood another chapel dedicated to St Bartholomew. It existed in 1150 when the land was owned by the Priory of Smithfield, but was unmentioned in the 1254 Norwich Tax. Claude Morley claimed to have found a dressed stone from this ancient chapel in 1930 in a copse just S of Mill Heath.

Medieval Heaths.

The heaths and commons of north Suffolk are fragments of the Suffolk Sandlings which stretched from Ipswich to Lowestoft. The L-shaped Church Common lay E of the church; the small, square Blowers Common further E by Narrow Way; Bickers Heath was triangular and N of the village; Mill Heath covered the junction of Bartholomews Lane and Heath View NW of the village; whilst parts of the extensive Blackheath remain S of the village and W of the modern A12 road.

Deserted Medieval Village.

The hamlet of Mells was once a considerable manor and separate parish. The main manor of three carucates (c360 acres) contained an area 10 furlings long and 7 broad, running along the southern bank of the river Blyth which forms the northern boundary of Wenhaston. It was held by the freeman Manning at Domesday

WENHASTON *(continued)*

and worked by 8 villeins, 12 borders and 3 serf. There was woodland for 100 swine and 5 acres of meadow. The ruins of the old Norman chapel (*see above*), Mells Bridge, Mells Cross Roads, Mells Hill Farm, Melles Court Farm and Mells Wood mark the extent of the former parish.

Ancient Mills.
Mells Domesday name of *Mealla* comes from the Anglo-Saxon 'Mealewes' meaning flour, an obvious reference to the water mill said to have existed here on the river Blyth in 1065, but gone by 1086. Formerly sited a mile up river, Mells watermill was moved to its current position at Watermill Farm in 1758, where, before 1793, it was topped by a windmill. A post mill which stood on Blackheath in 1783 was down by c1896.

Medieval Stocks & Whipping Post..
The leg-irons and handcuffs from the village stocks which once hung in the church had been destroyed by 1923. The stocks and whipping post were in existence between 1705 and 1814. There is also an entry in the 1717 records for 8d. paid for a ducking stool.

Free School.
A bequest for education was made by William Pepyn and Reginald Lessey in 1562. A schoolmaster was recorded in 1660 and a schoolmaster and school chamber in 1722. By 1818, 21 children were attending the endowed school and rethatching and repairs were carried out c1838.

Guildhall.
A Guildhall existence here in 1726. White tells of 'The Town Estate . . . comprises a building in four tenaments, anciently called the Guildhall, granted by the prior and convent of the Priory of Blythburgh.'

Almshouses.
An almshouse accommodated 15 poor persons in 1674. In 1686 Church House was occupied by the poor.

Historic Houses & Former Grange.
Wenhaston Grange, 2 miles W of the village, is Elizabethan with a later exterior dating from Queen Anne. It probably stands on the site of a grange to Sibton Abbey dating from the C13/C14. Wenhaston Hall and the Old Hall are both of ancient origin.

WESTERFIELD *(NE of and now partly in the borough of Ipswich)*

Bosmere & Claydon Hundred. 'Westerly clearing' (OScand+OE) *Westrefelda* (DB). Morley suggests the parish was named by the Norwegian Vikings about 840 A.D.
Manors. Westerfield (C13 Sir William Weyland).

'Castle' (?)
Cox wrote in 1720 of the 'remains of an old Castle found in Westerfield', but this has never been substantiated nor the site identified.

Lost Medieval Green.
The Green is shown on Faden's map of 1783 as occupying the area S of the crossroads in the village and, for the most part, W of the Ipswich road (B1077). It was enclosed in 1808.

Site of old Windmill.
A smock Mill which stood by Mill Farm before 1795 was gone by 1880.

Free School.
A Free School taught six poor boys in 1675. In 1679 provision was made for poor girls, and a school mistress provided for the purpose. Bridget Collet's 1662 bequest for education was applied to the purchase of bonnets, cloaks, shoes and books in 1840.

Historic Houses.
Westerfield Hall was built in 1656, probably on the site of an earlier hall. Green Farm which bordered the green has Tudor origins.

WESTHALL *(3 miles NE of Halesworth)*

Blything Hundred. 'At the west shelter' (OE) *Westhala* (DB)
Manors. Westhall Hall (C13 Crown property granted to Nicholas de Donewic/Dunwich; c1243 Hubert de Burgh). *Sub-Manors.* Empoles; Barringtons; Bacon's al Wingfield.

Tumuli & Iron Age Settlement.
In a Field E of the Roman Stone Street a hoard of Late Iron Age iron and bronze artefacts including rings, pins and vessels were found c1854 at a depth of 2' by a farmer making drains. The area of dark soil also revealed fragments of mainly Roman pottery. Was there once a barrow here on which a postmill later stood, and perhaps 'Deadman's Grave' to the N at the crossing of Noller's Lane and Butt's Road (*see* Spexhall) marks an associated burial site.

Medieval Greens.
The parish extends for nearly two miles NW from the church with settlement originally along the margins of five medieval greens or commons which covered 125 acres. All parishioners had the right of pasture here according to the extent of their landholdings. The line of interconnecting greens ran W from the hall (now Westhall Farm) along what is now a new road called Bacon's Green Road. They comprised the tiny Goose Green at Downings Farm, the linear Bacons Green near Bacons Farm, Great Green (now Mill Common), and Cox Common (formerly West Hall Green) which ran from Paradise Farm to Moat Farm at the junction with Butt's Road. At the junction of Hares Lane and The Danger (S of Great Green), was the tiny Nethergate Green. The greens of Bacon, Great, Nethergate and West Hall were enclosed c1853; Goose Green had already gone by 1783.

Plague Pit.
The site of a C15 plague pit was discovered in 1965 at Lower Common near Belle Grove Farm.

Medieval Market & Fair.
Robert de Burgh, Earl of Kent and Lord of the Manor, obtained the grant for a market in 1229 and for a fair, formerly held in Sotherton.

Workhouse.
A workhouse was recorded with 10 inmates in 1776.

Historic Houses & Ancient Moated Sites.
Moat Yards on Mill Common comprised a double moat, (one within the other) with traces of other enclosures close by. The inner moat which is very deep and wide enclosed a square island on which stood an ancient hall. The outer moat was rectangular. Old maps show no sign of any access across either moat so it must be assumed this was via bridges. While the plan and purpose appear similar to a motte and bailey castle, its level squared appearance suggests a C14 fortified manor house. When all remains of the outer moat were destroyed in the early 1950s for the construction of old people's bungalows 'many loose worked stone and flint were taken out with several lumps of rubble wall.' It is likely that the first hall on the site was that of the de Aspalls who held the manor here. From the time of Henry VIII to the latter part of the 18th century it housed the residence of the de Bohun family. A C17 book written by one of the family *Diary and Autobiography of Edmund Bohan, Esq.* shows two illustrations of an earlier hall 'on the site of the present one' (built in 1570 and now destroyed). Paradise Farm, on the N side of Cox Common 1¾ miles NW of the village, dates from the C16. Moat Farm, on the western parish boundary at Cox Common, has two sides of its rectangular moat. Rookery Farm, SE of Cox Common, retains three sides of its rectangular moat, and a fragment of another (oblong) moat lies to the W of the Common. Beacon Farm, on Bacon's Green Road, has the remains of a moat with field systems and a further rectangular moated enclosure shown to the S on aerial photographs; a trackway is also shown running NE-SW. Further E on the N side of the same road, in a field named The Grove, is the site of another moat, now ploughed out but identified in aerial photographs in 1974. It was some 200' square with a raised platform on the W half of which is a midden area. The site was visited in 1975 when a large quantity of C13 pottery was found. On the southern parish boundary, S of Westhall Farm, nothing now remains of a moat described in 1665 as the 'situation of Empoles'. Empoles was a late medieval sub manor of Westhall. The platform was demolished in 1968 and the last of the moat (the S arm) destroyed some time after 1974.

WESTHORPE *(8 miles N of Stowmarket)*

Hartismere Hundred. 'Westerly outlying hamlet or farmstead' (OScand + OE) *Westtorp* (DB). Morley suggests a Viking origin for this settlement, initially of hamlet status, lying west of a more major settlement which he considers to have been Stoke Ash, though this is some distance E; Finningham would therefore seem more likely.

Manors. Westhorpe Hall (1240 Walter de Westhorpe; 1338 Robert Hovel).

Ancient Track.

The ancient Hundred Lane forms a part of the western parish boundary and the hundred boundary between Hartismere and Blackbourn. It is evident on the ground in the track from Botany Farm NE to the Finningham road, also in the Hundred Lane from West Farm SW to the parish boundary. This is also the ancient boundary between East and West Suffolk - the boundary of the Liberty of St Edmund. In its course to Botany Farm the hedge boundary contains ten species, evidence to it probably dating back at least ten centuries.

Medieval Strip Fields.

Four medieval strip fields - possibly now the only ones remaining in Suffolk - have been preserved at 'The Carrs' in Westhorpe Field. They are under the protection of the Lord of the Manor, Mr. Barker of Westhorpe Lodge, sadly one of the few landowners with a true understanding of the importance of preserving and recording Suffolk's historic countryside. The strips are numbered 240, 293, 239 and 164 on the 1840 tithe map.

Ancient Chapel.

A chapel dedicated to St Mary was mentioned in 1402. Although its site and history are unknown, it may, in fact, refer to the private chapel known to have existed at Westhorpe Hall *(see below)*.

Medieval Green.

The pleasant village green, which still survives at the road junction opposite the hall, is shown on Faden's 1783 map where it is named simply 'Green'.

Medieval Market.

William de Ellingham or Elmham obtained a grant for a market and fair here in 1371. The tomb of his father, Henry de Elmham, lies in the church.

Historic Houses & Ancient Moated Sites.

A modest Georgian farmhouse stands on the moated site of Westhorpe Hall, the former residence of Mary Tudor (1496-1533), sister of Henry VIII, widow of Louis XII of France, and wife of Charles Brandon, Duke of Suffolk. She had married Louis to become Queen of France when she was just 17, and he 52. He died after two years of marriage and Mary secretly married Brandon after paying her brother (who opposed the union) £24,000 to reconcile him. She died here and was buried in Bury Abbey. Only the 3-arch Tudor bridge spanning the moat, her arms (rescued and inserted above the present door), and part of the domestic wing survive from the original house where Henry VIII was entertained in 1522. The cloister, chapel and original furniture were kept up until c1764 when the whole building was dismantled and a small farmhouse built on the site. One who witnessed the demolition of the great mansion - described as having been of palace proportions with decorated panels and pinnacles - said it had been done in a careless manner 'all the fine chimneys and ornaments (in terracotta) being pulled down with ropes and crushed to pieces.' Extensive ponds to the S of the moated site may have once been fish-ponds. Moathill Barn, NW of the village, has the remains of a square moat with indications of an adjoining enclosure to the S.

WESTLETON *(5½ miles NNE of Saxmundham)*

Blything Hundred. 'Vestlithi's village or homestead' (OScand + OE) *Westledestuna* (DB). Morley has a different translation. He breaks up the Domesday word into *west*; *ledes* - 'man from the'; *tuna* - 'farmstead': 'Man from the west's farmstead'.

Manors. Westleton (1264 William de Criketot). *Sub-Manors.* Westleton Grange; Minsmere/Scot's Hall; Lenwale's/Lembalde's/Lymbolds; Claydons; Westleton Cleeve's/Cliff's, Hernethorne; Valeins; Rysings.

WESTLETON *(continued)*

Roman Road (?)

The original road from Westleton to Dunwich, which leaves the present road at the fork to continue straight on as a white track through the heath known as Sandy Lane, may follow (at least for a part of its length) the course of a Roman road thought to have once connected Peasenhall with the coast at Dunwich.

Roman Pottery Production Site.

A kiln waster found entangled in tree roots below Watermill Farm, beside the river Minsmere, along with a spread of pottery sherds and oyster shells 200 yards away, suggests the site of Roman pottery kilns in the area.

Tumulus.

A round barrow lies on the NW parish boundary, W of Fen Covert, S of Newdelight Walks.

Ancient Way.

An ancient Packway passed through the village heading for Blythburgh. On the southern parish boundary Rackford Bridge (Rackway Bridge on Faden's map of 1783 and obviously a misspelling of its former name, Packway Bridge) takes the way over Minsmere River.

Earthworks.

Three long parallel earthen banks running beside a track called 'Black Slough' on Westleton Common may be connected with a former rabbit warren. Also on the Common a circular earthen mound, located on the outskirts of the village and 33'-39' in diameter with a possible gap in the bank, may have been an animal pound.

Chapel.

There was formerly an ancient chapel in Dingle hamlet but its site and history are unknown.

Turbary.

John Ridgard suggests that at Minsmere are 'unquestionably flooded peat cuttings dating back in charter material to at least the C12'. The extent of this turbary is unknown but may be that defined on Faden's 1783 map as 'The Broad'. In 1237 this part of the coast as described as being the port of Minsmere.

Medieval Green & Common.

The village green shown on Faden's 1783 map still remains at the junction of several roads. Westleton Common (parts of which remain) is shown on the same map running for some distance SE from the church.

Site of Gallows.

Hangman's Hill at Tin Houses Corner is the likely site of a former gibbet.

Site of old Windmills.

Two windmills stood either side of the track which crossed Westleton Common in 1783. Rouse's Mill, an open-trestle post mill had stood there since before 1736; it was later burned down. Ralph's Mill, a smock mill, stood close by. This was demolished in 1969.

Medieval Grange.

The manor of Westleton Grange belonged to Sibton Abbey in 1299. Here they sited one of their five granges. The manor was granted at the Dissolution to Thomas, Duke of Norfolk.

Town House.

Seven poor persons occupied the Town House in 1674.

Historic Houses & Ancient Moated Sites.

Lyenball's Farm on the NW parish boundary once had an interesting double moat enclosing a large tract of land. The inner one remains a perfect parallelogram, but the outer moat has now been lost. The site of the ancient Scotts Hall shows in cropmarks as a small rectangular enclosure at the fork of the access roads to and from Minsmere RSPB Reserve Visitors' Centre. Barnabes Restaurant occupies a C16 beamed building. The site of Westleton Hall is believed to be near Old Hall Farm; it was described as a barn in 1851. Springdays Farm, often referred to as 'Smugglers Hall', contains secret storage places (for contraband) behind the brick bread oven and in a chamber under the kitchen floor.

WESTLEY *(1 mile W of Bury St Edmunds)*

Thingoe Hundred. 'West meadow or clearing' (OE) *Westlea* (DB)
Manors. Westley otherwise Sextens/Sextins in Westley (-1539 Abbot of St. Edmunds; 1539 Sir Thomas Kytson). *Sub-Manors.* Leo's Hall/Luce's Hall; Westley otherwise Pembroke al Dunham Hall; Fresels.

Tumuli.
'An early British cinerary urn containing human bones', was said to have been discovered in a shallow tumulus on Old Heath in Westley. This burial mound was partially excavated in 1883 and 1884 and its contents exhibited in 1890. Old Heath may have extended over the parish boundary into Fornham All Saints and the barrow sited in this parish. Another, at Westley Bottom, contained Roman remains.

Deserted Medieval Village (?)
There were four manors in Westley, the main one, given by the Abbot of St Edmundsbury to his sexton, became Westley Sextons. A tiny fragment of the C14 church dedicated to Thomas a Becket lies in total isolation, replaced in 1836 by St Marys on a new site given by the Marquis of Bristol. Here, too, are sited the hall and two farms, with another on the southern parish boundary by the river Linnet. Long in the hands of succeeding medieval abbots, the parish boundaries would appear to have been artificially 'adjusted' for their convenience, and Old Warren Wood, New Warren and Warren Lodge just beyond the boundary possibly testify to the fate of any earlier settlement here. Faden's map of 1783 still shows a network of roads (since removed) across the parish.

Site of Historic House.
The site of Westley Manor House adjoins the road from Westley to Fornham All Saints near the Newmarket Road.

WESTON *(2½ miles S of Beccles)*

Wangford Hundred. 'West farmstead' (OE) *Westuna* (DB)
Manors. Weston (1280 Hugh de Berry).

Ancient Woodland.
Sparrow's Thick in the SW corner of the parish is a part of ancient woodland.

Historic Houses & Ancient Moated Sites.
Weston Hall, NW of the church, is part of a large Elizabethan manor house built by John Rede in the mid C16. Opposite is the Dower House, a curious house (originally much loftier than now) built by Rede's brother in the time of Charles II. Hill Farm is C17 and Walpole Hall, SW of Weston Hall, is another house of ancient origin. NE of the church, Church Farm had three sides of a rectangular moat (c1958) with the original E side and NE corner filled in and built over. In 1989 an aerial photograph showed what appears to be cropmarks of a second moat to the N of the first. It shows as field boundaries but looks 'moat-like' on the 1840 tithe map.

WEST STOW *(5 miles NW of Bury St Edmunds)*

Blackbourn Hundred. 'Westerly place (of assembly) or holy place' (OE) *Stowa* (DB) *Westowe* (1254)
Manors. West Stow (-1539 Abbot of St. Edmunds; 1539 Sir John Croftes). *Sub-Manors.* Jenney's/Ginney's; Unnamed Manor (C11/C12 de Blakenham family).

Lower Palaeolithic Site.
Finds of the Lower Palaeolithic period were made in Beeches Pit.

Multi-Period Settlement Site.
The small island beside the river Lark, later occupied by the Anglo-Saxon village (*see below*), was first settled some 5000 years earlier by mesolithic hunters. Excavations in the SW corner of what is now a country park uncovered a complex of ditches, pits and post-holes and finds of Mesolithic, Neolithic, Iron-age, Roman and Saxon settlement, showing the site had been occupied for over 6,000 years.

Tumuli.
A Neolithic round barrow was discovered NW of the village in The King's Forest. It is c105' in diameter and 5' high with no visible ditch. The northern half has been truncated by ploughing. On Jennet's Hill, in the area of

WEST STOW *(continued)*

North Stow in The King's Forest, two barrows are shown on Faden's map of 1783. One appears to be that described as 90' in diameter and 3' high cross-trenched in 1961 when an inner mound of turf layers was revealed 50' in diameter and 2'6" thick. This contained stain tracings of inhumation burial and Bronze Age pottery fragments. There were two hearths with 1,500 calcinated flints and 200 flakes including scrappers. The other barrow was probably destroyed when the area was forested in the 1930s.

Ancient Way & Roman Roads (?)

The Icknield Way, one of the country's oldest routes, passes SW-NE through the corner of the country park and continues through The King's Forest as a track called Westrow Road. Due to its (now) straight alignment, Margary lists it as a road later adopted by the Romans (333). Another possible Roman road is visible on aerial photographs as a continuation of the road running ENE across Ramparts Field to meet the Icknield Way. A possible fork then heads off SSE towards the Roman pottery kiln site.

Roman Pottery Industry.

On the N bank of the Lark, on the edge of the sand dunes and just upstream from the church, nine kilns were discovered and examined by Basil Brown in 1941 and 1947. They produced imitation terra sigillata, kiln waste pits, ditches and evidence of a potter's hut covering the period from 80-150 A.D.

Anglo-Saxon Cemetery.

In 1851 some 100 skeletons, together with cinerery urns and stone coffins hewn from solid blocks of stone, were discovered. The cemetery was associated with a settlement discovered nearly one hundred years later.

Pagan Saxon Village.

Following Basil Brown's discovery of a Saxon settlement on the N side of the river Lark in 1940, Dr. Stanley West excavated an entire pagan Saxon village. He found evidence of a number of small family 'halls' 30-35' long with smaller thatched huts with vertical plank walls grouped around them, together with considerable quantities of pottery and objects and material providing an insight into their living environment. The village was established by at least 400 A.D. on an island in the marsh and co-existed for more than a generation with the local Romano-British settlement at nearby Icklingham. The settlement lasted until c650 A.D. The thatched huts have since been recreated and form part of the West Stow Country Park & Anglo Saxon Village and is open to the public.

Site of Saxon 'Temple' (?)

Claude Morley suggested that the place name which (may?) relate to a 'holy place' in the parish points to a possible Saxon heathen 'Temple' on the site of the Norman church.

Earthworks.

An earthen bank running from TL820 719 to TL818 735 through The King's Forest, with another section 33'-39' wide and 1½' high at TL819 758 which no doubt continued N and S to join the former, marks the line of an old road which ran from West Stow to join the Old London Road (Icknield Way) and the Coach Way (now a track called the Duke's Ride) from Euston near Old Elveden Gap.

Site of Battle (?)

Stow Heath is the suggested site of a battle between the Saxons and Danes.

Deserted Medieval Village (?)

The original parish was called Stowe and was subsequently divided into North Stow and West Stow. Only North Stow Hall remains of the former which now lies under the Forestry Commission's King's Forest, but it is possible there was once a settlement here.

Historic Houses & Ancient Moated Sites.

West Stow Hall was formerly a large quadrangular house of C15 date surrounded by a wide moat. It was almost entirely rebuilt by Sir John Crofts, Master of Horse to Mary Tudor, sister of Henry VIII, former Queen of France, and wife of Charles Brandon, Duke of Suffolk. Their coat of arms appears above the impressive gateway built in the first half of the C16. Later owners included Edward Progers (Groom to the Chamber of Charles II), the

WEST STOW *(continued)*

Rushbrooke family and the 1st Marquis of Cornwallis. A circular water-filled moat(?) shown on the 1839 Culford tithe map on the eastern parish boundary N of the church and E of the road, is now incorporated in a playing field. The site of another moat lies immediately E of the church and road, again on the eastern parish boundary.

WETHERDEN *(4 miles NW of Stowmarket)*

Stow Hundred. 'Valley where wether-sheep (castrated rams) are kept' (OE) *Wederdena* (DB)
Manors. Wetherden (C12 de Scales family). *Sub-Manors.* Pulham Hall (C13 Abbot of St. Edmunds claimed free warren).

Roman Road (?)

The western parish boundary - seen on the ground as a public footpath N from Warren Mill House to the railway, and along a length of country road passing Botany Bay Bungalow to its sharp right turn at Willow Wood - traces the possible line of a Roman road. This also marks the Hundred boundary between Stowe and Blackbourn and the former county boundary between East and West Suffolk.

Ancient Tracks.

A footpath from just S of Bacton Hall to Willow Farm provides the Hundred boundary between Stowe and Hartismere. Another from Warren Mill House in the S of the parish, N to the railway, divides Stowe from Thedwastre.

Medieval Green.

Two very small greens were situated at Base Green near Batts Farm, and N of the church at Hunters Lodge.

Site of old Windmill.

Warrens Mill, by Warrens Mill House on the western parish boundary with Elmswell in 1764, was demolished c1907.

Historic Houses & Ancient Moated Sites.

Wetherden Hall, N of Base Green and about one mile NE of the village, has a perfect large rectangular moat. It occupies the site of an earlier hall and was formerly the seat of the Sulyards, one of whom, Sir John, was Lord Chief Justice of England. Sulyard was a loyal supporter of Mary, and she is thought to have stayed a night here on her way from Farmingham to London to claim the throne. Despite Sulyard's presence in his role as lord of the manor, a house in the village is thought to have been the meeting place of the supporters of Lady Jane Grey. The house was said to still exist in 1927 with a room where mass was celebrated in secret. Mutton Hall, NW of the village, was also owned by a Protestant, Robert Rosier. He was thought to have been arrested by Sir John in or around 1556 and burned at the stake in a field on the Wetherden to Woolpit road at Brennen (Burning) Hill (possibly Rush Green, *see* Harleston). Ironically, in a further twist, the hall, which retains detached fragments of its moat, was reputedly once the property of the Abbot of St. Edmunds. At Upper Lodge in the hamlet of Wetherden Upper Town there is one side and an angle of a small moat. Brickwall Farm on the SE parish boundary dates from the C16, as does The Maypole Inn.

WETHERINGSETT-CUM-BROCKFORD *(6 miles SW of Eye)*

Hartismere Hundred. 'Settlers of Weder's tribe' by the 'Ford over the brook' (OE) *Wederingaseta* (DB) - *Brocfort* (DB). At Brockford the A140 Ipswich to Norwich turnpike (Roman) road once forded a tributary of the river Dove.
Manors. Wetheringsett (-1528 St. Etheldreda; 1528 Crown property); Brockford Hall (Abbot of St. Edmunds).
Sub-Manors. Stoneham's.

Roman Road.

The Roman road from Coddenham to Caister-by-Norwich (the present A140) forms almost the entire western parish boundary from Brook Lane in the S to just S of Brockford Street in the N (where the boundary takes a western loop to take in Brockford hamlet).

Multi-period Settlement Site.

A site with evidence of long multi-period settlement covering Iron Age, Roman and Saxon was discovered W of Wetheringsett Lodge.

WETHERINGSETT-CUM-BROCKFORD *(continued)*

Ancient Ford.

At Brockford - 'The ford over the brook' - *Brocfort* (DB), the A140 Ipswich to Norwich (Roman) road once forded a tributary of the river Dove.

Ancient Track.

The old Hundred Lane (here called Brook Lane) formed the southern parish boundary ENE from the A140 road, and the Hundred boundary between Hartismere and Claydon.

Shrunken Settlement.

There may once have been a major settlement at Brockford Street - the point where the main road forded the Dove rivulet and prior to the ford being bridged - for Domesday Book shows 17 families here and there were 31 taxpayers in 1524 and 34 households by 1674. A church was mentioned in the writings of Joceline de Brakelond in 1189 but its dedication and site are unknown.

Earthworks.

The remains of a mound named Mill Mount is situated on the extreme SE parish boundary. Its name confirms its use as a windmill base but its origins may be earlier.

Medieval Greens.

The site of Brockford Green (enclosed 1849) is shown on the OS map of 1837 and Fadens of 1783. Its southern extent is Green Farm where it is traced by Town Lane. Its eastern side is shown by a public footpath ending just N of Brockford Green hamlet which included the tiny Knaves Green. Wetheringsett Green (enclosed 1849) and Great Green occupied a large area extending from Wetherup Street in the S to Wetheringsett Hall in the N; its eastern boundary marked today in the names of hamlets and properties which line the country road known (to the N of Wetheringsett) as High Lane: Broad Green, Page's Green, Blacksmith's Green and Moore's Green.

Site of old Windmill.

A post mill stood on Old Mill Green in 1783. It was demolished in 1919.

Workhouse.

A workhouse is recorded in Wetheringsett with 25 inmates in 1776.

Historic Houses & Ancient Moated Sites.

Wetheringsett Hall retains two sides of a (square?) moat with old field boundaries to the NE. Topography and cropmarks suggest there are sides of a larger moat to the NE and E; a fish-pond lay to the S. Shrubland House (now a farmhouse) was for over 300 years the home of the Revett family. The ancient Brames Hall, E of the village, was former home of the Prettimans and is surrounded by a large curved moat and complex series of moated yards. It is thought to have been the main medieval house for Wetheringsett Manor. Immediately S of Brames Hill Cottages which lie to the E at the northernmost end of the former Blacksmith's Green, soilmarks suggest at least two sides of a moated enclosure; the area is named 'Coopers Gate' on a 1950s map. There are parts of a small square moat on the W side of Blacksmith's Green, whilst Green Farm has a square moat. There are cropmarks of a square enclosure (probably a moat) shown as Talbot's Barn on the 1st edition OS map; the S and W sides are shown wet and the N and E sides dry. The same map shows a moat at Wetherup Street SE of the road junction with all but the E side wet. There are fragments of a possible moat on the E side of the A140 next to Brockford House; the NE angle and length of S arm were mapped as water-filled in 1985. Faden's 1783 map shows a possible moat to the S of Wickham Skeith Town House, destroyed during the construction of the second world war airfield. A similar fate befell Roses Farm which is probably represented by aerial photographs showing cropmarks of two rectangular enclosures with a possible moat to the S; the 1st Ed. OS map names the site Roses Farm and shows it surrounded by ponds (some linear) with, just to the W, an unoccupied moat with N, W, and half the S sides wet. Wetheringsett Lodge may be associated with a deer park; there are medieval fish-ponds to the W of the lodge and also within the park. The timber-framed Griffin Inn once stood beside the old ford at Brockford.

WEYBREAD *(8½ miles ENE of Eye)*

Hoxne Hundred. 'The wayside plantation' or 'Broad stretch of land by a (Roman) road' (OE) *Weibrada* (DB). Includes the Domesday vill of Istead.
Manors. Weybread Hall (1215 Nicholas de Shelton; 1281 Sir Oliver de Ingham). *Sub-Manors.* Istead al Hovell's al Weybread in Weybread Eithane/Earsham al Essam (1225 Robert Hovel); Finges in Istead; Weybread Rectory.

Roman Road.
The Roman road (Margary 35) from Peasenhall passes NW through the parish traced by the B1116. It enters the parish just SE of Rookery Farm in the hamlet of Weybread Street, and when the modern road turns N just beyond Middleton's Farm to cross the river Waveney into Norfolk via Shotford Bridge, the Roman road continues NW now lost in arable fields to cross the river at Needham on its way to Pulham St Mary.

Ancient Ford.
Shotford Bridge now carries the B1116 road over the river Waveney. Here was anciently a ford known as Scotford (now misspelt 'Shot') whereat one paid *scot* (toll) to cross.

Medieval Pottery Industry.
Evidence of a considerable medieval pottery industry in the form of a kiln, large quantities of kiln waste and pottery from C13-C16, have been found in the parish mainly in the area of Weybread Street and also around the main village.

Medieval Heath.
Shotford Heath is shown and named on Faden's map of 1783 lying S of the bridge (which carries the B1116 road) across the river Waveney on the northern parish boundary. The entire heath has now been flooded to create a reservoir.

Site of old Windmill.
A post mill stood on Shotford Heath in 1736. Its fate is unknown.

Lost Medieval Settlement (?)
Instead, or *Isteda* as it was formerly known, formed a small but distinct estate of 10½ acres at Domesday - *Istede juxta Weybred* - and Faden's map of 1783 shows that the major settlement in the parish was centred, not by the church and Roman road, but just SW of Instead Manor House at Upper Weybread on the junction of Wingfield Road and the road to Earsham Street.

Historic Houses & Ancient Moated Sites.
The Manor House of Instead Manor, just SE of the Waveney, was the ancient seat of the Hobarts and Astleys. Standing beside the church, Weybread Hall (on the site of an earlier hall) has a square moat with two rounded corners. Rookery Farm on the SE parish boundary had a moat now represented by two arms. Poppys Farm has a rectangular moat (the W arm now infilled) from which C14 pottery has been found, and the moat at Old Farm, beside Weybread Hall, has revealed a midden with kiln waste and late C15 to early C16 pottery. Church Farm, S of the parish, has the remains (in the form of the southern arm) of an oblong moat. The small oval moat NE of the vicarage with a central island 62' by 29' is the possible site of a former dovecot.

WHATFIELD *(3 miles NE of Hadleigh)*

Cosford Hundred. 'Open land where wheat is grown' (OE) *Watefelda* (DB). This must always have been celebrated for the quality of its wheat as the name implies a felled part of the forest where wheat is grown.
Manors. Whatfield Hall (1314 Thomas de Cokefield). *Sub-Manors.* Berrards Hall; Peyton's/Mannors; Hornham; Furneaux; Cosfords.

Ancient Woodland.
Calves Wood on the northern parish boundary is a part of ancient woodland.

Historic Houses & Ancient Moated Sites.
Four footpaths converge at the site of Peyton Hall (demolished in the 1950s) which lies just SE of the village.

WHATFIELD *(continued)*

It was timber-framed with documentary evidence going back to the C15. The hall and buildings were shown on the 1838 tithe map but by 1973 only three ponds remained and these have now been infilled and the site levelled. The ancient rectory still has a very strong rectangular moat in good condition with entrances on the W and N sides. The house is timber-framed but heavily restored. It had been partly rebuilt in 1657 by Rev Samuel Backler who was ejected five years later. The manor house of Barrard's Hall, S of the village, has a complete rectangular moat with an entrance to the E. The hall, which was the seat of the Barard family in 1385 and later the Martins, is timber-framed but again heavily restored externally in the C18; SE is a possible fish-pond. Two arms survive of the moat at Whatfield Hall near the NW parish boundary, former seat of the Veseys; one is wet, the other dry. There are remains of a moat at Whitehouse Farm on the eastern parish boundary; a 1958 map shows a trapezoidal moat with only the N arm infilled, but by 1973 only the W arm remained, the rest built over.

WHEPSTEAD *(4½ miles S of Bury St Edmunds)*

Thingoe Hundred. 'Place where brushwood grows' (OE) *Wepstede* (942-51) *Huepestede* (DB)
Manors. Whepstead (Abbot of St. Edmunds; 1202 leased to Benedict de Blakenham; 1539 Sir William Drury).
Sub-Manors. Doveton Hall/Dorrington/Duffin Hall; Cage's/Overcage Hall; Manston Hall.

Ancient Woodland.

The parish still retains much of its ancient woodland: Hay Wood, Jackson's Grove, Plumton Wood, Haws Wood, Woolmer Wood, and Rushbottom (formerly Woodlands) Wood in the SW of the parish, and Cages Wood in the SE.

Ancient Chapel.

'The Maiden Chapel' was founded by the Saxon Eric de Manston in the C11. It was said that many pilgrimages were made to "the Maiden of Manston". Although Manston Hall had its own private chapel (*see* below), it is unlikely this would have been the pilgrims' chapel the site of which is unknown.

Medieval Greens.

Whepstead had several greens: Hay Green represented by Haygreen Farm and its immediate enclosure running to Poulter's Lane on the eastern parish boundary; Stone Cross Green on the E side of Rede Road, which has now been enclosed and built upon (the buildings outlining its boundaries); Cages Green, a former 'entry' which has been replaced by Tuffields Road running between Cages Farm and Manston Hall; Melons Green, now replaced by Straight Road from the junction with Folly Lane W to Hawks Farm; and Mickley Green which occupied the N and E sides of the road junction, extending along Bull Lane.

Medieval Cross.

A boulder 4½' x 3' x 3' in the hamlet of Stonecross Green is Grade II listed by the DOE as the base of a medieval Cross, though it retains no surface workings or shaft socket.

Site of old Windmill.

The post mill with roundhouse which stood on Mickley Green in 1783 was burned down in 1894.

Historic Houses & Ancient Moated Sites.

Doveden (Doveton/Dorrington/Duffen) Hall, NW of the village, was a sub-manor of Whepstead. All rights were released to the Abbot of St Edmunds by Thomas Everard in 1292. Sir George Somerset owned it in 1545, Thomas Bacon in 1548 and Roger Frost in 1550. The house contains a C15 core comprising a 3-cell open hall house and retains its square moat. Manston Hall, by Tuffield's Road S of the village, was another sub-manor and originally had its own chapel. The present house is late C15 timber-framed and still has two sides of its square moat. The manor was held for the abbot by Eric de Manston in the C11 and owned by John de Brockley in 1428. A strange-shaped irregular and incomplete moat NW of Cages Farm in the S of the parish is the probable site of Cages (or Over Cages) Hall. This was another sub-manor of Whepstead held for the abbot by Richard Cage in 1246 and absorbed into the main manor in 1539 when owned by Sir Wiliam Drury. In total isolation by a tributary of the Lark, cropmarks of an enclosure shown on the 6" OS map may be those of a ploughed-out moat. A track runs E from the B1066 road to the site at TL8368 5910.

WHERSTEAD *(1½ miles S of Ipswich)*

Samford Hundred. 'Place by a wharf or landing-place' (OE) *Weruesteda* (DB). Includes the Domesday vills of Beria and Pannington.

Manors. Wherstead Hall (1203 Gilbert de Reymes/Raimes). *Sub-Manors.* Pannington Hall (1202 Gerard de Wachesham; C13 transferred to St. Peters Priory, Ipswich); Bowen Hall (Vill of Beria - transferred to St. Peters Priory, Ipswich); Thorington Hall.

Ancient Woodland.

Spring Wood near the northern parish boundary, and Spinney Wood on the eastern boundary, are ancient woodland.

Tumuli (?) and Early Settlement.

Aerial photographs have identified cropmarks of many ring ditches, enclosures, trackways and field systems showing very early settlement in the parish which lies on the W bank of the river Orwell. Three of the ring ditches which probably represent ploughed-out round barrows are: 153 yds S of Belstead Brook - 157' in diameter; at the top of Bourne Hill - 52' in diameter with Iron Age finds; and NE of Bluegate Farm - 98' in diameter with Iron Age and Roman finds.

Roman Road (?)

While digging an air raid shelter at the rear of Sunny View, Bourne Hill, workmen are said to have come across the foundations of a 'Roman road' at the base of a hole; the shelter is now infilled and covered by a patio. It is possible that the hard *(see below)* from which Wherstead takes its name may have provided the link with the E bank for the Roman road from Stratford St Mary which passed to the S of Ipswich and crossed the river on its way to the Roman fort at Walton (by Felixstowe). Known as Redgate Hard it lies opposite evidence of the continuation of the road at Nacton.

Pottery Production Sites.

SW of Bourne Hall Farm and W of the 'Roman camp' (*see below*), two pottery kilns which overlaid a Late Iron Age enclosure ditch were excavated in 1989. There was also part of a later C2 Roman enclosure. The kilns were probably used within the period 50-80 A.D. While digging in the garden of the Ostrich Inn near Bourne Bridge in 1829, workmen came upon the foundations of a kiln with old broken brick and pottery ware, though the date of the pottery has not been recorded. In 1882 upwards of 400 pieces of pottery were dug up from a depth of 3' to 4' in the orchard of the old vicarage.

Roman Coin Hoards.

In the early C19, two hoards of Roman coins were found in the parish. In the first an ancient pot containing 2,000 Roman coins of very debased metal were turned up by the plough, and in another a hoard of 117 Roman coins ranging from Gallienus to Tetricus were unearthed, probably deposited in the 270s A.D.

Site of Roman Camp (?) and Building.

A single ditched enclosure with a smaller one in the NE corner, showing as a shadow mark c109 yds by 77 yds in a grass meadow, S of Bourne Hall Farm, was noted in 1962 as a possible 'Roman earthwork or camp'. An area of woodland to the N is named Camp Yard (though this may relate to the game of Camping (*see below*). S of Wherstead Hall, aerial photographs show cropmarks of postholes defining a long, narrow and rectangular building with a number of linear field boundaries nearby.

Site of Ancient Ferry or River Hard.

In olden times when the draft of the river Orwell was too shallow for them to get closer, ships anchored just short of Downham Bridge ('bridge' in this instance meaning a hard beside the river) and lightered their cargo into smaller sailing hoys or barges for the final journey into Ipswich. The Saxons named the place *Weruesteda* meaning 'wharf or landing place' and this is no doubt a reference to this hard which would have been a prominent feature when they arrived.

Roman (?) Salt Industry.

Remains of salt pans have been discovered along the Orwell river bank in the parish. These may date back to Roman times.

WHERSTEAD *(continued)*

Earthworks.
The outline of a 'banjo' type oval enclosure with entrance on the W lies by a footpath SW of Bluegate Farm. These ancient enclosures with a funnel entrance were used as cattle pens.

Monastery (?)
An undated deed to which Gerard, Prior of Ipswich, is one of the witnesses, mentions that (before 1225) a monastery of Wervestede was granted to the priory of St Peter and St Paul, Ipswich. Although not mentioned by other sources, Taylor's *Index Monasticus* Map of Suffolk does show a monastery at Wherstead which had been destroyed. This may have paralleled the history of the small Benedictine cell at Wickham Skeith which had an early foundation but a short life, having its endowments withdrawn during the reign of Stephen in the late C12.

Ancient Bridge.
Belstead Brook, a tributary of the river Orwell, is crossed by Bourne Bridge which was mentioned in writings as early as 1352 and shown on both Bowen's map of 1755 and Faden's of 1783. The bridge, which must originally have been of timber, was widened and re-built in brick and stone in 1891.

Medieval Heath.
Wherstead Heath, a small area of common, lay on the W side of the present A137 road to Brantham between Pannington Hall and Constables Masts Manor in the S, and Chapmans Grove in the N.

Medieval Recreation.
A 'Camping' match (medieval ball game) was held in a field near The Ostrich Inn in 1791.

Town House.
A Town House was in existence c1729.

Historic Houses & Ancient Moated Sites.
Bourn Hall is C16 timber-framed with a C16 barn. A moat remains at Wherstead Hall c109 yds by 77 yds, wet on the NW and NE sides with the remainder infilled; a causeway leads across the NW arm and ponds to the SW may be fish-ponds. The White Horse public house is C16 and The Ostrich (now The Oyster Reach) dates from c1612. While this new name seems more apt and may perhaps define its original lost title, it has been suggested that the name Ostrich came from the crest of a former lord of the manor, Lord Chief Justice Coke of Bourn Hill.

WHITTON-CUM-THURLSTON *(NW of and now a part of Ipswich)*

Bosmere & Claydon Hundred. 'Hwita's (or White's) family's farmstead' (OE) *Widituna* (DB) *Witton* (1212). Includes the Domesday vill of Thurleston 'The farm of Thurulfr or Thorolfr', a Saxonised Norseman *Thurulfestun* (DB).
Manors. Barnes al Berives (C12 Priory of St. Peter, Ipswich). *Sub-Manors.* Dalehall al Daleshall (1332 Thomas de la Dale).

Roman Villa.
In Castle Field at Castle Hill (previously part of the parish but now in Ipswich) a large corridor-type Roman villa originally discovered in 1854 was excavated in 1931, and again prior to residential development of the area in 1949-50. A superb mosaic floor was uncovered (now preserved in Ipswich Museum) along with an extensive range of finds comprising building material, a hypocaust, furnaces, painted plaster, pottery and coins from the early part of the C2 through to the C4, indicating a family of considerable wealth. Amongst evidence of several other buildings in the complex, one was used for industrial purposes such as corn drying.

Lost Medieval Settlement.
Thurlston has been incorporated into Whitton, itself now lost in the ever expanding Ipswich suburbs. St Botolph's Church, Thurlston (or 'Thorlestone' [C12]) was still in use in 1500 but after being amalgamated with Whitton it was utilised as a barn before falling into ruin. It was taken down in 1862 and much of the material used to build a S aisle and tower for Whitton Church. Faden's map of 1783 shows the islolated church on a bend in the road NE of Datchet House right on the Ipswich borough boundary, and names the whole area Thurlston Chapel.

WHITTON-CUM-THURLSTON *(continued)*

Historic Houses & Ancient Moated Sites.

Dale Hall (formerly Deal Hall) in NW Ipswich, lost to C20 residential development, was mentioned as a Whitton manor in Domesday and belonged to the Dale family in the C13. It passed to the Wollascots in 1542 and later the Baxters and Bohuns. Whitton White House, Whitton's ancient Saxon place-name, stood on the site of the White Horse (mistranslation) public house, itself now lost to a new road scheme. It also gave name to a housing development on the Whitton borders with Ipswich. Both houses are shown and named by Faden in 1783.

WICKHAMBROOK *(10 miles SW of Bury St Edmunds)*

Risbridge Hundred. 'Homestead by a brook associated with a 'vicus' (an earlier Romano-British settlement - possibly a dairy farm)' (OE) *Wicham* (DB) *Wichambrok* (1254). 'Brook' was added after 1086 to distinguish it from the other Wickams. Includes the Domesday vill of Badmondisfield.

Manors. Badmondisfield Hall (C12 Baldwin de Boulers/Bulers with Honor of Montgomery; 1292 Robert de Bures). *Sub-Manors.* Gaynes Hall al Attilton; Giffords Hall (C13 Peter Gifford); Clopton Hall/Chappeley Manor (C12 William Clopton).

Ancient Woodland.

Spring Wood, and the extensive Easter Wood in the N of the parish, with the fragment of Garbs Grove in the extreme SE, are parts of ancient woodland.

Roman Road & Settlement (?)

The place name is suggestive of a Roman settlement in the parish, and although finds of the period have been unearthed, no settlement as such has to date been unearthed. It is more likely its associations were connected with a road, and the course of a Roman road from Cambridge to Bridge Street, Long Melford may pass through the parish - though there is no obvious evidence on the ground. However, Wickham Street in the S of the parish is suggestive of a likely site as 'street' can mean Roman road, and the hamlet lies beside a brook, a tributary of the Glem, possible site of the earliest settlement.

Ancient Track.

An extension of Bury Lane, running NE from Genesis Green to Lady's Green, forms part of the northern parish boundary and would appear to be of ancient origin.

Ancient Chapels.

There were two ancient chapels in the parish. A free chapel known as St Edmunds Chapel is said to have stood on the little island called St Edmund's Island within the moated site of Badmondisfield Hall *(see below)* 'before the hall door on the right hand side'. It was built of timber, panelled with brick and covered with tiles. A witness described it as in decay in 1591 and pulled down by Sir George Somerset *(see below)*. The other free chapel in the same manor was mentioned in 1254 and again in 1291. In 1369/70 a grant of land was given to Walter Amyas, guardian of the chantry in the chapel of the manor of Bademundesfeld. The chapel, dedicated to St Mary, was granted to William Mansey, Ironmonger of London, in 1583. While its site is unknown, a footings trench being dug in 1952 for a new bungalow called Sunset Bungalow at Meeting Green N of the village had to be abandoned when workmen came upon massive foundations including large immovable stone blocks. They exposed much (probably re-used) stonework including a large 'church' window with 'primrose-shaped' top complete except for one corner. A large portion of a stone coffin lid was also found suggesting the site of a religious building, possibly the lost chapel of St Mary?

Medieval Park.

The park (possibly for deer) may have been created by Henry Engaine around 1592 the year he obtained free warren here. Custody of the Parks of Cropley and Badmondesfield was granted to William Atte Lee in 1387-8. The following year keepership of parks of Badmondisfield and Lidgate was granted to Thomas Upton. A map of 1598 apparently shows the park extending into Lidgate parish. Part was later converted into a landscaped park for the hall.

Ancient Well.

A well situated by Bullocks Mill, Thorns Corner, reputedly never ran dry.

WICKHAMBROOK *(continued)*

Medieval Greens.

This large parish was once one of the richest ecclesiastical livings in England and in 1840, £22,000 was paid to redeem part of the tithes. It consists of twelve small hamlets, many of which appear to have originated as manors of greater or lesser importance. Today there are few remains of the greens which gave name to the many hamlets, and most must have already disappeared by 1783 when Faden shows only Farley Green - a long green running N from Moat Farm and replacing the present road between the two road junctions; Clopton Green - a small triangular green where Clopton Green House stands; Genesis Green, shown and named on a five-way junction W of Easter Wood; Ashfield Green, NE of the village on the road to Hargrave - now infilled but whose property boundaries still trace its form; Attleton Green, small and just S of the village on a 3-way junction by Grove Farm; Lady's Green on the northern parish boundary - unnamed by Faden but shown as a tiny triangular area in a road fork; and Nunnery Green a larger triangular green to the S of the last where Queens Cottage now stands. Baxters Green, N of Easter Wood, is named but not shown.

Medieval Deer Park.

Badmondisfield Hall was the residence of Henry Engaine in 1252 when he claimed free warren here and may possibly have enclosed a park for deer. The park was mentioned in 1387.

Site of Civil War Incident.

Badmondisfield Hall was reputedly attacked during the Civil War and the site of a burial mound of soldiers.

Site of old Mills.

Great Mill, dated 1740, stood at Wickham Street near the A143 road until 1966.

Almshouses.

Sparrow Almshouses, near the churchyard, were built by Anthony Sparrow in 1612 for six poor people.

Workhouse.

The village workhouse is believed to have been built at Attleton Green in 1737 by the deed of James Vernon. It had 42 inmates in 1776.

Historic Houses & Ancient Moated Sites.

On a remote site one mile SE of the village, Gifford's Hall stands on a fully moated rectangular island site c300' by 240' accessible only by a single triple-arched brick bridge - the 1841 tithe map suggests that there may have been a small gatehouse on the island end of the bridge. A short distance WSW in Moat Plantation is Moat Yard, the remains of a large irregular circular moat (now dry) with earthen ramparts which must have enclosed the ancient fortified hall of the Giffords, who held the manor as tenants of the Earl Warren in the first half of the C14. Later that century it became the residence of the Cloptons and later, Sir Hugh Francis. The present Giffords Hall was probably built by Clement Heigham c1485-90; his family lived here until 1630 making further alterations c1590. A massive fish-pond associated with the hall and known as Wickham Stew lies to the E. The Clopton family built a new residence, Clopton Hall at Clopton Green near the parish boundary E of the village c1500. Another great fortified manor house stands in its own park on the NW parish boundary two miles N of the village at Genesis Green (a corruption of Gesyns Green?). This is Badmondisfield Hall. The present hall has double cross wings separated by a great aisled hall built in the late C14 when it was a hunting lodge for the earls of Pembroke. It is encircled by a deep and ancient moat crossed by a two-arched C18 brick bridge. To the N of the moat is a large six acre enclosure (named Dovehouse Meadow on the 1841 tithe map) bordered on the N by large (fish-?)ponds. To the NW of the moat is another linear (fish-?)pond, possibly formalised in the mid C19. Domesday records a substantial (royal) manor with 10 caracates (c1,200 acres) of land at Bademondesfelda, formerly held by Earl Algar and at that time held in the keeping of Picot the Sheriff. The manor of Badmondisfield (or Barnsfield) was mentioned in Domesday when it housed a church, and a chapel dedicated to St Edmund on its own island site NW of the hall - the ruins of which were still standing in 1591. The first builder of an aisled hall house on this site may have been the Fitzurse or de Curtenais family but the site was certainly known to be the residence of Henry Engaine in 1252. First of the really important families here were the de Hastings; John de Hastings, 1st Lord of Hastings held in 1273 and the fourth earl became Earl of Pembroke in 1339. SW of

WICKHAMBROOK *(continued)*

Badmondisfield Hall lies the manor site of The Gesyns, with its irregular moat with enclosures. The chief manor house was in Wickham Street, a hamlet near the church on the Bury Road and now perhaps represented by the Vicarage, an old house dating from the C16. Maltings End, W of the church, and Attleton Green close by have interesting houses including Butlers Hall and Gaines Hall. The Gesyns, another former manor house N of Boyden End, has an extensive but irregular moat. At Farley Green on the SW parish boundary, Moat Farm retains a trapezoidal moat. Nunnery Green, Meeting Green and Coltsfooot Green are close together and have interesting C17 houses. Ashfield Green is NE with Aldersfield Hall on the eastern parish boundary.

WICKHAM MARKET *(5 miles NNE of Woodbridge)*

Wilford Hundred. 'Homestead associated with a 'vicus' (an early Romano-British settlement) (OE) *Wikham* (DB). 'Market' was added later *(see below)*. Includes the Domesday vill of Harpole.
Manors. Wickham Market/Wickham with the Members (1275 de Ufford family; C14 Campsey Priory). *Sub-Manors.* Harpole (C13 Hovel family; 1389 Campsey Priory); Gelham/Gelham Hall.

Ancient Woodland.
Potsford Wood, on the western parish boundary by the course of a Roman road, is part of ancient woodland.

Roman Road.
A Roman road makes a northerly curve in its E-W route crossing the ford over Potsford Brook to meet the W edge of the town at Simons Cross. It passes through the centre before leaving by crossing the Deben at Wickham Bridge near Wickham Mill. The route is traced by the present B1078 road as far as the bypass.

Roman Settlement.
The 'early Romano-British settlement' to which the place-name refers is in neighbouring Hacheston (*see* Hacheston).

Ancient Chapel.
A hermit's chapel formerly stood near Wickham Market watermill - itself probably with ancient origins. The area was once marshland and the dangers in crossing at flood-time necessitated the erection of a building in which the traveller could pray for safe passage and to provide home to a man employed to ferry them across.

Medieval Bridge.
Wickham Bridge is shown on Saxton's map of 1575, Speede's of 1610 and Faden's of 1783. All but Saxton place it in the same position as today, so his siting further upstream may have been an error.

Deserted Medieval Village.
Remains of moats (*see below*) originally enclosed the old manorial hall of Thorpe which was approached by a driftway now called California Lane, and previously White Gate Lane, passing by the E side and continuing N by Thorpell Wood. Thorpe Hall, one mile W of the town and SW of Valley Farm, was a small hamlet of Wickham Market and formed a separate manor called Harpole 'hare's pool' (Horpole 'muddy pool') or Thorp until the C17. At one time it had 27 households in addition to the small manor house with 100 acres. Its situation beside the Roman road suggests that it may possibly have originated from a Danish settlement. It had a church with 20 acres, the site and dedication of which is unknown. The manor was held by the Hovel family from 1225 until 1389 when it was granted to Campsea Abbey, and at the Dissolution, to Sir Anthony Wingfield. Pottery sherds from the site confirm a settlement here from at least the early C13 to the late C14 and it is likely to have continued until the development of Wickham Market in the C16-C17.

Medieval Market & Fairs.
There appears to have been no early grant of a market to Wickham but Claude Morley thinks it may have existed from Saxon times. Redstone states that Edward I granted Robert de Ufford the right to hold a market in the town before 1308 (probably c1286), and by 1360 it had become commonly known as Wycham 'Market'. Henry VI confirmed the market in 1440 and also granted two fairs. Later the town boasted a Shire Hall in which Quarter Sessions were held. The even faster growth of neighbouring Woodbridge, however, eventually brought

WICKHAM MARKET *(continued)*

about Wickham's demise and the Shire Hall was eventually pulled down (the materials used for the rebuilding of Letheringham Hall) and the Sessions and market moved to its great rival.

Medieval Crosses.
Three Crosses are recorded in Wickham Market. In his will dated 1481, John Symonds had erected a 'large stone Market Cross'. This stood in the market place to the rear of the Crown Inn until destroyed by the Puritans in the C17. Palme Cross was said to have been built at the expense of John Hobbys in 1447, and at the same time, Dettons Cross was said to have stood by the meadow of Thomas Smith Spicer.

Medieval Stocks.
The village stocks were situated near the Crown Inn.

Gallows.
The decaying main post of Posford Gibbet stands to a height of c8' on Potchards Hills by the eastern edge of Potsford Wood beside the B1078 (the course of the old Roman road). It was said to have been last used in 1699.

Medieval Recreation.
Camping Close, a four acre field near the church, was probably used for medieval ball-games. It was purchased for glebe land in 1723.

Site of old Windmills.
Two windmills stood either side of Mill Lane, SE of the Street, in the latter part of the C18. The tower mill was demolished in 1868, and the smock mill c1885.

Guildhall.
The mid-C15 Guildhall which held the Guild of St. John in 1517 is said to have been pulled down.

Historic Houses & Ancient Moated Sites.
Parts of the former White Hart Hotel in the centre of the village date from the C15 when it was known as 'The Harte'. A coaching inn from 1743, it was a stopping place on the Yarmouth to London via Ipswich run. The old Manor House is now known as '64 The Hill'. To the SW of Valley Farm is Thorpe Hall where there are remains of moated enclosures which were formerly associated with the hall and its grounds; a small piece of a moat is by the site of the hall; to the NE an angle of another; and to the S, at the end of a connecting channel, is a quadrangular moat. The Crown Inn was in existence in 1640 and closed in 1950. The George and The Blue Boar (now gone) public houses were recorded in 1652/3.

WICKHAM SKEITH *(5 miles SW of Eye)*

Hartismere Hundred. 'Homestead associated with a 'vicus' (an earlier Romano-British settlement)' (OE) 'Skeith' the Danish suffix means 'race-course' *Wichamm* (DB) *Wicham Skeyth* (1368)
Manors. Wickham Skeith (1120 Robert de Sackville granted to the Abbey of St. John, Colchester; 1542 Sir Richard Freston). *Sub-Manors.* Wickham called Skeith's/Skeith Hall.

Roman Settlement.
The place-name 'Wickham' is suggestive of a Romano-British settlement within the vicinity - probably that suspected but yet to be confirmed at Stoke Ash. A site producing artefacts of the period has been identified in the area of Wickham Hills, but this site may simply relate to the close proximity to the A140 Roman road.

Danish Settlement.
The Scandinavian place-name 'Skeith' suggests a place where horses were raced or exercised. The village green with its pond or mere and anciently known as the 'Grimmer' (a name of possible Danish origin) is the most likely site, but another is the long meadow in front of the church and hall.

Witchcraft.
When suspected people refused to confess to witchcraft they were often 'swum' to extort a confession. This involved their thumbs and big toes being tied together before they were thrown into a river or pond. If they

WICKHAM SKEITH *(continued)*

floated they were guilty and put to death, if they sank they were pronounced innocent! The fact that they sometimes drowned in the process made their acquittal academic. The swimming of Isaac Stebbings in the Grimmer (*see above)* in 1825, was claimed to be the last recorded in England - though this may have been a case of the light-hearted playing out of an old tradition to a local villain.

Saxon Hoard.

A great number of coins of Harold and Edward the Confessor (now in the British Museum) were found under an ancient oak tree in the parish.

Benedictine Priory.

A small priory was founded in the parish in 1140 by Sir Robert de Sackville who gave it as a cell (along with the manor) to the Abbey of St John's in Colchester on the condition that four Benedictine monks (Black Monks) should be settled here 'to pray for his soul' - the monks using the parish church. However, the priory was short-lived as his son, Jordon, consented to the endowments being transferred to Colchester to maintain four additional monks there. Wickham Skeith thus stripped of its only income was forced to close. The abbey still had a grant of free warren here, and at Benningham in Occold in 1252/3 suggesting that their lands were being run as a grange of the abbey. Walter, keeper of the manor of Wickham and a monk of the abbey, is recorded here c1260, and William le Graunger (of the grange) occurs as a taxpayer in Wickham in 1327. The actual site is not known but tradition places it in the area of Abbey Farm where brick foundations have been ploughed up in an adjacent field. The farm thereby took its name from this tradition but the construction of the priory would not have been brick at such an early date and the site is marked as a dovecot on the 1st OS map (*see below)*. An alternative site is by the church which was also granted to St John's.

Travellers' Chapel (?)

A round painting of St James and a Traveller - part of a leather traveller's purse - is said to have come from a wayside chapel which was once attached to Street Farm, an old timber-framed house which stands in the hamlet of Wickham Street beside a main pilgrims route.

Medieval Greens.

Wickham Green remains edged by old properties and incorporating its ancient pond or mere (*see above*). The tiny Daisy Green lay to the S at a bend in the narrow country lane leading to Wickham Abbey Farm. It is shown but unnamed on Faden's 1783 map which also apparently shows another unnamed small rectangular green at Wickham Street running between the two road junctions at Street Farm and The Broadway. Now infilled, properties are shown on the map edging the green to the N and S.

Historic Houses & Ancient Moated Sites.

The Vicarage, W of the church, has been much rebuilt but dates back to 1570. At Wickham Abbey Farm (*see above*), a small moated island was excavated by Basil Brown c1937. The island revealed a floor of greenish clay 3' thick and Brown considered this the site of a dovecot. There were no finds at the time and the site was destroyed in 1976 to create modern piggeries, when a scatter of Medieval peg tiles were found.

WILBY *(6 miles NNW of Framlingham)*

Hoxne Hundred. 'A circle of willow trees' (OE) *Wilebey* (DB). The site may be identified in Willow Farm which lies near the church. Morley considers it the Norwegian *Wila (Vila) bor - Wilabor*, meaning 'Wili's building', the '*a*' being dropped and the '*or*' corrupted with time to become 'y'.

Manors. Wilby (1282 M. de Crek; 1314 William de Bovile). *Sub-Manors.* Russels; Jordans; Goods.

Earthworks.

S of Rectory Farm is an oval mound c4' high enclosed by a ditch and ponds.

Medieval Greens.

Foals Green on the SE parish boundary originally formed a small roughly rectangular area bordered by Foals Green Farm, a lane on the W and S, and a public footpath on the E. Another green, the 'L' shaped Wilby

WILBY *(continued)*

Green, lay just to the W of Wilby Hall, bordered by Wilby Lane on its W and S sides, its outline still marked in field boundaries. Russels Green to the N of Messuage Farm is bordered on its eastern side by Stradbroke Road.

Historic Houses & Ancient Moated Sites.
Church Farm, immediately NE of the church, has a very ancient and complete circular moat with an entrance on the SE. At one time another rectangular enclosure lay immediately on its eastern arc. The Rectory, 600 yds SE of the church, has a rectangular moat subdivided into two enclosures. Wilby Hall, on the eastern parish boundary and dating back to 1579, has the remains of a double rectangular moat. Just SW of this, Moat Farm has one side and an angle left of its moat. Rookery Farm, near the western parish boundary, has three sides of a large rectangular moat. There are two arms of a moat on the southern edge of Wilby Green.

WILLINGHAM ST MARY *(4 miles S of Beccles)*

Wangford Hundred. 'Willa's family's home' (OE) plus church dedication *Wellingaham* (DB)
Manors. Willingham (1531 Playters family).

Ancient Woodland.
Willingham Wood in the N of the parish, and Likely Wood in the centre of the parish, are ancient woodland.

Deserted Medieval Village.
Now merged with Sotterley, Willingham St Mary, listed in Beresford's *Deserted Medieval Villages*, was included in the lands of Hugh de Montfort at Domesday when he had a church with 40 acres. This church was in use until 1526 when the living was united with North Cove, but was marked as 'in ruins' on Faden's map of 1783 and placed in the area of Willingham Wood. All that remained in 1951 was 'some rubble around the root of a tree'. Any early settlement appears to have centred on the banks of the Hundred River which forms part of the northern parish boundary, with the early church built on the high land above the valley.

Almshouse.
An almshouse is recorded housing 12 poor people in 1674.

Historic Houses & Ancient Moated Sites.
Willingham Hall stands on the Ellough road near the ruined church. Moat Farm, situated near the western parish boundary, still has part if its rectangular moat.

WILLISHAM *(7½ miles NW of Ipswich)*

Bosmere & Claydon Hundred. 'Wiglaf's homestead' (OE) *Wilagesham* (1198)
Manors. Willisham Hall (c1182 Albert Greilly; 1304 William de la Mote).

Ancient Woodland.
Chaffinch Wood on the NE parish boundary is a fragment of ancient woodland.

Medieval Green.
Since the late 1960s a residential development known as North Acres has occupied the triangular-shaped former Willisham Green at Willisham Tye. A silver penny of Alexander III, King of Scotland (1249-1286), was dug up in one of the gardens. Evidence has been unearthed of C11-C14 Medieval activity on the former green edge.

Medieval Market (?)
Willisham obtained a grant for a market in 1227 although it is not known if this was ever implimented.

Historic House & Ancient Moated Site.
The Manor House of Willisham Hall stands by the church on the site of an earlier hall destroyed by fire in 1934. It was listed as having 11 hearths in 1674 when occupied by Robert Brownrigge. Part of the moat from the first hall on the site, owned by the intriguingly named William de la Mote in 1304, is shown on an early OS map in the form of water-filled remains to the SW and a ditch(?) to the NW; the rest appears to have been built over.

WINGFIELD *(7 miles E of Eye)*

Hoxne Hundred. 'Winga's clearing' or 'Temple field' (OE) *Wingefeld* (1035) *Wighefelda* (DB). Includes the Domesday vill of Chickering.
Manors. Wingfield/Wingfield Castle (c1335 Sir John Wingfield; 1375 Michael de la Pole). *Sub-Manors.* Wingfield Old Hall; Chickering Hall/Chickering with Wingfield (1311 Jeffrey de Chickering).

Ancient Chapels.
'The church called the Chapel of St Faith which I believe stood in the field opposite to the turning known as Syleham Hall Lane; for a little more than a hundred years ago the last stones of an old ruin, which had apparently once been an ecclesiastical building, were removed from that very field, in the manor of Esham.' (1936). This would suggest a site just N of Yew Tree Farm on the road from the hamlet of Earsham (Esham) Street to Upper Weybread. Two buildings are shown in this position on Faden's map of 1783 and one on the OS 1st Edition map of 1837. In 1291 the benefice of a portion of St Faith's was valued at 10s. In 1362 the Manor of Esham, together with the Chapel of St Faith, was given by Alianore de Wingfield to the College of Priests which she had founded at Wingfield. It passed to the Crown in 1542. Our Lady Chapel at Chickering, mentioned 1502-37, is thought to have been sited in Chickering hamlet on the western parish boundary in the area of The Slades. The site was granted to William Boldero and Robert Parker in 1545.

Castle.
Wingfield Castle was built by Michael de la Pole, Earl of Suffolk, who was granted a licence by Richard II to crenellate his hall in 1384. He had married Katherine, daughter and heiress of Sir John Wingfield whose family had been seated at Wingfield since the Conquest. The building is of the period between a defensive castle and a fortified manor house although its outward appearance is very much the image of how a castle should appear, with an impressive curtain wall and three-storeyed gatehouse rising straight from the enclosing moat, 25-40' in breadth. The original wooden doors are in position with the grooves of the portcullis clearly scored in the stonework. The drawbridge was removed in 1750 and replaced with a red-brick bridge. None of the original buildings within remain. The present house, part brick, part timber-framed, was built by the Catelyns (tenants of Charles Brandon, Duke of Suffolk) c1544 using material from the ancient walls. The moated site covers 1½ acres.

College.
Wingfield College Farm, situated on the S side of the churchyard, was built c1760, but at the rear are the remains of the great hall (c1300) and a range of domestic buildings belonging to the C14 priests' college. This had been originally established in the parish church in 1362, dedicated to St Mary, St John the Baptist and St Andrew, for a master and nine priests under the will of Sir John Wingfield. It was dissolved in 1542. E of the house two water-filled features set at right angles to each other at the western edge may be the remains of an earlier moated site or of fish-ponds connected with the College; remains of a flint/brick wall have also been uncovered, perhaps forming part of the College's quadrangle.

Medieval Grange (?)
Abbey Farm, situated NE of the village in Earsham (Esham) Street hamlet, is said to stand on the moated site of a former grange or religious house, perhaps connected with the college which lies to the SW.

Medieval Park.
Michael de la Pole was granted a licence to enclose and empark all woods and lands belonging to Wingfield Manor c1383.

Medieval Market and Fair.
Richard de Brews, Lord of the sub-Manor of Wingfield Old Hall, obtained the grant for a fair here in 1328 and a market in 1338.

Medieval Greens.
E of the castle Wingfield Green remains complete and unenclosed though crossed by roads. Battlesea Green, a large green on the W side of the road from Stradbroke to Hoxne (B1118), and S of the junction with the road to

WINGFIELD *(continued)*

Fressingfield, formerly lay across the southern boundary extending into Stradbroke parish. It is marked and named on Faden's map of 1783 and was probably part of the 132 acres in Stradbroke enclosed under a private act of 1811. The Ist edition OS map of 1837 shows the green reduced to a triangular portion in Wingfield parish with a windmill mound in the centre.

Historic Houses & Ancient Moated Sites.
Abbey Farm (*see above)* has a rectangular moat plus fragments of others. Chickering Hall, situated in the hamlet of Chickering on the western parish boundary, dates from c1500 and has remains of a much mutilated moat now without form. There is a large portion of a rectangular moat by Boundary Cottage on the northern parish boundary. Hillhouse Farm, on the southern boundary, has two adjoining square moated enclosures, and at Moat House Farm (the possible site of the former manor house of Esham) are the remains of small rectangular moats adjoining the road. Part of another moat remains at the site of Evans Barn, N of the castle, near the northern parish boundary.

WINSTON *(1½ miles S of Debenham)*

Thredling Hundred. 'Wynhere's farmstead' (OE) *Winestuna* (DB)
Manors. Winston Hall/Winston cum Pulham (Abbot of St. Etheldreda; 1651 Richard Moyse). *Sub-Manors.* Bocking Hall.

Roman Occupation.
There is evidence of former Roman occupation in the parish.

Site of old Windmill.
A shallow, roughly circular ditch c4 yds wide, cut on two sides by field ditches, encloses an area c18 yds in diameter with a slight depression in the centre. The adjacent Mill Field suggests the site of a former windmill.

Medieval Green & Settlement Movement.
The triangular Winston Green on Debenham Road is still clearly defined and may at one time have accommodated the main village settlement. Faden's map of 1783 clearly shows a number of properties around the margins - fieldwalking has identified at least five sites of C12-C14 date with another a little later on the Debenham road - whilst the area around the church was, and still is, virtually unoccupied.

Historic Houses & Ancient Moated Sites.
Winston Hall stands next to the church. Park Farm has the greater part of a strong moat enclosing an oval site on the S side of Winston Green - C12-C14 pottery has been found here. On the N side of Winston Green are fragments of another moat.

WISSETT *(2 miles NW of Halesworth)*

Blything Hundred. The origins are debatable. It has been suggested as meaning 'fold of a man called Witta' or 'willow sticks for making a fold', and then again 'settlers by the heathen temple' or 'settlers who had previously (elsewhere) dwelt by the heathen temple' (OE) *Wisseta* (DB) *Witseta* (1165)
Manors. Wisset (c1325 Sir Robert de Ufford). *Sub-Manors.* Wissett/Wissett le Roos (1229 Sir John de Vallibus); Blenche's.

Roman Occupation.
Finds of pottery and artifacts suggest former Roman occupation in the parish.

Medieval Common.
The southern end of Rumburgh Common covered the northern tip of the parish traced by field boundaries either side of Nunn's Hill as far S as Rumburghplace Farm. Its western side is edged by four farms; Hor's, Red House, Whitehouse and Bank's.

Medieval Market & Fair.
Sir John de Vallibus had grants for a market and fair in 1229 (renewed in 1267) for his Manor of Wissett le Roos,

WISSETT *(continued)*

but is not known if these were ever taken up.

Historic Houses & Ancient Moated Sites.

The timber-framed Grange, c250 yds NW of the village on the road to Rumburgh, incorporates a small hall house which may date from the C14. Bleach Farm, NE of the village, has a narrow trapezoid moat with near vertical sides enclosing a large area. Pottery sherds of Early Medieval date have been found on the site. The larger part of another trapezoid-shaped moat, divided into two unequal parts, lies at Brookhall Farm on the northern parish boundary.

WISSINGTON (formerly Wiston) *(1½ miles W of Nayland)*

Babergh Hundred. 'Wigswith's (or Wigswip's) farm' or 'Osier-meadow farm' (OE) *Wiswythetun* (c995)
Manors. Wissington (Part of the Honor of Rayleigh at Domesday; C13 Godebold family). *Sub-Manors.* Wiston Grange (-1537 Thetford Priory; 1537 Sir Thomas Seymour).

Once a part of the great Domesday lordship of Eiland along with Nayland, Stoke, and the Horkesleys in Essex, it was united in 1884 with Nayland which had grown into a wealthy town in the C15 and C16 through the cloth-making industry.

Ancient Woodland.

Rowley Grove and Grange Wood in the N of the parish are sections of ancient woodland.

Roman Pottery Production Site.

A possible kiln group with Late C1-Early C2 pottery was found E of Malting Farm House in the S of the parish.

Historic Houses & Ancient Moated Sites.

In Grange Wood, NW of the present Wissington Grange, is a sub-rectangular earthworks internally 103 yds by 87 yds with a rampart, outer ditch and entrances on the E and W. A similar size bank and ditch run 55 yds NE from the NE corner. This may be the now dry moated enclosure associated with an earlier grange. Wiston (Wissington) Hall, built in 1791 by Samuel Beechcroft, Director of the Bank of England, would appear to stand on the ancient site of an earlier hall. Two adjoining moats partially enclose a large area N and E of the Hall and Wissington Church, close to the southern parish boundary. The system appears to be linked to the adjacent river Stour.

WITHERSDALE *(6½ miles NE of Stradbroke)*

Hoxne Hundred. 'Valley where wether-sheep are kept' or 'Wether's dale' referring to a man's nickname derived from a sheep and not taken directly from the sheep itself. (OE) *Weresdel* (DB) *Wideresdala* (1184)
Manors. Withersdale (1275 Ranulph de Arderne; 1316 Oliva de Ingham).

Deserted Medieval Village (?)

Once a separate parish S of the river Waveney and the Mendham Marshes, Withersdale (or Wethersdale) is now a hamlet of Mendham. It still has its tiny isolated church dedicated to St Mary Magdalen - with evidence of Saxon long-and-short work on its S doorway - and the moated site of an early hall (*see below*) standing in a well-laned area which possibly housed an original village. A small settlement called Withersdale Street (formerly Withersdale Cross) has since developed by the main junction of the roads from Mendham and Metfield.

Medieval Green.

The former Cocker's Green lay SE of Thorpe Hall. Although not shown, and probably long gone by the time of Faden's 1783 map, it may be that the rectangular field edged by ponds, with a footpath running down its eastern side and with Thorpe Hall Cottage to the S, traces its former outline and extent.

Historic Houses & Ancient Moated Sites.

Adjoining Withersdale Hall, SW of the church, is a curious quadrant-shaped moat, no doubt associated with an earlier hall. In the vicinity C13-C14 pottery has been found. SE of Thorpe Hall the W side of a small square moat adjoins the former Cocker's Green, the S side being formed by a field boundary. A scatter of C14-C15 pottery came from the site.

WITHERSFIELD *(2 miles NW of Haverhill)*

Risbridge Hundred. 'Open land where wether-sheep are kept' or 'Wether's clearing' (OE) *Wedresfelda* (DB). Includes the Domesday vill of Hanchet.

Manors. Withersfield Pellegrues al Pettigrues (C13 William de Stutevile).

Ancient Woodland.

The extensive Lawn Wood on the NW parish boundary, North Wood and Littley Wood in the N, Norney Plantation in the E, and Howe Wood S of the village, and the fragment of Markhams Wood on the SW boundary, are all sections of ancient woodland.

Ancient Settlements.

A Late Bronze Age hoard plus pottery of Late Bronze Age/Early Iron Age and Roman metalwork, postholes and small shallow pits were discovered N of the Withersfield road, whilst a survey at Hanchet End found evidence of Late Iron-Age/Belgic activity including two possible post-holes and a length of ditch. Both sites point to very early settlement of the area.

Roman Road.

A Roman road (possibly Margary 24 from Cambridge to Colchester via Wixoe) passes WNW-ESE through the southern part of the parish probably crossing the Stour Brook near Meldham Bridge. It is identified in Silver Street Farm just to its N, but nowhere evident on the ground except as a gravel spread unearthed in 1971. The Cambridge section is known as 'Wool Street'.

Roman Cemetery.

Cremations, several large glass urns, and a complete skeleton are alleged to have been found in 1759 during quarrying for gravel, adjoining a field called Osterfield (or Nosterfield) S of Meldham Bridge and just S of the line of the Roman road. One find was recorded in the 'Annual Register' under 31st October 1764: 'There has been discovered at Withersfield a Roman burying-place, a glass urn of a good colour, and of an elegant make, with a fluted handle. It contains 2½ gallons wine measure and is thought to be the largest that ever was discovered, at least in England . . .'

Medieval Green.

The area of the present village of Withersfield (Wethersfield) was once a linear green called Button Green which extended from the church to the three-way road junction of Highnoon Lane, Thurlow Road and Withersfield Road. Since enclosure the main road now passes down the centre and infilling has taken place along its entire length. The name is retained (though misquoted) in Burton Green and Bitton's Farm at its NE end, and Town Green at the SW end near the church.

Site of old Windmill.

A track (now leading nowhere) once led to the site of an open-trestle post mill which stood in an elevated position SE of Hall Farm in 1783. It was demolished c1910.

Deserted Medieval Settlement.

A survey and subsequent trial-trenching at Hanchet End - 'place settled by Henna's family' (*Haningehet* (DB) - on the parish boundary with Haverhill, indicated the site of a deserted medieval settlement. Small ditches, post-holes, possible pits cut into the clay sub-soil, and pottery suggested occupation from the C12 to C14.

Medieval Guildhall (?)

There are no guilds on record as operating in Withersfield, but a C16 building is believed to represent a former Guildhall.

Historic Houses & Ancient Moated Sites.

There are remains of a rectangular manorial moat at Hall Farm on the SE end of Town Green. The moat was 20' wide and c3' deep. It is open to the SW where a causeway leads to an earthwork hollow. The NE side is no longer visible and may have been replaced by a small rectangular moat shown on the 1841 tithe map but presumably since destroyed by ploughing. Many musket balls and pottery of unknown date were found on the

WITHERSFIELD *(continued)*

site in 1993. The remains of the original C15 timber-framed hall are now used as a barn. Tudor House is also timber-framed and C16, whilst White Hall, from the same period, has been converted into cottages. The site of a former manor house by Highnoon Lane on the NW corner of the former Button Green is represented by a dry moat comprising three sides of a rectangle standing in what was formerly known as Gatesbury Wood or Copse.

WITNESHAM *(3½ miles NE of Ipswich)*

Carlford Hundred. 'Hwitel's (or White's) homestead' (OE) *Witdesham* (DB) *Witnesham* (1254). The correct spelling and pronunciation of this township is thought by some to be 'Wittlesham'.
Manors. Burwash (C13 John de Weyland). *Sub-Manors.* Curdon's/Cardews Hall; Redhall al Brampton al Brompton.

Iron Age Settlement.
Basil Brown investigated two sandpits near Redhouse Farm which showed indications of two hut sites with fire holes and animal bones. Pottery dated to Belgic/Iron Age, and included Roman Samian ware.

Roman Road.
The modern B1078 traces the course of the Roman road from Coddenham to form the northern parish boundary with Ashbocking.

Ancient Ford.
The river Fynn which joined the Deben at Martlesham has a Saxon name, and *Finesford* 'the ford through the river Fynn' had five entries in Domesday Book suggesting a large estate here. The ford was where the present B1077 road crosses the river and Wash Lane E of the church and marked 'Finnbridge' on the early OS map.

Ridge & Furrow.
There appears to be signs of ancient ridge and furrow ploughing in the meadow by the corner of Hall Lane.

Site of Ancient Chapel.
A free Chapel of Ease was built by Richard Weyland and dedicated to St Thomas. Though there is no date for its erection, a right to celebrate Divine Service here was granted by the Priory at Norwich in 1262. This right was suspended and the chapel demolished sometime between 1484 and 1505. The Witnesham Church register states : "The ruines of ye long sought for chapel of St Thomas may be found probably in Burwash (Berghersh) Farm. There is a piece of ground between the Mote (moat) and Burwash Lane which still goes by ye name of Chappel Field or Chappel Meadow." This description probably refers to Berghersh Meadow where a low circular mound c49' in diameter and 5' high, boundered by a shallow ditch c6½' by 1½' to N, S and E and by a shapeless pond to the W lay to the SW of the moated site of the former Berghersh House *(see below)*. Kirby in his 'Suffolk Traveller' speaks of the free chapel 'the ruins of which appeared not long since in a meadow called Burghersh.' It is generally thought that the Weyland Arms, now in the W window of the church, came from the chapel when it was demolished.

Mills.
Two windmills are recorded here in 1340 and one in 1647. There is also mention of a watermill in 1675.

Medieval Market.
It may have been one of the Berghersh family who obtained Witnesham's market grant in 1227.

Free School.
William Arnold is recorded as teaching a school here in 1597, and a schoolhouse was built on the road to the church sometime before 1710. A Charity School was founded by Robert Beaumont Creiton in 1753.

Historic Houses & Ancient Moated Sites.
Witnesham Hall, seat of the Meadows family from the time of Edward III until 1858, is a C16 timber-framed building encased in red brick in 1842 with, nearby, a fragment of its former moat. The Rectory, adjoining the churchyard, still has slight remains of its former curved moat. Redhouse Farmhouse, ½ mile SE of the village,

WITNESHAM *(continued)*

dates from c1450. Some distance N of the village, a large square water-filled moat in good condition in an isolated position c200 yds E of the present Berghersh House Farm (enlarged in 1819), is the site of the ancient Berghersh House. A causeway runs to entrances in the SE and SW. Cropmarks were noted on the island site in dry weather but the interior has since (1987) been ploughed producing a large amount of building material dating from C13-C15. The Berghersh family were long seated here and in the C14 Sir Bartholomew Berghersh obtained a grant of free warren. Brome Hall, first mentioned in 1652, is now The Barley Mow which has been an inn since c1760.

WIXOE *(4 miles WSW of Clare)*

Risbridge Hundred. 'Hwittuc's hill-spur' (OE) *Wlteskeou* (DB) *Widekeshoo* (1205). The Saxon church stands at the south apex of this hill-spur or hoh overlooking the Stour valley and marks the later Saxon settlement site in this tiny parish.

Manors. Wixoe al Wickesher al Waterhall in Wixoe (C12 Chevre/Capra family).

Roman Settlement.

The parish appears to have provided a major settlement site throughout the Roman period above the Stour valley and beside the important road from Cambridge to Colchester. In a ploughed field near a ford, an extensive C1-C4 Roman settlement and cremation site was discovered in 1952, with much Samian ware and local pottery together with Roman brick, artefacts and oyster shells. Coins included Nero and Constans. Cropmarks of a road/track with associated ditched plots and pit groups have since been recognised in aerial photographs.

Site of Roman Villa (?)

A small excavation, following the discovery of a scatter of pottery and building debris including box tiles and tesserae on the Wixoe/Kedington parish boundary, revealed traces of flint and mortar foundations at a depth of 18" associated with a building. Coins dated the site to the C1 A.D. Cropmarks identified a possible Roman villa site.

Ancient Watermill.

The present watermill on the Stour near Baythorne Bridge was formerly in Suffolk, but is now in Essex - the county boundary for some reason has left the river at this point to take a bite out of Suffolk to include the mill. It stands on an ancient site, for in 1195 it was stated that the head of the Essex priory of St Leonard had laid claim to a mill in Wixoe belonging to William de Capra, presumably because the priory had been founded and endowed by a Michael de Capra and his wife.

Historic Houses & Ancient Moated Sites.

The Old Rectory probably stands on the site of the former manor house. Floriston Hall stands on an elevated knoll to the N, and Water Hall near Sturmer Mere is C17 behind a Georgian facade. At the rear is the rectangular moated enclosure of an earlier manor house built in the C15 of which only the S arm survives wet. A surviving building contract has left details of the hall's construction.

WOODBRIDGE

Loes Hundred. *wudu bricge* 'Bridge near the wood' or 'Wooden bridge' (OE) *Oddebruge* (1050) *Wudebrige* (DB) The origins of Woodbridge's place-name are a matter of debate. Some consider that the 'wooden bridge' refers to 'a wooden bridge built over a hollow between two parks near the road to Ipswich where, in Kirby's time, there was a house called Dry Bridge'. However, it may not refer to a bridge at all, but a 'hard' for ferries by the river Deben near Kyson Wood. Morley, with his usual enterprise and imagination, surmised that it could mean 'forest ridge, crowning the acclivity above the town and visible for many miles round' or that, with the ship burial at Sutton Hoo across the water, it may apply to a pagan Saxon god and mean 'Woden ridge'. Whatever its true place-name origin the town, delightfully situated on the banks of the lovely river Deben, grew up from the important Royal Saxon settlement situated to the S at Kyson *(see below)*. The river is tidal to this point and from early days shipbuilding was an important industry. The town is first mentioned in 970 A.D. when King

WOODBRIDGE *(continued)*

Eadgar made a grant of the town to the abbey of Ely, being the original Liberty of St Ethedreda for which the town became the centre. Woodbridge was visited by the plague in 1666 when over 300 of the townspeople perished. At one time five ferries plied their trade on the Deben, and later warehouses were built for the storage of salt collected from salt pans set up along the river, and coprolite (fossilised animal dung) used as a fertiliser and dug up in great quantities along the shore. These industries have long gone but the town still prospers and now provides a picturesque yachting centre.

Ancient Settlement.

Many finds of worked flint, arrow heads, hand axes, etc., have been made in the town from the pre-historic period.

Roman Settlement & Tile Production Site.

Evidence of a C1-C4 Roman tile production site were discovered N of Kingston hamlet and E of the railway track and, along with frequent finds of pottery and tile, strongly suggest that there was once a Roman settlement here within the town boundaries.

Royal Saxon Manor.

The Royal Saxon Manor of Kyson (still remembered in Kyson Hill and Kyson Point) was established in what is now Kingston ('King's town') hamlet S of the present town on the W bank of the river Deben and along Martlesham Creek. The Royal burial ground of the Wuffingas at Sutton Hoo lay across the river on the eastern bank and was connected by a ferry.

Tumulus (?)

An Anglo-Saxon male skeleton, an 18" long spearhead, and part of a bronze vessel were found in 1873 by two men 'raising stones about 3' below the surface'. The site was near Haugh Lane where 'there were traces of a mound'. Woodbridge School now occupies the site.

Ancient Way.

A section of Earl Bigod's Path (sometimes known as Walton Lane), a medieval way which connected the Bigods' castles at Walton (Felixstowe), Framlingham and Bungay, survives in a lane leading to Gazebo Farm.

Augustinian Priory.

On the S side of the parish church of St Mary, on a site now partly occupied by a C16 manor house called The Abbey (*see below*), a Priory for Augustinian canons was founded in 1193 by Ernald Rufus. It was never an important or wealthy institution. On a visitation in 1532, just prior to its dissolution, Bishop Nykke heard the grievances of a number of canons. They informed him that: the prior was remiss and a poor administrator; the priory gates were not shut at proper times; the house was in debt £10; they had neither corn nor barley in store for the next autumn; the south porch of the church was in ruins on account of defects in the timber; the house was over-burdened with the pension to the ex-prior Coke; there was not sufficient income to discharge the burdens and to do the repairs to the priory; the prior had incurred great expense in making a water-mill, and that both house and mill were in bad repair; and that the priory suffered from penury and want - but that otherwise all was well!

Site of Ancient Tide Mill.

The present picturesque timber tide mill at Ferry Quay is probably C17 in origin and was working until 1956 when the water-wheel's 22" square oak shaft broke. It stands on the site of earlier tide mills, the first belonging to the priory, was mentioned in 1170.

Beacon.

Woodbridge Beacon, formerly situated on high ground above the town on the site of Gazebo Farm, was superseded in Napoleon's time by a tower or 'gaze-about' which was in signalling communication with a Martello tower at Bawdsey.

Medieval Market.

In 1227 the priory obtained a grant for a market on Market Hill, the same site it occupies today.

WOODBRIDGE *(continued)*

Almshouses.

Elizabethan Almshouses in Seckford Street were created from the estate of Thomas Seckford, the town's great benefactor, who died childless in 1587. Income from the charity based on an estate in Clerkenwell rose to such an extent that the original allowance for thirteen elderly men was increased by the addition of eight women and eight married couples. Now known as Seckford Hospital it had additional western and eastern ranges added in 1840 and 1869.

Free Grammar School.

Woodbridge School dates back to 1577 when Thomas Annott founded a Free Grammar School. The venture failed through lack of funds but it was refounded in 1662. Until 1864 it occupied what is now the Seckford Library.

Historic Houses & Ancient Moated Sites.

The Abbey, occupying part of the site of the priory (*see above*) and probably incorporating part of the western range of the cloister buildings, was the Manor House of Woodbridge. Whilst much altered, the three-storeyed porch dates from 1564. It was the seat of Thomas Seckford. Priory Lodge close by stands on the site of the priory gatehouse, and the half-timbered Kings Head public house on Market Hill dating from the late C14, is said to incorporate parts of the C13 farm buildings associated with the priory. Shire Hall on Market Hill was built by Thomas Seckford c1570 as a Sessions Hall for the Liberty of St Etheldreda. The lower part was originally open and formed a covered market. The Crown is an old coaching inn and the Bull dates from c1500. The Old Bell & Steelyard in New Street, complete with its curious weighing machine which projects over the road, is now a public house, but in former days was used for weighing wagons complete with their loads of hay or corn - one of only two *in situ* in the country. In Cumberland Street, Barton Cottage, The Manor House, and the Hermitage date from the C16, whilst Brook House is mid-C17. The Captains Table restaurant in Quay Street dates from the C15 and the Anchor Inn to the C16. The Cross Quays on the corner of The Thoroughfare is recorded as a public house in 1652, but the building is much older. The Crown was a posting inn during the C17.

WOOLPIT *(6 miles NW of Stowmarket)*

Thedwestry Hundred. 'Pit for trapping wolves' (OE) *Wlpit* (C10) *Wlfpeta* (DB)

Manors. Woolpit/Cold Hall (-1541 Abbot of St. Edmundsbury; 1541 John, Lord Russell). There may have been two manors in Woolpit prior to the C16.

Ancient Woodland.

Great Wood on the southern parish boundary, and the extensive Woolpit Wood on the eastern boundary - still retaining its ancient boundary banks and ditches - are tracts of ancient woodland and must once have been inhabited by wolves.

Roman Roads.

There are two possible Roman roads crossing Woolpit. One enters by Corner Farm on the southern parish boundary traced by the road N from Rattlesden. It is lost at Woolpit Green (where the present road bears left to bypass The Grange) and is not picked up again until traced by the A1088 N to Ixworth from the Tostock junction. The missing section would need to have turned half left at some point, perhaps at the ancient Holy Well *(see below)*. Another road appears to have forked NNE from Rattlesden and is possibly traced on the ground by a footpath heading NE for Poplar Farm, and by a straight lane from the road passing Heathgate House and under the present A14 to reach Wood Road by The Warren. From here it is undetected as it passes through a section of Woolpit Wood to the parish boundary by Lawn Farm (*see below*).

Roman Encampment (?)

A reference to Woolpit in 1856 states that ' . . . certain large and deep (Roman) ditches, and Roman coins are frequent here.' Another in 1907 appears to identify the same site: 'Within the remains of an encampment on Warren Farm in this parish (Woolpit) were found a small spiked ornament of ivory, bronze fragments of horse

WOOLPIT *(continued)*

furniture and two Roman coins. These were exhibited in 1855 as found within 'The Roman Encampment on Warren Farm.' Warren Farm is now called Lawn Farm and lies by the course of a possible Roman road (*see above*). Nothing further is known of these findings and there is no trace of ditches or earthworks on the OS 1st Ed. 6" map or on the Woolpit or Elmswell tithe maps. The site may be confused with Warren Farm in the adjoining parish of Wetherden - also by the course of the suggested Roman road - where the site may have been lost in disused sand and gravel workings which possibly extended into Woolpit parish. Woolpit is one of the suggested sites of the Roman Station *Sitomagus.*

Ancient Holy Shrine & Chapel.
In 1501 Queen Elizabeth, wife of Henry VII, ordered a pilgrimage to be undertaken for her to 'Oure Lady of Wolpitte'. The earliest reference to pilgrims at Woolpit occurs in a mandate of the Bishop of Norwich issued between 1211 and 1214. The shrine was probably similar to that at Walsingham and whilst it may have been housed within a chapel on the moated site of Holy Well (*see below*), no evidence for this has been found . Two of the earliest references to a chapel and shrine, in 1390 and 1443, describe the chapel as being 'in the churchyard at Woolpit' which can often mean within the church rather than a separate building, and references after 1467 refer merely to the 'Chapel of Our Lady'. It may have stood on the N side of the chancel on the site of the present vestry. The image was removed in 1538 following the Dissolution but the chapel remained standing until 1551 when a warrant was issued for its demolition and sale.

Ancient Holy Well & Moated Site.
The Well of Our Lady of Woolpit is situated at the base of the S portion of a moat in a meadow NE of the church and village. The moat measures c72 yds by c44 yds internally, the NE, N and W sides are water-filled but the S and SE sides are dry and the SE angle now infilled. There is no evidence of any former building (chapel? *see above*) on the island. The ancient well was a favourite resort of pilgrims travelling to the shrine of Our Lady of Woolpit during the Middle Ages, its water said to be beneficial for sore eyes. Abbot Samson journeyed to Rome to secure the revenues from this well for his abbey at Bury St Edmunds to which Woolpit belonged. The earliest reference to the well occurs in a survey of the Manor in 1573-76 when the Rev John Cobbold of Woolpit wrote to Suffolk antiquarian David Elisha Day that 'Our Lady's Well is in great request with the antiquated females of the parish for its numerous virtues.' It was described in 1827 as being 'a perpetual spring about 2' deep of beautifully clear water and so cold that a hand immersed in it very soon benumbed. It is used occasionally for the immersion of weakly children, and much resorted to by persons of weak eyes.' Anglian Water tested it in 1978 and revealed a high sulphur content - similar to most 'spa' waters. In 1971 the well was encased in brickwork with a metal capping and the site is now part of a small nature reserve.

Ancient Franchise Boundary & Hundred Bank.
A deep ditch and bank, now providing a boundary between property gardens and Woolpit Wood along Wood Lane, Borley Green, are the remains of the ancient Franchise Bank shown on a map of c1568 which marked the extent of the Franchise of St Edmund. It also provided the boundary between Thedwastre and Stowe. Further N, the Procession Way dividing the parishes of Elmswell and Wetherden.

Medieval Green & Heath.
Woolpit Green, shown and named on Faden's 1783 map, lay to the S of the village. It has been partially infilled with a small modern development but its former limits would appear to be formed N and S by The Grange and Abbey Farm, and E and W by two Green Farms. The map also shows Woolpit Heath covering the area on the W side of Wood Lane from its junction with the Woolpit road in the hamlet of Borley Green, N to Kiln Lane. Borley Green formed a small green edged by the ancient boundary bank and ditch of Woolpit Wood. Woolpit Heath and Woolpit Green were enclosed in 1847.

Site of old Windmills.
Three post mills are recorded in the parish in the C18. In 1568 one stood E of The Warren and Wood Road; Pyke's Mill, dated 1644, stood to the N of Woolpit Green and was demolished in 1924; and Elmer's Mill stood on the W side of Broomhill Lane until 1963 when it collapsed.

WOOLPIT *(continued)*

Medieval Market & Fair.
Woolpit received a C13 grant for a market and fair held in the Market Place. In 1481 the Fair was said to be very popular. By 1792 there were two fairs, but records of drunkenness and disorderly behaviour were probably contributary factors in their subsequent demise for both had gone by 1878. The Market Place still survives and a Street Market was revived in 1877 and a Fairs Week in 1978.

Medieval Guildhall (?)
With the guilds of Our Lady and Trinity operating in Woolpit in the C15 and C16, there may at one time have been a guildhall here.

Historic Houses & Ancient Moated Sites.
Woolpit's main street contains a number of timber-framed houses dating from the C14/C15 including The Cottage and Doorways both of which retain timber-framed sections of medieval open hall structures. Hill House is a C15 former schoolhouse and The Swan public house has a C16 core.

WOOLVERSTONE *(3½ miles SE of Ipswich)*

Samford Hundred. 'Wulfhere's farmstead' (OE) *Uluerestuna* (DB)
Manors. Woolverstone Manor/Woolverstone Hall (C13 Crown demesne land; 1291 Hamonde Wolfreston had grant of free warren).

Ancient Woodland.
Glebe Wood, S of the village, and Bylam Wood on the SE parish boundary, are ancient woodland.

Tumuli (?)
Two mounds now of insignificant height in Lower Park Field, one 128 yds. in circumference, the other 140 yds and planted with trees which appear about 150 years old, may be C19 landscape features beside the former carriageway drive to Woolverstone Hall, created in 1861. However, an earlier origin may be suggested by the nearby croft which was called Newcroft or, more significantly, The Hills in 1501 when covering an area of some nine acres.

Earthworks.
An impressive Iron Age earthwork, hidden by a conifer plantation, crowns a hilly area known as Elbury Down. Aerial photography has shown that the church stands on the edge of a rectangular embanked enclosure, possibly Roman and connected with the Downham Bridge river crossing.

Medieval Tile Production Industry.
In 1991 a Late Medieval/Post Medieval tile kiln was exposed in the bank of the river Orwell, N of Whinnyfield Wood on the parish boundary with Freston. There was also a large quantity of peg-tile spread over the beach. In 1997 further erosion of the bank destroyed part of this kiln but exposed further sections. According to a C15 document this area was known as 'Old Tileyard', and numerous small depressions and irregularities evident in the adjoining pasture would suggest this former use. An C18 tile kiln was revealed on the Orwell shore immediately to the SE in 1953. A deep hole evident in Woolverstone Park nearby was probably the clay pit.

Historic House & Deer Park.
Woolverstone Hall and Park was built in 1776 by William Berners. The original house is believed to have occupied the site of the stables. The park was extended to 400 acres and stocked with spotted deer.

WORDWELL *(5 miles NNW of Bury St Edmunds)*

Blackbourn Hundred. Early analysis of the place-name suggested 'twisting stream' or 'thicket by a stream' (OE), however, Morley noted the later discovery of a well *(see below)* and proposed, with justifiable conviction, 'well by the saplings'. *Wridewella* (DB)
Manors. Wordwell (c1200 William de Wordwell held 4th part of a knight's fee of the Abbot of St. Edmunds; 1375 Sir John Holbroke).

WORDWELL *(continued)*

Tumuli.

Travellers Hill is a bowl barrow covered in trees on the S side of a track called Chalk Lane in the Kings Forest, with smaller bowl barrows on either side. It is flat topped, 115' in diameter and 4' high. Basil Brown noted in 1950 that silver bells were found here in 1942. Another barrow lies S of the same track further NW near the modern B1106 road. It has been ploughed but still remains 30 yds N-S and 26 yds E-W, c1½' high with no trace of a ditch.

Earthworks.

The C19 tithe map appears to show that earthwork banks in Forestry Commission woodland (in places 11½' wide) mark the boundaries between heathland (to the N) and arable (to the S) prior to the forestation of the heath.

Ancient Well.

An ancient well, discovered in the churchyard in 1868 may provide the answer to the origins of the place-name (*see above*).

Deserted Medieval Village.

Soil marks, undulations and medieval pottery mark the site of the former village E of All Saints Church which still retains elements of its former Saxon origins. Listed as one of Beresfield's *Lost Villages of England* it is one of the few known to have been depopulated by the Black Death. Lay Subsidies of 1283 and 1327 list 20 taxpayers representing 20 families suggesting a population of over 90. Following the plague the 1381 Poll Tax lists only 9 taxpayers, halving the population. Only 4 dwellings were shown on the 1674 Hearth Tax and by 1757 Tom Martin recorded: 'The village is now so reduced as to have no more buildings in it than the church, manor house, and one dwelling for the shepherd.' The area was ploughed out c1970.

Medieval Green & Heath.

Although almost the entire parish was formerly under heathland and used for sheep and rabbits, there is evidence to suggest the site of a former village green. Most of the land is now under the Forestry Commission and has been planted with conifers.

Town (Poor) House.

A Glebe Terrier of 1686 speaks of a 'pightle lying next the street (S of the churchyard) and occupied with a Tenement of the Town', probably the Poorhouse.

Historic Houses & Ancient Moated Sites.

Wordwell Hall occupies the site of the C13 manor house of the de Wordwell family. The remains of the water-filled sub-rectangular moat, c131' by 82', shown on the OS maps of 1882 and 1884 and linked to a water course flowing S to the river Lark c550 yds from Wordwell Hall and 437 yds from the road, now lies in the NW corner of an arable field.

WORLINGHAM *(1 mile SE of Beccles)*

Wangford Hundred. 'The homestead of Werel's people' (OE) *Werlingaham* (DB)
Manors. Worlingham (1281-1539 Abbot of St. Edmunds; 1539 Bokenham family). *Sub-Manors.* Little Worlingham (absorbed by Cove's Manor [North Cove]).

Deserted Medieval Village.

The former parish of Worlingham Parva to the E has long been lost. It included the ancient Wade Hall which is now included in North Cove. Its church, dedicated to St Peter, was last mentioned in 1492. During the construction of the Beccles bypass, 20 burials from its churchyard were unearthed and footings of the church itself showed that it was single celled (nave and chancel in one) with a round tower. Pottery dating from Thetford ware to the C15 confirmed the period of the building's existence.

Quaker Burial Ground.

A Quaker Burial Ground was in use in the parish in the C18.

WORLINGHAM *(continued)*

Guildhall.

A medieval document has been revealed which refers to 'messuage in Worlingham called the Guildhall'. The Guild of John Baptist was operating in the parish and the guildhall was later used by the Town Estate.

Town House.

The Town House held 6 poor persons in 1674.

Medieval Common.

Faden's 1783 map shows the wedge-shaped Worlingham Common extending N from the Lowestoft road opposite the church. Recent encrouchment in the form of new residential properties has taken place along the roadside.

Historic House.

In a park E of Beccles, Worlingham Hall, remodelled c1800, stands on the site of an ancient hall, formerly the seat of the Feltons.

WORLINGTON *(1 mile WSW of Mildenhall)*

Lackford Hundred. 'Farmstead by the winding stream' or 'Wrethel's (Wridewella's) family's farm' (OE) *Wirilintona* (DB) *Wridelingeton* (1201). The winding stream described above could well refer to the river Lark which does take a very meandering course whilst forming the northern parish boundary with Mildenhall and West Row. The place-name could equally have applied to the site of Wamil Hall which, although strictly in the adjoining parish of Mildenhall, is a site is of very ancient origin and could at one time have been within the parish and 'Wrethel's family's home'.

Manors. Worlington, Abergavenny/Bergavenny (C13 Agnes de Wichentan ne de Rivill). *Sub-Manors.* Worlington Scales/Tindalls.

With two fisheries listed here at Domesday it suggests the parish (at that time) lay on the edge of the Old Fen Sea.

Tumulus.

S of Swale's Plantation, on the W side of the road to Red Lodge, is a Late Neolithic round barrow called Swale's Tumulus. It was later modified by raising a larger mound over the former smaller one for another burial rite during the Bronze Age. The site has now been ploughed.

Romano-British Settlement & Saxon Hoard.

Extensive finds of pottery including Samian and Caister ware, tiles, brick, coins, etc., have been found over a spread of dark soil NW of the village with, further S, iron objects and bronze-headed iron agricultural implements, axes, hammers, chisels and sickles, suggestive of a Romano-British farming community. A hoard of Saxon coins in the same area may point to an extended settlement here.

Ancient Mill.

A mill was listed here at Domesday, and 'miller' as an occupation in 1340.

Medieval Cross.

In the churchyard of All Saints Church is the base of a Medieval Cross.

Medieval Market & Fair.

There were two manors in Worlington and, although from the C14 Bergavenny became the most important, Scales or Tindalls had earlier prominence. It was Robert de Scales who, in 1258, obtained the grant of a market in his manor of Worlington Scales. A Fair is said to have been held in the village until 1899.

Historic Houses & Ancient Moated Sites.

SE of the Bell Inn and W of Manor Farm is a large irregular moated site. The platform which was distinctly higher in the NW quarter was levelled off in the 1940s-50s. A bulb-like extension of the ditch to the moat island was referred to by old residents as the 'fish-ponds'. C14-C15 pottery has been found on the site which probably once contained a manor house.

WORLINGWORTH *(6 miles NW of Framlingham)*

Hoxne Hundred. 'The enclosure of Wilhere's people' (OE) *Wilrincgawertha* (c1035) *Wyrlingwortha* (DB)
Manors. Worlingworth (-1539 Abbot of St. Edmunds; 1539 Anthony Rous).

Ancient Chapel.
A 'Chapel at Worlingworth' is mentioned in 1254 but its history and site are unknown.

Medieval Greens.
A large triangular green formerly occupied the area known as Newtown, N of Mill Road. It was shown on Faden's map of 1783 and named Worlingworth Green, though an estate map of 1606 calls it Great Green. It extended to join Southolt Green to the W. There is documentary evidence for its suggested creation in the mid C13 and it was enclosed in 1831-2 leaving only a fraction surviving as pasture in the SE corner near Paradise Farm. Another green shown on the same map was called Stanway Green and lay on the northern parish boundary; a square-shaped green, its site is now marked by Stanway Green Farm. The church also stood beside a small green called Church Green.

Medieval Crosses.
A map of c1355 shows three medieval crosses: on Stanway Green; at the T-junction in 'Sudden Strete' (a White Cross opposite the inn); and on the SW corner of Great Green.

Site of old Windmills.
A mill is shown NW of the church on a map of c1355. A post mill known as Old Mill stood in Mill Road, Newtown in 1783. It was dismantled c1924.

Free School.
The Baldry Charity Trust for the support of a schoolmaster and the education of poor children of the parish in 1689 was aided by the Godbold Charity in 1698. 56 children were attending the Free School in 1818. A new school was built by John Cordy c1825.

Guildhall & Workhouse.
The parish's guildhall, situated N of the church and shown on a map of c1355, once had a rectangular moat. It held the Guild of St. Trinity in 1503. Later it was used as the parish workhouse, housing 35 inmates in 1776.

Historic Houses & Ancient Moated Sites.
A courthouse (*le letecote*) was disused by the C14 but had been situated in a field to the S of Great Green called 'Walhel'. It has been suggested that the original Saxon settlement was not by the church, hall and guildhall, but in the area of the Swan Inn ('newly built' in 1543) by the junction with Swan Road. Worlingworth Hall, NE of the church, stands on the site of Worlingworth Manor, formerly part of the possessions given by Bishop Alfric to Bury Abbey. Three sides of its rectangular moat survived until recently. On the northern parish boundary Honeypots Farm retains a fragment of an asymetrical enclosure. A map of 1686 by Thomas Hornebye names it 'Godbolds in the Wood', the property of William Godbold. The house is shown with a bridge or causeway crossing its irregular moat. Stanway Green Farm, again near the northern boundary with Wilby, has one side of a square moat, and Hill Farm, just to the S, has the southern side (with two arms partly gone) of a probable square moat. Grange Farm has three 'L' shaped fragments of moats (all relatively small) which seem to represent two copyhold tenements of Worlingworth Manor. Three sides of a rectangular moat just E of Wood Farm represent a free tenement of the same manor, as does another former moated site E of this.

WORTHAM *(6 miles NW of Eye)*

Hartismere Hundred. 'Homestead with an enclosure' (OE) *Wrtham* (c950) *Wortham* (DB)
Manors. Wortham Hall (1182 Abbot of St. Edmunds; 1247 De Wachesham family held of the Abbot; 1384 Sir George Felbrigg was granted free warren). *Sub-Manors.* Wortham Abbots.
There were formerly two parishes here: Wortham Everard (or Southmore) and Wortham Jervis (or Eastgate).

Ancient Woodland.
The scandalous and wilful destruction of our landscape heritage continues apace and is nowhere more evident

WORTHAM *(continued)*

than in Wortham which has seen the loss of two sections of ancient woodland since the 1950s - Great Wood and Little Wood. Only Gittin Wood remains.

Tumulus.

A long barrow in the NW corner of Wortham Ling on the northern parish boundary by the river Waveney, is c160' long and 45' wide. The site forms part of an old rifle range.

Iron Age (& Saxon?) Settlement Site.

On Spears Hill, ¾ mile NW of the village, an Iron Age settlement is marked by a group of hut circles bounded by V-section ditches and a scatter of pottery sherds. Another possible occupation site was excavated by Basil Brown E of Beans Lane in the S of the parish and close to Roman and multi-period settlement sites. Of two hut sites, one was definitely Iron Age; the other, with a hearth, he thought 'possibly Saxon'.

Roman Roads.

A Roman road was unearthed by Basil Brown in 1955 running N-S along Beans Lane. It was cambered and 30' wide overall made of packed flints over a chalk/clay base bordered by ditches. Another (minor?) Roman road was found W of Spears Hill Farm near the western parish boundary. It was some 15' wide, running E-W, cambered with V-shaped ditches approx 3' wide either side.

Roman Settlement Site

A Roman occupation site was found during pipe-laying near the southern parish boundary in 1955. It comprised six (hut?) sites in groups of three, all with hearths. The immediate area was strewn with pottery sherds and burnt clay.

Roman Cemetery (?)

A Roman tomb and urns were said to have been found in a field W of Low Farm in 1843 and marked on the OS map of 1903. Although Basil Brown found no evidence on a visit in 1954, he thought a ridge running across the field may have been an ancient track and the field is known locally as Roman Field where 'pieces of old pottery are said to have been found'.

Multi-Period Settlement Site.

Just N of the Roman site another multi-period site was excavated by Brown in 1955. It covered Prehistoric, Iron Age, Roman, Saxon and Medieval periods. A Roman ditch runs W-E across the field to intersect with the Roman Road (*see above*). Smaller ditches intersect and in one of these the complete skeleton of a deer was excavated.

Coin Hoard.

A hoard of 160 silver-plated bronze contemporary forgeries of denarii of Caludius I, struck between 46-51 A.D. and including numerous die links, was found in the parish in 1995.

Ancient Watch Tower (?)

The ruined C11 round church tower, 30' in diameter and the largest of its kind in England, has two fireplaces and is thought to have once been a watch tower for the abbots of Bury. The upper stage of the tower fell in c1780.

Earthworks.

'The Mount', E of Church Road, is shown as a circular mound on the OS map. Its original date and purpose are unknown but it may have (later?) provided the site for a windmill.

Medieval Greens & Common.

Wortham Green - with its northern extension Magpie Green - survives today as one of the largest green areas in the county. Wortham Common butting on the river Waveney on the northern parish boundary also survives as Wortham Ling. The green appears to have been encompassed by a large ditch or moat, several sections of which survive either side of the minor road running W to Spears Hill.

Cloth Industry.

Hemp and flax were grown here 1555-59: Wortham servants 'slept between sheets made of hemp cloth' (1784).

Deserted Medieval Village.

There were formerly two parishes here: Wortham Southmore (or Everard) - the southerly moor or the part of

WORTHAM *(continued)*

which the Everards were lords, and Wortham Eastgate (or Jervis) - at the east entrance or the part of which the Jervis family were lords. The two parishes were consolidated on 28 January 1769. During excavation of the multi-period site near Beans Lane, Basil Brown discovered remains of a building overlaid by a moated Tudor house (*see below*). These earlier building foundations were made of clay and thought by him to be the remains of St. Thomas's Church of Wortham Everard, one of the two churches previously in Wortham parish. Along with C13 pottery, he also found a tooled stone which he described as Norman and apparently part of a window or door surround.

Site of old Windmill.

A post mill stood on Wortham Ling in 1783. It was demolished in 1917.

Workhouse.

The Hartismere Union Workhouse on Ling Common held 30 inmates in 1776.

Historic Houses & Ancient Moated Sites.

NW of the church of St Thomas and St Mary on the banks of the river Waveney, stands the C16 Wortham (formerly Abbots) Hall, and beside it an irregular moat which formerly surrounded the original Wortham Abbots Manor House of the de Wacheshams (the Manor reverted to the Crown following the death of Sir Robert in 1366). The C16 Manor House, seat of the Betts family since 1590, is the manor house of Wortham Hall Manor and stands on a wooded and formerly moated site. The Rookery, SE of The Marsh, is a large house with ancient features. The remains (in the form of footings) of a late Tudor building, 142' by 64' surrounded by a courtyard and enclosed by a moat, were discovered during excavating the multi-period site E of Beans Lane (*see above*). Substantial wall footings included stone steps leading down to the moat which was over 6' deep. Pottery covered the period C15-C17. The hall may have been the manor house connected with the lost village of Southmore (*see above*). In the C17 there was a public house here called Tumble-down-Dick. The name refers to the death of Oliver Cromwell and the succession of his son, Richard. A verse under the old pub sign read: 'Now the far famed Diagenes is dead, the tumble down Dick is come in his sted.'

WRENTHAM *(5 miles N of Southwold)*

Blything Hundred. 'Wrenta's homestead' (OE) Wrenta may be a nickname meaning 'to grumble'. Morley suggests an Old Icelandic personal name 'Hrani' *Wretham* (DB) *Wrentham* (1228)

Manors. Wrentham, Perpounds al South Hall (c1486 Sir Richard Fienes, Lord Dacre). *Sub-Manors.* Wrentham, Northall/Poinings.

Ancient Woodland.

Wrentham Great Wood and Kitchen Wood NE of the parish are ancient woodland.

Roman Road (?)

Pyes Hall Farm (named Pye Hall on Faden's 1783 map) stands beside what may be the course of the Roman road (traced in sections by the present A12) to Caister.

Hollow Way & Former Settlement.

Faden's map of 1783 shows a road running between the Henstead road N of the church and the present A12 opposite Lock's Lane. This remains today as a hollow way in permanent pasture S of Kitchen Wood. The present Wrentham village is modern - developing beside the busy A12. It is likely that the original medieval village was instead centred on the church and former hall, radiating out along Guildhall Lane, Chapel Road and Priory Road, with the hollow way forming its northern boundary.

Site of old Windmill.

An open-trestle post mill stood in Mill Lane in 1736. It was moved to a new site on the E side of the A12 road S of the village and named Fletcher's Mill. It collapsed in 1931.

Guildhall (?)

Though no guilds are recorded here, Guildhall Lane suggests a guildhall was formerly sited in the parish.

WRENTHAM *(continued)*

Medieval Green & Common.

Wrentham Common formed a triangular shape from the 5-ways crossing on the present A12 road, southwards, flanked by the A12 and B1127, beyond the southern parish boundary to Gipsy Lane. Most of the common was probably enclosed around 1797, some 14 years after it was shown on Faden's 1783 map. Cuckold's Green, which lay W of the church, is not shown by Faden and may already have gone by this time.

Historic Houses & Ancient Moated Sites.

Wrentham Hall, which stood near the church and is shown on Faden's map of 1783, was built by the Brewster family. Humphrey Brewster had acquired the Manor of Wrentham Pierrepoint (or South Hall) in 1576 - Robert de Pierrepoint had held the manor at Domesday for Earl Warren - and the Manor of Wrentham Northall or Poinings in 1577. The hall which was listed as having 18 hearths in 1674 was demolished in 1810. Portions of a very weak moat - more ditches than homestead moat - remain at Moat Farm, West End, near the western parish boundary; the farmhouse dates from 1636.

WYVERSTONE *(7 miles N of Stowmarket)*

Hartismere Hundred. 'Wigfrith's farmstead' (OE) *Wiuerthestune* (DB)

Manors. Wyverstone (C11 Robert Hovel held under Robert Malet; C13 Hovel family). *Sub-Manors.* Hovells.

Ancient Track.

Hundred Lane forms the western parish boundary and the ancient Saxon Hundred boundary between Blackbourn and Hartismere from E of Slough Farm to just S of the junction with a track joining from the W named Madge's Lane. The point where the road to Badwell Ash crosses the lane is named Cuttings Hole on Faden's map of 1783.

Medieval Market & Fair.

The Hovel family had the grant for a market and 3-day fair in 1231, renewed in 1272.

Medieval Green.

The narrow Wyverstone Green ran down the N side of the Westhorpe-Long Thurlow road W from the church and widening to Crooksell Pond at the junction with the road to Earls Green, Bacton.

Historic Houses & Ancient Moated Sites.

The site of Wyverstone Hall is marked by Old Hall Barn and curved fragments of its former ancient moat. Faden's map shows a most impressive avenue curving away to the W from the hall site to meet The Grange (now a farmhouse) by Potash Road. A small park, no doubt associated with the hall, is also shown. The earliest moated hall may have been the seat of the Ewers who held the manor for some time. A small square moat remains isolated at Moat Hill SW of Wyverstone Green.

YAXLEY *(1½ miles W of Eye)*

Hartismere Hundred. 'Cuckoo meadow' (OE) *Jacheslea* (DB)

Manors. Yaxley (1294 Chapel of Ringshall settled on this manor by Prior of Norwich; C16 Anthony Yaxley). *Sub-Manors.* Bull's Head with Blodgates al Boles Manor (Bishop of Thetford; C14 William Bull/Bole).

Pre-historic Field Pattern.

Norman Scarfe has recognised that on the tithe and early C19 estate maps of the area the Roman road cuts through the co-axial landscape of field boundaries and tracks. It would therefore seem likely that they pre-date the Roman period. A large section has been lost through the creation of the World War II airfield.

Roman Road.

The Roman road to Caister-by-Norwich (*Venta Icenorum*) enters the parish from the S traced by the present A140. Although the modern road now forks NE to bypass the village, the old road continues through the village still on the line of the Roman road, crossing a tributary of the river Dove and rejoining the A140 N of Whitehouse Farm where it forms part of the NE parish boundary.

YAXLEY *(continued)*

Mound - Site of Ancient Beacon (?)

A mound known as 'Beacon Hill' lies SE of the church. Ogibly's map of 1675 shows a beacon on the site. The main turnpike road from Ipswich to Norwich lies on the Roman road to Caister-by-Norwich and passes to the W of the site.

Medieval Greens.

Lengths of unnamed green are shown along either side of the Roman road (the present A140) N of the village on Faden's 1783 map, and continuing into Broome Common.

Medieval Fair.

The grant of a fair in 1225/6 to the Jackell family, possibly relates to Yaxley.

Guildhall.

White mentions a guildhall in existence in the village but its site is unknown. The Guild of St. Thomas was sited here in 1524. It was used as a poor house in 1840.

Historic Houses & Ancient Moated Sites.

Immediately S of Yaxley Hall - an Elizabethan-style mansion said to have a C15 doorway - a rectilinear moated enclosure c240 yds by 230 yds is dry except for a pond extending to the interior from the E arm; the N arm is not visible. The moat, which is shown on the OS 1st Ed. map of 1838, probably held an earlier hall. Yaxley Manor House on the western parish boundary is an ancient building. On the W side of the road junction in the village is a weak sub-rectangular moat where C13-C14 pottery was found in 1968. The present Bull Inn built in the C17 and now a motel and restaurant, possibly occupies the site of Bull/Bole Manor House.

YOXFORD *(4 miles N of Saxmundham)*

Blything Hundred. 'Yoke's ford' - ford wide enough for a yoke of oxen (OE) *Gokesford* (DB). Includes the Domesday vill of Strickland. A bridge now carries the main road (A12) over the river Yox E of the village - a spot where no doubt an ancient ford once gave rise to the place-name.

Manors. Yoxford (C12 William de Pirnho). *Sub-Manors.* Cockfield Hall; Murrills; Stikingland (1322 Roger de Eveningham).

Ancient Woodland.

Yoxford Wood and Willowmarsh Wood in the N of the parish are parts of ancient woodland.

Roman Roads & Ancient Ford.

Two Roman roads met to cross the river Yox here, a spot no doubt referred to in the place-name. One was on the line of the present A12, the other came in from Peasenhall to the W, making a southwards curve (traced by the present street) to connect with the former at right angles to cross the ford as one - probably at the same point where the A12 is now carried over the river by a bridge. The medieval Cockfield Hall lies to the NW of this ancient road junction.

Medieval(?) Brick Industry.

Earthworks in permanent pasture on the site of Brick Kiln Farm probably identify former brick kilns.

Deer Park.

A former deer park was situated N of Kelsale Hall and defined by the surveyor John Middleton in 1616 when he showed: 'the late disparked park of Kelsale and Yoxford now divided in divers enclosures.' Its northern limit is still defined by a stretch of bank and dense hedge (of at least five species including stout oak) providing a curving field boundary running E from the corner of Coe Wood. Kelsale Lodge, to the SE of which is a remaining section of the park pale, lies on the southern parish boundary (*see also Kelsale*).

Site of old Windmill.

Two windmills were standing in the parish in the late C18. One stood E of Bark Barn and the A12 in 1764, and the other opposite the junction with the A1120 in the centre of the village in 1783.

YOXFORD *(continued)*

Historic Houses & Ancient Moated Sites.

Cockfield Hall was the manor house and former residence of the Brook and Blois families. The N wing and a gatehouse remain from c1540 along with two arms of an earlier square moat in the grounds - the river Yox may have provided the southern arm. Lady Catherine Grey, sister of Lady Jane Grey, who had married the Earl of Hertford without the Queen's consent, was brought to Cockfield Hall in 1567 in the hope that 'she would there recover from the privations she had suffered in the Tower where she had been imprisoned'. Sadly she died shortly after her arrival and was buried in the Cockfield Chapel in the church. Later her body was exhumed and buried with her husband in Salisbury Cathedral. Her heart was left at Yoxford and said to be buried under a stone slab hidden by tiles in front of the lectern. A small copse called Bush Corner, N of the village, is the site of Yoxford Manor. A manorial survey of 1471 states that the manor was 'walled about with walls and a moat, which said site was formerly built upon, and was then called the inner court of the manor. Men now living have seen jambs and posts.' The site was approximately square, the main entrance due S along a ditched causeway known as the Old Entry. A linear pond shown on the OS map may be part of the moat. Satis House, standing in three acres of grounds and now an hotel and restaurant, is mentioned in Charles Dicken's 'Great Expectations'. The timber-framed Church House stands on the S side of the churchyard. The half-timbered Drum House is the former manor House of Muriell's Manor; it was once used as 'The Fife & Drum' public house. The Griffin and The Three Tuns public houses were recorded as inns in 1624 and 1628. The latter was burned down in 1926.

Notes . . .

Notes . . .

Notes . . .